THIRD-PARTY COUNTE
IN INTERNATION.

The use of third-party countermeasures is an increasingly common phenomenon in international relations, yet their legal position remains uncertain. Providing the first systematic and comprehensive study of this key concept in international law, Martin Dawidowicz explores the position of third-party countermeasures and their safeguards regime based on the development of ideas on countermeasures in the UN International Law Commission and a thorough examination of State practice. The book clarifies the position of third-party countermeasures in international law, and in doing so it challenges some widely held assumptions about the likely impact of a regime of third-party countermeasures on international relations. It will be of interest to international law and relations scholars and students, diplomats, policy makers, international civil servants and NGOs in the field of human rights.

MARTIN DAWIDOWICZ was formerly Departmental Lecturer in Public International Law at the University of Oxford, and is currently Visiting Lecturer in Public International Law at the University of Stockholm. He was previously an associate at LALIVE in Geneva, where he practiced public international law and international arbitration, and before that he worked in the UN Office of Legal Affairs in New York.

CAMBRIDGE STUDIES IN INTERNATIONAL
AND COMPARATIVE LAW: 131

Established in 1946, this Series produces high quality, reflective and innovative scholarship in the field of public international law. It publishes works on international law that are of a theoretical, historical, cross-disciplinary or doctrinal nature. The series also welcomes books providing insights from private international law, comparative law and transnational studies which inform international legal thought and practice more generally.

The series seeks to publish views from diverse legal traditions and perspectives, and of any geographical origin. In this respect it invites studies offering regional perspectives on core *problématiques* of international law, and in the same vein, it appreciates contrasts and debates between diverging approaches. Accordingly, books offering new or less orthodox perspectives are very much welcome. Works of a generalist character are greatly valued and the Series is also open to studies on specific areas, institutions or problems. Translations of the most outstanding works published in other languages are also considered.

After 70 years, *Cambridge Studies in International and Comparative Law* remains the standard-setter for international legal scholarship and will continue to define the discipline as it evolves in the years to come.

General Editors   Larissa van den Herik
                     *Professor of Public International Law, Law School
                     Leiden University*

                     Jean D'Aspremont
                     *Professor of Public International Law, Manchester
                     International Law Centre, University of Manchester*

A list of books in the series can be found at the end of this volume.

THIRD-PARTY
COUNTERMEASURES IN
INTERNATIONAL LAW

MARTIN DAWIDOWICZ

CAMBRIDGE
UNIVERSITY PRESS

CAMBRIDGE
UNIVERSITY PRESS

University Printing House, Cambridge CB2 8BS, United Kingdom

One Liberty Plaza, 20th Floor, New York, NY 10006, USA

477 Williamstown Road, Port Melbourne, VIC 3207, Australia

314-321, 3rd Floor, Plot 3, Splendor Forum, Jasola District Centre, New Delhi - 110025, India

79 Anson Road, #06-04/06, Singapore 079906

Cambridge University Press is part of the University of Cambridge.

It furthers the University's mission by disseminating knowledge in the pursuit of education, learning and research at the highest international levels of excellence.

www.cambridge.org
Information on this title: www.cambridge.org/9781108717007
DOI: 10.1017/9781139046602

© Martin Dawidowicz 2017

First published 2017
First paperback edition 2018

A catalogue record for this publication is available from the British Library

Library of Congress Cataloging in Publication data
Names: Dawidowicz, Martin, author.
Title: Third-party countermeasures in international law / Martin Dawidowicz.
Description: Cambridge, United Kingdom ; New York, NY, USA : Cambridge University Press, 2017. | Series: Cambridge studies in international and comparative law ; 131 | Includes bibliographical references and index.
Identifiers: LCCN 2017007127 | ISBN 9781107014794 (hardback)
Subjects: LCSH: Third party countermeasures (International law) | United Nations. International Law Commission. Draft Articles on the Responsibility of States for Internationally Wrongful Acts. | BISAC: LAW / International.
Classification: LCC KZ4085 .D39 2017 | DDC 341.5–dc23
LC record available at https://lccn.loc.gov/2017007127

ISBN 978-1-107-01479-4 Hardback
ISBN 978-1-108-71700-7 Paperback

CONTENTS

v

FOREWORD

In this study, Martin Dawidowicz examines one of the great, unresolved questions of current international law: the position of third-party countermeasures. The topic is a difficult and controversial one. The construction of a multilateral public order is based not so much on logic as some mixture of high hope and limited experience. The construction may rest on the imposing pseudo-Roman columns of *jus cogens* and obligations *erga omnes* – *les grandes verticales* – but these were largely based on assertion rather than actual performance. It seems that this ambitious construction may have reversed the Roman scheme that it is society that requires and generates the law: *ubi societas, ibi jus.* Nowadays it may seem that international law seeks to develop more rapidly than international society may allow, including in the field of communitarian law enforcement. However, as this study shows, the position is not quite so bleak – the present state of play embodies hope, no doubt, but also a deal of experience.

For the use of otherwise unlawful unilateral sanctions of a peaceful character taken in defence of communitarian norms – i.e. third-party countermeasures – is an increasingly common phenomenon in international relations. They are often resorted to by a large (and increasingly diverse) number of States acting in concert as part of a broader strategy to deal with major assaults on multilateral public order. There is much here that requires careful, thorough and sober analysis. Martin Dawidowicz provides all this.

This is – remarkably – the first study on third-party countermeasures in international law which addresses the topic in a systematic and comprehensive way, based on the turbulent and even occasionally idiosyncratic development of ideas on countermeasures in the International Law Commission, resulting in the compromise 'solution' found in Article 54 ARSIWA. Both sides of the argument in this fraught debate are given due consideration. The study rightly places emphasis on the greatest area of uncertainty – State practice – which has received too little attention.

This approach has yielded a substantial harvest which is presented for the reader's consumption in a lucid, thoughtful and convincing manner. It makes a significant contribution to our understanding of the position of third-party countermeasures in international law. In doing so, it successfully challenges some widely held assumptions about the likely impact of a regime of third-party countermeasures on international relations.

Peace Palace, The Hague   *James Crawford*
May 2016

PREFACE

Popular legend has it that Jack Kerouac wrote *On the Road* in three weeks, typing it almost nonstop in one big coffee-fuelled burst of creative energy on a 120-foot scroll – replacing regular sheets of paper just interrupted his flow – cooped up in a New York City apartment in 1951. At least this is what Kerouac said in 1959 when asked by TV talk-show host Steve Allen about how long it had taken to write it: 'Three weeks'. '*How* many?' replied Allen, adding, in disbelief, 'That's amazing!' In reality, Kerouac's book had a much longer and bumpier journey, complete with multiple rewrites. And there were always roadblocks slowing down his creative flow – sometimes even to a complete halt – before sputtering off and gradually gaining steam again towards the final destination. And so it is with this book. It has spent many years on the road: from Oxford to Cambridge, Paris, New York, Washington, DC, Geneva and, finally, back to Oxford.

This personal journey has benefitted from the guidance of many companions along the way to whom I am much indebted. At Oxford, Catherine Redgwell supervised the incipient seed of this work as a master's thesis with great care and infectious charm, and set me on my way, in a northeasterly direction, on the X5 bus to Cambridge.

My arrival in Cambridge to complete a PhD thesis – of which this book is an updated and substantially revised version – was generously supported by the Gates Cambridge Trust and Trinity College, for which I am most thankful. To add to my good fortune, I had the great privilege of being supervised by Professor James Crawford, then Whewell Professor of International Law (now judge of the ICJ). James opened up ever-new horizons in characteristically succinct, but deeply profound and mean-ingful, ways. He is an inspirational figure in many ways and not only in matters of international law. I am deeply grateful for his guidance and generous support.

My PhD thesis was examined by Professors Giorgio Gaja (now judge of the ICJ) and Guglielmo Verdirame, who subjected it to a thorough and searching analysis, and made thoughtful and perceptive comments which are gratefully acknowledged. I would also like to extend my gratitude to Santiago Villalpando, from whom, during my time in the UN Office of Legal Affairs, I learnt a great deal about the workings of the Sixth (Legal) Committee of the General Assembly and the International Law Commission.

The book was completed during my time as Departmental Lecturer in Public International Law at the University of Oxford. I am most thankful to my Oxford colleagues Catherine Redgwell, Frank Berman, Dan Sarooshi, Dapo Akande and Antonios Tzanakopoulos for providing such a welcoming and intellectually stimulating environment in which to complete this work. My gratitude also extends to Finola O'Sullivan, Elizabeth Spicer and others at Cambridge University Press, not least for so patiently allowing a seed of inspiration to take root and grow into a tree of publication.

Finally, I am especially grateful to my family for their love and support throughout the years and for making all of this possible. Above all, I am grateful to Paz whose love and friendship has been the greatest gift of this journey. This book is dedicated to her.

Oxford   *Martin Dawidowicz*
May 2016   *m.dawidowicz@law.oxon.org*

TABLE OF CASES

ABBREVIATIONS

ACHR	American Convention on Human Rights, 22 November 1969, 1144 UNTS 123
ACP	African, Caribbean and Pacific Group of States
ADP	ILC Articles on Diplomatic Protection, ILC Report (2006), UN Doc. A/61/10, 24
ADP Commentary	Commentary to the ILC Articles on Diplomatic Protection, ILC Report (2006), UN Doc. A/61/10, 26
AFDI	Annuaire français de droit international
Ago, Second Report	R. Ago, Second Report on State Responsibility, YbILC (1970), vol. II, 177
Ago, Third Report	R. Ago, Third Report on State Responsibility, YbILC (1971), vol. II/1, 199
Ago, Fifth Report	R. Ago, Fifth Report on State Responsibility, YbILC (1976), vol. II/1, 3
Ago, Eighth Report	R. Ago, Eighth Report on State Responsibility, YbILC (1979 and 1980), vol. II/1, 3, 13
AJCIL	African Journal of International and Comparative Law
AJIL	American Journal of International Law
AJPIL	Austrian Journal of Public International Law
Ann. IDI	Annuaire de l'Institut de droit international
Arangio-Ruiz, Third Report	G. Arangio-Ruiz, Third Report on State Responsibility, YbILC (1991), vol. II/1, 1
Arangio-Ruiz, Fourth Report	G. Arangio-Ruiz, Fourth Report on State Responsibility, YbILC (1992), vol. II/1, 1
Arangio-Ruiz, Fifth Report	G. Arangio-Ruiz, Fifth Report on State Responsibility, YbILC (1993), vol. II/1, 1
Arangio-Ruiz, Sixth Report	G. Arangio-Ruiz, Sixth Report on State Responsibility, YbILC (1994), vol. II/1, 3
Arangio-Ruiz, Seventh Report	G. Arangio-Ruiz, Seventh Report on State Responsibility, YbILC (1995), vol. II/1, 3

ARSIWA	ILC Articles on Responsibility of States for Internationally Wrongful Acts, ILC Report (2001), UN Doc. A/56/10, 26
ARSIWA Commentary	Commentary to the ILC Articles on Responsibility of States for Internationally Wrongful Acts, ILC Report (2001), UN Doc. A/56/10, 31
ARV	Archiv des Völkerrecht
ASIL Proc.	American Society of International Law Proceedings
AU	African Union
BIT	Bilateral Investment Treaty
BYIL	British Yearbook of International Law
CESCR	Committee on Economic, Social and Cultural Rights (ICESCR)
Chinese JIL	Chinese Journal of International Law
CJICL	Cambridge Journal of International and Comparative Law
CLJ	Cambridge Law Journal
Crawford, First Report	J. Crawford, First Report on State Responsibility, YbILC (1998), vol. II/1, 1
Crawford, Second Report	J. Crawford, Second Report on State Responsibility, YbILC (1999), vol. II/1, 3
Crawford, Third Report	J. Crawford, Third Report on State Responsibility, YbILC (2000), vol. II/1, 3
Crawford, Fourth Report	J. Crawford, Fourth Report on State Responsibility, YbILC (2001), vol. II/1, 1
CSCE	Conference on Security and Cooperation in Europe
CTS	Consolidated Treaty Series
CYIL	Canadian Yearbook of International Law
DARIO	ILC Draft Articles on the Responsibility of International Organizations, ILC Report (2011), UN Doc. A/66/10, 54
DARIO Commentary	Commentary to the ILC Draft Articles on the Responsibility of International Organizations, ILC Report (2011), UN Doc. A/66/10, 69
Dept. of State Bulletin	Department of State Bulletin (US)
Diss. Op.	Dissenting Opinion
Draft Articles [1996]	ILC Draft Articles on Responsibility of States for Internationally Wrongful Acts, as adopted on first reading in 1996, ILC Report (1996), UN Doc. A/51/10, 58

Draft Articles Commentary	Commentary to the ILC Draft Articles on Responsibility of States for Internationally Wrongful Acts, as adopted on first reading in 1996:

	Art. 1	YbILC (1973), vol. II, 173
	Art. 3	YbILC (1973), vol. II, 179
	Art. 19	YbILC (1976), vol. II/2, 95
	Art. 30	YbILC (1979), vol. II/2, 115
	Art. 37	YbILC (1983), vol. II/2, 42
	Art. 39	YbILC (1983), vol. II/2, 43
	Art. 40	YbILC (1985), vol. II/2, 25
	Arts. 47–48	YbILC (1996), vol. II/2, 65
	Arts. 49–50	YbILC (1995), vol. II/2, 64
	Arts. 51–53	YbILC (1996), vol. II/2, 65
	Art. 58	YbILC (1995), vol. II/2, 78

DRC	Democratic Republic of the Congo
Dugard, First Report	J. Dugard, First Report on Diplomatic Protection, YbILC (2000), vol. II/1, 205
EC	European Community
EC Bull.	Bulletin of the European Community
ECHR	European Convention for the Protection of Human Rights and Fundamental Freedoms, 4 November 1950, 213 UNTS 221
ECOWAS	Economic Community of West African States
ECtHR	European Court of Human Rights
ed(s).	edition/editor(s)
EEC	European Economic Community
EJIL	European Journal of International Law
EU	European Union
EU Bull.	Bulletin of the European Union
FCN	Friendship, Commerce and Navigation (treaties)
FCO	Foreign and Commonwealth Office
Fitzmaurice, Second Report	G. Fitzmaurice, Second Report on the Law of Treaties, YbILC (1957), vol. II, 16
Fitzmaurice, Fourth Report	G. Fitzmaurice, Fourth Report on the Law of Treaties, YbILC (1959), vol. II, 37
FRY	Federal Republic of Yugoslavia
FYROM	Former Yugoslav Republic of Macedonia
G7	Group of 7
G77	Group of 77
GA	United Nations General Assembly

GATS	General Agreement on Trade in Services, Marrakesh Agreement Establishing the World Trade Organization, Annex 1B, 15 April 1994, 1869 UNTS 183
GATT	General Agreement on Tariffs and Trade, Marrakesh Agreement Establishing the World Trade Organization, Annex 1A, 15 April 1994, 1867 UNTS 187 (GATT 1994); 30 October 1947, 55 UNTS 187 (GATT 1947)
GYIL	German Yearbook of International Law
HILJ	Harvard International Law Journal
HRC	Human Rights Council (United Nations)
HRQ	Human Rights Quarterly
ICAO	International Civil Aviation Organization
ICC	International Criminal Court
ICCPR	International Covenant on Civil and Political Rights, 16 December 1966, 999 UNTS 171
ICESCR	International Covenant on Economic, Social and Cultural Rights, 16 December 1966, 993 UNTS 3
ICJ	International Court of Justice
ICJ Rep.	Reports of Judgments, Advisory Opinions and Orders of the International Court of Justice
ICJ Statute	Statute of the International Court of Justice, 26 June 1945, 15 UNCIO 355
ICLQ	International and Comparative Law Quarterly
ICSID	International Centre for the Settlement of Investment Disputes
ICTY	International Criminal Tribunal for the Former Yugoslavia
IDI	Institute of International Law (Institut de droit international):

> IDI, 1880 Oxford Resolution, 'Manuel des lois de la guerre sur terre', available at www.justitiaet pace.org
>
> IDI, 1887 Heidelberg Resolution, 'Déclaration concernant le blocus en dehors de l'état de guerre', available at www.justitiaetpace.org
>
> IDI, 1934 Paris Resolution, 'Régime des représailles en temps de paix', available at www.justitiaet pace.org

	IDI, 1989 Santiago de Compostela Resolution, 'The Protection of Human Rights and the Principle of Non-Intervention in Internal Affairs of States', available at www.justitiaetpace.org
	IDI, 2005 Krakow Resolution, 'Obligations *Erga Omnes* in International Law', available at www.justitiaetpace.org
IJMCL	International Journal of Marine and Coastal Law
ILC	International Law Commission
ILC Report	Annual Report of the International Law Commission
ILM	International Legal Materials
ITLOS	International Tribunal for the Law of the Sea
IYIL	Italian Yearbook of International Law
JCSL	Journal of Conflict and Security Law
Keesing's	Keesing's Contemporary Archives / Keesing's Record of World Events
LJIL	Leiden Journal of International Law
LNOJ	League of Nations Official Journal
LNTS	League of Nations Treaty Series
Mich. JIL	Michigan Journal of International Law
NAFTA	North American Free Trade Agreement
NATO	North Atlantic Treaty Organization
NILR	Netherlands International Law Review
NYIL	Netherlands Yearbook of International Law
NYJILP	New York University Journal of International Law and Politics
OAS	Organization of American States
OAU	Organization of African Unity (now AU)
OIC	Organisation of Islamic Cooperation (previously Organization of the Islamic Conference)
OJ	Official Journal (European Union)
OSCE	Organization for Security and Co-operation in Europe
ÖZÖR	Österreichische Zeitschrift für Öffentliches Recht
PCIJ	Permanent Court of International Justice
QIL	Questions of International Law
RBDI	Revue belge de droit international
RdC	Recueil des cours de l'Académie de droit international de la Haye
RDI	Rivista di diritto internazionale

RDILC	Revue de droit international et de législation comparée
Res.	Resolution
RGDIP	Revue générale de droit international public
RIAA	United Nations Reports of International Arbitral Awards
Riphagen, Preliminary Report	W. Riphagen, Preliminary Report on State Responsibility, YbILC (1980), vol. II/1, 107
Riphagen, Second Report	W. Riphagen, Second Report on State Responsibility, YbILC (1981), vol. II/1, 79
Riphagen, Third Report	W. Riphagen, Third Report on State Responsibility, YbILC (1982), vol. II/1, 22
Riphagen, Fourth Report	W. Riphagen, Fourth Report on State Responsibility, YbILC (1983), vol. II/1, 3
Riphagen, Fifth Report	W. Riphagen, Fifth Report on State Responsibility, YbILC (1984), vol. II/1, 1
Riphagen, Sixth Report	W. Riphagen, Sixth Report on State Responsibility, YbILC (1985), vol. II/1, 1
Riphagen, Seventh Report	W. Riphagen, Seventh Report on State Responsibility, YbILC (1986), vol. II/1, 1
SADC	Southern African Development Community
SC	United Nations Security Council
SELA	Latin American and Caribbean Economic System (Sistema Económico Latinoamericano y del Caribe)
Sep. Op.	Separate Opinion
SFRY	Socialist Federal Republic of Yugoslavia
Sixth Committee	UN General Assembly, Sixth (Legal) Committee
UK	United Kingdom
UN	United Nations
UNC	Charter of the United Nations, 26 June 1945
UNCC	United Nations Compensation Commission
UNCHR	Commission on Human Rights (United Nations)
UNCLOS	United Nations Convention on the Law of the Sea, 10 December 1982, 1833 UNTS 3
UNHCHR	United Nations High Commissioner for Human Rights
UNJY	United Nations Juridical Yearbook
UNTS	United Nations Treaty Series
UNYB	United Nations Yearbook
US	United States
U.S.C.	United States Code

USD	United States dollar
VCCR	Vienna Convention on Consular Relations, 24 April 1963, 596 UNTS 261
VCDR	Vienna Convention on Diplomatic Relations, 18 April 1961, 500 UNTS 95
VCLT	Vienna Convention on the Law of Treaties, 23 May 1969, 1155 UNTS 331
VJIL	Virginia Journal of International Law
VJTL	Vanderbilt Journal of Transnational Law
Waldock, Second Report	H. Waldock, Second Report on the Law of Treaties, YbILC (1963), vol. II, 36
Wood, Second Report	M. Wood, Second Report on Identification of Customary International Law, 22 May 2014, UN Doc. A/CN.4/672
Wood, Third Report	M. Wood, Third Report on Identification of Customary International Law, 27 March 2015, UN Doc. A/CN.4/682
Wood, Fourth Report	M. Wood, Fourth Report on Identification of Customary International Law, 8 March 2016, UN Doc. A/CN.4/695
WTO	World Trade Organization
Yale LJ	Yale Law Journal
YbECHR	Yearbook of the European Convention of Human Rights
YbILC	Yearbook of the International Law Commission
ZaöRV	Zeitschrift für ausländisches öffentliches Recht und Völkerrecht

1

Introduction

1.1 The Object of the Study

Modern international law has witnessed the emergence of a fledgling multilateral public order based not so much on logic as 'some mixture of hope and experience'.[1] Indeed the general life of the law in the international system (as in the municipal system) is not logic but experience – even if, in this particular case, the amount of that experience is limited and mixed with a great deal of hope. The construction of a multilateral public order is based on the hope that law – more precisely, the law of State responsibility – would come to play an increasingly important role in the settlement of collective problems.[2] Experience nonetheless shows that tools of communitarian law enforcement are limited and highly contested. Moreover, even insofar as they do exist, they are rarely used. So has this multilateral construction been based merely on normative means?[3] Might Shakespeare's King Claudius have exclaimed, 'My words fly up, my thoughts remain below: Words without thoughts never to heaven go'?[4] What – if anything – can States do 'between war and words'[5] in defence of multilateral public order when confronted with massive human rights violations and other international crises?

Judicial or quasi-judicial means of settlement – even when available under human rights treaties – are rarely (if ever) used. The inter-State complaint procedure under Article 41 ICCPR has never been used and

---

[1] Crawford (2012), 591–593 (with further references).
[2] Compare UN Doc. A/C.6/56/SR.14, 5, para. 28 (Greece).
[3] See YbILC (2000), vol. I, 311, para. 78 (Mr. Brownlie); ILC Report (2000), UN Doc. A/55/10, 60, para. 365 ('developments in the international legal order depended on progress in the international community and not just in the development of norms'). Compare Crawford (2013a), 362 (noting that the Roman scheme of society and law famously expressed in Cicero's maxim (*Ubi societas, ibi jus*) may have been reversed – that is, 'international law develops more rapidly than international society does').
[4] Shakespeare, *Hamlet*, Act 3, Scene 3.
[5] UN Doc. A/59/2005, Report of the Secretary-General, *In Larger Freedom: Towards Development, Security and Human Rights for All*, 30, para. 109.

remains a dead letter: the enforcement mechanism in the ICCPR appears to be in serious need of CPR.[6] What is more, even if somehow resuscitated, it is no Sleeping Beauty: the 'sad reality' is that enforcement mechanisms in many human rights treaties are optional, cumbersome and ineffective.[7] As for the ICJ, States have rarely knocked on the door of the Court to enforce a communitarian norm, and even when they have done so, the Court has been reluctant to open it. Indeed the ICJ has only once opened its door to a claim involving the enforcement of a communitarian norm.[8] The Grotian notion of humanitarian intervention – whatever its pre-Charter status – is widely regarded today as unlawful.[9] The notion of the responsibility to protect is little more than a rhetorical device.[10] The enforcement mechanism in Chapter VII UNC is highly contingent: the UN Security Council has considerable (albeit not unlimited)[11] discretion to respond to breaches of communitarian norms and – given the limitations of its institutional design – it is (too) often paralyzed by political disagreements.[12] Thus it has been observed that 'leaving it up to the "organized international community", i.e. the United Nations, to react to breaches of obligations *erga omnes* border[s]

---

[6] See 'Human Rights Bodies – Complaints Procedures', Office of the High Commissioner for Human Rights, www.ohchr.org/EN/HRBodies/TBPetitions/Pages/HRTBPetitions .aspx#interstate. Compare *Obligation to Prosecute or Extradite*, ICJ Rep. (2012), 422 at 484, para. 20 (Sep. Op. Judge Skotnikov).

[7] Meron (2003), 298; Tams (2011), 383–384. Also: 1989 IDI Santiago de Compostela Resolution (Art. 7).

[8] See *Obligation to Prosecute or Extradite*, ICJ Rep. (2012), 422; and further Section 2.1.

[9] For limited support see UN Doc. S/PV.3988 (23 March 1999), 12 (United Kingdom); *Legality of Use of Force (Yugoslavia v. Belgium)*, Provisional Measures, ICJ Rep. (1999), 124, Verbatim Record, 10 May 1999, CR.1999/15, 15–17 (Belgium); 'Chemical weapon use by Syrian regime: UK government legal position' (29 Aug. 2013), www.gov.uk/ government/publications/chemical-weapon-use-by-syrian-regime-uk-government-legal-position; and already Grotius (1646), Book II, Chapters XX, §40, XXV, §8. For widespread opposition see UN Docs. S/PV.3988 (24 March 1999), 12–13 (China), 13 (Russia), 15 (Belarus), 15–16 (India); S/PV.3989 (26 March 1999), 5 (Russia), 9 (China), 16 (India); Declaration on the Occasion of the Twenty-Third Annual Ministerial Meeting of the Group of 77 (New York, 24 Sept. 1999), para. 69, www .g77.org/doc/Decl1999.html. Also: *Nicaragua* case, ICJ Rep. (1986), 14 at 134–135, para. 268. Further: Brownlie (1963), 338–342; Chesterman (2001); Lowe and Tzanakopoulos (2011); Crawford (2012), 752–754 (all with many further references).

[10] See GA Res. 60/1 (16 Sept. 2005) (2005 World Summit Outcome), paras. 138–139; SC Res. 1674 (28 Apr. 2006); SC Res. 1373 (17 March 2011). Further: Stahn (2007), 99; Crawford (2013b), 355–357; Zifcak (2014), 509.

[11] See e.g. Frowein and Krisch (2002), 719–720 MN 4–5 (with further references).

[12] See e.g. UN Doc. A/59/565 (2 Dec. 2004), *A More Secure World: Our Shared Responsibility*, Report of the High-Level Panel on Threats, Challenges and Change, 56–57, paras. 197, 202.

on cynicism'.[13] Instead it seems that States frequently react by way of third-party countermeasures.

The third-party countermeasures taken by Western States against Russia in response to its military intervention in Ukraine provide a recent example.[14] The humanitarian calamity in Syria provides another apt reminder: the Security Council has repeatedly vetoed draft resolutions authorizing the adoption of non-military sanctions against Syria for the many atrocities President Al-Assad's regime stands accused.[15] This has not prevented the EU, the League of Arab States and many others from taking third-party countermeasures against Syria. In January 2012, France criticized the 'scandalous silence' of the Security Council. It explained:

> Of course, we have continued our efforts despite the Council's silence. The European Union has 11 times increased the sanctions on the [Syrian] regime and its leaders ... However, the actions of the European Union or the Arab League, no matter how resolute, cannot replace action by the Council.[16]

In the last decade, the Security Council has also vetoed the adoption of non-military sanctions against Burma and Zimbabwe for the continuing serious human rights abuses taking place there.[17] In all these cases (as in many others), States have responded in a multitude of ways, including by way of third-party countermeasures.

The following questions arise: does international law allow individual States to act as self-appointed guardians of communitarian norms by way of third-party countermeasures? And if so, what are the safeguards against abuse? The object of this study is to answer these questions. The issues raised concern one of the great, unresolved questions of contemporary international law.[18]

1.2 Sources of Controversy

The terminology of countermeasures is relatively recent, but the concept itself (under the traditional term 'reprisals', to which I will return below)

---

[13] YbILC (2000), vol. I, 305, para. 31 (Mr. Simma). Similarly: YbILC (2001), vol. I, 41, para. 49 (Mr. Pellet).
[14] See further Section 4.2.21.   [15] See further Section 4.2.20.
[16] UN Doc. S/PV.6710 (31 Jan. 2012), 15 (France).
[17] See further Sections 4.2.16 and 4.2.17.
[18] Compare Tams (2011), 390 ('one of contemporary international law's great debates'). Also: Alland (2002), 1223 ('one of the more crucial questions in the development of public international law').

refers to a form of unilateral measure of self-help which has long been recognized as a feature of a decentralized international system in which the judicial settlement of disputes is still not guaranteed and injured States may take otherwise unlawful action against the responsible State in order to seek enforcement of their rights.[19] Still, as a unilateral self-help measure which entitles the State to act as judge and sheriff in its own cause, countermeasures are ripe with the potential for abuse, and this potential is exacerbated by the factual inequalities between States.[20]

The first modern reprisals date back to Ancient Greece. The Megarian Decree of 433/32 BC entailed the imposition of a trade embargo by the Athenian Empire and its leader Pericles on Megara, an ally of Sparta, in response to a trumped-up charge of illegality; it appears the real reason was to pressure Megara to abandon its military alliance with Sparta. The trade embargo barred the Megarians from the ports of the Athenian Empire and the market of Athens, resulting in the economic strangulation of Megara and starvation among its population. It is widely recognized that the Megarian Decree was a significant factor in triggering the Second Peloponnesian War (431–404 BC).[21] The distant echoes of Thucydides' realist account of the Melian Dialogue of 416 BC relating to the lessons of that war – 'the strong do what they can and the weak suffer what they must'[22] – still reverberate. Thus it is not surprising that, in more recent times, the topic of countermeasures – and especially its modern congener, third-party countermeasures – is extremely

---

[19] See 1934 IDI Paris Resolution (preamble); ARSIWA Commentary, Introductory Commentary to Chapter II of Part Three, §1; Art. 52, §2. This basic rationale for countermeasures can be traced back to at least da Legnano (1360), 307, who (following Bartolus) explained that reprisals were necessary as a 'subsidiary remedy' in the event of a denial of justice. Further: Grewe (2000), 116–118; Grabher O'Brien (2002), 25.

[20] See ARSIWA Commentary, Art. 22, §2; Introductory Commentary to Chapter II of Part Three, §2 (with further references); Topical Summary of Government Comments in the Sixth Committee, UN Doc. A/CN.4/513 (2000), 29, paras. 149–150. Also: Dickinson (1920), 269–274; Simpson (2004), 45–47, 57.

[21] The Megarian Decree was a blunt and ineffective instrument that did not achieve its aims; the war that ensued was a complete disaster for Athens. Further: Aristophanes, *The Acharnians* (425 BC), ln. 530–543 (ridiculing Pericles for having 'enacted laws, which sounded like drinking songs, "That the Megarians must leave our land, our market, our sea and our continent"'); Kagan (1969), 251–272; Hufbauer, Schott and Elliot (1990), 4–5; Lowe and Tzanakopoulos (2013), paras. 4–6.

[22] Thucydides, *The History of the Peloponnesian War* (trans. R. Crawley and R.C. Feetham, Avon, CT: Cardavon Press, 1974), Book V, 294. The dialogue did not have a happy ending: the men of Melos were executed, and the women and children sold into slavery. See also Crawford (2013b), 27–28 (discussing the realist challenge to international law ever since the Melian Dialogue).

controversial: it is inextricably linked to an ignominious past indelibly marked by empire, power politics and gunboat diplomacy.[23]

The topic of reprisals was discussed in many classical texts based on an underlying (if somewhat crude) conception of legal responsibility; however, discussions about basic principles of State responsibility in any recognizable modern form only emerged in the literature from the mid-nineteenth century onwards.[24] These writings on State responsibility were mostly concerned with the practical question of their time; namely, the treatment of aliens within the territory of the host State.[25] In addition to the technically distinct category of a formal state of war, various modes of redress by way of forcible self-help (known as 'measures short of war')[26] were subsumed – without a clear distinction between them – under the broad rubric of 'intervention' covering such notions as pacific blockades, hostile embargoes and reprisals.[27] The nineteenth century was 'the classic epoch of reprisals',[28] which often took the form of gunboat diplomacy.[29]

The infamous practice of gunboat diplomacy often involved the use of armed reprisals by the Great European Powers purportedly seeking to enforce the law on the treatment of aliens by way of diplomatic protection.[30] The so-called Don Pacifico affair of 1850 – in which the

---

[23] See Colbert (1948), 60–103; Brownlie (1963), 28–37; Grewe (2000), 525–530 (for a review of State practice during the nineteenth and early twentieth century). Also: Jennings (1961), 157–159; Crawford (2013a), 684.

[24] See Brownlie (1983), 1–9. Generally: Crawford (2013a), 3–44 (with many further references).

[25] Brownlie (1983), 8–9. This focus on the treatment of aliens and their property remained in the ILC's early work on the law of State responsibility until the Ago revolution of the 1960s: see further Section 3.1.

[26] See e.g. Hall (1890), 361; Westlake (1913), Pt. II, 1; Brownlie (1963), 45–47. Also: Oppenheim (1905), Vol. II, 29.

[27] See generally Brownlie (1963), 26–40, 44–47, 50, 219–225, 344 (at ibid., 47, noting the *ex post facto* and illogical nature of these classifications characterized by a 'hopeless confusion of terminology'). Similarly: Westlake (1913), Pt. II, 6; Parry (1938), 682–683; Jennings (1961), 158. Further: 1887 IDI Heidelberg Resolution; Hall (1890), 361–373; Rivier (1896), Vol. II, 189–199; Hogan (1908); Lawrence (1911), 334–344; Stowell (1921); Fauchille (1926), Pt. III, 685–713; 1934 IDI Paris Resolution (Art. 3); Neff (2005), 215–249; Farrall (2007), 47–52.

[28] de Visscher (1968), 296. Also: Colbert (1948), 60 (n. 1).

[29] See Bradford (2006), 574–575 (on the term 'gunboat diplomacy'). Some twenty pacific blockades were adopted from 1827 to 1927 almost exclusively by the Great European Powers against weaker ones: see Giraud M., 'A Memorandum on Pacific Blockade up to the Time of the Foundation of the League of Nations', LNOJ (July 1927), App. II, 841 (for a complete list of practice). Further: Hogan (1908).

[30] Compare Phillimore (1857), Vol. III, 12 ('It most commonly happens that *Reprisals* are resorted to for the purpose of redressing injuries inflicted upon the right of Individuals')

United Kingdom imposed a naval blockade on Piraeus following Greece's refusal to compensate a British subject for injuries inflicted by a violent mob – provides a notorious example.[31] Many other examples of gunboat diplomacy by powerful Western States during this period, especially against weaker countries in Latin America and East Asia, could also be mentioned.[32] In 1902–1903, a coalition of three European States (Great Britain, Germany and Italy) imposed a naval blockade and bombardment of Venezuelan ports in response to a controversy which arose over certain pecuniary claims of their subjects against Venezuela.[33] The incident prompted the Argentinean Foreign Minister, Luis María Drago, to request the diplomatic support of the United States based on the principle that public debts could not be enforced by military force – known as the Drago Doctrine.[34] A modified version of the doctrine influenced the first (albeit modest) step away from abusive uses of armed reprisals: the 1907 Hague Peace Conference adopted a multilateral treaty (the Drago-Porter Convention) prohibiting the employment of force for the recovery of contract debts unless an attempt to settle the dispute by international arbitration had failed.[35]

The use of force was gradually curtailed during the inter-war period (notably in the Covenant of the League of Nations and the

---

(emphasis in original); Borchard (1915), 331 (noting 'the all too frequent abuse, by strong States, of the rights of weaker countries' by way of armed reprisals); Hindmarsh (1932), 320 ('Under the guise or pretext of seeking redress for an international delinquency, states have resorted to the use of embargoes, pacific blockades, seizures of property, occupation of territory, bombardments, and intimidation by display or threat of force'); Colbert (1948), 61, 64–68.

[31] See Oppenheim (1905), Vol. II, 36; Colbert (1948), 69–71; Grewe (2000), 526; Paulsson (2005), 15–17. Further: Great Britain-Greece, Convention for the Settlement of Claims (18 July 1850), 104 CTS 159; Phillimore (1857), Vol. III, 29–33; Hogan (1908), 105–114; Ralston (1929), 228. It was doubtful whether Greece had actually committed a wrongful act since Mr. Pacifico had not even sought to exhaust local remedies: see e.g. Phillimore (1857), Vol. III, 29–33; Rivier (1896), Vol. II, 197; Oppenheim (1905), Vol. II, 36; Colbert (1948), 70; Brownlie (1963), 220 (n. 3).

[32] See generally Colbert (1948), 60–103; Brownlie (1963), 28–37; Grewe (2000), 525–530.

[33] The underlying dispute was ultimately settled by arbitration on terms favourable to the blockading powers: see *The Venezuelan Preferential Case (Germany, Great Britain and Italy v. Venezuela)* (1904), RIAA, vol. IX, 99. Further: Basdevant (1904), 362; Jennings (1961), 159; Brownlie (1963), 35–36.

[34] See Drago (1907), 692; Benedek (2007). Further: Hershey (1907), 26.

[35] See Convention respecting the Limitation of the Employment of Force for the Recovery of Contract Debts (The Hague, adopted 18 Oct. 1907, entry into force 26 Jan. 1910) (Art. 1), 205 CTS 250. Further: Brown (1908), 78; Borchard (1915), 308–332; Benedek (2007).

Kellogg-Briand Pact),[36] but the legal status of armed reprisals in situations other than those contemplated in the Drago-Porter Convention was somewhat unclear.[37] In 1923, the Italian Navy bombarded and occupied Corfu in response to the assassination of Italian officials in Greece by way of reprisals. A Special Commission of Jurists was established by the Council of the League of Nations to determine whether such armed reprisals were consistent with Articles 12 to 15 of the Covenant of the League of Nations. The Commission provided a cryptic answer: armed reprisals 'may or may not be consistent' with the Covenant.[38] A proposal by Sweden to add some clarity on the matter by referring it to the PCIJ for an advisory opinion was unsuccessful.[39] The legal situation has since changed dramatically. In the modern period, the general prohibition of the unilateral use of force embodied in the UN Charter unambiguously excluded recourse to armed reprisals – a point repeatedly reaffirmed in categorical terms.[40] Still, these normative developments have only partially alleviated concerns about the possible role of third-party countermeasures in contemporary international relations.

The situation of colonial days is no longer relevant, and the use of force is generally prohibited; but the light which history shines on the topic is a lantern on the stern that nonetheless continues to 'colour the whole international approach to countermeasures'.[41] This light has illuminated but, at times, also blinded or even obscured the modern approach to countermeasures – especially, third-party countermeasures. This is perhaps not surprising given the passions stirred

---

[36] Covenant of the League of Nations (entry into force 10 Jan. 1920) (Arts. 10–16), 225 CTS 195; General Treaty for the Renunciation of War as an Instrument of National Policy (entry into force 5 July 1929) (Arts. I-II), 94 LNTS 57.

[37] See e.g. *Naulilaa (Responsibility of Germany for damage caused in the Portuguese colonies in the south of Africa) (Portugal/Germany)* (1928), RIAA, vol. II, 1011 at 1025–1028; Brownlie (1963), 84–92, 222 (with further references); Draft Articles Commentary, Art. 30, §10 (n. 589). Also: Giraud M., 'A Memorandum on Pacific Blockade up to the Time of the Foundation of the League of Nations', LNOJ (July 1927), App. II, 841–845 (with many further references). Compare 1934 IDI Paris Resolution (preamble; Arts. 3–4); de Visscher (1924), 382. For criticism of armed reprisals as a somewhat artificial category of justification, see e.g. Westlake (1913), Pt. II, 18; Brierly (1932), 308–309.

[38] See 'Interpretation of Certain Articles of the Covenant and Other Questions of International Law: Report of the Special Commission of Jurists', 5 LNOJ (Apr. 1924), 523 at 524. Further: Wright (1924), 536; de Visscher (1924), 213, 387; Politis (1924), 5; Strupp (1924), 255; Fauchille (1926), Pt. III, 695–696; Colbert (1948), 81–87; Brownlie (1963), 220–222; Neff (2005), 298–300.

[39] See 5 LNOJ (Apr. 1924), 523 at 525 (Mr. Branting).   [40] See further Section 6.2.1.1.

[41] YbILC (2000), vol. I, 282, para. 46 (Mr. Sreenivasa Rao).

by experience. In the *Barcelona Traction* case, Judge Padilla Nervo summed it up thus:

> The history of the responsibility of States in respect to the treatment of foreign nationals is the history of abuses, illegal interference in the domestic jurisdiction of weaker States, unjust claims, threats and even military aggression under the flag of exercising rights of protection, and the imposing of sanctions in order to oblige a government to make the reparations demanded.[42]

Critics have raised several policy objections against third-party countermeasures. They have notably feared that third-party counter-measures would provide a 'further pretext for power politics in international relations' contrary to the traditional principle that countermeasures can only be taken by States directly injured by an internationally wrongful act.[43] In particular, they have expressed the concern that third-party countermeasures might be used as a pretext for the adoption of unilateral measures such as armed reprisals and other forms of intervention.[44] Thus it is said that legal recognition of third-party countermeasures would add a new and dangerous category of justification that might eventually extend to the use of force – a development which would threaten the collective security system of the UN Charter and provide a superficial legitimacy for the bullying of small States on the claim that human rights or other communitarian norms must be respected.[45]

The modern practice of unilateral humanitarian intervention and implied UN Security Council authorization as alleged justification for the use of force appears to have reinforced these concerns. For example, during the debate in the Sixth Committee, Cameroon, seemingly alarmed by the unilateral action taken by Western States against the FRY during the Kosovo crisis, expressed concern that recognition of third-party countermeasures would create overlapping legal regimes that

---

[42] *Barcelona Traction*, ICJ Rep. (1970), 3 at 246 (Sep. Op. Judge Padilla Nervo). See also Dugard, First Report, 212; ADP Commentary, Art. 1, §8.

[43] Topical Summary of Government Comments in the Sixth Committee, UN Doc. A/CN.4/513 (2000), 33, para. 175. Further: UN Doc. A/CN.4/515, 69–70 (China).

[44] Topical Summary of Government Comments in the Sixth Committee, UN Doc. A/CN.4/513 (2000), 29, para. 149.

[45] See e.g. YbILC (2001), vol. I, 35, para. 2 (Mr. Brownlie); Koskenniemi (2001), 340; and further Section 3.2.1.3(i). Also: Brownlie (1963), 220.

could weaken the [UN] as a whole or marginalize the Security Council, particularly in the light of the recent and disturbing tendency of some States to take action, including armed intervention, without the Council's consent.[46]

In February 2013, Russia officially adopted foreign policy guidelines that, in relevant part, state:

Another risk to world peace and stability is presented by attempts to manage crises through unilateral sanctions and other coercive measures, including armed aggression, outside the framework of the Security Council.[47]

Russia appears to suggest that the adoption of third-party counter-measures outside the framework of the Security Council would even be a 'risk to world peace'. At a minimum, others have objected that the relationship between the Security Council and third-party countermeasures is unclear.[48]

Critics have also expressed the closely related concern that third-party countermeasures – even if limited to non-forcible means of enforcement – might encourage ill-founded or spurious actions based on ulterior motives. Such actions would pose a serious threat to sovereignty by way of coercive interference with the *domaine réservé* of target States contrary to the principle of non-intervention.[49] The said principle is 'one of the most potent and elusive of all international principles',[50] and this is especially so in the controversial debate on third-party countermeasures.

---

[46] UN Doc. A/C.6/55/SR.24, 11, para. 64 (Cameroon); Topical Summary of Government Comments in the Sixth Committee, UN Doc. A/CN.4/513 (2000), 33, para. 176. See further Section 3.2.1.3(ii).

[47] 'Concept of the Foreign Policy of the Russian Federation' (12 Feb. 2013) (unofficial translation), para. 15, http://archive.mid.ru/ns-osndoc.nsf/osnddeng. In the words of President Putin, 'unilateral sanctions that circumvent the United Nations Charter have almost become the norm': UN Doc. A/70/PV.13 (28 Sept. 2015), 26 (Russia). See also 'The Declaration of the Russian Federation and the People's Republic of China on the Promotion of International Law' (25 June 2016), para. 6, http://www.mid.ru/en/foreign_policy/news/-/asset_publisher/cKNonkJE02Bw/content/id/2331698 ('The adoption of unilateral coercive measures by States in addition to measures adopted by the United Nations Security Council can defeat the objects and purposes of measures imposed by the Security Council, and undermine their integrity and effectiveness').

[48] See Topical Summary of Government Comments in the Sixth Committee, UN Doc. A/CN.4/513 (2000), 35, para. 190; Crawford (2013a), 706; and further Section 3.2.1.3(ii).

[49] See above n. 45. For a definition of prohibited intervention see *Nicaragua* case, ICJ Rep. (1986), 14 at 108, 126, paras. 205, 245. Generally: Jennings and Watts (1996), 427–430, §128. Jamnejad and Wood (2009), 345; Ziegler (2012).

[50] Lowe (2007) 104.

In the Sixth Committee, Botswana observed a 'glaring problem': third-party countermeasures were 'open to abuse by powerful States against a weaker State that they might particularly dislike for other reasons'.[51] More specifically, the key implication is seemingly that recognition of third-party countermeasures might facilitate 'the exploitation and distortion of human rights issues as a means of interference in the internal affairs of States'.[52] Target States have regularly protested that the adoption of third-party countermeasures against them – supposedly 'in the name of certain noble doctrines or ideals'[53] – is merely a thinly veiled 'political tool'[54] based on 'trumped-up claims'[55] and 'unavowed objectives'.[56] These problems are compounded by the indeterminacy of communitarian norms (the content of the category of obligations *erga omnes* being far from settled), which invites further abuse of third-party countermeasures.[57] It thus seems that serious concerns about a possible erosion of the basic organizing principles of non-use of force, collective security and non-intervention largely explain the normative pull away from the legitimation of third-party countermeasures as a possible means of enforcement for communitarian norms.

Commentators have warned that a regulation of third-party counter-measures would constitute a '*lex horrenda*'.[58] It has been claimed that 'the stability of the international legal order would be threatened'[59] by legitimizing third-party countermeasures. Crawford has cautioned that empowering States to take third-party countermeasures 'could generate pernicious effects for political stability and undermine the function of international law as a system that regulates interstate relations'.[60] Put differently, in the words of Brownlie, 'in certain political circumstances, the result may be to give the appearance of legitimacy to questionable

---

[51] UN Doc. A/C.6/55/SR.15, 10, para. 63 (Botswana). Compare Topical Summary of Government Comments in the Sixth Committee, UN Doc. A/CN.4/513 (2000), 27–28, para. 144.

[52] GA Res. 36/103 (9 Dec. 1981), Principle II(l). See also Section 6.1.3.1.

[53] UN Doc. S/PV.3692 (28 Aug. 1996), 6 (Burundi).

[54] UN Docs. A/66/138 (14 July 2011), 11 (Burma); A/HRC/20/G/3 (15 June 2012) (Syria); A/68/211 (22 July 2013), 6 (Syria). See further Sections 4.2.16 and 4.2.20.

[55] UN Doc. S/2012/242 (Belarus). Also: UN Doc. S/2008/199 (Cuba on behalf of the Non-Aligned Movement). See further Section 4.2.18.

[56] UN Docs. S/PV.3692 (28 Aug. 1996), 3–5; S/1996/788, 2 (Burundi). See further Sections 4.2.13; 6.1.3.1; and 6.2.

[57] See Topical Summary of Government Comments in the Sixth Committee, UN Doc. A/CN.4/513 (2000), 26, 33, paras. 137, 175. Further: Sections 3.2.1.3(ii) and 5.2.6.

[58] YbILC (2001) vol. I, 35, para. 2 (Mr. Brownlie).   [59] Hutchinson (1988), 202.

[60] Crawford (2012), 584 (and also 589).

policies based on objectives collateral to the enforcement of the law'.[61] It is further suggested in sibylline terms that legitimizing third-party countermeasures would be 'an invitation to chaos' which would result in 'mob-justice', 'the rule of the jungle' and 'vigilantism'.[62] In short, 'under the banner of law, chaos and violence would come to reign among states'.[63]

Others have supported third-party countermeasures as a 'useful and necessary' tool of law enforcement for communitarian norms and an 'essential consequence' of their breach without which States would be 'powerless' to defend multilateral public order, given the limitations of the UN Security Council in doing so.[64] The essentially Austinian argument has been made that the emergence of a multilateral public order would be meaningless without effective tools of enforcement such as third-party countermeasures. For example, Gaja has observed:

> The risk of States making an improper use of counter-measures cannot be discarded, but the alternative may well be that common interests of international society are not protected by law. Were States not even allowed to adopt counter-measures that are otherwise lawful, one would probably have to conclude that law rather protects the infringements of those interests.[65]

Third-party countermeasures have been considered a 'significant factor' in making obligations *erga omnes* 'more effective'.[66] Similarly, Fox has argued that third-party countermeasures should be given legal recognition as otherwise the value of obligations *erga omnes* would be reduced to a 'moral exhortation'; the availability of third-party countermeasures providing a 'litmus paper' as to the whole value of obligations *erga omnes*.[67] Others have made statements to the same effect.[68]

---

[61] Brownlie (2008), 515. Similarly: Crawford (2012), 603.

[62] Jimenez de Aréchaga (1978), 275; Marek (1978–1979), 481; YbILC (1983), vol. I, 143, paras. 27–28 (Mr. McCaffrey); Graefrath (1984), 68; McCaffrey (1989), 244; YbILC (2000), vol. I, 277, para. 6 (Mr. Kateka).

[63] Weil (1983), 433.

[64] ILC Report (2001), UN Doc. A/56/10, 23, para. 54. Between 1945 and 1992, the United Nations was 'rendered powerless' to act in most international crises because of a total of 249 vetoes cast in the Security Council: see An Agenda for Peace, Report of the Secretary-General, UN Doc. A/47/277-S/2411 (17 June 1992), 4, para. 14. The Council may since have become more active, but the examples of Burma, Belarus, Zimbabwe, Syria and Russia (among others) demonstrate that the cogency of this argument remains largely intact (on which see generally Chapter 4).

[65] Gaja (1989), 156. See also Gaja (2005), 148.   [66] Gaja (2013), 130.

[67] Fox (2005), 158–159.

[68] See e.g. Frowein (1994), 423; YbILC (2001), vol. I, 107, para. 24 (Mr. Pellet); Alland (2002), 1239; Meron (2003), 288; Tomuschat (2005), 162; Villalpando (2005), 371, 410;

The hope has also been expressed that a regime of non-forcible third-party countermeasures could be a viable alternative to the use of force to induce a return to legality; in other words, legitimizing third-party countermeasures 'might have the effect of reducing the risk of a spillover into military sanctions'.[69] Disallowing third-party countermeasures 'may place further pressure on States to intervene in other, perhaps less desirable ways', notably by way of humanitarian intervention.[70] Simply put, international law should offer to States some means of securing compliance with communitarian norms which does not involve the use of force.[71] On this view, third-party countermeasures – much like non-military sanctions under Chapter VII UNC – would constitute 'a necessary middle ground between war and words',[72] but one available to individual States under general international law. Some have even suggested that, in view of the limitations of the Security Council in taking resolute action, a parallel regime of third-party countermeasures 'may prove a saving grace for international law'.[73]

In sum, third-party countermeasures raise a serious normative dilemma. Opponents suggest that legitimizing third-party countermeasures might encourage the use of unilateral force contrary to the UN Charter and the bullying of weaker States contrary to the principle of non-intervention – and all in the guise of humanitarian ideals. Supporters suggest that third-party countermeasures could be an effective tool of communitarian law enforcement in an otherwise limited toolbox – and one that could potentially discourage the use of unilateral force, especially on humanitarian grounds. In terms of policy considerations, the potential for abuse must be balanced against the effective protection of community interests in international law. There is an inherent tension between the need for a more effective legal order in spite of decentralization and the risks of abuse relating to the allocation of enforcement authority to individual States, even if limited to

Orakhelashvili (2006), 272; Katselli Proukaki (2010), 10, 281–282. Compare Zemanek (2000), 17; Tams (2005), 158.

[69] YbILC (2001), vol. I, 35, para. 4 (Mr. Simma); and also YbILC (2000), vol. I, 305, para. 33 (Mr. Simma); ILC Report (2000), UN Doc. A/55/10, 60, para. 368.

[70] Crawford, Third Report, 106, para. 405.   [71] Ibid. See further Section 3.2.1.3.

[72] UN Doc. A/59/2005, Report of the Secretary-General, *In Larger Freedom: Towards Development, Security and Human Rights for All*, 30, para. 109. This argument may be understood as a particular application of the traditional view that a key function of reprisals is to avoid the greater evil of war: see e.g. Vattel (1758), Book II, Chapter XVIII, §354; Hall (1890), 367, 371–372; Lawrence (1911), 343–344; Maccoby (1929), 69; Lauterpacht (1933), 139–140.

[73] Bederman (2002), 831.

the most serious illegalities. The degree of polarization is evident in the debate summarized above: at one extreme, third-party countermeasures are denounced as a 'risk to world peace'; at the other extreme, they are hailed as a possible 'saving grace for international law'.

The ILC, in its work on State responsibility, had the delicate task of finding an appropriate balance between competing legal and policy considerations.[74] There was, in 2000, a 'significant level of approval' for third-party countermeasures in the ILC – as reflected in the provisional adoption of Draft Article 54 [2000].[75] The extreme controversy of the topic nonetheless ultimately prompted the ILC, in adopting ARSIWA in 2001, to leave open the question of whether any individual State could adopt third-party countermeasures in order to induce compliance with communitarian norms. The ILC did so by adopting the following saving clause:

> **Article 54**
> **Measures taken by States other than an injured State**
> This chapter [i.e. Chapter II of Part Three on countermeasures] does not prejudice the right of any State, entitled under article 48, paragraph 1, to invoke the responsibility of another State, to take lawful measures against that State to ensure cessation of the breach and reparation in the interest of the injured State or of the beneficiaries of the obligation breached.

The resolution of the matter was accordingly left to the future development of international law.

1.3 Factors Contributing to Uncertainty

Aside from being controversial on normative grounds, the topic of third-party countermeasures is also marked by legal uncertainty. Three factors contributing to uncertainty merit particular attention. The first factor concerns the paucity of relevant case law and the limited guidance it provides.[76] The second factor (already alluded to above) concerns the limited guidance provided by the ILC.[77] During the ILC debate, critics claimed that 'there was no existing foundation for article 54 [2000] as law or its potential progressive development because of the inconsistent practice and the absence of *opinio juris*'.[78] Supporters insisted that recognition of third-party countermeasures would at least have been 'a

---

[74] See ARSIWA Commentary, Introductory Commentary to Chapter II of Part Three, §2 (also ibid., §6).

[75] ILC Report (2000), UN Doc. A/55/10, 62, para. 385 (and also ibid., 70).

[76] See further Chapter 2.   [77] See further Chapter 3.

[78] ILC Report (2001), UN Doc. A/56/10, 23, para. 54.

legitimate form of progressive development of international law'.[79]
The ILC commentary to Article 54 ARSIWA explains that the limited
and uncertain character of State practice on third-party countermeasures
was a key consideration in the adoption of the saving clause. It was
apparently 'not appropriate' to use affirmative language as there appeared
to be 'no clearly recognised entitlement' of the States referred to in Article
48 ARSIWA to take third-party countermeasures under international
law.[80] The limited guidance provided by the ICJ and the ILC calls
attention to the crucial importance of State practice in this area of the
law. But herein also lies the key problem.

The third (and most important) factor contributing to uncertainty
concerns the obscurity of State practice.[81] States will rarely (if ever)
officially designate otherwise unlawful unilateral action taken in defence
of communitarian norms by reference to third-party countermeasures
(or some equivalent expression) to justify their conduct in legal terms.[82]
Indeed – beyond references to violations of human rights or other
communitarian norms as part of the underlying rationale – there is
typically conspicuous silence with respect to the specific international
legal basis for the relevant conduct. State practice on third-party countermeasures appears to be deliberately obscure on grounds of political and
strategic interest in order to allow States greater room to manoeuvre in
this highly sensitive area of the law.[83] It might therefore be said that
a third-party countermeasure is the sanction that dare not speak its
name. In short, as observed during the ILC debate, the topic of third-
party countermeasures is a difficult one 'deeply enmeshed with policy'; it
belongs to 'an area in which the borderline between international law
per se and foreign relations [is] fairly indistinct'.[84] It must be emphasized,
however, that this observation does not vitiate the law-making capacity

---

[79] Ibid.

[80] ARSIWA Commentary, Art. 54, §§6–7. See also ILC Report (2000), UN Doc. A/55/10, 58, para. 356.

[81] See further Sections 4.1 and 5.1.

[82] See Crawford, Third Report, 104, para. 396(b); YbILC (2001), 35, para. 2 (Mr. Brownlie); and further Sections 5.1.1 and 5.1.3.

[83] This might also partially explain the minimalist approach to regulation of countermeasures, including third-party countermeasures, favoured in the ILC by some powerful Western States that are otherwise among those States that have in practice most frequently adopted third-party countermeasures: see UN Doc. A/CN.4/515 (2001), 76 (United Kingdom), 76–77 (United States); and further Section 3.2.1.3(ii). Compare Lesaffre (2010), 470–471.

[84] YbILC (2000), vol. I, 282, para. 46 (Mr. Sreenivasa Rao), 296, para. 46 (Mr. Opertti Badan). To the same effect see also ibid., 333, para. 20 (Mr. Rodríguez Cedeño); Petman (2004), 376.

of the relevant practice; it simply underlines some of the difficulties involved in identifying and assessing it.[85]

There is no shortage of studies on the role of obligations *erga omnes* and peremptory norms in an evolving construction of multilateral public order in international law.[86] The study of third-party countermeasures has also received some attention in the literature as a possible building block in that construction.[87] The area of greatest uncertainty – State practice – has nevertheless received insufficient attention.[88] A closer examination of State practice is warranted for two main reasons. First, it is necessary in order to provide greater clarity regarding the position of third-party countermeasures in international law. Second, policy arguments made about third-party countermeasures have too often been divorced from actual practice. It may be that the prominence of policy considerations in the debate can be explained by the legal uncertainty of the topic. In any event, practice will need to be examined more closely in order to assess the opposing policy arguments outlined above.[89]

1.4   Countermeasures and Cognate Concepts

Over a century ago, Lawrence observed that the term reprisals was used 'in a bewildering variety of senses'.[90] In 1948, Colbert noted that the

---

[85] Compare Petman (2004), 376 ('Most of this practice is, however, heavily motivated by considerations of power and policy and lawyers have been reluctant to see in it any general rule enabling community reactions to violations of norms of great importance . . . [I]n few of the cases has the reacting State itself invoked any general right to take community measures under customary international law. This is not to say that the cases could not be evidence of practice contributing to the emergence of such right – nothing definite can be generalized from them, however'). Further: Section 5.1.3.

[86] See e.g. Tomuschat (1993), 195; Simma (1994a), 217; Frowein (1994), 345; Ragazzi (1997); Kolb (2001); Tams (2005); Villalpando (2005); Tomuschat and Thouvenin (2006); Orakhelashvili (2006); Gaja (2013); Picone (2013).

[87] See generally Akehurst (1970), 1; Schachter (1982), 167–187; Leben (1982), 9; Dupuy (1983), 505; Malanczuk (1983), 705; Zoller (1984a); Zoller (1984b), 361; de Guttry (1985); Elagab (1988); Hutchinson (1988), 151; Sicilianos (1990), 110–175; Boisson de Chazournes (1992); Focarelli (1993), 52; Alland (1994); Focarelli (1994); Frowein (1994), 405–422; Simma (1994a), 313–317; Dzida (1997); Koskenniemi (2001), 337; Alland (2002), 1221; Tams (2005); Sicilianos (2005), 447; Gaja (2005), 146–149; Villalpando (2005), 365–378, 409–413, 448–450, 470–472; Hillgruber (2006), 265; Dawidowicz (2006), 333; Orakhelashvili (2006), 270–272; Katselli Proukaki (2010); Sicilianos (2010), 1137; Gaja (2013), 128–133; Crawford (2013a), 684–686, 703–706; White and Abass (2014), 537; Dawidowicz (2015), 340.

[88] For notable exceptions see Sicilianos (1990), 155–169; Tams (2005), 198–251; Dawidowicz (2006), 333–418; Katselli Proukaki (2010), 90–209. Also: Dawidowicz (2016), 3–15.

[89] See above Section 1.2.   [90] Lawrence (1911), 334. See also above n. 27.

meaning ascribed to the terms 'retaliation', 'retorsion' and 'reprisal' 'seem at times to be as varied as the writers dealing with them'.[91] For his part, during the ILC debate, Reuter pointed to 'an astonishing confusion with regard to the measures a State might be led to take in response to the conduct of another State', and considered that the term countermeasures 'meant nothing'.[92] Indeed the term 'countermeasures' has sometimes been used as convenient shorthand for a general category covering an assortment of measures that a State (or international organization) might take in response to the conduct of another State. Countermeasures should notably be distinguished from the suspension or termination of treaty relations under Article 60 VCLT (or other treaty-law doctrines), reprisals, self-defence, measures taken under Chapter VII UNC and retorsion.[93] The concept of countermeasures is a term of art that denotes a narrow legal category. It is not an umbrella concept for a rainy day. Difficulties have nevertheless occasionally arisen because of the overlapping nature of countermeasures and cognate concepts. These difficulties have also compounded the problems related to the obscurity of State practice noted in the previous section. It thus becomes necessary to distinguish these cognate concepts so that the term countermeasures – and more specifically, the term third-party countermeasures – may be properly understood.

1.4.1 Countermeasures, Reprisals and Self-Defence

The institution of reprisals has an ancient pedigree: it dates back to at least the thirteenth century and is closely associated with the concept of just war – that is, both entailed the pursuit of justice by force of arms.[94]

---

[91] Colbert (1948), 2–3 (n. 1). The term 'retaliation' was used as a generic non-technical term to cover both retorsion and reprisal (ibid.). On 'retaliation', see below Section 1.4.4; and Section 6.1.3.1.

[92] YbILC (1983), vol. I, 102, para. 23 (Mr. Reuter). To the same effect: YbILC (1981), vol. I, 214, para. 25 (Mr. Reuter); Leben (1982), 16–17.

[93] See e.g. ILC Report (1992), UN Doc. A/47/10, 21–23, paras. 139–152; and already 1934 IDI Paris Resolution (preamble; Art. 2).

[94] Brownlie (1963), 7; Grewe (2000), 116–118. As already observed, this is not to suggest that reprisals did not exist in Antiquity; however, the establishment of the Roman Empire appears to have reduced the frequency of their use in territory under Roman rule. It was only with the disintegration of the Roman Empire and its centralized authority of government with a functioning system for the administration of justice that the practice of reprisals was revived in the more decentralized and disorderly medieval period that followed: see da Legnano (1360), 307; Nys (1894), 68–69; Rivier (1896), Vol. II, 193; Fauchille (1926), Pt. III, 690–691; Hindmarsh (1932), 316; Colbert (1948), 10–12. For the

Grotius (following the post-glossator Bartolus) recognized 'the right of reprisals' for 'the enforcement of right', which occurred 'where a right is denied'.[95] Vattel observed that '[r]eprisals are used between nation and nation to do justice to themselves, when they cannot otherwise obtain it'.[96] In the *Naulilaa* arbitration, which concerned the use of armed reprisals, the tribunal explained:

> Reprisals are an act of taking the law into its own hands (*Selbsthilfehandlung*) by the injured State . . . in response to an act contrary to the law of nations by the offending State. Their effect is to suspend momentarily, in the relations between the two States, the observation of a particular rule of the law of nations . . . They would be illegal if an earlier act, contrary to the law of nations, had not furnished the motive.[97]

Thus the term 'reprisals' was traditionally used to describe otherwise unlawful action – whether forcible or non-forcible[98] – taken by way of self-help in response to a prior breach of international law.[99]

---

earlier practice of reprisals in Ancient Greece (including in its original primitive form of *androlepsia*), see Oppenheim (1905), Vol. II, 37; Phillipson (1911), Vol. II, 349–364; Bederman (2001), 122–123; and also above n. 21.

[95] Grotius (1646), Book III, Chapter II, §4. See also Brownlie (1963), 7.

[96] Vattel (1758), Book II, Chapter XVIII, §342. This modern conception of public reprisals gradually replaced the medieval practice of private reprisals; that is, letters of marque or reprisal by which the sovereign authorized its subjects to enforce for themselves their otherwise unsatisfied claims (following a denial of justice) against foreigners. Further: Grotius (1646), Book III, Chapter II, §4; Bynkershoek (1737), Vol. II, Chapter XXIV, 133–137; Vattel (1758), Book II, Chapter XVIII, §346; Phillimore (1857), Vol. III, 12–13; Wheaton (1866), 309–311; de Mas Latrie (1875); Hall (1890), 368; Nys (1894), 62–77; Winthrop (1894), 116; Rivier (1896), Vol. II, 191–198; Oppenheim (1905), Vol. II, 37; Lawrence (1911), 335–336; Westlake (1913), Pt. II, 7–10; Maccoby (1924), 60; Fauchille (1926), Pt. III, 689–696; de la Brière (1928), 251–256; Clark (1933), 694; Hindmarsh (1933), 43–56; Colbert (1948), 9–59; Brownlie (1983), 3–5; Grewe (2000), 116–118, 201–203; Neff (2005), 76–82. The Declaration of Paris (signed and entered into force 16 Apr. 1856, with fifty-five States Parties) declared that '[p]rivateering is, and remains, unlawful': see www.icrc .org/ihl/INTRO/105?OpenDocument. Private reprisals had effectively disappeared by the end of the eighteenth century: see e.g. Oppenheim (1905), Vol. II, 37; Hindmarsh (1932), 318; Colbert (1948), 3–4, 31–32; Grewe (2000), 201–202. For the historical link between denial of justice and reprisals, see generally Spiegel (1932), 63; Freeman (1938), 53–67; Paulsson (2005), 13–20; Paparinskis (2008), 270–272.

[97] *Naulilaa (Responsibility of Germany for damage caused in the Portuguese colonies in the south of Africa) (Portugal/Germany)* (1928), RIAA, vol. II, 1011 at 1026. See also *Cysne (Responsibility of Germany for acts committed subsequent to 31 July 1914 and before Portugal entered the war) (Portugal/Germany)* (1930), RIAA, vol. II, 1035 at 1056; 1934 IDI Paris Resolution (Art. 1). Further: Politis (1934), 1.

[98] See e.g. 1934 IDI Paris Resolution (Art. 3).

[99] See ARSIWA Commentary, Introductory Commentary to Chapter II of Part Three, §3.

In the modern era of the UN Charter, the term 'reprisals' developed a 'pejorative connotation'[100] due to its close historical association with measures involving the use of force. As already noted, Article 2(4) UNC prohibited armed reprisals; however, that prohibition did not extend to unarmed reprisals, which remained lawful in principle.[101] More recently, the use of the term 'reprisals' has been limited to action taken by belligerents in time of international armed conflict, i.e. belligerent reprisals.[102] And so, for socio-legal reasons, the term 'reprisals' – which once had covered both forcible and non-forcible measures – was replaced by the term 'countermeasures' and, in the words of the ILC commentary, accordingly 'covers that part of the [traditional] subject of reprisals not associated with armed conflict'.[103] In other words, countermeasures are, first and foremost, a peaceful unilateral self-help measure.[104]

The origin of the term countermeasures has been disputed in the literature. Some have claimed that British government lawyers coined the term in 1915 in a postal dispute with Sweden; others have pointed to the literal translation of the term in German (*Gegenmaßnahmen*) coined by Swiss government lawyers in 1928 with respect to a dispute involving taxation matters.[105] Whatever the sporadic early references to the term, it is widely accepted that it only gained currency in the late 1970s following the award in the *Air Services* arbitration.[106] The *Air Services* tribunal in relevant part stated:

> If a situation arises which, in one State's view, results in the violation of an international obligation by another State, the first State is entitled, within the limits set by the general rules of international law pertaining to the use of armed force, to affirm its rights through 'counter-measures'.[107]

The placing of 'countermeasures' in quotation marks was an indication of the novelty of the term and reflected its repeated usage

---

[100] YbILC (1979), vol. I, 59, para. 61 (Mr. Francis).

[101] See e.g. Draft Articles Commentary, Art. 30, §11. Thus there was continuity with the situation prevailing under the League Covenant (where the legality of unarmed reprisals likewise remained intact): see e.g. de Visscher (1924), 386; Colbert (1948), 85.

[102] See ARSIWA Commentary, Art. 22, §3; Introductory Commentary to Chapter II of Part Three, §3; Art. 50, §8; and further Section 6.2.1.3.

[103] ARSIWA Commentary, Introductory Commentary to Chapter II of Part Three, §3.

[104] See Alland (2010), 1130; Crawford (2013a), 684–685.

[105] See Elagab (1988), 2 (and also ibid., 24); Sicilianos (1990), 5 (n. 21); Zoller (1984a), xvi (n. 8); Alland (1994), 24 (n. 73). Compare Leben (1982), 16 (n. 24).

[106] *US-France Air Services Agreement* (1978), RIAA, vol. XVIII, 417. See further ARSIWA Commentary, Art. 22, §3; Introductory Commentary to Chapter II of Part Three, §3.

[107] *US-France Air Services Agreement* (1978), RIAA, vol. XVIII, 417 at 443, para. 81.

(as synonymous with non-forcible reprisals) by the United States in its pleadings in that case.[108] As Reuter (himself a member of the tribunal) later explained in the ILC, the choice of terminology was rather fortuitous:

> For its part, the United States had started using the word 'countermeasure', which meant nothing but had established itself by being adopted by an arbitral tribunal seeking to avoid the words 'reciprocal obligations' or 'reprisals'.[109]

The ILC endorsed the term countermeasures in 1979;[110] and it was shortly thereafter given the imprimatur of the ICJ in the *Tehran Hostages* case.[111]

In traditional international law, the legal relations arising from wrongful conduct were 'essentially bilateral'; in other words (except where rights were granted by treaty in terms which entitled third States to invoke their breach),[112] they concerned only the relations between the responsible State and the injured State *inter se*.[113] This bilateral enforcement model meant that only the State injured by the wrongful act could seek redress by way of countermeasures against the responsible State.[114] It is this classical bilateral conception of countermeasures that is embodied in Articles 22 and 49 ARSIWA.[115] In other words, a countermeasure is essentially a non-forcible measure of an injured State not in conformity with an international obligation owed towards a responsible State. The countermeasure would otherwise be unlawful if it was not taken by the injured State in response to an internationally wrongful act by the responsible State in order to achieve a specific objective, namely, to procure cessation and reparation.[116] Accordingly, a countermeasure 'provides a shield against an otherwise well-founded claim for the breach of an international obligation' by operating as a circumstance precluding

---

[108] See Nash (1980), 769 et seq.   [109] YbILC (1983), vol. I, 102, para. 23 (Mr. Reuter).

[110] See Draft Articles Commentary, Art. 30, §21; and further Section 3.1.1.

[111] See *United States Diplomatic and Consular Staff in Tehran*, ICJ Rep. (1980), 3 at 27, para. 53. Further: *Nicaragua* case, ICJ Rep. (1986), 14 at 106, para. 201; *Gabčíkovo Nagymaros Project*, ICJ Rep. (1997), 7 at 55, para. 82; *Application of the Interim Accord of 13 September 1995*, ICJ Rep. (2011), 644 at 691, para. 164.

[112] See *South West Africa*, ICJ Rep. (1966), 6 at 32, para. 44.

[113] ARSIWA Commentary, Art. 1, §§3–4; Draft Articles Commentary, Art. 1, §6.

[114] See Vattel (1758), Book II, Chapter XVIII, §§338–354.

[115] ARSIWA Commentary, Introductory Commentary to Chapter II of Part Three, §8.

[116] ARSIWA Commentary, Art. 22, §1; Introductory Commentary to Chapter II of Part Three, §1; Art. 49, §1. Compare Alland (2010), 1135; Crawford (2013a), 685 (noting that the ARSIWA do not contain a definition of countermeasures as such).

wrongfulness in the law of State responsibility.[117] For convenience, as distinct from the category of third-party countermeasures, countermeasures taken by an injured State (as defined in Article 42 ARSIWA) will, as appropriate, be referred to in this study as 'bilateral countermeasures'.

An injured State has broad (but by no means unlimited) discretion in its choice of countermeasures based on considerations of effectiveness:[118] there is no requirement limiting their use to the suspension of performance of the same or a closely related obligation.[119] A key reason for this – which is especially relevant for the category of third-party countermeasures – is that for some obligations, such as those concerning the protection of human rights, countermeasures of a reciprocal nature are 'inconceivable'.[120] The broad discretion afforded to States in taking countermeasures – coupled with the risks of abuse already outlined above – underline the need for adequate safeguards against abuse in order to ensure, by appropriate conditions and limitations, that countermeasures are 'kept within generally acceptable bounds'.[121] And so, recourse to countermeasures is limited under international law by several substantive and procedural conditions, which are codified in Articles 49–53 ARSIWA.[122]

Finally, it will be apparent that countermeasures are also distinct from the notion of self-defence. Whereas the former is a non-forcible self-help measure that can be taken in response to all manner of breaches of international law, the latter is a forcible self-help measure that applies only in case of a very specific breach – that is, an 'armed attack'.[123] Moreover, their purposes are different: countermeasures are a law enforcement tool, whereas self-defence is a defensive reaction designed to restore a certain military balance vis-à-vis an attacking State. Still, the concepts might nevertheless overlap in practice insofar

---

[117] ARSIWA Commentary, Introductory Commentary to Chapter V of Part One, §§1–2; Art. 22, §§1–6. Further: Lesaffre (2010), 469–473; Crawford (2013a), 274–283, 292–295 (with further references).

[118] See Simma (1970), 21.

[119] ARSIWA Commentary, Introductory Commentary to Chapter II of Part Three, §5. The performance of certain obligations may not be suspended by way of countermeasures in any circumstances. For all other obligations '[t]he test is always that of proportionality': see ARSIWA Commentary, Art. 49, §6; and further Sections 6.2 and 6.3.

[120] ARSIWA Commentary, Introductory Commentary to Chapter II of Part Three, §5. See further Section 6.2.

[121] ARSIWA Commentary, Introductory Commentary to Chapter II of Part Three, §§2, 5–6.

[122] See further Chapter 6.

[123] See Crawford (2012), 586; and already 1934 IDI Paris Resolution (Art. 2).

as an otherwise unlawful non-forcible reaction to an armed attack may fall into either category – at least based on an *a fortiori* reading of Article 51 UNC.[124]

1.4.2 Countermeasures and the Suspension of Obligations

Countermeasures must be distinguished from the suspension or termination of treaty relations under Article 60 VCLT (or other treaty-law doctrines). Unlike the latter, the legal effect of a countermeasure is not to temporarily extinguish the obligation, still less to permanently extinguish it. Rather, the obligation remains in force, and the effect is to temporarily suspend its performance. As a result, if the conduct is justified as a countermeasure, the obligation continues to apply and the wrongfulness of the conduct in question is only precluded for as long as the circumstance justifying its adoption obtains and the necessary conditions for taking countermeasures are satisfied. As soon as the justification for the countermeasure ceases to exist, the duty to comply with the obligation revives and the countermeasure must accordingly be terminated forthwith.[125] Their purposes are also different: a suspension under Article 60 VCLT is a protective measure designed to restore a certain contractual balance (the *quid pro quo*); by contrast, a countermeasure, in the words of Grotius recalled above,[126] is intended for 'the enforcement of right'.[127]

1.4.3 Countermeasures and Sanctions

Countermeasures must also be distinguished from the term 'sanctions'. In a general (Kelsenian) sense, a countermeasure is clearly a 'sanction' if

---

[124] See Frowein (1994), 370; Tams (2005), 21–22, 300–302; Hillgruber (2006), 281; Dawidowicz (2006), 372–373; Crawford (2013a), 290. Also: UN Doc. A/ES-10/PV.21 (20 Oct. 2003), 6 (Israel). Compare *Wall* case, ICJ Rep. (2004), 136 at 194, paras. 138–139; and contrast ibid., 215, para. 35 (Sep. Op. Judge Higgins). Generally: 1934 IDI Paris Resolution (Art. 2(4)); ARSIWA Commentary, Art. 21, §§1–6; Crawford (2013a), 289–292. For an example of an overlap in practice see Section 4.2.8.

[125] See generally ARSIWA Commentary, Introductory Commentary to Chapter V of Part One, §§2–3; Art. 22, §4; Art. 27, §§1–6; Introductory Commentary to Chapter II of Part Three, §4; Art. 49, §§6–7; Art. 53, §§1–2. Further: Sicilianos (1993), 341; Crawford, Third Report, 86–87, paras. 324–325; Simma and Tams (2011), 1354, 1376–1377; Crawford (2013a), 682–684.

[126] See above n. 95.

[127] See Simma (1970), 20–21; Tams (2005), 21–22; Simma and Tams (2011), 1354; Crawford (2013a), 676, 684. Also: 1934 IDI Paris Resolution (Art. 2(2)); Simma (1970), 24–25.

that term is used to mean a coercive reaction to illegality. As a unilateral self-help measure, a countermeasure may accordingly (if only in Kelsenian terms) be described as a 'unilateral sanction'.[128] However, as the ILC commentary explains, the term 'sanction' has acquired a specific meaning in modern international law: it is reserved for a wide range of institutional reactions (including the use of force) taken in the framework of international organizations, notably under Chapter VII UNC. Still, the term is imprecise: the UN Charter uses the term 'measures' (or 'enforcement measures'), not 'sanctions'.[129] Thus sanctions are distinct from countermeasures in several respects.

First, sanctions constitute a centralized reaction taken by States acting in a collective or institutional capacity through a corporate organ, whereas countermeasures constitute a decentralized or unilateral reaction taken by one State or a group of States, with each acting in an individual capacity through their own organs.[130] Second, as opposed to countermeasures, sanctions in the form of measures taken under Chapter VII UNC need not necessarily respond to a prior wrongful act – even if the Security Council in practice frequently does make findings of State responsibility.[131] In principle,

---

[128] See Kelsen (1950), 706; Kelsen (1952), 20–25; Kelsen (1961), 328–330; Kelsen (1967), 111. Also: Alland (2010), 1134; Pellet and Miron (2011), paras. 4–11; Tzanakopoulos (2015), 146–147. The ILC does not appear to have adopted a Kelsenian view of international law (or its sanctions): see ARSIWA Commentary, Art. 1, §3; Draft Articles Commentary, Art. 1, §5.

[129] ARSIWA Commentary, Art. 22, §3; Introductory Commentary to Chapter II of Part Three, §3; Art. 54, §2; Draft Articles Commentary, Art. 30, §21 (and also ibid., §§12–14); and further Section 3.1.1. Further: Supplement to an Agenda for Peace, UN Doc. A/50/60-S/1995/1, 16; Abi-Saab (2001), 29–41; Crawford (2001b), 57–68; Gowlland-Debbas (2010), 126–133; Pellet and Miron (2011); Gowlland-Debbas (2012), 225–269; Crawford (2013a), 706–707; White and Abass (2014), 552–555. Also: GA Res. 60/1 (16 Sept. 2005) (2005 World Summit Outcome), para. 106.

[130] ARSIWA Commentary, Art. 54, §2. Sanctions may be 'comprehensive' or 'targeted' (also known as 'smart' or 'intelligent') in character. However, as the former are widely considered as a blunt instrument, they have since the 1990s normally taken the form of the latter. Further: Supplement to an Agenda for Peace, UN Doc. A/50/60-S/1995/1, 16; GA Res. 60/1 (16 Sept. 2005) (2005 World Summit Outcome), para. 106; Cortright, Lopez and Stellingwerf (2007), 349; Carish and Rickard-Martin (2011); Pellet and Miron (2011), paras. 33–38. Third-party countermeasures are likewise also often targeted in character, notably in the form of asset freezes (on which see generally Chapter 4).

[131] The question whether measures under Chapter VII UNC necessarily respond to a wrongful act (i.e. whether Article 39 UNC imposes a pre-existing general treaty obligation on States not to threaten the peace of which commands in relevant Security Council resolutions constitute an ad hoc elaboration) is contested in the literature: see generally YbILC (1999), vol. I, 162, para. 79 (Mr. Simma); Frowein and Krisch (2002),

their functions are different: measures under Chapter VII UNC have a broad aim to maintain or restore international peace and security, whereas countermeasures are a tool of law enforcement within a narrow compass.

In any event, even if measures under Chapter VII UNC do respond to an illegality by an otherwise unlawful act, their justification – unlike countermeasures – does not derive from general international law but from the supremacy clause in Article 103 UNC.[132] What is more, measures under Chapter VII UNC may include intrinsically lawful conduct (i.e. acts of retorsion),[133] whereas countermeasures by definition only refer to otherwise unlawful conduct. In short, there is more to the distinction between measures under Chapter VII UNC and countermeasures than simply their centralized as opposed to decentralized character. In analytical terms, measures under Chapter VII UNC are distinct from countermeasures, and they should not be conflated.[134] This point was never clarified by the ILC; but, as Simma proposed during the debate, it would (ideally) have been useful to do so.[135] The distinction between countermeasures and sanctions prompts some observations concerning two overlapping situations relevant to this study.

---

705 MN 12, 739 MN 7; d'Argent, d'Aspremont, Dopagne and van Steenberghe (2005), 1137–1140; Forteau (2006), 58–71 (also ibid., 449–452); Gowlland-Debbas (2010), 126–133; Pellet and Miron (2011), paras. 15–25; Orakhelashvili (2011), 170–175; Tzanakopoulos (2011), 76–79; Gowlland-Debbas (2012), 225–269; Crawford (2013a), 706–709; White and Abass (2014), 554–555. Also: UN Doc. A/CN.4/515 (2001), 92 (Spain); ARSIWA Commentary, Art. 30, §4; Art. 40, §9; Art. 59, §1.

[132] See e.g. Bernhardt (2002), 1298–1299 MN 21; Thouvenin (2005), 2140–2142; ILC Report on Fragmentation of International Law, UN Doc. A/CN.4/L.682 (2006), 175–178, paras. 344–350; Kolb (2010), 161–164 (the UN Charter prevails over conflicting treaty obligations and customary international law, subject to the overriding limits imposed by peremptory norms). Also: ARSIWA Commentary, Art. 59, §1 (which appears to leave open whether Article 103 UNC trumps customary law); Alland (2010), 1135; and compare DARIO Commentary, Art. 22, §3. Further: Kolb (2013), 9.

[133] See e.g. Draft Articles Commentary, Art. 30, §13.

[134] See Forteau (2006), 449–452; Orakhelashvili (2011), 188–189; Tsagourias and White (2013), 227. Also: 1934 IDI Paris Resolution (Art. 2(3)); DARIO Commentary, Art. 22, §3. Contrast Tzanakopoulos (2011), 77–79 (and also ibid., 199 n. 357).

[135] YbILC (1999), vol. I, 162, para. 79 (Mr. Simma). See also UN Doc. A/CN.4/515 (2001), 92 (Spain); Forteau (2006), 449–452 (with further references). The ILC's silence on this point was nevertheless understandable given the extreme controversy of third-party countermeasures, including their unclear relationship to Chapter VII UNC (ultimately safeguarded by Article 59 ARSIWA): see Crawford, Third Report, 102, para. 387; Crawford, Fourth Report, 18, para. 73.

1.4.3.1   Countermeasures and Measures
under Chapter VII UNC

First, even where conceptual boundaries are clearly demarcated, functional and practical ones may not be. It was observed above that the Security Council – as part of its Charter mandate to maintain or restore international peace and security – frequently adopts measures under Chapter VII UNC as a tool of law enforcement aimed at ensuring the cessation of wrongful conduct and/or reparation for any injury caused. In such cases, there is inevitably a point of convergence with the law of State responsibility, including countermeasures. It follows that measures under Chapter VII UNC – to the extent that they overlap with the law of State responsibility – may limit (or even entirely extinguish) any entitlement to take countermeasures by affecting the conditions (notably necessity and proportionality) governing their use.[136] The extent to which a resolution under Chapter VII UNC may do so in a given case is essentially a question of interpretation[137] – and one on which there is at least some useful guidance from State practice.[138] This question, it may be recalled, forms an integral part of the controversy of third-party countermeasures – that is, their unclear relationship to Chapter VII UNC.[139] In sum, measures under Chapter VII UNC may be distinct from countermeasures, but in circumstances where they overlap, the former may still be relevant in assessing the permissibility of the latter.

1.4.3.2   Countermeasures by International Organizations
and Member States

Second, reactions by international organizations do not qualify as 'sanctions' simply by virtue of their institutional character.[140] Insofar as Articles 25 and 103 UNC cannot justify such reactions (e.g. because they go beyond a Chapter VII UNC resolution or simply in the complete absence thereof),[141] they require an independent justification. Countermeasures provide such a justification. As it happens, international organizations most frequently adopt third-party countermeasures

---

[136] Compare the slightly different perspective in Tzanakopoulos (2011), 77–83 (discussing the 'functional analogy' between sanctions and countermeasures). Also: Orakhelashvili (2011), 188–189.

[137] See notably Forteau (2006), 468–481.   [138] See further Sections 5.2.1; 6.3; and 6.4.1.

[139] See above Section 1.2.

[140] For a (non-exhaustive) definition of an 'international organization', see DARIO Commentary, Art. 2, §§1–15.

[141] Compare Alland (2010), 1135. Also: Reisman (1980), 904; Alland (1994), 322–325.

as opposed to bilateral countermeasures.[142] For its part, the EU does not actually use the language of countermeasures, but instead it refers interchangeably to the terms 'restrictive measures' and 'autonomous sanctions' to denote such action (as well as acts of retorsion).[143]

The manner in which international relations are conducted means that the State practice examined in this study will inevitably overlap with actions taken by international organizations by way of third-party countermeasures. The question whether the conduct that may constitute a breach of an international obligation in a given case should be considered the conduct of the international organization or the individual Member States, or both, is a question of attribution.[144] This observation prompts the following clarification: the present study concerns the adoption of third-party countermeasures under the law of State responsibility. It does not concern the adoption of third-party countermeasures under the law of responsibility of international organizations – a subject worthy of examination in its own right.[145] Still, it might be useful to make a few brief general comments on attribution relevant to this study and its examination of practice.

First, the normative conduct involved in the suspension of a treaty to which an international organization is a party will clearly be directly attributable to it. However, so-called 'mixed agreements'[146] – i.e. those concluded by the international organization (almost invariably the EU)[147] and one or more of its Member States with a third State – would appear to be attributable to both the organization (Article 6 DARIO) and its Member States (Article 4 ARSIWA).[148] To illustrate,

---

[142] See generally DARIO Commentary, Arts. 22, 51–57. Further: European Commission, EU Guidelines on Implementation and Evaluation of Restrictive Measures (2008), 1 (third-party countermeasures – a form of 'autonomous sanctions' – 'have been frequently imposed by the EU in recent years'), http://eeas.europa.eu/cfsp/sanctions/docs/index_en.pdf; Dopagne (2010); Tzanakopoulos (2015), 145.

[143] See European Commission, EU Guidelines on Implementation and Evaluation of Restrictive Measures (2008), 1, http://eeas.europa.eu/cfsp/sanctions/docs/index_en.pdf.

[144] See Article 2 ARSIWA; Article 4 DARIO. Attribution of conduct is a first necessary step analytically distinct from its possible characterization (in a second step) as internationally wrongful (and, if in the affirmative, in a third step, its possible preclusion of wrongfulness as a countermeasure): see e.g. ARSIWA Commentary, Art. 2, §§5–8, 11; Introductory Commentary to Chapter II of Part One, §4.

[145] See notably Dopagne (2010). [146] See e.g. Möldner (2011).

[147] See Klabbers (2009), 263 (for some rare examples of mixed agreements outside the EU context).

[148] For a useful discussion see Tzanakopoulos (2015), 153–154 (with further references). Also: DARIO Commentary, Art. 48, §1 (on attribution of responsibility in case of mixed agreements).

the Lomé Conventions (later replaced by the Cotonou Agreement) – a series of development assistance treaties concluded by the (then) EC and its Member States with the ACP States – would be one such example.[149] A second example would be 1962 EEC-Greece Association Agreement.[150] A third example in the EU context would be the WTO covered agreements (notably, the GATT and the GATS).[151]

Second, the adoption by an international organization of a normative act that imposes a strict obligation on its Member States to take certain action for which it does not itself have operational capacity (such as the freezing of assets held in Member States' financial institutions by way of third-party countermeasures), and as such requiring implementation by Member States' own organs, may arguably be attributed to it insofar as it may be deemed to exercise 'effective control'[152] over that conduct – that is, to be more precise, even if it does not do so in factual terms (by controlling the State organs on the ground), but only does so in normative terms (by operation of law). It could on that basis be understood as another case of dual attribution.[153] In any event, what really matters here is this: the conduct of Member States' own organs in implementing the freeze order will be attributed to each of them in line with the basic principle in Article 4 ARSIWA.[154] Conversely, in the absence of effective normative control by the international organization (e.g. where the conduct consists merely in a recommendation to adopt an asset freeze),

---

[149] The otherwise unlawful action taken by the (then) EC and its members with respect to those treaties in relation to Uganda, the Central African Republic and Liberia may accordingly (also) be characterized as third-party countermeasures taken by States: see further Sections 4.2.3–4.2.5. Similar action taken with respect to Nigeria and Zimbabwe did not require justification as third-party countermeasures following the introduction of human rights conditionality clauses in the relevant agreements: see further Sections 4.2.12 and 4.2.17.

[150] See further Section 4.2.2.

[151] For relevant examples, see generally Chapter 4. For its part, the EU has been a WTO member since 1 January 1995: see https://www.wto.org/english/thewto_e/whatis_e/tif_e/org6_e.htm.

[152] See *Nicaragua* case, ICJ Rep. (1986), 14 at 64–65, para. 115; *Application of the Convention on the Prevention and Punishment of the Crime of Genocide (Bosnia and Herzegovina v. Serbia and Montenegro)*, ICJ Rep. (2007), 43 at 208–211, paras. 399–407.

[153] See Tzanakopoulos (2015), 154–155 (with further references). Compare DARIO Commentary, Art. 7, §§1–16 (which appears to preclude dual attribution on normative – as distinct from factual – grounds).

[154] The point appears to be confirmed by ARSIWA Commentary, Art. 57, §2 (and also above n. 130). For numerous examples of asset freezes emanating from international organizations (such as the EU, the Commonwealth and the Arab League), see generally Chapter 4.

any implementing measures that might follow will clearly only be attributable to the relevant Member States.[155]

Third, even if a certain normative act may be attributable to an international organization, it will not engage its responsibility unless the conduct in question is actually in breach of some international obligation binding upon it. Thus an international organization may – in the absence of any relevant international obligation incumbent upon it – direct (or simply recommend) its Member States to adopt certain conduct against a third State such as suspending various treaty obligations binding only upon them (e.g. bilateral air services agreements, bilateral investment treaties or the GATT/GATS).[156] Finally, the suspension of membership in an international organization by way of third-party countermeasures may arguably – albeit in strictly limited circumstances – be attributed on a dual basis to the Member States. At the very least, it may reasonably be assumed that Member States accept the use of third-party countermeasures in such circumstances.[157] In all cases of attributed conduct, the general principle applies by which each reacting State remains responsible for its own conduct vis-à-vis the injured (target) State in case of the unlawful use of third-party countermeasures.[158]

1.4.4   Countermeasures, Retorsion and Other Miscellaneous Concepts

Countermeasures must also be contrasted with retorsion. Unlike the former category of unilateral self-help measures, which involves otherwise unlawful conduct, the latter category concerns intrinsically lawful conduct that does not infringe the target State's rights under international law. At least in Kelsenian terms, retorsion accordingly does not qualify as a sanction.[159] Retorsion may be described as '"unfriendly" conduct which is not inconsistent with any international obligation of the State engaging in it, even though it may be a response to an internationally wrongful act'.[160] As the ICJ explained in the *Nicaragua* case,

---

[155] Ibid.

[156] Compare Tzanakopoulos (2015), 155. See generally Chapter 4 for relevant examples.

[157] See further Section 4.2.5 (ECOWAS/Liberia); Section 4.2.12 (Commonwealth/Nigeria); Section 4.2.17 (Commonwealth/Zimbabwe); Section 4.2.19 (Arab League/Libya); Section 4.2.20 (Arab League/OIC/Syria).

[158] See ARSIWA Commentary, Art. 1, §6.

[159] See Kelsen (1952), 25 (and above n. 128). Also: Tzanakopoulos (2015), 148.

[160] ARSIWA Commentary, Introductory Commentary to Chapter II of Part Three, §3. Generally: Vattel (1758), Book II, Chapter XVIII, §341; Phillimore (1857), Vol. III,

there is no obligation under international law for States to maintain friendly relations 'in a vague general sense'.[161] Retorsion is widely regarded as the exercise of a freedom – as distinct from the exercise of a right to which certain limitations may apply[162] – in other words, a self-help measure that is, within the meaning of the PCIJ's famous dictum in the *Lotus* case, largely unregulated by international law in the absence of any prohibitive rule to the contrary.[163] In short, unlike countermeasures, retorsion does not require legal justification and falls outside the law of State responsibility.[164]

It follows that the motive behind acts of retorsion, unless in actual violation of an international obligation of the State(s) taking them vis-à-vis the target State, is irrelevant: they may respond to illegality or express disapproval of policy by way of retaliation or otherwise.[165] Thus retorsion may have a punitive or retributive function, whereas countermeasures must have an instrumental function the principal object of which is to induce a return to legality. This points to a further difference with countermeasures: there is no legal (as distinct from political or moral) requirement for acts of retorsion to be temporary or reversible. In the words of Vattel, 'there is nothing in this [the law of retorsion], but what is conformable to just and sound politics'.[166] As it happens, States normally

---

8–9; Wheaton (1866), 309–312; Hall (1890), 364; Rivier (1896), Vol. II, 189–191; Oppenheim (1905), Vol. II, 31–33; Westlake (1913), Pt. II, 6–7; Rapisardi-Mirabelli (1914), 223; Fauchille (1926), Pt. III, 687–689; Zoller (1984a), 5–13; Alland (2010), 1131–1132; Giegrich (2011); Crawford (2013a), 676–678.

[161] *Nicaragua* case, ICJ Rep. (1986), 14 at 136, para. 273. Indeed acts of retorsion in the economic field may not even violate the object and purpose of a FCN treaty: see ibid., 138, para. 276; and further Section 2.1.4. Also: *Oil Platforms*, ICJ Rep. (1996), 803 at 815, para. 31.

[162] See Schachter (1982), 185–187; Zoller (1984a), 12–13; Cassese (2005), 310; Giegrich (2011), para. 8 (referring to proportionality and abuse of rights as possible limitations on retorsion). Also: ILC Report (1992), UN Doc. A/47/10, 23, para. 150; White and Abass (2014), 544.

[163] *S.S. 'Lotus'* (1927), PCIJ Ser. A, No. 10, 18–19. See also Zoller (1984a), 5–9; Crawford (2013a), 677. For possible procedural and substantive limits on retorsion see generally Giegrich (2011), paras. 14–27; Crawford (2013a), 677.

[164] See ARSIWA Commentary, Introductory Commentary to Chapter II of Part Three, §3. Also: 1934 IDI Paris Resolution (Art. 2(1)); Draft Articles Commentary, Art. 30, §3 (n. 581).

[165] See ARSIWA Commentary, Introductory Commentary to Chapter II of Part Three, §3. Also: Schachter (1982), 185–186; Giegrich (2011), paras. 24–27; Crawford (2013a), 677. Compare *Railway Traffic Between Lithuania and Poland* (Adv. Op., 15 Oct. 1931), PCIJ Ser. A/B No. 42, 108 at 113–114.

[166] Vattel (1758), Book II, Chapter XVIII, §341.

follow the dictates of just and sound politics in their actual use of retorsion.[167]

It will be apparent from the above that the scope of application of retorsion is vast and covers innumerable acts: from the symbolic renaming in 1986 by Glasgow City Council (as an organ of the United Kingdom under Article 4 ARSIWA) of St George's Place – the address of the South African Consulate – as Nelson Mandela Place during the apartheid era, to general denials of the voluntary benefits of international cooperation (e.g. in the diplomatic, economic, development, cultural, scientific, transportation, migration or military spheres) and so on.[168] Unsurprisingly, retorsion is by far the most frequently used unilateral self-help measure in State practice, including in the enforcement of communitarian norms.[169] This raises at least two issues of overlap.

First, countermeasures are limited to an instrumental function whereas retorsion is not so limited. However, in practice, countermeasures and retorsion are frequently used simultaneously as broadly related to the enforcement of communitarian norms. Based on this overall rationale for the action as a whole, instrumental and punitive elements are often mixed together in a manner that may be difficult to disentangle. Their concurrent use may accordingly complicate the analysis of the permissibility of countermeasures.[170] Second, the distinction between countermeasures and retorsion may sometimes be difficult to make in practice, and it is especially so for communitarian law enforcement involving recourse to third-party countermeasures by many different States. This is so because each State enjoys different legal relations with the target State and it may not be entirely clear that a particular action consists of otherwise unlawful conduct taken in response to a previous wrongful act; the characterization of the conduct will depend upon the myriad of specific treaty relations applicable between the relevant parties and the state of general international law on any given day.[171]

Countermeasures should additionally be distinguished from unilateral trade restrictions, notably those based on the national security exception

---

[167] See generally Chapter 4. Also: Giegrich (2011), paras. 5–6, 8.
[168] See 'Why did Nelson Mandela thank Glasgow?', BBC News, 6 December 2013, www.bbc .co.uk/news/uk-scotland-22976781. For further examples of retorsion, see ARSIWA Commentary, Introductory Commentary to Chapter II of Part Three, §3; Cassese (2005), 310; Giegrich (2011), para. 10.
[169] See generally Giegrich (2011), para. 4; Crawford (2013a), 676; and further Chapter 4.
[170] See further Section 6.1.3.1.
[171] See Sicilianos (1990), 8; Tams (2005), 228–229, 231; Dawidowicz (2006), 349–350; Giegrich (2011), para. 7; Crawford (2013a), 676.

in Article XXI GATT (or Article XIV *bis* GATS).[172] Countermeasures are also distinct from the principles of collective non-recognition (whether optional or obligatory) and non-assistance within the meaning of Article 41 ARSIWA.[173] The term 'economic coercion' is commonly used by the UN General Assembly and is also recurrent in the literature; however, it is not a term of art. It is best understood as a descriptive term essentially related to a specific concern with the legal category of countermeasures; namely, the relationship between (economic) countermeasures and non-intervention. The reliance on this notion has only served to muddy the waters of an already obscure area of international law. The concerns raised by 'economic coercion' are best addressed by the existing law of countermeasures.[174] The same applies *mutatis mutandis* to the descriptive term 'unilateral coercive measures', which is frequently used – notably by the UN General Assembly and the Human Rights Council – in a confusing manner without a clear distinction being drawn between countermeasures and acts of retorsion.[175] Countermeasures and retorsion may be considered coercive in a broad sense insofar as they are concerned with unilateral measures, whether taken by a State acting

---

[172] It should be noted that there is a distinct reluctance in the WTO context to formally invoke the national security exception in Article XXI GATT, which adds a further layer of obscurity to the assessment of State practice. The approach taken in this study is that, even if *arguendo* Article XXI GATT has a self-judging character, its application surely cannot be triggered in the abstract without even being formally invoked as a treaty-based defence, notably by way of notification to the target State. In such cases, an otherwise unlawful unilateral trade restriction will require independent justification. See also the discussion in Section 4.2.1 (esp. text accompanying n. 28 in that section).

[173] See Crawford (2013a), 676. For the suggestion that collective non-recognition amounts to 'the classic countermeasure taken by third States', see Talmon (2004), 174 (and generally ibid., 162–179). Also: Schachter (1982), 184; YbILC (1992), vol. I, 190, para. 36 (Mr. Arangio-Ruiz); Cassese (1995), 158.

[174] See e.g. Topical Summary of Government Comments in the Sixth Committee, UN Doc. A/CN.4/513 (2000), 30–31, para. 160; GA Res. 70/185 (22 Dec. 2015). Further: Sections 4.2.18; 6.2; and 6.3.1. Generally: Bowett (1972), 1; Elagab (1988), 190–213; Jennings and Watts (1996), Vol. I, 428–429, 432–434 (nn. 13–16); Carter (2009); Boisson de Chazournes (2010), 1209–1211; White and Abass (2014), 550–552. Also: Art. 16 OAS Charter (119 UNTS 48); GA Res. 2625 (XXV) (24 Oct. 1970), Principle III; GA Res. 3281 (XXIX) (12 Dec. 1974) (Art. 32). On the related non-technical term 'economic warfare', see further Lowe and Tzanakopoulos (2011).

[175] The term 'unilateral coercive measures' is notably used in relation to their possible adverse consequences on the enjoyment of human rights by civilian populations in target States. See e.g. HRC Res. 27/21 (26 Sept. 2014); GA Res 70/151 (17 Dec. 2015); and generally UN Docs. A/HRC/19/33 (11 Jan. 2012), 2–11; A/HRC/28/74 (10 Feb. 2015), 4–6; Jazairy, Report of the Special Rapporteur on the negative impact of unilateral coercive measures on the enjoyment of human rights, A/HRC/30/45 (10 Aug. 2015). Further: Section 6.2.1.2(iii).

alone or by a group of States acting collectively, to compel a change of policy by another State.

With the aforementioned caveat in mind, the non-technical term 'unilateral coercive measures' will be used in this study as convenient shorthand for conduct involving both countermeasures and retorsion.

1.4.5 Third-Party Countermeasures

It is now finally convenient to discuss the central concept of this study: third-party countermeasures. It was noted above that the underlying concept of countermeasures has long been firmly established in international law. However, countermeasures were traditionally concerned only with bilateral situations of responsibility arising between the directly injured State and the responsible State.[176] By contrast, the concept of third-party countermeasures is a relatively recent one, even if it is broadly associated with a long history of debate about the possible invocation of responsibility for breaches of communitarian norms. Grotius affirmed a right of sovereigns to resort to war in response to violations of natural law in circumstances where they were not directly injured:

> [K]ings, and those who possess rights equal to those kings, have the right of demanding punishments not only on account of injuries committed against themselves or their subjects, but also on account of injuries which do not directly affect them but excessively violate the law of nature or of nations in regard to any persons whatsoever.[177]

For his part, Vattel excluded reprisals by third States based on an essentially bilateral conception of responsibility:

> [T]o grant reprisals against a nation in favour of foreigners, is to set himself up for a judge between that nation and the foreigners, which no sovereign has a right to do ... England having in 1662 granted reprisals against the United Provinces, in favour of the Knights of Malta, the States of Holland said, with reason, that, according to the law of nations, reprisals could only be granted to maintain the right of the subjects of the State, and not for an affair in which the nation had no concern.[178]

Bynkershoek suggested that such reprisals were lawful, '[f]or if you permit reprisals on behalf of subjects, there seems no reason why you

---

[176] See above Section 1.4.1.

[177] Grotius (1646), Book II, Chapter XX, §40. See also ibid., Chapter XXV, §8 (on humanitarian intervention).

[178] Vattel (1758), Book II, Chapter XVIII, §348. See, however, ibid., Chapter V, §70.

should deny them on behalf of foreigners'.[179] Still, the Vattelian conception of responsibility as a bilateral matter was predominant in the literature of the nineteenth century – even if it was sometimes contested. Heffter and Bluntschli introduced lists of obligations 'owed to the international community as a whole' (such as the putative obligation not to attempt world domination or the obligations to suppress piracy and the slave trade) the violation of which was deemed an injury to all States that should be suppressed by their joint efforts.[180] For his part, Heffter affirmed a limited right for third States to take reprisals:

> [U]ne tierce puissance pourrait participer aux représailles d'une autre, lorsque sa coopération aurait pour but de mettre un terme aux violations du droit international ou à des procédés contraire à l'humanité et à la justice. En ce cas les États ne font que remplir une mission commune qui leur est tracée naturellement. Organes suprêmes et multiples de l'humanité, ils sont appelés à en faire respecter les lois partout où elles sont violées.[181]

In more general terms, Hall stated:

> When a state grossly and patently violates international law in a matter of serious importance, it is competent to any state, or to the body of states, to hinder the wrong-doing from being accomplished, or to punish the wrong-doer ...
>
> Whatever may be the action appropriate to the case, it is open to every state to take it. International law being unprovided with the support of an organised authority, the work of police must be done by such members of the community of nations as are able to perform it.[182]

Manning, Phillimore, Halleck and von Martens (following Vattel) observed that reprisals by third States were unlawful, while von Bulmerincq cautioned against them, as he feared their use would lead to a Hobbesian *bellum omnium contra omnes*.[183] In short, by the early twentieth century, the bilateral conception of responsibility was widely accepted in the literature with only sporadic support for third-party countermeasures.

---

[179] Bynkershoek (1744), Ch. XXII, 120–121. See also Tams (2005), 49.
[180] Heffter (1857), 207–208, §104; Bluntschli (1868), 263–265, §§471–473. Further: Ago, Fifth Report, 41–42; Frowein (1994), 406–407; Nolte (2002), 1085–1086; Crawford (2013a), 21–22.
[181] Heffter (1857), 217, §110.   [182] Hall (1890), 57–58.
[183] Manning (1839), 110–111; Phillimore (1857), Vol. III, 22 (and also ibid., Vol. I, 442); Halleck (1861), 309–310, §29; von Martens (1864), 198–199, §261; von Bulmerincq (1889), 84–85.

During the course of the twentieth century, two ruinous world wars resulted in a growing recognition of communitarian norms. In particular, the gradual emergence of international obligations in the field of human rights exposed deficiencies in the traditional bilateral model of responsibility based on direct injury and individual right-duty relationships. Under such a regime, in case of violations of the human rights of non-nationals, there was simply no directly injured State with standing to invoke the responsibility of the wrongdoing State. In 1966, by the casting vote of President Spender, the ICJ's much-criticized judgment in the second phase of *South West Africa* highlighted the limitations of the bilateral model of responsibility.[184] A few years later, the ICJ in *Barcelona Traction* famously took a 'significant step' in the direction of a multilateral dimension of responsibility by its affirmation of the category of obligations *erga omnes* – that is, obligations of a State towards the international community as a whole, the protection of which is in the legal interest of all States.[185] Still, the ICJ was silent on the specific means by which obligations *erga omnes* could be enforced under international law. Even prior to the Court's judgment in *Barcelona Traction*, a nascent practice had emerged in the 1960s by which several States, based on the rationale of third-party counter-measures, took unilateral action against South Africa in response to its illegal policy of apartheid and against Greece for serious human rights violations committed in that country.[186]

The ILC has recognized a broader conception of responsibility which, although it includes traditional bilateral situations of responsibility, is not limited to them – as witnessed by Articles 40, 41, 48 and 54 ARSIWA.[187] In 2000, Special Rapporteur Crawford introduced a proposal concerned with the enforcement of 'collective obligations' which, 'for the sake of simplicity', he discussed under the rubric of '"collective countermeasures"'.[188] As this category was not necessarily limited to situations where States responded collectively (i.e. it covered responses adopted by one State or by several States), Crawford

---

[184] *South West Africa*, ICJ Rep. (1966), 6 (and above n. 112). See further Section 2.1.1.1.
[185] ARSIWA Commentary, Art. 1, §4. See further Section 2.1.1.
[186] See further Sections 4.2.1 and 4.2.2.
[187] ARSIWA Commentary, Art. 1, §4; Draft Articles Commentary, Art. 1, §6.
[188] Crawford, Third Report, 101–102, para. 386; and already YbILC (1992), vol. I, 154, para. 30 (Mr. Crawford). See also Riphagen, Fourth Report, 12, para. 62; Focarelli (1993), 52; Talmon (2004), 162; Sicilianos (2010), 1137; Crawford (2013a), 703; White and Abass (2014), 547. Further: Section 3.2.1.3.

acknowledged that '"collective" countermeasures' was a 'somewhat ambiguous term' and that the term '"multilateral" countermeasures might well be preferable'.[189] The Drafting Committee in 2000 adopted a modified version of Crawford's proposal as Draft Article 54 [2000] entitled 'Countermeasures by States other than the injured State'.[190] As already noted, however, the ILC in 2001 ultimately reserved its position by the adoption of a saving clause in Article 54 ARSIWA using the expression 'lawful measures' rather than 'countermeasures' in order to safeguard all points of view on the matter.[191]

Several other terms have also been used to refer to the same legal category, including 'third-party countermeasures',[192] 'third-State countermeasures',[193] 'countermeasures of general interest',[194] 'countermeasures *omnium*',[195] 'solidarity measures'[196] and 'multilateral sanctions'.[197] The diverse terminology provides a further illustration of the uncertainty surrounding this legal category: it does not only denote the sanction that dare not speak its name, but in fact, it does not even have a settled name. This study uses the term 'third-party countermeasures' as it seems to best reflect the rationale of Article 48 ARSIWA. A third-party countermeasure may thus be described as an otherwise unlawful act of a peaceful character taken by a State other than an injured State in response to a breach of a communitarian norm owed to it (as defined in Article 48 ARSIWA) in order to obtain cessation and reparation.[198]

---

[189] YbILC (2000), vol. I, 337, para. 56 (Mr. Crawford); Crawford (2002), 54. See also YbILC (2000), vol. I, 336, para. 46 (Mr. Pellet); Alland (2002), 1222 (for criticism of the term 'collective countermeasures'); and Crawford, Bodeau and Peel (2000), 672; YbILC (2000), vol. I, 323, para. 12 (Mr. Kamto), 329, para. 59 (Mr. Galicki) (for the term 'multilateral countermeasures').

[190] ILC Report (2000), UN Doc. A/55/10, 70; YbILC (2000), vol. I, 399–400, paras. 86–91 (Chairman of the Drafting Committee, Mr. Gaja).

[191] See above Section 1.3; and YbILC (2001), vol. I, 112–113, para. 64 (Chairman of the Drafting Committee, Mr. Tomka); ARSIWA Commentary, Art. 54, §7.

[192] See e.g. Simma (1989), 306 (n. 94), 308, 314; Simma (1994a), 295; Tams (2002a), 781, 789–790; Meron (2003), 296; Orakhelashvili (2006), 270; Dawidowicz (2006), 333; Tams (2011), 391–392; Crawford (2013a), 703 (n. 176).

[193] See e.g. Charney (1989), 75; Katselli Proukaki (2010), 2–3; Bird (2010), 899; Hakimi (2014), 119.

[194] See e.g. Alland (2002), 1221; Tams (2005), 199, 242.   [195] See Villalpando (2005), 366.

[196] See e.g. Koskenniemi (2001), 337; Katselli Proukaki (2010), 2–3.

[197] See YbILC (2000), vol. I, 311, para. 81 (Mr. Brownlie), 312, para. 11 (Mr. Momtaz).

[198] See ARSIWA Commentary, Art. 22, §6; Introductory Commentary to Chapter II of Part Three, §8; Art. 54, §6.

1.5 Outline of the Study

This study is composed of six chapters. Chapters 2 and 3 consider the contribution made by the ICJ and the ILC, respectively, to the development of third-party countermeasures in international law. Chapter 4 examines State practice on third-party countermeasures. Chapter 5 assesses whether States are entitled to resort to third-party countermeasures under international law. In the light of State practice, it also examines more closely the main policy arguments made about the concept as well as some other salient features related thereto. Finally, Chapter 6 examines the safeguards regime applicable to third-party countermeasures.

2

Third-Party Countermeasures and the ICJ

The notion of third-party countermeasures, as embodied in Article 54 ARSIWA, is generally understood as a possible means of implementation of responsibility for breaches of communitarian norms, i.e. obligations *erga omnes (partes)*[1] within the meaning of Article 48 ARSIWA.[2] Responsibility may arise by operation of law, but its implementation is by no means automatic. Implementation of responsibility requires invocation (or standing) by way of a claim of a relatively formal character, including one made, in the terminology of Article 48 ARSIWA, by 'a State other than the injured State' in defence of a communitarian norm.[3] Simply put, standing is primarily a 'normative concept' which seeks to distinguish a State's legally enforceable interests from other non-enforceable ones based on notions such as 'right', 'injury' and 'legal interest'.[4] The invocation or implementation of responsibility can take various forms; it may involve the presentation of a claim in a diplomatic setting, the commencement of proceedings before an international court or tribunal, or even the taking of (third-party) countermeasures.[5]

The notion of standing is relevant in analytical terms to all such forms of law enforcement even if it does not necessarily apply in the same way. An entitlement to invoke responsibility in response to breaches of communitarian norms (whether by judicial proceedings or otherwise) may

---

[1] The terminology of 'obligations *erga omnes (partes)*' was deliberately avoided by the ILC but it is nevertheless used (as appropriate) throughout this study – interchangeably with the term 'communitarian norms' – as convenient shorthand for either (or both) of the two sets of communitarian norms embodied in Article 48(1)(a) and (b) ARSIWA: see further ARSIWA Commentary, Art. 48, §9.

[2] See generally ARSIWA Commentary, Introductory Commentary to Chapter II of Part Three, §3. Also: Crawford, Third Report, 77–78, paras. 285, 291. For examples of obligations *erga omnes (partes)*, see ARSIWA Commentary, Art. 48, §§7, 9.

[3] See ARSIWA Commentary, Introductory Commentary to Part Three, §1; Art. 42, §2; Art. 43, §2.

[4] See Tams (2005), 28–31 (with further references).

[5] See ARSIWA Commentary, Art. 42, §2.

not automatically translate into an entitlement to take third-party countermeasures.[6] The ILC affirms in Article 48 ARSIWA that States have standing to invoke breaches of communitarian norms, but in Article 54 ARSIWA, it leaves open the question of whether – and if so, in which circumstances – States may do so by way of third-party countermeasures. Indeed, standing to take third-party countermeasures – insofar as it exists at all[7] – may well be subject to different and more stringent conditions (e.g. regarding the possible condition of a serious breach) than other less coercive forms of invocation of responsibility for breaches of communitarian norms. The basic point nevertheless remains intact: the general notion of standing in defence of community interests provides the analytical basis for an assessment of the contours of a possible entitlement to take third-party countermeasures.

The ICJ in its famous *Barcelona Traction* dictum was the catalyst for the modern formulation of the *erga omnes* concept as a tool of law enforcement for communitarian norms.[8] The Court's affirmation of obligations *erga omnes* in that case marked a 'significant step'[9] away from the traditional bilateral model of enforcement towards a regime of communitarian law enforcement. Much of the debate about the *Barcelona Traction* dictum has centred on the issue of third-party countermeasures. Thus it marks the analytical starting point for the debate on third-party countermeasures in the modern period. As will be shown in the following chapters, the Court's affirmation of obligations *erga omnes* almost immediately influenced the ILC's work on State responsibility and also, *inter alia*, gradually influenced State practice concerning the increasing enforcement of communitarian norms by way of third-party countermeasures – in short, in the words of Judge Weeramantry, 'the

---

[6] See Tams (2005), 25–27.

[7] This basic question cannot be answered in the abstract but requires an assessment of practice. For a detailed assessment see Chapters 3–5.

[8] *Barcelona Traction*, ICJ Rep. (1970), 3 at 32, para. 33. The *erga omnes* applicability of communitarian norms (especially in the form of jurisdictional clauses under multilateral treaties expressly granting States parties standing in defence of community interests) has a long history and was not a novel idea unknown to international law pre-*Barcelona Traction*: for a useful historical overview see Tams (2005), 69–94 (with many further references). Also: ILC Report on Fragmentation of International Law, UN Doc. A/CN.4/ L.682 (2006), 193, para. 381; Crawford (2013a), 363–364; Villalpando (2013), 623.

[9] ARSIWA Commentary, Art. 1, §4. Similarly: Simma (1994a), 293 ('A great leap forward'); Tams and Tzanakopoulos (2010), 792 ('a giant leap for the ICJ'). By evading the issue of peremptory norms – 'a leap too far' – it has also been described as 'a great leap sideways': Crawford (2006b), 411; Crawford (2012), 583. Also: Villalpando (2013), 636.

notion of obligations *erga omnes* developed apace thereafter'.[10] The ICJ has in this way acted as a 'powerful agent of legal development'[11] in the field of communitarian law enforcement. It thus seems appropriate to start the analysis of third-party countermeasures as a possible tool of communitarian law enforcement by an assessment of the ICJ's contribution to this matter.

The present chapter will do so by examining the ICJ's jurisprudence relevant to third-party countermeasures;[12] however, before embarking on that analysis, a few preliminary remarks of a general character relevant to the Court's contribution are warranted (2.1). This will be followed by an examination of the *Barcelona Traction* (2.1.1), *Namibia* (2.1.2), *Tehran Hostages* (2.1.3) and *Nicaragua* (2.1.4) cases before some concluding observations are made (2.2).

2.1   The ICJ's Contribution

In *East Timor*, Judge Weeramantry observed that 'the *erga omnes* concept has been at the door of this Court for many years'.[13] In reality, States (especially those which are not specially affected by the breach of a communitarian norm) have rarely come knocking on that door. And in any event, it remains unclear whether the Court would actually open it, even if given the opportunity to do so. Obligations *erga omnes* have rarely been enforced by way of judicial proceedings.[14] This is perhaps unsurprising given the political ramifications and jurisdictional constraints under which such claims operate. As the ICJ held in *East Timor*, 'the

---

[10] *East Timor*, ICJ Rep. (1995), 90 at 215 (Diss. Op. Judge Weeramantry).

[11] Tams and Tzanakopoulos (2010), 800.

[12] The case law relevant to the applicable safeguards regime – which presupposes an affirmative answer to the antecedent question of possible standing to take third-party countermeasures – is considered separately in Chapter 6.

[13] *East Timor*, ICJ Rep. (1995), 90 at 216 (Diss. Op. Judge Weeramantry).

[14] See e.g. Tams (2005), 159; Gaja (2013), 100; and further Voeffray (2004), 73–90; Tams (2005), 158–197; Villalpando (2005), 270–293. As will be demonstrated in Chapter 4, such obligations are much more frequently enforced by way of third-party countermeasures – and this is so even where judicial (or quasi-judicial) avenues of redress are *prima facie* available. For example, States could have brought ICJ (or other inter-State) proceedings against the FRY for its actions in Kosovo, but they did not do so, instead preferring, *inter alia*, to take third-party countermeasures: see further Section 4.2.15. Similarly, such proceedings could also in many cases potentially have been brought, *inter alia*, under the Torture Convention (Arts. 22 and 30) and the International Convention on the Elimination of All Forms of Racial Discrimination (Arts. 11 and 22) in lieu of (or in parallel with) the adoption of third-party countermeasures against target States. For relevant examples, see generally Chapter 4.

erga omnes character of a norm and the rule of consent to jurisdiction are two different things'[15] – in many cases, there simply is no judicial door to knock on. A few rare instances may briefly be recalled.

In the *Nuclear Tests* cases, Australia and New Zealand brought proceedings against France following nuclear tests carried out by the latter in the South Pacific Ocean.[16] Australia sought to establish the admissibility of its claim on the basis that the 'rule prohibiting atmospheric nuclear testing' was 'couched in terms of an *erga omnes* obligation and not in terms of an obligation owed to particular States'.[17] New Zealand likewise expressly based the admissibility of its claim on France's nuclear testing being in violation of an obligation *erga omnes*.[18] The ICJ dismissed both claims as moot when, during the proceedings, French President Giscard d'Estaing made a unilateral undertaking by way of a public statement to terminate the nuclear tests in the South Pacific.[19]

In *East Timor*, Portugal brought a case against Australia concerning its dealings with Indonesia over the continental shelf of East Timor. Portugal, in order to establish standing, based the admissibility of its claim on the *erga omnes* character of the right of self-determination and on its (individual) status as the former administrating power.[20] The ICJ found that it could not exercise jurisdiction relying on a strict (perhaps

---

[15] *East Timor*, ICJ Rep. (1995), 90 at 102, para. 29. See also *Armed Activities (New Application: 2002) (DRC v. Rwanda)*, ICJ Rep. (2006), 6 at 32, para. 64 (noting that the same principle applies with respect to peremptory norms). This distinction is generally undisputed: see e.g. 2005 IDI Krakow Resolution (Art. 3).

[16] *Nuclear Tests (Australia v. France)*, ICJ Rep. (1974), 253; *Nuclear Tests (New Zealand v. France)*, ICJ Rep. (1974), 457.

[17] *Nuclear Tests (Australia v. France)*, ICJ Rep. (1974), 253 at 256; Australia's Memorial on Jurisdiction and Admissibility (27 Nov. 1973), 334, paras. 447–448. Australia also claimed to be specially affected by France's nuclear testing: see ibid., 331, paras. 430–433.

[18] *Nuclear Tests (New Zealand v. France)*, ICJ Rep. (1974), 457 at 460; New Zealand's Memorial on Jurisdiction and Admissibility (29 Oct. 1973), 203–204, paras. 190–193 (also claiming individual legal injury, at ibid.).

[19] *Nuclear Tests (Australia v. France)*, ICJ Rep. (1974), 253 at 269–272, paras. 49–59, 62; *Nuclear Tests (New Zealand v. France)*, ICJ Rep. (1974), 457 at 474–478, paras. 51–62, 65. For criticism of the Court's narrow interpretation of the object of the claims (rendering them moot), see generally ibid., 312 and 494 (Joint Diss. Op. Judges Onyeama, Dillard, Jiménez de Aréchaga and Waldock). They added that the possible judicial enforcement of obligations *erga omnes* was 'capable of rational legal argument and a proper subject of litigation before this Court' (ibid., 370, para. 117; 521, para. 52).

[20] *East Timor*, ICJ Rep. (1995), 90 at 94–95; Portugal's Reply (1 June 1992), 237–248, paras. 8.01–8.17. For its part, Australia (seemingly contrary to its earlier position in *Nuclear Tests*) denied the existence of an individual right of public interest standing to bring an *erga omnes* claim with respect to the principle of self-determination: see ibid., Australia's Counter-Memorial (1 June 1992), 119, paras. 262–263.

too strict) application of the indispensable third-party rule: it could not decide on the matter without ruling on the lawfulness of the conduct of an absent third State, Indonesia, vis-à-vis East Timor.[21] In sum, States rarely knock on the Court's door for the enforcement of obligations *erga omnes*; and on the odd occasion that they summon the political will to do so, the Court appears reluctant to open it. Some twenty years later, Judge Weeramantry's observation in *East Timor* that 'the *erga omnes* obligation has not thus far been the subject of judicial determination' still holds true.[22]

By contrast, it is more surprising that States, in the absence of individual injury, have made such little use of the many treaty provisions recognizing public interest standing to bring judicial (or quasi-judicial) claims in response to breaches of obligations *erga omnes partes*.[23] The *South West Africa* cases provide a well-known example of an unsuccessful attempt to do so.[24] In *Obligation to Prosecute or Extradite*, Belgium brought (partly) successful proceedings against Senegal for various alleged violations of the Torture Convention and customary international law regarding the latter State's failure to bring criminal proceedings against Mr. Habré, a former president of Chad.[25] Belgium

---

[21] *East Timor*, ICJ Rep. (1995), 90 at 102, para. 29. See also ibid., 238 (Diss. Op. Judge Skubiszewski) ('concerned with the possibility that the Judgment might revive past fears regarding a restrictive concept of the Court's function'). For critical comment see further Simma (1994a), 297–298; Lowe (1995), 484; Dugard (1996), 549; Chinkin (1996), 712; Gaja (2005), 197. See also Tams (2005), 185 (for the suggestion that the Court would have allowed Portugal standing to enforce its *erga omnes* claim, absent the indispensable third-party rule as a procedural bar).

[22] *East Timor*, ICJ Rep. (1995), 90 at 216 (Diss. Op. Judge Weeramantry). See also Simma (1994a), 298 ('[O]bligations *erga omnes* do exist in the world of international law, even if its paramount judicial institution appears hitherto to only pay lip-service to this manifestation of community interest'); *Armed Activities (DRC v. Uganda)*, ICJ Rep. (2005), 168 at 339–340, paras. 17–19 (Sep. Op. Judge Simma) (lamenting that, as a result of the 'somewhat careless' presentation of Uganda's second counterclaim – rightly dismissed as a diplomatic protection claim – 'the Court's reasoning ... finished at this point', and thereby did not clarify that 'no gaps exist in the law' with respect to the judicial protection of non-nationals).

[23] See e.g. Tams (2011), 383–388; and also Section 6.1.3.1(i) (text accompanying nn. 67–70, with further references).

[24] *South West Africa*, ICJ Rep. (1966), 6. Contrast the early successful attempt in *S.S. 'Wimbledon'*, PCIJ Ser. A, No. 1 (1923), 15 at 23; and also (perhaps more straightforwardly), *Interpretation of the Statute of the Memel Territory*, Preliminary Objection, PCIJ Ser. A/B, No. 47 (1932), 243 at 248; Merits, PCIJ Ser. A/B, No. 49 (1932), 294 at 337. Further: *South West Africa*, ICJ Rep. (1966), 6 at 375–377 (Diss. Op. Judge Jessup); Voeffray (2004), 47–54; Tams (2005), 75–79.

[25] *Obligation to Prosecute or Extradite*, ICJ Rep. (2012), 422.

based the admissibility of its claim on the *erga omnes partes* character of certain obligations under the Torture Convention and, for this purpose, relied on Article 48(1)(a) ARSIWA. Belgium also relied (less persuasively) on being specially affected under Article 42(b)(i) ARSIWA by reason of its own criminal proceedings and an extradition request. In addition, Belgium based its standing under customary international law on Article 48(1)(b) ARSIWA and the *erga omnes* character of the *aut dedere aut judicare* obligation with respect to crimes against humanity, war crimes and genocide.[26]

The Court dismissed the *erga omnes* claim under customary international law for lack of jurisdiction on exceedingly narrow grounds: no dispute existed between the parties on this point prior to the date of the filing of the case – it only arose subsequently.[27] The Court did, however, uphold the admissibility of the *erga omnes partes* claim under the Torture Convention. Relying on the broader rationale of the *Barcelona Traction* dictum, the Court concluded:

> The common interest in compliance with the relevant obligations under the Convention against Torture implies the entitlement of each State party to the Convention to make a claim concerning the cessation of an alleged breach by another State party. If a special interest were required for that purpose, in many cases no State would be in a position to make such a claim. It follows that any State party to the Convention may invoke the responsibility of another State party with a view to ascertaining the alleged failure to comply with its obligations *erga omnes partes*, such as those under Article 6, paragraph 2, and Article 7, paragraph 1, of the Convention, and to bring that failure to an end.[28]

The Court, on that basis, concluded that Belgium, in its capacity as self-appointed guardian of the Torture Convention, had standing to

---

[26] *Obligation to Prosecute or Extradite*, ICJ Rep. (2012), 422 at 428–429, 448–449, paras. 12–14, 65–66; Belgium's Memorial (1 July 2010), 79, paras. 5.14–5.18. For a rejection of the customary law basis of such an obligation, see *Obligation to Prosecute or Extradite*, ICJ Rep. (2012), 422 at 476–480, paras. 21–40 (Sep. Op. Judge Abraham).

[27] *Obligation to Prosecute or Extradite*, ICJ Rep. (2012), 422 at 444–445, paras. 53–55. For strong criticism see ibid. at 472–476, paras. 6–20 (Sep. Op. Judge Abraham), 541–544, paras. 134–144 (Sep. Op. Judge Cançado Trindade). It has been suggested that the Court's restrictive approach to jurisdiction under the optional clause resulted from its twofold concern to simplify the dispute and to avoid pronouncing on the delicate issue of the customary law status of the putative *aut dedere aut judicare* obligation for core international crimes: see ibid., 610, para. 18 (Diss. Op. Judge *ad hoc* Sur). Also: Hernández (2013), 48–49.

[28] *Obligation to Prosecute or Extradite*, ICJ Rep. (2012), 422 at 450, para. 69 (see also ibid., para. 68).

invoke the responsibility of Senegal for violations of its obligations thereunder.[29] This implied affirmation of Article 48(1)(a) ARSIWA merits attention: it is the *first time* that the Court has given concrete effect to a communitarian norm[30] – a point not lost on Judges Skotnikov and Xue.[31] Still, the Court only left its door ajar; communitarian norms had made their entrance with just one foot in the door. And yet even this much was not without controversy.[32]

Crawford has concluded that the Court's handling of the dispute in *Obligation to Prosecute or Extradite* as exclusively one under the Torture Convention – with its limited affirmation of obligations *erga omnes partes* – and not also under customary international law is 'significant' insofar as it suggests that 'it may be more parsimonious with *erga omnes* obligations in future'.[33] Based on the above review, this seems

---

[29] Ibid., 450, para. 70.

[30] A second example – *sub silentio* – may be found in the *Whaling in the Antarctic* case. Australia successfully brought proceedings against Japan and implicitly based the admissibility of its claim on alleged breaches of obligations *erga omnes partes* under the International Convention for the Regulation of Whaling (161 UNTS 74) and other obligations for the preservation of marine mammals and the marine environment; however, the matter was curiously not in dispute and wholly absent in the judgment: see *Whaling in the Antarctic*, ICJ Rep. (2014), 226. The Court's silence on this point is unfortunate. It had another (rare) opportunity to consider the evolving law on the enforcement of communitarian norms under Article 48 ARSIWA, and (yet again) failed to seize it. See also Crawford (2013a), 373; and *Obligations concerning Negotiations relating to Cessation of the Nuclear Arms Race and to Nuclear Disarmament (Marshall Islands v. United Kingdom; Marshall Islands v. Pakistan; Marshall Islands v. India)*, ICJ, Judgment, 5 Oct. 2016, Marshall Island's Application (24 Apr. 2014), 15, 17, 30, paras. 35, 40, 85, respectively (basing its standing on the claim that Article VI of the Nuclear Non-Proliferation Treaty (729 UNTS 161) amounts to an obligation *erga omnes*).

[31] *Obligation to Prosecute or Extradite*, ICJ Rep. (2012), 422 at 484, para. 20 (Sep. Op. Judge Skotnikov) ('The Judgment cites no precedent in which a State has instituted proceedings before this Court or any other international judicial body in respect of alleged violations of an *erga omnes partes* obligation simply on the basis of it being a party to an instrument similar to the Convention against Torture. Nor does it mention the fact, which might be worth noting as a reflection of State practice – or rather the absence of it – that the inter-State human rights complaints mechanisms (including the one provided for in Article 21 of the Convention against Torture) have never been used'), 575–576, paras. 16, 18 (Diss. Op. Judge Xue).

[32] For strong criticism of the affirmation of Article 48(1)(a) ARSIWA, see *Obligation to Prosecute or Extradite*, ICJ Rep. (2012), 422 at 482–485, paras. 10–22 (Sep. Op. Judge Skotnikov) (voting in favour of the relevant part of the *dispositif*, but submitting that the Court had erred as to the proper ground – special injury – to base its finding of admissibility, ibid., 481, paras. 1–2) (Diss. Op. Judge Xue), 574–577, paras. 13–23 (Diss. Op. Judge Xue), 613–619, paras. 26–46 (Diss. Op. Judge *ad hoc* Sur). Further: Thirlway (2014), 150–153.

[33] Crawford (2013a), 370. Compare *Obligation to Prosecute or Extradite*, ICJ Rep. (2012), 422 at 468, para. 15 (Dec. Judge Owada), explaining his vote in favour of the relevant part of the *dispositif* thus: 'Nevertheless, I wish to underline that this finding of the Court is

a reasonable conclusion. To summarize, the *erga omnes* concept has rarely been at the door of the Court; and on the odd occasion that it has, the Court has only *once* (discounting the anomalous *Whaling in the Antarctic* case)[34] opened its door to a claim involving the enforcement of obligations *erga omnes partes*. And the Court is still to open its door to a claim involving the enforcement of obligations *erga omnes*. For the rest, following *Barcelona Traction*, the *erga omnes* concept has only found its way onto the judicial stage in a relatively small number of cases, as a sort of cameo appearance with a minor supporting role, with little or no relevance for the outcome. The Court has in these cases (as in the others already discussed) treated the *erga omnes* concept with parsimony and provided little by way of elaboration of its possible legal effects, including in the field of law enforcement.[35]

It follows that there is not much concrete guidance in the ICJ's jurisprudence on the possible enforcement of communitarian norms. The Court's contribution is limited.[36] This is especially so for the concept of third-party countermeasures: with the possible exception of the *Nicaragua* case, which is discussed below, it has never been the proper subject of a dispute before the Court.[37] States have simply not brought

---

built on its reasoning that Belgium's entitlement to this standing derives from its status as a State party to the Convention, and *nothing else*') (emphasis added).

[34] See above n. 30.

[35] See *Namibia* case, ICJ Rep. (1971), 16 at 56, para. 126; *Application of the Convention on the Prevention and Punishment of the Crime of Genocide (Bosnia and Herzegovina v. Yugoslavia)*, ICJ Rep. (1996), 595 at 616, para. 31; *Wall* case, ICJ Rep. (2004), 136 at 199, paras. 155–157; *Armed Activities (New Application: 2002) (DRC v. Rwanda)*, ICJ Rep. (2006), 6 at 31–32, para. 64; *Application of the Convention on the Prevention and Punishment of the Crime of Genocide (Bosnia and Herzegovina v. Serbia and Montenegro)*, ICJ Rep. (2007), 43 at 104, para. 147. Generally: Hernández (2013), 13–60 (noting the Court's role as 'a reluctant guardian' of communitarian norms).

[36] Some further guidance can be found in the individual opinions of ICJ judges (see n. 78 below).

[37] This does not necessarily mean that such judicial claims could not have been brought. For example, the ten ICJ cases brought by the FRY against various NATO Member States in 1999 focused exclusively (and perhaps understandably so) on *Operation Allied Force* in Kosovo; the FRY did not once impugn the multitude of third-party countermeasures adopted against it by the said States. See however Section 4.2.15 (text accompanying nn. 461–463) for vehement FRY protests about their illegality outside the courtroom. See also YbILC (2000), vol. I, 329, para. 60 (Mr. Galicki) (noting the aborted arbitration proceedings following the US adoption of third-party countermeasures against Poland in 1981); and further Section 4.2.7. For its part, Uganda could have brought ICJ proceedings under the optional clause in response to the third-party countermeasures adopted against it by Western States in the late 1970s (though in the circumstances that option was perhaps somewhat theoretical): see further Section 4.2.3.

disputes about third-party countermeasures to the door of the Court. Thus the Court's contribution to the debate on third-party counter-measures in the analysis that follows is both limited and indirect: it results almost exclusively from inferences drawn from a general assessment of the Court's jurisprudence on the *erga omnes* concept. To conclude, the ICJ in its famous *Barcelona Traction* dictum may have been avant-garde in articulating the *erga omnes* concept as a general category, but – especially in terms of drawing specific consequences for the enforcement of obligations *erga omnes* – it has been 'at the rearguard of current international legal debate' ever since.[38] That said, the Court's jurisprudence on the *erga omnes* concept constitutes the *fons et origo* of the modern debate on third-party countermeasures in analytical terms and certainly cannot be ignored.

2.1.1   *The* Barcelona Traction *Case*

The judgment of the ICJ in *Barcelona Traction* is the 'classic judicial text'[39] on the subject of the enforcement of communitarian norms.[40] The Court's contribution on the issue was nevertheless purely by way of dictum with little (if any)[41] relevance to the actual dispute before it. That dispute concerned the rules governing the diplomatic protection of corporations and the treatment of aliens under customary international law. Belgium had brought a claim against Spain for alleged injury done to Belgian shareholders in the Barcelona Traction, Light and Power Company, Ltd., a company that operated in Spain – at one stage as a major supplier of electricity in Catalonia – but was incorporated in Canada, in whose territory it also had its registered office. The Belgian claim for reparation was based on certain allegedly internationally wrongful acts (amounting to a series of denials of justice) by administrative and judicial organs of the Spanish State, which involved a declaration adjudging the company bankrupt and certain subsequent judicial and other acts that led to its total spoliation.[42] The key issue

---

[38] Hernández (2013), 13. The Court has so far not taken the opportunity to endorse the ILC's interpretation of its case law as articulated in ARSIWA Commentary, Art. 48, §8.
[39] Thirlway (2014), 147.   [40] *Barcelona Traction*, ICJ Rep. (1970), 3.
[41] For an interesting discussion see Villalpando (2013), 623, esp. at 634–636.
[42] See *Barcelona Traction*, ICJ Rep. (1970), 3 at 6–30, paras. 1–25 (for a summary of the facts and the submissions of the parties). The bankruptcy proceedings were allegedly part of a wider orchestrated effort to illegally wrest control of the company for the benefit of important Spanish financial interests, controlled by Mr. Juan March, an influential financier closely associated with the Franco regime (compare ibid., 17, para. 25).

before the Court concerned Spain's third preliminary objection related to the admissibility of the claim: namely, the question of whether Belgium had standing to exercise diplomatic protection of Belgian shareholders in a Canadian company.[43]

The ICJ answered the above question in the negative. In essence, the Court rejected the admissibility of the Belgian claim, as the alleged injury was done to the company itself and did not cause any direct injury to the rights of the Belgian shareholders. The nationality of corporations is determined by national incorporation rules:[44] under the law of diplomatic protection, the espousal of a claim of a Canadian company was thus a matter held in right of Canada, not of Belgium or any other State.

2.1.1.1 The Dictum Revisited

In a famous dictum, introduced in paragraphs 33 and 34 of the judgment, the Court added the following to its negative answer on the admissibility of the Belgian claim:

> [A]n essential distinction should be drawn between the obligations of a State towards the international community as a whole, and those arising vis-à-vis another State in the field of diplomatic protection. By their very nature the former are the concern of all States. In view of the importance of the rights involved, all States can be held to have a legal interest in their protection; they are obligations *erga omnes*.
>
> Such obligations derive, for example, in contemporary international law, from the outlawing of acts of aggression, and of genocide, as also from the principles and rules concerning the basic rights of the human person, including protection from slavery and racial discrimination. Some of the corresponding rights of protection have entered into the body of general international law (*Reservations to the Convention on the Prevention and Punishment of the Crime of Genocide, Advisory Opinion, I.C.J. Reports 1951, p. 23*); others are conferred by international instruments of a universal or quasi-universal character.[45]

---

[43] Ibid., 32, para. 32. Spain had raised four preliminary objections against Belgium's claim. In its earlier judgment (*Barcelona Traction*, ICJ Rep. (1964), 6) the Court had rejected the first two of them and joined the third and fourth (related to lack of standing based on the rules governing nationality of claims and exhaustion of local remedies) to the merits (see ICJ Rep. (1970), 3 at 6, para. 3).

[44] *Barcelona Traction*, ICJ Rep. (1970), 3 at 42, para. 70. In 2006, the ILC codified this rule (subject to a limited exception) in Article 9 ADP: see ADP Commentary, Art. 9, §4.

[45] *Barcelona Traction*, ICJ Rep. (1970), 3 at 32, paras. 33–34. Judge Lachs is often credited as the author of the dictum (though no hint of this is found in his brief declaration appended to the judgment, ibid., 52–53): see McWhinney (1995), 37–38; Higgins (1995), 19. Schachter (1986), 892, considers it likely that, based on his earlier strong dissent in

The Court did not, however, elaborate on the specific legal consequences of its affirmation that, with respect to obligations *erga omnes*, 'all States can be held to have a legal interest in their protection'.[46] No elaboration was provided with respect to whom specifically obligations *erga omnes* – defined as 'obligations of a State towards the international community as a whole' – are owed.[47] Neither did the Court elaborate on the 'corresponding rights of protection' of the *erga omnes* concept under international law.[48] Nor did it elaborate on the question of identifying obligations *erga omnes* beyond providing a non-exhaustive list of examples based on 'the importance of the [correlative] rights involved'.[49] Thus statements (mostly) infused by Delphic vapours were emitted from the courtroom. This is not surprising. After all, the dictum was essentially 'a pretext for an apology' for its earlier decision in the second phase of *South West Africa* – it was 'law as politics'.[50]

As a result, the dictum still 'continues to fascinate and puzzle commentators (including at times the Court and its members)';[51] and the two paragraphs have 'taken on a life of their own'.[52] For her part, Judge Higgins rightly observed in the *Wall* case that the famous *Barcelona Traction* dictum is 'frequently invoked for more than it can bear'.[53] Leaving aside the perennial question of identification, the answers to the other questions raised by the dictum nonetheless seem, on closer inspection, reasonably clear.

It may be recalled that the key issue in *Barcelona Traction* concerned Belgium's standing before the ICJ – as evident from paragraph 32 of the judgment. The Court, in paragraphs 33 and 34, introduced its analysis of this issue. For the purposes of determining whether Belgium had

---

South West Africa, Judge Jessup also played an important role in its drafting – a point alluded to (but not confirmed) by Lachs' own reminiscences: see Lachs (1986), 897–898.

[46] *Barcelona Traction*, ICJ Rep. (1970), 3 at 32, para. 33.   [47] Ibid.

[48] Ibid., para. 34. That is, beyond alluding (somewhat paradoxically) to the restriction on making treaty reservations as a right of protection of the *erga omnes* concept under general international law. Compare *Obligation to Prosecute or Extradite*, ICJ Rep. (2012), 422 at 613–614, para. 28 (Judge *ad hoc* Sur).

[49] *Barcelona Traction*, ICJ Rep. (1970), 3 at 32, para. 34. It is not the purpose of this study to seek an answer to this vexed question, except to suggest that State practice on third-party countermeasures may prove a fertile terrain for such an enquiry: see e.g. for a brief discussion Section 5.2.6. Also: ARSIWA Commentary, Art. 48, §9; 2005 IDI Krakow Resolution (preamble).

[50] Crawford, in Tams (2005), xiii.   [51] Tams and Tzanakopoulos (2010), 791.

[52] Tams (2005), 2 (and also ibid., 9–11, for examples in the fields of jurisdiction and the use of force).

[53] *Wall* case, ICJ Rep. (2004), 136 at 216, para. 37 (Sep. Op. Judge Higgins).

standing to bring its claim, the Court made 'an essential distinction' between obligations *erga omnes* and obligations in the field of diplomatic protection. With respect to the latter, the Court added in the next paragraph:

> Obligations the performance of which is the subject of diplomatic protection are not of the same category. It cannot be held, when one such obligation in particular is in question, in a specific case, that all States have a legal interest in its observance. In order to bring a claim in respect of the breach of such an obligation, a State must first establish its right to do so.[54]

It concluded the same paragraph by recalling its earlier jurisprudence that for this distinct category of (bilateral) obligations 'only the party to whom an obligation is due can bring a claim in respect of its breach'.[55] It seems clear from the relevant parts of the judgment that the 'essential distinction' introduced between the two different categories of obligations was concerned with the general rules governing standing to institute ICJ proceedings. Judge Ammoun, albeit alone in the instant case to elaborate on this particular point, expressly confirms this reading.[56] Thus it appears that the Court, in line with Article 34 of the ICJ Statute, acknowledged that the institution of ICJ proceedings by a State (in the event of there being a jurisdictional link) is a corresponding right of protection of the *erga omnes* concept.[57] Two observations suffice to reinforce this conclusion.

First, it is widely regarded as an 'open secret'[58] that the Court's dictum in *Barcelona Traction* was intended as a reversal of its restrictive – and

---

[54] *Barcelona Traction*, ICJ Rep. (1970), 3 at 32, para. 35. For criticism of the distinction between 'rights' and 'mere interests', see ibid., 340 (Diss. Op. Judge *ad hoc* Riphagen). The ILC ultimately refrained from making this distinction as individually injured States also have legal interests: see ARSIWA Commentary, Art. 48, §2; and further Chapter 3.

[55] *Barcelona Traction*, ICJ Rep. (1970), 3 at 32, para. 35.

[56] See ibid., 325, (Sep. Op. Judge Ammoun), where he distinguished between a diplomatic protection claim and 'an action brought in defence of a collective or general interest, the objective being to safeguard legality or the respect due to principles of an international or humane nature, translated into imperative legal norms *(jus cogens)*'. Judge Ammoun appears further to have alluded to the dictum by adding (at ibid.): 'This *distinction* has seemed to me *essential* for the purposes of this discussion, in particular in order to avoid the confusion between individual interest and general interest to which the Respondent has pointed ...') (emphasis added); and also ibid., 326 (criticizing the Court's narrow approach to public interest standing in its 1966 judgment in *South West Africa*). See also ibid., 338–340 (Diss. Op. Judge *ad hoc* Riphagen).

[57] See e.g. Gaja (1989), 154–155; de Hoogh (1996), 50–51; Tams (2005), 163, 174–175.

[58] Thirlway (1989), 94 (also ibid., 98).

much criticized – interpretation of the rules governing standing that had been adopted four years earlier in the second phase of *South West Africa*. That case concerned the question of whether Liberia and Ethiopia, absent any individual injury, had standing under the compromissory clause in Article 7(2) of the Mandate for South West Africa Agreement to institute ICJ proceedings against South Africa. The Court's answer turned on treaty interpretation – an exercise that included the applicable rules on standing under general international law. Departing from its earlier judgment in 1962,[59] the Court adopted a restrictive interpretation (effectively a strong negative presumption)[60] which held that public interest standing, in order to exist, had to be 'clearly vested' in the applicants.[61] In short, the *South West Africa* and *Barcelona Traction* cases were both concerned with the issue of standing to bring ICJ proceedings. In the former case, the Court had declined to affirm the equivalent of an *actio popul005ris* but, in the words of Judge Schwebel in *Nicaragua*, 'that holding was rapidly and decisively displaced by the Court's Judgment in *Barcelona Traction*'.[62] For its part, the ILC has noted that Article 48 ARSIWA, which is explicitly based on the dictum in *Barcelona Traction*, is a 'deliberate departure' from *South West Africa*.[63]

---

[59] *South West Africa*, ICJ Rep. (1962), 319 at 343, 347 ('The language used [in Art. 7(2) of the Mandate Agreement] is broad, clear and precise: it gives rise to no ambiguity and it permits of no exception . . . the dispute is one which is envisaged in the said Article 7 . . .'). The Court (rather unpersuasively) claimed that it had not departed from its earlier judgment: see ibid., 36–38, paras. 59–61. For widespread criticism based on the principle of *res judicata* see e.g. ibid., 333 (Diss. Op. Judge Jessup); Higgins (1966), 577–582; Dugard (1973), 332–346.

[60] See e.g. Brownlie (2008), 470 (noting the alternative view that, in the process of treaty interpretation, public interest standing should not be 'ruled out as an eccentric possibility').

[61] *South West Africa*, ICJ Rep. (1966), 6 at 32, para. 44.

[62] *Nicaragua* case, Provisional Measures, ICJ Rep. (1984), 169 at 197 (Diss. Op. Judge Schwebel). Contrast Gray (1990), 214; Ragazzi (1997), 210–214; Talmon (2004), 172–173. In affirming obligations *erga omnes*, the Court was not necessarily 'announcing a new rule as much as a category, a general idea, an alternative way of establishing legal relations in international law, contrasted with the classic bilateral relation of several rights and duties': see Crawford (2006b), 423; and *Nuclear Tests (Australia v. France)*, ICJ Rep. (1974), 253 at 290, para. 24 (Sep. Op. Judge Gros) (referring to the dictum 'as a sort of benchmark for subsequent use'). But even this much was arguably a rapid and decisive displacement of its earlier holding.

[63] ARSIWA Commentary, Art. 48, §7 (n. 725) (but for a useful clarification see Gaja (2010), 959); and compare Draft Articles Commentary, Art. 19, §10. On the relation between the two cases see e.g. Charpentier (1970), 12; Thirlway (1989), 94, 98; Simma (1994a), 295; Crawford (1996), 588–589; Dugard (1996), 549, 554; Tams (2005), 15, 163; Orakhelashvili (2006), 518–527; Wittich (2007), para. 26; Crawford (2013a), 552. Also: UN Doc. A/C.6/

Second, a contextual reading of paragraph 33 suggests that obligations *erga omnes* are owed to States, which all have an individual legal interest in their protection. Opponents of this view rely on a mixture of legal and policy arguments,[64] including the Court's description of obligations *erga omnes* as being owed 'towards the international community as a whole', in support of the general proposition that their enforcement requires a collective response (whether by competent UN organs or a group of States acting together). Put differently, on this view, individual States simply lack the requisite standing to enforce. For example, Ago stated:

> It is not all States, but rather the international community that is envisaged as the possible bearer of a right of reaction to this particular serious form of internationally wrongful act. Accordingly, the whole idea of obligations *erga omnes* is bound up not only with the fact of recognition of the existence of that community as such, but also with the fact of more advanced institutionalization of that community.[65]

Similar conclusions informed his proposals as ILC Special Rapporteur; as a consequence, individual standing to take third-party countermeasures was seemingly excluded.[66]

In the *Bosnian Genocide* case, Judge Oda argued as follows with respect to the judicial enforcement of the obligations to prevent and punish genocide embodied in Article 1 of the Genocide Convention:

> [T]hese legal obligations are borne in a general manner *erga omnes* by the Contracting Parties in their relations with all the other Contracting Parties to the Convention – or, even, with the international community as a whole – but are *not* obligations in relation to any specific and particular signatory Contracting Party.[67]

56/SR.12, 4–5, para. 22 (South Africa on behalf of SADC). See however *Obligation to Prosecute or Extradite*, ICJ Rep. (2012), 422 at 574–575, para. 15 (Diss. Op. Judge Xue).

[64] See generally Chapter 3 (for an overview of the ILC debate on what became Articles 40, 41, 48 and 54 ARSIWA).

[65] Ago (1989), 238. To similar effect see e.g. Sachariew (1988), 282–285; Graefrath (1989), 167–168.

[66] See Sections 3.1.1; and also 3.1.2 and 3.1.3 (for the unsuccessful proposals by ILC Special Rapporteurs Riphagen and Arangio-Ruiz concerning the institutional enforcement of so-called 'international crimes of State').

[67] *Application of the Convention on the Prevention and Punishment of the Crime of Genocide (Bosnia and Herzegovina v. Serbia and Montenegro)*, ICJ Rep. (1996), 595 at 626, para. 4 (Dec. Judge Oda) (emphasis in the original).

Thus, in Judge Oda's view, Bosnia-Herzegovina lacked standing to institute ICJ proceedings. He added:

> The failure of any Contracting Party 'to prevent and to punish' such a crime may only be rectified and remedied through (i) resort to a competent organ of the United Nations (Art. VIII) or (ii) resort to an international penal tribunal (Art. VI), but not by invoking the responsibility of States in inter-State relations before the International Court of Justice.[68]

Australia, albeit seemingly limiting itself to the principle of self-determination, made a similar point in *East Timor* by stressing the requirement of 'a collective decision by the international community' for any communitarian law enforcement action, as otherwise 'the result would be practically chaotic and self-serving'.[69] Finally, in *Obligation to Prosecute or Extradite*, Judge Xue, after criticizing the Court's interpretation of the *Barcelona Traction* dictum, stated: '[T]here is no general standing resident with each and every State to bring a case in the Court for the vindication of a communal interest'.[70]

The proposition that, as a general matter, collective standing is required to enforce obligations *erga omnes* does not withstand closer scrutiny of the dictum. The use of the Latin term obligations *erga omnes* does not as such take matters further with respect to whom such obligations are owed: it literally means 'towards everyone'. The Court did, however, clarify the matter: the *omnes* refers to States. It first described obligations *erga omnes* as being owed 'towards the international community as a whole', and then equated this community to 'all States'.[71] As Weil observed, the alternative concept of collective standing 'would imply the possession by the international community of some organic representation capable of taking legal action for the protection of its rights, which is certainly not the case'.[72] In a similar vein, Gaja explains: 'It would anyway be difficult to imagine how the international community could exert a right other than through the action of individual States'.[73]

---

[68] Ibid.

[69] *East Timor*, ICJ Rep. (1995), 90, Australia's Counter-Memorial (1 June 1992), 119, paras. 262–263.

[70] *Obligation to Prosecute or Extradite*, ICJ Rep. (2012), 422 at 574–575, para. 15 (Diss. Op. Judge Xue); and also at 484–485, paras. 21–22 (Diss. Op. Judge Skotnikov), 614, paras. 30–31 (Judge *ad hoc* Sur).

[71] See e.g. Lachs (1980), 208; Gaja (1981), 281; Tomuschat (1999), 84; Tams (2005), 175; Gaja (2005), 124. Also: 2005 IDI Krakow Resolution (Art. 1).

[72] Weil (1983), 432. See however UN Doc. A/C.6/56/SR.14, 4, para. 22 (Greece).

[73] Gaja (1981), 281. See also Tams (2005), 175.

Gaja further observes that a requirement that all States must act collectively would make obligations *erga omnes* 'meaningless' as enforcement action agreed to by all States is 'in practice impossible'.[74] And a requirement of collective standing involving a lesser number of States acting jointly would become a vague and indeterminate concept.[75] In short, the reference in the dictum to obligations *erga omnes* being owed to 'all States' necessarily means that they are owed to each State on an individual basis.[76] Indeed the ILC explains in this regard that the use of the term '[a]ny State' in Article 48 ARSIWA is 'intended to avoid any implication that these States have to act together or in unison'.[77]

Several individual opinions by ICJ judges since *Barcelona Traction*, on balance, support this conclusion with respect to the judicial enforcement of obligations *erga omnes* as a corresponding right of protection.[78] To conclude, it seems reasonably clear that the dictum refers to the entitlement of each State individually to bring judicial proceedings in order to ensure compliance with obligations *erga omnes*.

---

[74] Gaja (2005), 125–126; and also Gaja (2013), 97–98 (noting that this effect-oriented reading conforms with treaty practice, including the inter-State complaint procedure in Article 41 ICCPR). Others have made similar statements: see e.g. Zoller (1984a), 117; Meron (2003), 287–288; Fox (2005), 158–159; Skubiszewski (2005), 181; ILC Report on Fragmentation, UN Doc. A/CN.4/L.682 (2006), 200, para. 396. Also: Tomuschat (2005), 162; but contrast YbILC (1985), vol. I, 127 (Mr. Tomuschat).

[75] Gaja (2005), 126. See also the discussion in Sections 5.2.3 and 6.4.2 (on the putative requirement of a widely acknowledged breach as a condition of third-party countermeasures); and generally Chapter 3 and Sections 6.3.1 and 6.4.2 (on the putative requirement of cooperation as a condition of third-party countermeasures).

[76] Gaja (2005), 126. See also e.g. Annacker (1994a), 160; Simma (1994a), 295; Voeffray (2004), 25.

[77] ARSIWA Commentary, Art. 48, §4. See also Gaja (2010), 958; Crawford (2013a), 550.

[78] See *Nuclear Tests (Australia v. France)*, ICJ Rep. (1974), 253 at 303 (Sep. Op. Judge Petrén), 369–370, para. 117 (Joint Diss. Op. Judges Onyeama, Dillard, Jiménez de Aréchaga and Waldock), 437 (Judge ad hoc Barwick); *Nuclear Tests (New Zealand v. France)*, ICJ Rep. (1974), 457 at 521, para. 52 (Joint Diss. Op. Judges Onyeama, Dillard, Jiménez de Aréchaga and Waldock); *East Timor*, ICJ Rep. (1995), 90 at 131–132 (Sep. Op. Judge Ranjeva), 215–216 (Diss. Op. Judge Weeramantry); *Nicaragua* case, Provisional Measures, ICJ Rep. (1984), 169 at 196–198 (Diss. Op. Judge Schwebel); *Gabčíkovo Nagymaros Project*, ICJ Rep. (1997), 7 at 117–118 (Sep. Op. Judge Weeramantry); *Wall* case, ICJ Rep. (2004), 136 at 216, para. 37 (Sep. Op. Judge Higgins); *Armed Activities (DRC v. Uganda)*, ICJ Rep. (2005), 168 at 346–350, paras. 32–41 (esp. at para. 40) (Sep. Op. Judge Simma); *Application of the International Convention on the Elimination of All Forms of Racial Discrimination*, ICJ Rep. (2011), 70 at 272, para. 74 (Diss. Op. Judge Cançado Trindade). Contra: *Nuclear Tests (Australia v. France)*, ICJ Rep. (1974), 253 at 387 (Diss. Op. Judge de Castro); and above nn. 67–68, 70.

2.1.1.1(i) Third-Party Countermeasures: A Corresponding Right of Protection?   The dictum, by contrast, is silent on the question of third-party countermeasures as a possible corresponding right of protection of the *erga omnes* concept. This seems unsurprising, not least because State practice on third-party countermeasures at the time of the judgment was still very much in its infancy.[79] And yet it is often suggested that an entitlement to take third-party countermeasures is necessarily implied by the dictum. This conclusion is said to follow automatically from the Court's affirmation in paragraph 33 that, with respect of obligations *erga omnes*, 'all States can be held to have a legal interest in their protection'.

For example, in the words of Schachter:

> It would plausibly follow from this principle that all States – and not only those directly affected – would be entitled to take counter-measures against a State that allegedly violated one of the obligations owed to the community as a whole.[80]

Schachter nonetheless immediately added: 'To my knowledge, no third State has claimed a right to take reprisals (in the strict sense) on grounds that an offending State has violated an *erga omnes* obligation'.[81] Similarly, Orakhelashvili concludes:

> The logical and consequential link between the nature of the relevant violations and the standing of third States to take countermeasures is quite clear ... The conceptual link between the nature of certain breaches of international law and the faculty to take third-party countermeasures, in other words the conceptual incompatibility between *erga omnes* obligations and the restriction of the standing to take countermeasures to the contexts of bilateralism, is the factor that can outweigh the lack of uniformity in State practice. In practical terms, limiting the standing to take countermeasures to bilateral contexts is effectively to leave many breaches without redress.[82]

State practice is evidently not decisive. The normative consideration of effectiveness appears central to this conclusion.[83]

Others have not read the dictum in this mechanical fashion. Sicilianos observes:

---

[79] For State practice pre-1970 see Sections 4.2.1 (South Africa) and 4.2.2 (Greece).
[80] Schachter (1982), 183.   [81] Ibid.
[82] Orakhelashvili (2006), 271–272. See also Kuyper (1982), 157; Elagab (1988), 58–59, 63; Erasmus (1992), 133–134; Annacker (1994a), 86–88; Delbrück (1995), 152–153; Byers (1997), 238.
[83] See e.g. Villalpando (2005), 371.

Ce serait cependant aller un peu vite en besogne que de vouloir déduire de cet *obiter dictum* que chaque Etat serait habilité à réagir unilatéralement face aux violations des obligations y énoncées. La CIJ ne s'est pas prononcée sur ce point. Il est dès lors difficile de tirer de l'affaire *Barcelona Traction* une conclusion définitive quant à la question qui nous préoccupe.[84]

Alland likewise notes: 'Il serait très audacieux, sur la seule base de ce *dictum*, d'inclure dans ces 'droits de protection' la faculté pour des Etats indirectement lésés de prendre des contre-mesures'.[85] This must surely be correct. It is one thing to say that the affirmation in the dictum of States' legal interest in the protection of obligations *erga omnes* – their 'common interest in compliance' in the Court's modern parlance – is postulated in broad terms and is of general application. It is quite another to say *a priori* that this general legal interest can be enforced by way of third-party countermeasures. These are different things.[86] The dictum simply did not elaborate on the corresponding rights of protection of the *erga omnes* concept under international law. That said, as already demonstrated, it seems reasonably clear that the Court, by way of the dictum, implicitly affirmed one such right of protection: the entitlement of each State individually to bring judicial proceedings.

To conclude, third-party countermeasures are not an automatic consequence of the *erga omnes* concept. What is more, the dictum clearly did not recognize third-party countermeasures as a corresponding right of protection. At most, by affirming the general legal interest of each State individually to ensure compliance with obligations *erga omnes*, the Court recognized – albeit in indirect and strictly analytical terms – the mere possibility of third-party countermeasures as a corresponding right of protection. Thus with respect to third-party countermeasures, the dictum stands for two key propositions. First, the *erga omnes* concept is relevant in analytical terms to third-party countermeasures. Second, the *erga omnes* concept is based on individual standing and it can be presumed that, as a possible corresponding right of protection, the same would therefore apply to third-party countermeasures. Whether third-party countermeasures have indeed emerged as a right of protection – and, if so, potentially subject to different or more stringent conditions of standing than those which appear to follow from the *erga omnes* concept – will, however, ultimately depend on an assessment of State practice.[87]

---

[84] Sicilianos (1990), 151.   [85] Alland (1994), 364. See also Hillgruber (2006), 270–272.
[86] See Tams (2005), 202–204 (also ibid., 39–40).
[87] For a similar conclusion see Tams (2005), 201.

2.1.1.1(ii) An Empty Statement? In a subsequent passage introduced in paragraph 91 of the judgment, the Court expressly referred to the earlier dictum as follows:

> With regard more particularly to human rights, to which reference has already been made in paragraph 34 of this Judgment, it should be noted that these also include protection against denial of justice. However, on the universal level, the instruments which embody human rights do not confer on States the capacity to protect the victims of infringements of such rights irrespective of their nationality. It is therefore still on the regional level that a solution to this problem has had to be sought; thus, within the Council of Europe, of which Spain is not a member, the problem of admissibility encountered by the claim in the present case has been resolved by the European Convention on Human Rights, which entitles each State which is a party to the Convention to lodge a complaint against any other contracting State for violation of the Convention, irrespective of the nationality of the victim.[88]

The relationship between this passage and the earlier dictum has been much discussed and is still the source of confusion.[89] One interpretation suggests that paragraph 91 directly contradicted the affirmation in paragraphs 33 and 34 concerning the enforcement of obligations *erga omnes* in the field of human rights, because 'on the universal level, the instruments which embody human rights do not confer on States the capacity to protect the victims of infringements of such rights irrespective of their nationality'. In *Nuclear Tests*, Judge Gros considered that these two passages were 'inconsistent'.[90] Judge Petrén regretted the absence – alluded to in paragraph 91 – of an effective system of jurisdictional clauses for the settlement of human rights disputes and considered that paragraph 91 had left 'the impression of a self-contradiction'.[91] Others have also expressly invoked the same contradiction.[92] But the contradiction is more apparent than real.

---

[88] *Barcelona Traction*, ICJ Rep. (1970), 3 at 47, para. 91.
[89] See generally Charpentier (1970), 312; Bollecker-Stern (1973), 84–88; Marek (1978–1979), 479–480; Lachs (1980), 341 (n. 795); Schachter (1982), 196–197; Meron (1986), 10–12; Mbaye (1988), 307–308; Thirlway (1989), 99–100; Gaja (1989), 152 (n. 5); de Hoogh (1991), 197–199; Weil (1992), 286–287; Kamminga (1992), 154–156, 181; Frowein (1994), 406; Simma (1994a), 296–297; de Hoogh (1996), 52–53; Ragazzi (1997), 211–212; Tomuschat (1999), 84; Meron (2003), 281; Talmon (2004), 172–173; Voeffray (2004), 76–78; Villalpando (2005), 284–285; Tams (2005), 176–179, 268–272; Crawford (2006b), 424–425; Okowa (2014), 497–498.
[90] *Nuclear Tests (Australia v. France)*, ICJ Rep. (1974), 253 at 290 (Sep. Op. Judge Gros).
[91] Ibid., 303 (Sep. Op. Judge Petrén).
[92] See. e.g. Marek (1978–1979), 480; Mbaye (1988), 307–308; Weil (1992), 286–287. Also: Bollecker-Stern (1973), 84–88.

As Lachs (the supposed author of the dictum)[93] himself explained, the apparent contradiction appears to be based on a 'misunderstanding'.[94] There is no real contradiction. Paragraph 91 is concerned exclusively with the treaty-based enforcement of obligations *erga omnes partes* in the field of human rights. Specifically, the passage is limited to the question of 'denial of justice' and the protection under 'the instruments which embody human rights' of 'victims of infringements of such rights irrespective of their nationality'.[95] The Court appears to have taken a restrictive view of the protection of human rights by clarifying that denial of justice was not considered to be part of 'the principles and rules concerning the basic rights of the human person'; in other words, the obligation not to deny justice did not qualify in 1970 as an obligation *erga omnes* within the meaning of the dictum. Standing to invoke an alleged breach of the obligation not to deny justice could accordingly only be based on a right of protection specifically conferred by treaty.[96]

The Court's implicit reference in paragraph 91 to the ICCPR, by which it alluded to the inapplicability of Article 41 ICCPR concerning an optional inter-State complaint procedure for the protection of non-nationals, was correct: the ICCPR had not yet entered into force at the time of judgment in 1970.[97] The Court concluded its discussion of standing in paragraph 91 by noting that the problem of the admissibility encountered by Belgium's claim concerning denial of justice could have been resolved under the ECHR; however, Spain was not a party to that treaty. As Tams observes, the key issue addressed by the dictum was thus a different one: it was whether obligations *erga omnes* could be enforced even '*in the absence of express treaty provisions*'.[98] In sum, it is difficult to see how the foundation stone laid by the Court in paragraphs 33 and 34 in support of a construction of a multilateral regime of enforcement for obligations *erga omnes* could possibly have been shaken – still less undermined – by paragraph 91.

The same line of interpretation nonetheless suggests that, at least with respect to human rights law, the Court in paragraph 91 intended to

---

[93] See above n. 45.   [94] Lachs (1980), 341 (n. 795).

[95] See e.g. Lachs (1980), 341 (n. 795); Meron (1986), 10–11; Kamminga (1992), 155–156; Frowein (1994), 406; Villalpando (2005), 285–286; Tams (2005), 138 (n. 91), 271–272; Crawford (2006b), 425.

[96] Ibid.

[97] The ICCPR entered into force on 23 March 1976, except for the optional inter-State complaint procedure envisaged in its Article 41 which entered into force on 28 March 1979: see further https://treaties.un.org.

[98] Tams (2005), 178 (emphasis in the original). See also Weil (1992), 285.

qualify the earlier dictum. In *Nuclear Tests*, Judge Gros considered that the dictum could not be read without taking account of paragraph 91, which was 'in fact intended to qualify and limit the scope of the earlier pronouncement'.[99] This interpretation, which is based on the Court's implied reference in paragraph 91 to special enforcement mechanisms in 'the instruments which embody human rights', raises an issue of a general character: the relationship between means of enforcement under treaties and customary international law.[100] It has been suggested that what the Court intended to say was that obligations *erga omnes* under customary international law are unenforceable except insofar as they are embodied in a treaty that specifically confers a right of enforcement. For example, in the words of Weil:

> Le passage a fait l'effet d'une bombe dans le monde juridique, même si sa portée se trouvait quelque peu affaiblie par la présence dans le même arrêt d'un passage qui lui contredisait de front. Quelques pages plus loin, en effet, la Court jugera nécessaire de préciser que c'est *seulement en vertu et dans le cadre d'instruments conventionnels* que les Etats ont qualité pour protéger les victimes de violations des droits de l'homme indépendamment de leur nationalité.[101]

Talmon appears to make a very similar point:

> [T]he ICJ held that a legal interest in the protection of human rights alone does not confer on States a general right of action (*jus standi*) in order to protect such rights irrespective of the nationality of the victim. Such *jus standi* can only derive from relevant universal or regional human rights treaties. The judgment thus affirms the dictum in the much criticized *South West Africa* case.[102]

Furthermore, in cases where treaty-based mechanisms of enforcement do exist, it has been suggested that the Court meant to exclude the corresponding rights of protection of the *erga omnes* concept under customary international law. For his part, Thirlway considered that this 'qualification' of the dictum amounted to an 'apparent withdrawal on the question of human rights'.[103] The dictum was, in his view, 'little more than an empty gesture' with obligations *erga omnes* reduced to 'a purely

---

[99] *Nuclear Tests (Australia v. France)*, ICJ Rep. (1974), 253 at 290 (Sep. Op. Judge Gros). See also ibid., 387 (Diss. Op. Judge de Castro).

[100] See generally ARSIWA Commentary, Art. 55, §§1–6 (on *lex specialis*).

[101] Weil (1992), 286–287 (emphasis added).

[102] Talmon (2004), 172–173. See also e.g. Schachter (1982), 196–197; de Hoogh (1991), 197–199; Ragazzi (1997), 212; Okowa (2014), 497–498. Compare Kamminga (1992), 181.

[103] Thirlway (1989), 99–100.

theoretical category'.[104] This interpretation has already been implicitly rejected: it presupposes a real contradiction (which does not exist) between the dictum and paragraph 91. Thus paragraph 91 does not support an interpretation according to which treaty-based mechanisms of enforcement generally exclude recourse to means of enforcement under customary international law, including third-party countermeasures.[105] The same point applies *a fortiori* in the absence of an enforcement mechanism specifically conferred by treaty. It may be added that any conclusion to the contrary would indeed make the affirmation of obligations *erga omnes* in the dictum seem rather pointless.[106] It would also appear to contradict the *pacta tertiis* principle embodied in Article 35 VCLT.[107]

A less categorical interpretation of paragraph 91 is that the Court merely alluded to the possibility that the existence of treaty-based mechanisms of enforcement could in limited circumstances exclude recourse to the corresponding rights of protection of the *erga omnes* concept under customary international law. For example, Simma has suggested that enforcement mechanisms specifically conferred by treaty could 'exclud[e] the possibility of recourse to the classical means of self-help [i.e. countermeasures] under general international law to a certain extent, that is, as far as these agreements are self-contained'.[108] Leaving aside the terminology of self-contained regimes,[109] this may well be correct as a matter of treaty interpretation.[110] But it seems difficult to read this into paragraph 91.

All that can be said is that the Court in *Barcelona Traction* raised but did not answer the broader question concerning the relationship between competing enforcement mechanisms under treaty and custom. Two such relationships of relevance to third-party countermeasures should be distinguished: the relationship between treaty-based

---

[104] Ibid.

[105] See e.g. Meron (1986), 11–12; Gaja (1989), 152 (n. 5); Frowein (1994), 406; Tomuschat (1999), 84; Tams (2005), 176–179, 268–272.

[106] See Simma (1994a), 296–297; Tams (2005), 271; Crawford (2006b), 425.

[107] See Tams (2005), 275.

[108] Simma (1994a), 296. See also Bollecker-Stern (1973), 84–88.

[109] The term is apt to mislead. It seems difficult to describe any treaty regime as truly self-contained in the sense of it operating in complete clinical isolation of general international law: see further ARSIWA Commentary, Art. 55, §5; ILC Report on Fragmentation of International Law, UN Doc. A/CN.4/L.682 (2006), 64, para. 120; Simma and Pulkowski (2010), 139.

[110] See generally ARSIWA Commentary, Art. 55, §4.

mechanisms of enforcement of obligations *erga omnes* (e.g. Article IX of the Genocide Convention or potentially Chapter VII UNC), on the one hand, and obligations *erga omnes partes* (e.g. Article 41 ICCPR and certain substantive ICCPR obligations, with no corresponding extra-conventional *erga omnes* status) on the other.[111] In particular, with respect to the latter, the Court in *Barcelona Traction* did not even remotely contemplate the question of whether third-party counter-measures could potentially be adopted in response to breaches of obligations *erga omnes partes*.[112]

To summarize, the Court's dictum in *Barcelona Traction* is often invoked for more than it can bear. The Court did not recognize third-party countermeasures as a corresponding right of protection of the *erga omnes* concept. At most, by affirming the general legal interest of each State individually to ensure compliance with obligations *erga omnes*, the Court recognized the mere possibility of third-party countermeasures as a corresponding right of protection. Thus the Court – albeit indir-ectly – affirmed two points of relevance to third-party countermeasures. First, the *erga omnes* concept is relevant in analytical terms to the debate on third-party countermeasures. Second, the *erga omnes* concept is based on the notion of individual standing and it can therefore be presumed that, in principle, each State individually would be entitled to adopt third-party countermeasures.

2.1.2   *The* Namibia *Case*

The ICJ in *Namibia* did not address the question of third-party countermeasures.[113] It has nonetheless sometimes been suggested that the *Namibia* case may be understood as an implicit endorsement of third-party countermeasures. This suggestion can be dismissed rather summarily. In October 1966, a few months after the Court's debacle in the *South West Africa* cases, the UN General Assembly, convinced that

---

[111] See also more generally the *Tehran Hostages* case (Section 2.1.3 below) with respect to the extra-conventional enforcement of bilateral obligations.

[112] The Court did, however, provide some further guidance on all these issues in the *Nicaragua* case: see below Section 2.1.4.

[113] *Namibia* case, ICJ Rep. (1971), 16. See generally Dugard (1973), 376–542; Schachter (1982), 184; Zoller (1984a), 115–117; Zoller (1984b), 374; Charney (1989), 69–70; Thirlway (1989), 98–99; Sicilianos (1990), 151–152; Alland (1994), 364; Thirlway (1996), 4–5; Ragazzi (1997), 165–173; Talmon (2004), 166; Tams (2005), 107–109, 204; Orakhelashvili (2006), 448; Ronen (2011), 38–46; Crawford (2013a), 377.

South Africa had administered South West Africa (Namibia)[114] in flagrant violation of fundamental principles of international law, declared
that South Africa had disavowed the Mandate Agreement for South West
Africa and on that basis decided to terminate it.[115] The General Assembly
accordingly decided that South Africa no longer had any right to admin-
ister Namibia, and resolved to discharge that responsibility itself until its
independence.[116] The Security Council adopted a series of resolutions
under Chapter VI UNC by which, *inter alia*, it recognized the termination of the mandate and considered that South Africa's continued presence in Namibia was illegal; it called upon South Africa to immediately
withdraw its administration from Namibia.[117]

As South Africa remained intransigent, the Security Council declared
that, in the absence of any legal title, all acts taken by South Africa on
behalf of or concerning Namibia after the termination of the mandate
would be illegal and invalid. In particular, the Security Council called on
all States 'to refrain from any dealings' with South Africa inconsistent
with that declaration.[118] To this end, among others, the Security Council
decided to establish a subsidiary organ to study the ways and means
by which this policy could be effectively implemented.[119] As a result, the
Security Council, based on the recommendation of its subsidiary organ,
decided to submit the following question to the ICJ for an advisory
opinion: 'What are the legal consequences for States of the continued
presence of South Africa in Namibia, notwithstanding Security Council
resolution 276 (1970)?'[120]

The Court first concluded that, seemingly on the basis of the principles embodied in Article 60(2)(a) and 60(3) VCLT, the mandate had
been lawfully terminated by the General Assembly.[121] The Court then
concluded that, albeit adopted under Chapter VI UNC, Security
Council resolution 276 was *intra vires* and binding under Articles 24
and 25 UNC.[122] The Court, having reached these conclusions, finally
addressed the question of the legal consequences arising for States

---

[114] See GA Res. 2372 (XXII) (12 June 1968).   [115] See GA Res. 2145 (XXI) (27 Oct. 1966).
[116] Ibid.   [117] See SC Res. 264 (20 March 1969). Also: SC Res. 269 (12 Aug. 1969).
[118] See SC Res. 276 (30 Jan. 1970), op. paras. 2 and 5.   [119] Ibid., op. para. 6.
[120] SC Res. 284 (29 July 1970). See also SC Res. 283 (29 July 1970) (which outlined certain
    proscribed acts implying non-recognition). The Court was, however, not called upon to
    advise on the legal effects of that resolution.
[121] *Namibia* case, ICJ Rep. (1971), 16 at 45–50, paras. 87–103. See however Simma and Tams
    (2011), 1362 (n. 67) (noting that GA Res. 2145 (XXI) was not adopted unanimously, as
    Article 60(2)(a) VCLT requires).
[122] *Namibia* case, ICJ Rep. (1971), 16 at 51–54, paras. 106–116.

from the continued presence of South Africa in Namibia.[123] With respect to UN Member States, the Court concluded that, based on Security Council resolution 276, these States were under a dual obligation of non-recognition and non-assistance related to South Africa's occupation of Namibia. In other words, these States were obligated not to recognize as lawful the situation created by South Africa's presence in Namibia and to refrain from any acts lending support or assisting it to maintain that situation.[124] Specifically, UN Member States had to refrain from any dealings with South Africa that 'may imply a recognition that South Africa's presence in Namibia is legal'.[125] The Court observed that the precise determination of what this entailed was a matter for the political organs of the UN; it accordingly confined itself to giving advice 'under the Charter of the United Nations and general international law' on those dealings with South Africa which should be considered as implied recognition in the instant case.[126] The Court observed that UN Member States would be required, *inter alia*, to abstain from invoking or applying certain existing treaties vis-à-vis South Africa.[127]

The Court added:

> As to non-member States, although not bound by Articles 24 and 25 of the Charter, they have been called upon in paragraphs 2 and 5 of resolution 276 (1970) to give assistance in the action which has been taken by the United Nations with regard to Namibia. In the view of the Court, the termination of the Mandate and the declaration of the illegality of South Africa's presence in Namibia are opposable to all States in the sense of barring *erga omnes* the legality of a situation which is maintained in violation of international law ... The Mandate having been terminated by decision of the international organization in which the supervisory authority over its administration was vested, and South Africa's continued presence in Namibia having been declared illegal, it is for non-member States to act in accordance with those decisions.[128]

Sicilianos has suggested that the Court's reference in the above passage to 'non-member States' having to 'act in accordance' with the relevant resolutions, including by way of suspending certain existing treaties in a manner not contemplated therein, and in the absence of any obligation to do so under the UN Charter, may be understood as an implied

---

[123] Ibid., 54–56, paras. 117–126.   [124] Ibid., 54–56, paras. 119–125.
[125] Ibid., 55, para. 121.   [126] Ibid., 55, paras. 120–121.
[127] Ibid., 55–56, paras. 122–125.   [128] Ibid., 56, para. 126.

entitlement to adopt third-party countermeasures against South Africa.[129] This conclusion seems very difficult to sustain.

It seems clear from the above passage that, in referring to certain States as having to 'act in accordance' with the relevant UN resolutions, the Court was simply concerned with the objective legal effect – i.e. the opposability *erga omnes* – of the termination of the mandate and the declaration of the illegality of South Africa's presence in Namibia.[130] The Court concluded on that basis that it was 'incumbent' upon these States – i.e. they were seemingly under an obligation based on customary international law – not to recognize as lawful the situation created by South Africa's presence in Namibia and to refrain from any acts lending support or assisting it to maintain that situation.[131] Thus the Court in *Namibia* did not implicitly endorse third-party countermeasures. By contrast, the Court effectively endorsed what later became Article 41(2) ARSIWA.[132]

2.1.3 *The* Tehran Hostages *Case*

The *Tehran Hostages* case by implication provides some (albeit limited) guidance on third-party countermeasures.[133] On 29 November 1979, the United States instituted ICJ proceedings against Iran in respect of a dispute concerning alleged grave violations of diplomatic and consular law arising from the seizure and holding as hostages of members of the United States diplomatic and consular staff and certain other US nationals.[134] The Court, in holding Iran responsible for egregious violations of basic principles of diplomatic and consular law, stressed the 'imperative character of the legal obligations incumbent upon the Iranian Government'.[135] Furthermore:

---

[129] Sicilianos (1990), 151–152. Compare Schachter (1982), 184; Zoller (1984b), 374; Talmon (2004), 166.

[130] See *Namibia* case, ICJ Rep. (1971), 16 at 73 (Sep. Op. Judge Ammoun), 219 (Sep. Op. Judge de Castro); Thirlway (1996), 4–5; Tams (2005), 107–109, 204 (with further references); Orakhelashvili (2006), 448.

[131] *Namibia* case, ICJ Rep. (1971), 16 at 58, para. 133 (third operative paragraph).

[132] See ARSIWA Commentary, Art. 41, §§8, 10–11; Crawford (2013a), 377. Also: *Wall* case, ICJ Rep. (2004), 136 at 200, para. 159; Crawford (2013a), 370–371 (for the suggestion – somewhat unlikely – that the *Wall* case can be seen as going so far as to endorse a positive duty to take third-party countermeasures, as distinct from the conceptually separate putative obligations of non-recognition and non-assistance under Article 41(2) ARSIWA).

[133] *United States Diplomatic and Consular Staff in Tehran*, ICJ Rep. (1980), 3.

[134] Ibid., 12–15, paras. 17–26 (for a summary of the facts).   [135] Ibid., 41, para. 88.

[T]he Court considers it to be its duty to draw the attention of the entire international community . . . to the irreparable harm that may be caused by events of the kind now before the Court. Such events cannot fail to undermine the edifice of law carefully constructed by mankind over a period of centuries, the maintenance of which is vital for the security and well-being of the complex international community of the present day, to which it is more essential than ever that the rules developed to ensure the ordered progress of relations between its members should be constantly and scrupulously respected.[136]

It has sometimes been suggested that the Court in this passage implied that the obligations violated by Iran amounted to obligations *erga omnes* within the meaning of the *Barcelona Traction* dictum and, as such, entailed a right to take third-party countermeasures in order to protect 'the edifice of [diplomatic] law'.[137] This interpretation should be rejected. The Court did not concern itself with the affirmation of obligations *erga omnes* in the field of diplomatic and consular law, let alone third-party countermeasures. It seems that the Court simply meant to stress the exceptionally serious character of Iran's wrongful conduct – involving exclusively 'reciprocal obligations'[138] in the field of diplomatic and consular law – vis-à-vis the United States.[139]

By contrast, the Court by implication provided some additional guidance on the relationship between treaty-based mechanisms of enforcement and countermeasures. Prior to the institution of ICJ proceedings, the United States responded to the hostage crisis by bringing the matter before the UN Security Council. The United States also adopted several unilateral coercive measures against Iran, including countermeasures by way of freezing all of its assets held in the country.[140] During the pendency of the ICJ proceedings, the Security Council adopted two resolutions under Chapter VI UNC urgently calling on Iran to release the hostages, but to no avail.[141] An order by the Court indicating

---

[136] Ibid., 43, para. 92. See also ibid., 48 (Sep. Op. Judge Lachs) (stressing the essential character of diplomatic and consular law).

[137] See e.g. Hailbronner (1992), 4; Annacker (1994b), 21–22; Frowein (1983), 244–245; Frowein (1987), 74. Also: Stein (1992), 47.

[138] *United States Diplomatic and Consular Staff in Tehran*, ICJ Rep. (1980), 3 at 42, para. 91.

[139] See Gaja (1989), 153–154; Sicilianos (1990), 152; Tams (2005), 204–205. Also: Zoller (1980), 1024; Simma (1989), 287 (n. 15); Alland (1994), 356 (n. 169); Ragazzi (1997), 191–193. Contrast e.g. *East Timor*, ICJ Rep. (1995), 90 at 214 (Diss. Op. Judge Weeramantry).

[140] *United States Diplomatic and Consular Staff in Tehran*, ICJ Rep. (1980), 3 at 15–17, paras. 28–30.

[141] See SC Res. 457 (4 Dec. 1979); SC Res. 461 (31 Dec. 1979).

provisional measures was not complied with.[142] A draft Security Council resolution calling for the adoption of non-military sanctions against Iran under Chapter VII UNC was vetoed by the Soviet Union.[143] Finally, a month before the Court rendered its judgment, the United States launched an unsuccessful military operation ('Operation Rice Bowl') to rescue the hostages.[144]

The United States appears to have considered that countermeasures against Iran could be adopted even prior to the institution of the ICJ proceedings, notwithstanding the available treaty-based enforcement mechanism in Article 1 of the Optional Protocol concerning the Compulsory Settlement of Disputes under the VCCR and the VCDR, respectively, which provided the main basis for the Court's jurisdiction in the case.[145] In addition, the United States adopted countermeasures while the Security Council was seized of the matter, and they remained in place after the vetoed resolution under Chapter VII UNC. With respect to Operation Rice Bowl, the Court stated emphatically: '[A]n operation undertaken in those circumstances, from whatever motive, is of a kind calculated to undermine respect for the judicial process in international relations'.[146] Thus the Court conspicuously failed to criticize the United States for the adoption of countermeasures against Iran. This silence is 'noteworthy'[147] and suggests that the Court implicitly accepted that the existence of treaty-based enforcement mechanisms, notably in the form of judicial proceedings, does not as such exclude recourse to (third-party) countermeasures.[148]

This interpretation is reinforced by the dissenting opinions of two of the judges in the case, which specifically criticized the Court's failure *proprio motu* to hold the United States responsible for the adoption of

---

[142] *United States Diplomatic and Consular Staff in Tehran*, Provisional Measures, ICJ Rep. (1979), 7.

[143] *United States Diplomatic and Consular Staff in Tehran*, ICJ Rep. (1980), 3 at 17, para. 31. See also UN Doc. S/13735 (10 Jan. 1980) (for the draft resolution). EC Member States, based on the enforcement action envisaged in the vetoed draft resolution, adopted a range of unilateral coercive measures (amounting to acts of retorsion) against Iran: see further e.g. EC Bull. No. 4 (1980), paras. 1.2.6–1.2.9; Frowein (1987), 74–75; Sicilianos (1990), 159–160; Frowein (1994), 416–417; Tams (2005), 226–227; Dawidowicz (2006), 402–403.

[144] *United States Diplomatic and Consular Staff in Tehran*, ICJ Rep. (1980), 3 at 17–18, para. 32. Further: Stein (1982), 499.

[145] *United States Diplomatic and Consular Staff in Tehran*, ICJ Rep. (1980), 3 at 24–25, paras. 45–46.

[146] Ibid., 43, para. 93.   [147] Schachter (1982), 173–174.

[148] See Tams (2005), 297. Also: Schachter (1982), 173–175.

unlawful countermeasures against Iran.[149] Judge Morozov stated that the US countermeasures were 'incompatible with ... the provisions of general international law, including the Charter of the United Nations', as they had been adopted in disregard of the respective roles of the ICJ and the Security Council both of whom were concurrently actively seized of the dispute.[150] Judge Morozov noted that the Security Council had even vetoed enforcement action under Chapter VII UNC and yet the US countermeasures still remained in place.[151] Judge Tarazi made a statement to similar effect.[152] To conclude, the Court in the *Tehran Hostages* case did not pronounce itself on third-party countermeasures as a possible right of protection of the *erga omnes* concept. The Court, however, suggested that the adoption of (third-party) countermeasures would not *per se* be excluded simply by virtue of the existence of a competing treaty-based enforcement mechanism.

2.1.4   *The* Nicaragua *Case*

The *Nicaragua* case provides important additional guidance on third-party countermeasures.[153] In April 1984, Nicaragua instituted ICJ proceedings against the United States in respect of a dispute concerning responsibility for military and paramilitary activities in and against Nicaragua. Specifically, Nicaragua alleged that the United States had provided various forms of support to an armed opposition group (the *contras*) and taken other military actions against it in violation of the principles of non-use of force and non-intervention under customary

---

[149] See Schachter (1982), 174.

[150] *United States Diplomatic and Consular Staff in Tehran*, ICJ Rep. (1980), 3 at 52 (and also ibid., 54–57) (Diss. Op. Judge Morozov).

[151] Ibid., 54 (Diss. Op. Judge Morozov). Further: Reisman (1980), 904; Alland (1994), 320–322.

[152] *United States Diplomatic and Consular Staff in Tehran*, ICJ Rep. (1980), 3 at 63–65 (Diss. Op. Judge Tarazi). See also ibid., 48 (Sep. Op. Judge Lachs) ('[T]he Applicant, having instituted proceedings, is precluded from taking unilateral action, military or otherwise, as if no case is pending').

[153] *Nicaragua* case, ICJ Rep. (1986), 14. See generally de Guttry (1986–1987), 186–189; Frowein (1987), 76–77; Hutchinson (1988), 193–194; Sachariew (1988), 286; Charney (1989), 74–75; Thirlway (1989), 100–102; Sicilianos (1990), 152–154; Frowein (1994), 371–376; Alland (1994), 175–176, 337–338; Meron (2003), 297–298; *Oil Platforms*, ICJ Rep. (2003), 161 at 331–332 (Sep. Op. Judge Simma); Noortmann (2005), 37; Tams (2005), 205–207, 272–276, 301; Gaja (2005), 147, 191; Dawidowicz (2006), 378–383; Simma and Pulkowski (2010), 158–159; Crawford (2012), 588; Gaja (2013), 131.

international law.[154] In the economic field, Nicaragua also alleged that the United States had adopted unilateral coercive measures against it, including a general trade embargo, in violation of a bilateral FCN treaty and the principle of non-intervention.[155]

To legally justify its conduct involving the use of force, the United States explicitly relied on the right of collective self-defence by which it had allegedly responded to requests from the neighbouring countries of El Salvador, Honduras and Costa Rica for assistance in their self-defence against armed aggression by Nicaragua. Furthermore, the United States appeared to suggest that certain human rights violations by Nicaragua against its own population might justify its conduct.[156] The Court established that Nicaragua had supplied arms to guerrillas in El Salvador and carried out certain trans-border military incursions into Honduras and Costa Rica. Thus Nicaragua was found responsible for conduct involving the unlawful use of force against its neighbours.[157] The Court, however, distinguished the most serious forms of the use of force (those constituting an armed attack) from other less serious forms.[158] The Court only found Nicaragua responsible for the latter; accordingly, it did not qualify the forcible conduct as an armed attack triggering a right of collective self-defence.[159] But the Court did not stop there.

The Court, in the discharge of its duty under Article 53 of the ICJ Statute following the non-participation of the United States in the merits phase of the proceedings, enquired whether other rules of customary international law could exclude the unlawfulness of the forcible action taken by the Unites States. Specifically, the Court considered the question of 'whether there is any justification for the [forcible] activities in question, to be found not in the right of collective self-defence against an armed attack, but in the right to take counter-measures in response to

---

[154] The conduct in question notably included the arming, training and financing of the *contras*, the laying of mines in Nicaraguan waters and attacks on ports, oil installations and a naval base: see *Nicaragua* case, ICJ Rep. (1986), 14 at 48, 50, 53, paras. 80–81, 86, 93.

[155] Ibid., 22, 69–70, paras. 22–23, 123–125. Further: United States-Nicaragua Treaty of Friendship, Commerce and Navigation, 367 UNTS 3 (entry into force 24 May 1958).

[156] *Nicaragua* case, ICJ Rep. (1986), 14 at 70, para. 126.

[157] Ibid., 86–87, paras. 160, 164.

[158] Ibid., 101, para. 191. Further: Gray (2008), 147–148, 179–181; Ruys (2010), 139–157.

[159] *Nicaragua* case, ICJ Rep. (1986), 14 at 119–120, paras. 230–231. The justification of collective self-defence was also unavailable on other grounds: see ibid., 120–123, paras. 232–238. For criticism see Frowein (1994), 372–373 (nn. 57–58) (with further references).

conduct of Nicaragua which is not alleged to constitute an armed attack'.[160] The Court answered in the negative:

> [U]nder international law in force today – whether customary international law or that of the United Nations system – States do not have a right of 'collective' armed response to acts which do not constitute an 'armed attack'.[161]

Forcible (third-party) countermeasures were evidently deemed unlawful. In more general terms, the Court concluded:

> While an armed attack would give rise to an entitlement to collective self-defence, a use of force of a lesser degree of gravity cannot, as the Court has already observed (paragraph 211 above), produce any entitlement to take collective countermeasures involving the use of force. The acts of which Nicaragua is accused, even assuming them to have been established and imputable to that State, could only have justified proportionate countermeasures on the part of the State which had been the victim of these acts, namely El Salvador, Honduras or Costa Rica. They could not justify countermeasures taken by a third State, the United States, and particularly could not justify intervention involving the use of force.[162]

Beyond reaffirming the legality of bilateral countermeasures, the Court appears to have suggested that third-party countermeasures could only – if at all – be justified if taken in response to a *serious* breach of an obligation *erga omnes* (e.g. an act of aggression). Specifically, the Court seemingly held that 'a use of force of a lesser degree of gravity ... [than an armed attack] could not justify countermeasures taken by a third State'.[163]

---

[160] *Nicaragua* case, ICJ Rep. (1986), 14 at 106, para. 201 (also ibid., 110, para. 210).

[161] Ibid., 110, para. 211.

[162] Ibid., 127, para. 249. See further Section 6.2.1.1 (for a discussion of forcible countermeasures).

[163] Ibid. For the same conclusion see notably Gaja (2013), 131. Contra: Alland (1994), 337–338; UN Doc. A/C.6/56/SR.16, 4, para. 15 (Iran); Crawford (2012), 588 (suggesting that the Court categorically ruled out third-party countermeasures in response to breaches of obligations *erga omnes*). Compare *Oil Platforms*, ICJ Rep. (2003), 161 at 331–332 (Sep. Op. Judge Simma); Tams (2005), 188 (n. 135), 269 (n. 64), 301 (suggesting that the Court was not concerned with the possible justification of pacific countermeasures within the meaning of Articles 49–54 ARSIWA, but with defensive military action short of full-scale self-defence). Although the Court was primarily concerned with forcible conduct – 'the Court ... has primarily to consider whether a State has a right to respond to intervention with intervention going so far as to justify a use of force ...' (ICJ Rep. (1986), 14 at 110, para. 210) – this reading seemingly fails to consider that it was also, albeit to a lesser extent, concerned with the possible justification of third-party countermeasures for non-forcible conduct (involving the illegal financing of the *contras*), as the use of the word 'particularly' in paragraph 249 of the *Nicaragua* judgment

The Court, having rejected the possible justifications of collective self-defence and third-party countermeasures in response to Nicaragua's forcible conduct, considered 'whether there is anything [else] in the conduct of Nicaragua which might legally warrant counter-measures by the United States'.[164] In particular, the United States Congress had in July 1985 accused Nicaragua of various human rights violations; notably, that its government had not been 'freely elected under conditions of freedom of the press, assembly and organization', and linked support to the *contras* to those alleged human rights violations.[165] As for this possible justification, the Court stated:

> The Court also notes that Nicaragua is accused by the 1985 finding of the United States Congress of violating human rights . . . [W]here human rights are protected by international conventions, that protection takes the form of such arrangements for monitoring or ensuring respect for human rights as are provided for in the conventions themselves . . . The Court has noted above (paragraph 168) that the Nicaraguan Government has since 1979 ratified a number of international instruments on human rights, and one of these was the American Convention on Human Rights . . . The mechanisms provided therein have functioned. The Inter-American Commission on Human Rights in fact took action and compiled two reports . . . following visits by the Commission to Nicaragua at the Government's invitation. Consequently, the Organization was in a position, if it so wished, to take a decision on the basis of these reports.
>
> In any event, while the United States might form its own appraisal of the situation as to respect for human rights in Nicaragua, the use of force could not be the appropriate method to monitor or ensure such respect . . .
> The Court concludes that the argument derived from the preservation of

suggests. A variation of this argument (on which see Hutchinson (1988), 194; Sicilianos (1990), 153; Arango-Ruiz, Fourth Report, 48, para. 147 (n. 323); Villalpando (2005), 368 (n. 1267)) suggests that paragraph 249 cannot be interpreted as supporting the inadmissibility, in general terms, of third-party countermeasures as it was concerned with bilateral obligations and not obligations *erga omnes*. Put differently, the Court did not address the issue of non-forcible third-party countermeasures. This argument is equally unconvincing as it appears to neglect that the Court referred to the prohibition of the use of force as a conspicuous example of a rule in international law having the character of *jus cogens* (presumably with corresponding *erga omnes* status): see *Nicaragua* case, ICJ Rep. (1986), 14 at 100–101, para. 190; and *Nicaragua* case, Provisional Measures, ICJ Rep. (1984), 169 at 198 (Diss. Op. Judge Schwebel); Tams (2005), 206 (n. 36). By contrast, the ICJ did not address, by way of analogy with the law of collective self-defence, whether (if at all) non-forcible third-party countermeasures could only be adopted at the request and on behalf of a directly injured State: see further Sections 5.2.5 and 6.1.3.1(i).

[164] *Nicaragua* case, ICJ Rep. (1986), 14 at 130, para. 257.

[165] Ibid., 90–91, para. 169. The United States Congress also in general terms referred to alleged Nicaraguan 'atrocities against its citizens' (ibid.).

human rights in Nicaragua cannot afford a legal justification for the conduct of the United States.[166]

The Court's statement, 'where human rights are protected by international conventions, that protection takes the form ... provided for in the convention themselves', appears to generally exclude recourse to extra-conventional means of enforcement, including third-party countermeasures, wherever a treaty-based enforcement mechanism exists for their protection.[167] The Court, however, immediately added the qualification that treaty-based mechanisms of enforcement in the field of human rights were not exclusive *per se*, but only to the extent that 'the mechanisms provided therein have functioned'.[168] The question is whether such a qualified exclusion of extra-conventional means of enforcement would apply to all human rights obligations or only to some of them.

As in paragraph 91 of the judgment in *Barcelona Traction*, the Court was seemingly not concerned with the enforcement of obligations *erga omnes* under customary international law in the field of human rights, but with the treaty-based enforcement of obligations *erga omnes partes* in that field; namely, the ACHR obligations related to 'freedom of the press, assembly and organization'.[169] Thus the Court's suggestion in an earlier part of the judgment that third-party countermeasures could only be taken – if at all – in response to serious breaches of obligations *erga omnes* remains intact.[170] By contrast, the Court does appear to have excluded extra-conventional means of enforcement in response to breaches of obligations *erga omnes partes*, but only to the extent that effective or functioning treaty-based mechanisms of enforcement exist. That said, within the strict limits of the *pacta tertiis* principle in Article 35 VCLT, the same rationale should logically apply to obligations *erga omnes* protected by treaties. Whether treaty-based mechanisms of enforcement are deemed effective and thereby exclude extra-conventional means of

---

[166] Ibid., 134–135, paras. 267–268.

[167] Ibid, 134, para. 267. To this effect see e.g. Frowein (1987), 76–77; Thirlway (1989), 100–101; Frowein (1994), 399–400; Gaja (2005), 191 (albeit disagreeing with such a conclusion as a matter of *lex lata*).

[168] *Nicaragua* case, ICJ Rep. (1986), 14 at 134, para. 267. See Tams (2005), 274; Simma and Pulkowski (2010), 158–159.

[169] See Tams (2005), 272–276. The Court did not pronounce on the alleged human rights 'atrocities' – possibly involving breaches of obligations *erga omnes* – alluded to by the United States Congress: see above n. 165.

[170] See text above accompanying nn. 162–163.

enforcement, including third-party countermeasures, is essentially a matter of treaty interpretation.[171]

However, given the Court's earlier position on third-party countermeasures with respect to obligations *erga omnes* (involving a proposition already controversial enough), it seems unlikely that the Court meant to extend their application further by implicitly affirming that they could in certain circumstances also be adopted in response to breaches of obligations *erga omnes partes*. At most, it can be said that the Court did not exclude the possibility that in certain circumstances third-party countermeasures might be permissible in order to enforce obligations *erga omnes partes*. As such, the Court arguably affirmed that the *erga omnes partes* concept (in addition to its congener under customary international law, *erga omnes*) is at least conceptually relevant to the debate on third-party countermeasures.

In the present case, the Court explained (somewhat unpersuasively) that the compilation of two reports by a treaty body meant that the enforcement mechanisms provided under the ACHR had functioned. More fundamentally, the United States lacked standing to enforce obligations *erga omnes partes*, whether by way of third-party countermeasures or otherwise, since, unlike Nicaragua, it had not ratified the ACHR.[172] In the circumstances of the case, there was accordingly not 'anything in the conduct of Nicaragua which might legally warrant counter-measures by the United States'.[173] In any event, the use of force was not an appropriate method to ensure respect for human rights.

Finally, the Court considered whether the adoption of certain unilateral coercive measures in the economic field by the United States against Nicaragua, including a general trade embargo, could be justified under a bilateral FCN treaty. In particular, the Court found that the trade

---

[171] See Tams (2005), 272–279 (and further ibid., 120–128, 252–299, esp. at 286–299). It may be recalled from Chapter 1 (n. 7) that treaty-based mechanisms of enforcement, at least in the human rights field, are mostly optional and ineffective. As a result, recourse to third-party countermeasures is rarely excluded as a general matter. Indeed third-party countermeasures have in practice frequently been adopted to enforce obligations under human rights treaties – notably the ICCPR – whether in situations where the optional inter-State complaint procedure in Article 41 ICCPR was unavailable (see e.g. Sections 4.2.7 (Poland and the Soviet Union); 4.2.12 (Nigeria); 4.2.14 (Sudan); 4.2.15 (FRY); 4.2.20 (Syria)) or available (see e.g. Sections 4.2.17 (Zimbabwe); 4.2.18 (Belarus)). For an assessment of the controversial relationship between third-party countermeasures and Security Council enforcement measures see Section 5.2.1.

[172] Compare Tams (2005), 273–274. The United States signed the ACHR on 1 June 1977 but has still not ratified it: see further https://treaties.un.org.

[173] See above n. 164.

embargo constituted a violation of the obligation not to defeat the object and purpose of the FCN treaty.[174] The question was then whether the trade embargo was nevertheless justified by reference to the national security exception in Article XXI of the FCN treaty. The Court answered in the negative: the trade embargo had not been 'necessary' to protect the essential security interests of the United States within the meaning of Article XXI.[175] It has been suggested that, in having rejected the treaty-based defence in Article XXI, the Court should have discharged its duty under Article 53 of the ICJ Statute by considering whether the trade embargo could still have been justified as a third-party countermeasure in response to violations of human rights law and the prohibition against the use of force. The Court's supposed failure to do so has been described as 'quite astonishing' and 'remarkable' suggesting that the justification of third-party countermeasures was unavailable under international law.[176] But this line of reasoning seemingly fails to take into account that the Court had already in an earlier part of the judgment ruled out third-party countermeasures in response to the non-serious breaches of obligations *erga omnes* at issue in the case.

To conclude, the Court in *Nicaragua* suggested that third-party countermeasures could only be taken – if at all – in response to serious breaches of obligations *erga omnes*. The Court also seemingly did not exclude the possibility that third-party countermeasures might be permissible in order to enforce obligations *erga omnes partes* to the extent that treaty-based mechanisms of enforcement are ineffective. In other words, as a minimum, the Court affirmed that the *erga omnes partes* concept (in addition to its congener under customary international law, *erga omnes*) is conceptually relevant to third-party countermeasures.

2.2   Conclusion

The Court's contribution to the development of communitarian norms has largely been borne of exigency. The Court in *Barcelona Traction*

---

[174] *Nicaragua* case, ICJ Rep. (1986), 14 at 138, para. 276.

[175] Ibid., 140–142, paras. 280–282 (and also ibid., 115–117, paras. 221–225). For criticism see ibid., 252–253 (Diss. Op. Judge Oda), 540–542 (Diss. Op. Judge Jennings); Frowein (1994), 374–376. The Court had earlier held that none of the unilateral coercive measures taken in the economic field contravened the principle of non-intervention (ICJ Rep. (1986), 14 at 125–126, paras. 244–245). Compare *Oil Platforms*, ICJ Rep. (2003), 161 at 178–199, paras. 31–78 (regarding the scope of national security exceptions).

[176] Frowein (1994), 373–374; Tams (2005), 205–206.

affirmed the category of obligations *erga omnes* by way of dictum as an apology for its ignominious handling of the second phase of *South West Africa*. Ever since, the Court has been reluctant to open its door to claims involving communitarian norms and provided little by way of elaboration of the specific legal consequences arising from their breach. It follows that there is not much concrete guidance in the Court's jurisprudence on the possible enforcement of communitarian norms. This is especially so for the concept of third-party countermeasures which has simply not been litigated before the Court. Four conclusions may nevertheless be identified. First, the *erga omnes* concept is relevant in analytical terms to the debate on third-party countermeasures. Second, the same appears to be true for the *erga omnes partes* concept. Third, the *erga omnes* concept is based on individual standing and it can be presumed that, as a possible corresponding right of protection, the same would therefore apply to third-party countermeasures. Fourth, third-party countermeasures may only – if at all – be justified if taken in response to a *serious* breach of a communitarian norm.

The Court may have been avant-garde in affirming the *erga omnes* concept but it has been at the rearguard of the debate ever since. The Court's affirmation of the *erga omnes* concept almost immediately influenced the ILC's work on State responsibility and also gradually influenced State practice concerning the enforcement of communitarian norms by way of third-party countermeasures. Thus developments outside the Court have proved far more important for the possible entitlement to enforce communitarian norms by way of third-party countermeasures – as will become apparent from the chapters that follow.

Third-Party Countermeasures in the ILC

This chapter will examine the contribution made by the ILC to the concept of third-party countermeasures in its lengthy work on the law of State responsibility.[1] The ILC did not on first reading give serious attention to the question of third-party countermeasures and only considered it indirectly in the broader context of its effort to construct a multilateral public order. For decades, that construction remained a building site with essential works staying incomplete and resting on shaky foundations. It was only on second reading that the question of third-party countermeasures emerged as a discrete issue and was addressed squarely as part of a construction of a multilateral public order resting on more solid foundations. Thus, the building block of third-party countermeasures can only be properly understood as part of that broader construction. The relevant contribution made in this respect by the ILC on first reading (3.1) and on second reading (3.2) will be examined. This will be followed by some concluding observations (3.3).

3.1 The ILC's Contribution on First Reading (1963–1996)

The post-Charter era witnessed the emergence of several fundamental norms which transformed international law, including the principles of non-use of force and self-determination. In 1963, the ILC provisionally recognized the concept of peremptory norms in its work on the law of treaties – later adopted in 1969 as Articles 53, 64 and 71 of the VCLT.[2] The question of the legal consequences of breaches of peremptory norms

---

[1] The present chapter is concerned only with the basic question of the possible entitlement to adopt third-party countermeasures, not with the conditions governing their use. The procedural and substantive limitations applicable to third-party countermeasures (i.e. the safeguards regime) are examined separately in Chapter 6. For an assessment of the ILC's work on countermeasures, see generally Sicilianos (2005), 447.

[2] See YbILC (1963), vol. II, 198 (Draft Art. 37), 211 (Draft Art. 45), 216 (Draft Art. 53); YbILC (1966), vol. II, 247–249 (Draft Art. 50), 261 (Draft Art. 61), 266 (Draft Art. 67).

beyond the VCLT remained largely unexplored.[3] The ILC (in the form of its Sub-Committee on State Responsibility, chaired by Ago) thus also decided in 1963 that, as part of its study of State responsibility, 'careful attention should be paid to the possible repercussions which [these] new developments in international law may have had on responsibility'.[4] As possible forms of responsibility, 'reprisals' and 'collective sanctions' would also be studied in this respect.[5] The question of responsibility for the most serious violations of international law evidently merited particular attention. As a guide to the future work of the ILC, it was agreed that, in a first stage, the origin of responsibility should be examined, followed, in a second stage, by the forms or consequences of responsibility.[6]

The 1960s and 1970s was a period marked by decolonization and a Cold War stalemate in the UN Security Council. These developments exposed the limitations of the traditional bilateral model of State responsibility. Indeed such limitations were never far removed from the centre of the 'storm of indignation'[7] which swept through the UN General Assembly in the aftermath of the ICJ's judgment in the second phase of the *South West Africa* cases. The Court soon offered an 'apology'[8] in the *Barcelona Traction* case. It was clear that the traditional bilateral enforcement model was being 'hotly disputed'.[9] A 'burning question'[10] following the *South West Africa* cases concerned the issue of enforcement of fundamental norms. In 1963, Roberto Ago was appointed Special

---

[3] Compare Gaja (1981), 271.

[4] Ago, Report by the Chairman of the Sub-Committee on State Responsibility, YbILC (1963), vol. II, 228; and for the ILC's approval see YbILC (1963), vol. I, 86, para. 75 (Chairman of the ILC, Mr. Jiménez de Aréchaga). The ILC's work on State responsibility began in 1956 under García-Amador as Special Rapporteur with a focus on the responsibility for injuries to aliens and their property. His approach prompted substantial criticism and the topic was abandoned in 1963 when, following the recommendation of the Sub-Committee on State Responsibility, the ILC decided to shift its focus to 'the definition of the general rules governing the international responsibility of the State' (ibid.). Further: Müller (2010), 69.

[5] Ago, Report by the Chairman of the Sub-Committee on State Responsibility, YbILC (1963), vol. II, 228.

[6] Ibid. The UN General Assembly explicitly endorsed the ILC's approach: see GA Res. 1902 (XVIII) (18 Nov. 1963).

[7] Klein (1981), 266. For a survey of the strongly negative reception of the judgment among (mostly developing) States see further the statements reproduced in *Namibia*, ICJ Rep. (1971), 16, South Africa's Written Statement, 427–433.

[8] Crawford (2013a), 491. The ILC at the time referred to the apparent reversal simply as 'a clarification of great importance': see Draft Articles Commentary, Art. 19, §10.

[9] Ago, Fifth Report, 26, para. 80.   [10] YbILC (1967), vol. I, 227, para. 2 (Mr. Ustor).

Rapporteur and laid the foundations of the subsequent debate in the ILC on these issues while also offering some preliminary answers of his own.

3.1.1   Special Rapporteur Ago's Proposals

Following the ILC's plan of work, Special Rapporteur Ago's proposals addressed the question of the origin of responsibility. In 1971, influenced by the ICJ's recent dictum in *Barcelona Traction* (in which he was counsel for Spain) on obligations *erga omnes*,[11] Ago proposed, as a first step, to move away from the exclusively bilateral model of enforcement by defining responsibility more broadly to include all forms of new legal relationships arising from the commission of a wrongful act:

> irrespective of whether they are limited to a relationship between the State which commits the wrongful act, or extend to other subjects of international law as well, and irrespective of whether they are centred on the guilty State's obligation to restore the rights of the injured State and to repair the damage caused, or whether they also involve the faculty of the injured State itself, or of other subjects, of imposing on the guilty State a sanction permitted by international law.[12]

The ILC in 1973 provisionally adopted Ago's proposal as Draft Article 1 [1996].[13]

Special Rapporteur Ago, again influenced by the ICJ's dictum in *Barcelona Traction*, further proposed in 1976 to make a distinction between different types of internationally wrongful acts on the basis of the relative importance of the obligation breached.[14] Such a distinction would be 'absurd'[15] if it did not involve the application of different regimes of responsibility. Ago accordingly proposed in his draft article 18 to distinguish between two completely different regimes of responsibility. One regime would apply in the case of a serious breach by a State of a limited category of obligations – called 'international crimes'[16] – whose respect is of fundamental importance to the international community. The other regime would apply in the case of a breach by a State of a much broader category of obligations – called 'international delicts'[17] – of lesser

---

[11] Ago, Third Report, 210–211, para. 41. See also Ago, Second Report, 184, paras. 22–23.

[12] Ago, Third Report, 211, para. 43. See also ibid., 214, para. 48 (for his draft article 1).

[13] Draft Articles Commentary, Art. 1, §§5–10. Compare ARSIWA Commentary, Art. 1, §§4–5.

[14] Ago, Fifth Report, 26, 28–29, paras. 79–80, 89–90.   [15] Ibid., 26, para. 79.

[16] Ibid., 53–54, para. 153.   [17] Ibid.

importance.[18] Given the envisaged serious consequences to be attached to the commission of a State crime (to be specified at the second stage of the ILC's work), Ago proposed that the UN Security Council or the ICJ should be tasked with the establishment of such a breach.[19] Ago noted, however, that it was 'not very clear' whether States could invoke those serious consequences individually or only do so as a member of an international organization (i.e. the UN) which alone would be competent to decide on the action to be taken, but his preference for the latter was clear.[20]

Although there were grave reservations regarding the terminology of crimes,[21] the ILC agreed with Ago that the integrity of the most fundamental norms required a distinct regime of responsibility. The ILC in 1976 provisionally adopted Special Rapporteur Ago's proposal on State crimes as Draft Article 19 [1996].[22] The concept of a State crime effectively corresponded to a serious breach of a peremptory norm.[23] The ILC explained that, at the second stage of its work, the distinction between internationally wrongful acts, based on their relative importance to the international community, would be reflected in the legal consequences attached to them and the State(s) entitled to implement them.[24] In any event, the regime applicable to State crimes would in no way encroach upon the powers of the Security Council under Chapter VII UNC.[25]

In 1979, Special Rapporteur Ago proposed in his draft article 30 ('Legitimate application of a sanction') that the wrongfulness of certain 'sanctions' should be precluded.[26] By the term 'sanction', Ago referred to two distinct cases: countermeasures under general international law and enforcement measures taken by the Security Council under Chapter VII

---

[18] Ibid., 26, 54, paras. 80, 155 (for his draft article 18). For Ago's proposal, see further ibid., 24–54, paras. 72–155; and for a useful discussion, Nolte (2002), 1083.

[19] Ago, Fifth Report, 53, para. 152.

[20] Ago, Third Report, 211, para. 41. Compare Ago, Second Report, 184, paras. 22–23.

[21] In the bulk of the commentary to Draft Article 19 [1996], the term 'crime' was placed in quotation marks as an indication of its deeply controversial nature: see generally Draft Articles Commentary, Art. 19. Following a suggestion by Crawford, a footnote was later added to Draft Article 40(3) [1996] (concerning the 'Meaning of injured State' in case of an international crime), which indicated that the issue of terminology was left open: see YbILC (1996), vol. I, 29, para. 44 (Mr. Crawford), 137, para. 11 (Chairman of the Drafting Committee, Mr. Calero Rodrigues); ILC Report (1996), UN Doc. A/51/10, 62–63.

[22] See Draft Articles Commentary, Art. 19, §§7, 51–54. For a very useful summary of the debate in the ILC and Sixth Committee, see generally Spinedi (1989), 7 (with many further references).

[23] Draft Articles Commentary, Art. 19, §§62, 66, 70.   [24] Ibid., §§6–7, 58.   [25] Ibid., §55.

[26] See Ago, Eighth Report, 39–43.

UNC.[27] However, Ago seemed to rule out the possibility of third-party countermeasures. It is worth reproducing his rationale for doing so in full:

> [T]he former monopoly of the State directly injured by the internationally wrongful act of another State, as regards the possibility of resorting against that other State to sanctions which would otherwise be unlawful, is no longer absolute in modern international law. It probably still subsists in general international law, even if, *in abstracto*, some might find it logical to draw certain inferences from the progressive affirmation of the principle that some obligations – defined in this sense as obligations *erga omnes* – are of such broad sweep that the violation of one of them is to be deemed an offence committed against all members of the international community, and not simply against the State or States directly affected by the breach. In reality, one cannot underestimate the risks that would be involved in pressing recognition of this principle the chief merit of which, in our view, is that it affirms the need for universal solidarity in dealing with the most serious assaults on international order to the point where any State would be held to be automatically authorized to react against the breach of certain obligations committed against another State and individually to take punitive measures against the State responsible for the breach. It is understandable, therefore, that a community such as the international community, in seeking a more structured organization, even if only an incipient 'institutionalization', should have turned in another direction, namely towards a system vesting in international institutions other than States, the exclusive responsibility, first, for determining the existence of a breach of an obligation of basic importance to the international community as a whole, and thereafter, for deciding what measures should be taken in response and how they should be implemented.
>
> Under the United Nations Charter, those responsibilities are vested in the competent organs of the Organization.[28]

In short, Ago opposed third-party countermeasures on the dual basis that, notwithstanding the recent affirmation of obligations *erga omnes*, the prohibition against them 'probably still subsist[ed] in general international law' and that, in any event, the risk of abuse involved in pressing recognition of such a principle would be too great. The enforcement of State crimes was exclusively a matter for the UN Security Council. Based on Ago's rationale, the ILC provisionally adopted his proposal as Draft Article 30 [1996] ('Countermeasures in respect of an internationally

---

[27] Ibid. The adjective 'legitimate' referred to the applicable safeguards regime: see ibid., 39, para. 80; Draft Articles Commentary, Art. 30, §2.

[28] Ago, Eighth Report, 43, paras. 91–92. Compare Draft Articles Commentary, Art. 30, §12.

wrongful act').[29] In doing so, the ILC replaced Ago's unitary term 'sanction' with the terms 'countermeasures' and 'measures' 'as a means of preventing any misunderstanding' between the two distinct cases covered by the provision, i.e. countermeasures under general international law and enforcement measures under Chapter VII UNC.[30] The term 'sanction' was reserved for the latter type of action.[31]

Some doubts were expressed in the Sixth Committee as to whether enforcement measures adopted under Chapter VII UNC could really be considered a form of State responsibility: such action could be taken even against States that had not committed any wrongful act. The additional point was also made that it would be inappropriate to assign a decisive role to the Security Council in relation to issues of responsibility for international crimes since the Council was a political and not a judicial organ.[32] For example, Spain observed that the voting procedure in the Security Council 'might in fact impede, and in many cases even preclude, the effective and just imposition of sanctions'.[33]

Few States in the Sixth Committee at this stage explicitly addressed the issue of possible third-party countermeasures in response to State crimes. Finland and Japan stressed the risk of abuse by powerful States and expressed their opposition to third-party countermeasures.[34] In contrast, the Federal Republic of Germany stated that in response to a State crime, 'third States, although not immediately involved, might well be entitled to take countermeasures'.[35] Indonesia stated in seemingly unequivocal terms that in the case of a State crime, 'an injured State can take reprisals, and the other States can do the same'.[36] The legal consequences of State crimes and delicts, including the possibility of

---

[29] See generally Draft Articles Commentary, Art. 30, §§1–23.

[30] Ibid., §21. See also YbILC (1979), vol. I, 171, para. 8 (Chairman of the Drafting Committee, Mr. Riphagen); and ibid., 55–63 (for the debate among ILC members).

[31] Draft Articles Commentary, Art. 30, §21. See also ibid., Art. 19, §§16, 22–29 (for a review of Security Council practice in response to State crimes and Chapter VII UNC action as a special form of responsibility).

[32] UN Docs. A/C.6/31/SR.21, para. 8 (Japan); A/C.6/31/SR.26, para. 5 (France); A/C.6/31/SR.27, para. 20 (Australia). See also UN Doc. A/C.6/31/SR.23, paras. 11–12 (Greece).

[33] YbILC (1982), vol. II/1, 17 (Spain).

[34] UN Docs. A/C.6/31/SR.18, para. 68, A/C.6/36/SR.48, paras. 13, 15 (Finland); A/C.6/31/SR.21, para. 8, A/C.6/35/SR.48, para. 35 (Japan). Brazil and Trinidad and Tobago expressed more general doubts about the admissibility of countermeasures: see UN Docs. A/C.6/34/SR.45, para. 28 (Brazil); A/C.6/34/SR.49, para. 23 (Trinidad and Tobago).

[35] YbILC (1981), vol. II/1, 75, and along similar lines UN Doc. A/C.6/35/SR.45, para. 11 (Federal Republic of Germany). See also UN Doc. A/C.6/31/SR.22, para. 5 (Netherlands).

[36] UN Doc. A/C.6/31/SR.30, para. 33 (Indonesia).

third-party countermeasures, would be further considered by Special Rapporteur Ago's successor, Willem Riphagen.

3.1.2   Special Rapporteur Riphagen's Proposals

Special Rapporteur Riphagen was the first to introduce proposals concerning the second stage of the ILC's work on State responsibility, i.e. the consequences of an internationally wrongful act based on the two distinct regimes of responsibility for State crimes and delicts. In order to determine those consequences, it was necessary to define the State(s) entitled to implement them. Riphagen acknowledged that the enforcement model under traditional international law was 'essentially bilateral-minded'; however, modern international law increasingly seemed to recognize a notion of standing with respect to State crimes and the protection of collective interests under multilateral treaties.[37] In his view, exceptions to the bilateral model of enforcement had developed precisely because such breaches of communitarian norms could not adequately be redressed by it. Collective enforcement was required to ensure the integrity of such norms, including measures taken by States not specially affected by the breach.[38]

In 1984, based on these considerations, Riphagen introduced his draft article 5 on the meaning of the 'injured State'.[39] Under his proposal, an 'injured State' notably referred to any State party to a multilateral treaty in case of a breach of an obligation thereunder established to protect a collective interest or fundamental human rights (i.e. obligations *erga omnes partes*). In case the breach constituted a State crime, all States were deemed injured.[40] In terms of the consequences of the breach of a collective obligation and the new legal relationships arising therefrom, Riphagen distinguished between 'three parameters': the obligations of the responsible State (the first parameter), the rights of the injured State (the second parameter) and the obligations of all States to take a 'non-neutral position' (the third parameter).[41] Riphagen's proposals on

---

[37] Riphagen, Third Report, 36, paras. 91–92.
[38] Riphagen, Fourth Report, 21–22, para. 115.
[39] Riphagen, Fifth Report, 3; Riphagen, Sixth Report, 5–8 (for commentary to his draft article 5).
[40] Ibid.
[41] Riphagen, Preliminary Report, 112, 122, paras. 28, 74; and also ibid., 121–122, paras. 68–73 (on the general requirement of a collective decision taken with respect to the wrongful conduct of the responsible State).

third-party countermeasures (somewhat confusingly) concerned both the second and third parameters. Riphagen proposed in his draft article 9 that the injured State was entitled to adopt third-party countermeasures in response to breaches of obligations *erga omnes partes*.[42] However, in response to a State crime, each injured State could not, in principle, adopt third-party countermeasures on an individual basis. As Riphagen explained:

> [T]here is little chance that States generally will accept a legal rule along the lines of article 19 [1996] ... without a legal guarantee that they will not be charged by any or all other States of having committed an international crime, and be faced with demands and countermeasures of any or all other States without an independent and authoritative establishment of the facts and the applicable law ...
>
> On the other hand, the international community will not accept, if there is such an authoritative establishment of the facts and the applicable law and if the conclusion thereof is that an international crime was committed, that the matter of sanctions be left to the willingness of each individual State to make the sacrifices inevitably involved. And finally, the individual States will not accept a duty to support countermeasures taken by another State, or a duty to participate in collective counter-measures, without such an independent and authoritative statement and a collective discussion and decision on the sharing of the burden of implementation.[43]

By a 'duty to participate in collective countermeasures' in the above passage, Riphagen was alluding to the additional threefold obligations (i.e. cooperation, non-recognition and non-assistance) – based on 'a minimum of required solidarity'[44] – on all States following a State crime embodied in his draft article 14.[45] Under Riphagen's scheme, their enforcement was subject to the procedures in the UN Charter

---

[42] Riphagen, Fifth Report, 3; Riphagen, Sixth Report, 11 (for commentary to his draft article 9). It should be added however that, among other safeguards, the injured State could not adopt third-party countermeasures until it had exhausted the dispute settlement procedures available to it to resolve the dispute with the allegedly responsible State. See Riphagen, Sixth Report, 11 (for his draft article 10, with accompanying commentary).

[43] Riphagen, Fourth Report, 12, para. 65.

[44] Riphagen, Sixth Report, 14, para. 6 (commenting on his draft article 14). See further Dawidowicz (2010), 677; Jørgensen (2010), 687 and 695 (for a brief discussion of the obligations later embodied in Article 41 ARSIWA).

[45] See e.g. Riphagen, Third Report, 44, paras. 133–134, and 49, para. 8 (commenting on his draft article 6, later replaced by his draft article 14); Riphagen, Fifth Report, 5 (for his draft article 14); Riphagen, Sixth Report, 13–14 (for commentary to his draft article 14).

related to the maintenance of international peace and security.[46] Although Riphagen proposed a broad definition of injury, a State indirectly injured by a State crime could only implement the responsibility of the wrongdoing State 'within the framework of the organized community of States'.[47] Thus, '[a] single State cannot take upon itself the role of "policeman" of the international community'.[48] However, as a possible exception, Riphagen tentatively suggested that in response to a State crime, all injured States nevertheless had an individual right to take 'limited' action by way of non-recognition and non-assistance (such as the suspension of treaties) – described as a right to take 'countermeasures' – 'pending a decision of the competent organ of the United Nations'.[49]

The ILC in 1985 provisionally adopted Riphagen's provision on the meaning of the injured State as Draft Article 5 (later adopted on first reading as Draft Article 40 [1996]), albeit with some changes. Most importantly, the ILC replaced Riphagen's original language, which had defined the 'injured State' in terms of the breach of an obligation by the responsible State, with a reference to the infringement of a right. The ILC commentary explained that '[t]his was done on the assumption that to each and every obligation corresponds *per definitionem* a right of at least one other State'.[50] The notion of injury was also broadened to include breaches of communitarian norms arising under customary international law.[51] In so doing, the ILC notably extended the protection of human rights obligations. As the ILC commentary explained with respect to Draft Article 5(2)(e)(iii) (later Draft Article 40(2)(e)(iii) [1996]):

> The interests protected by such provisions are not allocatable to
> a particular State. Hence the necessity to consider in the first instance

---

[46] Riphagen, Sixth Report, 14, paras. 10–11. See also Riphagen, Third Report, 48, para. 5. For an incisive analysis of Riphagen's scheme, see further Forteau (2006), 528–541, who concludes that it clearly violated the UN Charter.

[47] Riphagen, Sixth Report, 14, para. 10 (commenting on his draft article 14).

[48] Riphagen, Third Report, 45, para. 140.

[49] Ibid., 45, paras. 140–143 (Riphagen suggested that as an additional safeguard such action could only be taken by a group of States acting collectively); Riphagen, Sixth Report, 14, para. 6 (commenting on his draft article 14).

[50] Draft Articles Commentary, Art. 40, §2. See already Ago, Second Report, 192, para. 46 ('[I]t seems perfectly legitimate, in international law, to regard the idea of the breach of an obligation as the exact equivalent of the idea of the impairment of the subjective rights of others'). See also Draft Articles Commentary, Art. 3, §9.

[51] See YbILC (1985), vol. I, 307–314.

every other State party to the multilateral convention, or bound by the relevant rule of customary law, as an injured State.[52]

Draft Article 5(2)(f) (later Draft Article 40(2)(f) [1996]) provided in general terms for standing with respect to obligations *erga omnes partes*. In addition, although the ILC adopted the principle that all States were injured in case of a State crime in Draft Article 5(3) (later Draft Article 40(3) [1996]), it explicitly did so without taking any position on Riphagen's draft article 14 and the consequences attached to such unlawful conduct, including the possibility of third-party countermeasures.[53] The ILC also did not take a position on Riphagen's draft article 9 on countermeasures. Thus, the possibility for injured States to take third-party countermeasures in response to breaches of obligations *erga omnes partes* was likewise left open.[54] The next Special Rapporteur, Gaetano Arangio-Ruiz, would consider these issues further.

3.1.3 Special Rapporteur Arangio-Ruiz's Proposals

Special Rapporteur Arangio-Ruiz was especially concerned with the inherent risk of abuse associated with countermeasures and proposed to deal with the regime governing countermeasures in two different ways based on the distinction in Draft Article 19 [1996] between crimes and delicts. In the case of a delict, Arangio-Ruiz proposed in his draft article 11 that an 'injured State', as broadly defined in Draft Article 40 [1996], could adopt third-party countermeasures in response to breaches of obligations *erga omnes (partes)*.[55] However, among the most stringent safeguards against abuse, Arangio-Ruiz initially proposed that an injured State could not adopt such third-party countermeasures prior to the exhaustion 'of all the amicable settlement procedures available under general international law, the Charter of the United Nations or any other dispute settlement instrument to which it is a party' – a proposal he subsequently limited to an obligation to seek a settlement of the dispute under a binding third-party settlement procedure or, in the

---

[52] Draft Articles Commentary, Art. 40, §20 (and see also the qualification with respect to the seriousness of the breach, at ibid., §22). To the same effect: *Obligation to Prosecute or Extradite*, ICJ Rep. (2012), 422 at 450, para. 69 (with respect to obligations *erga omnes partes*).

[53] Draft Articles Commentary, Art. 40, §§26–28.

[54] See ILC Report (1985), UN Doc. A/40/10, 24, paras. 162–163.

[55] Arangio-Ruiz, Fourth Report, 22, para. 52 (for his draft article 11); Arangio-Ruiz, Sixth Report, 17, para. 81 (for his revised draft article 11).

absence of such a possibility, to offer to resolve the dispute by such means.[56] As an additional safeguard, Arangio-Ruiz proposed that the State(s) taking third-party countermeasures would be required to have recourse to certain post-dispute settlement procedures (notably, compulsory arbitration) under a future convention on State responsibility or any other binding dispute settlement procedure in force between itself and the target State.[57] In short, the adoption of third-party countermeasures would be subject to judicial scrutiny. The ILC in 1996, albeit with some changes, provisionally adopted, among other articles, Arangio-Ruiz's proposals as Draft Articles 47 ('Countermeasures by an injured State'), 48 ('Conditions relating to resort to countermeasures') and 58 ('Arbitration') [1996].[58]

With respect to State crimes, Arangio-Ruiz stressed that the risks of abuse arising from a universalization of the status of the injured State were necessarily greater than in the case of delicts.[59] In his view, 'the most crucial problem' concerning the consequences of State crimes 'relate[d] to the determination of the existence of any such wrongful act and its attribution to one or more States'.[60] To address this problem, Arangio-Ruiz proposed an elaborate and extremely ambitious institutional safeguards regime for the adoption of third-party countermeasures based on 'the indispensable role of international institutions'.[61]

As a preliminary matter, Arangio-Ruiz considered Riphagen's proposal ill-advised and unworkable: 'The Council has neither the constitutional function nor the technical means to determine, on the basis of law, the existence, the attribution or the consequences of any wrongful act [other than aggression], whether "delict" or "crime"'.[62] For his part, Arangio-Ruiz proposed a scheme based on a two-phase procedure embodied in his draft articles 17 and 19 by which, prior to the adoption of any third-party countermeasures, the UN General Assembly or the Security

---

[56] Ibid. (for his (revised) draft article 12(1)). The ILC after an extensive debate adopted a modified version of Arangio-Ruiz's draft article 12 (requiring simply an initial obligation to attempt to settle the dispute by negotiation) as Draft Article 48 [1996]. See further Section 6.4.1.

[57] Arangio-Ruiz, Fifth Report, 28–30, para. 106 (his draft articles 1–5 of Part Three, with accompanying dispute settlement annex).

[58] See generally YbILC (1996), vol. I, 166–176, 180–182, 184–193; Draft Articles Commentary, Arts. 47–48, 58.

[59] Arangio-Ruiz, Seventh Report, 17, paras. 70–73.   [60] Ibid., 20, para. 87.

[61] See Arangio-Ruiz, Seventh Report, 17–30, paras. 70–140. Further: Forteau (2006), 549–565 (for a critical assessment of Arangio-Ruiz's proposal).

[62] Arangio-Ruiz, Fifth Report, 48, para. 211.

Council would make a political assessment (under Chapter VI UNC), and the ICJ a decisive legal determination. Any UN Member State making a claim about the commission of a State crime would be required, under a future convention on State responsibility to which it was a contracting party, to bring the matter to the attention of the General Assembly or the Security Council. If either of these political organs resolved (by qualified majority) that the allegation was sufficiently substantiated to justify the grave concern of the international community, any such State could then in contentious proceedings bring the matter before the ICJ by unilateral application. A decision by the Court that a State crime had indeed been committed would serve as judicial authorization to adopt third-party countermeasures.[63]

The ILC and Sixth Committee rejected Arangio-Ruiz's proposed scheme, mainly on the basis of it being perceived as 'too broad to be realistic and as revolutionary and unattuned to States' sense of international law'.[64] His 'set of grand utopian principles'[65] was also rejected as being inconsistent with the UN Charter.[66] The Drafting Committee in 1996 concluded that the normal countermeasures regime (as embodied in Draft Articles 47–50 [1996]) 'applied without exception or modification to international crimes'.[67] In terms of the initial determination that a State crime had been committed, the Drafting Committee concluded that that determination was, in the first instance, a matter for the injured State(s). If the allegedly responsible State protested against this determination of responsibility, the resulting dispute between the parties would be subject to the post-dispute settlement obligations mentioned above.[68] In addition, the Drafting Committee believed that the allegedly

---

[63] Arangio-Ruiz, Seventh Report, 29–30, para. 140 (for his draft articles 17 and 19). It may be added that Arangio-Ruiz's scheme nevertheless allowed for the possibility of certain urgent or interim third-party countermeasures: see his draft article 17(2) (at ibid.).

[64] ILC Report (1995), UN Doc. A/50/10, 47, para. 250; Topical Summary of Government Comments in the Sixth Committee, UN Doc. A/CN.4/472/Add.1 (1995), 25–27, paras. 86–97.

[65] Pellet (2010), 81. Compare YbILC (1995), vol. I, 113, para. 26 (Mr. Rosenstock) (dismissing the proposal as 'a castle in the sky').

[66] See ILC Report (1995), UN Doc. A/50/10, 47, 53–57, paras. 250, 297–319 (for a summary of the debate); Topical Summary of Government Comments in the Sixth Committee, UN Doc. A/CN.4/472/Add.1 (1995), 25–27, paras. 86–97. Also: Draft Articles Commentary, Art. 51, §§7–13. In an apparent bout of disillusionment, Arangio-Ruiz promptly resigned as Special Rapporteur: see YbILC (1996), vol. I, 30–31, 46–47, paras. 59–63.

[67] YbILC (1996), vol. I, 178, para. 63 (Chairman of the Drafting Committee, Mr. Calero Rodrigues).

[68] See above nn. 57–58.

responsible State had the option of invoking Article 35 UNC, thereby bringing the dispute to the attention of the General Assembly or the Security Council. Thus the Drafting Committee concluded that these procedures provided an adequate safeguard against abuse concerning the individual characterization of a wrongful act as a State crime; it would be unnecessary to design any new procedures for that purpose.[69]

The ILC in 1996 on first reading provisionally adopted Draft Articles 51–53 [1996] (concerning the regime governing State crimes), Draft Articles 54–60 [1996] (concerning general post-dispute settlement obligations) and Draft Article 39 [1996] (concerning the privileged role of the Security Council under the UN Charter) based on this rationale.[70] As the ILC explained with respect to State crimes:

> In practice, it is likely that [a] collective response will be coordinated through the competent organs of the United Nations. It is not the function of the present draft articles to regulate the extent or exercise of the constitutional power and authority of UN organs – nor, in view of article 103 of the Charter, is it even possible to do so.[71]

It thus appears from a combined reading of the broad definition of injury in Draft Article 40 [1996] and the right of the injured State to take countermeasures in Draft Article 47 [1996] (and the accompanying commentary) that the ILC on first reading recognized the individual right of any State to adopt third-party countermeasures in response to breaches of obligations *erga omnes (partes)* (including State crimes). It should be stressed, however, that this provisional conclusion resulted more from the poor drafting of Draft Article 40 [1996] (which had completely failed to distinguish between directly and indirectly injured States) than any explicit approval of a regime of individual third-party countermeasures.[72] As a result, States simply did not pay much attention to the issue.[73] This conclusion is evidenced by the limited comments provided by States.

---

[69] See YbILC (1996), vol. I, 178–180, paras. 64–65, 70–73 (Chairman of the Drafting Committee, Mr. Calero Rodrigues).
[70] See Draft Articles Commentary, Art. 51, §§2, 5–6.
[71] Draft Articles Commentary, Art. 53, §3. To the same effect: ARSIWA Commentary, Art. 40, §9.
[72] See YbILC (1993), vol. I, 141, para. 7 (Chairman of the Drafting Committee, Mr. Mikulka); and compare YbILC (1985), vol. I, 307–314; Draft Articles Commentary, Art. 40, §§26–28. Further: Bederman (1998), 291; Kawasaki (2000), 17; Crawford (2000), 27; Tams (2005), 243–244.
[73] Compare Crawford, Fourth Report, 15, para. 59.

Only three States at this stage explicitly opposed a regime of third-party countermeasures.[74] Japan stressed that the right to take countermeasures provided in Draft Articles 30 and 47 [1996]:

> must be understood as individual measures taken by an individual State whose interests have been damaged directly by the internationally wrongful act of another State, and thus do not include collective measures or sanctions that international organizations such as the United Nations would take.[75]

For its part, the Czech Republic stated:

> [It] does not believe that the regime of countermeasures in the cases of State 'crimes' should be individualized, i.e., liberalized ... The taking of countermeasures can give rise to abuses and would probably be even more likely to do so if one yielded to the temptation to establish a less strict regime for resort to countermeasures in response to a State crime.[76]

France made a statement to similar effect.[77] In contrast, Ireland was concerned that the regime of countermeasures should not 'unduly restrict a State's ability to take effective countermeasures in respect of certain wrongful acts involving obligations *erga omnes*, for example, violations of human rights'.[78] On second reading, Special Rapporteur James Crawford brought much needed attention to this issue and introduced a number of proposals explicitly designed, among other things, to limit the apparent entitlement to take third-party countermeasures.

3.2   The ILC's Contribution on Second Reading (1997–2001)

It soon became clear on second reading that the ILC's 'construction of a multilateral public order'[79] rested on shaky foundations. The single most controversial issue on first reading concerned the distinction between crimes and delicts. The ILC's original vision in 1976 of formulating Draft Article 19 [1996] based on two completely different regimes of responsibility had not been realized.[80] The lofty notion of State crimes

---

[74] It should be added that the notion of State crimes in Draft Article 19 [1996] and the unitary notion of injury in Draft Article 40 [1996] elicited much debate and strong criticism in the Sixth Committee: see Tams (2005), 243–244; Crawford (2013a), 390–394 (both with a brief summary of the debate, with further references).
[75] UN Doc. A/CN.4/492, 11–12 (Japan).
[76] UN Doc. A/CN.4/488, 137–138 (Czech Republic).   [77] Ibid., 141 (France).
[78] Ibid., 126 (Ireland).   [79] YbILC (2000), vol. I, 311, para. 78 (Mr. Brownlie).
[80] See Section 3.1.1 above.

turned out to be little more than a rhetorical device (albeit a powerful one). No special rules applied to the establishment of responsibility for crimes. The special legal consequences attached to crimes were ultimately thin on the ground; they were barely followed through in Draft Articles 51–53 [1996]. In fact, those consequences were not even special to crimes. In short, 'the mountain gave birth to a ridiculous mouse'.[81] But there was more.

The ILC's whole approach to operationalize the enforcement of communitarian norms was paradoxical in that it effectively relied on the traditional bilateral model of enforcement to do so. The aggregation of 'injury' in Draft Article 40 [1996] meant that all States were deemed equally injured in the case of breaches of obligations *erga omnes (partes)* (including State crimes) and could make individual claims for cessation and reparation on their own behalf, irrespective of their proximity to the breach. Any State was entitled to enforce these broad claims by way of third-party countermeasures without any apparent limitation. Some structural engineering work would be required on second reading to ensure that the ILC's construction of a multilateral public order rested on more solid foundations. In 1997, the ILC appointed a new architect, Special Rapporteur Crawford, to urgently attend to the essential works. The two building blocks of peremptory norms and obligations *erga omnes* – '*les grandes verticales*'[82] of the construction – were soon brought back to replace the stone of State crimes which was crumbling from its own weight.

3.2.1   Special Rapporteur Crawford's Proposals

Special Rapporteur Crawford characterized the ILC's approach on first reading as 'unsatisfactory on nearly all accounts' in its construction of a multilateral public order.[83]

Three issues required special attention: (1) international crimes of State; (2) invocation of responsibility for breaches of communitarian norms; and (3) third-party countermeasures.[84] These will be dealt with in turn.

---

[81] YbILC (1996), vol. I, 179, para. 69 (Mr. Arangio-Ruiz). Similarly: Crawford (2001b), 65.
[82] Crawford (2006b), 397, 452.   [83] YbILC (1998), vol. I, 148, para. 13 (Mr. Crawford).
[84] Crawford, First Report, 11, para. 51. Another controversial issue (of a more general character) concerned the settlement of disputes under a possible future convention on State responsibility (ibid., 5, para. 6).

3.2.1.1   International Crimes of State

The first issue that Special Rapporteur Crawford had to consider was how to deal with the extremely controversial and much debated concept of international crimes of State.[85] Albeit not without its strong supporters, it had been widely criticized on multiple grounds in both the ILC and the Sixth Committee.[86] Crawford broadly shared these criticisms, noting that the terminology of crimes in Draft Article 19 [1996] was potentially misleading as it merely amounted to a pejorative way of describing serious breaches of fundamental norms.[87] Simply put, there was nothing 'criminal' about 'crimes'.[88]

In search of a compromise solution, Crawford outlined five possible alternatives to dealing with State crimes.[89] His own preference was to exclude it altogether and thereby decriminalize the law of State responsibility: 'The present draft articles do not do justice to the concept or its implications for the international legal order, and cannot be expected to do so'.[90] In Crawford's view, 'the most appropriate and coherent solution' to try to resolve the pressing issues raised by State crimes would be to concentrate on the existing cognate concepts of obligations *erga omnes* and peremptory norms based on one single regime for all internationally wrongful acts.[91] In 1998, following an extensive debate, the ILC decided to provisionally set consideration of Draft Article 19 [1996] aside and, as a compromise solution, agreed to consider whether

> ... the systematic development in the draft articles of key notions such as obligations (*erga omnes*), peremptory norms (*jus cogens*) and a possible category of the most serious breaches of international obligation could be sufficient to resolve the issues raised by article 19 [1996].[92]

---

[85] See generally Crawford, First Report, 9–23, paras. 43–95. Further: Crawford (2006b), 452–478.

[86] See ILC Report (1998), UN Doc. A/53/10, 118–147, paras. 241–331; UN Docs. A/CN.4/488, 51–66, 133–141; A/CN.4/488/Add.1, 5–6; A/CN.4/488/Add.2, 3–7; A/CN.4/492, 8–9, 16; and also above n. 21. Further: Crawford, First Report, 11–14, paras. 52–54 (for a summary of comments provided by States).

[87] Crawford, First Report, 13–14, 22, paras. 54, 84.

[88] Ibid., 10–11, 19–22, paras. 46–51, 76–80, 83–86. For a brief discussion see Ollivier (2010), 703 (with many further references). Also: Crawford (2010), 405.

[89] Crawford, First Report, 18–23, paras. 70–95.   [90] Ibid., 23, para. 94.

[91] Ibid., 23, paras. 92–93.

[92] ILC Report (1998), UN Doc. A/53/10, 77, para. 331 (and for a summary of the debate, see ibid., 67–76, paras. 260–321). To the same effect, see also UN Doc. A/CN.4/488, 137 (Germany).

Special Rapporteur Crawford sought to give effect to this mandate by disaggregating the notion of State crimes into its various component parts. On that basis, Crawford's draft article 51 (a consolidated version of Draft Articles 51–53 [1996]) proposed that, in response to a 'serious and manifest breach by a State of an obligation owed to the international community as a whole', the responsible State would be under an obligation to pay 'aggravated' damages.[93] The threefold obligations for third States embodied in Draft Article 53 [1996] with respect to non-recognition, non-assistance and cooperation were also included; they were 'broadly acceptable, but only as long as they do not carry *a contrario* implications for other breaches which may not be egregious, systematic or gross'.[94] The possibility of any future additional consequences of serious breaches was reserved.[95]

The Drafting Committee in 2000 provisionally adopted Crawford's proposal, including damages reflecting the gravity of the breach, with only minor changes as Draft Article 42 [2000].[96] The proposal provoked much debate.[97] As a result, the Drafting Committee in 2001 introduced two changes as a compromise solution; first, the concept of 'aggravated' damages was abandoned; second, the implied reference to a serious breach of an obligation *erga omnes* was replaced by a reference to a serious breach of a peremptory norm. The latter change was introduced to avoid confusion by clarifying that obligations *erga omnes* were primarily concerned with the invocation of responsibility, not the status of the norm breached.[98] The ILC adopted the proposal as Articles 40–41 ARSIWA.[99] The ICJ in the

---

[93] This proposal replaced Draft Article 52 [1996] under which certain limitations upon the obtaining of restitution or satisfaction did not apply in the case of State crimes: see further Draft Articles Commentary, Art. 52; Crawford, Third Report, 107, para. 408.

[94] Crawford, Third Report, 107, para. 410.

[95] Ibid., 106–108, paras. 407–413 (his draft article 51). See also Crawford, Fourth Report, 12–14, paras. 43–53. Further: Wittich (2010), 667; Crawford (2013a), 523–526 (on the ILC's treatment of punitive damages).

[96] YbILC (2000), vol. I, 392–393, paras. 40–46 (Chairman of the Drafting Committee, Mr. Gaja); ILC Report (2000), UN Doc. A/55/10, 69 (for the text of Draft Article 42 [2000]).

[97] For a summary of the debate see ILC Report (2000), UN Doc. A/55/10, 59–60, 62–63, paras. 359–363, 374–383; ILC Report (2001), UN Doc. A/56/10, 22, paras. 45–49.

[98] YbILC (2001), vol. I, 104–105, paras. 14–19 (Chairman of the Drafting Committee, Mr. Tomka). See also ARSIWA Commentary, Introductory Commentary to Chapter III of Part Two, §7. For the debate in the Sixth Committee, see Topical Summary of Government Comments in the Sixth Committee, UN Doc. A/CN.4/513 (2000), 19–24, paras. 89–121; UN Doc. A/CN.4/515, 44–58.

[99] See generally ARSIWA Commentary, Arts. 40–41. For a contemporaneous assessment see further Sicilianos (2002), 1127; Wyler (2002), 1147; Tams (2002b), 1161; Gattini (2002), 1181.

Wall case implicitly endorsed Articles 40–41 ARSIWA, and in the *Bosnian Genocide* case, it unequivocally confirmed that 'international law does not recognize the criminal responsibility of the State'.[100]

3.2.1.2 Invocation of Responsibility for Breaches of Communitarian Norms

In fulfilment of his mandate to systematically develop obligations *erga omnes*,[101] Special Rapporteur Crawford next considered Draft Article 40 [1996] and that part of the construction of a multilateral public order which concerned the invocation of responsibility for breaches of multilateral obligations.[102] There was broad agreement in the ILC and Sixth Committee that Draft Article 40 [1996] was defective in several respects in its treatment of multilateral responsibility (as well as others).[103] As Crawford explained, the key difficulty with the provision was that it completely failed to distinguish between bilateral and multilateral obligations. In so doing, it reduced all relations of responsibility to a single form: the traditional bilateral model of right-duty relations. Thus even multilateral responsibility exhausted itself in bundles of bilateral relations between States *inter se*. The result was somewhat paradoxical: the ILC's construction of a multilateral public order rested on a bilateral model of enforcement.[104] It may be recalled that Draft Article 40 [1996] was based precisely on the assumption that 'to each and every obligation corresponds *per definitionem* a right of at least one other State'.[105] Crawford stressed that this assumption of 'exact equivalence'[106] was contradicted by the alternative way of conceptualizing relations of responsibility affirmed by the ICJ in *Barcelona Traction* and raised a series of problems.[107]

---

[100] *Wall* case, ICJ Rep. (2004), 136 at 200, paras. 159–160; *Application of the Convention on the Prevention and Punishment of the Crime of Genocide (Bosnia and Herzegovina v. Serbia and Montenegro)*, ICJ Rep. (2007), 43 at 115, para. 170. Further: Crawford (2010), 405.

[101] See above n. 92.

[102] See generally Crawford, Third Report, 25–39, 99–100, 108, paras. 66–119, 373–379, 413 (n. 828); Crawford, Fourth Report, 10–11, paras. 35–42. Also: Crawford (2006b), 421–451.

[103] See ILC Report (2000), UN Doc. A/55/10, 30, para. 119; Topical Summary of Government Comments in the Sixth Committee, UN Doc. A/CN.4/504 (1999), 18–19, paras. 62–66; Crawford, Third Report, 27–29, paras. 77–81 (for a useful summary of comments by States).

[104] See Crawford, Third Report, 29–32, paras. 82–96. Also: Crawford (2001a), 319–321.

[105] Draft Articles Commentary, Art. 40, §2 (as discussed above in n. 50).

[106] Ibid., Art. 3, §9. Compare ARSIWA Commentary, Art. 2, §8.

[107] See Crawford, Third Report, 27, 29–30, 32, paras. 74, 83–85, 96(b).

Draft Article 40 [1996] treated all injured States in exactly the same way, with all being entitled to the same remedies. For example, in a conspicuous departure from the logic of Article 60(2) VCLT, the provision failed with respect to multilateral obligations to take account of the position of the directly injured or specially affected State(s) (e.g. the victim of an unlawful armed attack). It translated human rights into States' rights by failing to distinguish between the victims as right-holders and States as mere representatives of those victims with a legal interest in the responsible State's compliance with its human rights obligations. It also failed to consider other multilateral obligations whose breach did not affect the individual rights of any State (e.g. pollution of the high seas). Each State injured by the breach of a multilateral obligation was entitled on an individual basis to claim cessation and reparation and (if required) to do so by way of third-party countermeasures.[108] It was observed that 'absurd results' could follow from 'a competitive or cumulative competence of States to invoke legal consequences of a violation'.[109] Indeed 'it could become chaotic if a number of States began demanding different things under the rubric of State responsibility'.[110]

Crawford proposed a solution to the many problems raised by Draft Article 40 [1996] based on the alternative way of establishing relations of responsibility affirmed by the ICJ in *Barcelona Traction*. The Court in that case had very clearly drawn an 'essential distinction'[111] between the individual rights of States arising in a bilateral context and the legal interests of all States in respect of obligations *erga omnes*. Thus there was, for purposes of the invocation of responsibility, an essential distinction between breaches of bilateral obligations and breaches of multilateral obligations. This required a separate treatment of States that had suffered 'injury' and those that had only a 'legal interest' in compliance.[112]

In order to delimit the notion of the 'injured State' in respect of multilateral obligations, Crawford distinguished between three subcategories of such obligations: (1) obligations owed to the international community as a whole (obligations *erga omnes*), (2) obligations owed to a group of States and established for the protection of a collective interest of the group (obligations *erga omnes partes*, including those

---

[108] Ibid., 29–32, paras. 83–96.
[109] UN Doc. A/CN.4/488, 96 (Austria). See also ibid., 98–99, 101 (United States), 100 (Germany); UN Doc. A/C.6/54/SR.23, 8, para. 59 (Israel).
[110] ILC Report (2000), UN Doc. A/55/10, 57, para. 352.
[111] *Barcelona Traction*, ICJ Rep. (1970), 3 at 32, paras. 33, 35.
[112] See Crawford, Third Report, 32–33, paras. 97–98.

requiring integral performance within the meaning of Article 60(2)(c) VCLT and Draft Article 40(2)(e)(ii) [1996]), and (3) obligations *erga omnes (partes)* involving a specially affected State.[113] Based on an analogy with Article 60(2) VCLT, only breaches of multilateral obligations requiring integral performance or involving a specially affected State should be assimilated to cases of individual injury arising in a purely bilateral context. Put differently, States could clearly be affected in different ways in respect of the same breach of a multilateral obligation.[114] Thus a distinction was required between the primary victim of the breach of a multilateral obligation and other States which are party to same obligation and have only a legal interest in its performance. In such cases, the position of the latter States would to some extent have to be secondary with respect to the invocation of responsibility and its possible implementation by way of third-party countermeasures.[115]

In terms of the extent to which differently affected States should be able to invoke the legal consequences of a breach of a multilateral obligation, Crawford proposed that a State injured by such a breach should be entitled to make claims for cessation and reparation on its own behalf and (if necessary) do so by way of countermeasures. Any State party to a multilateral obligation with only a legal interest in its performance should, as a minimum, be entitled to claim cessation (and assurances and guarantees of non-repetition). In addition, any such State should be able to claim reparation on behalf of and with the consent of the injured State. In the absence of an injured State, any State party to a multilateral obligation with a legal interest in its performance should be able to claim restitution – but not other forms of reparation – in the interests of the victims of the breach.[116] These proposals formed the basis of Crawford's draft article 40 *bis* ('Right of a State to invoke the responsibility of another State').[117]

The Drafting Committee in 2000 provisionally adopted the substance of Crawford's proposal, albeit with some changes, as Draft Articles 43 and 49 [2000].[118] Crawford's draft article 40 *bis* had raised too many

---

[113] Ibid., 34–35, paras. 106–107.   [114] Ibid.
[115] Ibid., 36, paras. 108–109. The possible enforcement of claims for cessation and reparation by way of third-party countermeasures is discussed separately as part of the safeguards regime in Section 6.1.3.1(i).
[116] Ibid., 36–37, 99–100, paras. 110–113, 375–379.
[117] Ibid., 38–39, 108, paras. 119, 413 (n. 828) (for his draft article 40 *bis*).
[118] See YbILC (2000), vol. I, 393–394, 396, paras. 47–54, 61 (Chairman of the Drafting Committee, Mr. Gaja); ILC Report (2000), UN Doc. A/55/10, 69–70 (for the text of Draft Articles 43 and 49 [2000]).

important and difficult issues; in the interest of clarity, they were dealt with individually in two separate provisions.[119] The distinction between 'injured' States and States having a 'legal interest' was unsatisfactory since 'all injured States also had legal interests'.[120] This language was replaced by the categories of 'injured State' and 'States other than the injured State'. Finally, it was considered that the latter States should be entitled to seek all forms of reparation (and not only restitution) in the interests of the injured State or of the beneficiaries of the obligation breached.[121] Draft Articles 43 and 49 [2000] were extensively debated in the ILC and Sixth Committee.[122] Although broad support was expressed for their underlying rationale, Article 49 [2000] was somewhat controversial. In particular, a minority of States criticized the notion of obligations *erga omnes (partes)* as being indeterminate, alleging that its lack of precision might result in serious abuse in the form of collective sanctions or collective interventions.[123] Several States questioned whether the right of third States to demand reparation was recognized by international law.[124] There was also some concern that, in the absence of a provision for cooperation, the responsible State might be subject to contradictory demands.[125]

The Drafting Committee in 2001 did not revisit these issues and proposed only minor changes to Draft Articles 43 and 49 [2000], which the ILC finally adopted as Articles 42 ('Invocation of responsibility by an injured State') and 48 ('Invocation of responsibility by a State other than an injured State') ARSIWA.[126] Article 48 ARSIWA reads as follows:

---

[119] YbILC (2000), vol. I, 393, para. 49 (Chairman of the Drafting Committee, Mr. Gaja).

[120] Ibid., 394, para. 50. See also ARSIWA Commentary, Art. 48, §2. Further: Tams (2005), 28–36.

[121] YbILC (2000), vol. I, 396, para. 61 (Chairman of the Drafting Committee, Mr. Gaja).

[122] See ILC Report (2000), UN Doc. A/55/10, 30–34, paras. 119–150; Topical Summary of Government Comments in the Sixth Committee, UN Doc. A/CN.4/513 (2000), 25–27, paras. 124–130, 136–143.

[123] See Topical Summary of Government Comments in the Sixth Committee, UN Doc. A/CN.4/513 (2000), 26–27, paras. 137, 140. Further: UN Docs. A/C.6/55/SR.15, 5–6, para. 31 (India); A/C.6/55/SR.18, 11, para. 59 (Cuba); A/CN.4/515, 69–70 (China); and Section 5.2.6 (for an assessment of the risk of abuse associated with the indeterminacy of communitarian norms).

[124] Topical Summary of Government Comments in the Sixth Committee, UN Doc. A/CN.4/513 (2000), 27, paras. 140, 142.

[125] Ibid., 27, para. 143. For a proposal to include an obligation to negotiate a joint request, see UN Doc. A/CN.4/515, 73 (Austria).

[126] See YbILC (2001), vol. I, 108–110, paras. 34–37, 45–47 (Chairman of the Drafting Committee, Mr. Tomka); ARSIWA Commentary, Arts. 42 and 48. Generally: Gaja (2010), 941, 957; Crawford (2013a), 362–378.

Article 48
Invocation of responsibility by a State other than an injured State

1. Any State other than an injured State is entitled to invoke the responsibility of another State in accordance with paragraph 2 if:
   (a) the obligation breached is owed to a group of States including that State, and is established for the protection of a collective interest of the group; or
   (b) the obligation breached is owed to the international community as a whole.
2. Any State entitled to invoke responsibility under paragraph 1 may claim from the responsible State:
   (a) cessation of the internationally wrongful act, and assurances and guarantees of non-repetition in accordance with article 30; and
   (b) performance of the obligation of reparation in accordance with the preceding articles, in the interest of the injured State or of the beneficiaries of the obligation breached.
3. The requirements for the invocation of responsibility by an injured State under articles 43, 44 and 45 apply to an invocation of responsibility by a State entitled to do so under paragraph 1.

The ILC commentary to Article 48 ARSIWA makes clear that it is based on the ICJ's dictum in *Barcelona Traction* and constitutes a 'deliberate departure' from the second phase of *South West Africa*.[127] With respect to 48(2)(b) ARSIWA, the commentary acknowledges that it involves 'a measure of progressive development', but emphasizes that, in cases where no State is individually injured, it is 'highly desirable that some State or States be in a position to claim reparation, in particular restitution'.[128] The ICJ in the *Obligation to Prosecute or Extradite* case implicitly endorsed Article 48(1)(a) ARSIWA.[129]

3.2.1.3   Third-Party Countermeasures

Special Rapporteur Crawford finally considered the vexed question of third-party countermeasures.[130] It was already suggested above that the

---

[127] ARSIWA Commentary, Art. 48, §§2, 7 (n. 725), 8–9.   [128] Ibid., Art. 48, §12.
[129] *Obligation to Prosecute or Extradite*, ICJ Rep. (2012), 422 at 449–450, paras. 68–69; and Section 2.1 (text accompanying nn. 28–32). See also *Responsibilities and Obligations of States Sponsoring Persons and Entities with Respect to Activities in the Area*, ITLOS Case No. 17 (Adv. Op., 1 Feb. 2011), para. 180 (for an affirmation of Article 48(2)(b) ARSIWA).
[130] See generally Crawford, Third Report, 101–106, 108–109, paras. 386–406, 413; Crawford, Fourth Report, 17–19, paras. 70–74, 76. Although not wedded to terminology, Crawford discussed the issue under the rubric of 'collective countermeasures' (Crawford, Third Report, 101-102, para. 386).

ILC's treatment of this issue on first reading had been deficient since the overbroad conception of injury in Draft Article 40 [1996], read in conjunction with Draft Article 47 [1996], effectively recognized an individual right to resort to third-party countermeasures without any apparent limitation. Crawford found this solution 'wholly untenable'.[131] For his part, broadly in line with his proposals on invocation of responsibility in what became Article 48 ARSIWA, Crawford proposed to limit the circumstances in which third-party countermeasures might be adopted.[132] Crawford briefly examined State practice on third-party countermeasures, but this review did not allow clear conclusions to be drawn with respect to the existence of a right to adopt third-party countermeasures. State practice was apparently limited, inconsistent, dominated by Western States and lacked clear evidence of *opinio juris*.[133] Practice nevertheless suggested that recourse to third-party countermeasures might be envisaged in two different situations. To allow third-party countermeasures in those situations would also be normatively desirable.

First, in cases involving a directly injured State, it seemed that other States had sometimes adopted third-party countermeasures at the request of and on behalf of that State. In doing so, they appeared to have treated the injured State's own reaction as legally relevant.[134] This practice was analogous to that of collective self-defence. In the *Nicaragua* case, the ICJ had observed that action by way of collective self-defence could only be taken by a third State at the request of the State directly injured by the breach of an obligation *erga omnes* (i.e. the State victim of the armed attack).[135] Thus practice appeared to support the view that a State directly injured by a breach of an obligation *erga omnes (partes)* 'should not be left alone to seek redress for the breach'.[136] If third States could invoke responsibility for such breaches on the basis of what became Article 48 ARSIWA, it did not seem inconsistent with principle that they should also be recognized as entitled to take third-party countermeasures

---

[131] YbILC (2000), vol. I, 302, para. 2 (Mr. Crawford).

[132] Crawford, Third Report, 102, para. 390.

[133] Ibid., 102–105, paras. 391–397. See also YbILC (2000), vol. I, 303, para. 7 (Mr. Crawford).

[134] Crawford, Third Report, 105, para. 400. As examples, Crawford referred to the unilateral coercive measures adopted by Western States against Argentina and Iran in response to the Falklands conflict and the Tehran hostage crisis, following requests for assistance by the United Kingdom and the United States (ibid.). See further Sections 5.2.5 and 6.1.3.1(i).

[135] Crawford, Third Report, 105, para. 400.

[136] Ibid., 105, para. 401. See also Dawidowicz (2006), 337; Crawford (2013a), 703–704; and further Section 5.2.5.

with the consent of the directly injured State (subject to any conditions laid down by the latter State and to the extent that it was itself entitled to take those countermeasures).[137]

Second, in the case of a breach of an obligation *erga omnes* which did not directly injure any State (notably breaches of international human rights or humanitarian law affecting only nationals of the responsible State), practice also tentatively supported the conclusion that an individual entitlement to take third-party countermeasures should be recognized.[138] Crawford acknowledged that such unilateral action, based on the auto-interpretation of wrongful conduct, raised an important issue of 'due process' for the allegedly responsible State and might serve to exacerbate (rather than resolve) individual disputes.[139] Those concerns were, however, 'substantially reduced' where the breach concerned was 'gross, well attested, systematic and continuing'.[140] Practice demonstrated that States had not adopted third-party countermeasures in response to minor or isolated violations of obligations *erga omnes*. On the contrary, practice was limited to 'some of the major political crises of recent times' involving serious breaches of obligations *erga omnes*.[141] Crawford found it 'difficult to envisage' that States should have no entitlement to take third-party countermeasures in such circumstances.[142] With the example of humanitarian intervention in mind, Crawford suggested that to disallow third-party countermeasures in response to gross and well-attested breaches of obligations *erga omnes* 'may place further pressure on States to intervene in other, perhaps less desirable ways'.[143] Accordingly:

> [I]nternational law should offer to States with a legitimate interest in compliance in such obligations, some means of securing compliance which does not involve the use of force.[144]

These two situations formed the basis of Crawford's draft articles 50 A ('Countermeasures on behalf of an injured State') and 50 B ('Countermeasures in cases of serious breaches of obligations to the international community as a whole').[145] The latter provision also

---

[137] Crawford, Third Report, 105, para. 401.   [138] Ibid., 106, para. 403.

[139] Ibid., 37, 106, paras. 115, 403.   [140] Ibid., 106, para. 405 (also ibid., 37, para. 115).

[141] Ibid., 105, para. 399.   [142] Ibid., 106, para. 403.   [143] Ibid., 106, para. 405.

[144] Ibid.

[145] Ibid., 105–106, 108–109, paras. 401–402, 406, 413. It may be added that Crawford's proposals on countermeasures rejected any link to compulsory post-dispute settlement obligations by way of arbitration as envisaged in Draft Article 58(2) [1996]: see Crawford, Second Report, 94–95, paras. 386–389; and generally Crawford, Fourth Report, 4–6, paras. 12–20; ILC Report (2001), UN Doc. A/56/10, 23, paras. 56–60.

included an obligation of cooperation in cases where several States adopted third-party countermeasures in order to ensure that the general conditions for the taking of countermeasures (notably, proportionality) would be fulfilled.[146] It may be noted that, although practice also suggested that third-party countermeasures had occasionally been taken in response to serious breaches of obligations *erga omnes partes*,[147] Crawford did not propose to endorse their application in such cases, seemingly out of a concern to avoid 'the undue licensing of individual responses to third States'.[148]

Although various concerns were expressed with respect to Crawford's proposed draft articles 50 A and 50 B during the ILC debate in 2000, including the relationship between third-party countermeasures and the Security Council, his proposals nevertheless found a 'significant level of approval' in the Commission.[149] The Drafting Committee in 2000 accordingly provisionally adopted Crawford's proposals, albeit with some changes, as Draft Article 54 [2000] ('Countermeasures by States other than the injured State'). Crawford's two draft articles were merged into one as they did not cover all situations and partly overlapped. In the case of a serious breach of an obligation *erga omnes*, third-party countermeasures could be adopted irrespective of the wishes of the injured State.[150] Draft Article 54 [2000] read as follows:

1. Any State entitled under article 49, paragraph 1 [i.e. what became Article 48(1) ARSIWA], to invoke the responsibility of a State may take countermeasures at the request and on behalf of any State injured by the breach, to the extent that that State may itself take countermeasures under this chapter.
2. In the cases referred to in article 41 [i.e. what became Article 40 ARSIWA], any State may take countermeasures, in accordance with the present chapter in the interest of the beneficiaries of the obligation breached.

---

[146] Crawford, Third Report, 108-109, para. 413.

[147] Ibid., 105, para. 398. Crawford appears here to have referred to the action taken by Western States against Poland in 1981–1982 in response to the widespread suspension of internationally protected civil and political rights in that country (ibid., 102, para. 391). See further Section 4.2.7.

[148] Crawford, Third Report, 37, para. 116 (also ibid., para. 117, for his 'Table 2'). Compare YbILC (2000), vol. I, 8, para. 45 (Mr. Crawford).

[149] ILC Report (2000), UN Doc. A/55/10, 62, para. 385 (and for a summary of the debate, ibid., 60–61, paras. 364–373). Further: YbILC (2000), vol. I, 302–317, 321–338, 399–400.

[150] See YbILC (2000), vol. I, 399–400, paras. 86–91 (Chairman of the Drafting Committee, Mr. Gaja).

3. Where more than one State takes countermeasures, the States concerned shall cooperate in order to ensure that the conditions laid down by this chapter [i.e. what became Articles 49–53 ARSIWA] for the taking of countermeasures are fulfilled.[151]

The Drafting Committee explained that it had adopted this provision notwithstanding its inability to reach agreement on the relationship between third-party countermeasures and the Security Council. This issue raised complex questions which had not been considered by the ILC or Special Rapporteur Crawford; and it was in any event deemed outside the scope of the topic.[152]

This provision – and especially its second paragraph – turned out to be 'extremely controversial'[153] and prompted a lively debate in the ILC and Sixth Committee. This will be examined in turn.

3.2.1.3(i) Draft Article 54: The Debate in the ILC

Opinion in the ILC was evenly divided on the merits of Draft Article 54 [2000].[154] Supporters favoured the retention of Draft Article 54 [2000] based essentially on the following arguments. Among others, Economides expressed support for Draft Article 54 [2000] as an 'extremely useful' and 'necessary' provision, especially for dealing with serious breaches of obligations *erga omnes*.[155] Pellet likewise observed that the provision was 'one of the essential consequences' of serious breaches of obligations *erga omnes* without which States would be 'powerless' to deal with such breaches given that the UN Security Council frequently failed to do so because of political disagreements.[156] Thus Draft Article 54 [2000] was 'crucial to the balance of the draft and paragraph 2, in particular, was vital'.[157]

---

[151] ILC Report (2000), UN Doc. A/55/10, 70. The words 'in the interest of the beneficiaries of the obligation breached' implicitly referred to the interests of the injured State: see YbILC (2000), vol. I, 399, para. 89 (Chairman of the Drafting Committee, Mr. Gaja).

[152] YbILC (2000), vol. I, 399–400, para. 91 (Chairman of the Drafting Committee, Mr. Gaja).

[153] YbILC (2001), vol. I, 73, para. 47 (Mr. Crawford). To the same effect: ibid., 110, para. 48 (Chairman of the Drafting Committee, Mr. Tomka).

[154] For a summary of the debate, see ILC Report (2001), UN Doc. A/56/10, 23, paras. 54–55. Further: YbILC (2001), vol. I, 6, 30, 34–42, 44–47, 50, 52–57, 73, 107, 110, 112–113.

[155] YbILC (2001), vol. I, 40, para. 41 (Mr. Economides) (albeit proposing to add a fourth paragraph to Draft Article 54 [2000] indicating that third-party countermeasures should be impermissible in cases where 'the organized international community itself takes action or authorizes the taking of action against the responsible State').

[156] Ibid., 41, para. 49 (Mr. Pellet). On the question of whether individual third-party countermeasures were permissible in response to serious breaches (such as genocide), Pellet answered 'emphatically in the affirmative': see YbILC (2000), vol. I, 336, para. 46 (Mr. Pellet).

[157] YbILC (2001), vol. I, 41, para. 49 (Mr. Pellet).

Simma also emphasized that 'leaving it up to the "organized international community", i.e. the United Nations, to react to breaches of obligations *erga omnes* bordered on cynicism'.[158] The main purpose of a regime of pacific third-party countermeasures was that it could serve as a viable alternative to the use of force to induce a return to legality. As Simma explained:

> The Commission must not forget that it was devising a regime of non-forcible countermeasures which would help avoid situations where States claimed that they had exhausted all peaceful means and adopted the attitude which had been taken by the United Kingdom in the context of the collective measures adopted against Yugoslavia in 1998. If the Commission defined a feasible regime of pacific collective countermeasures, States would be less likely to adopt another course, such as the regrettable one taken in Kosovo.[159]

He later added:

> The example of Kosovo showed that a State, in that case the United Kingdom of Great Britain and Northern Ireland, could consider economic sanctions illegal and then resort to the use of force. Thus legitimizing economic sanctions might have the effect of reducing the risk of a spillover into military sanctions.[160]

In addition, 'it was not true that economic countermeasures, whether individual or collective, were in breach of the Charter of the United Nations'.[161] Practice also showed that third-party countermeasures had not been used as a pretext for unavowed objectives: 'not directly injured States were far from abusing countermeasures in the event of a breach of human rights or other obligations *erga omnes* . . . they were in fact hardly concerned with such breaches, in respect of which selectivity was widespread'.[162] Finally, as Dugard explained, supporters believed that 'article 54, paragraph 2, could be included as an example of legitimate progressive development of international law'.[163]

Opponents called for the deletion of Draft Article 54 [2000] based essentially on the following counter-arguments, neatly summarized in rather scathing terms by Brownlie. There was no existing foundation for

---

[158] YbILC (2000), vol. I, 305, para. 31 (Mr. Simma).
[159] Ibid., 305, para. 33 (Mr. Simma). See also ILC Report (2000), UN Doc. A/55/10, 60, para. 368.
[160] YbILC (2001), vol. I, 35, para. 4 (Mr. Simma). See further Section 4.2.15.   [161] Ibid.
[162] YbILC (2000), vol. I, 305, para. 31 (Mr. Simma).
[163] YbILC (2001), vol. I, 45, para. 18 (Mr. Dugard); ILC Report (2001), UN Doc. A/56/10, 23, para. 54.

third-party countermeasures. Practice was extremely inconsistent, and there was no evidence of *opinio juris*. Thus 'article 54 constituted neither the law nor its potential progressive development'.[164] But that was not all. As Brownlie observed:

> In any case, leaving aside practice, article 54 was flawed in other respects. First, it provided a superficial legitimacy for the bullying of small States on the claim that human rights must be respected. Although article 54 referred only to non-forcible countermeasures, it would install a 'do-it-yourself' sanctions system that would threaten the security system based on Chapter VII of the Charter of the United Nations. It added to circumstances precluding wrongfulness a new category that sooner or later might extend to the use of force.
>
> In reality, article 54 was not about countermeasures: it was about sanctions, it was incompatible with the Charter and it was neither *lex lata* nor *lex ferenda*. Perhaps a new category would need to be invented for it: *lex horrenda*.[165]

Similarly, Sepúlveda-Amor noted:

> Suffice it to say that determination of the existence of a serious breach by a State of an obligation owed to the international community of States as a whole and essential for the protection of its fundamental interests was, in principle, a matter regulated by Chapter VII of the Charter of the United Nations, which established a universally accepted legal system governing the adoption of enforcement measures.[166]

There was a risk of creating overlapping legal regimes with no clear demarcation between them. Moreover, there was seemingly 'no imperative need to create a parallel system', alongside the Charter system, for dealing with serious breaches.[167] As Tomka indicated, in order not to disadvantage small States, it was thus better to leave such matters to the United Nations in its capacity as guardian of the international community.[168] Elaraby likewise remarked that Draft Article 54 [2000] 'extended to questions which fell under Article 41 of the Charter of the

---

[164] YbILC (2001), vol. I, 35, para. 2 (Mr. Brownlie). See also ibid., 35, para. 5 (for his rejection of third-party countermeasures as 'a neologism that designated a category which itself had had to be completely invented' based on an *ex post facto* classification of practice).

[165] Ibid.; and also Brownlie (2008), 515. To similar effect: YbILC (1992), vol. I, 152, paras. 16–17 (Mr. Bennouna); and also ibid., 88, para. 32 (Mr. Shi).

[166] YbILC (2001), vol. I, 30, para. 34 (Mr. Sepúlveda-Amor).

[167] YbILC (2000), vol. I, 336, para. 44 (Mr. Sepúlveda-Amor); and generally his comments at ibid., 335–336, paras. 36–43.

[168] YbILC (2001), vol. I, 54, para. 26 (Mr. Tomka).

United Nations, while circumventing the security system which the latter had set up to safeguard the rights of all States'.[169] Other ILC members made statements to similar effect.[170]

3.2.1.3(ii) Draft Article 54: The Debate in the Sixth Committee   The
debate in the Sixth Committee raised essentially the same issues as the one in the ILC.[171] In terms of support for Draft Article 54 [2000], Finland (on behalf of the Nordic countries) 'commended the efforts to establish a public law enforcement system in the case of a breach of obligations owed to the international community as a whole'.[172] Chile observed that Draft Article 54 [2000] articulated an 'extremely significant rule'.[173] Argentina, Costa Rica and New Zealand found the provision 'acceptable'.[174] For its part, Argentina added that it 'may be regarded as progressive development' and would call for further study.[175] Spain was 'generally positive' about the countermeasures regime, including Draft Article 54 [2000], the second paragraph of which it found acceptable.[176] Slovenia, while acknowledging the risk of abuse, noted that the provision 'could certainly be justified'.[177] France likewise supported the provision but proposed to limit its application to demands for cessation in response to serious breaches of obligations *erga omnes*.[178] South Africa (on behalf

---

[169] Ibid., 35, para. 3 (Mr. Elaraby).

[170] See ibid., 35, para. 6 (Mr. Rosenstock), 37, para. 14 (Mr. Yamada), 45, para. 22 (Mr. Sreenivasa Rao), 46, para. 36 (Mr. He), 47, para. 40 (Mr. Opertti Badan), 47, para. 42 (Mr. Addo), 53, para. 22 (Mr. Kamto). Others called in general terms for the deletion of Draft Article 54 [2000]: ibid., 56, para. 35 (Mr. Idris), 57, para. 47 (Mr. Kabatsi), 114, para. 75 (Mr. Kateka).

[171] See generally Topical Summary of Government Comments in the Sixth Committee, UN Doc. A/CN.4/513 (2000), 20–21, 27–29, 32–35, paras. 94, 96, 144–151, 174–182, 189–190.

[172] UN Doc. A/C.6/56/SR.11, 5, para. 30 (Finland on behalf of the Nordic countries). They later considered it 'unfortunate' that Article 54 ARSIWA was reduced to a simple saving clause: see UN Doc. A/C.6/56/SR.11, 6, para. 33 (Finland on behalf of the Nordic countries).

[173] UN Doc. A/C.6/55/SR.17, 8, para. 48 (Chile).

[174] UN Docs. A/C.6/55/SR.15, 10, para. 66 (Argentina); A/C.6/55/SR.17, 11, para. 63 (Costa Rica); A/C.6/56/SR.11, 8, para. 46 (New Zealand).

[175] UN Doc. A/CN.4/515/Add.3, 9 (Argentina). However, it later 'welcomed' the adoption of Article 54 ARSIWA: see UN Doc. A/C.6/56/SR.15, 8, para. 53 (Argentina). South Korea also called for Draft Article 54(2) [2000] to be studied further: see UN Doc. A/CN.4/515, 89 (South Korea).

[176] UN Doc. A/C.6/55/SR.16, 3, paras. 13, 16 (Spain) (albeit on condition of a link to a dispute settlement procedure). See also UN Doc. A/CN.4/515, 54 (Spain).

[177] UN Docs. A/CN.4/515, 54 (Spain); A/C.6/55/SR.18, 6, para. 27 (Slovenia).

[178] UN Doc. A/CN.4/515/Add.2, 15–16, 18 (France).

of SADC) generally 'welcomed' the limitations imposed on countermeasures on second reading, including in relation to Draft Article 54 [2000].[179] With respect to its second paragraph, South Africa (on behalf of SADC) noted that there was 'clearly support for such action' even if practice was 'still at an early stage'.[180] Other States such as Australia, Italy, Mongolia and Switzerland expressed support for the provision in general terms.[181] Germany, while noting the danger of disproportional unilateral acts, still appears to have cautiously supported Draft Article 54 [2000].[182]

Austria recognized the basic entitlement to adopt third-party countermeasures and proposed some minor changes to Draft Article 54 [2000]. It pointed out, however, that the relationship between third-party countermeasures and the Security Council, as embodied in what became the saving clause in Article 59 ARSIWA ('Charter of the United Nations') seemed 'rather ambiguous'.[183] The Netherlands respected the 'innovative nature' of Draft Article 54 [2000] but, 'in the interests of being systematic', proposed to add a subparagraph to what became Article 52(3) ARSIWA suggesting that third-party countermeasures would not be permitted 'if the Security Council has taken a binding decision with regard to the dispute'.[184] In a similar vein, Greece proposed to add a provision to Draft Article 54 [2000] to make it clear that 'countermeasures should not be taken unilaterally by any State if the organized international community was seized of the matter through the Security Council'.[185]

Poland stated that 'the Security Council should enjoy the monopoly of deciding on possible countermeasures (sanctions)'; however, the situation was 'less clear' in cases where the Council was unable to take

---

[179] UN Doc. A/C.6/55/SR.14, 6, paras. 24–25 (South Africa on behalf of SADC). Two SADC Member States – Botswana and Tanzania – strongly opposed the provision (on which see nn. 213–214 below).

[180] UN Doc. A/C.6/56/SR.12, 5, para. 23 (South Africa on behalf of SADC).

[181] UN Docs. A/C.6/55/SR.16, 5, para. 28 (Italy), 7, para. 41 (Australia); A/C.6/55/SR.18, 14, para. 81 (Switzerland); A/C.6/56/SR.14, 9, para. 56 (Mongolia). Bahrain also appears to have expressed some support; however, it later called for the deletion of what became Article 54 ARSIWA: see UN Docs. A/C.6/55/SR.19, 14, para. 87, A/C.6/56/SR.12, 7–8, para. 39 (Bahrain).

[182] UN Doc. A/C.6/55/SR.14, 10, para. 54 (Germany).

[183] UN Doc. A/CN.4/515, 88–92 (Austria). To the same effect see also UN Doc. A/C.6/55/ SR.17, 13, paras. 76–80 (Austria).

[184] UN Doc. A/CN.4/515, 87 (Netherlands).

[185] UN Doc. A/C.6/55/SR.17, 14, para. 85 (Greece). Compare UN Doc. A/C.6/54/SR.28, 2, para. 4 (Greece) ('[T]he adoption of countermeasures should not be left to individual States, but should be the prerogative of the Security Council, acting under Chapter VII of the Charter').

action.[186] It was such cases that Draft Article 54(2) [2000] was intended to regulate. Practice demonstrated that there was 'a trend in that direction' but it 'hardly reflected the general practice of States'.[187] Poland nevertheless appears to have concluded that in such circumstances, third-party countermeasures should be permissible, at least in order to enforce claims for cessation (as distinct from reparation).[188] Finally, with respect to the relationship between countermeasures and Security Council enforcement measures, Jordan stated:

> [T]he countermeasures regime should not be interpreted as an encroachment on the authority of the Security Council under Chapter VII of the Charter of the United Nations. Draft article 59 should provide the necessary guarantees in that respect to those who considered that there was an overlap between the two regimes of measures. Countermeasures could in fact be necessary to ensure that the State committing the internationally wrongful act ceased its action and made reparation for the damage caused.[189]

Although Jordan found the first paragraph of Draft Article 54 [2000] 'acceptable', it was sceptical about its second paragraph which 'needed to be studied further', in particular as it was 'hard to envisage' how the principle of proportionality could be respected if any State was entitled to take third-party countermeasures on an individual basis.[190]

Other States strongly opposed Draft Article 54 [2000] and called for its deletion on several grounds. Mexico objected principally on the basis that the notion of third-party countermeasures was unsupported by international law and incompatible with the collective security system enshrined in the UN Charter. It stated:

> [T]he position expressed in article 54 is not supported by international law and raises serious difficulties since it encourages States to take unilateral countermeasures where they have not suffered any specific and objective injury as a result of an internationally wrongful act. The many countermeasures that could be taken under this article would have disruptive effects and would give rise to a series of complex relationships. [...]
>
> The consequences of the existence of a serious breach by a State of an obligation owed to the international community as a whole and essential to the protection of its fundamental interests would seem, in principle, to be a matter covered by Chapter VII of the Charter of the United Nations.

---

[186] UN Docs. A/CN.4/515/Add.2, 18–19, A/C.6/55/SR.18, 9, para. 48 (Poland).   [187] Ibid.
[188] Ibid.
[189] UN Doc. A/C.6/55/SR.18, 4, para. 15 (Jordan). The same basic point was made with respect to Article 41 ARSIWA: see UN Doc. A/C.6/56/SR.15, 5, para. 24 (Jordan).
[190] UN Doc. A/C.6/55/SR.18, 4, para. 17 (Jordan). See also UN Doc. A/C.6/56/SR.15, 4, para. 21 (Jordan).

The response to a serious violation of this type has already been clearly defined in the legal order established by the Charter itself. In a regime of State responsibility, it would be unacceptable to introduce a mechanism that would change the collective security system enshrined in the Charter and allow for the taking of collective countermeasures, unilaterally decided, without the intervention of the central organ of the international community, and leaving it up to each State, if a grave violation has occurred, to determine the nature of the countermeasure to be taken and how that countermeasure will be terminated. The latitude provided by a system of this kind is incompatible with the institutional system created in 1945, whose norms and procedures are binding; it is therefore inadmissible to establish saving clauses such as those being proposed through collective countermeasures.[191]

Mexico also noted that the indeterminacy of obligations *erga omnes* invited abuse of third-party countermeasures.[192] Cuba likewise stated:

[T]he recognition in article 54, paragraph 2, of the right of any State to take countermeasures in the interest of the beneficiaries of the obligation breached went well beyond the progressive development of international law. The lack of precision in the provisions proposed in the draft articles [i.e. what became Articles 40, 41 and 48 ARSIWA] might lead to the justification of collective sanctions or collective interventions.[193]

It added that third-party countermeasures ran counter to the UN Charter, the principle of proportionality and 'often served as pretext for the adoption of unilateral measures such as armed reprisals and other types of intervention'.[194] Libya objected that the scope of Draft Article 54 [2000] seemed 'vague and imprecise' and was liable to abuse; a coercive response to serious breaches 'could be legitimate only in the context of intervention by the competent international or regional institutions'.[195] Algeria, Colombia and Iran similarly opposed Draft Article 54 [2000] on the basis that it contravened the UN Charter.[196]

---

[191] UN Doc. A/CN.4/515/Add.1, 9–10 (Mexico). It may be added that even Mexico's proposal for redrafting Draft Article 50 [2000] on bilateral countermeasures included a requirement to inform the Security Council (ibid.).

[192] UN Doc. A/C.6/56/SR.14, 3, para. 12 (Mexico).

[193] UN Doc. A/C.6/55/SR.18, 11, para. 59 (Cuba).

[194] Ibid., 11, paras. 60–62 (Cuba). See also UN Doc. A/C.6/47/SR.29, 14, para. 59 (Cuba) ('despite the stipulation that the regime of countermeasures would exclude the use of military force, it contained the seeds of aggression because ... political coercion and economic pressure were as much forms of aggression as was military force').

[195] UN Doc. A/C.6/55/SR.22, 8, para. 52 (Libya).

[196] UN Docs. A/C.6/55/SR.15, 3, para. 17 (Iran); A/C.6/55/SR.18, 2, para. 5 (Algeria); A/C.6/56/SR.16, 7, para. 40 (Colombia). It may be added that Algeria, although expressing

A number of States also stressed the unclear relationship between third-party countermeasures and the collective security regime under the UN Charter, which entailed the risk of parallel action and a marginalized Security Council. As Cameroon explained:

> [It] was concerned that draft article 54, which had not been included in the text adopted on first reading, might lead to the taking of multilateral or collective countermeasures simultaneously with other measures taken by the competent United Nations bodies; the draft articles must not be allowed to create overlapping legal regimes that could weaken the Organization as a whole or marginalize the Security Council, particularly in the light of the recent and disturbing tendency of some States to take action, including armed intervention, without the Council's consent. The situations envisaged in draft article 54 were adequately dealt with under Articles 39 to 41 of the Charter of the United Nations, which was the best expression of the will of the community of States.[197]

It added that the relationship between third-party countermeasures and Security Council enforcement measures was not resolved by the saving clause in what became Article 59 ARSIWA 'since the Charter itself did not establish whether Council-mandated measures automatically entailed the cessation of countermeasures by States or whether the two types of measures could be implemented simultaneously without violating the principle of proportionality'.[198] Morocco made the same point:

> A question not settled in the draft articles was whether individual counter-measures should cease as soon as collective countermeasures [i.e. enforcement measures] were taken by an international organization such as the United Nations. The draft articles were to be interpreted in conformity with the Charter of the United Nations, but the Charter itself was silent on the point with respect to measures not involving the use of armed force.[199]

Brazil also would have 'welcomed greater guidance' on this point.[200]

Russia thus observed that Draft Article 54 [2000] had 'excited considerable opposition, not least because the scope for countermeasures seemed to be virtually unrestricted and could mean that they would be taken to

serious doubts, nevertheless concluded that the issue 'deserved further discussion and analysis' (ibid.).

[197] UN Doc. A/C.6/55/SR.24, 11, para. 64 (Cameroon).

[198] UN Doc. A/C.6/56/SR.14, 10, para. 62 (Cameroon).

[199] UN Doc. A/C.6/56/SR.11, 7, para. 39 (Morocco). Morocco suggested that 'by analogy with Article 51 of the Charter concerning the right of self-defence, a State should cease its own countermeasures once the Security Council had ordered collective economic sanctions' (ibid.). For a discussion see further Section 5.2.1.

[200] UN Doc. A/C.6/56/SR.16, 2, para. 4 (Brazil).

protect a collective interest even while action taken by the competent organs of the United Nations was in progress'.[201] Although the provision had some merit in terms of "'stimulating'" the responsible State to return to legality, any individual entitlement to take third-party countermeasures 'could too easily have been abused, however, and that risk had outweighed its practical advantages'.[202] In addition, Russia dismissed Draft Article 54(1) [2000], as '[i]t would be unacceptable for any State to take countermeasures at the request of any injured State, because that would give the big Powers the opportunity to play the role of international policemen'.[203]

Israel stated that Draft Article 54 [2000] 'went beyond existing law' and was 'unwarranted', as it would have 'a destabilizing effect by creating a parallel mechanism for responding to serious breaches which lacked the coordinated, balanced and collective features of existing mechanisms'.[204] It further explained that the notion of 'serious breaches' was so general that it was 'open to dangerous abuse by States purporting to act in the interests of the international community'.[205] In more general terms, the United States observed:

> There are already existing international institutions and regimes to respond to violations of international obligations that the Commission would consider 'serious breaches'. For example, the efforts under way to establish an International Criminal Court, and the Security Council's creation of the international criminal tribunals of the former Yugoslavia and Rwanda, are examples of special regimes of law better suited than the law of State responsibility to address serious violations of humanitarian law. Indeed, responsibility for dealing with violations of international obligations which the Commission interprets as rising to the level of 'serious breaches' is better left to the Security Council rather than to the law of State responsibility ... The articles on State responsibility are an inappropriate vehicle for making such distinctions.[206]

It added that the indeterminacy of the notion of 'serious breaches' – which might simply serve to incentivize unwarranted action by third States – provided an additional strong reason for the proposed deletion of what became Articles 40 and 41 ARSIWA.[207] Thus dealing with serious

---

[201] UN Doc. A/C.6/56/SR.14, 7, para. 44 (Russia).   [202] Ibid.
[203] UN Doc. A/C.6/55/SR.18, 9, para. 51 (Russia).
[204] UN Doc. A/C.6/55/SR.15, 5, para. 25 (Israel).   [205] Ibid., 4, para. 24 (Israel).
[206] UN Doc. A/CN.4/515, 52–53 (United States). See already UN Doc. A/CN.4/488, 62 (United States).
[207] UN Doc. A/CN.4/515, 53 (United States).

breaches was apparently better left to the Security Council rather than to the law of State responsibility, presumably including third-party countermeasures. It seems reasonable to infer that this rationale partly explained the calls of the United States for Draft Article 54 [2000] to be deleted.[208]

India stressed that countermeasures were 'open to serious abuse' by powerful States, and this was especially so, as obligations *erga omnes* were indeterminate; countermeasures were merely 'sanctions under another name' and were regulated by the UN Charter.[209] The relationship between the law of State responsibility and the UN Charter called for in-depth consideration.[210] China emphasized that Draft Article 54 [2000] ran counter to the basic principle that only bilateral countermeasures were permissible under international law. More seriously, and bearing in mind the indeterminacy of obligations *erga omnes* as a source of abuse, third-party countermeasures could become 'one more pretext for power politics in international relations, for only powerful States and blocs of States are in a position to take countermeasures against weaker States'.[211] In addition, third-party countermeasures were deemed inconsistent with the principle of proportionality.[212] Botswana likewise rejected Draft Article 54 [2000] because of the 'glaring problem' that it was 'open to abuse by powerful States against a weaker State that they might particu-larly dislike for other reasons'.[213] Tanzania made the same point.[214]

Japan stated that Draft Article 54(1) [2000] had some value in that 'unlawful situations will not be left unresolved' in case the injured State could not itself take countermeasures; however, such a 'subrogation system of countermeasures' had no basis in international law.[215] With respect to Draft Article 54(2) [2000], Japan opined that it went 'far beyond the progressive development of international law'; and consid-ered that 'it should be called an "innovative" or "revolutionary" devel-opment of international law'.[216] Finally, the United Kingdom was sceptical of Draft Article 54 [2000] on the basis that it would be 'poten-tially highly destabilizing of treaty relations [and] questioned whether

---

[208] Ibid., 76–77. See also UN Doc. A/C.6/55/SR.18, 12–13, para. 70 (United States).
[209] UN Doc. A/C.6/55/SR.15, 5–6, paras. 29, 31 (India). See also UN Doc. A/C.6/56/SR.14, 7, para. 40 (India).
[210] UN Doc. A/C.6/55/SR.15, 5, para. 27 (India).
[211] UN Docs. A/CN.4/515, 69–70; A/C.6/56/SR.11, 10, paras. 59, 62 (China).   [212] Ibid.
[213] UN Doc. A/C.6/55/SR.15, 10, para. 63 (Botswana).
[214] UN Doc. A/C.6/55/SR.14, 9, paras. 46–47 (Tanzania).
[215] UN Doc. A/CN.4/515, 79 (Japan).   [216] Ibid., 89 (Japan).

a State should really be able to contravene any of its treaties, including, for example, those of a technical character, such as postal service agreements, in response to any serious breach by another State of any *erga omnes* obligations'.[217] The United Kingdom concluded that Draft Article 54 [2000] raised a difficult problem with no obvious solution and proposed that, as a compromise to accommodate the different views of States, one possibility might be to replace the provision with a saving clause.[218]

3.2.1.3(iii) Article 54 ARSIWA: The Compromise Solution   Special Rapporteur Crawford had, in 2000, called for the ILC to provisionally adopt his proposals on third-party countermeasures on the basis that there was 'no need to be prudent unless the Sixth Committee so required'.[219] The proposal met with a significant level of approval in the ILC as the Drafting Committee adopted Draft Article 54 [2000].[220] As it happened, notwithstanding considerable support, the provision provoked 'strong opposition' in the Sixth Committee.[221] And so like the Grand Old Duke of York, having courageously and painstakingly marched his troops up the hill, Crawford promptly marched them back down again. Crawford explained that this tactical retreat had become necessary since 'the thrust of government comments is that article 54, and especially paragraph 2, has no basis in international law and would be destabilising'.[222] Many governments had also objected to the unclear relationship between Draft Article 54 [2000] and Chapter VII UNC.[223]

Crawford noted that the latter objection would be difficult to resolve. It would certainly be possible to subordinate Draft Article 54(2) [2000] to enforcement action duly taken under Chapter VII UNC; however, that would not deal with all situations.[224] More generally, it was unclear how the ILC – beyond the general and necessarily vague obligation of cooperation in Draft Article 54(3) [2000] – could resolve the question of the interface between individual action by way of third-party countermeasures and collective action taken by the Security

---

[217] UN Doc. A/C.6/55/SR.14, 7, para. 31 (United Kingdom). Compare UN Doc. A/CN.4/488, 116 (United Kingdom).

[218] UN Doc. A/C.6/55/SR.14, 7, para. 32 (United Kingdom).

[219] YbILC (2000), vol. I, 303, para. 7 (Mr. Crawford).   [220] See above nn. 149–150.

[221] See Topical Summary of Government Comments in the Sixth Committee, UN Doc. A/CN.4/513 (2000), 33, para. 175.

[222] Crawford, Fourth Report, 18, para. 72.   [223] Ibid., 18, para. 73.

[224] Ibid. See above nn. 184–185 (for proposals to this effect by the Netherlands and Greece).

Council. It was not possible for the ILC to stray into the territory of primary norms and move beyond the saving clause in what became Article 59 ARSIWA.[225] The former objection also raised a difficulty. On the one hand, the mere deletion of Draft Article 54 [2000] would suggest that only bilateral countermeasures were permissible under international law with little prospect for the law in this area to develop. It would also suggest that, contrary to emerging practice, States had relinquished their individual right of response in respect of obligations *erga omnes (partes)* with the result that such obligations would be perceived as '"second-class"' by comparison with bilateral treaty obligations.[226] On the other hand, the limited amount of relevant State practice meant that the status of third-party countermeasures under international law was 'uncertain'.[227] As a way forward, based on the compromise proposal by the United Kingdom, Crawford concluded that, if Draft Article 54 [2000] were deleted, it would need to be replaced by a saving clause.[228]

The Drafting Committee in 2001 decided that Draft Article 54 [2000], which had been 'highly controversial', would be deleted and replaced by a saving clause 'which took account of all the positions on that issue'.[229] This solution had thus been adopted as part of a compromise in the ILC 'reserving the position of all those who believed that the right to take countermeasures should be granted to States other than the injured State with regard to the breaches of obligations established to preserve collective interests and those who believed that only injured States should have the right to take countermeasures'.[230] The expression 'lawful measures' was used in lieu of 'countermeasures' in order to 'respect all points of view'.[231] Thus the ILC ultimately did not take a position on third-party countermeasures and left the resolution of the matter to the future development of international law.[232] It did so in the following terms:

> **Article 54**
> **Measures taken by States other than an injured State**
> This chapter does not prejudice the right of any State, entitled under article 48, paragraph 1, to invoke the responsibility of another State, to

---

[225] Ibid. See also Crawford, Third Report, 110–111, paras. 422–426, 429 (on what became Article 59 ARSIWA); and further Crawford (2013a), 706–711.
[226] Crawford, Fourth Report, 18, para. 74.   [227] Ibid. See also Crawford (2013a), 705.
[228] Crawford, Fourth Report, 18, para. 74.
[229] YbILC (2001), vol. I, 110, para. 48 (Chairman of the Drafting Committee, Mr. Tomka).
[230] Ibid., 112, para. 64.   [231] Ibid. See also ARSIWA Commentary, Art. 54, §7.
[232] ARSIWA Commentary, Art. 54, §6. Contrast 2005 IDI Krakow Resolution (Art. 5).

take lawful measures against that State to ensure cessation of the breach
and reparation in the interest of the injured State or of the beneficiaries of
the obligation breached.

The commentary to Article 54 ARSIWA explains that institutional
reactions in the framework of international organizations, including
where it occurs under Chapter VII UNC, are excluded from the
scope of this provision.[233] The commentary further affirms that, from
a review of State practice, it appeared that the legal status of third-party
countermeasures was 'uncertain' with 'no clearly recognised entitlement' for States referred to in Article 48 ARSIWA to take such action in
response to breaches of obligations *erga omnes (partes)*. It was accordingly 'not appropriate' to include a provision to that effect.[234] It is
noteworthy that the saving clause in Article 54 ARSIWA, albeit based
on a review of State practice almost exclusively concerned with serious
breaches of obligations *erga omnes*, is worded in general terms.[235] Thus
it concerns all possible cases covered by Article 48 ARSIWA, i.e. both
obligations owed to a group of States and established for the protection
of the collective interest of the group (*erga omnes partes*) and those
owed to the international community as a whole (*erga omnes*). It even
covers cases where there is no serious breach.

3.3   Conclusion

The issue of third-party countermeasures proved extremely controversial
in the ILC. On the one hand, there was considerable support for third-
party countermeasures as a legitimate progressive development of international law and as a necessary tool of law enforcement, especially for
dealing with serious breaches of obligations *erga omnes*. Third-party
countermeasures were deemed consistent with the UN Charter and
crucial in those frequent situations where the Security Council failed to
take action in response to such breaches. Third-party countermeasures
would serve as a viable alternative to the use of force to induce a return to
legality and thereby reduce the risk of a spillover into military sanctions.
Furthermore, practice, albeit limited, demonstrated that third-party
countermeasures had not been used in an abusive manner by States
purporting to act in the interests of the international community.

---

[233] ARSIWA Commentary, Art. 54, §2. See also Crawford, Third Report, 98, para. 372.
[234] ARSIWA Commentary, Art. 54, §6. See also ibid., §§3–5 (for a review of practice).
[235] Compare Gaja (2010), 962.

On the other hand, there was strong opposition against third-party countermeasures. It was suggested that the notion of third-party counter-measures was unsupported by international law and incompatible with the collective security system enshrined in the UN Charter. It was also noted that the relationship between third-party countermeasures and the Security Council was unclear. A parallel regime of third-party counter-measures would marginalize the Security Council and have a destabilizing effect. Indeed there was no pressing need to establish such a regime: the response to serious breaches of international law was better left to the Security Council. It was further suggested that third-party countermeasures would add a new legal category that sooner or later might extend to the use of force. In addition, and especially given the indeterminacy of obligations *erga omnes* and the auto-interpretation of wrongful conduct, there was concern that third-party countermeasures could become one more pretext for power politics and the bullying of small States on the claim that human rights or other communitarian norms had been violated. The notion of a serious breach was also indeterminate and did not alleviate the concerns about the dangers of abuse.

The ILC was ultimately 'caught between a rock and a hard place'[236] which resulted in the adoption of the saving clause in Article 54 ARSIWA – a compromise solution motivated by the kind of pragmatism that so often characterizes the international law-making process. Thus the ILC left the resolution of the question of third-party countermeasures to the future development of international law. Notwithstanding its brief review of State practice, which was almost exclusively concerned with serious breaches of obligations *erga omnes*, the ILC did so in terms which suggested that the law might evolve to include all the situations covered by Article 48 ARSIWA (even without any additional requirement of a serious breach).

The following two chapters will examine State practice in order to determine, in the first instance, whether international law recognizes an entitlement of States to resort to third-party countermeasures in response to breaches of obligations *erga omnes (partes)* (and if so, whether such action can only be taken in case of a serious breach). The normative considerations discussed above, as well as some other salient features of practice, will also be examined.

---

[236] Crawford (2013a), 705.

4

Third-Party Countermeasures in State Practice

The true extent of State practice on third-party countermeasures has not always been fully appreciated.[1] Already in 2001, at the time of the adoption of the saving clause in Article 54 ARSIWA, relevant instances of practice on third-party countermeasures greatly exceeded the rather limited examples identified by the ILC. And this practice has since only continued to grow. The present chapter will make a number of preliminary observations about some of the complex issues involved in assessing the substantial body of practice concerning third-party countermeasures (4.1) before evaluating, in chronological order, instances in which States have adopted *prima facie* unlawful unilateral coercive measures in response to breaches of obligations *erga omnes (partes)* (4.2).

4.1 Some Problems in the Assessment of Practice

The assessment of State practice and *opinio juris* concerning third-party countermeasures raises some problems. In order to properly assess this practice it is necessary to distinguish third-party countermeasures from several cognate concepts that might equally justify unilateral action in defence of communitarian norms. Third-party countermeasures must, *inter alia*, be clearly distinguished from retorsion, the suspension and termination of treaties under Article 60 VCLT (and other treaty-law doctrines), self-defence, collective non-recognition and non-assistance (whether under Article 41 ARSIWA or otherwise) and the right to adopt unilateral trade restrictions based on the national security exception in

---

[1] For a notable example see Hillgruber (2006), 283 (lamenting that '[t]here is very little "material" that can be used to assess whether customary law permits reprisals by third States'). See however Tams (2005), 198–251; Dawidowicz (2006), 333–418; Katselli Proukaki (2010), 90–209; Dawidowicz (2016), 3–15. Sicilianos (1990), 155–169, remains a useful (albeit somewhat dated) survey. Further: Dopagne (2010), 79–143 (for a review of the practice of international organizations).

Article XXI GATT (or Article XIV *bis* GATS).[2] Distinguishing between these cognate concepts is not always straightforward.[3] The difficulty in identifying third-party countermeasures is compounded by the obscurity of practice: States rarely explain in clear terms which of the aforementioned categories they actually rely on in a given case.[4] Above all, the distinction between retorsion and third-party countermeasures may sometimes be difficult to draw in practice.[5] As Special Rapporteur Arangio-Ruiz observed, 'international practice does not always distinguish clearly between measures constituting violations of international obligations and those which do not cross that threshold'.[6]

The obscurity of State practice means that the actual legal basis for unilateral action taken in defence of a communitarian norm may be difficult to determine with confidence. While these difficulties should not be exaggerated, they cannot be ignored. Any study of practice on third-party countermeasures should therefore take into account the possibility in a particular instance of alternative justifications based on cognate concepts. The assessment that follows attempts to impose order on an otherwise disorderly and unwieldy practice in the hope of facilitating a clearer understanding of it.

4.2   An Assessment of Practice

The entry into force of the UN Charter in 1945 provides a useful starting point for the analysis of State practice concerning third-party countermeasures in the modern period. In the UN Charter era, States have, on a large number of occasions, adopted *prima facie* unlawful unilateral coercive measures in order to induce compliance with communitarian norms. Such action has included trade, investment and financial embargoes, suspension of air services, development aid, sale of agricultural commodities, membership in international organizations, military assistance and fishing rights in *prima facie* violation of responding States' treaty obligations towards the responsible State. The assets of the responsible State, including those belonging to high-ranking officials such as

---

[2] For a discussion see Section 1.4.
[3] See YbILC (2000), vol. I, 335, paras. 37–43 (Mr. Sepúlveda); ILC Report (2000), UN Doc. A/55/10, 60, para. 366.
[4] See Tams (2005), 21–22; Dawidowicz (2006), 349–350; Crawford (2013a), 676. Also: Section 1.3.
[5] See Section 1.4.4 (text accompanying n. 171).
[6] Arangio-Ruiz, Third Report, 11, para. 19.

Heads of State and Prime Ministers, as well as central banks, have also regularly been frozen in *prima facie* violation of general international law.[7] Let us now turn to the following examples where such conduct has been adopted.[8]

4.2.1 Developing Countries – South Africa (1960–1964)

South Africa's illegal policy of apartheid and racial segregation, initially instituted in 1948, continued with increasing force during the 1960s. In a period marked by rapid decolonization, developing countries took various actions against South Africa at the UN, including by bringing proceedings before the ICJ.[9] During this period, developing countries also adopted a variety of unilateral coercive measures against

---

[7] In the *Arrest Warrant* case, the ICJ found it 'firmly established' that at least such high-ranking officials (also including Foreign Ministers) enjoy immunity from the jurisdiction of other States, both civil and criminal: *Arrest Warrant of 11 April 2000 (DRC v. Belgium)*, ICJ Rep. (2002), 3 at 20–21, para. 51. The freezing of assets belonging to central banks is also prohibited under international law: see the principle codified in Article 21(1)(c) of the UN Convention on Jurisdictional Immunities of States and Their Property (not yet in force), https://treaties.un.org/doc/source/RecentTexts/English_3_13.pdf. The freezing of assets belonging to, among others, Vice-Presidents, Foreign Ministers, Ministers of Defence and Ministers of the Interior have also occurred but (with the possible exception of Foreign Ministers) it is unclear whether their assets are protected by State immunity: see further below Sections 4.2.17 (Zimbabwe) and 4.2.20 (Syria).

[8] A possible example of some complexity not included below concerns the decision by EU Member States in January 2012, *inter alia*, to freeze assets of the Central Bank of Iran in response to the controversy over Iran's nuclear programme. The precise international obligation allegedly violated by Iran – i.e. the basis on which this action was taken – remains somewhat unclear. Insofar as EU Member States were concerned with Iran's obligations under the IAEA-Iran Safeguards Agreement (INFCIRC/214, 13 Dec. 1974, www.iaea.org /Publications/Documents/Infcircs/Others/infcirc214.pdf) and/or Articles II and III(1) of the Nuclear Non-Proliferation Treaty (729 UNTS 161), it is doubtful whether any breach has actually been committed. In any event, the former concerns a bilateral treaty between the IAEA and Iran; as a result, EU Member States clearly lack standing to take countermeasures thereunder. As to the latter, even if *arguendo* a violation has occurred, the action could only be justified – if at all – as a bilateral countermeasure based on Article 42(b)(ii) ARSIWA. The action thus falls outside the scope of this study. See Council of the European Union, 'Conclusions on Iran' (1 Dec. 2011), para. 1, www.consilium.europa.eu/uedocs/cms_Data/ docs/pressdata/EN/foraff/126493.pdf (EU Member States referring in rather vague terms to their 'grave concern posed by Iran's continued refusal to comply with its international obligations and to fully co-operate with the IAEA'); Council Decision 2012/35/CFSP (23 Jan. 2012), OJ 2012 L 19/22 (24 Jan. 2012). Further: Calamita (2009), 1393; Dupont (2012), 301; Joyner (2013), 237; Orakhelashvili (2015), 3 (esp. at 17); 'International Sanctions on Iran are Lifted', *BBC News*, 16 January 2016, www.bbc.co.uk/news/world-middle-east-35335163.

[9] See further Sections 2.1.1.1 and 2.1.2.

South Africa.[10] In March 1960, thousands of protesters famously gathered in Sharpeville to demonstrate against apartheid; there, South African police opened fire on the crowd, killing scores of protesters. In April 1960, the UN Security Council deplored the Sharpeville massacre but took no immediate enforcement action against South Africa.[11]

In June 1960, the Second Conference of African Independent States responded by recommending that all African States impose a comprehensive trade embargo against South Africa in response to its illegal policy of apartheid.[12] In November 1962, the UN General Assembly adopted a resolution by which it strongly condemned 'the continued and total disregard by the Government of South Africa of its obligations under the Charter of the United Nations'.[13] By the same resolution, notwithstanding its appeal to the Security Council to take appropriate action, including sanctions, the General Assembly requested individual members 'separately or collectively, in conformity with the Charter, to bring about the abandonment of [apartheid]' through the adoption of various unilateral coercive measures against South Africa.[14] The recommended measures included a comprehensive trade embargo and a suspension of landing rights for all South African aircraft.[15] In August 1963, the Security Council responded to the request made by the General Assembly and, following its earlier condemnation of the Sharpeville massacre, called on all States to impose an arms embargo against South Africa.[16]

The debate on the resolution adopted by the General Assembly was largely concerned with the question of whether the Assembly (as distinct from the Security Council) was institutionally competent under the UN Charter to recommend the adoption of unilateral coercive measures. Although General Assembly resolutions do not have any

---

[10] See e.g. Focarelli (1994), 39–40; Tomaševski (2000), 48–54.

[11] SC Res. 134 (1 Apr. 1960).

[12] Rousseau (1960), 804; Tomaševski (2000), 49. These annual conferences were a predecessor to what became the OAU (later the AU) founded in 1963.

[13] GA Res. 1761 (XVII) (6 Nov. 1962).

[14] Ibid. The General Assembly later characterized South Africa's apartheid policy as a crime against humanity and a violation of the principle of self-determination: see GA Res. 2202A (XXI) (16 Dec. 1966); GA Res. 2775E (XXVI) (29 Nov. 1971). The latter qualification related to the policy of bantustanization – a central aim of apartheid. See further Crawford (2006a), 338–341.

[15] GA Res. 1761 (XVII) (6 Nov. 1962).

[16] SC Res. 181 (7 Aug. 1963). See also SC Res. 182 (4 Dec. 1963).

intrinsic legal force, the possible justification for the adoption of these unilateral coercive measures under general international law was not discussed.[17] Some of the unilateral coercive measures recommended by the General Assembly (such as the call to suspend diplomatic relations) were mere acts of retorsion and, as such, required no justification. Still, at least the trade embargo appeared to require justification given that many States were parties to the GATT during the relevant period.

In May 1963, at the first meeting of the newly created OAU, the African sanctions regime was extended to include the call for the adoption of the unilateral coercive measures requested some months before by the UN General Assembly.[18] Several (mainly) African States imposed flight and port entry bans against South African ships and aircraft.[19] In the absence of any rights under general international law or specific treaty commitments, these unilateral coercive measures can be categorized as acts of retorsion.[20] Many States (including South Africa), however, were already parties to the GATT; the call for a trade embargo in the resolutions therefore expressed at least the willingness of those States to engage in conduct in *prima facie* violation of international law. In the absence of relevant bilateral treaties, any such violation would have to be justified either under the exceptions in Articles XIX–XXI GATT or on the basis of general international law.

In 1960, following the recommendation of the Second Conference of African Independent States, Ghana and Malaysia had imposed a trade embargo against South Africa.[21] Over the next four years, seven other States followed the OAU and UN recommendations and imposed individual trade embargoes against South Africa. Embargoing States included

---

[17] See UN Docs. A/PV.1164 (6 Nov. 1962), 659; A/PV.1165 (6 Nov. 1962), 677; UNYB (1962), 93.

[18] *Keesing's* (1963–1964), 19463, 19699; Resolutions Adopted by the First Conference of Independent African Heads of State and Government, Addis Ababa, 22–25 May 1963, 'Resolution A' (esp. op. para. 9), available at http://archive.au.int/collect/auassemb/import/English/Res1963%20_E.pdf. See also Dawidowicz (2006), 400–401, 403–404 (for additional OAU support for the adoption of unilateral coercive measures against South Africa).

[19] *Keesing's* (1963–1964), 19699; Dugard (1967), 159–160 (with further references).

[20] It is widely agreed that, with the exception of a right for ships in distress, there is no general right of entry into ports under customary international law: see Lowe (1977), 597; de La Fayette (1996), 1.

[21] Rousseau (1960), 804–806.

Indonesia, Kuwait, Nigeria, Pakistan, Sierra Leone, Tanganyika[22] (now Tanzania) and Uganda.[23]

In terms of possible justifications, the *Nicaragua* case makes it clear that, in the absence of specific treaty commitments, a trade embargo does not as such violate international law.[24] For their part, South Africa and the embargoing States were all parties to the GATT during the relevant period.[25] The GATT regime, by virtue of Articles XI and XIII in particular, prohibits the use of qualitative and discriminatory trade restrictions such as embargoes.[26] Moreover, the embargoing States did not invoke any of the exceptions in Articles XIX–XXI GATT. This may be contrasted with Ghana's explicit invocation of Article XXI GATT in 1961 as justification for its trade embargo against Portugal in response to its responsibility for the colonial uprising against it in Angola.[27] There is some authority for the view that such notification is required in order to validly invoke the security exception in Article XXI GATT.[28] The trade embargo against South Africa therefore cannot be categorized as an act of retorsion based on a treaty right. It would have to be justified on the basis of general international law.

For their part, Ghana and Malaysia both acknowledged that the trade embargo violated their respective GATT obligations towards South Africa, but even so, they admittedly did not attempt to justify their actions on the basis of general international law.[29] Still, it does not seem that they considered their actions to be unlawful.[30] All that can be said in this instance is that States appear to have relied on the rationale of

---

[22] The Republic of Tanganyika imposed its trade embargo in 1963 at a time when it had gained independence from the United Kingdom and was no longer a trust territory administered by the UN.

[23] *Keesing's* (1961–1962), 18027 (Nigeria); *Keesing's* (1961–1962), 18186 (Sierra Leone); *Keesing's* (1963–1964), 19699 (Tanganyika and Uganda); *Keesing's* (1963–1964), 19757 (Kuwait and Indonesia); *Keesing's* (1964), 20421 (Pakistan). For examples of acts of retorsion by a large number of other States, see further Focarelli (1994), 39–40; Tomaševski (2000), 51, 53 (tables 2.2–2.3).

[24] *Nicaragua* case, ICJ Rep. (1986), 14 at 138, para. 276.

[25] On GATT membership see www.wto.org/english/thewto_e/gattmem_e.htm.

[26] See Porges (1994), 285–326, 363–382.

[27] See GATT Doc. SR.19/12 (9 Dec. 1961), 196; Porges (1994), 600. Also: Hahn (1996), 322–324.

[28] See Decision of the GATT Council of Representatives, Decision Concerning Article XXI of the General Agreement (30 Nov. 1982), GATT Doc. L/5426, www.wto.org/gatt_docs/English/SULPDF/91000212.pdf; Porges (1994), 605–606. Also: Hahn (1990–1991), 574–575; Boisson de Chazournes (1992), 143–146; Reiterer (1997), 191; Mavroidis (2005), 214–223; Desierto (2014); and discussion below at Section 4.2.8.

[29] See Rousseau (1960), 805–806.

[30] Ibid. Compare Frowein (1994), 383, 433; YbILC (2001), vol. I, 44–45, para. 17 (Mr. Dugard).

the concept of third-party countermeasures and done so in response to serious breaches of obligations *erga omnes*; namely, those concerning apartheid, crimes against humanity and self-determination.[31] These *prima facie* unlawful unilateral coercive measures were adopted at a time when the Security Council had simply called on all States to impose an arms embargo against South Africa.

4.2.2 European States – Greece (1967–1970)

On 21 April 1967, a group of Greek army officers led by Colonel Papadopoulos seized power in Greece in a *coup d'état* and immediately declared a state of emergency, suspending several provisions of the Greek Constitution by royal decree. Political parties were dissolved and thousands of dissidents were interned, among other repressive measures.[32] On 23 June 1967, the Consultative Assembly of the Council of Europe adopted a resolution by which it expressed 'its grave concern at the present situation in Greece and at the many serious reported violations of human rights and fundamental freedoms'.[33] By the same resolution, the Assembly also expressed the wish that the States Parties to the ECHR 'refer the Greek Case either jointly or separately to the European Commission of Human Rights in accordance with Article 24 of the Convention'.[34]

On 20 September 1967, Denmark, Norway, Sweden and, a week later, the Netherlands, brought complaints against Greece before the European Commission of Human Rights requesting it to declare Greece responsible for the following violations of the ECHR: (1) prohibition of torture (Article 3); (2) right to liberty and security of person (Article 5); (3) right to a fair trial (Article 6); (4) no punishment without law (Article 7); (5) right to respect for private and family life (Article 8); (6) freedom of thought, conscience and religion (Article 9); (7) freedom of expression (Article 10); (8) freedom of assembly and association (Article 11); (9) right to an effective remedy (Article 13); and (10) prohibition of discrimination (Article 14).[35]

---

[31] For a similar conclusion see Dzida (1997), 252; Weschke (2001), 109–110; YbILC (2001), vol. I, 44–45, para. 17 (Mr. Dugard); Tams (2005), 90. Contra: Rosenstock (1994), 330 (for whom the trade embargo amounted to an act of retorsion).

[32] *Keesing's* (1967–1968), 22023–22027. [33] 12 YbECHR (1969), 3, para. 6 (n. 1).

[34] Ibid.

[35] 'The Greek Case' (*Denmark, Norway, Sweden and the Netherlands v. Greece*), Report of the European Commission of Human Rights, in ibid., 1, para. 3. The applicants also relied on violations of Articles 1 and 3 of the First Protocol to the ECHR (protection of property;

On 5 November 1969, the European Commission of Human Rights issued its report in *'The Greek Case'* and found Greece responsible for systematic human rights violations under the ECHR, as alleged by the complaints.[36] On 12 December 1969, Greece gave notice to the Secretary General of the Council of Europe of its intention to denounce the ECHR, effective within six months pursuant to Article 65 ECHR (now Article 58 ECHR).[37] A few days later, in his reply, the Secretary General took note of the Greek denunciation but stressed that, in accordance with Article 65(2) ECHR (now Article 58(2) ECHR), it was without any legal effect in relation to the pending proceedings brought against Greece for its various human rights violations.[38]

EC Member States responded to Greece's continuing human rights violations by partially suspending the 1962 EEC-Greece Association Agreement.[39] In particular, EC Member States suspended financial assistance owed to Greece under Protocol 19 of the Association Agreement, which formed an integral part thereof under Article 74 of the Association Agreement.[40] For example, on 21 September 1967, a Greek request for a USD 10 million loan was denied in apparent breach of Protocol 19.[41]

Article 2 of the Association Agreement explained:

> 1. The aim of this Agreement of Association is to promote the continuous and balanced strengthening of trade and economic relations between the Parties, while taking full account of the need to ensure an accelerated development of the Greek economy and to improve the level of employment and the living conditions of the Greek people.
> 2. In order to attain the objectives set out in paragraph 1, the Association shall entail, as provided in this Agreement and in accordance with the timetable set out therein:
> ... (c) the making available to the Greek economy within the framework of the Financial Protocol to this Agreement, of resources which will assist it to develop at a higher rate.[42]

right to free elections), and rejected Greece's reliance on Article 15 ECHR (derogation in time of emergency) as justification for its actions (ibid., 2, para. 4).

[36] Ibid.   [37] Ibid., 78–82.   [38] Ibid., 82–84.

[39] Agreement establishing an Association between the European Economic Community and Greece, OJ 1963 294/63 (18 Feb. 1963) (entry into force 1 Nov. 1962); *Keesing's* (1961–1962), 18168; *Keesing's* (1963), 19260; *Keesing's* (1969–1970), 24170. See also Coufoudakis (1977–1978), 114.

[40] Protocol No. 19 to the Agreement establishing an Association between the European Economic Community and Greece, Financial Protocol, OJ 1963 340/63 (18 Feb. 1963). See also Coufoudakis (1977–1978), 114.

[41] See Buergenthal (1968), 448 (with further references).

[42] OJ 1963 294/63 (18 Feb. 1963).

The obligation to provide financial assistance under the Association Agreement was not conditioned by compliance with human rights obligations. It therefore does not seem possible to explain this action in terms of a treaty suspension.[43]

Moreover, even if in the absence of a denunciation clause in the Association Agreement, the suspension of financial assistance might be explained in legal terms as a unilateral denunciation under general international law (itself a doubtful proposition), no reasonable notice was provided to Greece as required by customary international law. The *prima facie* unlawful suspension of financial assistance may, however, be explained in legal terms by the rationale of the concept of third-party countermeasures taken in response to the systematic violation of several human rights obligations under the ECHR.[44]

4.2.3 United States and European States – Uganda (1971–1978)

On 25 January 1971, General Idi Amin deposed then President Obote and seized power in Uganda through a *coup d'état*. His military dictatorship, which came to an end by Tanzania's invasion in April 1979, was infamous for its gross and systematic violations of basic human rights, including widespread extra-judicial killings, ethnic cleansing and acts of torture. In August 1972, General Amin ordered Uganda's Asian community to leave the country within three months. Around 75,000 Asians (mostly of Indian descent) had their property confiscated and were forcibly expelled from Uganda through the implementation of a deliberate governmental policy that bore all the hallmarks of ethnic cleansing. It is estimated that at least some 300,000 people were brutally killed by Idi Amin's murderous regime.[45]

In June 1977, the Commonwealth Heads of Government condemned Uganda for its egregious human rights violations in the following terms:

> Cognisant of the accumulated evidence of sustained disregard for the sanctity of life and of massive violation of basic human rights in Uganda, it was the overwhelming view of Commonwealth leaders that these excesses were so gross as to warrant the world's concern and to

---

[43] Compare Buergenthal (1968), 449; Katselli Proukaki (2010), 120–121.

[44] For a similar conclusion see Dzida (1997), 252; Tams (2005), 91; Katselli Proukaki (2010), 116–122.

[45] See Oestreich (1990), 44; Tomaševski (2000), 100–106. In September 1979, Ugandan President Binaisa estimated that at least 500,000 people had been killed by Idi Amin's regime: see UN Doc. A/34/PV.14 (28 Sept. 1979), 269, para. 8.

evoke condemnation by Heads of Government in strong and unequivocal terms. Mindful that the people of Uganda were within the fraternity of Commonwealth fellowship, Heads of Government looked to the day when the people of Uganda would once more fully enjoy their basic human rights which now were being so cruelly denied.[46]

Apart from this verbal condemnation, the international community took no concerted action against Uganda during Idi Amin's eight years in power.[47] Instead, towards the end of General Amin's rule, the United States and EC Member States adopted unilateral coercive measures against Uganda in order to put an end to the appalling human rights situation in the country.[48]

On 10 October 1978, the United States Congress adopted the Uganda Embargo Act by which it imposed a trade embargo against Uganda.[49] The Uganda Embargo Act explained:

> [T]he Government of Uganda, under the regime of General Idi Amin, has committed genocide against Ugandans ... It is the sense of the Congress that the Government of the United States should take steps to dissociate itself from any foreign government which engages in the international crime of genocide.[50]

It further explained that the trade embargo would remain in force 'until the President determines and certifies to the Congress that the Government of Uganda is no longer committing a consistent pattern of

---

[46] Final Communiqué London CHOG Meeting, 15 June 1977, The Commonwealth at the Summit: Communiqués of Commonwealth Heads of Government Meetings 1944–1986, Commonwealth Secretariat, London (1987), 192. See further Ullman (1977–1978), 530; Arts (2000), 84.

[47] For General Assembly action on Uganda following the immediate overthrow of Idi Amin, see GA Res. 34/122 (14 Dec. 1979). Also: Tomaševski (2000), 101–102 (with further references).

[48] Keesing's (1979), 29669. The US action against Uganda was in line with President Carter's more proactive stance against serious human rights violations: see further e.g. Schachter (1977), 53; Cohen (1982), 246; Zoller (1985), 104–118.

[49] Uganda Embargo Act, 22 USC s. 2151 (1978). The United States had previously terminated all of its development assistance to Uganda. For the various unilateral coercive measures adopted by the United States, see United States-Uganda Relations: Hearings Before the Subcommittee on Africa, International Organizations and International Economic Policy and Trade of the House Committee on Foreign Relations, 95th Cong., 2nd session (1978), app. 3, 59–60 (statement by W.C. Harrop) [hereinafter Uganda Hearings]. On measures adopted by other States (mostly relating to the termination of development assistance), see Hufbauer, Schott and Elliott (1985), 455; Tomaševski (2000), 103–105.

[50] Uganda Embargo Act, 22 USC s. 2151 (1978) (s. 5(a) and (b)).

gross violations of human rights'.[51] During the legislative drafting process, US administration officials acknowledged before Congress that the adoption of such a trade embargo would violate US trade obligations owed to Uganda under the GATT; in particular, Articles XI and XIII GATT prohibiting quantitative and discriminatory trade restrictions.[52] The United States also recognized that, unlike its previous trade embargoes that had either been justified on the basis of the national security exception in Article XXI GATT or adopted pursuant to a Security Council resolution, the trade embargo against Uganda could not be justified on such a basis.[53] It could only be justified on the basis of general international law, i.e. as a third-party countermeasure.[54]

In 1977, EC Member States also adopted unilateral coercive measures against Uganda.[55] The EC Council of Ministers criticized Uganda's systematic violations of basic human rights and decided to review development assistance owed to Uganda under the then applicable Lomé I Convention.[56] In June 1977, upon the insistence of the United Kingdom, the EC Council of Ministers adopted the so-called 'Uganda Guidelines' which, without formally suspending the Lomé I Convention, declared that development assistance henceforth provided under it should not contribute to the serious and continuing human rights violations in Uganda. The 'Uganda Guidelines' stated:

> The Council deplores the consistent denial of basic human rights to the people of Uganda. The Council agrees to take steps within the framework of its relationship with Uganda under the Lomé Convention to ensure that any assistance given by the Community to Uganda does not in any way have as its effect a reinforcement or prolongation of the denial of basic human rights to its people.[57]

---

[51] Ibid., (s. 5(c)).

[52] Uganda Hearings (above n. 49), 61 and 64 (statements by W.C. Harrop and R.H. Meyer). In October 1978, the United States and Uganda were both parties to the GATT.

[53] Uganda Hearings (above n. 49), 98–100, 105–106 (statement by J.L. Katz). For the history of the Uganda Embargo Act see Fredman (1979), 1149, and esp. 1156–1165 (for the congressional hearings); Talkington (1979), 206; de Guttry (1985), 96–100.

[54] For a similar conclusion see Zoller (1985), 101; Sicilianos (1990), 156; Rucz (1992), 604; YbILC (2000), vol. I, 316, para. 41 (Mr. Kabatsi); ARSIWA Commentary, Art. 54, §3; Tams (2005), 210; Katselli Proukaki (2010), 126–132. On 15 May 1979, after a military invasion by Tanzania resulted in the overthrow of Idi Amin's regime, the United States lifted its trade embargo against Uganda: see Grove (1979), 704.

[55] Tomaševski (2000), 104.

[56] For the text of the Lomé I Convention (entry into force 1 Apr. 1976), see Council Regulation (EEC) No. 199/76, OJ 1976 L 25/2 (30 Jan. 1976).

[57] EC Bull. No. 6 (1977), para. 2.2.59. See further King (1997), 55.

The problem for EC Member States was that the Lomé I Convention did not explicitly condition the right to development assistance on the observance of human rights obligations. A compromise was therefore reached by the Council of Ministers to redirect rather than formally suspend development assistance. As a result of this redirection, only 5 per cent of the development assistance owed to Uganda under the Lomé I Convention was actually paid out by EC Member States. This substantial reduction seemingly constituted a *de facto* suspension of development assistance owed to Uganda under the Lomé I Convention.[58]

As for possible justifications, Article 40 of the Lomé I Convention stated that the purpose of development assistance was to 'contribute essentially to the economic and social development of the [African, Caribbean and Pacific] States . . . [and] consist in particular in the greater well-being of the population'.[59] In March 1977, a statement by the Commissioner for Development, Mr. Cheysson, made clear, however, that no lawful action under the Lomé I Convention could be taken against Uganda. As Commissioner Cheysson explained:

> The *Convention* does not provide *any* measures which we could take at the present time against Uganda: we are linked with that country, as with the other ACP countries, by an international agreement which has been duly ratified by all the contracting parties . . .[60]

It is clear from Cheysson's statement that the Lomé I Convention itself could not justify any action against Uganda based on human rights concerns. This conclusion is underlined by the European Commission's decision not to invoke the treaty doctrine of fundamental change of circumstances (Article 62 VCLT).[61] The wording of Cheysson's statement even appears to exclude the possibility of denunciation upon six

---

[58] For a similar conclusion see Oestreich (1990), 304–307; Arts (1995), 268; Bartels (2005), 10–11; Tams (2005), 211; Tzanakopoulos (2015), 150 (n. 26).

[59] Lomé I Convention, Council Regulation (EEC) No. 199/76, OJ 1976 L 25/2 (30 Jan. 1976).

[60] OJ Supp. 214/71 (1977–1978) (emphasis added). The same argument was reaffirmed by the European Commission as grounds for not suspending application of the Lomé II Convention in response to human rights violations committed by Zaire and Surinam in 1980 and 1982, respectively. See further OJ 1980 C 49/47 (27 Feb. 1980); OJ 1984 C 148/40 (6 June 1984); Fierro (2003), 55; Bartels (2005), 12–13.

[61] See Answer to Written Question No. 115/78 by Mr. Adams to the Commission of the European Communities, 18 July 1978, OJ 1978 C 199/27 (21 Aug. 1978); Kamminga (1992), 51.

months' notice as envisaged in Article 92 of the Lomé I Convention.[62] More significantly, the statement suggests that it was limited to purely conventional responses; it did not appear to exclude resort to extra-conventional measures. In sum, by Commissioner Cheysson's own admission, a *de facto* suspension of development assistance would violate the Lomé I Convention. In the absence of any treaty-based justifications, it seems that this action could only be justified as a third-party countermeasure.[63]

In October 1978, Ugandan forces occupied a part of bordering Tanzania. In November 1978, Tanzania launched its own offensive and invaded Uganda resulting in the overthrow of the Amin regime in April 1979.[64] During the eight-year period of Idi Amin's brutal reign, no action was ever taken by the UN. On 28 September 1979, newly appointed Ugandan President Binaisa expressed before the General Assembly that his country was 'deeply disappointed' with the UN for having 'looked on with embarrassed silence as the Uganda tragedy unfolded [and] the Amin régime continued with impunity to commit genocide against our people'.[65] Following the overthrow of Idi Amin's regime, President Binaisa now simply asked the international community to provide financial assistance for the reconstruction of the country.[66] On 14 December 1979, the General Assembly adopted a resolution by which it belatedly expressed that it was 'deeply concerned at the tragic loss of life, widespread destruction of property and severe damage to the economic and social infrastructure of Uganda during the past eight years', and urged the international community to contribute to the reconstruction of the country.[67]

4.2.4 European States – Central African Republic (1979)

On 1 January 1966, Colonel Bokassa assumed power in the Central African Republic through a military *coup d'état* which deposed then

---

[62] For a similar conclusion see Kamminga (1992), 50–51 (for whom the failure to mention the possibility of denunciation in Article 92 of the Lomé I Convention suggests that the EC was unwilling for political reasons to contemplate the use of such a strong sanction).

[63] Compare Oestreich (1990), 442–443; Tams (2005), 210–211; Katselli Proukaki (2010), 130–131; Tzanakopoulos (2015), 150. Also: King (1997), 91–92.

[64] *Keesing's* (1979), 29669–29673; UNYB (1979), 262–263. The invasion has sometimes been characterized as a humanitarian intervention. For an assessment of this claim, see Chesterman (2001), 77–79; Franck (2002), 143–145.

[65] UN Doc. A/34/PV.14 (28 Sept. 1979), 270, para. 13.   [66] Ibid., 272, paras. 47–48.

[67] GA Res. 34/122 (14 Dec. 1979); UNYB (1979), 259.

President Dacko. Colonel Bokassa shortly thereafter abolished the constitution and, in December 1976, crowned himself 'emperor' of a new monarchy called the Central African Empire.[68] His dictatorial reign, which was ended by French military intervention in September 1979,[69] was marred by serious human rights abuses such as the widespread use of torture and extra-judicial killings. On 18 April 1979, Bokassa's personal guard arrested and later brutally killed scores of schoolchildren in response to a demonstration in the capital, Bangui, against the use of school uniforms. On 22 May 1979, at the Sixth Franco-African Summit in Kigali, a judicial inquiry was established to investigate the incident. On 16 August 1979, it published a damning report which concluded that Bokassa had 'almost certainly' participated, alongside his security forces, in a massacre which ended up killing between 50 and 200 children.[70]

In August 1979, EC Member States responded to the Bangui massacre by recalling the 'Uganda Guidelines'[71] and accordingly decided to freeze the further allocation of development assistance owed to the Central African Republic under the Lomé I Convention.[72] Admittedly, while EC Member States, as in the Ugandan case examined above, did not formally suspend the Lomé I Convention, the action nevertheless constituted a *de facto* suspension of development assistance thereunder. Moreover, as also observed in the above Ugandan example, the Lomé I Convention itself did not explicitly condition the provision of development assistance on the observance of human rights obligations.

As for possible justifications, the EC debate on the legal basis for a suspension of development assistance to the Central African Republic under the Lomé I Convention provides at least some guidance. In July 1978, in response to a question from the European Parliament, the European Commission concluded that

> [O]n the question of respect for human dignity and basic human rights in relations with the ACP States [under the Lomé I Convention] . . . the *rebus sic stantibus* clause can be invoked only where there has been

---

[68] Rousseau (1979), 361–362.

[69] On 'Operation Barracuda', see Rousseau (1980), 364–365. For an assessment of the claim that the military operation amounted to humanitarian intervention, see Chesterman (2001), 81–82; Franck (2002), 151–152.

[70] *Keesing's* (1979), 29750–29751; Rousseau (1980), 363–365.

[71] See Fierro (2005), 46 (with further references); and above Section 4.2.3 (text accompanying n. 57).

[72] *Keesing's* (1979), 29751. See also Oestreich (1990), 316; Bartels (2005), 11–12.

a fundamental and unforseeable change in the circumstances that existed when a treaty was concluded.[73]

In short, as already acknowledged by Commissioner Cheysson in relation to the earlier *de facto* suspension of development assistance to Uganda,[74] the Commission had in March 1978 again observed that

[T]he Community is linked to the ACP States by an International Agreement, duly ratified by all the parties. It is, therefore, bound to honour the commitments entered into *vis-à-vis* every one of those States under the Convention of Lomé.[75]

These repeated conclusions remained intact in August 1979 when EC Member States decided to freeze development assistance owed to the Central African Republic under the Lomé I Convention. No treaty-law doctrine could apparently justify this conduct in legal terms. The action therefore appears to have constituted a violation of the Lomé I Convention. In the absence of any other possible justifications, the action can seemingly only be explained in legal terms by reference to the concept of third-party countermeasures.[76]

In terms of other unilateral coercive measures, France decided on 17 August 1979 to suspend the provision of development assistance to the Central African Republic apparently owed to it under a bilateral treaty.[77] Given the absence of clear documentation, however, it is unclear whether this action amounted to a third-party countermeasure.[78] On 23 May 1979, likewise in response to the Bangui massacre, France had also decided to suspend the application of the 1960 Agreement Concerning Technical Military Assistance.[79] While no military assistance had been provided under this bilateral treaty since 1976, it remained in force at the time France suspended its application.[80] The 1960 Agreement did not condition the provision of military assistance on the observance of human rights or include a denunciation clause. The French conduct

---

[73] Answer to Written Question No. 115/78 by Mr. Adams to the Commission of the European Communities (18 July 1978), OJ 1978 C 199/27 (21 Aug. 1978).

[74] See above Section 4.2.3 (text accompanying n. 60).

[75] Answer to Written Question No. 943/77 by Mr. Adams to the Commission of the European Communities (6 March 1978), OJ 1978 C 74/18 (28 March 1978).

[76] For a similar conclusion see Katselli Proukaki (2010), 132–133.

[77] *Keesing's* (1979), 29933; Rousseau (1980), 363–365. In doing so, France exempted development assistance with respect to health, education and foodstuffs (ibid., 364).

[78] Ibid.; Arangio-Ruiz, Fourth Report, 31, para. 80 (n. 205); Draft Articles Commentary, Art. 50, §21.

[79] 821 UNTS 266 (entry into force 27 Jan. 1961).   [80] *Keesing's* (1979), 29750.

could therefore not be justified as a treaty suspension based on the principle codified in Article 60 VCLT.

There is also nothing to suggest that the French conduct could be justified by reference to any other treaty-law doctrine. As observed above, the principle of fundamental change of circumstances codified in Article 62 VCLT was explicitly discarded by EC Member States in relation to obligations owed to the Central African Republic under the Lomé I Convention. That principle seems equally inapplicable here, not least given the very strict conditions for its application. And even if France might conceivably be understood to have denounced the 1960 Agreement – i.e. an agreement on military cooperation of an impermanent nature and therefore in principle subject to denunciation[81] – the short period of time that passed between the Bangui massacre and the suspension strongly suggests that no reasonable notice was provided as required by the principle embodied in Article 56(2) VCLT. Again, it seems that the French action could only be justified by the rationale of third-party countermeasures.

4.2.5   European and African States – Liberia (1980)

On 12 April 1980, Master Sergeant Samuel Doe seized power in a bloody *coup d'état* killing then President Tolbert. On 22 April 1980, among other repressive measures, thirteen ministers and high-ranking officials of the ousted government were summarily executed on Doe's orders after show trials.[82] ECOWAS and EC Member States responded to the situation by adopting unilateral coercive measures against Liberia.

On 27 April 1980, ECOWAS Member States decided not to allow President Doe's participation at an ECOWAS summit in Lomé.[83] This action may be considered a *de facto* suspension of Liberia's rights as a member of the organization. ECOWAS was founded by treaty as an international organization in 1975 with corresponding rights and

---

[81] There is a strong presumption against the possibility of unilateral denunciation in the absence of a specific treaty right. However, treaties on military cooperation and treaties otherwise not intended to be of a permanent nature such as commercial, cultural or technical treaties have been singled out as examples of exceptions to the general prohibition on unilateral denunciation. See further e.g. Waldock, Second Report, 64 (his draft article 17(3)(ii) referring to a treaty of military cooperation); Widdows (1982), 85–88, 106–108; Bastid (1985), 202; Aust (2013), 255–257.

[82] *Keesing's* (1980), 30405–30407; Rousseau (1980), 1144–1145.

[83] Rousseau (1980), 1145. Liberia protested against the decision by breaking off diplomatic relations with the Ivory Coast, Senegal and Nigeria (ibid.).

obligations for its members.[84] An example of a membership right is the right to vote. The right to vote seemingly presupposes a derivative right to participate in meetings of the organization.[85] However, the 1975 ECOWAS Treaty, the explicit aim of which was to promote cooperation and development in all fields of economic activity, did not include any provision on the suspension of membership rights. It would seem to follow that Liberia's *de facto* suspension was in breach of the 1975 ECOWAS Treaty and as such could not be characterized as an act of retorsion.

In the absence of a specific power of suspension it is doubtful whether an international organization can suspend membership.[86] It is unclear whether the decision to suspend Liberia was formally taken by an organ of ECOWAS (such as the Authority of Heads of State and Government or the Council of Ministers, as envisaged in Articles 5 and 6 of the 1975 ECOWAS Treaty) or whether it was directly attributable to individual members. At least in the latter case, the suspension might be categorized as a third-party countermeasure.[87] As a minimum, ECOWAS Member States expressed support for such action.

In July 1980, the European Commission condemned Liberia for its human rights violations and announced that development assistance owed to it under the Lomé 1 Convention would be suspended.[88] As in the above cases of Uganda and the Central African Republic, this action finds no support in the Lomé I Convention and could seemingly only be justified by way of third-party countermeasures.[89]

4.2.6 Western Countries – Soviet Union (1980)

On 24 December 1979, Soviet troops invaded Afghanistan. The government in Afghanistan, then led by President Amin, was at

---

[84] Treaty of the Economic Community of West African States, 1010 UNTS 17 (provisionally in force 28 May 1975).

[85] Sands and Klein (2001), 545–546. To the same effect: UNJY (1970), 170 (UN Legal Counsel concluding that the rejection of South Africa's credentials to the General Assembly – which prevented its participation in Assembly meetings – effectively amounted to a suspension of membership rights in breach of Article 5 UNC). Also: Schachter (1982), 230.

[86] Sands and Klein (2001), 545–546.   [87] Compare ibid.

[88] Statement by Commissioner Cheysson, 8 July 1980, Europe, vol. 28, No. 2495 (new series), 11. See further Oestreich (1990), 320–322 (with further references); Hoffmeister (1998), 17–18.

[89] Compare Oestreich (1990), 447–449; Tams (2005), 211; Katselli Proukaki (2010), 135; Tzanakopoulos (2015), 150.

the time in the throes of a civil war against anti-government rebels.[90] An urgent meeting of the UN Security Council was convened to discuss the situation in Afghanistan and its implications for international peace and security.[91]

On 5 January 1980, the Soviet Union claimed in the debate before the Security Council that the military intervention was justified by the 1978 Afghanistan-USSR Treaty of Friendship, Good-Neighbourliness and Co-operation,[92] following repeated requests from the Afghan government for military assistance in order to repel armed intervention from outside. The Soviet Union also insisted that its military intervention was fully compatible with the right of individual and collective self-defence under Article 51 UNC.[93] Afghanistan strongly insisted on the same point.[94] But the invitation was a mere pretext; it came from an Afghan puppet regime (headed by Babrak Karmal) forcibly installed on 27 December 1980 in a bloody Soviet-engineered *coup* which had killed then President Amin in the first days of the invasion.[95] As Pakistan, among many others, pithily observed before the Security Council: 'It does not stand to logic that a Government should have invited foreign troops to liquidate itself'.[96] The invocation of Article 51 UNC was also largely dismissed in similarly scathing terms.[97]

During the debate in the Security Council, the Soviet military intervention was widely denounced as an 'act of aggression' and an unlawful use of force under the UN Charter.[98] The invasion was also commonly

---

[90] *Keesing's* (1979), 30229. For a summary of events see Rousseau (1980), 826; Hufbauer, Schott and Elliott (1985), 655–657.

[91] Report of the Security Council (1979–1980), UN Doc. A/35/2, 49. See further UN Doc. S/13724 (3 Jan. 1980).

[92] 1145 UNTS 332 (entry into force 27 May 1979).

[93] See UN Doc. S/PV.2185 (5 Jan. 1980), 2–3, paras. 16–17 (USSR). For a summary of events, see UNYB (1980), 296–306. Also: *Keesing's* (1978), 29459.

[94] UN Doc. S/PV.2185 (5 Jan. 1980), 11, paras. 100–105 (Afghanistan).

[95] UNYB (1980), 298. See also Gray (2008), 92–94.

[96] UN Doc. S/PV.2185 (5 Jan. 1980), 8–9, para. 76 (Pakistan). To the same effect see further: UN Docs. S/PV.2186 (6 Jan. 1980), 5–6, para. 37 (China), 7–8, para. 51 (United Kingdom); S/PV.2187 (6 Jan. 1980), 2, para. 17 (United States), 5, paras. 42–43 (Singapore), 6, para. 61 (Spain), 8, para. 87 (Malaysia), 9, paras. 94–95 (Costa Rica); S/PV.2187 (6 Jan. 1980), 13, para. 125 (Liberia); S/PV.2190 (7 and 9 Jan. 1980), 5, para. 39 (Zaire).

[97] See e.g. UN Docs. S/PV.2185 (5 Jan. 1980), 13, para. 121 (Japan); S/PV.2186 (6 Jan. 1980), 3, para. 21 (United States), 16, para. 131 (New Zealand); S/PV.2187, 10–11, para. 108 (Italy), 12–13, paras. 119–130 (Liberia); S/PV.2190 (7 and 9 Jan. 1980), 14, para. 129 (France).

[98] See e.g. UN Docs. S/13717 (31 Dec. 1979) (China); S/13727 (4 Jan. 1980) (Kampuchea); S/PV.2185 (5 Jan. 1980), 13, para. 127 (Egypt); S/PV.2186 (5 Jan. 1980), 8, para. 52 (United Kingdom), 9, para. 62 (Colombia), 13–14, paras. 109–110 (Saudi Arabia), 16,

denounced as a violation of the principles of non-intervention and self-determination.[99] On 6 January 1980, a draft Security Council resolution, which deplored the armed intervention in Afghanistan as a violation of the UN Charter on these grounds and called for the immediate withdrawal of foreign troops from the country, was vetoed by the Soviet Union.[100] On 9 January 1980, a revised Security Council resolution was nevertheless adopted by which it was decided to call an emergency special session of the General Assembly to consider the situation in Afghanistan.[101] On 14 January 1980, the General Assembly adopted a resolution by which it 'strongly deplore[d] the armed intervention in Afghanistan' as inconsistent with the fundamental Charter principles of non-use of force, non-intervention and self-determination.[102] The resolution also called for the immediate withdrawal of foreign troops from Afghanistan in order to enable its people to determine their own form of government free from outside intervention.[103]

Several Western States adopted numerous acts of retorsion and third-party countermeasures against the Soviet Union as a means of inducing a return to international legality.[104] The United States – in response to a 'gross and blatant violation of the most important principles of international law and of the Charter of the United Nations'; notably, the principles of non-use of force, non-intervention and self-determination[105] – adopted the most comprehensive regime of unilateral coercive measures.[106] On 4 January 1980, the United States announced that it was limiting Aeroflot flights to the country.[107] This action contravened the 1966 US-USSR Civil Air Transport Agreement

---

para. 132 (New Zealand); S/13728 (6 Jan. 1980) (Chile); S/PV.2187 (6 Jan. 1980), 2, para. 8 (United States), 4, para. 34 (Australia), 5, para. 44 (Singapore), 6, para. 62 (Spain), 7, para. 72 (Somalia), 9, paras. 92–93 (Costa Rica); S/PV.2190 (7 and 9 Jan. 1980), 4, para. 33 (Panama).

[99] See generally UN Docs. S/PV.2185–2190 (5–9 Jan. 1980).

[100] UN Doc. S/13729 (6 Jan. 1980). Only the German Democratic Republic joined with the Soviet Union in voting against the resolution.

[101] SC Res. 462 (9 Jan. 1980).

[102] GA Res. ES-6/2 (14 Jan. 1980). For a brief summary, see further Rousseau (1980), 840–841.

[103] Ibid.

[104] See Moyer and Mabry (1983), 43–47; Rousseau (1980), 837–840; and more generally Peles-Bodson (1984–1985), 202.

[105] UN Doc. S/PV.2187 (6 Jan. 1980), 3, para. 20 (United States).

[106] See Rousseau (1980), 832–837, 1069–1072; 80 Dept. of State Bulletin (Apr. 1980), 45–52. Also: Moyer and Mabry (1983), 27–41; Katselli Proukaki (2010), 135–137.

[107] 80 Dept. of State Bulletin (March 1980), 48.

under which the Soviet Union's national airline, Aeroflot, enjoyed landing rights.[108] Article 17 of the 1966 Agreement provided for a right of denunciation upon six months' prior notice; the US action could therefore not be justified under the terms of the treaty.

On 4 January 1980, 'in response to an act of Soviet aggression',[109] the United States also decided to suspend shipments of agricultural commodities, including wheat and corn, to the Soviet Union. However, shipments of grain would be allowed to continue up to the eight million tons of wheat and corn per year covered by Article I of the 1975 US-USSR Agreement on the Supply of Grain.[110] It seems that the reason for this can be found in Article II of the 1975 Agreement, which 'guarantee[d]'[111] the supply of these eight million tons of grain to the Soviet Union under Article I thereby making suspension impermissible. Still, as the United States recognized, '[t]he most significant effect of the control on U.S. exports relates to the 17 million tons of grain previously authorized for the Soviet Union, valued at $2.3 billion'.[112]

The cancellation of this sale of grain appears to have violated Article VI of the 1975 Agreement, which envisaged the additional sale of grain on the basis of mutual agreement beyond the guaranteed amount covered by Articles I and II of the 1975 Agreement.[113] As the US Department of State explained, 'sales in excess of 8 mmt were not covered by the safeguards against embargoes [under the 1975 Agreement]'.[114] Article IX of the 1975 Agreement provided that it would remain in force until at least 30 September 1981; there was no denunciation clause. In sum, the restriction of US grain exports to the Soviet Union beyond eight million tons seemingly required justification under general international law. Several European States (at least initially) expressed support for the US grain embargo,[115] which may be categorized as a third-party countermeasure.[116]

---

[108] 675 UNTS 3 (entry into force 4 Nov. 1966); as subsequently modified, see 7 ILM (1968), 571.

[109] 80 Dept. of State Bulletin (March 1980), 46.

[110] 1020 UNTS 365 (entry into force 20 Oct. 1975). See also Keesing's (1976), 27641; 80 Dept. of State Bulletin (March 1980), 45–46, 48. Further: Paarlberg (1980), 144.

[111] 82 Dept. of State Bulletin (Oct. 1982), 41.

[112] 80 Dept. of State Bulletin (March 1980), 46.

[113] 82 Dept. of State Bulletin (Oct. 1982), 40–42. It thus appears that the additional sale of grain was not based on a unilateral US commitment (as has sometimes been alleged: see notably Sicilianos (1990), 157–158 (n. 309); Crawford, Third Report, 104, para. 393) but was instead based on Article VI of the 1975 Agreement.

[114] 82 Dept. of State Bulletin (Oct. 1982), 41.

[115] 80 Dept. of State Bulletin (March 1980), 49. See also Keesing's (1980), 30235; Katselli Proukaki (2010), 140 (with further references, noting an apparent reversal of European States' policy in relation to their position on the US grain embargo).

[116] Compare Sicilianos (1990), 157–158; Frowein (1994), 417; Focarelli (1994), 49; Petman (2004), 363; Katselli Proukaki (2010), 136–137. Also: Crawford, Third Report, 104, para. 393.

On 11 June 1980, the United States announced that it had withheld fishery allocations owed to the Soviet Union under the 1977 US-USSR Agreement Concerning Fisheries off the Coasts of the United States,[117] and reallocated to other countries approximately 200,000 tons of fish that would otherwise have gone to the Soviet Union.[118] This action *prima facie* violated Article III of the 1977 Agreement, which granted the Soviet Union fishing rights in United States' waters subject only to a determination of the quota allocated in a given year based on criteria related to the conservation of fish stocks. Moreover, Article XV of the 1977 Agreement provided that it was by its terms effective until 1 July 1982 unless terminated in writing with twelve months' prior notice. It appears that, at least in June 1980 when the relevant US action was taken, denunciation of the 1977 Agreement was not possible. The United States' suspension of Soviet fishing rights should be understood as a third-party countermeasure.[119]

On 15 January 1980, EC Member States condemned the Soviet military intervention in Afghanistan as a 'serious violation of the principles of international relations enshrined in the Charter of the United Nations . . . [and] a flagrant interference in the internal affairs of [Afghanistan]'.[120] More specifically, recalling the resolution on the Afghan crisis just adopted by the General Assembly the day before, EC Member States urged the Soviet Union to immediately withdraw all its troops and to allow the Afghan people, in conformity with the UN Charter and the principle of self-determination, to decide on their own future without outside interference.[121] The European Council of Ministers was, however, reluctant for mainly economic reasons to adopt unilateral coercive measures against the Soviet Union.[122] On 11 February 1980, the European Parliament nevertheless urged the Council of Ministers to 'immediately reconsider *all* economic relations'[123] with the Soviet Union – a wording that implied, *inter alia*, a call for the adoption of third-party countermeasures.[124]

On 11 January 1980, in response to 'a gross violation of international law',[125] namely, the principles of non-use of force, non-intervention and

---

[117] 1069 UNTS 307 (entry into force 28 Feb. 1977).
[118] Nash (1986), 601–602. See also *Keesing's* (1980), 30234.
[119] For a similar conclusion see Katselli Proukaki (2010), 136. Also: Sicilianos (1990), 157.
[120] UN Doc. S/13760 (17 Jan. 1980).   [121] Ibid. See also UNYB (1980), 303.
[122] Rousseau (1980), 838.   [123] OJ 1980 C 34/28 (11 Feb. 1980) (emphasis added).
[124] For a similar conclusion see Sicilianos (1990), 159.
[125] UN Doc. S/PV.2190 (7 and 9 Jan. 1980), 7, para. 63 (Canada).

self-determination, Canada suspended Soviet fishing rights in its Exclusive Economic Zone.[126] These fishing rights had been granted to the Soviet Union under the 1976 Canada-USSR Agreement on Their Mutual Fisheries' Relations.[127] The suspension *prima facie* violated Article II of the 1976 Agreement under which the Soviet Union enjoyed fishing rights in Canadian waters subject only to a determination by Canada of the quota allocated in a given year based on criteria related to the conservation of fish stocks. The suspension could not be justified on the basis of Article VII of the 1976 Agreement, which provided that any such action was impermissible for six years following its entry into force, and thereafter required at least twelve months' prior notice.

On 23 February 1980, in response to 'an act of aggression',[128] as well as violations of the principles of non-intervention and self-determination, New Zealand similarly suspended the 1978 New Zealand-USSR Agreement on Fisheries.[129] Again, the suspension *prima facie* violated Articles II and III of the 1978 Agreement under which the Soviet Union enjoyed fishing rights in New Zealand waters. Moreover, Article XII of the 1978 Agreement provided that it would remain in force until 30 June 1982 unless terminated in writing with twelve months' prior notice. In the absence of alternative treaty-based justifications, the actions taken by Canada and New Zealand should be understood as third-party countermeasures.[130]

Finally, on 29 January 1980, the OIC met in extraordinary session and adopted a resolution which 'condemn[ed] the Soviet military aggression against the Afghani people ... as a flagrant violation of international law ...' and expressed grave concern at the breaches of the principles of non-intervention and self-determination.[131] Moreover, the resolution 'urge[d] all countries and peoples to secure the Soviet withdrawal through *all* possible means'[132] – a wording that may be understood as a call for, *inter alia*, the adoption of third-party countermeasures.

---

[126] Rousseau (1980), 837.   [127] 1132 UNTS 139 (entry into force 19 May 1976).

[128] UN Doc. S/PV.2186 (5 Jan. 1980), 16, para. 132 (New Zealand).

[129] 1151 UNTS 277 (entry into force 4 Apr. 1978). See also Rousseau (1980), 837; *Keesing's* (1980), 30241.

[130] See Sicilianos (1990), 158; Focarelli (1994), 112; Alland (1994), 178–179; Katselli Proukaki (2010), 139–140.

[131] 'Resolution No. 1/EOS on the Soviet Military Intervention in Afghanistan and on its Ensuing Effects', annexed to UN Doc. S/13810 (21 Feb. 1980), 16. See further Rousseau (1980), 844–846.

[132] Ibid. (op. para. 2) (emphasis added).

4.2.7   Western Countries – Poland and the Soviet Union (1981)

On 13 December 1981, the Polish government under the leadership of General Jaruzelski, allegedly under pressure from the Soviet Union, declared a state of emergency and imposed martial law in an attempt to thwart the rising influence of the trade union *Solidarność* and its popular calls for political reform in Poland. A widespread suspension of civil and political rights followed in the wake of continuing strikes and demonstrations taking place throughout the country, as a result of which around 12,500 political dissidents were arbitrarily arrested and interned without trial.[133]

On 10 March 1982, the UN Commission on Human Rights adopted a resolution by which it 'recall[ed] the principles enshrined in the Charter of the United Nations and in the Universal Declaration of Human Rights' and

> express[ed] deep concern at the continued reports of widespread violations of human rights and fundamental freedoms in Poland, including the arbitrary arrest and detention of thousands of persons, denial of the right to freedom of expression and the right of peaceful assembly, suspension of the right to form and join independent trade unions, and at the imposition of severe punishment on persons accused of violating martial law.[134]

The same resolution also 'affirm[ed] the right of the Polish people to pursue its political, economic, social and cultural development, free from outside interference'.[135] But aside from this verbal condemnation, no further action was taken by the UN. In fact, the humanitarian crisis in Poland was not even on the agenda of the General Assembly or the Security Council.

On 23 December 1981, the United States denounced Poland for the human rights violations observed above and announced the adoption of unilateral coercive measures against it.[136] The United States also accused the Soviet Union of direct involvement in the crisis and warned it of similar action. Indeed US President Reagan warned both countries that 'if the outrages in Poland do not cease, we cannot and will not conduct

---

[133] Rousseau (1982), 603–604. For a detailed summary of events, see *Keesing's* (1982), 31453–31467.

[134] UNCHR Res. 1982/26, Report of the Commission on Human Rights (38th session, 1 Feb. – 12 March 1982), UN Doc. E/1982/12, 143.

[135] Ibid. See further UNYB (1982), 1117.

[136] 82 Dept. of State Bulletin (Feb. 1982), 2–3. See also Nash (1982), 379–382; Rousseau (1982), 606, 608–609; Moyer and Mabry (1983), 64–75.

"business as usual" with the perpetrators and those who aid and abet them ... free men cannot and will not stand idly by in the face of brutal repression'.[137]

On the same day, President Reagan thus announced that the United States was, *inter alia*, taking immediate action to suspend the 1977 United States-Poland Agreement concerning Fisheries off the Coasts of the United States.[138] The suspension *prima facie* violated Article III of the 1977 Agreement, which granted Poland fishing rights in US waters subject to the specific allocation of possible surpluses of total allowable catches based on criteria related to the conservation of fish stocks. Article XVI of the 1977 Agreement provided that it would remain in force until 1 July 1982, unless terminated beforehand following twelve months' prior notice. As in the very similar cases already examined in the previous example above, the US suspension of Polish fishing rights under the 1977 Agreement may therefore also be categorized as a third-party countermeasure. President Reagan explained: 'We made it clear that these sanctions are reversible if and when Polish authorities restore the internationally recognized human rights of the Polish people'.[139]

On 23 December 1981, President Reagan also announced that the United States was taking immediate action to suspend the 1972 United States-Poland Air Transport Agreement under which the Polish national airline, LOT, enjoyed landing rights.[140] On the following day, the United States gave Poland notice of the suspension with effect from 29 December 1981.[141] The 1972 Agreement, as subsequently amended by an exchange of notes, was by its terms effective until 31 March 1982.[142] Article 15 of the 1972 Agreement, as amended, provided for termination thereafter upon twelve months' notice. This provision could accordingly not have provided a basis for the US suspension. Similarly, Article 4 of the 1972 Agreement, which provided for the possibility of suspension in the

---

[137] 82 Dept. of State Bulletin (Feb. 1982), 2–3.

[138] 1068 UNTS 3 (entry into force 28 Feb. 1977). Several measures of retorsion against Poland were also announced: see 82 Dept. of State Bulletin (Feb. 1982), 2–3. Further: Carter (1988), 55–56; Focarelli (1994), 113.

[139] 82 Dept. of State Bulletin (Aug. 1982), 64. See also 84 Dept. of State Bulletin (Jan. 1984), 54 ('[A]ny future allocation of fish at the end of the discussions will be contingent on the Polish Government's actions on human rights').

[140] 1279 UNTS 205 (entry into force 8 Dec. 1972). See also 82 Dept. of State Bulletin (Feb. 1982), 3; and for an analysis, see Malamut (1983), 190.

[141] Nash (1982), 380–381.

[142] 1279 UNTS 236 (entry into force 30 Jan. 1979, with retroactive effect from 1 Jan. 1979).

case of non-observance of safety regulations, was inapplicable. Other treaty-based defences were also unavailable.[143]

In proceedings before the US Civil Aeronautics Board, LOT representatives insisted that the action taken by the United States was ineffective as it violated Article 15 of the 1972 Agreement.[144] On 29 December 1981, the Civil Aeronautics Board issued its LOT suspension order by which it determined that the US government did not rely on a treaty-based right of suspension, but on a general right to suspend treaties with immediate effect as an 'extraordinary' response to 'exceedingly serious world events'.[145] It continued:

> Clearly, in such circumstances, there resides in the President and the Executive Branch of the U.S. Government ample authority to suspend application of an Executive Agreement [e.g. an air transport agreement] between the United States and a foreign country, whether or not such suspension is provided for under the specific terms of the Agreement. This is a political question which is clearly one for the President. That the President has made such a decision is reflected in his television speech of December 23, as confirmed by the letters of the Department of State attached to this Order.[146]

The suspension with immediate effect of LOT landing rights should be understood as a third-party countermeasure.[147] As President Reagan explained in a letter to General Jaruzelski, the 1972 and 1977 Agreements had been suspended in order to induce Poland 'to free those in arbitrary detention, to lift martial law, and to restore the internationally recognized rights of the Polish people to free speech and association'.[148] Finally, on 9 October 1982, in order to ensure compliance with internationally protected trade union rights following the disbandment of *Solidarność*, President Reagan also announced the imminent US suspension of Poland's most-favoured-nation-tariff status in *prima facie* violation of Article I GATT. It appears that this action was taken without any reference to possible treaty justifications for doing so such as Article XXI GATT.[149]

On 29 December 1981, President Reagan issued a statement regarding the responsibility of the Soviet Union which in relevant part read:

> The Soviet Union bears a heavy and direct responsibility for the repression in Poland. For many months the Soviets publicly and privately

---

[143] For a brief assessment see Malamut (1983), 191–192, 196–197.
[144] Nash (1982), 381 (with further references).   [145] Ibid.   [146] Ibid.
[147] See notably ARSIWA Commentary, Art. 54, §3.
[148] 82 Dept. of State Bulletin (Feb. 1982), 3.
[149] 82 Dept. of State Bulletin (Dec. 1982), 11.

demanded such a crackdown. They brought major pressures to bear through now-public letters to the Polish leadership, military maneuvers, and other forms of intimidation. They now openly endorse the suppression which has ensued.[150]

President Reagan had about a week before sent a letter to Soviet President Brezhnev urging him 'to permit the restoration of basic rights in Poland' and gave notice of the imminent adoption of unilateral coercive measures against the Soviet Union in case of a failure to comply.[151]

In the absence of an adequate response, the United States adopted a host of unilateral coercive measures against the Soviet Union.[152] The United States, *inter alia*, completely suspended with immediate effect the 1966 US-USSR Civil Air Transport Agreement under which the Soviet Union's national airline, Aeroflot, enjoyed landing rights.[153] The United States notified the Soviet Union of the immediate suspension by letter of the same day, notwithstanding Article 17 of the 1966 Agreement, which only provided for a right of denunciation upon six months' notice.[154] Thus the immediate suspension could not be justified under the terms of the treaty. It should be understood as a third-party countermeasure.[155]

On 14–15 December 1981, EC Foreign Ministers met in London to voice their concern at the proclamation of martial law in Poland.[156] On 4 January 1982, EC Foreign Ministers adopted a communiqué by which

> The Ten utterly disapprove[d] of the development of the situation in Poland [and] ... noted violations of the most elementary human and citizens' rights, contrary to the Helsinki Final Act, the United Nations Charter, and the Universal Declaration of Human Rights.[157]

EC Foreign Ministers also condemned the Soviet Union for the 'serious external pressure' directed against Poland.[158] No unilateral coercive

---

[150]   82 Dept. of State Bulletin (Feb. 1982), 8. The United States made clear in April 1982 that the Soviet military maneuvers amounted to a threat of force in violation of the UN Charter: see UN Doc. A/37/41 (27 July 1982), 14, para. 50 (United States).

[151]   82 Dept. of State Bulletin (Feb. 1982), 3, 8.

[152]   Ibid., 8. See also Nash (1982), 382; Rousseau (1982), 608–609; Moyer and Mabry (1983), 64–75.

[153]   675 UNTS 3 (entry into force 4 Nov. 1966); as subsequently modified, see 7 ILM (1968), 571. The earlier US suspension in January 1980 merely restricted Aeroflot landing rights but did not suspend them in full: see above Section 4.2.6 (text accompanying n. 107).

[154]   Nash (1982), 382–383.   [155]   See notably ARSIWA Commentary, Art. 54, §3.

[156]   EC Bull. No. 12 (1981), point 1.4.1.   [157]   Ibid., point 1.4.2.   [158]   Ibid.

measures were adopted at this point but the communiqué nevertheless envisaged the possibility of such action at a later stage.[159] Instead, for the time being, EC Foreign Ministers limited themselves to denouncing the developments in Poland as 'a grave violation of the principles of the Helsinki Final Act', and considered that the alleged violations thereunder should principally be discussed by the CSCE. On 9 February 1982, at the CSCE Madrid Conference, Belgium (on behalf of EC Member States), in close consultation with the United States,[160] elaborated on the specific breaches of international law for which the Soviet Union was deemed responsible. It stated:

> The serious external pressure brought to bear against the efforts at renewal in Poland is in flagrant contradiction to the obligations undertaken by the signatories of the agreements in question and, more specifically, the principles governing sovereignty, non-intervention, the threat or use of force, and the right of peoples to self-determination. No country has the right to determine the political and social course of another country, and that applies particularly to the Soviet Union in regard to Poland.[161]

On 11 January 1982, NATO Member States had already adopted a similar statement, which in relevant part read:

> 1. The Allied Governments condemn the imposition of martial law in Poland and denounce the massive violation of human rights and the suppression of fundamental civil liberties in contravention of the United Nations Charter, the Universal Declaration on Human Rights and the Final Act of Helsinki. [...]
> 4. The Allies deplore the sustained campaign mounted by the Soviet Union against efforts by the Polish people for national renewal and reform, and its active support for the subsequent systematic suppression of those efforts in Poland. These acts cannot be reconciled with the Soviet Union's international undertakings, and in particular with the principles of the Final Act of Helsinki, especially those dealing with sovereignty, non-intervention, threat of force and self-determination. The Soviet Union has no right to determine the political and social development of Poland. [...]
> 6. The Allies call upon the Soviet Union to respect Poland's fundamental right to solve its own problems free from foreign interference and

---

[159] Ibid. See also EC Bull. No. 1 (1982), points 2.2.38, 2.2.44; Council Regulation (EEC) No. 596/82 (15 March 1982), OJ 1982 L 72/15 (16 March 1982) (for some limited measures of retorsion later adopted against Poland and the Soviet Union). For a survey and evaluation of the unilateral coercive measures imposed on Poland and the Soviet Union, see Moyer and Mabry (1983), 78–86.

[160] 82 Dept. of State Bulletin (Feb. 1982), 12–13.

[161] European Political Cooperation (Press and Information Office, Bonn, Federal Republic of Germany, 4th ed. 1982), 307–308, available at http://aei.pitt.edu/5584/1/5584.pdf.

to respect the clear desire of the overwhelming majority of the Polish people for national renewal and reform. Soviet pressure, direct or indirect, aimed at frustrating that desire, must cease.[162]

In terms of inducing compliance with the above obligations, NATO Member States expressed general support for the host of unilateral coercive measures recently imposed by the United States against Poland and the Soviet Union, notably including the US suspension of fishing and aviation rights.[163]

For their part, NATO Member States declared that 'economic relations with Poland and the Soviet Union are bound to be affected'; they accordingly announced the adoption of their own measures of retorsion against Poland.[164] The suspension of air services agreements was among the measures contemplated.[165] As it happened, at least the United Kingdom and the Netherlands suspended, with immediate effect, application of their respective air services agreements with Poland.[166] In addition, Austria and Switzerland (both non-NATO Member States) likewise suspended application of their respective air services agreements with Poland.[167] All of these unilateral measures violated rights owed to Poland under the respective agreements and could not be justified by the suspension provisions contained therein.[168] Again, in the absence of alternative justifications, these suspensions may be characterized as third-party countermeasures.[169]

In terms of identifying actual Polish and Soviet breaches of international law, it appears that unilateral coercive measures were adopted against Poland mainly in order 'to free those in arbitrary detention, to lift martial law, and to restore the internationally recognized rights of the Polish people to free speech and association'.[170] Specific reference was also occasionally made to ensuring compliance with internationally protected trade union rights.[171] As observed above, Poland was widely deemed responsible for 'the massive violation of human rights and the suppression of fundamental civil liberties in contravention of the

---

[162] 82 Dept. of State Bulletin (Feb. 1982), 19.   [163] Ibid., 20.   [164] Ibid.   [165] Ibid.
[166] Rousseau (1982), 607.
[167] Ibid. See Austria-Poland Air Transport Agreement, 334 UNTS 211 (entry into force 1 Apr. 1956); Switzerland-Poland Civil Air Transport Agreement, 559 UNTS 249 (entry into force 13 May 1963).
[168] Netherlands-Poland Civil Air Transport Agreement, 497 UNTS 190 (entry into force 21 July 1960); United Kingdom-Poland Agreement Concerning Civil Air Transport, 385 UNTS 87 (entry in force 25 Oct. 1960).
[169] See notably ARSIWA Commentary, Art. 54, §3.   [170] See above n. 148.
[171] See above n. 149.

United Nations Charter, the Universal Declaration on Human Rights and the Final Act of Helsinki'.[172]

As also observed above, particular emphasis was placed on Poland's human rights commitments under the 1975 Final Act of Helsinki.[173] Principle VII of the Final Act of Helsinki exhorted respect for human rights with an explicit *renvoi* to the Universal Declaration of Human Rights, the UN Charter, and the specific obligations arising under the ICCPR and ICESCR. It thus appears that the relevant Polish human rights violations with which the United States and other Western countries were chiefly concerned included the following provisions of the ICCPR: (1) right to liberty and security of person (Article 9); (2) right to a fair trial (Article 14); (3) freedom of expression (Article 19); (4) freedom of assembly (Article 21); and (5) freedom of association (Article 22).

Poland ratified the ICCPR in March 1977 and was accordingly bound by the above mentioned human rights obligations during the relevant period. There is no indication that Poland invoked Article 4 ICCPR to justify any derogation in time of public emergency.[174] Likewise Austria, the Netherlands and the United Kingdom were all parties to the ICCPR at the time they suspended their respective air services agreements with Poland.[175] Their actions may therefore be understood as third-party countermeasures adopted in response to violations of obligations *erga omnes partes* within the meaning of what later became Article 48(1)(a) ARSIWA. By contrast, Switzerland and the United States were not parties to the ICCPR at the time they suspended their respective air services agreements with Poland.[176] As regards the violations which prompted the adoption of third-party countermeasures against the Soviet Union, it was widely deemed responsible for breaches of obligations relating to the non-threat of force, non-intervention and self-determination. It was also considered jointly responsible with Poland for the human rights violations taking place in that country.[177]

---

[172] See above n. 162.

[173] Helsinki Final Act (signed at Helsinki, 1 Aug. 1975), www.osce.org/mc/39501.

[174] See generally General Comment No. 29 (24 July 2001), 'States of Emergency (Article 4)', para. 17, UN Doc. CCPR/C/21/Rev.1/Add.11, para. 17; *Wall* case, ICJ Rep. (2004), 136 at 192, para. 136. Article 4(3) ICCPR requires immediate notification of any intention to derogate.

[175] Austria ratified the ICCPR on 10 September 1978; the Netherlands on 11 December 1978; and the United Kingdom on 20 May 1976.

[176] Switzerland acceded to the ICCPR on 18 June 1992. The United States signed the ICCPR on 5 October 1977, but only ratified it on 8 June 1992.

[177] See above n. 150; and Tams (2015), 312.

4.2.8   Western Countries – Argentina (1982)

On 2 April 1982, Argentina invaded the Falkland Islands (Islas Malvinas), a non-self-governing territory administered by the United Kingdom. The Argentinean invasion was swiftly condemned by the UN Security Council in a resolution adopted under Chapter VII UNC.[178] The Security Council, recalling the obligation to refrain from the threat or use of force, qualified the Argentinean action as an 'invasion',[179] determined that it constituted a 'breach of the peace', demanded an immediate withdrawal of all Argentinean forces from the Falkland Islands and called on the parties to seek a diplomatic resolution to the conflict.[180] No enforcement action was taken. During the debate in the Security Council, the invasion was widely condemned as an unlawful use of force under Article 2(4) UNC.[181] The United Kingdom invoked its inherent right of self-defence under Article 51 UNC and launched military operations against Argentina in the South Atlantic.[182] It also proceeded to freeze Argentinean assets within its jurisdiction as a bilateral countermeasure.[183]

Several Western countries adopted unilateral coercive measures against Argentina.[184] On 10 April 1982, in response to 'a flagrant violation of international law constituted by the armed action of Argentina', and at the express request of the United Kingdom,[185] EC Member States announced, *inter alia*, the imminent adoption of a temporary general import embargo on Argentinean goods.[186] As further justification, EC Member States added that Argentina was responsible for 'an intervention committed in violation of international law and the rights of the

---

[178]   SC Res. 502 (3 Apr. 1982). The resolution did not explicitly refer to Chapter VII UNC but the debate in the Security Council on a point of order raised by Panama in terms of Article 27(3) UNC made that intention clear: see UN Doc. S/PV.2350 (3 Apr. 1982), 17–18, paras. 189–202.

[179]   An 'invasion' is the principal act of aggression recognized in the 1974 Definition of Aggression: see GA Res. 3314 (XXIX) (14 Dec. 1974), Art. 3(a).

[180]   SC Res. 502 (3 Apr. 1982).

[181]   See generally UN Docs. S/PV. 2345–2346, 2349–2350 (1–3 Apr. 1982).

[182]   For a detailed summary of events, see UNYB (1982), 1320–1347. Also: Report of the Security Council (1981–1982), UN Doc. A/37/2, 43–57.

[183]   See Marston (1982), 509.

[184]   For an evaluation of arms embargoes and other measures of retorsion, see Rousseau (1982), 744–749; Charpentier (1982), 1025–1026.

[185]   *Keesing's* (1982), 31532.

[186]   UN Doc. S/14976 (14 Apr. 1982) (Belgium on behalf of EC Member States). For the initial EC condemnation, see UN Doc. S/14949 (3 Apr. 1982) (Belgium on behalf of EC Member States).

inhabitants of the Falkland Islands'.[187] EC Member States, characterizing the invasion as 'a matter of serious concern for the international community as a whole', called upon other States to take similar action 'in order to ensure, within the shortest possible time, the full implementation of Security Council resolution 502'.[188]

On 21 April 1982, the Vice-President of the European Commission, Mr. Davignon, explained that 'Europe's display of solidarity was the expression of the Community's attachment to compliance with international law and its wish to safeguard peace'.[189] France similarly explained that 'in this matter [it] has but one concern, but one aim: that hostilities should cease as early as possible, in respect for law'.[190] Put simply, the trade embargo adopted by EC Member States was concerned with the cessation of Argentina's wrongful conduct as implicitly demanded by the Security Council. The general import embargo came into effect on 16 April 1982.[191]

The import embargo *prima facie* violated GATT obligations (notably Article XI GATT) owed by EC Member States to Argentina. In addition, the import embargo amounted to a suspension, with immediate effect, of rights owed to Argentina under two sectoral agreements concerning trade in textiles and trade in mutton and lamb, respectively.[192] Article 16.3 of the former agreement provided for denunciation upon three months' notice; Article 14 of the latter agreement provided that it was by its terms effective until 31 March 1984, and thereafter subject to denunciation upon twelve months' notice.[193] The security exception in

---

[187] EC Bull. No. 4 (1982), point 1.1.7. The Falklands were recognized as a British territory (ibid.).

[188] UN Doc. S/14976 (14 Apr. 1982) (Belgium on behalf of EC Member States).

[189] EC Bull. No. 4 (1982), point 1.1.1.

[190] UN Doc. S/PV.2373 (4 June 1982), 7, para. 85 (France).

[191] See Council Regulation (EEC) No. 877/82 (16 Apr. 1982), OJ 1982 L 102/1 (16 Apr. 1982); as extended by Council Regulation (EEC) No. 1176/82 (18 May 1982), OJ 1982 L 136/1 (18 May); and Council Regulation (EEC) No. 1254/82 (24 May 1982), OJ 1982 L 146/1 (25 May 1982). The EC also imposed an arms embargo, see EC Bull. No. 4 (1982), point 1.1.5; as well as an embargo on Argentinean coal and steel imports by the European Coal and Steel Community, see Regulation 82/221/ECSC (16 Apr. 1982), OJ 1982 L 102/3 (16 Apr. 1982); as briefly extended by Regulation 82/320/ECSC (18 May 1982), OJ 1982 L 136/2 (18 May 1982). Also: *Keesing's* (1982), 31532.

[192] Agreement between the European Economic Community and the Argentine Republic on trade in textiles, OJ 1979 L 298/2 (26 Nov. 1979); Arrangement in the form of an exchange of letters between the European Economic Community and the Argentine Republic on trade in mutton and lamb, OJ 1980 L 275/14 (18 Oct. 1980).

[193] Ibid.

Article XXI GATT did not apply to these sectoral agreements.[194] In short, the general import embargo also violated rights owed to Argentina under these agreements.

On 8 April 1982, in response to 'the act of aggression that has been committed by the Argentine armed forces in clear violation of Article 2, paragraph 3 and paragraph 4, of the Charter of the United Nations', Australia likewise announced the adoption of a general import embargo on Argentinean goods in *prima facie* violation of Article XI GATT.[195] Australia added that Argentina was responsible for 'an action which cares nothing for the principle of self-determination'.[196] On 28 April 1982, Canada announced that, in response to 'the [Argentinean] use of force . . . in fundamental violation of the Charter of the United Nations', it had also (in *prima facie* violation of Article XI GATT) adopted a general import embargo on Argentinean goods.[197] Canada explained that the trade embargo was prompted by Argentina's continuing wrongful conduct, i.e. its failure to immediately withdraw all troops from the Falkland Islands as required by the Security Council. As Canada observed:

> This has not taken place. Canada has thus been compelled to impose certain economic sanctions against that country. We did this with great regret, because Canada greatly values its friendly relations with Argentina. More important, however, we believe that respect for the rule of law throughout the world, as embodied in the Charter, is fundamental in today's society and must take precedence.[198]

Following a request from the United Kingdom, New Zealand adopted a general trade embargo and suspended application of its air services agreement with Argentina in response to 'a clear [Argentinean] violation of the principles of the Charter'.[199] The Charter principles invoked concerned non-use of force and self-determination of peoples.[200] New Zealand's actions *prima facie* violated rights owed to Argentina under the GATT and the air services agreement. In a similar vein, in response to

---

[194] See Kuyper (1982), 154–156; Sicilianos (1990), 163–164; Tams (2005), 216. Also: ARSIWA Commentary, Art. 54, §3.
[195] 10 AYIL (1983), 573; UN Doc. S/PV.2349 (2 Apr. 1982), 2, para. 22 (Australia).
[196] 10 AYIL (1983), 572.
[197] de Mestral (1983), 337. An arms embargo against Argentina was also announced (ibid.). See also UN Docs. S/PV.2349 (2 Apr. 1982), 3, paras. 26–30 (Canada); S/PV.2362 (22 May 1982), 19, para. 209 (Canada).
[198] UN Doc. S/PV.2362 (22 May 1982), 19, para. 212 (Canada).
[199] *Keesing's* (1982), 31533; UN Doc. S/PV.2349 (2 Apr. 1982), 3, para. 33 (New Zealand).
[200] UN Doc. S/PV.2363 (23 May 1982), 7, paras. 55–57 (New Zealand).

conduct which ' ... violated ... the prohibition of the use of force in international relations',[201] the Federal Republic of Germany suspended its air services agreement with Argentina in *prima facie* violation of the agreement.[202] On 30 April 1982, the United States, in response to 'the use of unlawful force', adopted several measures of retorsion against Argentina.[203]

On 28 April 1982, OAS Foreign Ministers adopted a resolution by which it was resolved:

> To deplore the adoption by members of the European Economic Community and other states of coercive measures of an economic and political nature, which are prejudicial to the Argentine nation and to urge them to lift those measures, indicating that they constitute a serious precedent, inasmuch as they are not covered by Resolution 502 (1982) of the United Nations Security Council and are incompatible with the Charters of the United Nations and of the OAS and the General Agreement on Tariffs and Trade (GATT).[204]

A 'serious precedent' had apparently been established.[205] The Security Council was deemed to have exclusive authority under the UN Charter to decide on the adoption of coercive measures against Argentina. The OAS resolution was urgently brought to the attention of the Security Council for consideration.[206] For its part, the United Kingdom

> ... reject[ed] as unfounded the assertion that the adoption of legitimate counter-measures in the political and economic fields is in some unspecified way incompatible with the Charters of the United Nations and the Organization of American States and with the General Agreement on Tariffs and Trade.[207]

On 21 May 1982, an urgent meeting of the Security Council was convened to discuss a new resolution concerning the deteriorating

---

[201] UN Doc. S/PV.2368 (26 May 1982), 2, para. 11 (Federal Republic of Germany).

[202] Lindemann (1984), 557–558.

[203] 82 Dept. of State Bulletin (June 1982), 87–88. See also UN Doc. S/15028 (3 May 1982) for Argentina's protest. For a survey and assessment of US measures of retorsion, see 21 ILM (1982), 682–685; Azevedo (1984), 323.

[204] OAS Res. I 'Serious Situation in the South Atlantic', op. para. 6, annexed to UN Doc. S/15008 (28 Apr. 1982). See further UNYB (1982), 1324. The Member States of SELA also condemned the action against Argentina in similar terms: see UN Doc. S/15159 (4 June 1982); UNYB (1982), 1337.

[205] OAS Res. I 'Serious Situation in the South Atlantic', op. para. 6, annexed to UN Doc. S/15008 (28 Apr. 1982).

[206] Ibid., op. para. 8.   [207] UN Doc. S/15010 (29 Apr. 1982) (United Kingdom).

situation in the South Atlantic.[208] One of the issues discussed during the subsequent debate in the Security Council related to the unilateral coercive measures taken by western countries against Argentina and their legality under the UN Charter.

Several (mostly OAS) countries emphatically stated that the Security Council had a monopoly to decide on sanctions. For example, Mexico stated:

> [T]here is no legal basis for a Member of the United Nations unilaterally to arrogate to itself the right to implement a Security Council resolution without having received a specific mandate to that end from the Council itself . . .[209]

Poland denounced the 'legally unfounded and morally suspect policy of sanctions applied outside the system prescribed in the Charter of the United Nations'.[210] The Soviet Union stated:

> The economic sanctions imposed on 10 April against Argentina by the Western European countries are, among other things, in direct contradiction with the provisions of the Charter of the United Nations, in particular, Article 41, which provides that it is precisely the Security Council which may decide what measures not involving the use of armed force, and possibly including complete or partial interruption of economic relations, should be employed to give effect to its decisions.
>
> The imposition of economic sanctions against Argentina by the United States and the ten member States of the European Community demonstrates that the Governments of those countries, in violation of the requirements of the Charter, have undertaken unilateral acts without any authorization from the Council.[211]

In a similar vein, Panama stated:

> The European Economic Community has also obviously committed a flagrant violation of Articles 39 and 41 of the Charter of the United Nations by adopting sanctions or enforcement measures of an economic character against Argentina, since the Security Council, and the Security Council alone, is the only body competent to impose economic sanctions of this nature.[212]

---

[208] UN Doc. S/15044 (4 May 1982).

[209] UN Doc. S/PV.2362 (22 May 1982), 10, para. 120 (Mexico).

[210] UN Doc. S/PV.2363 (23 May 1982), 2, para. 15 (Poland).

[211] UN Doc. S/PV.2362 (22 May 1982), 9, paras. 101–102 (Soviet Union). To similar effect: UN Doc. S/PV.2371 (2 June 1982), 11, para. 111 (Soviet Union).

[212] UN Doc. S/14978 (14 Apr. 1982), 4 (Panama). See also UN Doc. S/PV.2362 (22 May 1982), 17, para. 190 (Panama).

Cuba added:

> The economic sanctions imposed–also unilaterally–against Argentina by the members of the European Community constitute a serious precedent. They are not provided for in the Charter and thus lack any vestige of legality.[213]

Argentina, Brazil, El Salvador and Venezuela made statements to similar effect.[214] Several other Latin American States denounced the trade embargo as 'a serious threat to international peace and security' which could only serve to aggravate the conflict.[215] A number of Eastern European States also protested against the illegality of the action, notably on the basis that it violated Chapter VII UNC.[216]

Belgium (in a statement on behalf of EC Member States) strongly disagreed:

> In many statements we have heard attacks on the economic sanctions decided upon by the members of the European Community. An entirely new idea, it seems, was even invoked whereby this decision was said to be a violation of Article 41 of the Charter, which it was claimed would give the Security Council a monopoly on deciding on sanctions. In joining in these sanctions, Belgium intended, like its partners, to give specific form to the grave view it takes of violations of the Charter, which have been condemned by a resolution of the Council, on the one hand, and above all to support the diplomatic efforts under way to find a negotiated solution, on the other hand.[217]

Article 41 UNC was evidently not considered to give the Security Council a 'monopoly on deciding on sanctions'.[218] The Federal Republic

---

[213] UN Doc. S/PV.2362 (22 May 1982), 13, para. 150 (Cuba).

[214] UN Docs. S/14968 (12 Apr. 1982), 1 (Argentina); S/PV.2360 (21 May 1982), 18, para. 190 (Brazil); S/PV.2362 (22 May 1982), 6–7, paras. 62, 75 (Venezuela); S/PV.2363 (23 May 1982), 11, para. 118 (El Salvador). For a similar conclusion see Azevedo (1984), 343.

[215] UN Doc. S/PV.2366 (25 May 1982), 10, para. 100 (joint declaration by Argentina, Nicaragua, Panama and Venezuela). See also UN Docs. S/14978 (14 Apr. 1982), 6 (Panama); S/PV.2363 (23 May 1982), 6, para. 46 (Nicaragua); GATT Docs. L/5317 (30 Apr. 1982), 2 (Argentina); L/5414 (12 Nov. 1982), 18 (Peru).

[216] UN Docs. A/37/PV.52 (3 Nov. 1982), 897, para. 148 (German Democratic Republic); A/37/PV.53 (3 Nov. 1982), 908, para. 100 (Bulgaria), 916, paras. 188–190 (Albania), 918, paras. 207–208 (Byelorussian Soviet Socialist Republic); A/37/PV.54 (4 Nov. 1982), 927, para. 31 (Czechoslovakia).

[217] UN Doc. S/PV.2363 (23 May 1982), 12, paras. 131–132 (Belgium on behalf of EC Member States).

[218] Ibid. Belgium also noted that the action taken against Argentina, including unilateral coercive measures, was not 'disproportionate to what was at stake'; namely, to induce Argentina to cease its unlawful use of force (ibid., paras. 128–129).

of Germany fully endorsed the above statement.[219] The debate in the Security Council culminated in the adoption of a resolution which requested the good offices of the UN Secretary General with a view to negotiating an end to the conflict; no position was taken on the trade embargo.[220] In parallel, the legality of the trade embargo was debated within the institutional context of the GATT.

On 29 April 1982, Argentina lodged a complaint before the GATT Council of Representatives (the GATT's main institutional organ) concerning the trade embargo adopted against it.[221] Aside from identifying several individual GATT violations for which the embargoing States were deemed to bear several responsibility, Argentina stressed that only the Security Council could decide on sanctions. Thus Argentina denounced the unilateral trade restrictions adopted against it (which it claimed had resulted in lost annual export revenue in excess of USD 2 billion) as unlawful on that basis:

> In the matter under reference, the Security Council has limited itself to recognizing that there was a breach of the peace in the region of the Islands and to making certain requests to the countries involved, but it has not requested nor authorized, explicitly or implicitly, and accordingly did not consider appropriate, any action on the part of third parties, as would be the case for economic measures of international coercion, nor have any such measures been requested in that forum by any country.
>
> The measures adopted inconsiderately by the countries of the EEC other than the United Kingdom, and by Australia and Canada are entirely without justification, whether within or outside the context of the GATT rules, and coming from countries with which the Argentine Republic has maintained relations free of all dispute they constitute a hostile act and a flagrant economic aggression, affecting the basic principles of international law.[222]

Argentina later explained that

> ... sanctions could only be adopted expressly in conformity with Article 41 of the Charter of the United Nations, and that no country or group of countries could, by itself, invoke decisions of the Security Council and adopt measures in breach of the United Nations Charter itself.[223]

---

[219] UN Doc. S/PV.2368 (26 May 1982), 2, para. 14 (Federal Republic of Germany).
[220] SC Res. 505 (26 May 1982).
[221] GATT Doc. L/5317 (29 Apr. 1982), www.wto.org/gatt_docs/English/SULPDF/90990459.pdf.
[222] Ibid., 2.
[223] GATT Doc. C/M/157 (7 May 1982), 3, www.wto.org/gatt_docs/English/SULPDF/90440042.pdf.

Argentina also denounced the action taken against it as abusive:

> [T]he measures were based on reasons of a political nature and were meant to exert political pressure on the sovereign decisions of Argentina in order to intervene in a conflict in which only one of the countries concerned was involved. The other contracting parties which had intervened in this case were foreign to the conflict, but nevertheless were applying financial, economic and trade measures against Argentina ... [I]t was much easier for a group of developed countries to impose measures against a developing country which did not have any power of retaliation. This [was] a new type of colonialism.[224]

Brazil similarly observed:

> While the motives for the trade sanctions against Argentina were clear, the justification was not; and this type of action set a dangerous precedent. The trade sanctions had no basis in either the Charter of the United Nations, the General Agreement or in Resolution 502 of the Security Council.[225]

On 4 May 1982, EC Member States, Australia and Canada acknowledged in a joint statement that the trade embargo affected Argentinean rights under the GATT, but insisted that it was nevertheless exceptionally justified 'on the basis of their inherent rights of which Article XXI of the General Agreement is a reflection'.[226] EC Member States later explained:

> The exercise of these rights constituted a general exception, and required neither notification, justification, nor approval, a procedure confirmed by thirty-five years of implementation of the General Agreement ... [I]n effect, this procedure showed that every contracting party was – in the last resort – the judge of its exercise of these rights.[227]

For its part, Australia stated:

> The Australian measures were in conformity with the provisions of Article XXI:(c) [GATT], which did not require notification or justification. Quoting from Article I of the UN Charter, [Australia] said that one of [its] obligations was to carry out the purposes for which the United Nations was created.[228]

Canada added that its 'actions were consistent with Canada's international obligations, including those under the General Agreement ...

---

[224] Ibid., 2. See also GATT Doc. L/5414 (12 Nov. 1982), 17, www.wto.org/gatt_docs/English/SULPDF/91000182.pdf.

[225] GATT Doc. L/5414 (12 Nov. 1982), 5.

[226] GATT Doc. 5319/Rev.1 (4 May 1982), www.wto.org/gatt_docs/English/SULPDF/90990462.pdf. For an analysis, see further Hahn (1996), 328–334.

[227] GATT Doc. C/M/157 (7 May 1982), 10. Contra: ibid., 2 (Argentina).   [228] Ibid., 11.

Canada's sovereign action was to be seen as a political response to a political issue'.[229] Finally, New Zealand explained that it 'had an inherent right to take such action as a sovereign State and that, in [its] view, these actions were in conformity with New Zealand's rights and obligations under the General Agreement'.[230]

The reference above to 'inherent rights', 'sovereignty' and 'general exception' suggests that EC Member States, Australia, Canada and New Zealand considered the adoption of unilateral trade restrictions on grounds of essential security interests, as codified in Article XXI GATT, permissible as an inherent right of States under general international law.[231] This conclusion is reinforced by the sectoral agreements on trade in textiles and trade in mutton and lamb discussed above for which Article XXI GATT did not apply; the suspension of these agreements could only be justified on the basis of general international law. This leaves the specific justification under general international law upon which the embargoing States actually relied to be determined.

A combined reading of Article XXI(c) GATT and Article 1 UNC (and presumably by implication, Article 2(5) UNC) suggests that Australia (rather unpersuasively) relied on an implied authorization to enforce the relevant Security Council resolutions on the Falklands Islands, *inter alia*, demanding an immediate withdrawal of Argentinean forces from the islands. As for EC Member States, Canada and New Zealand, they could potentially justify their action on the basis of the right of collective self-defence embodied in Article 51 UNC. After all, given that the Security Council had qualified Argentina's action as an illegal use of force, the United Kingdom was fully justified to invoke its right of self-defence and as such was entitled to request assistance (whether forcible or non-forcible) from other States. The conditions for such invocation certainly appear to have been met in this case:[232] the United Kingdom, the directly injured State, declared itself the victim of an armed attack and requested assistance from other States to restore international legality. EC Member States even reported the adoption of the trade embargo to the Security

---

[229] Ibid., 10.   [230] Ibid., 9.

[231] For a similar conclusion see Kuyper (1982), 152; Dewost (1982); Tams (2005), 215–216. For the view that the trade embargo could not be justified as a treaty-based exception under Article XXI GATT, see de Guttry (1985), 133–134; Sicilianos (1990), 163 (n. 342). See also the critical statements by Brazil and Spain during the GATT Council debate, GATT Doc. C/M/157 (7 May 1982), 5–6.

[232] *Nicaragua* case, ICJ Rep. (1986), 14 at 105, paras. 199–200; *Oil Platforms*, ICJ Rep. (2003), 161 at 186–187, para. 51.

Council.[233] Some commentators have on that basis suggested that the trade embargo should be understood as an act of collective self-defence under Article 51 UNC.[234]

Still, it is striking that the above statements make no explicit reference to the all-important principle of collective self-defence embodied in Article 51 UNC. If reliance were placed on Article 51 UNC, EC Member States, Canada and New Zealand did not say so openly and unequivocally. Rather, as a minimum, the explicit invocation of a 'general exception' seems to indicate that collective self-defence could not have been the only possible justification relied upon.[235] It seems significant in this context that the United Kingdom characterized the trade embargoes – adopted by third States upon its request – by reference to the notion of 'legitimate countermeasures'.[236] It is suggested that the statements by Belgium (on behalf of EC Member States) and the Federal Republic of Germany before the Security Council should be understood in the same vein.[237]

This conclusion is further reinforced by the debate in the Security Council, which revealed a concern more with the legality of non-forcible unilateral coercive measures than the proper exercise of the right of collective self-defence. The resolution adopted by the OAS points in the same direction. Thus at least the trade embargoes adopted by EC Member States, Canada and New Zealand may be understood as examples of third-party countermeasures in response to violations of the principles of non-use of force and self-determination. While the matter may not be 'undisputed'[238], it appears that the same can be said for the action taken by the Federal Republic of Germany and New Zealand to suspend their respective air services agreements with Argentina.[239]

4.2.9   Western Countries – Soviet Union (1983)

On 1 September 1983, a Soviet fighter jet shot down a Korean Air Lines passenger plane en route from New York to Seoul after it had

---

[233] UN Doc. S/14976 (14 Apr. 1982).
[234] Kuyper (1982), 159–162; Fischer and Hafner (1982), 389–392; Zoller (1984a), 104–105; Weschke (2001), 105.
[235] Tams (2005), 216.   [236] See above n. 207.   [237] See above nn. 217, 219.
[238] Tams (2005), 215.
[239] For a similar conclusion see Tams (2005), 216. Also: Tzanakopoulos (2015), 151. See already David (1984–1985), 164–165 (seemingly qualifying the EC trade embargo on textiles and mutton and lamb as a third-party countermeasure).

inadvertently strayed into Soviet air space off Sakhalin Island. The incident caused the death of all 269 passengers and crew.[240] The United States and South Korea immediately called for an urgent meeting of the UN Security Council in order to condemn 'the unprovoked resort to the use of force by the Soviet military authorities in contravention of international civil aviation organization standards and the basic norms of international law'.[241] The Security Council convened urgently to consider the matter.

During the debate in the Security Council, the United States, *inter alia*, denounced a Soviet violation of the prohibition of the use of force embodied in the UN Charter.[242] Portugal likewise emphasized: 'No argument relating to the security of States can be invoked as a pretext for the use of force in conditions which jeopardize the recognized principles of *jus cogens* and accepted norms of the international community'.[243] Other States made observations to similar effect.[244] Still, most States focused their condemnations on the breach of international law for which the Soviet Union was widely deemed responsible under the 1944 Chicago Convention on International Civil Aviation.[245] Australia identified the following breach:

> Standard procedures governing the situation where a civil aircraft may have strayed into another country's airspace are laid down in the 1944 Chicago Convention on International Civil Aviation to which both the Soviet Union and the Republic of Korea are parties. Annex 2 to that Convention, which covers the rules of the air, lays down in attachment A specific procedures to be followed in the event of interception, which itself is to be used only as a last resort.
>
> It is abundantly clear that the Soviet fighter aircraft involved failed to follow the procedures laid down by that Convention and instead chose to exercise a singularly brutal option.[246]

---

[240] UNYB (1983), 218–223; Rousseau (1984), 435–448. For a legal assessment see Dutheil de la Rochère (1983), 749; Jahn (1984), 444; Lakehal (1984–1985), 171.

[241] UN Docs. S/15947 (1 Sept. 1983) (United States); S/15948 (1 Sept. 1983) (Republic of Korea). Canada, Japan and Australia made similar calls: see UNYB (1983), 218.

[242] UN Doc. S/PV.2470 (2 Sept. 1983), 5, para. 39 (United States).

[243] UN Doc. S/PV.2476 (12 Sept. 1983), 2, para. 16 (Portugal).

[244] See e.g. UN Docs. S/PV.2470 (2 Sept. 1983), 10, para. 110 (Netherlands); S/PV.2471 (6 Sept. 1983), 10, para. 78 (Sweden).

[245] 15 UNTS 295 (entry into force 4 Apr. 1947).

[246] UN Doc. S/PV.2470 (2 Sept. 1983), 9, paras. 96–97 (Australia). Specifically, Australia (at ibid.) referred to International Civil Aviation Organization, Rules of the Air, Annex 2 to the 1944 Chicago Convention on International Civil Aviation, Attachment A, para. 2.1, in force at the time of the incident: see 22 ILM (1983), 1154.

These standard interception procedures were binding on the Soviet Union under Articles 37, 54(1) and 90 of the Chicago Convention. As the United States explained:

> Those internationally agreed upon standards call for serious efforts at identification, verification and warning and–if the case is serious–for intercepting the intruder and forcing it to land or to leave one's airspace. Sovereignty [as defined in Article 1 of the Chicago Convention] neither requires nor permits shooting down airliners in peacetime.[247]

In more general terms, the United Kingdom explained that '[t]he action of the Government of the USSR in shooting down an unarmed civilian aircraft . . . was contrary to a fundamental object and purpose of the Chicago Convention . . . which is to ensure the safety of civil aircraft in international flights'.[248] Most members of the Security Council condemned the same breach of the Chicago Convention in terms such as 'flagrant', 'gross', 'serious' or 'massive'.[249] Italy, by reference to the relevant 'international regulations and standards' under the Chicago Convention, observed that 'the issue before us today is not an event affecting a limited number of States but one that bears upon basic principles and needs shared by the whole international community'.[250] The Dominican Republic explained simply that 'this incident affects not only the parties directly involved but also the entire international community'.[251] Similarly, Ireland stated that the incident 'raises issues that have implications for all nations involved in international civil aviation and for the conduct of international relations generally'.[252] This suggests that, alongside a violation of the prohibition on the use of force under general international law, States also considered the Soviet

---

[247] UN Doc. S/PV.2471 (6 Sept. 1983), 5, para. 16 (United States).
[248] Marston (1983), 534.
[249] See UN Docs. S/15949 (1 Sept. 1983) (Canada); S/PV.2470 (2 Sept. 1983), 10, paras. 109–110 (Netherlands), 11–12, para. 124 (France), 14, paras. 155–156 (Federal Republic of Germany); S/PV.2471 (6 Sept. 1983), 8, para. 49 (Japan), 10, para. 70 (Liberia), 10–11, paras. 78–81 (Sweden); S/PV.2472 (6 Sept. 1983), 3, paras. 6–8 (Belgium), 4, paras. 17–18 (Togo), 4, paras. 26–27 (Italy), 8, para. 75 (Bangladesh); S/PV.2473 (7 Sept. 1983), 2, para. 9 (Singapore), 7, paras. 68–69 (Ecuador), 11, para. 139 (Kenya); S/PV.2474 (8 Sept. 1983), 3, para. 24 (Paraguay), 5, paras. 45–46 (Republic of Korea); S/PV.2476 (12 Sept. 1983), 2, para. 14 (Portugal), 9, para. 97 (China), 10, para. 101 (Jordan). Only Bulgaria, the German Democratic Republic, Poland and the Soviet Union denied that any responsibility was engaged: see UNYB (1983), 218–223.
[250] UN Doc. S/PV.2472 (6 Sept. 1983), 4, paras. 25–26 (Italy).
[251] UN Doc. S/PV.2473 (7 Sept. 1983), 11, para. 127 (Dominican Republic).
[252] Ibid., 10, para. 115 (Ireland).

Union responsible for a breach of an obligation *erga omnes partes* owed to them under the widely ratified Chicago Convention.

On 12 September 1983, a draft Security Council resolution was introduced, which in relevant part

> Reaffirm[ed] the rules of international law that prohibit acts of violence which pose a threat to the safety of international civil aviation; [and]
>
> Recogniz[ed] the importance of territorial integrity as well as the necessity that only internationally agreed procedures should be used in response to intrusions into the airspace of a State, [and]
>
> Declare[d] that such use of armed force against international civil aviation is incompatible with the norms governing international behaviour and elementary considerations of humanity.[253]

But the draft resolution was ultimately vetoed by the Soviet Union.[254]

On 16 September 1983, the ICAO Council met in emergency session and adopted a resolution condemning the Soviet Union for its wrongful conduct. Specifically, the ICAO resolution

> Recogniz[ed] that such use of armed force against international civil aviation is incompatible with the norms governing international behaviour and elementary considerations of humanity and with the rules, Standards and Recommended Practices enshrined in the Chicago Convention and its Annexes and invokes generally recognized legal consequences.[255]

The response against the Soviet Union went beyond mere verbal condemnations.[256] On 6 September 1983, the International Federation of Airline Pilots, a professional association of airline pilots, called for a ban on all flights to Moscow for an initial period of sixty days. The national pilot associations of Denmark, Finland, France, the Federal Republic of Germany, Italy, Japan, the Netherlands, Norway, Spain, Sweden, Switzerland and the United Kingdom carried out a ban

---

[253] UN Doc. S/15966/Rev.1 (12 Sept. 1983).

[254] See generally *Keesing's* (1983), 32513–32517; Rousseau (1984), 435–446.

[255] 22 ILM (1983), 1150–1151. Only Czechoslovakia and the Soviet Union voted against the resolution (ibid.). See also to the same effect: 23 ILM (1984), 837. Ultimately, following a French proposal (UN Doc. S/PV.2476 (12 Sept. 1983), 9, para. 94), a protocol relating to the amendment of the Chicago Convention was adopted Article 3 *bis* of which explicitly prohibited the use of force against civil aircraft in flight subject to the relevant rights and obligations of States embodied in the UN Charter (see 2122 UNTS 346, entry into force 1 Oct. 1998). Further: Nash (1984), 244–245.

[256] *Keesing's* (1983), 32513–32517; Rousseau (1984), 445–447; Lakehal (1984–1985), 171; Hufbauer, Schott and Elliott (1985), 563–567.

with effect from 12 September 1983 for about three weeks.[257] More significantly, on 7 September 1983, at a meeting of NATO Foreign Ministers in Madrid, NATO Member States agreed on the need for concerted action against the Soviet Union; notably, the immediate suspension of air services agreements with the Soviet Union.[258] By 17 September 1983, with the exception of France, Greece and Turkey, all NATO Member States had temporarily suspended civil aviation between their respective countries and the Soviet Union. Japan and Switzerland had also taken similar measures.[259] For its part, France explained that such a measure would not be permissible under its air services agreement with the Soviet Union.[260]

At least in the cases of Canada, Denmark, the Federal Republic of Germany, Japan, the Netherlands, Norway, Spain, Switzerland, the United Kingdom and the United States this conduct *prima facie* violated their respective air services agreements with the Soviet Union and could not be justified under the terms of the respective agreements.[261] Canada, Japan, the United Kingdom and the United States were all directly injured and thus adopted bilateral countermeasures. In the cases of Denmark, the Federal Republic of Germany, the Netherlands, Norway, Spain and Switzerland no bilateral injury was involved. The *prima facie* unlawful suspension of their respective air services agreements with the Soviet Union may therefore be understood as third-party countermeasures.[262] Several of the (third-party) countermeasures discussed above were adopted at the same time as the Security Council was actively considering the adoption of a resolution condemning the Soviet Union for its wrongful conduct. France appears to have been the

---

[257] 22 ILM (1983), 1218–1219. See also *Keesing's* (1983), 32516–32517; Rousseau (1984), 445–447.

[258] 83 Dept. of State Bulletin (Nov. 1983), 67.

[259] Ibid., 45. See also Dutheil de la Rochère (1983), 765; Rousseau (1984), 446; Hufbauer, Schott and Elliott (1985), 739, 741.

[260] 1578 UNTS 323; Rousseau (1984), 446. See also Lakehal (1984–1985), 175–176.

[261] 835 UNTS 54 (Canada); 259 UNTS 169 (Denmark); 972 UNTS 115 (Federal Republic of Germany); 12 Japanese Annual of Int'l Law (1968), 268 (Japan); 335 UNTS 99 (Netherlands); 259 UNTS 205 (Norway); 1063 UNTS 185 (Spain); Amtliche Sammlung (1968), 1068 (Switzerland); 351 UNTS 235 (United Kingdom); 675 UNTS 3 (United States). See further e.g. the statement by the United Kingdom, Marston (1983), 533–534; and for the statements by Canada, Japan and the United States, see 22 ILM (1983), 1200, 1202, 1206–1207.

[262] See e.g. Raub and Malanczuk (1985), 735 (for the German response); Rousseau (1984), 446; Linsi (1994), 232–235 (for the Swiss response). For a similar conclusion see Frowein (1994), 420; Tams (2005), 215.

only NATO Member State opposed to a civil aviation boycott while the Security Council and ICAO were seized of the matter.[263]

4.2.10   Western Countries – South Africa (1985–1986)

On 2 November 1983, a so-called 'new constitution' which further entrenched the apartheid system in South Africa was endorsed by the white minority in the country. The UN General Assembly swiftly condemned South Africa for these 'constitutional' reforms.[264] On 17 August 1984, the Security Council declared the 'new constitution' null and void and two months later characterized the apartheid system as a 'crime against humanity'.[265] Still, the South African government led by President Botha continued to brutally enforce the 'constitutional' reforms. Demonstrations, strikes and riots followed. The Botha regime responded with increasing repression, including wanton killings and arbitrary mass arrests and detentions without trial of opponents of the apartheid regime. The situation deteriorated further following the wanton killing of demonstrators protesting against the forcible removal of thousands of people at Crossroads. On 21 July 1985, the Botha regime declared a state of emergency in parts of the country to deal with the unrest – the first such draconian measure since the aftermath of the Sharpeville massacre in 1960.[266]

On 23 July 1985, EC Member States condemned the Botha regime for its latest acts of brutal repression and urged it to abolish apartheid and ensure respect for the legitimate civil and political rights of the black majority population in South Africa.[267] On 24 July 1985, France (and later Mali on behalf of African States) called for an immediate meeting of the Security Council to consider the deteriorating situation in South Africa.[268] France decried South Africa's 'flagrant violation of fundamental human rights'.[269] The following day, Denmark and France co-sponsored a draft Security Council resolution under Chapter VI UNC

---

[263] Lakehal (1984–1985), 180 (his n. 39) citing *Le Monde*, 9 Sept. 1983 (suppl.).

[264] GA Res. 38/11 (16 Nov. 1983); GA Res. 39/2 (28 Sept. 1984).

[265] SC Res. 554 (17 Aug. 1984); SC Res. 556 (23 Oct. 1984). See also SC Res. 560 (12 March 1985). The General Assembly had already qualified apartheid as a crime against humanity in 1966: see above Section 4.2.1 (n. 14).

[266] UNYB (1985), 128.

[267] UN Doc. S/17362 (26 July 1985) (Luxembourg on behalf of EC Member States).

[268] UN Docs. S/17351 (24 July 1985) (France); S/17356 (25 July 1985) (Mali on behalf of African States).

[269] UN Doc. S/PV.2602 (25 July 1985), 2, para. 20 (France).

which, *inter alia*, denounced the killings, mass arrests and forcible removals, strongly condemned the apartheid system in all its manifestations and called for its abolition, and urged UN Member States to adopt several measures of retorsion against South Africa, notably by way of sectoral economic boycotts and the suspension of cultural and sports relations.[270]

On 26 July 1985, a revised draft resolution followed which 'commended' those States which had already adopted unilateral coercive measures against South Africa and invited those which had not yet done so to follow suit.[271] A proposed amendment to the revised draft resolution, which threatened South Africa with enforcement measures under Chapter VII UNC in case it failed to abolish apartheid, was vetoed by the United Kingdom and the United States.[272] The revised draft resolution, absent the amendment, was nevertheless adopted by the Security Council.[273] On 4 November 1977, the Security Council had already imposed a mandatory arms embargo against South Africa under Chapter VII UNC.[274]

On 10 September 1985, upon the recommendation made earlier by the Security Council, EC Member States (as well as Spain and Portugal) adopted several measures of retorsion against South Africa.[275] On 16 September 1986, the EC sanctions regime was broadened to include a ban on the importation of iron, steel and gold coins from South Africa.[276] Aside from the latter, these unilateral coercive measures were not explicitly envisaged by the non-binding recommendation of the Security Council and could, in any event, only be justified on the basis of general international law.[277] The action taken was principally intended to ensure the total abolishment of apartheid.[278]

The deteriorating situation in South Africa was also considered at the 1985 Commonwealth Heads of Government Meeting in Nassau.

---

[270] UN Doc. S/17354 (25 July 1985) (Denmark and France). For the debate on the draft resolution see UN Docs. S/PV.2600–2602 (25–26 July 1985).

[271] UN Doc. S/17354/Rev.1 (26 July 1985) (Denmark and France).

[272] UN Doc. S/17363 (26 July 1985) (Burkina Faso et al.); Report of the Security Council (1985–1986), UN Doc. A/41/2, 55–56.

[273] SC Res. 569 (26 July 1985). The United Kingdom and the United States abstained from voting.

[274] SC Res. 418 (4 Nov. 1977); as reinforced by SC Res. 558 (13 Dec. 1984). See also SC Res. 591 (28 Nov. 1986).

[275] EC Bull. No. 9 (1985), para. 2.5.1. See also 24 ILM (1985), 1474–1482.

[276] EC Bull. No. 9 (1986), para. 2.4.2.   [277] See Frowein and Krisch (2002), 728 MN 31.

[278] EC Bull. No. 6 (1986), para. 1.1.18.

On 20 October 1985, Commonwealth Member States adopted the Nassau Accord, which provided for the adoption of several measures of retorsion which 'have as their rationale impressing on the authorities in Pretoria the compelling urgency of dismantling apartheid and erecting the structures of democracy in South Africa'.[279] Moreover, the Nassau Accord provided that, in the absence of adequate progress by South Africa in terms of the dismantling of its apartheid policy within a period of six months, some Commonwealth Member States would consider taking further action involving, *inter alia*, an aviation embargo and an import embargo on agricultural products.[280]

On 5 August 1986, Australia, the Bahamas, Canada, India, the United Kingdom, Zambia and Zimbabwe convened for the Commonwealth Heads of Government Review Meeting in London and (albeit with the disapproval of the United Kingdom) adopted a communiqué by which they agreed to adopt the unilateral coercive measures envisaged in the Nassau Accord in response to South Africa's continuing illegal policy of apartheid. In addition, they agreed to adopt further unilateral coercive measures against South Africa, including an import embargo on uranium, coal, iron and steel. They encouraged all States to take similar action.[281] This suggests that these six States considered resort to conduct that would otherwise be *prima facie* unlawful as permissible in exceptionally serious circumstances.

On 21 August 1986, Australia adopted, *inter alia*, an import embargo on agricultural products from South Africa.[282] On the same day, Australia also suspended the 1970 Australia-South Africa Agreement Relating to Air Services.[283] This action amounted to a breach of Article 12 of the 1970 Agreement, which provided for suspension upon twelve

---

[279] 'The Commonwealth Accord on Southern Africa – Nassau Accord' (Nassau, 20 Oct. 1985), The Commonwealth at the Summit: Communiqués of Commonwealth Heads of Government Meetings 1944–1986, Commonwealth Secretariat, London (1987), 267. For a discussion see Rousseau (1986), 176, 948–949.

[280] 'The Commonwealth Accord on Southern Africa – Nassau Accord' (Nassau, 20 Oct. 1985), The Commonwealth at the Summit: Communiqués of Commonwealth Heads of Government Meetings 1944–1986, Commonwealth Secretariat, London (1987), 269. See also Rousseau (1986), 948–949.

[281] 'Communiqué of the Commonwealth Heads of Government Review Meeting' (London, 5 Aug. 1986), The Commonwealth at the Summit: Communiqués of Commonwealth Heads of Government Meetings 1944–1986, Commonwealth Secretariat, London (1987), 291. See also Rousseau (1986), 947–949.

[282] Rousseau (1986), 949.

[283] 796 UNTS 155 (entry into force 2 Apr. 1970); Rousseau (1986), 949.

months' prior notice.[284] In the absence of any treaty-based justification, this action may be understood as a third-party countermeasure.[285]

As further examples, on 15 June 1986, Denmark had already adopted a comprehensive trade embargo against South Africa and did not appear to justify its action on the basis of any of the exceptions in Articles XIX–XXI GATT.[286] On 9 July 1986, Norway had similarly introduced a limited import embargo on certain South African agricultural products.[287] On 18 August 1986, New Zealand also decided to adopt an import embargo on South African agricultural products as well as on uranium, coal, steel and iron, affecting rights owed to South Africa under the GATT. In August 1986, Canada likewise adopted an import embargo on agricultural products from South Africa thereby withholding rights owed to South Africa under the GATT.[288]

The most comprehensive action against South Africa was taken by the United States. On 2 October 1986, the United States Congress, by overwhelming majority, overrode a presidential veto and adopted the Comprehensive Anti-Apartheid Act of 1986.[289] The Anti-Apartheid Act stated:

> The purpose of this Act is to set forth a comprehensive and complete framework to guide the efforts of the United States in helping to bring an end to apartheid in South Africa and lead to the establishment of a nonracial, democratic form of government.[290]

It further explained that US policy was designed, *inter alia*, to 'encourage' South Africa – through the imposition of a broad range of economic, political and diplomatic measures – to 'end military and paramilitary activities aimed at neighbouring states' in violation of the prohibition against the use of force in international law.[291]

In order for the United States to achieve these aims, many of the numerous unilateral coercive measures envisaged in the Anti-Apartheid

---

[284] See Sicilianos (1990), 166.
[285] Compare Sicilianos (1990), 166; Tams (2005), 218 (n. 99); Katselli Proukaki (2010), 176. In July 1985, Canada had already imposed an aviation embargo against South Africa but, in the absence of any specific treaty obligations, this amounted to a mere act of retorsion: see the statement of the Canadian Secretary of State for External Affairs, Mr. Clark, 24 ILM (1985), 1470–1471.
[286] Rousseau (1986), 950.
[287] Ibid., 951. Denmark, Norway and South Africa were all parties to the GATT in 1986.
[288] Rousseau (1986), 949. The examples provided above are merely illustrative. For a survey of further potentially relevant examples see Tomaševski (2000), 51–53.
[289] 26 ILM (1987), 79.   [290] Ibid., 81.   [291] Ibid.

Act went beyond those recommended earlier by the Security Council, and included, *inter alia, prima facie* unlawful import embargoes on textiles and certain raw materials and agricultural products from South Africa.[292] On 27 October 1986, President Reagan (albeit reluctantly) instructed the US government to implement the Anti-Apartheid Act.[293]

The Anti-Apartheid Act notably provided for the suspension of landing rights under the 1947 United States-South Africa Agreement Relating to Air Services Between their Respective Territories.[294] The suspension came into force on 16 November 1986, notwithstanding Article XI of the 1947 Agreement, which provided for suspension upon twelve months' notice.[295] Before the US Department of Transportation, South African Airways protested, *inter alia*, that the suspension violated Article XI of the 1947 Agreement but it was concluded in response that 'this argument ignores the extraordinary context within which this [suspension] order is being issued'.[296] As in the previous cases of the US suspension of LOT and Aeroflot landing rights, the US action here should likewise be explained by reference to the concept of third-party countermeasures.[297]

In terms of institutional action during this period, the UN General Assembly adopted a recurring resolution on 10 December 1985 by which it condemned South Africa for its illegal policy of apartheid (characterized as a crime against humanity), its continuing 'acts of aggression' against neighbouring African States, and its violations of the principle of self-determination.[298] The General Assembly repeated its call for the Security Council to urgently adopt comprehensive and mandatory sanctions against South Africa under Chapter VII UNC, including a comprehensive trade embargo.[299] However, in the meantime, the General Assembly requested all States that had not yet done so, 'pending action by the Security Council', to take action to ensure,

---

[292] For a survey of measures see Nash (1987), 201–205; 26 ILM (1987), 79.

[293] See President Reagan's Executive Order 12571 (27 Oct. 1986), 'Implementation of the Comprehensive Anti-Apartheid Act', 26 ILM (1987), 78. See also the statement by President Reagan of 2 Oct. 1986 (ibid.); and 86 Dept. of State Bulletin (Dec. 1986), 35–36.

[294] 26 ILM (1987), 86; 66 UNTS 234 (entry into force 23 May 1947).

[295] For the Implementation Order of the US Department of Transportation, see 26 ILM (1987), 104.

[296] Ibid., 108.

[297] See e.g. Sicilianos (1990), 166; UN Doc. A/C.6/56/SR.12, 5, para. 23 (South Africa on behalf of SADC); ARSIWA Commentary, Art. 54, §3; Tams (2005), 218; Katselli Proukaki (2010), 170–171.

[298] GA Res. 40/64(A) (10 Dec. 1985).   [299] Ibid., op. para. 7.

inter alia, the implementation of a trade embargo against South Africa.[300] This suggests that the General Assembly considered it permissible for States to adopt unilateral coercive measures otherwise unlawful even in circumstances where the Security Council was actively seized of the matter. The widespread adoption of *prima facie* unlawful unilateral coercive measures against South Africa points in the same direction.

4.2.11   Miscellaneous Countries – Iraq (1990)

On 2 August 1990, Iraqi troops invaded and occupied Kuwait. The UN Security Council immediately adopted a resolution under Chapter VII UNC by which it condemned the Iraqi invasion and called for the immediate withdrawal of Iraqi forces from Kuwait.[301] On the same day, EC Member States 'strongly condemn[ed] the use of force by a member State of the United Nations against the territorial integrity of another State [which] constitutes a breach of the Charter of the United Nations', and expressed support for the resolution adopted by the Security Council.[302]

On 4 August 1990, EC Member States adopted a statement which provided that, in the continued absence of Iraqi compliance with the demands of the Security Council, they would work for the adoption of a Security Council resolution under Chapter VII UNC imposing mandatory and comprehensive sanctions against Iraq.[303] However, in the meantime, EC Member States informed the Security Council that

> As of now, they have [*inter alia*][304] decided to adopt the following:
> [. . .]
> (b) Appropriate measures aimed at freezing Iraqi assets in the territory of member States.[305]

---

[300]   Ibid., op. para. 9. See also to similar effect during the relevant period, GA Res. 41/35(B) (10 Nov. 1986).

[301]   SC Res. 660 (2 Aug. 1990). In addition to the invasion, the UN General Assembly also condemned Iraq's violations of international humanitarian law and its 'serious violations of human rights' against the Kuwaiti people, including summary executions, torture, arrests and enforced disappearances: see GA Res. 45/170 (18 Dec. 1990).

[302]   UN Doc. S/21426 (2 Aug. 1990) (Italy on behalf of EC Member States).

[303]   UN Doc. S/21444 (6 Aug. 1990) (Italy on behalf of EC Member States).

[304]   Other unilateral coercive measures included arms and oil embargoes (ibid.).

[305]   Ibid. (emphasis added). For the national implementation measures of France, Italy, Luxembourg, the Netherlands and Spain, see Bethlehem and Lauterpacht (1991), 120–121, 178–179, 218, 232–233, 294.

The freezing of State assets constitutes a *prima facie* unlawful act which requires justification under international law. France explained before the Security Council simply that such action was justified in response to a 'major violation of international law'.[306]

On 2 August 1990, the United States, in response to a 'blatant use of military aggression and violation of the United Nations Charter',[307] had likewise adopted a variety of unilateral coercive measures against Iraq, including an import embargo and an asset freeze.[308] On the same day, Czechoslovakia imposed an arms embargo against Iraq.[309] On 3 August 1990, the Soviet Union and the United States adopted a joint statement by which they announced the adoption of unilateral coercive measures against Iraq, including the Soviet suspension of arms deliveries and the United States' freezing of assets.[310] They also called on States to adopt an arms embargo and 'to take *all possible steps*' to ensure implementation of the resolution of the Security Council and a return to international legality – a wording which suggests that third-party countermeasures were envisaged.[311]

On 5 August 1990, Japan adopted several unilateral coercive measures against Iraq, including a total export embargo.[312] Japan explained that '[w]hen a resolution on sanctions is approved by the Security Council, [it] will faithfully implement this resolution'.[313] On 6 August 1990, prior to any enforcement action by the Security Council, Australia condemned Iraq for 'a gross and indefensible violation of the United Nations Charter', and announced the adoption of several unilateral coercive measures against it, including an asset freeze.[314] It added:

> Australia was prepared to implement and support a Security Council resolution on sanctions against Iraq if the Iraqi Government failed to heed calls for the immediate withdrawal of its forces from occupied Kuwait. The Government was following closely the deliberations of the Security Council.[315]

---

[306] UN Doc. S/PV.2933 (6 Aug. 1990), 21 (France).
[307] UN Doc. S/PV.2932 (2 Aug. 1990), 13 (United States).
[308] UN Doc. S/21525 (15 Aug. 1990) (United States). President Bush's Executive Order 12722 (2 Aug. 1990), 'Blocking Iraqi Government property and prohibiting transactions with Iraq', is annexed at ibid., 3. See also Nash (1990), 903–905.
[309] UN Doc. S/21488 (10 Aug. 1990) (Czechoslovakia).
[310] UN Doc. S/21472 (9 Aug. 1990) (Soviet Union and United States).
[311] Ibid. (emphasis added).   [312] UN Doc. S/21449 (6 Aug. 1990) (Japan).   [313] Ibid.
[314] UN Doc. S/21520 (14 Aug. 1990) (Australia).   [315] Ibid.

On 6 August 1990, the Security Council adopted a further resolution under Chapter VII UNC by which it characterized Iraq's invasion as an 'armed attack' and affirmed Kuwait's inherent right of individual and collective self-defence under Article 51 UNC in response thereto.[316] By the same resolution, with the aim of ensuring the immediate withdrawal of Iraqi forces from Kuwait (i.e. to ensure cessation of Iraq's wrongful conduct), the Security Council also took enforcement action against Iraq, including a trade embargo and an asset freeze.[317]

During the debate in the Security Council, the United Kingdom appeared to suggest that the real issue was not whether unilateral coercive measures, including third-party countermeasures, were permissible in the circumstances, but whether they could be deemed sufficient. It observed:

> What should the international community do in such circumstances [i.e. the Iraqi invasion of Kuwait]? Some governments have already taken action. The twelve member countries of the European Community have already done so. But individual action by States or groups of States is not sufficient; we need a framework for international action, and we have it today in the form of the draft resolution.[318]

On 7 August 1990, Japan declared that 'for its part, [it] will faithfully respect this resolution, *in addition to carrying out its own measures*, as it announced earlier on 5 August'.[319]

Cuba opposed the resolution, *inter alia*, on the basis that 'we are asked to approve specific sanctions that have already been implemented unilaterally by the principal developed Powers of the world'.[320] But Cuba was alone in refusing to legitimize *ex post facto* States' adoption of unilateral coercive measures, including third-party countermeasures, against Iraq. As already observed, several States had, albeit by implication, clearly affirmed a legal entitlement to do so in response to gross and manifest breaches of international law irrespective of any action taken by the Security Council under Chapter VII UNC.

Finally, on 7 August 1990, Switzerland announced the adoption of a trade embargo against Iraq and a prohibition on financial transactions (amounting to an effective asset freeze) with Iraq.[321] Switzerland further

---

[316] SC Res. 661 (6 Aug. 1990).   [317] Ibid.

[318] UN Doc. S/PV.2933 (6 Aug. 1990), 26 (United Kingdom). See also ibid., 18 (United States).

[319] UN Doc. S/21461 (7 Aug. 1990) (Japan) (emphasis added).

[320] UN Doc. S/PV.2933 (6 Aug. 1990), 38 (Cuba).

[321] UN Doc. S/21585 (22 Aug. 1990) (Switzerland).

explained that, as a non-UN member, its action was taken independently of the Security Council as it was not legally bound to implement its sanctions regime.[322] Switzerland's coercive action therefore could not be justified by reference to the Security Council but requires explanation on the basis of general international law.[323]

The adoption of the coercive measures discussed above were, at least not initially, legitimized by the Security Council as enforcement action under Chapter VII UNC. Still, their adoption at a time when the Security Council was actively considering enforcement action against Iraq seemed uncontroversial. Permanent members of the Security Council such as France, the United Kingdom, the United States and the Soviet Union had adopted such measures and encouraged other States to do the same notwithstanding any potential future action taken by the Security Council. The sequence of events required that such measures be justified on the basis of general international law. In this regard, although the Security Council affirmed Kuwait's inherent rights under Article 51 UNC, the statements provided by States in which they announced the adoption of asset freezes and trade embargoes against Iraq did not refer to collective self-defence as a possible justification. Similarly, States did not explain their *prima facie* unlawful trade embargoes against Iraq by reference to Article XXI GATT. These unilateral coercive measures should be understood as third-party countermeasures.[324]

4.2.12   European and Commonwealth States – Nigeria (1995)

On 12 June 1993, presidential elections were held in Nigeria. Moshood Abiola declared himself president, but the democratic elections were annulled some ten days later by Nigeria's military ruler, Ibrahim Babangida, in response to alleged voting irregularities.[325] Democratically elected institutions were dissolved, political parties were banned and members of the opposition were arbitrarily detained. Violent protests followed and, in November 1993, General Sani Abacha seized power in a *coup* following which the brutal repression intensified. However, it was only after a Nigerian special military tribunal, in a hasty and flawed judicial

---

[322] Ibid. See, however, SC Res. 661 (6 Aug. 1990), op. para. 5.   [323] Tams (2005), 219.

[324] See Focarelli (1994), 35; Kawasaki (2000), 23–24; ARSIWA Commentary, Art. 54, §3 (noting that the action was taken with the consent of Kuwait); Tams (2005), 219; Katselli Proukaki (2010), 181.

[325] 'Nigerian Military Rulers Annul Election', *The New York Times*, 24 June 1993, www .nytimes.com/1993/06/24/world/nigerian-military-rulers-annul-election.html.

process which fell below international fair trial standards,[326] had imposed death sentences on the well-known author and Ogoni human rights and environmental campaigner, Ken Saro-Wiwa, and eight other fellow activists, sentences executed on 10 November 1995, that the international community decided to take action.

On 3 March 1995, France (on behalf of EU Member States), as well as several other co-sponsors, introduced a draft resolution to the UN Commission on Human Rights by which, recalling Nigeria's obligations under the ICCPR and the ICESCR, deep concern was expressed about Nigeria's manifold violations of human rights, including arbitrary detentions, severe restrictions on the freedom of expression, cases of torture, inhuman and degrading treatment of prisoners, summary and public executions, the abolition of habeas corpus and restrictions on the right to leave the country.[327] But the draft resolution was narrowly voted down.[328] However, on 22 December 1995, the UN General Assembly adopted a resolution by which, recalling Nigeria's obligations under the ICCPR, it condemned the arbitrary execution of Ken Saro-Wiwa and his co-defendants, following a flawed judicial process, and expressed deep concern about Nigeria's other numerous violations of human rights.[329] Specifically, the General Assembly called on Nigeria to comply with its obligations under the ICCPR and other human rights instruments. It also called on the UN Commission on Human Rights to give urgent attention to the situation of human rights in Nigeria. During the debate on the resolution, Nigeria protested that the resolution violated Article 2(7) UNC and denied any violation of its human rights obligations.[330]

On 22 April 1996, Italy (on behalf of EU Member States), joined by several other co-sponsors, introduced a further draft resolution to the UN Commission on Human Rights by which, recalling Nigeria's obligations, inter alia, under the ICCPR, the ICESCR and the African Charter of Human and Peoples' Rights, deep concern was expressed about

---

[326] UNYB (1996), 684.

[327] Report of the Commission on Human Rights (51st session, 30 Jan. – 10 March 1995), UN Doc. E/1995/23, 414–416. The draft resolution was co-sponsored by several other European States as well as by Australia, Canada and Japan (ibid.).

[328] Report of the Commission on Human Rights (51st session, 30 Jan. – 10 March 1995), E/1995/23, 416. See also UNYB (1995), 785–786.

[329] GA Res. 50/199 (22 Dec. 1995). To the same effect: GA Res. 51/109 (12 Dec. 1996); GA Res. 52/144 (12 Dec. 1997). The 'other violations of human rights' to which the General Assembly repeatedly referred were those identified by the Commission on Human Rights.

[330] UN Doc. A/50/PV.99 (22 Dec. 1995), 10–11 (Nigeria).

'reports of grave [Nigerian] violations of human rights, including arbitrary executions, arbitrary arrests and detention, failure to respect due process of law and excessive use of force against demonstrators'.[331] The resolution, which was adopted the following day, also called on Nigeria to comply with its obligations under the ICCPR and other human rights instruments.[332]

EU Member States, Commonwealth Member States and the United States all adopted several measures of retorsion against Nigeria, including arms embargoes and travel restrictions.[333] On 20 November 1995, EU Member States had 'condemn[ed] the human rights abuses perpetrated by the military regime ... express[ing] its particular concern at the detention without trial of political figures and the suspension of habeas corpus', and imposed several measures of retorsion against Nigeria, including an arms embargo and travel restrictions on senior regime officials. Development cooperation was also suspended, but this measure appears to have found some justification in Article 5 of the Lomé IV Convention.[334] Following a Swedish proposal, EU Member States also considered freezing Nigerian financial assets within their respective jurisdictions. However, EU Member States ultimately decided against it after most of the assets had already been transferred to Swiss bank accounts.[335] It thus appears that EU Member States considered taking action unlawful under international law but for the possible justification provided by third-party countermeasures.[336] For its part, the UN General Assembly explicitly took note of the decisions taken by EU Member States regarding unilateral coercive measures against Nigeria.[337]

---

[331] Report of the Commission on Human Rights (52nd session, 18 March – 26 Apr. 1996), UN Doc. E/1996/23, 360. The co-sponsors included several other European States as well as Argentina, Australia, Canada, Japan, South Africa and the United States (ibid.).

[332] UNCHR Res. 1996/79 (23 Apr. 1996), Report of the Commission on Human Rights (52nd session, 18 March – 26 Apr. 1996), UN Doc. E/1996/23, 261–263.

[333] Torelli (1996), 234–236; Tomaševski (2000), 288–293. The adoption of an oil embargo was rejected by the United Kingdom and the Netherlands (ibid.).

[334] EU Common Position 95/515/CFSP (20 Nov. 1995), OJ 1995 L 298/1 (11 Dec. 1995). For additional measures of retorsion, see EU Common Position 95/544/CFSP (4 Dec. 1995), OJ 1995 L 309/1 (21 Dec. 1995). For the Lomé IV Convention, see 1924 UNTS 3 (entry into force 1 Sept. 1991).

[335] Keesing's (1995), 40758; Torelli (1995), 236. See further Dzida (1997), 263–264 (with further references); Tams (2005), 220.

[336] See Dzida (1997), 263–264; Weschke (2001), 124–125; Tams (2005), 220; Katselli Proukaki (2010), 189.

[337] GA Res. 50/199 (22 Dec. 1995).

Commonwealth Heads of Government met in Auckland, New Zealand, from 10–13 November 1995 and adopted the Auckland Communiqué.[338] Ken Saro-Wiwa and his co-defendants had been arbitrarily executed in Nigeria on the first day of the summit. South African President Mandela responded by proposing that Nigeria should be suspended from its membership in the Commonwealth. In a similar vein, UK Prime Minister Major called the executions 'judicial murder' and expressed support for the same action.[339] On 11 November 1995, the Commonwealth decided, *inter alia*, to suspend Nigeria's membership in the organization 'in response to developments in Nigeria which constituted a serious violation of the principles set out in the Harare Commonwealth Declaration [which emphasizes the importance of fundamental human rights] ... pending the return to compliance with the principles of the Harare Declaration'.[340] The Auckland Communiqué added that, if no demonstrable progress were made in this regard, Nigeria would be expelled from the Commonwealth. Nigeria promptly protested against the 'unfortunate, unfair and baseless' suspension.[341]

On 19–20 December 1995, at the First Meeting of the Commonwealth Ministerial Action Group on the Harare Declaration in London, the adoption of unilateral coercive measures against Nigeria by States outside the Commonwealth was welcomed.[342] It was noted that, in the event of continued non-compliance by Nigeria, 'existing measures could be made more effective by better coordination and further measures would be necessary'.[343] Such further measures could notably include the freezing of assets of members of the Nigerian regime, presumably including

---

[338] Commonwealth Heads of Government Meeting: Auckland Communiqué (10–13 Nov. 1995), available at http://assets.thecommonwealth.org.

[339] '1995: Nigeria hangs human rights activists', *BBC News*, 10 November 1995, http://news .bbc.co.uk/onthisday/hi/dates/stories/november/10/newsid_2539000/2539561.stm.

[340] Commonwealth Heads of Government Meeting: Auckland Communiqué (10–13 Nov. 1995), op. para. 10; Marston (1995), 626; *Keesing's* (1995), 40806, 40850; 'Nigeria suspended from Commonwealth', *CNN*, 11 November 1995, http://edition.cnn.com /WORLD/9511/nigeria/11-11. See further Carmody (1996), 273; Magliveras (1999), 188–192; and for the Harare Commonwealth Declaration (20 Oct. 1991), see http:// thecommonwealth.org/history-of-the-commonwealth/harare-commonwealth-declaration.

[341] See 'Nigeria suspended from Commonwealth', *CNN*, 11 November 1995, http://edition .cnn.com/WORLD/9511/nigeria/11-11/. Also: Commonwealth Heads of Government Meeting: Auckland Communiqué (10–13 Nov. 1995), op. para. 10.

[342] See Concluding Statement by the First Meeting of the Commonwealth Ministerial Action Group on the Harare Declaration (London, 19–20 Dec. 1995), in: The Round Table – The Commonwealth Journal of International Affairs (1996), 253–254.

[343] Ibid., 254.

those of the Head of State, General Abacha.[344] Thus Commonwealth Member States seemed to express a willingness to resort to third-party countermeasures by contemplating conduct otherwise unlawful under international law. Again, the UN General Assembly explicitly took note of the decisions taken by the Commonwealth regarding unilateral coercive measures against Nigeria.[345]

In terms of Nigeria's suspension from the Commonwealth the situation is more complex. In order to be characterized as a third-party countermeasure, the suspension must be deemed to have affected membership rights belonging to Nigeria. Such rights may emanate from a treaty establishing an international organization or from declarations of a more informal association of States. At the December 1995 meeting of the Commonwealth in London, it was explained that Nigeria's suspension meant that its representatives were excluded from participation in all inter-governmental Commonwealth meetings and likewise affected other Nigerian rights associated with membership in the organization.[346]

Although the Commonwealth was not founded by treaty,[347] the dominant view among commentators is that it can nevertheless be characterized as an international organization.[348] More significantly, at least since the 1979 Lusaka Declaration, the Commonwealth refers to itself as an international organization.[349] As most international organizations, and as confirmed in the constitutionally significant 1971 Singapore Declaration, the Commonwealth grants voting rights to its members.[350] Against this background, the suspension, *inter alia*, affected Nigeria's voting rights and its derivative right to participate in intergovernmental meetings. It therefore required some form of legal justification.[351]

---

[344] Ibid. See also 'Commonwealth Proposes Further Measures against Military Regime in Nigeria', 2 Commonwealth Currents (1996), 3. On the political reasons for eventual non-implementation, see 3 Commonwealth Currents (1996), 7; *Keesing's* (1995), 40856. Further: Duxbury (1997), 375.

[345] GA Res. 50/199 (22 Dec. 1995).   [346] See above n. 342.

[347] The creation of the modern Commonwealth is often traced back to the 1949 London Declaration: see e.g. Dale (1982), 460, 463.

[348] See e.g. Fawcett (1963), 88; Dale (1982), 451; Duxbury (1997), 346–349; Sands and Klein (2001), 145–146.

[349] Lusaka Declaration on Racism and Racial Prejudice (7 Aug. 1979), http://thecommon wealth.org/history-of-the-commonwealth/lusaka-declaration-racism-and-racial-prejudice.

[350] Singapore Declaration of Commonwealth Principles (22 Jan. 1971), http://thecommon wealth.org/history-of-the-commonwealth/singapore-declaration-commonwealth-principles.

[351] Magliveras (1999), 192–194.

The two constitutional documents of the Commonwealth, the 1971 Singapore Declaration of Commonwealth Principles and the 1991 Harare Commonwealth Declaration, articulate the basic rules of the organization. They both place emphasis on the promotion and protection of democracy and fundamental human rights, but they do not refer to the question of suspension of membership.[352] It thus seems clear that, in the absence of an express provision in the Singapore or Harare Declarations, the suspension could not be justified by reference to the institutional rules of the organization. It would rather have to be justified on the basis of general international law, and as such could be categorized as a third-party countermeasure.[353] As a minimum, Commonwealth Member States expressed support for such action.

On 22 December 1995, the UN General Assembly

> welcome[d] the decisions by the Commonwealth and other States individually or collectively to take various actions designed to underline to the Government of Nigeria the importance of return to democratic rule and observance of human rights and fundamental freedoms, and expresse[d] the hope that these actions and other possible actions by other States, consistent with international law, will encourage the Government of Nigeria to achieve that specific purpose.[354]

In other words, it appears that the General Assembly shortly afterwards endorsed the adoption of third-party countermeasures against Nigeria as 'consistent with international law', and called on other States to also take action, including by way of third-party countermeasures, in order to ensure the cessation of Nigeria's wrongful conduct. It further appears that the General Assembly did so mainly in response to the following Nigerian violations of the ICCPR: (1) right of non-discrimination (Article 2); (2) right to life (Article 6); (3) freedom from torture (Article 7); (4) freedom from arbitrary detention (Article 9); (5) right to humane treatment of prisoners (Article 10); (6) freedom of movement (Article 12); (7) right to a fair trial (Article 14); (8) freedom of expression (Article 19); (9) freedom of association (Article 22); and (10) minority rights (Article 27).[355]

---

[352] On the significance of these declarations see Duxbury (1997), 353–357; Dale (1997), 463–465; Schiavone (1997), 67.

[353] For a similar conclusion see YbILC (2000), vol. I, 316, para. 39 (Mr. Kabatsi); Tams (2005), 221; Katselli Proukaki (2010), 189–190. For the possible qualification of such action as a countermeasure see generally Sands and Klein (2001), 545–546; Dopagne (2010), 80–104, 134–137.

[354] GA Res. 50/199 (22 Dec. 1995).

[355] As discussed above, see for more details on specific human rights violations GA Res. 50/199 (22 Dec. 1995); Report of the Commission on Human Rights (52nd session,

On 9 December 1998, the General Assembly welcomed the decision of EU Member States, Commonwealth Member States and the United States to start lifting their respective unilateral coercive measures against Nigeria in the light of the progress made towards the restoration of democratic government and respect for human rights.[356]

4.2.13   African States – Burundi (1996)

On 1 June 1993, Burundi held its first democratic elections since gaining independence in 1962 from its then colonial ruler, Belgium. Since independence, Burundi had been ruled by the ethnic Tutsi minority but, on 10 July 1993, Melchior Ndadaye, himself a member of the ethnic Hutu majority, was installed as president. A parliament was established following the legislative elections of 29 June 1993, marking Burundi's nascent transition to democracy.[357] On 21 October 1993, however, the situation changed dramatically following an attempted *coup d'état* during the course of which a group of soldiers from the ethnic Tutsi-dominated army took President Ndadaye and several other political leaders hostage and later assassinated them.[358] Old ethnic tensions were promptly revived resulting in a humanitarian catastrophe involving widespread inter-ethnic massacres across the country, as well as hundreds of thousands of refugees and internally displaced persons.[359]

The surviving members of the elected government, under the leadership of Prime Minister Kinigi, soon re-established some of its authority operating from the French Embassy compound where they had taken refuge.[360] On 25 October 1993, Burundi made an emotional appeal for the UN Security Council to intervene by taking 'urgent and energetic measures':

18 March – 26 Apr. 1996), UN Docs. E/1996/23, 261–263, 360; E/CN.4/L.52/Rev.1 (22 Apr. 1996); UNCHR Res. 1996/79 (23 Apr. 1996).

[356] GA Res. 53/161 (9 Dec. 1998). On 29 May 1999, Nigeria resumed its membership in the Commonwealth: see 'Nigeria Commonwealth ban lifted', *BBC News*, 19 May 1999, http://news.bbc.co.uk/1/hi/world/africa/347509.stm.

[357] UNYB (1993), 262.

[358] UN Doc. S/26628 (25 Oct. 1993); UNYB (1993), 262; *Keesing's* (1993), 39496–39497, 39672. See further Tomaševski (2000), 238–247.

[359] By May 1994, a UN fact-finding mission estimated the number of violent deaths at 50,000–100,000 people. The number of refugees was estimated at about 700,000 people and the number of internally displaced persons was estimated to be around 200,000: see UN Doc. S/1995/157, 20.

[360] UNYB (1993), 262.

[M]assacres of all kinds are taking place and if nothing is done to stop them, the country runs the risk of becoming engulfed in a civil war with incalculable consequences for international peace and security.[361]

More specifically, Burundi requested the establishment of an international force in order to stop the ongoing massacre of Hutus and stabilize the situation in the country.[362] On 25 October 1993, the Security Council merely denounced the *coup* and called for the immediate reinstitution of democracy and constitutional order.[363] On 27 October 1993, Burundi asked the UN General Assembly to take urgent action.[364] On 3 November 1993, the General Assembly, expressing serious concern that the *coup* was plunging Burundi into violence and causing mass displacement of the civilian population, similarly condemned the *coup* and called for an immediate return to constitutional order.[365]

On 5 February 1994, after prolonged negotiations, Cyprien Ntaryamira assumed the presidency in Burundi after having been elected to the office by the national assembly. However, on 6 April 1994, President Ntaryamira was killed, together with President Habyarimana of Rwanda, in a plane crash near Kigali airport after their plane had been shot down by rocket fire upon their return from a regional peace conference held in Dar es Salaam. The incident infamously sparked the genocide in Rwanda, and it also resulted in the deterioration of the situation in Burundi. The East African leaders at the regional summit in Dar es Salaam issued a communiqué which expressed deep concern that Burundi 'ha[d] again been plunged into ethnically motivated political turmoil'.[366] On 30 September 1994, amidst escalating inter-ethnic violence, the national assembly elected Sylvestre Ntibantunganya as President of Burundi.[367]

On 29 March 1995, the Security Council expressed grave concern that 'systematic, widespread and flagrant violations of international humanitarian law have been committed in Burundi'.[368] The Security Council also warned that 'if acts of genocide [and/or crimes against humanity] are committed in Burundi, it will consider taking appropriate measures to bring to justice under international law any who may have committed such acts'.[369] On 28 August 1995, the Security Council established an

---

[361] UN Doc. S/26626 (25 Oct. 1993) (Burundi).
[362] UN Docs. S/26703 (5 Nov. 1993) (Burundi); S/26745 (15 Nov. 1993).
[363] UN Doc. S/26631 (25 Oct. 1993).   [364] UN Doc. A/48/240 (28 Oct. 1993).
[365] GA Res. 48/17 (3 Nov. 1993).   [366] UN Doc. S/1994/406; UNYB (1994), 276.
[367] UNYB (1994), 278.   [368] S/PRST/1995/13.   [369] Ibid.

international commission of inquiry in order to determine the facts surrounding the deadly October 1993 *coup* and the atrocities and other serious acts of violence which followed.[370] The establishment of the commission of inquiry was precipitated by the submission of a report to the Security Council by a preparatory UN fact-finding mission which had, *inter alia*, concluded that some provincial governors as well as extremist elements of the army and even certain political leaders all shared responsibility for the atrocities, albeit in varying degrees.[371] In particular, the report concluded that

> The provincial administration, set up by the new Government, did not always live up to its responsibilities; some of its members incited or encouraged the Hutu population in the massacres.[372]

The report similarly denounced some political leaders for incitement to violence.[373]

The situation in Burundi had over several years been characterized by 'daily killings, massacres, torture and arbitrary detention'.[374] On 29 January 1996, the Security Council declared its readiness to consider the imposition of enforcement measures in the form of an arms embargo and travel bans against those leaders in Burundi who encouraged the violence.[375] This fell somewhat short of the UN Secretary General's request for the establishment of a multinational force under Chapter VII UNC, and the imposition of travel bans and asset freezes on extremists, in order to prevent 'full-scale civil war, ethnic violence and genocide'.[376]

On 25 July 1996, the UN Secretary General delivered the report of the international commission of inquiry to the Security Council.[377] The commission notably concluded that acts of genocide had been committed against the Tutsi minority on 21 October 1993 (the fateful day of the *coup*) at the instigation and with the participation of certain Hutu political officials (belonging to President Ndadaye's political party) and communal leaders. It was not possible, however, for the commission to determine with confidence whether or not these acts of genocide had been centrally planned or ordered by leaders at a higher level of government. Still, circumstantial evidence was sufficient to

---

[370] SC Res. 1012 (28 Aug. 1995).   [371] UN Doc. S/1995/127, 23.   [372] Ibid., 33.
[373] Ibid., 34.   [374] S/PRST/1996/1; SC Res. 1072 (30 Aug. 1996).
[375] SC Res. 1040 (29 Jan. 1996), op. para. 8.
[376] UN Docs. S/1996/116, 5–6; S/1995/163, 5–6; UNYB (1996), 77–78.
[377] UN Doc. S/1996/682; UNYB (1996), 88–89.

warrant the conclusion that some highly placed members within then President Ndadaye's political party had in advance planned for the very real eventuality of a *coup* by, most notably, instigating the acts of genocide that followed.[378]

Moreover, the commission concluded that some members of the Burundian army and police were responsible for the indiscriminate killing of Hutus. The commission took it as an established fact that no effort had been made by the military authorities at any level of command to prevent, stop, investigate or punish such heinous acts. The commission concluded that this failure to act engaged the responsibility of the Burundian military authorities with regard to the indiscriminate killing.[379] In short, acts of genocide (or at least a failure to prevent such acts) appeared to be attributable to the State. The Security Council expressed grave concern at the findings of the report but decided only to keep the matter under close review.[380]

The situation in Burundi reached a new crisis point on the same day as the report of the commission was delivered to the Security Council. On 25 July 1996, another *coup d'état* followed in which the country's former military dictator, Major Pierre Buyoya – reportedly also the instigator of the deadly October 1993 *coup*[381] – overthrew President Ntibantunganya's government and again seized power in the country. The national assembly was immediately suspended and political parties, strikes and demonstrations were banned.[382] The OAU immediately called for the imposition of sanctions against Burundi.[383] On 31 July 1996, at the Second Arusha Summit, East African leaders from Ethiopia, Kenya, Rwanda, Tanzania, Uganda and Zaire (now Democratic Republic of the Congo) adopted a joint communiqué, shortly thereafter communicated to the Security Council, by which they strongly condemned the illegal *coup* and called for the restoration of constitutional order and an end to killings and massacres. The joint communiqué added:

> The Regional Summit decided to exert maximum pressure on the [new] regime in Bujumbura, including the imposition of economic sanctions in

---

[378] UN Doc. S/1996/682, 74.

[379] Ibid. Among its recommendations to the Security Council, the commission proposed that an international criminal tribunal should be established in order to bring those responsible for the genocide to justice (ibid., 75–76).

[380] UN Doc. S/1996/780; UNYB (1996), 89.

[381] 'Burundi Leader Blamed for 1993 Coup', *The Independent*, 30 July 1996, www .independent.co.uk/news/world/burundi-leader-blamed-for-1993-coup-1331331.html.

[382] UNYB (1996), 82; *Keesing's* (1996), 41174, 41213–41214. [383] UN Doc. S/1996/594.

order to bring about conditions which are conducive to a return to normalcy in Burundi. In this regard, the Summit strongly appeals to the international community to support the efforts and measures taken by the countries of the region.[384]

The unilateral coercive measures adopted against Burundi included a total trade embargo.[385] Before the Security Council, Tanzania explained the purpose of the action:

> These sanctions are meant to shape the future prosperity of the people of Burundi. They are meant to articulate the fundamental principles of democracy in the country and, *above all, they are meant to stop genocide* by asking the Buyoya regime to retrace its footsteps to constitutional governance.[386]

A month later, Zambia followed suit and imposed a total trade embargo.[387] For its part, Rwanda suspended air and road links with Burundi.[388] With the exception of Ethiopia and Zaire, Burundi and the other embargoing States were members of the GATT/WTO in August 1996. Thus the trade embargo amounted to a *prima facie* violation of rights belonging to Burundi under Articles XI and XIII GATT. None of the embargoing States invoked Article XXI GATT as a possible justification for the violation of GATT obligations. As for Zaire and Rwanda, their trade embargoes *prima facie* violated obligations owed to Burundi under the 1976 Convention establishing the Economic Community of the Great Lakes Countries, which is aimed at promoting regional economic integration.[389] The 1976 Convention may have been defunct but it was nevertheless still in effect in August 1996.[390]

---

[384] UN Doc. S/1996/620, para. 11. See also to the same effect the joint communiqué adopted at the Third Arusha Summit, UN Doc. S/1996/857, para. 9 (referring to 'necessary pressure'). Further: 'As the West Hesitates on Burundi, Leaders in Africa Make a Stand', *The New York Times*, 24 August 1996, www.nytimes.com/1996/08/24/world/as-the-west-hesitates-on-burundi-leaders-in-africa-make-a-stand.html.

[385] *Keesing's* (1996), 41214; Angelet (2003), 226–227. See also e.g. Kenya's statement on its implementation of various unilateral coercive measures against Burundi, UN Doc. S/1996/651 (Kenya); and UN Doc. S/1997/319, para. 8 (Tanzania) (on the introduction of humanitarian exemptions to an otherwise comprehensive trade embargo).

[386] UN Doc. S/PV.3692 (28 Aug. 1996) (Tanzania), 10 (emphasis added). See also the explanation provided by East African leaders at the Third Arusha Summit: 'The objective of the sanctions was to serve as an effective means of securing a negotiated settlement between all the parties to the conflict in Burundi in an effort to avert a human disaster in that country' (UN Doc. S/1996/857, para. 6).

[387] *Keesing's* (1996), 41214.   [388] UN Doc. S/1996/668 (Rwanda).

[389] 1092 UNTS 49 (entry into force 17 Apr. 1978). On this treaty see further Schiavone (1997), 94–95.

[390] Schiavone (1997), 94–95; and Tams (2005), 222, for a brief analysis.

The only possibility for Zaire and Rwanda to justify the trade embargo under the 1976 Convention would have been to denounce it pursuant to its terms. However, a denunciation under Article 39 of the 1976 Convention would have required three years' notice; it could not therefore have served as justification for the trade embargo. As the Tanzanian and Ugandan ILC members Kateka and Kabatsi later concluded, the trade embargo should be categorized as a third-party countermeasure.[391] In any case, as Tams has correctly observed, the language of the joint communiqués adopted at the Second and Third Arusha Summits allowing for 'maximum pressure' or 'necessary pressure' suggests that the embargoing States considered otherwise unlawful acts to have been justified.[392]

On 25 August 1996, Burundi requested an urgent meeting of the Security Council:

> to discuss the total and illegal economic blockade, which is in all respects contrary to international law, imposed by the States of the Great Lakes Region and the threat of an imminent arms embargo to the very severe detriment of our country and our people.[393]

On 30 August 1996, the Security Council adopted a resolution by which it condemned the July 1996 *coup* and 'expresse[d] its strong support for the efforts of regional leaders, including at their meeting in Arusha on 31 July 1996'.[394]

In other words, the Security Council, albeit indirectly, strongly endorsed the adoption of *prima facie* unlawful unilateral coercive measures against Burundi.[395] As previously, the Security Council decided yet again that it would return to consider enforcement action against Burundi, i.e. an arms embargo and unspecified targeted measures against leaders of the regime, if within a few months the *status quo* in the country remained.[396] As a minimum, this indicates that the Security Council deemed unilateral coercive measures (including third-party

---

[391] YbILC (2000), vol. I, 304, para. 17 (Mr. Kateka) (citing the Burundi example in support of a regime of third-party countermeasures in a regional context), 316, para. 39 (Mr. Kabatsi). For a similar conclusion see also Tams (2005), 222; Katselli Proukaki (2010), 190.

[392] Tams (2005), 222. See also above n. 384.   [393] UN Doc. S/1996/690 (Burundi).

[394] SC Res. 1072 (30 Aug. 1996), op. paras. 1–2.

[395] The resolution (adopted unanimously) notably included the affirmative votes of the following States: Botswana, Chile, China, Egypt, Guinea-Bissau, Honduras, Indonesia, Poland, South Korea and Russia: see UN Doc. S/PV.3695 (30 Aug. 1996).

[396] SC Res. 1072 (30 Aug. 1996), op. para. 11.

countermeasures) permissible even as it was actively considering the adoption of its own enforcement measures.

The adoption of unilateral coercive measures against Burundi gave rise to some discussion in the Security Council. For its part, Burundi protested repeatedly and at length against the adoption of unilateral coercive measures against it. The protest merits closer examination, not least as it set out in clear terms some of the most common objections to third-party countermeasures. Among other things, Burundi complained that

> [T]he motives of our neighbouring countries remain unknown and, at best, are open to interpretation. However stealthily they are concealed, the measures taken against Burundi have been dictated by unavowed objectives.[397]

The adoption of unilateral coercive measures 'in the name of certain noble doctrines or ideals'[398] was simply interventionism disguised as humanitarianism: the conduct amounted, *inter alia*, to a violation of the principle of non-intervention under general international law.[399]
Burundi continued:

> It is important for the Security Council to consider whether the hasty economic sanctions are well founded . . . as regards the clear illegality and immorality of the economic blockade against Burundi, an utterly specious interpretation tends to support the thesis according to which each State is authorized to decree measures such as those that have now been decided upon against Burundi.[400]

In conclusion:

> [T]he Charter of the United Nations is gravely violated by the ordering of economic sanctions against Burundi. Indeed, judging by their nature and their excessive gravity, they are identical to those stipulated in Chapter VII of the United Nations Charter. Under the terms of Article 39 of the Charter, such sanctions can be imposed on a Member State of the Organization only when such a State has been guilty of a grave threat to the peace, a breach of the peace or an act of aggression. [. . .]
>
> Even supposing that a country deserved the economic sanctions recommended in Article 41 of the Charter, *their imposition requires prior authorization by the Security Council*, under the terms of Article 53 of the Charter.[401]

---

[397] UN Doc. S/PV.3692 (28 Aug. 1996), 3 (Burundi).   [398] Ibid., 6.
[399] Ibid., 5 ('From a legal standpoint, this embargo is a form of intervention in Burundi's internal affairs, a type of intervention that has been prohibited by the United Nations since the 1970s').
[400] Ibid., 4.   [401] Ibid., 5 (emphasis added).

In addition to a clear violation of the UN Charter and the principle of non-intervention, Burundi protested that the unilateral coercive measures adopted against it violated its rights under UNCLOS to innocent passage as well as its rights as a land-locked State. Burundi also placed particular emphasis on 'the cruel consequences of the economic blockade on the entire people of Burundi', which amounted to a violation of the African Charter on Human and Peoples' Rights.[402] Other violations of international law were also invoked.[403] Finally, Burundi denounced the fact that the Security Council had failed to condemn the illegal unilateral coercive measures adopted against it.[404]

It is significant that Burundi's position found no express support in the Security Council. On the contrary, Botswana, Canada, Chile, Germany, Guinea-Bissau, Indonesia, Russia, South Africa, South Korea, Tanzania, Uganda, the United Kingdom and the United States all expressed support for the unilateral coercive measures adopted against Burundi.[405] OAU Member States also expressed their 'full support' in a separate communication to the Security Council.[406] The European Parliament similarly expressed support.[407]

For its part, South Africa considered that the unilateral coercive measures adopted were 'the most effective and appropriate means of pressing for a speedy end to the strife in Burundi', as opposed to 'military intervention [which] should be considered only as a last resort if the situation deteriorates drastically'.[408] The United States likewise expressed 'strong support' for the unilateral coercive measures adopted against Burundi which, subject to due allowance for humanitarian relief, it hoped would ensure its objective. The United States added that 'if this does not work, the Security Council [was] willing to consider further action [such as an arms embargo and targeted sanctions]'.[409] Botswana observed that 'the boycott seemed ... to be

---

[402] Ibid., 5–6. Burundi later set out in more detail the adverse effects of the trade embargo in a letter addressed to the Security Council: see UN Doc. S/1996/788 (Burundi). Curiously, Burundi made no reference to any infringement of its rights under the GATT.

[403] UN Doc. S/1996/788, 2 (Burundi). These violations included the principles of self-determination, sovereign equality of States, non-use of force and the peaceful settlement of international disputes (ibid.).

[404] UN Doc. S/PV.3695 (30 Aug. 1996), 5 (Burundi).

[405] UN Doc. S/PV.3692 (28 Aug. 1996), 10 (Canada), 12 (South Africa and Uganda), 16–17 (Botswana), 18 (Chile), 21 (Indonesia), 23 (South Korea), 24 (United States), 26 (Guinea-Bissau), 28 (United Kingdom), 30 (Russia), 31 (Germany).

[406] UN Doc. S/1996/628.   [407] EC Bull. No. 9 (1996), para. 1.4.62.

[408] UN Doc. S/PV.3692 (28 Aug. 1996), 12 (South Africa).   [409] Ibid., 24 (United States).

the only option open to the regional leaders ... [and] deserve[d] the commendation of the international community'.[410] As observed above, this position found expression in the resolution adopted by the Security Council on 30 August 1996. Far from condemning the adoption of unilateral coercive measures (as Burundi had implicitly demanded), the Security Council instead expressed its strong support for the action taken.

On 16 April 1997, at the Fourth Arusha Summit, East African States decided to ease the otherwise comprehensive trade embargo against Burundi by excluding from its application items of humanitarian concern such as food and medicines – a decision welcomed by the Security Council.[411] By March 1998, the sanctions regime had been further limited but still included an arms embargo, a ban on exports and a ban on commercial flights to and from Burundi.[412] At this time, Burundi requested the support of the Security Council in the lifting of the unilateral coercive measures against it, but to no avail.[413] On 17 December 1998, following an improvement of the situation in Burundi, the OAU appealed to their fellow East African States to immediately lift all unilateral coercive measures in place against Burundi.[414] The sanctions regime was lifted shortly thereafter.[415]

4.2.14   United States – Sudan (1997–present)

From 1983 to 2005, Sudan was engulfed in a protracted civil war between the Government of Sudan and the Sudan People's Liberation Army. In January 2005, a Comprehensive Peace Agreement was finally signed between the parties resulting, in July 2011, in the establishment of a new State, South Sudan. The lengthy civil war that preceded these momentous developments was one of the bloodiest conflicts in recent history causing millions of civilian deaths and internally displaced persons. However, as

---

[410] Ibid., 16–17 (Botswana).
[411] UN Docs. S/1997/319, para. 8; S/PRST/1997/32. See also UNCHR Res. 1997/77, Report of the Commission on Human Rights (53rd session, 10 March – 18 Apr. 1997), UN Doc. E/1997/23, 258–259, op. para. 4 (encouraging the countries which imposed unilateral coercive measures against Burundi to continue to evaluate their effects).
[412] UN Doc. S/1998/276, 6 (Uganda); UNYB (1998), 96.
[413] UN Doc. S/1998/243, 5 (Burundi); UNYB (1998), 97.
[414] 'OAU Resolution on the economic sanctions imposed on Burundi', UN Doc. S/1998/1229; UNYB (1998), 99.
[415] 'World: Africa Burundi Sanctions Lifted', BBC News, 23 January 1999, http://news.bbc.co.uk/1/hi/world/africa/261258.stm.

the north-south situation in Sudan improved, the crisis in Sudan's western Darfur region escalated to a humanitarian catastrophe.

Since 1993, the UN General Assembly had condemned Sudan for its many grave human rights violations and called for their cessation.[416] For example, on 12 December 1996, the General Assembly

> expresse[d] deep concern at the serious, widespread and continuing human rights violations in the Sudan, including extrajudicial killings and summary executions, detentions without due process, violations of the rights of women and children, forced displacement of persons, enforced or involuntary disappearances, torture and other forms of cruel and unusual punishment, slavery, practices similar to slavery and forced labour, denial of the freedoms of expression, association and peaceful assembly and discrimination based on religion . . .[417]

In addition, the General Assembly called on Sudan to comply with its human rights obligations, in particular those under the International Covenants on Human Rights, the International Convention on the Elimination of All Forms of Racial Discrimination, the Convention on the Rights of the Child, the Slavery Convention (as amended) and the Supplementary Convention on the Abolition of Slavery, the Slave Trade and Institutions and Practices Similar to Slavery.[418] Finally, the General Assembly requested Sudan to immediately cease its many violations of international humanitarian law, including aerial bombardments of civilian targets.[419] However, aside from repeated verbal condemnations, no significant action was taken by the General Assembly or the Security Council as a result of these determinations.

It would take an assassination attempt in Addis Ababa on then Egyptian President Mubarak on 26 June 1995 to propel the Security Council into action against Sudan. Ethiopia informed the OAU and the UN that the operation had been carried out by a terrorist group with the full support and backing of Sudan, and denounced a violation of the UN Charter and the OAU Charter.[420] On 11 September 1995, the OAU condemned Sudan for a 'flagrant violation of the sovereignty and integrity of Ethiopia' related to its involvement in the assassination attempt, and called on Sudan to desist from such activities and extradite the terrorists suspected of involvement in the attack to Ethiopia to stand trial.[421] Sudan refused to comply and Ethiopia accordingly requested assistance from the Security Council.[422]

---

[416] GA Res. 48/147 (20 Dec. 1993).   [417] GA Res. 51/112 (12 Dec. 1996), op. para. 1.
[418] Ibid., op. para. 2.   [419] Ibid., op. paras. 8–9.   [420] UN Doc. S/1995/867.
[421] UN Doc. S/1996/10, Annex I.   [422] Ibid.

On 31 January 1996, the Security Council adopted a resolution by which it 'strongly deplored the flagrant violation of the sovereignty and integrity of Ethiopia and the attempt to disturb the peace and security of Ethiopia and the region as a whole'.[423] Sudan was asked to immediately comply with the request of the OAU to extradite the suspected terrorists to Ethiopia. In addition, the Security Council requested Sudan to

> Desist from engaging in activities of assisting, supporting and facilitating terrorist activities and from giving shelter and sanctuaries to terrorist elements and act in its relations with its neighbours and others in full conformity with the Charter of the United Nations and with the Charter of the Organization of African Unity.[424]

This admonition referred to complaints by several neighbouring States, notably Egypt, Eritrea, Ethiopia and Uganda concerning certain acts of cross-border violence in their respective territories for which Sudan was deemed responsible in apparent breach of the principles of non-use of force and non-intervention.[425]

On 26 April 1996, following non-compliance by Sudan, the Security Council adopted a resolution under Chapter VII UNC by which it instituted limited diplomatic and travel sanctions against Sudan and warned Sudan of possible further measures against it.[426] During the debate in the Security Council, the United States expressed support for the resolution, but emphasized:

> We do not believe that the sanctions outlined in this resolution are sufficient to convince the Government of Sudan to cease its sponsorship of international terrorism and return to the fold of responsible, law-abiding nations. [...]
> We favour the steps the Council is taking today, but we must say again that they are not big enough. We believe that firmer measures should be taken, not against the people of Sudan, but against their unresponsive Government.[427]

On 16 August 1996, the Security Council adopted a further resolution under Chapter VII UNC by which it decided, in principle, to institute an

---

[423] SC Res. 1044 (31 Jan. 1996), op. para. 2.   [424] Ibid., op. para. 4.

[425] UN Doc. S/1996/179, 2–4, 7–8; UNYB (1996), 129–130. See notably Uganda's repeated complaints about 'unprovoked acts of aggression' consisting, *inter alia*, in Sudan bombing and shelling Ugandan territory, and in providing support to the Lord's Resistance Army: UN Doc. S/1996/288 (Uganda).

[426] SC Res. 1054 (26 Apr. 1996).

[427] UN Doc. S/PV.3660 (26 Apr. 1996), 20, 22 (United States).

aviation embargo against Sudan in case of continued non-compliance.[428] For its part, the United States again stressed:

> Continued Sudanese non-compliance with the demands of the international community not only will bring these measures into force [i.e. the aviation embargo], but will compel consideration of further steps.[429]

However, notwithstanding Sudan's continued non-compliance, the Security Council never actually adopted the aviation embargo.

On 3 November 1997, the United States announced the immediate adoption of several unilateral coercive measures against Sudan, including a trade embargo and the freezing of all Sudanese government assets within its jurisdiction.[430] Since Sudan was not a member of the GATT/ WTO, and no other treaties were seemingly at issue, the trade embargo could be categorized as an act of retorsion. By contrast, the asset freeze required justification under general international law. It should be understood as a third-party countermeasure.

The United States adopted these unilateral coercive measures in response to Sudan's 'continued support for international terrorism; ongoing efforts to destabilize neighbouring governments; and the prevalence of human rights violations, including slavery and the denial of religious freedom'.[431]

The United States was here referring to Sudan's responsibility for various cross-border attacks notably carried out in Egypt, Eritrea, Ethiopia and Uganda, which seemingly violated the principles of non-use of force and non-intervention under international law.[432] In addition, although the United States placed particular emphasis on the prohibition of slavery and the denial of religious freedom, the Sudanese human rights violations with which it was concerned was broader, as the use of the above adverb 'including' clearly suggests. Indeed, as one of the co-sponsors of the resolution against Sudan adopted by the General Assembly in December 1996,[433] it can safely be assumed that the other human rights

---

[428] SC Res. 1070 (16 Aug. 1996).

[429] UN Doc. S/PV.3690 (16 Aug. 1996), 10 (United States).

[430] President Clinton's Executive Order 13067 (3 Nov. 1997), 'Blocking Sudanese Government Property and Prohibiting Transactions with Sudan', www.treasury.gov /resource-center/sanctions/Documents/13067.pdf. See further *Keesing's* (1997), 41900; 'New US Sanctions Imposed on Sudan', *BBC News*, 4 November 1997, http://news.bbc.co .uk/2/hi/22462.stm.

[431] Ibid.   [432] See text above accompanying nn. 424–425.

[433] See text above accompanying n. 417. For the draft resolution (which became GA Res. 51/112 (12 Dec. 1996)), see UN Doc. A/C.3/51/L.61 (22 Nov. 1996).

violations to which the United States made indirect reference included the many serious, widespread and continuing human rights violations identified earlier in that resolution. On 28 September 2001, the Security Council lifted sanctions against Sudan.[434] The United States nevertheless stressed that, in response to ongoing human rights abuses by Sudan, it would 'continue to demand that the Government of Sudan address these issues' notably by maintaining the unilateral coercive measures against it.[435]

On 21 September 2004, the justification for these unilateral coercive measures appears to have been broadened after US President Bush declared before the General Assembly that the humanitarian crisis in Darfur amounted to genocide for which Sudan was deemed responsible, and called on Sudan to stop the atrocities.[436] The United States has regularly renewed the unilateral coercive measures it first adopted against Sudan in 1997, which still remain in force.[437] Sudan immediately protested against the adoption of these unilateral coercive measures.[438] In 1998, Sudan observed that 'the freezing of $5 million of funds of the Government of the Sudan in United States of America banks was in contravention of international law'.[439] More recently, Sudan stated:

> Allowing individual countries to impose unilateral measures against other countries, which contradicts international law and undermines the raison d'être of the United Nations, should not be tolerated.[440]

---

[434] SC Res. 1372 (28 Sept. 2001). The United States abstained from voting.

[435] UN Doc. S/PV.4384 (28 Sept. 2001) (United States).

[436] UN Doc. A/59/PV.3 (21 Sept. 2004), 9 (United States). On 9 September 2004, US Secretary of State Powell stated that 'genocide has been committed in Darfur and the Government of Sudan and the Janjaweed bear responsibility and genocide may still be occurring': see 'Powell Declares Genocide in Sudan', BBC News, 9 September 2004, http://news.bbc.co.uk/2/hi/3641820.stm. The Security Council shortly thereafter requested the Secretary General to establish an international commission of inquiry to determine, inter alia, whether genocide had been committed in Sudan: see SC Res. 1564 (18 Sept. 2004), op. para. 12. The commission concluded that the Government of Sudan had not pursued a policy of genocide, but recognized that in some instances, individuals, including government officials, may have committed acts with genocidal intent: see UN Doc. S/2005/60, 4.

[437] See President Bush's Executive Order 13412 (27 Oct. 2006), 'Blocking Property and Prohibiting Transactions With the Government of Sudan', www.treasury.gov/resource-center/sanctions/Documents/13412.pdf; White House Press Release, 'Continuation of the National Emergency with Respect to Sudan' (31 Oct. 2016) https://www.whitehouse.gov/the-press-office/2016/10/31/letter-continuation-national-emergency-respect-sudan.

[438] See 'Sudan Denounces US Trade Embargo', BBC News, 6 November 1997, http://news.bbc.co.uk/2/hi/world/monitoring/23891.stm.

[439] UN Doc. A/53/293 (2 Nov. 1998), 7 (Sudan).

[440] UN Doc. A/66/138 (14 July 2011), 14 (Sudan).

Sudan has also protested that the unilateral coercive measures adopted against it by the United States has had 'long-term harmful consequences on the human rights of the Sudanese population'.[441] In April 1998, OIC Member States called on the United States to lift its unilateral coercive measures against Sudan 'in view of its harmful effects and the losses incurred at economic and social levels'.[442]

On 29 March 2005, in response to the crisis in Sudan's Darfur region, the Security Council adopted a resolution under Chapter VII UNC by which it took enforcement measures against Sudan in the form of an arms embargo, travel bans and asset freezes on designated individuals.[443] Thus the unilateral coercive measures, including third-party counter-measures, adopted by the United States since 1997 continue to operate in parallel with the Security Council sanctions regime adopted against Sudan under Chapter VII UNC. The debate in the Security Council in March 2005 leading up to the enforcement action taken against Sudan made no reference to the unilateral coercive measures already adopted by the United States.[444]

4.2.15 Miscellaneous Countries – Federal Republic of Yugoslavia (1998–2000)

The human rights situation in Kosovo, formerly a province of the Republic of Serbia within the Federal Republic of Yugoslavia (Serbia and Montenegro) (hereinafter FRY, as appropriate), had been a matter of concern since 1992 and the establishment of the International Conference on the Former Yugoslavia tasked with supervising the peace process in that war-torn region.[445] Already in December 1993, the UN General Assembly had strongly condemned 'large-scale repression committed by Serbian authorities' against ethnic Albanians in Kosovo, including arbitrary arrests, summary executions, acts of torture and other ill-treatment, as well as serious discrimination on a massive

---

[441] UN Doc. A/68/211 (22 July 2013), 6, para. 13 (Sudan).

[442] Final Communiqué of the Twenty-Fifth Session of the Islamic Conference of Foreign Ministers (Doha, 15–17 March 1998), UN Doc. S/1998/311, 26–27, para. 103.

[443] SC Res. 1591 (29 March 2005). On 31 March 2005, the Security Council referred the situation in Darfur to the ICC: see SC Res. 1593 (31 March 2005). On 12 July 2010, the ICC issued an arrest warrant for Sudanese President Al-Bashir on charges of genocide committed in Darfur: see *Prosecutor v. Omar Al-Bashir*, ICC Case No. ICC-02/05-01/09, Second Warrant of Arrest for Omar Al-Bashir, ICC, Pre-Trial Chamber I, 12 July 2010.

[444] UN Doc. S/PV.5153 (29 March 2005).   [445] UNYB (1998), 365.

scale aimed at ethnic Albanians in order to force their departure from the country, and called on the FRY to put an end to these serious illegalities.[446] In December 1994, the General Assembly noted that the FRY's unlawful actions amounted to 'a form of ethnic cleansing'.[447] An armed rebellion followed, led by the Kosovo Liberation Army, resulting in increased repression by FRY security forces. The General Assembly continued to repeatedly condemn the FRY for its widespread human rights violations in Kosovo until 1999. For example, in December 1997, recalling the ICCPR and the ICESCR, as well as other relevant human rights instruments, the General Assembly called on the FRY to

> bring to an immediate end all human rights violations against ethnic Albanians in Kosovo, including, in particular, discriminatory measures and practices, arbitrary searches and detention, the violation of the right to a fair trial and the practice of torture and other cruel, inhuman or degrading treatment.[448]

By early 1998, the scope and intensity of the ethnic conflict in Kosovo had increased dramatically resulting in an impending humanitarian catastrophe characterized by loss of life, a massive exodus of refugees, thousands of internally displaced persons and serious violations of international human rights law. On 4 March 1998, Albania requested an urgent meeting of the UN Security Council to discuss measures needed to avert a conflagration of the conflict following a recent massacre in which Serbian security forces had killed scores of ethnic Albanians. Specifically, Albania asked for the Security Council to request the intervention of the so-called Contact Group on the Former Yugoslavia in order to seek a resolution of the crisis.[449]

On 9 March 1998, the Foreign Ministers of the Contact Group, comprised of France, Germany, Italy, Russia, the United Kingdom and the United States, met in London to consider the deteriorating situation in Kosovo. The Contact Group adopted a statement by which it expressed

> particular concern [at] the recent violence in Kosovo, resulting in at least 80 fatalities, and condemn[ed] the use of excessive force by Serbian police against civilians, and against peaceful demonstrators in Pristina on 2 March.[450]

---

[446] GA Res. 48/153 (20 Dec. 1993), op. paras. 17–19; UNYB (1993), 947.
[447] GA Res. 49/204 (23 Dec. 1994). See also to similar effect GA Res. 50/190 (22 Dec. 1995).
[448] GA Res. 52/139 (12 Dec. 1997).
[449] UN Doc. S/1998/193 (Albania); UNYB (1998), 366.
[450] UN Doc. S/1998/223 (United Kingdom on behalf of the Contact Group), para. 2. See also UNYB (1998), 366-367.

In response to 'very serious allegations of extra-judicial killings', the Contact Group added:

> Our commitment to human rights values means that we cannot ignore such disproportionate means of control ... In light of the deplorable violence in Kosovo, we feel compelled to take steps to demonstrate to the authorities in Belgrade that they cannot defy international standards without facing severe consequences. The Contact Group has decided to take a broad range of actions to address the situation on an urgent basis.[451]

In terms of unilateral coercive measures, the Contact Group endorsed the immediate adoption of an arms embargo, a travel ban on senior FRY officials responsible for the repression and a suspension of export credits for trade and foreign investment in Serbia. Russia dissociated itself from the immediate adoption of the latter two measures of retorsion. In addition, the Contact Group called on the Security Council to adopt a comprehensive arms embargo against the FRY.[452] The Contact Group also called on FRY President Milosevic to take certain effective steps within a period of ten days to stop the repression in Kosovo, and gave notice that in case of a failure to do so:

> The Contact Group will move to further international measures, and specifically to pursue a freeze on the funds held abroad by the Federal Republic of Yugoslavia and Serbian Governments.[453]

At least at this stage, and unlike its express reservations regarding other unilateral coercive measures, Russia did not expressly dissociate itself from the possible imminent adoption of the asset freeze.[454] As a minimum, Russia therefore appears to have expressed some support for conduct otherwise unlawful under international law.

In a subsequent debate before the Security Council, Japan expressed its 'full support' for these unilateral coercive measures.[455] EU Member States, the Czech Republic, Hungary, Poland, Romania, Norway and Albania also expressed their full support.[456] Slovenia, Gambia, Turkey, Bulgaria and Macedonia likewise expressed support, albeit in more general terms.[457] For their part, OIC Member States 'strongly condemned the large scale repression and violations of human rights against the

---

[451] UN Doc. S/1998/223 (United Kingdom on behalf of the Contact Group), paras. 5–6.
[452] Ibid., para. 7.   [453] Ibid.   [454] Ibid.
[455] UN Doc. S/PV.3868 (31 March 1998), 3 (Japan).
[456] Ibid., 14 (United Kingdom on behalf of EU and associated States), 23 (Albania).
[457] Ibid., 8 (Slovenia), 14 (Gambia), 22 (Turkey); UN Doc. S/1998/234 (Bulgaria on behalf of South Eastern European States).

defenceless Muslims of Kosovo', and called on the international community to 'take *all* necessary measures' to bring these violations to an end; a wording which similarly seems to have indicated a degree of support.[458]

On 19 March 1998, EU Member States adopted the measures of retorsion against the FRY endorsed earlier by the Contact Group, and notified it of the impending freezing of all of its assets in case of continued repression.[459] On 25 March 1998, following continued repression in Kosovo, the Contact Group met in Bonn to announce the adoption of the measures of retorsion it had endorsed a few weeks earlier, and agreed to urgently seek the adoption of a mandatory arms embargo by the Security Council.[460] The FRY vehemently protested against the adoption of unilateral coercive measures, including the asset freeze. It stated:

> The positions taken by the Contact Group in London on 9 March 1998 and in Bonn on 25 March 1998 are tantamount to the pursuit of a policy of force and so-called gunboat diplomacy. Under the pressure of certain Powers, the Contact Group, by its policy, places itself above every Government and every principle.[461]

It continued:

> Sanctions are threatened, as well as military intervention, and the normal economic development and lives of millions of people are hampered – and all in the name of democracy and human rights. The Contact Group, by its policy, places itself over and above the Charter of the United Nations in an attempt to transform the Security Council, before the eyes of the world, into a body that merely executes decisions taken at some other place, and with a motivation that is different from the goals and objectives of the Charter.[462]

Put simply, the FRY protested that the unilateral coercive measures adopted against it were abusive and in violation of the UN Charter. The FRY also denounced them as 'unlawful, unilateral and an example of the policy of discrimination'.[463]

On 31 March 1998, the Security Council adopted a resolution under Chapter VII UNC by which, *inter alia,* condemning the use of excessive force by Serbian police forces against civilians and peaceful demonstrators

---

[458] Final Communiqué of the Twenty-Fifth Session of the Islamic Conference of Foreign Ministers (Doha, 15–17 March 1998), UN Doc. S/1998/311, 20–21, paras. 71–72 (emphasis added).

[459] Common Position 98/240/CFSP (19 March 1998), OJ 1998 L 95/1 (27 March 1998).

[460] UN Doc. S/1998/272.   [461] UN Doc. S/PV.3868 (31 March 1998), 16 (FRY).

[462] Ibid.

[463] Weller (1999), 227 (with further references); ARSIWA Commentary, Art. 54, §3.

in Kosovo, and calling on the FRY to end the repression, it adopted a comprehensive arms embargo.[464] No other enforcement action against the FRY was taken by the Security Council. On 29 April 1998, the Contact Group met in Rome and decided to freeze all assets held abroad by the FRY and Serbian Governments.[465] It was also decided that, by 9 May 1998, they would take action to ban new foreign investment in Serbia. Russia did not associate itself with the adoption of these unilateral coercive measures.[466]

On 7 May 1998, following their earlier announcement in March 1998, EU Member States announced their intention to freeze all assets belonging to the FRY and Serbian Governments. Following the earlier decision by the Contact Group, EU Member States also decided to ban new foreign investment in Serbia by 9 May 1998 if the repression continued.[467] On 9 June 1998, EU Member States expressed grave concern at a 'new wave of ethnic cleansing' in Kosovo characterized by 'widespread house-burning and indiscriminate artillery attacks on whole villages ... on the part of the Serb security forces'.[468] In response, EU Member States had the day before announced the impending adoption of a ban on new foreign investment in Serbia. They also decided that the asset freeze would be implemented as a matter of urgency.[469] EU Member States added that, in parallel with these unilateral coercive measures, all options available to the Security Council for enforcement action under Chapter VII UNC should be considered.[470] The EU associated countries of Bulgaria, Cyprus, the Czech Republic, Estonia, Hungary, Iceland, Latvia, Lichtenstein, Lithuania, Norway, Poland, Romania, Slovakia, Slovenia and Switzerland aligned themselves with the EU statement and thereby expressed support for the asset freeze and the investment ban.[471]

In the case of Austria, Bulgaria, France, Germany, Greece, the Netherlands, Poland, Romania, Slovakia and Sweden, the investment ban seemingly violated their respective bilateral investment treaties with the

---

[464] SC Res. 1160 (31 March 1998).

[465] UN Doc. S/1998/355, para. 9; UNYB (1998), 371.   [466] Ibid.

[467] Common Position 98/326/CFSP (7 May 1998), OJ 1998 L 143/1 (14 May 1998), Council Regulation (EC) No. 1295/98, OJ 1998 L 178/33 (23 June 1998). Some limited exceptions applied to the asset freeze, including payment of current expenses for Yugoslav diplomatic missions (see Arts. 3 and 7 of Council Reg. No. 1295/98).

[468] UN Doc. S/1998/554, 2 (United Kingdom on behalf of EU Member States).

[469] Ibid., 3; Common Position 98/374/CFSP (8 June 1998), OJ 1998 L 165/1 (10 June 1998), Council Regulation (EC) No. 1607/98 (24 July 1998), OJ 1998 L 209/16 (25 July 1998).

[470] UN Doc. S/1998/554 (United Kingdom on behalf of EU Member States), 3; UNYB (1998), 371-372.

[471] Ibid; EU Bull. No. 6 (1998), para. 1.4.24.

SFRY or its successor State, the FRY.[472] In principle, absent a treaty-specific justification, an investment ban would appear to contradict the object and purpose of such treaties, which is typically to promote and protect foreign direct investment. This is also the aim of the bilateral investment treaties considered here.[473] Moreover, the investment ban seemingly amounted to a *de facto* suspension which could only be justified by the terms of the relevant investment treaties. Immediate denunciation could not have served as a possible justification since denunciation was at best possible upon twelve months' notice.

On 12 June 1998, the Contact Group, together with Canada and Japan, met again in London to consider the serious deterioration of the situation in Kosovo. At the meeting, the Contact Group, with the exception of Russia, confirmed their decision to implement the investment ban and the asset freeze, and also agreed to take steps to ban flights by Yugoslav carriers between the FRY and their countries. Canada agreed to the same and Japan also expressed support and agreed to consider taking similar action.[474] In the case of the United States, the investment ban amounted to an act of retorsion as it did not affect any rights owed to the FRY. By contrast, the flight ban amounted to a violation of the 1977 United States-Yugoslavia Air Transport Agreement, which could not be justified thereunder.[475] The US flight ban thus required justification under general international law.

In the absence of any treaty obligations, investment and flight bans imposed by Japan would have amounted to mere acts of retorsion. By contrast, Japan's support for the asset freeze expressed at least

---

[472] France-Yugoslavia BIT, 974 UNTS 109 (entry into force 3 March 1975); Netherlands-Yugoslavia BIT, 1047 UNTS 369 (entry into force 1 Apr. 1977); Sweden-Yugoslavia BIT, 1254 UNTS 305 (entry into force 21 Nov. 1979); Germany-Yugoslavia BIT, 1707 UNTS 604 (entry into force 25 Oct. 1990); Austria-Yugoslavia BIT, 1893 UNTS 225 (entry into force 1 June 1991); Greece-Yugoslavia BIT (entry into force 13 March 1998), http://investmentpolicyhub.unctad.org/IIA/country/81/treaty/1814; Slovakia-Yugoslavia BIT (entry into force 16 July 1998), http://investmentpolicyhub.unctad.org/IIA/country/191/treaty/2891. The BITs involving Bulgaria, Poland and Romania were all in force at the time the investment ban was implemented in July 1998: see further http://investmentpolicyhub.unctad.org/IIA. The analysis which follows is based on the assumption that treaties originally entered into with the SFRY continued to apply in relation to the FRY: see further e.g. Marston (1999), 555; Tams (2005), 223 (n. 122). Contra: Wibaux (1998), 267.

[473] The BITs of Bulgaria and Poland are not publicly available (except for dates of signature and entry into force, above n. 472).

[474] UN Doc. S/1998/567, para. 8; UNYB (1998), 373–374. See also Penny (1998), 444–445.

[475] 1203 UNTS 205 (entry into force 15 May 1979). Denunciation was only possible upon twelve months' notice (see ibid., Art. 17).

a willingness to engage in conduct otherwise unlawful under international law. As for Canada, for whom it was, *inter alia*, 'clear that ... the actions of the Yugoslav leadership in Kosovo constitute a crime against humanity',[476] its support for the flight ban was seemingly contrary to its air services agreement with the FRY.[477] Canada's investment ban likewise appeared to violate a bilateral investment treaty with the FRY.[478] Canada's decision to implement the investment and flight bans, as well as the asset freeze, required justification under general international law.

On 29 June 1998, EU Member States announced that all flights to and from the FRY by its national airline JAT would be banned.[479] The EU flight ban came into effect on 8 September 1998 in response to 'indiscriminate violence and brutal repression against its own citizens, which constitute serious violations of human rights and international humanitarian law'.[480] At least with respect to Austria, Belgium, France, Germany, Greece, Luxembourg, the Netherlands, Spain, Sweden and the United Kingdom, the flight ban violated their air services agreements with the FRY and could not be justified thereunder.[481]

The United Kingdom was initially reluctant to adopt the flight ban other than in conformity with the United Kingdom-Yugoslavia

---

[476] Leir (1999), 329.

[477] Canada-Yugoslavia Air Transport Agreement, 1469 UNTS 18 (entry into force 21 March 1985). Denunciation was only possible upon twelve months' notice (see ibid., Art. 20).

[478] Canada-Yugoslavia BIT, 1469 UNTS 3 (entry into force 28 Oct. 1980). Denunciation was only possible upon six months' notice (see ibid., Art. V).

[479] Common Position 98/426/CFSP (29 June 1998), OJ 1998 L 190/3 (4 July 1998). For a discussion see Wibaux (1998), 262.

[480] Council Regulation (EC) No. 1901/98 (7 Sept. 1998), OJ 1998 L 248/1 (8 Sept. 1998).

[481] Greece-Yugoslavia Agreement Concerning Air Services, 187 UNTS 237 (entry into force 15 March 1951); Austria-Yugoslavia Agreement Concerning Air Services, 363 UNTS 149 (entry into force 11 Nov. 1953); Netherlands-Yugoslavia Agreement Relating to Scheduled Air Services, 327 UNTS 227 (entry into force 3 March 1958); Sweden-Yugoslavia Air Transport Agreement, 393 UNTS 226 (entry into force 18 Apr. 1958); Germany-Yugoslavia Air Transport Agreement, 463 UNTS 287 (entry into force 13 July 1959); United Kingdom-Yugoslavia Agreement Concerning Air Services, 359 UNTS 339 (entry into force 30 Sept. 1959); Belgium-Yugoslavia Air Transport Agreement, 1427 UNTS 347 (entry into force 20 Dec. 1960); Luxembourg-Yugoslavia Air Transport Agreement, 464 UNTS 294 (entry into force 19 March 1962); France-Yugoslavia Air Transport Agreement, 922 UNTS 74 (entry into force 20 July 1967); Spain-Yugoslavia Air Transport Agreement, 1162 UNTS 198 (entry into force 22 Oct. 1979). In *JAT v. Belgium*, the Brussels Court of Appeal held that the flight ban was justified as a third-party countermeasure: see *Jugoslovenski Aerotransport c. l' État Belge*, Cour d'appel de Bruxelles (9ème chambre), Decision of 10 June 1999 (No. 1998/ KR/528), 693 Journal des tribunaux (1999).

Agreement Concerning Air Services, which could only be denounced upon twelve months' notice.[482] Indeed the United Kingdom initially gave the FRY the required notice of termination of the air services agreement.[483] However, reportedly after pressure from its EU partners and the European Commission, the United Kingdom soon changed its position.[484] On 16 September 1998, following a notice of termination a week earlier, Foreign Secretary Cook (seemingly concerned to preserve his 'ethical foreign policy') announced that the flight ban would take immediate effect. He explained that

> President Milosevic's current behaviour, and in particular his worsening record on human rights, means that, *on moral and political grounds*, he has forfeited the right of his Government to insist upon the 12 months notice which would normally apply.[485]

The United Kingdom was evidently unwilling to justify the flight ban in legal terms by reference to third-party countermeasures. A leaked FCO memorandum of 7 September 1998 reportedly explained that

> The present case [i.e. Serbia's massive military attacks on civilians in Kosovo] concerns violations of human rights ... against local nationals. Though of considerable concern to EU member states, such actions do not ... justify taking reprisals ... [486]

Countermeasures could only be adopted by 'an injured State'.[487] A senior official from the European Commission apparently replied:

> This is really baffling from a government which claims it has an ethical foreign policy. We have not heard this line of argument [concerning the illegality of third-party countermeasures] from anyone else.[488]

In the event, Greece also expressed a reluctance to implement the flight ban other than in conformity with the Greece-Yugoslavia Agreement

---

[482] See Marston (1998), 580–581; 'Cook Reviews "Unethical" Policy on Serbia after EU Outrage', *The Independent*, 16 September 1998, www.independent.co.uk/news/cook-reviews-unethical-policy-on-serbia-after-eu-outrage-1198408.html. Further: United Kingdom-Yugoslavia Agreement Concerning Air Services, 359 UNTS 339 (entry into force 30 Sept. 1959).

[483] Marston (1998), 580.

[484] See 'Cook Reviews "Unethical" Policy on Serbia after EU Outrage', *The Independent*, 16 September 1998.

[485] Marston (1998), 581 (emphasis added). See also Marston (1999), 554–556.

[486] See 'Cook Reviews "Unethical" Policy on Serbia after EU Outrage', *The Independent*, 16 September 1998.

[487] Ibid.   [488] Ibid.

Concerning Air Services, which could only be denounced upon six months' notice.[489] It should be noted that no such reluctance was expressed by Greece or the United Kingdom in relation to the asset freeze and, in the case of Greece, the suspension of its bilateral investment treaty with the FRY.

On 23 September 1998, the Security Council adopted a further resolution under Chapter VII UNC by which, *inter alia*, it expressed grave concern at the rapid deterioration of the humanitarian situation in Kosovo marked by intense fighting and increasing violations of human rights and international humanitarian law. A ceasefire was demanded and the parties were called, with international involvement, to immediately enter into meaningful negotiations to reach a political solution to the Kosovo crisis. By the same resolution, the Security Council also took note 'with appreciation' of the statement made by the Contact Group (alongside Canada and Japan) on 12 June 1998.[490] In other words, the Security Council expressed general support for the *prima facie* unlawful unilateral coercive measures adopted against the FRY, notwithstanding its own active role in seeking a resolution to the crisis and the limited support within the Council for the adoption of sanctions beyond the arms embargo.[491] The following day, NATO Member States announced their intention to resort to the use of force if the brutal repression continued.[492]

On 9 December 1998, the General Assembly adopted a resolution by which, *inter alia*, it strongly condemned

> the overwhelming number of human rights violations committed by the Federal Republic of Yugoslavia (Serbia and Montenegro), the police and military authorities in Kosovo, including summary executions, indiscriminate attacks and widespread attacks on civilians, indiscriminate and widespread destruction of property, mass forced displacement of civilians, the taking of civilian hostages, torture and other cruel, inhuman or degrading treatment, in breach of international humanitarian law including article 3 common to the Geneva Conventions of 12 August 1949 and Additional Protocol II to the Conventions, relating to the protection of

---

[489] See Weller (1999), 220; Katselli Proukaki (2010), 195 (with further references). Further: Greece-Yugoslavia Agreement Concerning Air Services, 187 UNTS 237 (entry into force 15 March 1951).

[490] SC Res. 1199 (23 Sept. 1998). See further SC Res 1203 (24 Oct. 1998).

[491] The resolution, adopted with the abstention of China, notably included the affirmative votes of the following States: Bahrain, Brazil, Costa Rica, Gabon, Gambia, Japan, Kenya, Russia and Slovenia: see UN Doc. S/PV.3930 (23 Sept. 1998).

[492] NATO Press Release (24 Sept. 1998), www.nato.int/docu/pr/1998/p980924e.htm.

victims of non-international armed conflicts, and calls upon the authorities of the Federal Republic of Yugoslavia (Serbia and Montenegro) to
take all measures necessary to eliminate these unacceptable practices.[493]

By the same resolution, the General Assembly also notably called on
the FRY to respect minority rights, freedom of expression, freedom from
arbitrary detention, the right to a fair trial, and repeal its policy of mass
discrimination against Kosovo Albanians.

On 15 January 1999, FRY security forces committed a massacre by
summarily executing scores of Kosovo Albanian civilians in the village of
Racak. The Security Council swiftly condemned the Racak massacre but
took no enforcement action.[494] The massacre prompted NATO Member
States to issue a 'final warning' to President Milosevic concerning the
impending use of military force to resolve the crisis, barring the success
of peace talks at Rambouillet.[495] On 24 March 1999, following President
Milosevic's refusal to sign the Rambouillet Accords, NATO Member States
launched a military campaign against the FRY on humanitarian grounds.[496]

In doing so, NATO Member States explained that they had, *inter alia*,
'fully supported . . . the efforts of the Contact Group' – i.e. including the
adoption of *prima facie* unlawful unilateral coercive measures – and
regretted that these efforts had not succeeded leaving NATO to conclude
that 'no alternative is open but to take military action'.[497] As the United
Kingdom explained, '[e]very means short of force has been tried to avert
this situation'.[498] The Security Council met immediately to consider
NATO's military intervention; however, a draft resolution condemning
it as a violation of the UN Charter and calling for the immediate cessation
of the use of force and an urgent resumption of negotiations found little
support and was ultimately not adopted.[499]

On 13 April 1999, the UN Commission on Human Rights adopted
a resolution by which it strongly condemned 'the widespread and

---

[493] GA Res. 53/164 (9 Dec. 1998), op. para. 8.
[494] S/PRST/1999/2; UNYB (1999), 334–335.
[495] See notably UN Doc. S/1999/107 (FRY); NATO Press Release (28 Jan. 1999), www.nato
.int/docu/pr/1999/p99-011e.htm; UNYB (1999), 338–342 (with many further references). For criticism of this approach (i.e. peace through coercion) as inconsistent
with Article 52 VCLT, see Brownlie and Apperley (2000), 895–897.
[496] NATO Press Release (23 March 1999), www.nato.int/docu/pr/1999/p99-040e.htm;
UNYB (1999), 342.
[497] NATO Press Release (23 March 1999).
[498] UN Doc. S/PV.3988 (23 March 1998), 12 (United Kingdom).
[499] UN Doc. S/1999/328; UNYB (1999), 343–344. The draft resolution was co-sponsored by
Russia, Belarus and India (ibid.).

systematic practice of ethnic cleansing perpetrated by the Belgrade and Serbian authorities against the Kosovars ... [resulting in] ... massive criminal violations of international human rights and humanitarian law'; namely, 'war crimes and crimes against humanity'.[500] Most EU Member States were among the many co-sponsors of this resolution.[501]

On 23 April 1999, in parallel with NATO's ongoing military campaign, and in response to 'criminally irresponsible policies', EU Member States announced the adoption of an oil embargo against the FRY.[502] The Security Council was informed that EU Member States intended to continue to exert 'maximum pressure' on the FRY by urgently imposing additional unilateral coercive measures against it.[503] On 10 May 1999, EU Member States announced the adoption of several additional measures of retorsion against the FRY, including a travel ban against President Milosevic and other senior FRY officials.[504] In addition, EU Member States decided to extend the scope of the asset freeze to notably include assets belonging to President Milosevic, the FRY Head of State.[505] This action clearly required justification under international law. The investment ban was also broadened, as was the flight ban to cover all commercial flights between EU Member States and the FRY.[506]

On 10 June 1999, during the debate in the Security Council on an all-important post-conflict resolution on Kosovo following the end of NATO's military campaign,[507] the FRY requested that all existing sanctions and unilateral coercive measures adopted against it be lifted as a matter of urgency; but to no avail.[508] No other State raised the issue of the unilateral coercive measures still in force against the FRY. The human rights situation in Kosovo remained a matter of serious concern.[509] However, on 9 October 2000, following democratic elections held on 24 September 2000 in the FRY which saw Vojislav Koštunica

---

[500] UNCHR Res. 1999/2, Report of the Commission on Human Rights (55th session, 22 March – 30 Apr. 1999), UN Doc. E/1999/23, 33–34. Russia was alone in voting against the resolution (ibid., 315).

[501] Ibid., 315.

[502] Common Position 1999/273/CFSP (23 Apr. 1999), OJ 1999 L 108/1 (27 Apr. 1999), Council Regulation (EC) No. 900/1999 (1 May 1999).

[503] UN Doc. S/1999/490 (Germany on behalf of EU Member States). See also UNYB (1999), 345.

[504] Common Position 1999/318/CFSP (10 May 1999), OJ 1999 L 123/1 (13 May 1999).

[505] Ibid.   [506] Ibid.   [507] SC Res. 1244 (10 June 1999).

[508] UN Doc. S/PV.4011 (10 June 1999), 4 (FRY).   [509] GA Res. 54/183 (17 Dec. 1999).

elected as President, EU Member States announced the immediate lifting of the sanctions regime against the FRY.[510]

In conclusion, a large number of States adopted third-party counter-measures against the FRY by freezing its assets and those of its Head of State, as well as withholding rights owed to the FRY under relevant investment treaties and air services agreements without any conventional basis for doing so.[511] Many more States expressed support for the adoption of these third-party countermeasures, in terms ranging from 'full support' to support couched in more indirect and general terms. For its part, the Security Council took note 'with appreciation' of the adoption of third-party countermeasures against the FRY. By contrast, no State expressed support for the FRY's protest to the effect that the adoption of third-party countermeasures violated the UN Charter or otherwise interfered with the privileged role of the Security Council under the Charter regime.

It is difficult to determine with confidence whether all of the breaches of international law committed by the FRY, as affirmed in numerous resolutions by various UN organs and other international bodies during the relevant period, actually *in toto* motivated the adoption of third-party countermeasures against it. As recognized in the representative sample of UN resolutions examined above, these breaches arose under both general international law and under several international human rights and humanitarian law instruments, notably including the ICCPR and the 1949 Geneva Conventions and Additional Protocol II to the Conventions, to which the FRY was a contracting party.[512]

From the above survey, it nevertheless seems clear that the breaches of particular concern to the international community, in response to which a large number of States adopted third-party countermeasures, included the following: (1) right of non-discrimination (Article 2 ICCPR); (2) right

---

[510]   Common Position 2000/599/CFSP (9 Oct. 2000), OJ 2000 L 255/1 (9 Oct. 2000). The UN arms embargo was lifted in September 2001: see SC Res. 1367 (10 Sept. 2001).

[511]   See e.g. ARSIWA Commentary, Art. 54, §3; Tams (2005), 223; Katselli Proukaki (2010), 195; Tzanakopoulos (2015), 151 (regarding the asset freeze and the EU flight ban). Also: UN Doc. A/C.6/56/SR.12, 5, para. 23 (South Africa on behalf of SADC); Paasivirta and Rosas (2002), 214; Palchetti (2002), 219–220 (qualifying the EU flight ban as a third-party countermeasure).

[512]   Yugoslavia ratified the ICCPR on 2 June 1971. A state of emergency under Article 4 ICCPR was never invoked in relation to Kosovo, except for a brief period in 1989–1990 in relation to derogations from Articles 12 and 21 ICCPR (terminated on 18 April 1990). Yugoslavia ratified the 1949 Geneva Conventions on 21 October 1950, and Additional Protocol II on 11 December 1979.

to life (Article 6 ICCPR); (3) freedom from torture (Article 7 ICCPR); (4) freedom from arbitrary detention (Article 9 ICCPR); (5) right to a fair trial (Article 14 ICCPR); (6) freedom of expression (Article 19 ICCPR); (7) minority rights (Article 27 ICCPR); (8) war crimes; and (9) crimes against humanity.

4.2.16 Miscellaneous Countries – Burma (2000–present)

The history of Burma (or Myanmar) since gaining independence from British colonial rule in 1948 has been marked by an oppressive military dictatorship and a protracted internal armed conflict. By 1988, the dire situation in Burma triggered widespread pro-democracy protests against the military junta. Violent clashes erupted between protesters and the military resulting in the death of around 3,000 people, many of whom were summarily executed by the military or died from ill treatment in detention. The military junta nevertheless pledged to hold a referendum and put an end to one-party rule. On 27 May 1990, parliamentary elections were held in Burma. A transition to democracy seemed possible as the political party of the main opposition leader, Aung San Suu Kyi, won the elections after receiving overwhelming popular support. However, the Burmese military junta refused to relinquish power and arbitrarily detained many political leaders and other dissidents, including Aung San Suu Kyi.

The international community soon expressed concern at the grave humanitarian situation in Burma. Indeed the UN General Assembly has expressed its concern at ongoing international human rights and humanitarian law violations in Burma in annual resolutions since December 1991.[513] In March 1992, the UN Commission on Human Rights appointed a Special Rapporteur to report on the human rights situation in Burma.[514] A few months later, the Special Rapporteur presented a preliminary report to the General Assembly detailing well-documented accounts of widespread summary execution, torture, arbitrary arrest and detention, show trials and enforced disappearances (especially of the minority Muslim population).[515] In December 1992, taking note of the report by the Special Rapporteur, the General

---

[513] See GA Res. 46/132 (17 Dec. 1991).
[514] UNCHR Res. 1992/58 (3 March 1992), Report of the Commission on Human Rights (48th session, 27 Jan. – 6 March 1992), UN Doc. E/1992/22, 136–138.
[515] Preliminary Report of the Special Rapporteur of the Commission on Human Rights on the Situation of Human Rights in Myanmar, UN Doc. A/47/651 (13 Nov. 1992).

Assembly expressed grave concern about the human rights situation in Burma and called on it to comply with its obligations under international human rights and humanitarian law.[516]

Since 1993, the General Assembly has, based in part on a large number of reports from successive Special Rapporteurs, repeatedly condemned Burma for 'widespread', 'systematic' and 'serious' violations of international human rights and humanitarian law, including extra-judicial and summary executions, torture, arbitrary arrest and detention, deaths in custody, lack of fair trials and due process of law, forced (child) labour, forced displacement, enforced disappearances, freedom of expression, freedom of assembly, freedom of association, freedom of movement, freedom of religion, discrimination of ethnic and religious minorities, abuse of women (e.g. rape, other forms of sexual violence and human trafficking), enlistment of child soldiers, destruction of crops and arable lands, and dispossession of property. The General Assembly has also repeatedly called on Burma to comply with relevant international human rights and humanitarian law, including by recalling obligations embodied in the ICCPR to which Burma is not a contracting party.[517]

On 28 October 1996, following the detention a few weeks earlier of several hundreds of Aung San Suu Kyi supporters,[518] EU Member States adopted several unilateral coercive measures against Burma, including a travel ban on senior Burmese regime officials, and renewed diplomatic sanctions as well as an arms embargo already in effect since July 1991.[519] The action was justified on the following basis:

> The European Union is concerned at the absence of progress towards democratisation and at the continuing violation of human rights in

---

[516] GA Res. 47/144 (18 Dec. 1992).

[517] See generally GA Res. 48/150 (20 Dec. 1993); GA Res. 49/197 (23 Dec. 1994); GA Res. 50/194 (22 Dec. 1995); GA Res. 51/117 (12 Dec. 1996); GA Res. 52/137 (12 Dec. 1997); GA Res. 53/162 (9 Dec. 1998); GA Res. 54/186 (17 Dec. 1999); GA Res. 55/112 (4 Dec. 2000); GA Res. 56/231 (24 Dec. 2001); GA Res. 57/231 (18 Dec. 2002); GA Res. 58/247 (23 Dec. 2003); GA Res. 59/263 (23 Dec. 2004); GA Res. 60/233 (23 Dec. 2005); GA Res. 61/232 (22 Dec. 2006); GA Res. 62/222 (22 Dec. 2007); GA Res. 63/245 (24 Dec. 2008); GA Res. 64/238 (24 Dec. 2009); GA Res. 65/241 (24 Dec. 2010); GA Res. 66/230 (24 Dec 2011); GA Res. 67/233 (24 Dec. 2012); GA Res. 68/242 (27 Dec. 2013); GA Res. 69/248 (29 Dec. 2014); GA Res. 70/233 (23 Dec. 2015).

[518] EU Bull. No. 10 (1996), para. 1.4.91.

[519] Common Position 96/635/CFSP (28 Oct. 1996), OJ 1996 L 287/1 (8 Nov. 1996). A number of States associated with the EU aligned themselves with this statement: see EU Bull. No. 11 (1996), para. 1.4.15; EU Bull. No. 10 (2000), para. 1.6.7.

Burma/Myanmar. It deplores, in particular, the practice of torture, summary and arbitrary executions, forced labour, abuse of women, political
arrests, forced displacement of the population and restrictions on the
fundamental rights of freedom of speech, movement and assembly.[520]

More specifically:

> It condemns the detentions in May and September 1996 of members and
> supporters of the National League for Democracy (NLD). It calls for the
> immediate and unconditional release of all detained political prisoners.
> The NLD and other legitimate political parties, including those from
> ethnic minorities, should be allowed to pursue freely their normal activ-
> ities. It calls on the Slorc [i.e. the military junta] to enter into meaningful
> dialogue with pro-democracy groups with a view to bringing about
> national reconciliation.[521]

On 24 May 2000, in response to 'severe and systematic violations of
human rights in Burma, with continuing and intensified repression of
civil and political rights', the EU sanctions regime was broadened to
include the freezing of assets belonging to senior members of the
Burmese regime, including the then leader of the military junta,
General Than Shwe, the Burmese Head of State.[522] At least the freezing
of General Than Shwe's assets required justification under international
law.[523] Twenty-six countries aligned themselves with the EU sanctions
regime and duly pledged to ensure its implementation.[524] The EU

---

[520] Common Position 96/635/CFSP (28 Oct. 1996), OJ 1996 L 287/1 (8 Nov. 1996).

[521] Ibid.

[522] Common Position 2000/346/CFSP (26 Apr. 2000), Council Regulation (EC) No. 1081/
2000, OJ 2000 L 122/29 (24 May 2000). See also EU Bull. No. 4 (2000), paras.
1.6.61–1.6.62.

[523] The ILC in 2011 appears to have categorized the asset freeze as a third-party countermeasure attributable to the EU: see DARIO Commentary, Art. 57, §2 (n. 338). It is
unclear why the EU asset freeze against Burma was singled out for specific mention –
presumably, among other relevant practice of international organizations, the same EU
action against the FRY (4.2.15), Zimbabwe (4.2.17) and Belarus (4.2.18) could equally
have been mentioned. The ILC has previously also attributed asset freezes to individual
(EU) Member States: see ARSIWA Commentary, Art. 54, §3 (n. 808).

[524] Bulgaria, Cyprus, the Czech Republic, Estonia, Hungary, Iceland, Latvia, Lichtenstein,
Lithuania, Malta, Norway, Poland, Romania, Slovakia, Slovenia, Switzerland and
Turkey: see EU Bull. No. 4 (2001), para. 1.6.15. In addition, Albania, Armenia, Bosnia
and Herzegovina, Croatia, Georgia, Macedonia, Malta, Moldova, Serbia and
Montenegro later also aligned themselves, inter alia, with the asset freeze. See EU Bull.
No. 2 (2004), para. 1.6.33; Declaration by the High Representative on behalf of the
European Union on the alignment of certain third countries with the Council Decision
2011/239/CFSP amending Decision 2010/232/CFSP renewing restrictive measures
against Burma/Myanmar (28 Apr. 2011), http://www.consilium.europa.eu/uedocs/

sanctions regime was renewed on a regular basis and further broadened to include a limited investment ban, a ban on financial loans and the suspension of development assistance.[525] These unilateral coercive measures amounted to acts of retorsion as they did not affect any rights owed to Burma under international law.

On 19 November 2007, in response to 'continuing serious violations of human rights in Burma/Myanmar', the EU adopted several additional unilateral coercive measures against Burma by notably targeting the sources of revenue of the regime, including in the sectors where human rights abuses were common.[526] An export embargo was adopted on technology and equipment destined for use in the industry sectors of logging, timber, and mining of metals and minerals, as well as precious and semi-precious stones. A corresponding import embargo was also adopted, and the investment ban was strengthened.[527] In addition, EU Member States proceeded to freeze the assets of then newly appointed Burmese Prime Minister (later President), Thein Sein.[528] The trade embargo affected rights owed to Burma under the GATT/WTO,[529] and EU Member States did not explicitly justify these unilateral trade restrictions as exceptionally permissible; notably, under Article XXI GATT. The freezing of Thein Sein's assets clearly required justification under international law, at least once he became Head of State.

On 23 April 2012, EU Member States announced a one-year suspension of all unilateral coercive measures (except the arms embargo) against Burma. This decision was taken in response to alleged 'historic changes' and 'wide-ranging reforms' underway in Burma, including progress made in relation to freedoms of expression, assembly and association, the release of political prisoners, forced labour practices

cms_data/docs/pressdata/en/cfsp/121671.pdf; Declaration by the High Representative on behalf of the European Union on the alignment of certain third countries with Council Decision 2012/225/CFSP amending Decision 2010/232/CFSP concerning restrictive measures against Burma/Myanmar (8 June 2012), www.consilium.europa .eu/uedocs/cms_Data/docs/pressdata/en/cfsp/130740.pdf.

[525] Common Position 2003/297/CFSP (28 Apr. 2003), OJ 2003 L 106/36 (29 Apr. 2003); Common Position 2004/730/CFSP (25 Oct. 2004), OJ 2004 L 323/17 (26 Oct. 2004).

[526] Common Position 2007/750/CFSP (19 Nov. 2007), OJ 2007 L 308/1 (24 Nov. 2007). Also: EU Bull. No. 10 (2007), para. 1.34.34.

[527] Ibid.

[528] Ibid. See also Common Position 2011/239/CFSP (12 Apr. 2011), OJ 2011 L 101/24 (15 Apr. 2011) (renewing the application of the asset freeze to President Thein Sein).

[529] Burma became a WTO member on 1 January 1995.

and minority rights.[530] On 22 April 2013, the EU sanctions regime against Burma was lifted.[531]

In October 2000, Switzerland joined its EU partners and adopted similar unilateral coercive measures against Burma.[532] In June 2006, Switzerland broadened its sanctions regime by announcing that it was also freezing the assets of leading members of the Burmese military junta, including those belonging to President Thein Sein.[533] Although the Swiss sanctions regime, as its EU counterpart, was largely suspended in May 2012, the asset freezes still remain in force.[534]

In September 1988, following the violent suppression of the initial pro-democracy protests in Burma, the United States suspended development aid and imposed an arms embargo against Burma.[535] In May 1997, in response to a 'deepening pattern of severe [and] large-scale repression', including arbitrary arrests of dissidents, serious military abuses against ethnic minorities and forced

---

[530] Council of the European Union, 'Council Conclusions on Myanmar/Burma' (23 Apr. 2012), http://register.consilium.europa.eu/pdf/en/12/st09/st09008.en12.pdf; Council of the European Union, 'Burma/Myanmar: EU sanctions suspended' (14 May 2012), https://ec.europa.eu/europeaid/burmamyanmar-eu-sanctions-suspended-press-release-council-european-union_en; Common Position 2012/225/CFSP (26 Apr. 2012), OJ 2012 L 115/25 (27 Apr. 2012), Council Regulation (EC) No. 409/2012 (14 May 2012), OJ 2012 L 126/1 (15 May 2012).

[531] Council of the European Union, 'Council Conclusions on Myanmar/Burma' (22 Apr. 2013), www.consilium.europa.eu/uedocs/cms_data/docs/pressdata/EN/foraff/136918.pdf; Common Position 2013/184/CFSP (22 Apr. 2013), OJ 2013 L/111/75 (23 Apr. 2013), Council Regulation (EC) No. 401/2013 (2 May 2013), OJ 2013 L 121/1 (3 May 2013). See further 'EU Lifts Sanctions against Burma', BBC News, 22 April 2013, www.bbc.co.uk/news/world-asia-22254493.

[532] Swiss State Secretariat for Economic Affairs, 'Mesures à l'encontre du Myanmar (ex-Birmanie)', https://www.seco.admin.ch/seco/fr/home/Aussenwirtschaftspolitik_Wirtschaftliche_Zusammenarbeit/Wirtschaftsbeziehungen/exportkontrollen-und-sanktionen/sanktionen-embargos/sanktionsmassnahmen/massnahmen-gegenueber-myanmar–burma-.html.

[533] Ibid. See further 'Swiss Banks Freeze Burma Accounts', The Irrawaddy, 29 June 2006, www2.irrawaddy.org/article.php?art_id=5919.

[534] Swiss Federal Council, 'Myanmar: le Conseil fédéral concrétise ses décisions antérieures et lève partiellement les sanctions' (9 May 2012), www.news.admin.ch/message/index.html?lang=fr&msg-id=44492. See also 'Lifting Sanctions Seen as Key to Myanmar Reform', Swissinfo, 3 April 2012, www.swissinfo.ch/eng/lifting-sanctions-seen-as-key-to-myanmar-reform/32411654.

[535] 'Funds for Burma Suspended by U.S'., The New York Times, 23 September 1988, www.nytimes.com/1988/09/23/world/funds-for-burma-suspended-by-us.html; Martin (2013), 11 (with further references).

displacement, the United States banned new investment in Burma.[536] Specifically, the United States called on Burma to lift the restrictions imposed on dissidents and respect the rights of freedom of expression, assembly and association.[537]

On 28 July 2003, US President Bush signed into law the Burmese Freedom and Democracy Act.[538] The United States Congress thereby notably determined that the military junta in Burma was committing 'egregious human rights violations against Burmese citizens', including by government-sponsored forced labour, extra-judicial killings, arbitrary arrests, 'us[ing] rape as a weapon of intimidation and torture against women', and forcibly conscripting child soldiers.[539] It also made the following determination:

> [T]he SPDC [i.e. the military junta] is engaged in ethnic cleansing against minorities within Burma, including the Karen, Karenni, and Shan people, which constitutes a crime against humanity and has directly led to more than 600,000 internally displaced people living within Burma and more than 130,000 people from Burma living in refugee camps along the Thai-Burma border.[540]

In response to these egregious violations of international law, the United States Congress decided that a range of unilateral coercive measures should be adopted against Burma, including an import embargo and the freezing of assets belonging to all members of the military junta; notably, the then Burmese Head of State, General Than Shwe.[541] Finally, it was decided that unilateral coercive measures against Burma would only be lifted once 'the SPDC has made substantial and measurable progress to end violations of internationally recognized human rights', placing particular emphasis on workers rights (especially the use of forced (child) labour), conscription of

---

[536] President Clinton's Executive Order 13047 (20 May 1997), 'Prohibiting New Investment in Burma', www.treasury.gov/resource-center/sanctions/Documents/13047.pdf; discussed in Nash (1997), 714–717.

[537] Ibid.

[538] Burmese Freedom and Democracy Act of 2003, Public Law 108–61 (28 July 2003), www .treasury.gov/resource-center/sanctions/Documents/bfda_2003.pdf. See also Tom Lantos Block Burmese JADE (Junta's Anti-Democratic Efforts) Act of 2008, Public Law 110–286 (29 July 2008), www.treasury.gov/resource-center/sanctions/Documents/pl110_286_ja de_act.pdf.

[539] Burmese Freedom and Democracy Act of 2003, Public Law 108–61 (28 July 2003) (ss. 2(4)-(5)).

[540] Ibid. (s. 2(6)).   [541] Ibid. (ss. 3 and 4).

child soldiers, rape, arbitrary detention, and the rights of freedom of expression, association and religion.[542]

President Bush immediately took action against Burma as envisaged in the Burmese Freedom and Democracy Act. The actions taken included an import embargo and the freezing of assets of senior regime officials, such as those belonging to General Than Shwe.[543] In July 2012, President Obama expanded the US asset freezes.[544] At that time, the US sanctions regime (like its EU counterpart) had otherwise been mostly suspended following some improvements to the human rights situation in Burma.[545] On 19 September 2012, the United States also decided to lift the freeze on then Burmese President Thein Sein's assets.[546]

In October 2007, in addition to an arms embargo and a travel ban already in place, Australia announced that it was freezing the assets of senior Burmese leaders.[547] In June 2012, Australia announced the partial suspension of its sanctions regime and lifted the freeze on President Thein Sein's assets.[548] Australian Foreign Minister Carr explained that,

---

[542] Ibid. (s. 3(3)).

[543] President Bush's Executive Order 13310 (28 July 2003), 'Blocking Property of the Government of Burma and Prohibiting Certain Transactions', www.treasury.gov /resource-center/sanctions/Documents/13310.pdf. It may be noted (at ibid.) that an exemption was made to the import embargo to exclude from its scope of application the importation of goods protected by diplomatic privileges and immunities under relevant international instruments (e.g. the VCDR and the UN Headquarters Agreement).

[544] President Obama's Executive Order 13619 (11 July 2012), 'Blocking Property of Persons Threatening the Peace, Security, or Stability of Burma', www.treasury.gov/resource-center/sanctions/Programs/Documents/13619.pdf.

[545] 'US Suspends All Economic Sanctions on Burma', Voice of America, 17 May 2012, www .voanews.com/content/clinton-bruma-fm-meet-in-washington/667077.html; White House Press Release, 'Statement by the President on the Easing of Sanctions on Burma' (11 July 2012), www.whitehouse.gov/the-press-office/2012/07/11/statement-president-easing-sanctions-burma.

[546] US Dept. of the Treasury Press Release, 'Treasury Department Lifts Sanctions Against Burma's President and Lower House Speaker' (19 Sept. 2012), www.treasury.gov/press-center/press-releases/Pages/tg1715.aspx.

[547] 'Australia Fleshes Out Burma Sanctions', The Sydney Morning Herald, 24 October 2007, www.smh.com.au/news/National/Australia-fleshes-out-Burma sanctions/2007/10/24/ 1192941140707.html.

[548] Joint Press Statement by Trade Minister Emerson and Foreign Minister Carr, 'Australia Recognises Reform in Burma' (16 Apr. 2012), trademinister.gov.au/releases/2012/ ce_mr_120416.html; Press Statement by Foreign Minister Carr, 'Australia to Lift Sanctions against Myanmar' (7 June 2012), http://foreignminister.gov.au/releases/ 2012/bc_mr_120607.html. Further: 'Australia Eases Some Sanctions against Burma', BBC News, 16 April 2012, www.bbc.co.uk/news/world-asia-17724407.

although human rights challenges in Burma still remained, recent improvements meant that 'lifting sanctions is the best way to promote further progress'.[549]

In December 2007, Canada likewise announced the adoption of a range of unilateral coercive measures against Burma, including an arms embargo, a trade embargo, an investment ban and the freezing of assets of senior regime officials such as those belonging to then President Than Shwe and Prime Minister Thein Sein.[550] On 24 April 2012, Canada suspended most of its sanctions regime, but the arms embargo and the freeze on then President Thein Sein's assets remained in place.[551] Canadian Foreign Minister Baird, unlike his Australian counterpart, observed that 'limited sanctions may be useful in pressuring for continued progress'.[552] Foreign Minister Baird nevertheless noted that 'this is probably one of the best examples in the modern era where sanctions have proven very effective'.[553]

The UN Security Council has not taken any enforcement action against Burma. The dire situation in Burma has nevertheless provoked some debate in the Security Council. In September 2006, following a deterioration of the situation in Burma involving 'grave human rights and humanitarian conditions', including the arbitrary detention of over 1,100 political prisoners, the United States requested that the matter be put on the agenda of the Security Council.[554] In January 2007, a draft resolution introduced by the United Kingdom and the United States, which 'express[ed] deep concern at large-scale human rights violations in Burma ... including, violence against unarmed civilians by the Myanmar military, unlawful killings, torture, rape, forced labour, the militarization of refugee camps, and the recruitment of child soldiers', was vetoed by China and Russia.[555]

---

[549] Press Statement by Foreign Minister Carr, 'Australia to Lift Sanctions against Myanmar' (7 June 2012), http://foreignminister.gov.au/releases/2012/bc_mr_120607.html.

[550] Special Economic Measures (Burma) Regulations (SOR/2007–285) (13 Dec. 2007), http://laws-lois.justice.gc.ca/eng/regulations/SOR-2007-285/FullText.html.

[551] Regulations Amending the Special Economic Measures (Burma) Regulations (SOR/2012–85) (24 Apr. 2012), http://www.gazette.gc.ca/rp-pr/p2/2012/2012-05-09/html/sor-dors85-eng.html.

[552] Ibid.

[553] 'Canada to Lift Sanctions on Burma in Wake of Historic Vote', The Toronto Star, 24 April 2012, www.thestar.com/news/canada/2012/04/24/canada_to_lift_sanctions_on_burma_in_wake_of_historic_vote.html.

[554] UN Docs. S/2006/742 (United States); S/PV.5526 (15 Sept. 2006).

[555] UN Doc. S/2007/14. See further 'Russia, China Veto Resolution on Burma', The Washington Post, 13 January 2007, www.washingtonpost.com/wp-dyn/content/article/2007/01/12/AR2007011201115.html.

In August 2007, hundreds of thousands of peaceful protesters demonstrated nation-wide against the Burmese regime – the largest such uprising since the fateful events of 1988. The military junta responded by a brutal crackdown involving extra-judicial killings, arbitrary detention, enforced disappearances and torture. On 2 October 2007, the UN Human Rights Council met in special session and strongly condemned the Burmese regime for 'beatings, killings, arbitrary detentions and enforced disappearances'.[556] On 11 October 2007, the Security Council likewise condemned the violence against the protesters but took no action against Burma.[557]

During the debate in the Security Council, there was some discussion of the unilateral coercive measures taken against Burma. France, Belgium and Italy explained that EU Member States had responded, *inter alia*, by adopting third-party countermeasures against Burma and reaffirmed their support for such action.[558] For its part, the United States stated:

> What can the world do to incentivize the Burmese regime to take these necessary measures [i.e. to incentivize it to cease some of its wrongful conduct]? This is an issue for the entire international community. The United States has done its part to back up its words with actions that will serve to ratchet up pressure on the regime. Last week, the Department of the Treasury blocked the assets of 14 senior regime officials, and the Department of State identified senior regime officials and their immediate family members – over 200 individuals – as subject to a ban on entry into the United States. We are now exploring follow-up measures targeting the regime and those who provide financial support to it.
>
> The Security Council must not remain silent just because the people of Burma have been silenced by the violent repression carried out by the regime. We have an opportunity to be their voice, and we must.[559]

The United States added that if Burma did not take appropriate steps to cease its wrongful conduct it was prepared to introduce a draft resolution in the Security Council imposing sanctions against it.[560]

Costa Rica also expressed support for the use of unilateral coercive measures (such as third-party countermeasures) against Burma.[561] Singapore questioned whether additional unilateral coercive measures,

---

[556] HRC Res. S-5/1 (2 Oct. 2007). For subsequent condemnation by the General Assembly, see GA Res. 62/222 (22 Dec. 2007).
[557] S/PRST/2007/37.
[558] UN Doc. S/PV.5753 (5 Oct. 2007), 9 (France), 10 (Belgium), 15 (Italy).
[559] Ibid., 13 (United States).   [560] Ibid.
[561] UN Doc. S/PV.6161 (13 July 2009), 17 (Costa Rica).

including third-party countermeasures, would be helpful in assisting the role of the United Nations to resolve the situation in Burma, but concluded that 'we should not rule that out'.[562] China stated that 'sanctions will not help resolve the issue, but rather further complicate the situation'.[563] It called for unilateral coercive measures against Burma to be lifted in order 'to provide the people of that country with a fair and enabling environment for its economic development'.[564] Russia likewise objected to the use of unilateral coercive measures against Burma on policy grounds.[565] For its part, Burma has protested that

> [T]he unilateral sanctions currently imposed on Myanmar are unwarranted, and they are also against international law ... Sanctions are being employed as a political tool against Myanmar.[566]

The adoption of third-party countermeasures against Burma appears primarily concerned with the following breaches of international law: (1) forced (child) labour (Convention concerning Forced or Compulsory Labour);[567] (2) right to life (Article 6 ICCPR); (3) freedom from arbitrary arrest and detention (Article 9 ICCPR); (4) freedom from torture (Article 7 ICCPR); (5) right to a fair trial (Article 14 ICCPR); 6) freedom of expression (Article 19 ICCPR); (7) freedom of assembly (Article 21 ICCPR); (8) freedom of association (Article 22 ICCPR and the Convention concerning Freedom of Association and Protection of the Right to Organize);[568] (9) freedom of movement (Article 12 ICCPR); (10) freedom of religion (Article 18 ICCPR); (11) minority rights (Article 27 ICCPR); (12) crimes against humanity; and (13) various other violations of international humanitarian law.

Most of the unilateral coercive measures adopted against Burma have now been lifted. The human rights situation in Burma nevertheless remains a matter of serious concern. In December 2012, the UN General Assembly expressed concern about 'remaining human rights violations, including arbitrary detention, forced displacement, land confiscation, rape and other forms of sexual violence, and torture and cruel,

---

[562] UN Doc. S/PV.5753 (5 Oct. 2007), 19 (Singapore).
[563] UN Doc. S/PV.5777 (13 Nov. 2007), 10 (China).
[564] UN Doc. S/PV.6161 (13 July 2009), 15 (China).
[565] UN Doc. S/PV.5777 (13 Nov. 2007), 14 (Russia) ('We are convinced that threats, pressure and sanctions exerted from outside the country are counterproductive and will only hinder the effort to solve the problems facing the country today').
[566] UN Doc. A/66/138 (14 July 2011), 11 (Burma).
[567] 39 UNTS 55 (entry into force 1 May 1932).
[568] 68 UNTS 17 (entry into force 4 July 1950).

inhuman and degrading treatment, as well as violations of international humanitarian law'.[569] The Human Rights Council, including its Special Rapporteur on Burma, have continued to express similar concerns about serious human rights abuses.[570]

It is difficult to say whether, as suggested by Australian Foreign Minister Carr, 'lifting sanctions is the best way to promote further progress'[571] or whether, as Canadian Foreign Minister Baird has instead proposed, 'limited sanctions may be useful in pressuring for continued progress'.[572] Still, Foreign Minister Baird's assessment that '[t]his is probably one of the best examples in the modern era where sanctions have proven very effective'[573] demonstrates that, as a minimum, third-party countermeasures do have an important role to play within an otherwise limited toolbox of communitarian law enforcement.

4.2.17 Miscellaneous Countries – Zimbabwe (2002–present)

In April 1980, following a protracted civil war between a national liberation movement led by Robert Mugabe and Ian Smith's racist white-minority regime in Rhodesia, Zimbabwe gained independence from the United Kingdom as envisaged in the 1979 Lancaster House Agreement. A major stumbling block in the independence negotiations concerned the issue of land reform. At the time of independence, land ownership in Zimbabwe heavily favoured the white minority population. On the insistence of the United Kingdom, Zimbabwe's independence constitution (the 'Lancaster House Constitution') would for ten years ban the forcible redistribution of arable land pending a permanent solution to the thorny question of long-term land reform involving the provision of funds from

---

[569] GA Res. 67/233 (24 Dec. 2012), op. para. 6. Similarly: GA Res. 68/242 (27 Dec. 2013); GA Res. 69/248 (29 Dec. 2014); GA Res. 70/233 (23 Dec. 2015).

[570] See e.g. UN Docs. A/HRC/22/58 (17 Apr. 2013); A/HRC/25/64 (2 Apr. 2014); A/HRC/ 28/72 (23 March 2015); A/HRC/31/71 (18 March 2016); and HRC Res. 22/14 (21 March 2013); HRC Res. 25/26 (28 March 2014); HRC Res. 28/23 (27 March 2015); HRC Res. 29/21 (3 July 2015); HRC Res. 31/24 (24 March 2016).

[571] See above n. 549.   [572] See above n. 552.

[573] See above n. 553. On 8 November 2015, Burma voted in historic general elections in which Aung San Suu Kyi's political party (NLD) won a landslide victory. An orderly and peaceful transfer of power to a civilian government led by President Htin Kyaw followed shortly thereafter. Further: 'Myanmar Election: Suu Kyi's NLD Wins Landslide Victory', *BBC News*, 13 November 2015, www.bbc.co.uk/news/world-asia-34806439; 'Myanmar Swears in First Elected Civilian President in 50 Years', *BBC News*, 30 March 2016, http:// www.bbc.com/news/world-asia-35923083.

the United Kingdom and other international donors to compensate dispossessed white landowners.[574]

In February 2000, a constitutional referendum was held in Zimbabwe. The proposed new constitution notably envisaged a scheme of land redistribution which gave the Zimbabwean government, led by President Mugabe, the power to seize arable lands owned by white farmers, without compensation, and transfer the ownership to black farmers. The draft constitution was unexpectedly defeated in the referendum.[575] In March 2000, so-called war veterans initiated a sustained violent campaign of land redistribution by illegally occupying hundreds of white-owned farms in Zimbabwe. A law was subsequently passed by the Zimbabwean parliament allowing for the seizure of white-owned farmland without compensation. EU Member States quickly condemned the situation and urged Zimbabwe to ensure respect for law and public order.[576]

The political and humanitarian situation in Zimbabwe deteriorated sharply as a result of the presidential elections held in March 2002, which saw President Mugabe re-elected in controversial circumstances.[577] The elections were preceded by an escalation of violence, intimidation of political opponents and harassment of the independent press. Legislation was enacted which seriously infringed on the rights to freedom of expression, assembly and association.[578] On 18 February 2002, EU Member States decided, in response to continuing acts of violence and intimidation which amounted to 'serious human rights violations' as well as conduct which 'seriously infringe on the right to freedom of speech, assembly and association', to impose various unilateral coercive measures against Zimbabwe.[579] The action taken included an arms embargo and a travel ban on senior government officials – both acts of

---

[574] See Southern Rhodesia, Report of the Constitutional Conference, Lancaster House, London, Sept.–Dec. 1979, http://peacemaker.un.org/sites/peacemaker.un.org/files/ZW_791221_LancasterHouseAgreement.pdf. Also: SC Res. 460 (21 Dec. 1979).

[575] See EU Bull. No. 1/2 (2000), para. 1.6.33; 'Opposition Maintains Lead in Zimbabwe Referendum', *The Guardian*, 15 February 2000, www.theguardian.com/world/2000/feb/15/1.

[576] EU Bull. No. 3 (2000), para. 1.6.14; EU Bull. No. 4 (2000), para. 1.6.73.

[577] See 'Mugabe Victory Leaves West's Policy in Tatters', *The Guardian*, 14 March 2002, www.theguardian.com/world/2002/mar/14/zimbabwe.chrismcgreal.

[578] EU Bull. No. 1/2 (2002), para. 1.6.154.

[579] Common Position 2002/145/CFSP (18 Feb. 2002), OJ 2002 L 50/1 (21 Feb. 2002), Council Regulation (EC) No. 310/2002 (18 Feb. 2002), OJ 2002 L 50/4 (21 Feb. 2002). For an analysis of the EU sanctions regime, see further Pillitu (2003), 55.

retorsion.[580] In addition, EU Member States also decided to suspend financial aid and development assistance owed to Zimbabwe under the Cotonou Agreement (which replaced the earlier Lomé Conventions).[581] Article 96(c) of the Cotonou Agreement enables contracting parties to take 'appropriate measures' in case of the non-fulfilment of obligations relating to human rights, principles of democratic governance and the rule of law.[582] The suspension of financial assistance may therefore be categorized as another measure of retorsion.

Finally, EU Member States also decided to freeze the assets of several senior Zimbabwean officials such as those belonging to President Mugabe, Foreign Minister Mudenge and Defence Minister Sekeramayi.[583] As a minimum, the freezing of President Mugabe's assets required justification under general international law. It should be understood as a third-party countermeasure.[584] Twenty-five countries aligned themselves with the EU sanctions regime and pledged to ensure its implementation.[585]

On 10 April 2002, a draft resolution on the situation in Zimbabwe, whose many co-sponsors included EU Member States, Australia,

---

[580] Ibid.

[581] Council Decision 2002/148/EC (18 Feb. 2002), OJ 2002 L 50/64 (21 Feb. 2002). For the text of the Cotonou Agreement see OJ 2000 L 317/3 (15 Dec. 2002); and for the regime of transitional application see OJ 2000 L 195/46 (27 July 2000).

[582] On the development of human rights conditionality clauses in EU treaties with third States, see further Brandtner and Rosas (1998), 468; Riedel and Will (1999), 723; Bartels (2005).

[583] Common Position 2002/145/CFSP (18 Feb. 2002), OJ 2002 L 50/1 (21 Feb. 2002), Council Regulation (EC) No. 310/2002 (18 Feb. 2002), OJ 2002 L 50/4 (21 Feb. 2002); Council Decision 2002/148/EC (18 Feb. 2002), OJ 2002 L 50/64 (21 Feb. 2002); EU Bull. No. 1/2 (2002), paras. 1.6.155–1.6.156.

[584] Tams (2005), 224–225; Katselli Proukaki (2010), 198; Tzanakopoulos (2015), 152. Following the ICJ's judgment in *Arrest Warrant*, the freezing of Foreign Minister Mudenge's assets would also appear to require justification under international law. The situation concerning Defence Ministers (and indeed other high-ranking ministers) is more unclear (see above n. 7).

[585] Albania, Armenia, Bosnia-Herzegovina, Bulgaria, Croatia, the Czech Republic, Estonia, Georgia, Hungary, Iceland, Latvia, Liechtenstein, Lithuania, Macedonia, Malta, Moldova, Montenegro, Norway, Poland, Romania, Serbia, Slovakia, Slovenia, Turkey and Ukraine: see EU Bull. No. 3 (2002), para. 1.6.22; EU Bull. No. 10 (2002), para. 1.6.32; EU Bull. No. 1/2 (2006), para. 1.25.26; Council of the European Union Press Release (6 Feb. 2006), http://www.consilium.europa.eu/uedocs/cms_Data/docs/pressData/fr/cfsp/88341.pdf; Council of the European Union Press Release (28 March 2012), http://consilium.europa.eu/uedocs/cms_Data/docs/pressdata/en/cfsp/129316.pdf;

Council of the European Union Press Release (4 Apr. 2012), www.consilium.europa.eu/uedocs/cms_Data/docs/pressdata/en/cfsp/129416.pdf (for Georgia's support).

Canada, Switzerland and the United States, was introduced in the UN Commission on Human Rights.[586] It condemned

(b) the continuing violations of human rights in Zimbabwe, often committed with impunity by agencies and supporters of the Zimbabwean ruling party, and in particular condemn[ed]:

   (i) The role of State-sponsored 'youth-militia', so-called 'war veterans' and agencies of the State in the deaths of, among others, at least one hundred supporters of the opposition Movement for Democratic Change;

   (ii) The occurrences of cases of enforced and involuntary disappearance, summary execution, kidnapping, torture, beating, harassment, arbitrary arrest and detention without trial, including of journalists, opposition politicians and their supporters and human rights defenders;

   (iii) Attacks on the independence of the judiciary and the rule of law;

   (iv) Cases of sexual and other forms of violence against women;

   (v) Racially motivated intimidation of minority ethnic communities in Zimbabwe;

(c) The violations of the freedoms of expression, opinion, association and assembly in Zimbabwe, as evidenced by the recent Public Order and Security Act and Access to Information Act, and the disregard by the executive of court rulings . . .[587]

However, the draft resolution was not put to a vote.[588]

On 11 April 2003, a similar draft resolution was again (unsuccessfully) introduced in the Commission on Human Rights by many of the same co-sponsors.[589] The draft resolution expressed deep concern at continuing human rights violations in Zimbabwe, including

> numerous cases of assault and torture in a climate of impunity, cases of sexual and other forms of violence against women, including cases of politically motivated rape, incidents of arbitrary arrest, attempts to restrict the independence of the judiciary, and apparent political bias in the distribution of food provided through government channels . . . [as well as] violations of the freedoms of expression, opinion, association and assembly.[590]

---

[586] Report of the Commission on Human Rights (58th session, 18 March – 26 Apr. 2002), UN Doc. E/2002/23, 438–442.

[587] Ibid., 440 (op. para. 1).   [588] Ibid., 441–442; UNYB (2002), 785–786.

[589] Report of the Commission on Human Rights (59th session, 17 March – 24 Apr. 2003), UN Doc. E/2003/23, 376–380.

[590] Ibid., 377 (op. para. 1).

On 9 April 2004, a further draft resolution was introduced in the Commission on Human Rights but was yet again denied a vote.[591]

On 19 May 2005, the already dire humanitarian situation in Zimbabwe further deteriorated when President Mugabe initiated a forcible slum clearance programme known as Operation Murambatsvina (literally 'drive out rubbish') precipitating a humanitarian crisis.[592] On 18 July 2005, the Special Envoy on Human Settlement Issues in Zimbabwe, appointed by the UN Secretary General, reported that Operation Murambatsvina had resulted in 'enormous humanitarian consequences'; notably, the internal displacement of hundreds of thousands of people and wanton destruction of property.[593] EU Member States immediately denounced Operation Murambatsvina – carried out 'in contravention of international law on human rights' – and stressed that, while Zimbabwe continued to engage in 'serious violations', the unilateral coercive measures adopted against it would remain in place.[594] For his part, the UN Secretary General similarly denounced a 'catastrophic injustice' affecting some 700,000 people.[595]

The EU sanctions regime against Zimbabwe has been broadened and renewed on a regular basis since February 2002 and partially still remains in force.[596] On 25 March 2013, in response to a 'peaceful, successful and credible' referendum to approve a new constitution in Zimbabwe, the EU partially suspended its sanctions regime.[597] On 17 February 2014, the EU

---

[591] Report of the Commission on Human Rights (60th session, 15 March – 23 Apr. 2004), UN Doc. E/2004/23, 379–381.

[592] *Keesing's* (2005), 46611–46612, 46671, 46726.

[593] Report of the UN Special Envoy on Human Settlements Issues in Zimbabwe (18 July 2005), 8, 63, 67, www.un.org/News/dh/infocus/zimbabwe/zimbabwe_rpt.pdf.

[594] EU Bull. No. 7/8 (2005), para. 1.6.83; Council of the European Union Press Release (7 June 2005), www.consilium.europa.eu/ueDocs/cms_Data/docs/pressData/en/cfsp/85103.pdf.

[595] UNSG Press Release (22 July 2005), www.un.org/press/en/2005/sgsm10012.doc.htm.

[596] Council Decision 2016/220/CFSP (15 Feb. 2016), OJ 2016 L 40/11 (17 Feb. 2016). Also: Council Decision 2011/101/CFSP (15 Feb. 2011), OJ 2011 L 42/6 (16 Feb. 2011). In February 2007, the asset freeze (and travel ban) was extended to Vice-President Mujuru and Foreign Minister Mumbengegwi: see Council Common Position 2007/120/CFSP (19 Feb. 2007), OJ 2007 L 51/25 (20 Feb. 2007).

[597] Declaration by the High Representative, Catherine Ashton, on behalf of the European Union with regard to the successful Constitutional referendum in Zimbabwe and the review of EU restrictive measures (25 March 2013), www.consilium.europa.eu/uedocs/cms_data/docs/pressdata/en/cfsp/136501.pdf; Council Regulation (EU) No. 298/2013 (27 March 2013), OJ 2013 L 90/48 (28 March 2013). Also: 'Has the EU Lifted Sanctions against Zimbabwe Too Soon?', *The Guardian*, 26 March 2013, www.theguardian.com/world/2013/mar/26/eu-lifted-zimbabwe-sanctions-too-soon.

suspended the remaining sanctions regime with some exceptions.[598] In particular, the freeze on President Mugabe's assets still remains in force.[599] On 20 March 2002, Switzerland likewise adopted unilateral coercive measures against Zimbabwe, including the freezing of President Mugabe's assets, which also still remain in force.[600]

On 19 March 2002, Commonwealth Member States decided to suspend Zimbabwe's membership in the Commonwealth for twelve months with immediate effect.[601] The same argument developed above in relation to the Commonwealth suspension of Nigeria applies here.[602] Thus Zimbabwe's suspension violated its membership rights and could not be justified under the rules of the Commonwealth. It required justification under general international law and should be characterized as a third-party countermeasure.[603] As a minimum, Commonwealth Member States expressed support for the adoption of third-party countermeasures against Zimbabwe. In September 2002, Australia adopted its own sanctions regime against Zimbabwe. This sanctions regime, which included the freezing of President Mugabe's assets, still remains in force.[604] On 7 March 2003, the United States decided, *inter alia*, to impose a travel ban and freeze the assets of senior Zimbabwean government officials, including assets belonging to President Mugabe.[605] The US sanctions regime against Zimbabwe

---

[598] Council Decision 2014/98/CFSP (17 Feb. 2014), OJ 2014 L 50/20 (20 Feb. 2014); Declaration by the High Representative, Catherine Ashton, on behalf of the European Union on the review of EU-Zimbabwe relations (19 Feb. 2014), www.consilium.europa .eu/uedocs/cms_data/docs/pressdata/EN/foraff/141064.pdf.

[599] Ibid. See also above n. 596.

[600] Swiss Federal Council, 'Ordonnance du 19 mars 2002 instituant des mesures à l'encontre du Zimbabwe', www.admin.ch/opc/fr/classified-compilation/20020594/index.html. Further: 'Switzerland Imposes Sanctions on Zimbabwe', *Swissinfo*, 20 March 2002, www .swissinfo.ch/eng/Switzerland_imposes_sanctions_on_Zimbabwe.html?cid=2607990.

[601] 'Meeting of Commonwealth Chairpersons' Committee on Zimbabwe', Commonwealth News Release (19 March 2002), available at http://thecommonwealth.org. In December 2003, as the suspension was renewed, Zimbabwe immediately withdrew its membership: see 'Mugabe Quits Commonwealth', *The Guardian*, 8 December 2003, www .theguardian.com/world/2003/dec/08/zimbabwe.politics. For a brief discussion see Duxbury (2011), 210–211 (with further references).

[602] See above Section 4.2.12 (text accompanying nn. 346–353).

[603] See Tams (2005), 225; Katselli Proukaki (2010), 198.

[604] See Australian Department of Foreign Affairs and Trade, 'Sanctions Regimes: Zimbabwe', http://dfat.gov.au/international-relations/security/sanctions/sanctions-regimes/pages/zimbabwe.aspx.

[605] See President Bush's Executive Order 13288 (6 March 2003), 'Blocking Property of Persons Undermining Democratic Processes or Institutions in Zimbabwe', www .treasury.gov/resource-center/sanctions/Documents/13288.pdf. Further: 'US to Match

also still remains in force.[606] In September 2008, Canada adopted several unilateral coercive measures against Zimbabwe, including the freezing of President Mugabe's assets, which likewise still remain in force.[607] The Security Council has not taken any action against Zimbabwe. On 18 March 2002, a month after EU Member States had first adopted unilateral coercive measures against Zimbabwe, they informed the Security Council of the possibility of 'additional targeted measures' against the Mugabe regime.[608] On 27 July 2005, following a request by the United Kingdom, the Security Council convened in a private meeting to discuss the report of the Special Envoy on Operation Murambatsvina.[609] On 18 June 2008, Belgium requested a meeting of the Security Council to discuss the dire situation in Zimbabwe.[610] On 23 June 2008, ahead of presidential elections in Zimbabwe marred by political violence, the Security Council condemned

> the campaign of violence against the political opposition ahead of the second round of presidential elections scheduled for 27 June, which has resulted in the killing of scores of opposition activists and other Zimbabweans and the beating and displacement of thousands of people, including many women and children.
>
> The Security Council further condemns the actions of the Government of Zimbabwe that have denied its political opponents the right to campaign freely, and calls upon the Government of Zimbabwe to stop the violence, to cease political intimidation, to end the restrictions on the right of assembly and to release the political leaders who have been detained.[611]

On 11 July 2008, a draft Security Council resolution under Chapter VII UNC, the co-sponsors of which included several EU Member States,

EU Sanctions on Zimbabwe', *The Guardian*, 20 February 2002, www.guardian.co.uk/world/2002/feb/20/zimbabwe.davidpallister.

[606] See President Bush's Executive Order 13469 (25 July 2008), 'Blocking Property of Additional Persons Undermining Democratic Processes or Institutions in Zimbabwe', www.treasury.gov/resource-center/sanctions/Documents/13469.pdf; White House Press Release, 'Continuation of the National Emergency with Respect to Zimbabwe' (2 March 2016), www.whitehouse.gov/the-press-office/2016/03/02/message-continuation-national-emergency-respect-zimbabwe.

[607] See Special Economic Measures (Zimbabwe) Regulations (SOR/2008–248) (4 Sept. 2008), http://laws-lois.justice.gc.ca/eng/regulations/SOR-2008-248/FullText.html.

[608] UN Doc. S/2002/299 (Spain on behalf of EU Member States).

[609] UN Docs. S/2005/485; S/2005/489 (United Kingdom); Report of the Security Council (1 Aug. 2004 – 31 July 2005), UN Doc. A/60/2, 11.

[610] UN Doc. S/2008/407 (Belgium).

[611] S/PRST/2008/23. See also Council of the European Union Press Release (4 July 2008), www.consilium.europa.eu/ueDocs/cms_Data/docs/pressData/en/cfsp/101625.pdf.

Australia, Canada and the United States, was introduced.[612] The draft resolution notably demanded that the Mugabe regime:

> Immediately cease attacks against and intimidation of opposition members and supporters ... and in particular end the abuse of human rights, including widespread beatings, torture, killings, sexual violence, and displacement, and release all political prisoners.[613]

Moreover, the draft resolution provided for enforcement measures under Chapter VII UNC to be taken against Zimbabwe in the form of an arms embargo, a travel ban and the freezing of assets of senior regime officials, including assets belonging to President Mugabe. However, the draft resolution was vetoed by China and Russia.[614]

During the debate on the draft resolution, the EU sanctions regime was briefly discussed in the Security Council.[615] For its part, Zimbabwe assailed the unilateral coercive measures adopted against it, which had 'brought much suffering to the people of Zimbabwe'.[616] It added: 'The current sanctions against Zimbabwe are basically an expression of imperialist conquest and no amount of propaganda or denial can ever wish that away'.[617] While some States opposed the adoption of sanctions by the Security Council, no other State protested against the unilateral coercive measures, including third-party countermeasures, already adopted against Zimbabwe.[618] In July 2009, however, the Non-Aligned Movement called for 'the immediate lifting of arbitrary and unilateral sanctions by those states and parties that have imposed the economically crippling measures on Zimbabwe'.[619]

On 31 July 2013, President Mugabe was again re-elected in flawed elections. Following these elections, SADC likewise called for the lifting of unilateral coercive measures against Zimbabwe as the civilian population, in the words of Malawian President Banda, had 'suffered enough'.[620]

---

[612] UN Doc. S/2008/447.   [613] Ibid., op. para. 2(a).

[614] Ibid., op. paras. 4–9; Report of the Security Council (1 Aug. 2007 – 31 July 2008), UN Doc. A/63/2, 19–20; UN Press Release (11 July 2008), www.un.org/News/Press/docs/ 2008/sc9396.doc.htm. See further 'China and Russia Veto Zimbabwe Sanctions', *The Guardian*, 11 July 2008, www.guardian.co.uk/world/2008/jul/11/unitednations .zimbabwe.

[615] UN Doc. S/PV.5933 (11 July 2008), 10 (France).   [616] Ibid., 3 (Zimbabwe).

[617] Ibid.   [618] Ibid., 7 (Indonesia and Vietnam), 9 (Russia), 13 (China).

[619] UN Doc. S/2009/514 (Egypt on behalf of the Non-Aligned Movement), 82, para. 235.

[620] 'Zimbabwe's Mugabe Should Not Face Sanctions, SADC Says', *BBC News*, 19 August 2013, www.bbc.co.uk/news/world-africa-23754623.

Zimbabwe again lambasted the continuing resort to unilateral coercive measures against it:

> These are not from the UN, they are just from a club of white people who just don't like the fact that we are repossessing our land . . . The sanctions are illegal and they should be lifted yesterday, not tomorrow.[621]

It thus appears that a large number of States have adopted third-party countermeasures against Zimbabwe, including in response to the following breaches of the ICCPR:[622] (1) right of non-discrimination (Article 2); (2) right to life (Article 6); (3) freedom from torture (Article 7); (4) right to liberty and security of person (Article 9); (5) right to a fair trial (Article 14); (6) freedom of thought (Article 18); (7) freedom of expression (Article 19); (8) freedom of assembly (Article 21); and (9) freedom of association (Article 22).

4.2.18 European States and the United States – Belarus (2004–present)

In July 1994, Alexander Lukashenko was elected President of Belarus. President Lukashenko has since been re-elected on several occasions in deeply flawed elections marred by human rights abuses. The Lukashenko regime has repeatedly been condemned by the international community for its human rights violations.[623] On 17 April 2003, the UN Commission on Human Rights expressed deep concern at credible reports implicating senior Belarusian government officials in the forced disappearance and/or summary execution of several dissidents, as well as reports concerning the arbitrary arrest and detention of dissidents, harassment of civil society groups and independent media and restrictions on religious freedom.[624]

On 15 April 2004, the Commission on Human Rights appointed a Special Rapporteur to examine the situation of human rights in Belarus.[625]

---

[621] 'Robert Mugabe Election Victory Could Force West to Lift Zimbabwe Sanctions', *The Guardian*, 2 August 2013, www.theguardian.com/world/2013/aug/02/robert-mugabe-election-zimbabwe-sanctions.

[622] Zimbabwe acceded to the ICCPR on 13 May 1991. All responding States were parties to the ICCPR at the relevant time.

[623] See already UNYB (1998), 754.

[624] UNCHR Res. 2003/14, Report of the Commission on Human Rights (59th session, 17 March – 24 Apr. 2003), UN Doc. E/2003/23, 60–61; UNYB (2003), 824.

[625] UNCHR Res. 2004/14, Report of the Commission on Human Rights (60th session, 15 March – 23 Apr. 2004), UN Doc. E/2004/23, 51–54; UNYB (2004), 815. See further UNYB (2005), 901–902.

On 18 March 2005, the Special Rapporteur presented his first report to the Commission on Human Rights, which found, *inter alia*, that 'torture is routinely used as a means of extracting confessions from detainees' and also expressed concern about the 'systematic torture of detainees on death row'.[626] Other potential violations of international law included the right to a fair trial, and the rights to freedom of expression, assembly, association and religion.[627]

On 19 December 2006, the UN General Assembly adopted a resolution by which it expressed concern about the deeply flawed presidential elections held on 19 March 2006 which failed to meet international standards. It also expressed deep concern, *inter alia*, in relation to

> continuing reports of harassment, arbitrary arrest and detention of up to one thousand persons, including opposition candidates, before and after the election of 19 March 2006; [and] ... continuing and expanding criminal prosecutions, lack of due process and closed political trials of leading opposition figures and human rights defenders.[628]

In response, the General Assembly notably urged Belarus 'to respect the rights to freedom of speech, assembly and association, and to release immediately all political prisoners and other individuals detained for exercising those rights ... [and] to uphold the right to freedom of religion or belief'.[629] On 18 December 2007, the General Assembly again expressed concern about continuing 'systematic violations of human rights' as documented by the UN Special Rapporteur on Belarus.[630]

On 17 June 2011, the UN Human Rights Council expressed deep concern at the severe deterioration of the overall human rights situation in Belarus following yet another fundamentally flawed presidential election held on 19 December 2010. In addition to expressing deep concern as to 'credible allegations of torture' of dissidents, the Human Rights Council notably condemned

> the human rights violations occurring before, during and in the aftermath of the presidential elections of 19 December 2010, including the use of violence against, arbitrary arrest, detention and the politically motivated

---

[626] Report of the Special Rapporteur on the situation of human rights in Belarus, UN Doc. E/CN.4/2005/35, 8–9.

[627] Ibid., 9–16.

[628] GA Res. 61/175 (19 Dec. 2006), op. para. 1. The draft resolution was co-sponsored by a large number of States, including the United States, most EU Member States and Switzerland: see UN Doc. A/C.3/61/L.40.

[629] Ibid., op. para. 2. See also UNYB (2006), 961–963.

[630] GA Res. 62/169 (18 Dec. 2007). See also UNYB (2007), 822–824.

conviction of opposition candidates, their supporters, journalists and human rights defenders, as well as the abuses of due process rights, including the right to a fair trial for those involved in the demonstrations of 19 December.[631]

On 5 July 2012, the Human Rights Council adopted a further resolution by which it

express[ed] grave concern at the findings of the United Nations High Commissioner for Human Rights in her report that suggest the existence of a pattern of serious violations of human rights since 19 December 2010, that is of a systemic nature, and includes intensified restrictions on the fundamental freedoms of association, assembly, opinion and expression, including with regard to the media, as well as allegations of torture and ill-treatment in custody, impunity of perpetrators of human rights violations and abuses, harassment of civil society organizations and human rights defenders, violations of due process and fair trial safeguards, and pressure on defence lawyers.[632]

European States and the United States have not only co-sponsored the above-mentioned resolutions against Belarus. They have also responded to the systematic violations of international law identified in those resolutions by adopting various unilateral coercive measures against Belarus. On 24 September 2004, EU Member States announced the adoption of a limited travel ban on four senior members of President Lukashenko's regime deemed responsible for the involuntary disappearances of leading dissidents.[633] On 10 March 2005, the European Parliament strongly condemned acts of repression by Belarusian authorities against dissidents, including arbitrary arrests, ill treatment of detainees and involuntary disappearances and called on Belarus to comply with its obligations under the ICCPR. In order to induce such compliance, the European Parliament notably called on EU Member States 'to identify and freeze the personal assets of President Lukashenko'.[634] On 7 November 2005, at a meeting of the European Council, Poland, in particular, stressed the need for such an asset freeze. No decision on an asset freeze was taken at this stage but EU Member States nevertheless notified Belarus that such

---

[631] HRC Res. 17/24 (17 June 2011), op. para. 1.
[632] HRC Res. 20/13 (5 July 2012), op. para. 1. See also HRC Res. 23/15 (13 June 2013), op. para. 2 (expressing deep concern at continuing human rights violations in Belarus of a 'structural and endemic nature').
[633] Common Position 2004/661/CFSP (24 Sept. 2004), OJ 2004 L 301/67 (28 Sept. 2004). See also UN Doc. S/2004/417 (Ireland on behalf of EU Member States).
[634] EU Bull. No. 3 (2005), para. 1.2.4.

action could be taken against it at a later stage if it did not return to legality.[635]

On 10 April 2006, notably in response to the arrest of peaceful demonstrators exercising their right of free assembly to protest against the conduct of the presidential elections held in Belarus on 19 March 2006, the EU travel ban was extended to include President Lukashenko.[636] On 21 December 2006, EU Member States further extended the sanctions regime by means of a temporary withdrawal of certain discretionary trade preferences.[637] On 25 October 2010, EU Member States ultimately decided, among other unilateral coercive measures, to freeze President Lukashenko's assets.[638] On 1 November 2012, EU High Representative Ashton declared that eight countries had aligned themselves with the EU sanctions regime against Belarus and pledged to ensure its implementation.[639] On 29 October 2015, in response to the release of all political prisoners and presidential elections held in an environment free from violence, the EU suspended most of its sanctions regime for four months, including the freezing of President Lukashenko's assets.[640] On 25 February 2016, the EU decided to lift most its sanctions regime against Belarus.[641] On 28 June 2006, Switzerland adopted several

[635] EU Bull. No. 11 (2005), para. 1.6.73; 'Belarus: EU Threatens Sanctions, Urges Free And Fair Elections', *Radio Free Europe/Radio Liberty*, 8 November 2005, http://www.rferl.org /a/1062738.html.

[636] Common Position 2006/276/CFSP (10 Apr. 2006), OJ 2006 L 101/5 (11 Apr. 2006). See also 'EU Sanctions as Belarus Moves against Protesters', *The Guardian*, 24 March 2006, www.theguardian.com/world/2006/mar/24/1.

[637] Council Regulation (EC) No. 1933/2006 (21 Dec. 2006), OJ 2006 L 405/35 (30 Dec. 2006); EU Bull. No. 6 (2007), para. 1.29.11.

[638] Council Decision 2010/639/CFSP (25 Oct. 2010), OJ 2010 L 280/18 (26 Oct. 2010). See also Council Decision 2012/642/CFSP (15 Oct. 2012), OJ 2012 L 285/1 (17 Oct. 2012).

[639] Albania, Croatia, Iceland, Lichtenstein, Macedonia, Montenegro, Norway and Serbia: see Declaration by the High Representative on behalf of the European Union on the alignment of certain third countries with Council Decision 2012/642/CFSP concerning restrictive measures against Belarus (1 Nov. 2012), www.consilium.europa.eu/uedocs/ cms_Data/docs/pressdata/en/cfsp/133277.pdf.

[640] Council of the European Union Press Release (29 Oct. 2015), www.consilium.europa.eu/ en/press/press-releases/2015/10/29-belarus; Council Decision 2015/1957/CFSP (29 Oct. 2015), OJ 2015 L 284/149 (30 Oct. 2015). See also 'Belarus Poll: EU Lifts Sanctions on Lukashenko – "Europe's Last Dictator"', *The Guardian*, 13 October 2015, www.theguardian.com/world/2015/oct/13/belarus-poll-eu-lifts-sanctions-on-lukashenko- europes-last-dictator.

[641] Council of the European Union Press Release (25 Feb. 2016), www.consilium.europa.eu/en/ press/press-releases/2016/02/25-belarus-sanctions; Council Decision 2016/280/CFSP (25 Feb. 2016), OJ 2016 L 52/30 (27 Feb. 2016). See also Council of the European Union,

unilateral coercive measures against Belarus, including the freezing of President Lukashenko's assets.[642] On 1 March 2016, the Swiss asset freeze against him was lifted.[643]

On 20 October 2004, US President Bush signed into law the Belarus Democracy Act, which called for the adoption of several unilateral coercive measures against Belarus, including an investment ban, a travel ban and an asset freeze on leading members of the Lukashenko regime.[644] On 19 June 2006, the United States decided to freeze President Lukashenko's assets.[645] On 3 January 2012, the US sanctions regime was strengthened as President Obama signed into law the Belarus Democracy and Human Rights Act.[646] On 29 October 2015, the US sanctions regime was eased; however, the freezing of President Lukashenko's assets still remains in force.[647]

The UN has to date not taken any coercive action against Belarus. Some protests regarding the unilateral coercive measures adopted against Belarus have, however, been communicated to the General Assembly and the Security Council. In March 2008, the Non-Aligned Movement protested that the unilateral coercive measures adopted against Belarus violated international law as they were deemed to contravene the principle of non-intervention, amounted to a form of political and economic

---

'Council Conclusions on Belarus' (15 Feb. 2016), www.consilium.europa.eu/en/press/press-releases/2016/02/15-fac-belarus-conclusions; 'EU Lifts Most Sanctions against Belarus Despite Human Rights Concerns', *The Guardian*, 15 February 2016, www.theguardian.com/world/2016/feb/15/eu-lifts-most-sanctions-against-belarus-despite-human-rights-concerns.

[642] Swiss Federal Council, 'Ordonnance du 28 juin 2006 instituant des mesures à l'encontre du Bélarus', www.admin.ch/opc/fr/classified-compilation/20061656.

[643] Ibid.

[644] Belarus Democracy Act of 2004, Public Law 108-347 (20 Oct. 2004), www.gpo.gov/fdsys/pkg/PLAW-108publ347/pdf/PLAW-108publ347.pdf.

[645] See President Bush's Executive Order 13405 (19 June 2006), 'Blocking Property of Certain Persons Undermining Democratic Processes or Institutions in Belarus', www.treasury.gov/resource-center/sanctions/Documents/13405.pdf. Further: 'US May Consider New Belarus Sanctions', *The Washington Post*, 18 March 2006, www.washingtonpost.com/wp-dyn/content/article/2006/03/17/AR2006031701709.html.

[646] Belarus Democracy and Human Rights Act of 2011, Public Law 112-82 (3 Jan. 2012), https://www.congress.gov/112/plaws/publ82/PLAW-112publ82.pdf. See further 'US Toughens Sanctions over "Brutal" Belarus Crackdown', *BBC News*, 31 January 2011, www.bbc.co.uk/news/world-europe-12330051; 'Obama Signs Belarus Human Rights and Democracy Act', *Radio Free Europe/Radio Liberty*, 4 January 2012, http://www.rferl.org/a/obama_signs_belarus_democracy_act/24441624.html.

[647] See White House Press Release, 'Continuation of the National Emergency with Respect to Belarus' (10 June 2016), www.whitehouse.gov/the-press-office/2016/06/10/notice-continuation-national-emergency-respect-actions-and-policies.

coercion against a developing country, as proscribed in repeated resolutions of the General Assembly, and were not authorized by either the General Assembly or the Security Council.[648]

In April 2012, Belarus likewise strongly protested that the unilateral coercive measures adopted against it 'contravene[d] the Charter of the United Nations [and] principles and norms of international law'; namely, the principle of non-intervention and several resolutions of the General Assembly which proscribed economic coercion against a developing country 'in order to obtain from it the subordination of the exercise of its sovereign rights'.[649] Belarus added that 'the trumped-up nature of these claims [i.e. its alleged breaches of international law] is obvious'[650] – an allegation difficult to reconcile with the repeated condemnations of Belarus' serious human rights violations by several UN organs. As a matter of policy, Belarus emphasized that

> Acts of intimidation, economic pressure and coercion are utterly unacceptable in international affairs and serve only to escalate tensions between sovereign States and in the international arena generally.[651]

Belarus also denounced 'the insufficient response of the United Nations',[652] and (unsuccessfully) called on the UN to urge States to lift the unilateral coercive measures adopted against it.[653]

In sum, it appears that third-party countermeasures have been adopted against Belarus principally in response to the following breaches of the ICCPR:[654] (1) freedom from torture (Article 7); (2) right to liberty and security of person (Article 9); (3) right to a fair trial (Article 14); (4) freedom of expression (Article 19); (5) freedom of assembly (Article 21); and (6) freedom of association (Article 22).

4.2.19   Switzerland and the United States – Libya (2011)

On 17 February 2011, Libyan security forces killed scores of protesters demonstrating against Colonel Gaddafi's regime in Benghazi. This marked the beginning of a series of similar incidents across Libya.

---

[648] UN Doc. S/2008/199 (Cuba on behalf of the Non-Aligned Movement).

[649] UN Doc. S/2012/242 (Belarus). See also e.g. UN Docs. A/66/272 (5 Aug. 2011), 4–5; A/67/181 (25 July 2012), 3–4; A/68/211 (22 July 2013), 3 (Belarus).

[650] UN Doc. S/2012/242 (Belarus).

[651] Ibid. See also UN Doc. A/67/181 (25 July 2012), 3–4 (Belarus).

[652] UN Doc. A/67/181 (25 July 2012), 4 (Belarus).   [653] Ibid.

[654] Belarus became a party to the ICCPR on 12 November 1973. All responding States were parties to the ICCPR at the relevant time.

A bloody uprising followed which soon sparked a full-scale civil war in the country.[655] The international community took almost immediate action against Libya. On 21 February 2011, Switzerland decided with immediate effect to freeze the assets of the Libyan Central Bank as well as those of several senior Libyan officials involved in the violent repression of the civilian population, including assets belonging to Colonel Gaddafi, Libya's Head of State.[656] On 22 February 2011, the Council of the League of Arab States agreed by unanimous vote to suspend Libya from its membership in the Arab League – a decision 'welcomed' by the UN Security Council and the General Assembly.[657]

Article 18 of the Pact of the League of Arab States[658] provides that membership suspension is possible by unanimous vote (except the member targeted by such action) for 'any State that is not fulfilling the obligations resulting from this Pact'. However, the Pact of the League of Arab States does not refer to any obligation on States Parties to comply with international human rights and humanitarian law. Thus the decision to suspend Libya was *prima facie* wrongful as it seemingly lacked a substantive treaty-based justification. Still, the decision to suspend Libya, which was taken by an official organ of the Arab League (i.e. the League Council), was nevertheless valid in procedural terms. Although the matter is somewhat unclear given the paucity of relevant practice, the better view is probably that Libya's wrongful suspension was attributable to the organization (as distinct from its individual members) in terms of Article 58(2) DARIO.[659] Still, as a minimum, Arab League Member States expressed support for such

---

[655] See e.g. 'Libya's Day of Rage Met by Bullets and Loyalists', *The Guardian*, 17 February 2011, www.theguardian.com/world/2011/feb/17/libya-day-of-rage-unrest; 'Libya Protests: Defiant Gaddafi Refuses to Quit', *BBC News*, 22 February 2011, www.bbc .co.uk/news/world-middle-east-12544624.

[656] See Swiss Federal Council, 'Ordonnance instituant des mesures à l'encontre de certaines personnes originaires de la Libye' (21 Feb. 2011), www.admin.ch/opc/fr/classified-compilation/20110418/201103110000/946.231.149.82.pdf.

[657] 'Arab League Bars Libya From Meetings', *The Wall Street Journal*, 23 February 2011, http://blogs.wsj.com/dispatch/2011/02/23/arab-league-bars-libya-from-meetings; Security Council Press Statement on Libya (22 Feb. 2011), www.un.org/News/Press/docs/2011/ sc10180.doc.htm; GA Res. 65/265 (1 March 2011) (preamble); and also to the same effect, HRC Res. S-15/1 (25 Feb. 2011) (preamble). Libya was reinstated as a member of the Arab League in August 2011.

[658] 70 UNTS 237 (entry into force 10 May 1945).

[659] DARIO Commentary, Art. 58, §4. Compare Klein (2010), 307–308. The Arab League suspension of Libya seemingly amounted to a third-party countermeasure within the meaning of Article 57 DARIO: see DARIO Commentary, Art. 57, §2 (n. 338).

action and so it may reasonably be assumed that all Arab League Member States accept the use of third-party countermeasures in such circumstances.

On 25 February 2011, the United States decided to freeze with immediate effect the assets of the Central Bank of Libya as well as those of Colonel Gaddafi and his closest associates in response to the 'extreme measures taken against the people of Libya, including by using weapons of war, mercenaries, and wanton violence against unarmed civilians, all of which have caused a deterioration in the security of Libya and pose a serious risk to its stability'.[660]

On 25 February 2011, the UN Human Rights Council adopted a resolution on Libya by which it strongly condemned

> the recent gross and systematic human rights violations committed in that country, including the indiscriminate armed attacks against civilians, extra-judicial killings, arbitrary arrests, detention and torture of peaceful demonstrators, some of which may also amount to crimes against humanity.[661]

The resolution also called on Libya to immediately put an end to all human rights violations, including arbitrary arrests and denials of the freedoms of expression and assembly, and established an international commission of inquiry to investigate all alleged breaches of international human rights law committed in Libya since February 2011.[662]

On 26 February 2011, the UN Security Council adopted a resolution under Chapter VII UNC by which it deplored

> the gross and systematic violation of human rights, including the repression of peaceful demonstrators, expressing deep concern at the deaths of civilians, and rejecting unequivocally the incitement to hostility and violence against the civilian population made from the highest level of the Libyan government.[663]

The Security Council likewise stressed the need to respect the freedoms of expression and assembly, and condemned 'serious violations of human rights and international humanitarian law' considering that 'the widespread and systematic attacks currently taking place in the Libyan Arab

---

[660] See President Obama's Executive Order 13566 (25 Feb. 2011), 'Blocking Property and Prohibiting Certain Transactions Related to Libya', www.treasury.gov/resource-center /sanctions/Programs/Documents/2011_libya_eo.pdf. Further: 'U.S. Imposes Sanctions on Libya in Wake of Crackdown', *The New York Times*, 25 February 2011, www.nytimes .com/2011/02/26/world/middleeast/26diplomacy.html.
[661] HRC Res. S-15/1 (25 Feb. 2011).   [662] Ibid., op. paras. 2–3, 11.
[663] SC Res. 1970 (26 Feb. 2011).

Jamahiriya against the civilian population may amount to crimes against humanity'.[664] In response, the Security Council decided to take enforcement action against Libya by immediately referring the situation in the country to the ICC, and by imposing an arms embargo as well as travel bans and asset freezes on leading regime officials, including Colonel Gaddafi.[665]

On 1 March 2011, the UN General Assembly suspended Libya's membership in the Human Rights Council pursuant to the terms of an earlier resolution which entitled it to do so in cases of 'gross and systematic violations of human rights'.[666] On 17 March 2011, the Security Council adopted a further resolution under Chapter VII UNC by which it condemned 'gross and systematic violations of human rights, including arbitrary detentions, enforced disappearances, torture and summary execution' and again stressed that crimes against humanity may have been committed.[667] By the same resolution, the Security Council also took additional enforcement action against Libya by imposing a civil aviation embargo and a no-fly zone, broadening the asset freezes and authorizing air strikes to protect the civilian population in Libya. In late March 2011, NATO launched Operation Unified Protector, which a few months later resulted in the overthrow of Colonel Gaddafi's brutal regime.

On 12 January 2012, the international commission of inquiry presented its report to the Human Rights Council.[668] The detailed report confirmed the violations of international human rights and humanitarian law identified earlier in resolutions adopted by UN organs. It notably concluded that crimes against humanity and war crimes had been committed by Libyan government forces carried out as a result of policy decisions taken at the highest levels of the Libyan government.[669] These conclusions were confirmed two months later by the final report of the commission.[670]

---

[664] Ibid.   [665] Ibid., op. paras. 4, 9, 15 and 17.

[666] See GA Res. 65/265 (1 March 2011); GA Res. 60/251 (15 March 2008), esp. op. para. 8. Libya's membership rights were restored in November 2011 following the overthrow of Colonel Gaddafi's regime: see GA Res. 66/11 (18 Nov. 2011).

[667] SC Res. 1973 (17 March 2011).

[668] Report of the International Commission of Inquiry to investigate all alleged violations of international human rights law in the Libyan Jamahiriya, UN Doc. A/HRC/17/44 (12 Jan. 2012).

[669] Ibid., 67–68, paras. 246–250.

[670] Report of the International Commission of Inquiry on Libya, UN Doc. A/HRC/19/68, 20–12, paras. 118–119. The Human Rights Council later adopted a resolution by which it took note of the report: see HRC Res. 19/39 (23 March 2012).

In sum, the chronology of events indicates that, prior to the enforcement measures taken by the Security Council under Chapter VII UNC, Switzerland and the United States adopted third-party countermeasures against Libya by freezing the assets of Colonel Gaddafi and the Central Bank of Libya. As a minimum, Arab League Member States also expressed support for the adoption of third-party countermeasures against Libya by suspending its membership in the Arab League – a decision welcomed by the Security Council and the General Assembly. It appears that these third-party countermeasures were mainly taken in response to the following Libyan violations of international human rights and humanitarian law: (1) freedom from torture (Article 7 ICCPR); (2) right to liberty and security of person (Article 9 ICCPR); (3) freedom of expression (Article 19 ICCPR); (4) freedom of assembly (Article 21 ICCPR); (5) crimes against humanity; and (6) war crimes.[671]

4.2.20   Miscellaneous Countries – Syria (2011–present)

In March 2011, peaceful protests erupted in the Syrian city of Dar'a in response to the detention and torture of a group of children accused of painting anti-government graffiti on public buildings. After the Syrian security forces indiscriminately opened fire on the demonstrators, killing several of them, demonstrations against President Bashar Al-Assad's dictatorial regime spread across Syria.[672] The Assad regime responded to the popular calls for political reforms with increasing brutality and Syria soon descended into civil war – a conflict which by August 2015 was estimated to have caused at least 250,000 violent deaths and millions of internally displaced persons and refugees in what the UN Security Council has described as 'the largest humanitarian emergency crisis in the world today'.[673] Although the UN Security Council has to date not intervened in any meaningful way in this humanitarian calamity many States have nonetheless responded by adopting a multitude of unilateral coercive measures against Syria.

---

[671] Libya (15 May 1970), Switzerland (18 June 1992) and the United States (8 June 1992) were all parties to the ICCPR at the relevant time.

[672] See e.g. 'Middle East Unrest: Three Killed at Protest in Syria', BBC News, 18 March 2011, www.bbc.co.uk/news/world-middle-east-12791738; 'Daraa: The Spark That Lit the Syrian Flame', CNN, 1 March 2012, http://edition.cnn.com/2012/03/01/world/meast/syria-crisis-beginnings.

[673] S/PRST/2015/15. See further e.g. 'Syria: The Story of the Conflict', BBC News, 11 March 2016, www.bbc.co.uk/news/world-middle-east-26116868.

On 29 April 2011, the UN Human Rights Council adopted a resolution by which it expressed grave concern at 'alleged deliberate killings, arrests and instances of torture of peaceful protesters by the Syrian authorities' and urged Syria to immediately put an end to all human rights violations, including the denial of the freedoms of assembly and expression.[674] The Human Rights Council also requested the UN High Commissioner for Human Rights to dispatch a fact-finding mission to Syria in order to investigate all alleged human rights violations in the country.[675] On 22 August 2011, taking note of the preliminary report of the fact-finding mission, the Human Rights Council

> strongly condemned the grave and systematic human rights violations by the Syrian authorities, such as arbitrary executions, excessive use of force and the killing and persecution of protesters and human rights defenders, arbitrary detention, enforced disappearances, torture and ill-treatment of detainees, including of children . . .[676]

The Human Rights Council expressed particular concern about the existence of 'patterns of human rights violations that may amount to crimes against humanity' and decided to establish an international commission of inquiry to investigate all allegations of human rights violations in Syria since March 2011.[677]

The already dire human rights situation in Syria has only continued to deteriorate and has been repeatedly condemned in numerous international fora, including the UN General Assembly, the UN Security Council, the UN Human Rights Council, the League of Arab States and the Organisation of Islamic Cooperation.[678] Serious violations of international humanitarian law have also been condemned on numerous occasions. For example, the Human Rights Council has strongly condemned Syria for 'widespread and systematic violations' of international human rights and humanitarian law, including

> the shelling of populated areas with ballistic missiles, the use of heavy weapons and force against civilians, unlawful killings, extrajudicial executions, arbitrary arrest and detentions, massacres, enforced disappearances, widespread and systematic attacks against the civilian population, the use of torture and other forms of ill-treatment, sexual violence against

---

[674] HRC Res. S-16/1 (29 Apr. 2011).   [675] Ibid.   [676] HRC Res. S-17/1 (22 Aug. 2011).
[677] Ibid.
[678] See e.g. OIC Res. 2/4-EX (IS) (15 Aug. 2012); League of Arab States Res. 7523 (5 Sept. 2012); SC Res. 2165 (14 July 2014); GA Res. 70/234 (23 Dec. 2015).

women, men and children, indiscriminate shelling and aerial bombardment on civilian gatherings, and mass killings.[679]

More specifically, the international commission of inquiry established
by the Human Rights Council has concluded that Syria is responsible
for numerous violations of international law, including (1) right to life
(Article 6 ICCPR); (2) freedom from torture (Article 7 ICCPR); (3) right
to liberty and security of person (Article 9 ICCPR); (4) right to humane
treatment of prisoners (Article 10 ICCPR); (5) freedom of movement
(Article 12 ICCPR); (6) right to a fair trial (Article 14 ICCPR); (7)
freedom of expression (Article 19 ICCPR); (8) freedom of assembly
(Article 21 ICCPR); (9) crimes against humanity; and (10) war
crimes.[680] The conclusions of the commission have been implicitly
endorsed by the international community and form part of the 'grave,
widespread and systematic violations' of international human rights and
humanitarian law for which Syria has been condemned on multiple
occasions by UN organs.[681]

On 9 May 2011, EU Member States responded to the unfolding
humanitarian catastrophe by adopting a sanctions regime against Syria
involving an arms embargo, travel bans and the freezing of assets of
several leading regime officials.[682] On 23 May 2011, the EU sanctions
regime was broadened to include the freezing of assets belonging to
President Al-Assad, Vice-President Al-Sharaa and Interior Minister Al-
Sha'ar.[683] On 27 February 2012, the EU sanctions regime was further
broadened to include the freezing of assets belonging to the Central Bank
of Syria.[684] At least the freezing of the assets belonging to President Al-
Assad and the Central Bank of Syria requires justification under international law. These asset freezes should be characterized as third-party

[679] HRC Res. 22/24 (22 March 2013), op. para. 4.
[680] See First Report of the Independent International Commission of Inquiry on the Syrian
Arab Republic, UN Doc. A/HRC/S-17/2/Add.1, 7, 16–21; Third Report of the
Independent International Commission of Inquiry on the Syrian Arab Republic, UN
Doc. A/HRC/21/50, 23. Syria acceded to the ICCPR on 21 April 1969.
[681] See e.g. HRC Res. 21/26 (28 Sept. 2012), op. paras. 1 and 10.
[682] See Council Decision 2011/273/CFSP (9 May 2011), OJ 2011 L 121/11 (10 May 2011);
Council Decision 2011/782/CFSP (1 Dec. 2011), OJ 2011 L 319/56 (2 Dec. 2011).
[683] See Council Implementing Decision 2011/302/CFSP (23 May 2011), OJ 2011 L 136/91
(24 May 2011). Also: Declaration by the High Representative for Foreign Affairs and
Security Policy, Catherine Ashton, on behalf of the European Union, on the unfolding
situation in Syria (18 May 2011), www.consilium.europa.eu/uedocs/cms_data/docs/
pressdata/en/cfsp/121684.pdf.
[684] Council Decision 2012/122/CFSP (27 Feb. 2012), OJ 2012 L 54/14 (28 Feb. 2012).

countermeasures. On 15 October 2012, EU Member States announced the adoption of an aviation ban covering all flights operated by Syrian Arab Airlines 'without prejudice to the obligations of Member States under international law, in particular relevant international civil aviation agreements'[685] – i.e. a measure of retorsion.

Ten countries have aligned themselves with the EU sanctions regime and pledged to ensure its implementation.[686] EU Member States have 'urge[d] the international community to join its efforts, in taking steps to apply and enforce restrictive measures on the Syrian regime and its supporters'.[687] The EU sanctions regime against Syria has been renewed and broadened on numerous occasions to include various trade and financial restrictions and still remains in force.[688] Since Syria is not a member of the WTO, and no other treaties are seemingly at issue, these restrictions may be characterized as acts of retorsion.

On 18 May 2011, the United States also decided to freeze the assets of senior Syrian regime officials, including those belonging to President Al-Assad, Vice-President Al-Sharaa, Prime Minister Safar, Defence Minister Mahmoud and Interior Minister Al-Sha'ar.[689]

---

[685] Council Decision 2012/634/CFSP (15 Oct. 2012), OJ 2012 L 282/50 (16 Oct. 2012).

[686] Albania, Croatia, Georgia, Iceland, Lichtenstein, Macedonia, Moldova, Montenegro, Norway and Serbia: see Declaration by the High Representative on behalf of the European Union on the alignment of certain third countries with the Council Decision 2011/273/CFSP concerning restrictive measures against Syria, as implemented by Council Decision 2011/302/CFSP (9 June 2011), www.consilium.europa.eu/uedocs/cms_data/docs/pressdata/en/cfsp/122483.pdf; Declaration by the High Representative on behalf of the European Union on the alignment of certain third countries with the Council Decision 2012/634/CFSP amending Council Decision 2011/782/CFSP and Council Implementing Regulation (EU) No. 944/2012 concerning restrictive measures against Syria (1 Nov. 2012), www.consilium.europa.eu/uedocs/cms_data/docs/press data/en/cfsp/133276.pdf.

[687] Council of the European Union, 'Council Conclusions on Syria' (15 Oct. 2012), www.consilium.europa.eu/uedocs/cms_data/docs/pressdata/EN/foraff/132825.pdf.

[688] See Council Decision 2012/739/CFSP (29 Nov. 2012), OJ 2012 L 330/21 (30 Nov. 2012); Council Decision 2013/255/CFSP (31 May 2013), OJ 2013 L 147/14 (1 June 2013); Council Decision 2014/309/CFSP (28 May 2014), OJ 2014 L 160/37 (29 May 2014); Council Decision 2015/837/CFSP (28 May 2015), OJ 2015 L 132/82 (29 May 2015); Council Decision 2016/850/CFSP (27 May 2016), OJ 2016 L 141/25 (28 May 2016). Some humanitarian exemptions were introduced by Council Decision 2013/186 (22 Apr. 2013), OJ 2013 L 111/101 (23 Apr. 2013).

[689] See President Obama's Executive Order 13573 (18 May 2011), 'Blocking Property of Senior Officials of the Government of Syria', www.treasury.gov/resourcecenter/sanc tions/Programs/Documents/13573.pdf. Albeit based on a different rationale, it should be noted that the United States had already in May 2004 adopted several unilateral coercive measures against Syria, including the *prima facie* unlawful freezing of Syrian

On 18 August 2011, Syrian government funds were frozen and several acts of retorsion were also adopted.[690] In May 2011, Australia, Switzerland and Canada adopted their own unilateral coercive measures against Syria, followed by Japan in September 2011, all of which notably included the *prima facie* unlawful freezing of assets belonging to President Al-Assad and in some instances also those of Vice-President Al-Sharaa and Prime Minister Safar.[691]

On 12 November 2011, the Council of the League of Arab States suspended Syria's membership in the organization without any clear legal basis for doing so under Article 18 of the Pact of the League of Arab States.[692] As observed in the case of Libya above, a decision on such a suspension requires a unanimous vote (except the affected State) to the effect that a State has failed to fulfil its obligations as a member of the organization. It may be recalled that the Pact of the League of Arab States does not condition membership rights upon compliance with international human rights and humanitarian law. In this case, Syria, Lebanon

---

assets. Several reasons motivated this action such as Syria's (then) occupation of Lebanon and its active support for terrorist groups carrying out attacks against Israel in violation of the principles of non-use of force and non-intervention. Further: Syria Accountability and Lebanese Sovereignty Restoration Act of 2003, Public Law 108–175 (12 Dec. 2003), www.gpo.gov/fdsys/pkg/PLAW-108publ175/pdf/PLAW-108publ175 .pdf; President Bush's Executive Order 13338 (11 May 2004), 'Blocking Property of Certain Persons and Prohibiting the Export of Certain Goods to Syria', www.treasury .gov/resource-center/sanctions/Documents/13338.pdf; Dawidowicz (2006), 396–397.

[690] See President Obama's Executive Order 13582 (17 Aug. 2011), 'Blocking Property of the Government of Syria and Prohibiting Certain Transaction With Respect to Syria', www .treasury.gov/resource-center/sanctions/Programs/Documents/syria_eo_08182011.pdf. The US sanctions regime still remains in force: see White House Press Release, 'Continuation of the National Emergency with Respect to Actions of the Government of Syria' (3 May 2016), https://www.whitehouse.gov/the-press-office/2016/05/03/notice-continuation-national-emergency-respect-actions-government-syria.

[691] See Australian Department of Foreign Affairs and Trade, 'Sanctions Regimes: Syria' (13 May 2011), http://dfat.gov.au/international-relations/security/sanctions/ sanctions-regimes/pages/syria.aspx; Swiss State Secretariat for Economic Affairs, 'Mesures à l'encontre de la Syrie' (18 May 2011), www.seco.admin.ch/seco/fr/home/ Aussenwirtschaftspolitik_Wirtschaftliche_Zusammenarbeit/Wirtschaftsbeziehungen/ exportkontrollen-und-sanktionen/sanktionen-embargos/sanktionsmassnahmen/mass nahmen-gegenueber-syrien.html; Canadian Department of Foreign Affairs, Trade and Development, 'Canadian Sanctions Related to Syria' (24 May 2011), www.international .gc.ca/sanctions/countries-pays/syria-syrie.aspx; Ministry of Foreign Affairs of Japan, 'Implementation of Measures to Freeze the Assets of President Bashar Al-Assad and His Related Individuals and Entities in Syria' (9 Sept. 2011), www.mofa.go.jp /announce/announce/2011/9/0909_02.html (all sanctions currently in force).

[692] See League of Arab States Ministerial Res. 7438 on the Situation in Syria (12 Nov. 2011), available at www.lcil.cam.ac.uk/arab_spring/arab-spring-syria#docs.

and Yemen, with Iraq abstaining, voted against the membership suspension.[693] It thus appears that the decision to suspend Syria was unlawful both in substantive and procedural terms. Although, as in the case of Libya examined above, the seemingly illegal decision to suspend Syria was taken by an organ of the Arab League, it could arguably therefore be attributable to individual Arab League Member States in terms of the general rule of attribution embodied in Article 58(1) DARIO.[694] As a minimum, Arab League Member States expressed support for the adoption of third-party countermeasures. For its part, Syria protested that the suspension was in breach of the Pact of the League of Arab States and was 'serving a western and American agenda'.[695]

On 27 November 2011, the Arab League also decided to adopt a host of other unilateral coercive measures against Syria, including travel bans and asset freezes against senior regime officials, as well as the freezing of assets of the Syrian government (seemingly including the Central Bank of Syria), a trade embargo and a ban on civil aviation.[696] The Arab League flight ban was reportedly to come into effect on 15 December 2011; however, it does not appear to have been implemented.[697] The Arab League sanctions regime (including the *prima facie* unlawful asset freezes) otherwise came into effect almost immediately.[698] The decision to ban flights nevertheless indicates at least a willingness on the part of several Arab League Member States to suspend their respective air

---

[693] See 'Syria Suspended from Arab League', *The Guardian*, 12 November 2011, www .guardian.co.uk/world/2011/nov/12/syria-suspended-arab-league.

[694] DARIO Commentary, Art. 58, §4. Compare Klein (2010), 307–308; and text above accompanying n. 659.

[695] See 'Syria Suspended from Arab League', *The Guardian*, 12 November 2011, www .theguardian.com/world/2011/nov/12/syria-suspended-arab-league. France 'commend-[ed]' the Arab League for its suspension of Syria: see UN Doc. S/PV.6710 (31 Jan. 2012), 14 (France).

[696] See League of Arab States Ministerial Res. 7442 on the Follow Up of the Development of the Situation in Syria (27 Nov. 2011), available at www.lcil.cam.ac.uk/arab_spring/arab-spring-syria#docs. The sanctions regime included a humanitarian exemption. Iraq and Lebanon abstained from voting, but at least Lebanon has reportedly implemented parts of the resolution by freezing Syrian government assets within its jurisdiction. Further: 'Syria Isolated after Unprecedented Arab League Sanctions', *The Telegraph*, 27 November 2011, www.telegraph.co.uk/news/worldnews/middleeast/syria/8919029/Syria-isolated-after-unprecedented-Arab-League-sanctions.html.

[697] See 'Arab League Places Sanctions against 17 Syrian Officials and Includes a Ban on Flights', *Al-Arabiya News*, 1 December 2011, www.alarabiya.net/articles/2011/12/01/180249.html.

[698] See 'Syria Given 24 Hours to Sign Arab League Deal or Face Sanctions', *The Guardian*, 4 December 2011, www.guardian.co.uk/world/2011/dec/04/syria-arab-league-sanctions.

services agreements with Syria without any clear conventional basis for doing so.[699]

On 30 November 2011, Turkey, in concert with the Arab League, announced the adoption of its own unilateral coercive measures against Syria, including the freezing of assets belonging to President Al-Assad and the Syrian government.[700] As Turkish Foreign Minister Davutoğlu explained, '[n]obody can expect Turkey and the Arab League to remain silent on the killings of civilians and the Syrian regime's increasing oppression of innocent people'.[701] Additionally, on 15 August 2012, the OIC suspended Syria from its membership in the organization with a doubtful legal basis for doing so in the OIC Charter.[702] Although the preamble and Article 2(7) of the OIC Charter refer to the importance of upholding human rights, Article 3(3) of the OIC Charter provides in categorical terms that '[n]othing in the present Charter shall undermine the present Member States' rights or privileges relating to membership or any other issues'. The decision to suspend Syria thus seemingly lacked a legal basis in the OIC Charter. Still, this *prima facie* illegal decision was taken by one of the main organs of the organization (i.e. the Islamic Summit) and was valid in procedural terms under Article 33 of the OIC Charter.[703] The *prima facie* illegal decision to suspend Syria from the OIC therefore does not appear to be attributable to the individual OIC Member States pursuant to Article 58(2) DARIO. Still, as a minimum,

---

[699] See e.g. Agreement For the Liberalization of Air Transport Between the Arab States (entry into force 18 Feb. 2007), available at www.icao.int/sustainability/Documents/RegionalAgreements.pdf. The agreement is in force for the following Arab League Member States: Bahrain, Iraq, Jordan, Lebanon, Palestine, Somalia, Sudan, Syria, Tunisia and Yemen (ibid.).

[700] See 'Turkey Imposes Sanctions on Syria', *The Guardian*, 30 November 2011, www.guardian.co.uk/world/2011/nov/30/turkey-imposes-sanctions-on-syria.

[701] 'Isolating Syria, Arab League Imposes Broad Sanctions', *The New York Times*, 27 November 2011, www.nytimes.com/2011/11/28/world/middleeast/arab-league-prepares-to-vote-on-syrian-sanctions.html.

[702] Charter of the Organisation of the Islamic Conference (as amended), www.oic-oci.org/is11/english/Charter-en.pdf. Also: Final Communiqué adopted by the Fourth Extraordinary Session of the Islamic Summit Conference (Mecca, 14–15 Aug. 2012), 7–8, www.oic-oci.org/english/conf/is/ex-4/is_ex4_fc_en_w_links.pdf; OIC Res. 2/4-EX (IS) on the Situation in Syria (15 Aug. 2012), www.oic-oci.org/english/conf/is/ex-4/is_ex4_res_en.pdf; 'Organization of Islamic Cooperation Suspends Syria', *CNN*, 16 August 2012, http://edition.cnn.com/2012/08/15/world/meast/syria-unrest.

[703] If consensus cannot be reached, a two-thirds majority vote is required for a valid decision. Only Iran and Algeria voted against Syria's suspension. See further 'Organization of Islamic Cooperation Suspends Syria', *CNN*, 16 August 2012, http://edition.cnn.com/2012/08/15/world/meast/syria-unrest.

OIC Member States expressed support for such action and so it may reasonably be assumed that all OIC Member States accepted the use of third-party countermeasures in such circumstances.

The UN Security Council has not taken any enforcement action against Syria.[704] On 3 August 2011, the Security Council 'condemn[ed] the widespread violations of human rights and the use of force against civilians by the Syrian authorities ... [and] call[ed] on the Syrian authorities to fully respect human rights and to comply with their obligations under applicable international law'.[705] On 4 October 2011, a draft Security Council resolution that had threatened Syria with the possible adoption of enforcement measures under Chapter VII UNC was vetoed by China and Russia – the first such double veto since the earlier blocking of sanctions against Zimbabwe and Burma.[706]

During the debate on the draft resolution, France explained that EU Member States had already adopted several rounds of unilateral coercive measures against Syria but nevertheless stressed that 'a united response from the international community was, and continues to be, necessary'.[707] The United States made a similar statement, pointing out that 'several of us on the Council and many throughout the international community have voiced our condemnation and imposed sanctions on the Al-Assad regime'.[708] For its part, Russia explained that a reason for its strong opposition to the draft resolution was that it would 'not get involved with legitimizing previously adopted unilateral sanctions or attempts at violent regime change'.[709]

On 4 February 2012, another Security Council draft resolution, which endorsed an Arab League sponsored peace plan for Syria and the possibility of further measures in case of non-compliance, was vetoed by

---

[704] See however SC Res. 2118 (27 Sept. 2013) by which the Security Council decided to dismantle Syria's arsenal of chemical weapons. The Security Council has also demanded that Syria facilitate humanitarian relief operations to assist the civilian population: see e.g. S/PRST/2013/15 (2 Oct. 2013); SC Res. 2139 (22 Feb. 2014), op. para. 4; SC Res. 2165 (14 July 2014), op. para. 2; SC Res. 2258 (22 Dec. 2015), op. para. 2; SC Res. 2332 (21 Dec. 2016), op. para. 2.

[705] See S/PRST/2011/16 (3 Aug. 2011). Also: SC Res. 2042 (14 Apr. 2012); SC Res. 2043 (21 Apr. 2012).

[706] See UN Doc. S/2011/612, op. para. 11. Further: 'Russia and China Veto UN Resolution against Syrian Regime', The Guardian, 5 October 2011, www.theguardian.com/world/2011/oct/05/russia-china-veto-syria-resolution.

[707] See UN Doc. S/PV.6627 (4 Oct. 2011), 2 (France).   [708] Ibid., 8–9 (United States).

[709] Ibid., 5 (Russia). China considered that any enforcement measures against Syria would be inopportune and might even further complicate the situation (ibid.). See also UN Doc. S/PV.6711 (4 Feb. 2012), 7 (United Kingdom).

China and Russia.[710] During the debate on the draft resolution, the Arab League informed the Security Council of its sanctions regime and called on the Council to take the same action against Syria.[711] France criticized the 'scandalous silence' of the Security Council in response to what it considered crimes against humanity for which President Al-Assad's regime bore responsibility.[712] As France explained:

> Of course, we have continued our efforts despite the Council's silence. The European Union has 11 times increased the sanctions on the regime and its leaders . . . However, the actions of the European Union or the Arab League, no matter how resolute, cannot replace action by the Council. By virtue of the legitimacy conferred on it by the United Nations Charter, it is the Council that can express authoritatively the will of the international community. The Security Council is the keystone of international peace and security. If it is to remain so, it has the responsibility to pronounce cases as serious as Syria's.[713]

France nevertheless cautioned the Security Council: 'We will continue to up the pressure [on Syria] by imposing further sanctions of the European Union'.[714] Finally, on 19 July 2012, a further draft Security Council resolution threatening Syria with possible enforcement measures under Chapter VII UNC was vetoed by China and Russia.[715]

In February 2012, US Secretary of State Clinton called for 'friends of democratic Syria' to unite against President Al-Assad based on the following rationale:

> Faced with a neutered security council, we have to redouble our efforts outside of the United Nations with those allies and partners who support the Syrian people's right to have a better future.[716]

French President Sarkozy agreed and took a leading role in the establishment of the so-called 'Group of Friends of the Syrian People' – a large

---

[710] UN Doc. S/2012/77, op. para. 15. See also 'Syria Resolution Vetoed by Russia and China at United Nations', *The Guardian*, 4 February 2012, www.theguardian.com/world/2012/feb/04/assad-obama-resign-un-resolution.

[711] UN Doc. S/PV.6710 (31 Jan. 2012), 6 (Qatar on behalf of the League of Arab States).

[712] Ibid., 14–15 (France).   [713] Ibid., 15.

[714] UN Doc. S/PV.6711 (4 Feb. 2012), 4 (France).

[715] UN Doc. S/2012/538, op. para. 14. See also 'Friction at the U.N. as Russia and China Veto Another Resolution on Syria Sanctions', *The New York Times*, 19 July 2012, www.nytimes.com/2012/07/20/world/middleeast/russia-and-china-veto-un-sanctions-against-syria.html.

[716] See 'Clinton Calls for "Friends of Democratic Syria" to Unite against Bashar Al-Assad', *The Guardian*, 5 February 2012, www.theguardian.com/world/2012/feb/05/hillary-clinton-syria-assad-un.

and diverse diplomatic coalition of States and international organizations created as a direct response to the failure of the Security Council to take resolute action on Syria.[717]

On 24 February 2012, the First Conference of the Group of Friends of the Syrian People was held in Tunis with the participation of more than sixty States and several regional organizations. It was there decided that, in response to Syria's 'ongoing, widespread and systematic human rights violations', amounting in some cases to 'crimes against humanity', a host of unilateral coercive measures should be adopted against Syria, including the freezing of assets of senior regime officials.[718] On 1 April 2012, at the Second Conference of the Group of Friends of the Syrian People held in Istanbul, attended by eighty-three States, as well as several regional organizations, the International Working Group on Sanctions (IWGS) was formed

> in order to achieve greater effectiveness in the enforcement of the restrictive measures already put in force by states or international organizations including the measures [such as the freezing of assets of senior Syrian regime officials] stipulated in the Chairman's Conclusions of the first meeting of the Friends' Group.[719]

On 17 April 2012, the IWGS held its first meeting in Paris at which it

> welcome[d] the sanctions adopted by the EU, the Arab League, the United States of America, Turkey, Norway, Switzerland, Monaco, Croatia, Iceland, Canada, Australia and Japan, and call[ed] upon all States of the group of Friends of the Syrian People and all states that have not yet exerted the necessary pressure to join these efforts and further isolate the Syrian regime.[720]

On 6 June 2012, some sixty States attended the second meeting of the IWGS held in Washington, DC. Support was there expressed for taking

---

[717] See 'Sarkozy: France, Partners Plan Syria Crisis Group', *The Jerusalem Post*, 4 February 2012, www.jpost.com/Middle-East/Sarkozy-France-partners-plan-Syria-crisis-group.

[718] See Chairman's Conclusions of the International Conference of the Group of Friends of the Syrian People (Tunis, 24 Feb. 2012), www.state.gov/r/pa/prs/ps/2012/02/184642.htm.

[719] See Chairman's Conclusions of the Second Conference of the Group of Friends of the Syrian People (Istanbul, 1 Apr. 2012), para. 18, www.mfa.gov.tr/chairman_s-conclusions-second-conference-of-the-group-of-friends-of-the-syrian-people_-1-april-2012_-istanbul.en.mfa.

[720] See Final Statement by the Co-Chairs of the International Working Group on Sanctions (Paris, 17 Apr. 2012), www.state.gov/e/eb/tfs/spi/syria/documents/211643.htm.

steps towards the adoption of a Security Council resolution under Chapter VII UNC instituting sanctions against Syria. The IWGS nevertheless also called on all States to unilaterally freeze the assets of senior Syrian regime officials as well as those of the Central Bank of Syria. An oil and arms embargo was also called for.[721] In subsequent meetings, the IWGS observed that the unilateral coercive measures adopted against Syria, including the asset freezes, were having a 'significant impact': they had 'seriously affected' the Syrian regime by depriving it of substantial revenue that would have been used to fund the violence against the Syrian people.[722] As a minimum, the IWGS noted that at least 'these resources are no longer available to the Syrian regime to finance the repression of the Syrian people'.[723] More generally:

> The Group reiterated its resolve to ensure that sanctions against the Syrian regime and its designated supporters are coordinated, effective and implemented robustly in order to hasten the end of the regime's oppression of the Syrian people.[724]

The IWGS also 'welcomed the increasing pressure placed on the [Syrian] regime by the wide range of sanctions [e.g. the freezing of State and Head of State assets] adopted by different states and organisations', and added that '[t]he members of the Group have adopted effective, proportional and coordinated sanctions'.[725]

In November 2012, at its meeting in Tokyo in which sixty-three States participated, the IWGS again 'welcomed the targeted and coordinated sanctions implemented by Group member countries and organizations to increase pressure on the Syrian regime and isolate it from the

---

[721] See Statement by the Friends of the Syrian People International Working Group on Sanctions (Washington, DC, 6 June, 2012), www.treasury.gov/press-center/press-releases/Pages/tg1606.aspx.

[722] See Statement by the Friends of the Syrian People International Working Group on Sanctions (Doha, 19 July 2012 and The Hague, 20 Sept. 2012), www.state.gov/e/eb/tfs/spi/syria/documents/211642.htm; www.government.nl/files/documents-and-publica tions/reports/2012/09/20/statement-by-the-friends-of-the-syrian-people-international-working-group-on-sanctions/statement-eng.pdf.

[723] See Statement by the Friends of the Syrian People International Working Group on Sanctions (The Hague, 20 Sept. 2012). See also Statement by the Friends of the Syrian People International Working Group on Sanctions (Tokyo, 30 Nov. 2012), op. para. 8, www.government.nl/documents-and-publications/leaflets/2012/12/10/joint-statement-tokyo-30-nov-2012.html.

[724] Statement by the Friends of the Syrian People International Working Group on Sanctions (The Hague, 20 Sept. 2012), para. 2.

[725] Ibid., paras. 5, 7.

international community as a means of ending the repression in Syria'.[726] The IWGS also repeated its call to action noting that it was necessary for all States to work in a 'continued concerted multinational effort' in order to coordinate the adoption of unilateral coercive measures against Syria, notably through the freezing of assets belonging to senior regime officials and the Central Bank of Syria.[727] More recent meetings of the IWGS have reaffirmed the same point in almost identical terms.[728]

These repeated statements, at least insofar as they relate to the freezing of assets belonging to President Al-Assad and the Central Bank of Syria, are indicative of a willingness of a very large number of States to adopt *prima facie* unlawful unilateral coercive measures for which the justification can seemingly only be explained in legal terms by reference to third-party countermeasures. Syria has vehemently protested against the illegality of this practice, *inter alia*, on the basis that it is merely a 'political tool used by foreign powers to put pressure on and create an internal political change in another country', and adversely affects the civilian population.[729]

4.2.21 Western States – Russia (2014–present)

On 28 February 2014, Russia militarily invaded Ukraine and occupied Crimea.[730] The following day the Russian Parliament adopted a resolution by which it authorized the use of force on the territory of the Ukraine following a request from President Putin to do so in order to address 'the extraordinary situation in Ukraine [involving] the threat to the lives of citizens of the Russian Federation, our compatriots [and] the personnel of the military contingent ... deployed in [Crimea]'.[731]

---

[726] See Statement by the Friends of the Syrian People International Working Group on Sanctions (Tokyo, 30 Nov. 2012).

[727] Ibid.

[728] See Communiqués by the Friends of the Syrian People International Working Group on Sanctions (Sofia, 26 Feb. 2013; Ottawa, 25 June 2013), www.government.nl/documents/ publications/2013/02/27/communique-by-the-friends-of-the-syrian-people-interna tional-working-group-on-sanctions; www.government.nl/documents-and-publica tions/publications/2013/06/25/communique-by-the-friends-of-the-syrian-people-inter national-working-group-on-sanctions.html.

[729] See UN Docs. A/HRC/20/G/3 (15 June 2012); A/68/211 (22 July 2013), 6 (Syria).

[730] See 'Russian "Invasion" of Crimea Fuels Fear of Ukraine Conflict', *The Guardian*, 1 March 2014, www.theguardian.com/world/2014/feb/28/russia-crimea-white-house.

[731] 'Federation Council Committees Support Putin's Letter on Use of Army in Ukraine', *Itar-Tass*, 1 March 2014, www.itar-tass.com/en/russia/721589. The authorization was later withdrawn (without much apparent effect): see 'Vladimir Putin Revokes

Russian troops massed on the Ukrainian border seemingly threatening to invade.[732] On 16 March 2014, a spurious independence referendum, organized by the newly installed puppet regime led by (then) 'Prime Minister' Aksyonov, was held in Sevastopol as a result of which Russia a few days later formally annexed Crimea.[733] Other self-proclaimed 'People's Republics' in Eastern Ukraine soon claimed their own independence following sham referenda and sought union with Russia.[734] A full-blown civil war erupted across Eastern Ukraine between pro-Russian separatists (allegedly supported by Russia) and the central government in Kiev.

On 2 March 2014, leaders of the G7 adopted a statement by which they 'condemn[ed] the Russian Federation's clear violation of the sovereignty and territorial integrity of Ukraine, in contravention of Russia's obligations under the UN Charter and its 1997 basing agreement with Ukraine'.[735] G7 leaders initially responded cautiously by agreeing simply to suspend their participation in the planned G8 summit in Sotchi – an act of retorsion.[736]

On 3 March 2014, EU Foreign Ministers adopted a statement by which

> The European Union strongly condemn[ed] the clear violation of Ukrainian sovereignty and territorial integrity by acts of aggression by the Russian armed forces as well as the authorisation given by the Federation Council of Russia on 1 March for the use of the armed forces on the territory of Ukraine. These actions are in clear breach of the UN Charter and the OSCE Helsinki Final Act, as well as Russia's specific commitments to respect Ukraine's sovereignty and territorial integrity under the Budapest Memorandum of 1994 and the bilateral Treaty on Friendship, Cooperation and Partnership of 1997. [. . .]
>
> The EU call[ed] on Russia to immediately withdraw its armed forces to the areas of their permanent stationing, in accordance with the

---

Russia's Mandate for Use of Military Force in Ukraine', *The Telegraph*, 24 June 2014, www.telegraph.co.uk/news/worldnews/europe/ukraine/10922531/Vladimir-Putin-revokes-Russias-mandate-for-use-of-military-force-in-Ukraine.html.

[732] See 'Russian Troops Mass at Border with Ukraine', *The New York Times*, 13 March 2014, www.nytimes.com/2014/03/14/world/europe/ukraine.html.

[733] See 'Ukraine Crisis: Putin Signs Russia-Crimea Treaty', *BBC News*, 18 March 2014, www .bbc.co.uk/news/world-europe-26630062; 'Ukraine: Putin Signs Crimea Annexation', *BBC News*, 21 March 2014, www.bbc.co.uk/news/world-europe-26686949.

[734] See 'East Ukraine Separatists Seek Union with Russia', *BBC News*, 12 May 2014, www .bbc.co.uk/news/world-europe-27369980.

[735] 'G-7 Leaders Statement' (2 March 2014), www.whitehouse.gov/the-press-office/2014/03/ 02/g-7-leaders-statement.

[736] Ibid.

Agreement on the Status and Conditions of the Black Sea Fleet stationing on the territory of Ukraine of 1997.[737]

Limited diplomatic sanctions were likewise adopted against Russia with the possibility of imminent further action being taken such as travel bans and asset freezes in case negotiations between the parties to resolve the crisis did not produce results within the next few days.[738] EU Member States also cautioned Russia that any further steps taken by it to destabilize the situation in Ukraine would 'lead to additional and far-reaching consequences for relations in a broad range of economic areas'.[739] On 17 March 2014, recalling their earlier statements, EU Member States decided to take action against Russia by imposing travel bans and asset freezes on a range of Russian officials and other individuals deemed responsible for the destabilization of Ukraine.[740] A few days later, additional persons were added to the EU sanctions list, including Russian Deputy Prime Minister Rogozin.[741] These actions are best understood as acts of retorsion.

On 22 July 2014, following the downing of Malaysian Airlines Flight MH17 in pro-Russian rebel-held territory in Ukraine a few days earlier killing all 298 people on board,[742] EU Member States 'urge[d] Russia to stop the increasing flow of weapons, equipment and militants across the border in order to achieve rapid and tangible results in de-escalation'.[743] EU Member States also urged Russia 'to withdraw its additional troops from the border area', and reaffirmed their readiness to introduce further 'significant' unilateral coercive measures against key sectors of the

---

[737] Council of the European Union, 'Council Conclusions on Ukraine' (3 March 2014), www.consilium.europa.eu/uedocs/cms_data/docs/pressdata/EN/foraff/141291.pdf.

[738] Ibid.; Council of the European Union, 'Statement of the Heads of State or Government on Ukraine' (6 March 2014), www.consilium.europa.eu/uedocs/cms_data/docs/press data/en/ec/141372.pdf.

[739] Council of the European Union, 'Statement of the Heads of State or Government on Ukraine' (6 March 2014).

[740] Council Decision 2014/145/CFSP (17 March 2014), OJ 2014 L 78/16 (17 March 2014), Council Regulation (EU) No. 269/2014 (17 March 2014).

[741] Council Implementing Decision 2014/151/CFSP (21 March 2014), OJ 2014 L 86/30 (21 March 2014). It is doubtful whether a Deputy Prime Minister enjoys personal immunity while in office: see above n. 7.

[742] See 'Malaysia Airlines Flight MH17 Crashes in East Ukraine', *The Guardian*, 17 July 2014, www.theguardian.com/world/2014/jul/17/malaysia-airlines-plane-crash-east-ukraine. For the action taken by the Security Council, see SC Res. 2166 (21 July 2014).

[743] Council of the European Union, 'Council Conclusions on Ukraine' (22 July 2014), www .consilium.europa.eu/uedocs/cms_data/docs/pressdata/EN/foraff/144090.pdf.

Russian economy (i.e. the financial, energy and defence sectors) if it failed to comply with their demands.[744] Put differently, Russia was seemingly urged (in all but name) to comply with the principles of non-use of force and non-intervention. As the President of the European Council, Mr. Van Rompuy, explained:

> The [sanctions] package ... is meant as a strong warning: illegal annexation of territory and deliberate destabilisation of a neighbouring sovereign country cannot be accepted in 21st century Europe.[745]

On 31 July 2014, EU Member States, in the absence of an adequate response, adopted the aforementioned unilateral coercive measures against Russia.[746] With respect to the defence sector, an arms embargo (covering dual-use goods) was introduced – an act of retorsion. As for the financial sector, the action taken consisted in denying certain Russian financial institutions access to European capital markets by banning them from selling newly issued bonds, shares or similar financial instruments there. In the energy sector, an export embargo was introduced on certain sensitive goods and technologies (such as certain pipe used in the oil and gas industry) destined for deep-water oil exploration and production, arctic oil exploration and production or shale oil projects.[747]

---

[744] Ibid. See further 'MH17 Plane Crash: EU to Widen Russia Sanctions', *BBC News*, 22 July 2014, www.bbc.co.uk/news/uk-28415248; 'Ukraine Crisis: EU to Impose Toughest Sanctions Yet on Russian Banks and Energy Firms', *The Independent*, 28 July 2014, www.independent.co.uk/news/world/europe/ukraine-crisis-eu-to-finalise-toughest-sanctions-yet-on-russian-banks-and-energy-firms-9634117.html.

[745] Statement by the President of the European Council Herman Van Rompuy and the President of the European Commission in the Name of the European Union on the agreed additional restrictive measures against Russia (29 July 2014), www.consilium.europa.eu/uedocs/cms_data/docs/pressdata/en/ec/144158.pdf.

[746] Council Decision 2014/512/CFSP (31 July 2014), OJ 2014 L 229/13 (31 July 2014), Council Regulation (EU) No. 833/2014 (31 July 2014), OJ 2014 L 229/1 (31 July 2014). The EU sanctions regime has subsequently been expanded and amended further: see Council Decision 2014/659/CFSP (8 Sept. 2014), OJ 2014 L 271/54 (12 Sept. 2014), Council Regulation (EU) No. 960/2014 (8 Sept. 2014), OJ 2014 L 271/3 (12 Sept. 2014); Council Decision 2014/872/CFSP (4 Dec. 2014), OJ 2014 L 349/58 (5 Dec. 2014), Council Regulation (EU) No. 1290/2014 (4 Dec. 2014), OJ 2014 L 349/20 (5 Dec. 2014); Council Decision 2015/1764/CFSP (1 Oct. 2015), OJ 2015 L 257/42 (2 Oct. 2015), Council Regulation (EU) No. 2015/1797 (7 Oct. 2015), OJ 2015 L 263/10 (8 Oct. 2015); Council Decision 2015/2431/CFSP (21 Dec. 2015), OJ 2015 L 334/22 (22 Dec. 2015); Council Decision 2016/1071/CFSP (1 July 2016), OJ L 178/21 (2 July 2016).

[747] Council Decision 2014/512/CFSP (31 July 2014), OJ 2014 L 229/13 (31 July 2014), Council Regulation (EU) No. 833/2014 (31 July 2014), OJ 2014 L 229/1 (31 July 2014). For the list of prohibited energy-related goods and technologies, see ibid., Annex II.

On 30 August 2014, the European Council adopted a further statement by which

> It condemns the increasing inflows of fighters and weapons from the territory of the Russian Federation into Eastern Ukraine as well as the aggression by Russian armed forces on Ukrainian soil. It calls upon the Russian Federation to immediately withdraw all its military assets and forces from Ukraine.[748]

A week later, the EU sanctions regime was extended by the introduction of additional restrictions on access to the European capital markets for certain Russian financial institutions and companies in the defence and energy sectors.[749] It was later clarified that the extension of loans or credit to such entities was essentially prohibited.[750]

The financial measures taken by EU Member States against Russia are covered by Article I(2)(b) GATS and as such appear to violate the general obligation to provide MFN treatment in Article II GATS. No exemption to the application of Article II GATS seems applicable.[751] EU Member States also did not invoke the national security exception in Article XIV *bis* GATS. The limited export embargo applicable to energy-related goods also amounts to a quantitative trade restriction which is *prima facie* unlawful under Article XI GATT. Again, EU Member States did not invoke the national security exception in Article XXI GATT as possible justification for their otherwise unlawful conduct. All States concerned are members of the WTO.[752] These actions may thus be understood as third-party countermeasures. For its part, Switzerland has also (somewhat reluctantly) taken action

---

The three biggest (State-owned) banks in Russia are among the financial institutions on the EU sanctions list (ibid., Annex III).

[748] Council of the European Union, 'Special Meeting of the European Council – Conclusions' (30 Aug. 2014), para. 8, www.consilium.europa.eu/uedocs/cms_data/docs/pressdata/en/ec/144538.pdf. See further: 'NATO: Russia Had Illegally Crossed Ukraine's Border', *BBC News*, 29 August 2014, www.bbc.co.uk/news/world-europe-28978065; 'Putin Admits Russian Military Presence in Ukraine for First Time', *The Guardian*, 17 December 2015, www.theguardian.com/world/2015/dec/17/vladimir-putin-admits-russian-military-presence-ukraine.

[749] Council Decision 2014/659/CFSP (8 Sept. 2014), OJ 2014 L 271/54 (12 Sept. 2014), Council Regulation (EU) No. 960/2014 (8 Sept. 2014), OJ 2014 L 271/3 (12 Sept. 2014).

[750] Council Decision 2014/872/CFSP (4 Dec. 2014), OJ 2014 L 349/58 (5 Dec. 2014), Council Regulation (EU) No. 1290/2014 (4 Dec. 2014), OJ 2014 L 349/20 (5 Dec. 2014).

[751] See GATS Annex on Article II Exemptions; GATS Annex on Financial Services, www.wto.org/english/docs_e/legal_e/26-gats.pdf.

[752] For its part, Russia has been a WTO member since 22 August 2012.

against Russia in order to prevent the circumvention of the EU sanctions regime.[753]

The United States has in close coordination with its EU and other international partners taken broadly the same action against Russia.[754] On 11 September 2014, in announcing additional unilateral coercive measures against Russia, President Obama stated:

> The international community continues to seek a genuine negotiated solution to the crisis in Ukraine ... As I said last week, if Russia fully implements its commitments, these sanctions can be rolled back. If, instead, Russia continues its aggressive actions and violations of international law, the costs will continue to rise.[755]

In addition, Australia has, in coordination with the United States, Canada and Europe, taken action against Russia, including by imposing an arms embargo, a limited export embargo in the energy sector and

---

[753] See Swiss Federal Council, 'Ordonnance instituant des mesures visant à empêcher le contournement de sanctions internationales en lien avec la situation en Ukraine' (27 Aug. 2014), www.admin.ch/opc/fr/classified-compilation/20142202/index.html. Further: 'Switzerland Adopts Russia Blacklist over Ukraine Crisis', BBC News, 5 August 2014, www.bbc.co.uk/news/world-europe-28659402; 'Swiss Sanctions Dilemma over Russia', BBC News, 19 August 2014, www.bbc.co.uk/news/business-28833360; 'Switzerland Extends Sanctions on Five Russian Banks', The Wall Street Journal, 27 August 2014, www.wsj.com/articles/switzerland-extends-sanctions-on-five-unnamed-russian-banks-1409151869.

[754] See President Obama's Executive Orders 13660–13662 (6, 17 and 20 March 2014; as amended on 16 July and 12 Sept. 2014), 'Blocking Property of Certain (Additional) Persons Contributing to the Situation in Ukraine', available at www.treasury.gov/resource-center/sanctions/Programs/Pages/ukraine.aspx; US Dept. of the Treasury Press Release, 'Announcement of Additional Treasury Sanctions on Russian Financial Institutions and on a Defense Technology Entity' (29 July 2014), www.treasury.gov/press-center/press-releases/Pages/jl2590.aspx; 'G-7 Leaders Statement on Ukraine' (30 July 2014), www.whitehouse.gov/the-press-office/2014/07/30/g-7-leaders-statement-ukraine; White House Press Release, 'Statement by the President on New Sanctions Related to Russia' (11 Sept. 2014), www.whitehouse.gov/the-press-office/2014/09/11/statement-president-new-sanctions-related-russia; US Dept. of the Treasury Press Release, 'Announcement of Expanded Treasury Sanctions within the Russian Financial Services, Energy and Defense or Related Materiel Sectors' (12 Sept. 2014), www.treasury.gov/press-center/press-releases/Pages/jl2629.aspx; White House Press Release, 'Continuation of the National Emergency with Respect to Ukraine' (2 March 2016), www.whitehouse.gov/the-press-office/2016/03/02/notice-continuation-national-emergency-respect-ukraine. Also: Ukraine Freedom Support Act of 2014, Public Law 113–272 (18 Dec. 2014), https://www.congress.gov/113/plaws/publ272/PLAW-113publ272.pdf.

[755] White House Press Release, 'Statement by the President on New Sanctions Related to Russia' (11 Sept. 2014), www.whitehouse.gov/the-press-office/2014/09/11/statement-president-new-sanctions-related-russia.

denying certain Russian banks access to Australian capital markets.[756] Canada has also taken the same action against Russia.[757] Japan has (albeit reluctantly), among other unilateral coercive measures, limited the access of certain Russian banks to its capital markets.[758]

For its part, Russia has repeatedly protested against the unilateral coercive measures adopted against it, stressing that they are 'invented and illegitimate'[759] and that 'sectorial sanctions are against the WTO rules'.[760] In addition, President Putin has stated:

> This contradicts international law because sanctions can only be imposed within the framework of the United Nations and its Security Council.[761]

---

[756] Australian Department of Foreign Affairs and Trade, 'Sanctions Regimes: Russia' (19 March 2014), http://dfat.gov.au/international-relations/security/sanctions/sanctions-regimes/Pages/russia.aspx. See also 'Australia to Adopt Tougher Sanctions against Russia over Ukraine', *The Guardian*, 1 September 2014, www.theguardian.com/world/2014/sep/01/australia-to-adopt-tougher-sanctions-against-russia-over-ukraine.

[757] Special Economic Measures (Russia) Regulations (SOR/2014–58) (17 March 2014), http://laws.justice.gc.ca/eng/regulations/SOR-2014-58/FullText.html. For amendments to the sanctions regime see further www.international.gc.ca/sanctions/countries-pays/russia-russie.aspx.

[758] See 'Statement by the Minister for Foreign Affairs of Japan on the Additional Measures Imposed on Russia in Connection with the Ukraine Situation' (25 Sept. 2014), www.mofa.go.jp/press/release/press4e_000445.html. Further: 'Japan Imposes New Sanctions on Russia but Keeps a Diplomatic Door Open', *The New York Times*, 5 August 2014, www.nytimes.com/2014/08/06/world/asia/japan-keeps-door-to-russia-open-while-imposing-sanctions.html; 'Japan Steps Up Sanctions as Tensions Rise with Russia', *BBC News*, 24 September 2014, www.bbc.co.uk/news/world-asia-29345451.

[759] 'Comment by the Russian Ministry of Foreign Affairs regarding the Continuing Anti-Russian Sanctions of the United States' (30 July 2014), available at www.mid.ru/brp_4.nsf/main_eng.

[760] 'Comment by the Russian Ministry of Foreign Affairs regarding Further Anti-Russian Sanctions Agreed by the European Union' (30 July 2014), available at www.mid.ru/brp_4.nsf/main_eng; 'Russia's Putin Says Sanctions Violate Principles of WTO', *Reuters*, 19 September 2014, www.reuters.com/article/2014/09/19/us-ukraine-crisis-putin-idUSKBN0HD17V20140919. This objection has not prevented Russia from taking 'counter-countermeasures' against Western States on rather spurious grounds: see 'Russia Hits West with Food Import Ban in Sanctions Row', *BBC News*, 7 August 2014, www.bbc.co.uk/news/world-europe-28687172; 'Russia Reacts to EU Sanctions with Further Western Trade Embargos', *The Guardian*, 11 September 2014, www.theguardian.com/world/2014/sep/11/russia-eu-sanctions-west-trade-embargos-cars-ukraine.

[761] 'G20 Summit: Russia Sanctions "Undermine Trade" – Putin', *BBC News*, 14 November 2014, www.bbc.co.uk/news/world-europe-30051352. Also: UN Doc. A/70/PV.13 (28 Sept. 2015), 26 (Russia) ('[U]nilateral sanctions that circumvent the United Nations Charter have almost become the norm'). Generally: 'Concept of the Foreign Policy of the Russian Federation' (12 Feb. 2013), para. 15 ('Another risk to world peace and stability is presented by attempts to manage crises through unilateral sanctions and other coercive

By December 2014, Russia was facing a full-blown economic crisis with a rapidly depreciating currency.[762] President Putin has estimated that the action taken by Western States accounts for up to 30 per cent of Russia's economic problems.[763] Whether the action taken by Western States will ultimately have the effect of ensuring a return to legality is an open and multifaceted question, but it nonetheless seems clear that, in the words of US President Obama, the 'costs' of Russia's intransigence are 'continu[ing] to rise'.[764]

measures, including armed aggression, outside the framework of the UN Security Council') (unofficial translation), http://archive.mid.ru/ns-osndoc.nsf/osnddeng. Contrast 'Turkey-Russia Jet Downing: Moscow Announces Sanctions', *BBC News*, 28 November 2015, www.bbc.co.uk/news/world-europe-34954575 (for the adoption of Russian countermeasures outside the framework of the Security Council).

[762] See 'Russian Rouble in Free-Fall Despite Shock 17% Rate Rise', *BBC News*, 16 December 2014, www.bbc.co.uk/news/business-30492518.

[763] See 'Putin Predicts Economic Recovery But Warns West against Pressuring Russian "Bear"', *The Washington Post*, 18 December 2014, www.washingtonpost.com/world/putin-predicts-economy-recover-in-two-years/2014/12/18/6b81bb70-8689-11e4-9534-f79a23c40e6c_story.html. Also: 'Russia Faces Full-Blown Crisis, Says Kudrin', *Financial Times*, 22 December 2014, www.ft.com/cms/s/0/d8bf5266-89cb-11e4-9dbf-00144feabdc0.html#axzz3MovE2gPX; 'Russian Economy Shrinks 2% as Sanctions Bite – Medvedev', *BBC News*, 21 April 2015, www.bbc.co.uk/news/world-europe-32396792; 'IMF Says Western Sanctions Could Cut 9 Percent Off Russia's GDP', *Reuters*, 3 August 2015, http://uk.reuters.com/article/uk-russia-economy-imf-idUKKCN0Q81E220150803.

[764] See above n. 755.

5

Permissibility of Third-Party Countermeasures: Evaluation

It is now convenient to assess whether the substantial body of practice examined in previous chapters is indicative of an emerging rule of customary international law entitling States to resort to third-party countermeasures in defence of communitarian norms. Although Judge Read in the *Fisheries* case appeared to suggest otherwise, the actual conduct of States clearly does not amount to the 'only convincing evidence'[1] of State practice. Account must be taken of all available State practice.[2] The body of actual practice – i.e. 'the conduct of States "on the ground"'[3] examined in Chapter 4 – should, as appropriate, be assessed alongside the statements made by States in the UN General Assembly's Sixth Committee during the ILC's work on State responsibility examined in Chapter 3. Contradictory practice in this respect must also be given appropriate weight.

As Judge Tanaka observed in the *North Sea Continental Shelf* cases, it is sometimes a 'delicate and difficult matter'[4] to determine with confidence whether an alleged rule of customary international law has come into existence. The answer may, in the final analysis, boil down to a matter of appreciation or judgment to be exercised by an informed observer based on flexible legal criteria.[5] In short, as Judge Tanaka reminds us, the various elements of a rule of custom 'cannot be mathematically and uniformly decided'.[6] These points seem especially apt for practice concerning third-party countermeasures. The added layers of complexity

---

[1] *Fisheries* case, ICJ Rep. (1951), 116 at 191 (Diss. Op. Judge Read).
[2] Wood, Second Report, 35, para. 48 (his Draft Conclusion 7); as provisionally adopted by the ILC Drafting Committee, UN Doc. A/CN.4/L.869 (14 July 2015) (Draft Conclusion 6).
[3] Ibid.
[4] *North Sea Continental Shelf*, ICJ Rep. (1969), 3 at 175 (Diss. Op. Judge Tanaka).
[5] Compare Lauterpacht (1958), 377, 386–387; Sørensen (1960), 38–39; Waldock (1962), 46–47, 49; Akehurst (1974–1975), 1; Mendelson (1998), 224; Boisson de Chazournes (2004), 13; Lowe (2007), 37; Crawford (2012), 24.
[6] *North Sea Continental Shelf*, ICJ Rep. (1969), 3 at 175 (Diss. Op. Judge Tanaka).

involved in the assessment of this practice (especially its somewhat obscure and overlapping nature) have already been noted in Chapters 1 and 4.[7]

Beyond the pragmatic reasons against third-party countermeasures examined in Chapter 3, it appears that the ILC – motivated by the thrust of opinion in the Sixth Committee – was reluctant to recognize the concept precisely because of some of these complexities. The ILC essentially advanced three legal arguments in support of its conclusion. The present chapter will assess these arguments and consider whether the ILC's position is actually borne out by State practice (5.1). This will be followed by an assessment of a number of other salient considerations emerging from practice (5.2) before some concluding observations are made (5.3).

5.1   The ILC's Arguments against Third-Party Countermeasures

It was already observed in Chapter 3 that the ILC concluded that there was insufficient evidence in State practice to support the inclusion of a right to take third-party countermeasures in Article 54 ARSIWA as a matter of progressive development of international law. The current state of international law on third-party countermeasures was deemed to be 'uncertain'; accordingly, there was 'no clearly recognised entitlement' to resort to third-party countermeasures under general international law.[8] This decision was mainly motivated by three legal arguments: (1) the absence of a widespread and representative practice; (2) the absence of a consistent practice; and (3) the absence of a practice accepted as law.[9] These arguments will now be considered in turn.

5.1.1   The Absence of a Widespread and Representative Practice

A first reason for the adoption of the saving clause in Article 54 ARSIWA was that practice was not deemed sufficiently widespread and representative: the ILC identified only six examples of State practice on third-party countermeasures in the period from 1978 to 1998. Although only

---

[7] See Sections 1.3–1.4; 4.1.

[8] See ARSIWA Commentary, Art. 54, §6. In Crawford's view, 'the legal position ... *remains uncertain*': Crawford (2013a), 703 (emphasis added).

[9] Crawford, Fourth Report, 18, paras. 71–74. Compare Crawford, Third Report, 104, para. 396; ARSIWA Commentary, Art. 54, §§3, 6.

reviewing 'some examples of recent experience',[10] the ILC concluded that practice on third-party countermeasures was 'limited and rather embryonic'.[11] Moreover, practice involved only 'a limited number of States'; mostly, if not exclusively, Western States.[12] Indeed the examples of practice provided by the ILC were exclusively Western oriented.[13] Practice was on that basis not deemed sufficiently 'extensive'[14] to form the basis of a general rule of customary international law.[15]

In terms of the generality of practice, there is certainly no requirement of universality.[16] At the same time, a change in custom – like fashion, as Mendelson explains – cannot be reduced to a 'magic number' of converts.[17] The ICJ in *North Sea Continental Shelf* required a 'very wide-spread and representative participation' in the relevant practice.[18] As Judge Lachs emphasized in that case, the geographical representative-ness of practice is an 'essential factor' which must be taken into account:

> No more can a general rule of international law be established by the fiat of one or of a few, or – as it was once claimed – by the consensus of European States only.[19]

This seems especially true, in light of the debate in the ILC and Sixth Committee, for an enforcement tool with universal aspirations as fraught with controversy as third-party countermeasures.

Although a greater quantity of practice will likely be required to effect a change in an existing rule of custom[20] – such as the prohibitive rule on

---

[10] Crawford, Third Report, 102, para. 390.

[11] See ARSIWA Commentary, Art. 54, §§3–5; Crawford, Third Report, 105, para. 401; YbILC (2000), vol. I, 303, para. 7 (Mr. Crawford). Also: YbILC (2000), vol. I, 336, para. 42 (Mr. Sepúlveda) ('the examples provided were extraordinarily few in number').

[12] See ILC Report (2000), UN Doc. A/55/10, 60, para. 367; ARSIWA Commentary, Art. 54, §6. Also: Topical Summary of Government Comments in the Sixth Committee, UN Doc. A/CN.4/513 (2000), 29, para. 149; Crawford, Third Report, 105, para. 401; Crawford, Fourth Report, 14, para. 55.

[13] Some ILC members emphasized this point: see e.g. YbILC (2000), vol. I, 336, para. 42 (Mr. Sepúlveda). However, as observed in Chapter 4, even these examples of practice include significant elements of non-Western practice in support of third-party countermeasures.

[14] *North Sea Continental Shelf*, ICJ Rep. (1969), 3 at 43, para. 74.

[15] See Crawford, Third Report, 104, para. 396(a). Generally: Wood, Second Report, 36–38, 40–45, paras. 52–53, 55–59 (his Draft Conclusion 9); as provisionally adopted by the ILC Drafting Committee, UN Doc. A/CN.4/L.869 (14 July 2015) (Draft Conclusion 8).

[16] See Wood, Second Report, 36–37, para. 52.   [17] Mendelson (1998), 224.

[18] *North Sea Continental Shelf*, ICJ Rep. (1969), 3 at 42, para. 73.

[19] Ibid., 227 (Diss. Op. Judge Lachs).

[20] See e.g. Akehurst (1974–1975), 19; Mendelson (1998), 222–223.

third-party countermeasures inherent in the traditional bilateral model of State responsibility – it may be doubted whether the ILC's conclusion was truly warranted.[21] All that can be said with confidence is that where the occasions for acting only arise sporadically, the repetitive element required for the practice would necessarily be less strict.[22] In any event, the extensive analysis of twenty-one examples in the previous chapter strongly suggests that State practice on third-party countermeasures can today hardly be described as neither limited nor embryonic. Indeed practice is considerably more widespread and representative than the ILC had assumed.

States such as Ghana, India, Indonesia, Kuwait, Malaysia, Nigeria, Pakistan, Sierra Leone, Tanzania, Uganda, Zambia and Zimbabwe adopted (or at least strongly supported) third-party countermeasures in the form of a trade embargo against South Africa.[23] Kenya, Rwanda, Zaire (now the DRC), Tanzania, Uganda and Zambia likewise adopted third-party countermeasures by way of a trade embargo against Burundi. States such as Botswana, Chile, China, Egypt, Guinea-Bissau, Honduras, Indonesia, Poland, Russia, South Africa and South Korea expressed support for that action before the Security Council; the OAU also expressed its full support.[24] Commonwealth Member States have adopted (or supported) third-party countermeasures against Nigeria and Zimbabwe by suspending them from their membership in the organization and by expressing a willingness to freeze the assets of then Nigerian Head of State, General Abacha.[25] The UN General Assembly expressed its support for the action taken against Nigeria.[26] Bahrain, Brazil, Costa Rica, Gabon, Gambia and Kenya expressed support for the third-party countermeasures adopted against the FRY.[27]

Arab League Member States have endorsed the adoption of third-party countermeasures against Libya and Syria by suspending them from their membership in the organization.[28] OIC Member States have likewise endorsed the adoption of third-party countermeasures against Syria by

---

[21] For some ILC members, the answer to the question of the permissibility of third-party countermeasures was even 'emphatically in the affirmative': YbILC (2000), vol. I, 336, para. 41 (Mr. Pellet). See also Alland (2002), 1239; Tams (2005), 231; Dawidowicz (2006), 408–409; Katselli-Proukaki (2010), 201–202; Pellet and Miron (2011), para. 58; others have been left 'puzzled': Sicilianos (2010), 1145–1146.

[22] See Waldock (1962), 44; Thirlway (2014), 65; Wood, Second Report, 41–42, para. 56.

[23] See Sections 4.2.1 (nn. 21, 23); 4.2.10 (n. 281).

[24] See Section 4.2.13 (nn. 384–385, 387, 395, 405–406, 408, 410).

[25] See Sections 4.2.12 (nn. 340, 344); 4.2.17 (n. 601).   [26] See Section 4.2.12 (n. 354).

[27] See Section 4.2.15 (nn. 490–491).   [28] See Sections 4.2.19 (n. 657); 4.2.20 (n. 692).

suspending its membership in the organization.[29] Arab League Member States have also adopted, or expressed strong support for, third-party countermeasures against Syria by freezing assets and expressing a willingness to suspend air services agreements.[30] Moreover, a very large number of States, as members of the so-called 'Group of Friends of the Syrian People', have adopted or repeatedly strongly supported third-party countermeasures against Syria in the form of asset freezes against President Al-Assad and the Central Bank of Syria.[31]

A considerable number of (mostly) Eastern European States have adopted or otherwise expressed support for third-party countermeasures by EU Member States. Albania, Bulgaria, Cyprus, the Czech Republic, Estonia, Hungary, Iceland, Latvia, Lichtenstein, Lithuania, Norway, Poland, Romania, Slovakia and Slovenia did so against the FRY in relation to asset freezes, suspensions of air services agreements and investment bans.[32] In the case of Bulgaria, Poland, Romania and Slovakia, among others, this action seemingly involved the unlawful suspension of bilateral investment treaties.[33] In addition, Bosnia and Herzegovina, Croatia, Georgia, Macedonia, Malta, Moldova, Montenegro, Serbia, Turkey and Ukraine have on one or more occasions adopted (or expressed support for) third-party countermeasures against Burma, Zimbabwe, Belarus and Syria.[34]

It is true that Western States still dominate practice; however, as the above survey shows, it is certainly not limited to Western States. Indeed the sheer volume and diversity of practice is striking. In addition to Western States, a very large number of States from Eastern Europe, Eurasia, the Middle East, Asia and Africa have contributed to practice in both word and deed – many of them repeatedly – over several decades. As Sepúlveda has observed, it is true that no State from Latin America has adopted third-party countermeasures,[35] – and, as will be discussed below, many of them have even strongly protested against their use – but Argentina, Costa Rica and Chile have nevertheless on occasion expressed some support for the concept.[36]

---

[29] See Section 4.2.20 (n. 702).   [30] Ibid. (nn. 696–699).   [31] Ibid. (nn. 718–728).
[32] See Section 4.2.15 (nn. 456, 471).   [33] Ibid. (n. 472).
[34] See Sections 4.2.16 (n. 524); 4.2.17 (n. 585); 4.2.18 (n. 639); 4.2.20 (n. 686). Croatia and Malta expressed their support prior to gaining EU membership in 2004 and 2013, respectively.
[35] See YbILC (2000), vol. I, 336, para. 42 (Mr. Sepúlveda).
[36] See Sections 3.2.1.3(ii) (nn. 173–174); 4.2.13 (nn. 395, 405); and below Section 5.1.2 (nn. 68–70).

To complete the picture, diplomatic protests should also be taken into account. A further striking – perhaps even 'astonishing'[37] – feature of practice concerns the relative absence of diplomatic protests against third-party countermeasures. The following examples may be mentioned. The OAS deplored the adoption of third-party countermeasures against Argentina on the basis that the Security Council has a monopoly to decide on sanctions under Chapter VII UNC.[38] Several States added strongly worded individual protests to the same effect.[39] Cuba also opposed the adoption of third-party countermeasures against Iraq.[40] Nigeria, Burundi, Sudan, the FRY, Burma, Zimbabwe, Belarus, Syria and Russia have all opposed the use of third-party countermeasures against them on several grounds, notably including violations of Chapter VII UNC, the principle of non-intervention and international human rights law.[41]

The OAU called on East African States to lift the third-party countermeasures taken against Burundi on humanitarian grounds.[42] The OIC has likewise called on the United States to lift its third-party countermeasures against Sudan on the same basis.[43] China and Russia have opposed Western States' use of third-party countermeasures against Burma on policy grounds.[44] The Non-Aligned Movement and SADC have called on Western States to lift their third-party countermeasures against Zimbabwe on essentially humanitarian grounds.[45] The Non-Aligned Movement has also called on Western States to lift their third-party countermeasures against Belarus on the basis that they violate the principle of non-intervention and Chapter VII UNC.[46] Finally, Russia has refused to legitimize the use of third-party countermeasures against Syria seemingly on the basis that such action contradicts Chapter VII UNC.[47]

It thus appears that it is only the protests made with respect to violations of Chapter VII UNC that impugn the basic entitlement to take third-party countermeasures (as distinct from the protests related

---

[37] Tams (2005), 236.   [38] See Section 4.2.8 (n. 204).   [39] Ibid. (nn. 209–216).
[40] See Section 4.2.11 (n. 320).
[41] See Sections 4.2.12 (n. 341); 4.2.13 (nn. 393, 397–404); 4.2.14 (nn. 439–441); 4.2.15 (nn. 461–463); 4.2.16 (n. 566); 4.2.17 (nn. 616–617); 4.2.18 (nn. 649–651); 4.2.20 (n. 729); 4.2.21 (nn. 759–761).
[42] See Section 4.2.13 (n. 414); and further Section 6.2.1.2(iii).
[43] See Section 4.2.14 (n. 442); and further Section 6.2.1.2(iii).
[44] See Section 4.2.16 (nn. 563–565).
[45] See Section 4.2.17 (nn. 619–620); and further Section 6.2.1.2(iii).
[46] See Section 4.2.18 (n. 648).   [47] See Section 4.2.20 (n. 709).

simply to the conditions governing their use in a particular case).[48] In any event, these protests do not significantly detract from the widespread and representative affirmative practice on third-party countermeasures. To conclude on this point, practice is considerably more extensive and representative than the ILC had assumed. Even the stringent standard applied by the ICJ in *North Sea Continental Shelf* regarding the extent and diversity of practice appears to have been met.

5.1.2   The Absence of a Consistent Practice

A second reason for the ILC's position was that it considered practice too selective and inconsistent. As Special Rapporteur Crawford observed:

> [P]ractice is selective; in the majority of cases involving violations of collective obligations, no reaction at all has been taken, apart from verbal condemnations;
>
> [E]ven if coercive measures were taken, they were not always designated as countermeasures. The decision of the Government of the Netherlands to rely on fundamental change of circumstances in order to suspend its treaty with Suriname seems to imply a preference for other concepts.[49]

In more poignant terms, Brownlie stressed that

> State practice in the area was highly selective, i.e. effective in some cases and merely verbal in others, and that it was not always officially designated as countermeasures. In reality, article 54 [2000] constituted neither the law nor its potential progressive development. Progressive development related to some existing foundations, but practice was inconsistent in the extreme. Faced with the same allegation, State A risked economic

---

[48] Protests concerning the principle of non-intervention typically involve assertions that no prior wrongful conduct has been committed and/or that the action taken is motivated by unavowed objectives unrelated to the instrumental function of countermeasures (Article 49 ARSIWA). Protests concerning adverse humanitarian consequences on the civilian population in the target State are based either on the exclusion of fundamental human rights obligations (Article 50(1)(b) ARSIWA) or (more persuasively) on the principle of proportionality (Article 51 ARSIWA). Action taken by the Security Council is also relevant in assessing the proportionality (and necessity) of third-party countermeasures. The suggestion that third-party countermeasures are *a priori* incompatible with Chapter VII UNC is not borne out by practice. See further below Section 5.2.1; and Sections 6.1.3.1; 6.2.1.2(iii); 6.3.2.

[49] Crawford, Third Report, 104, para. 396(b). For an assessment of States' occasional reliance on alternative justifications see Dawidowicz (2006), 404–407 (with further references).

sanctions and even armed attack, whereas State B would not even have to accept the presence of observers.[50]

Previously, Brownlie had observed that 'double standards were rampant' – third-party countermeasures (like humanitarian intervention) were 'nearly always dictated by political and strategic interest'.[51] For his part, Simma lamented that 'selectivity was widespread' in response to human rights violations.[52] Other commentators have pointed to the 'caractère aléatoire'[53] of practice – as exemplified by the complete absence of any third-party countermeasures adopted against Cambodia or Rwanda for the genocides committed in those countries in the 1970s and 1990s.[54] Koskenniemi has expressed a broader concern with third-party countermeasures:

> Interested and powerful States would be transformed into a kind of world police, or almost. Because there would be no *duty* to take measures, they could – unlike the police – create a world order of their liking by choosing between violations they enforce and violations they do not, as well as deciding on the manner and intensity of their reaction. With some systematic bias in one direction or another, the law would soon become indissociable from Great Power policy.[55]

During the Cold War, States occasionally made similar arguments decrying variants of arbitrary 'imperialist solidarity'.[56] Such reservations appear to reflect broader concerns among many States regarding an alleged link between unilateral coercive measures and the politicization of human rights.[57] In short, as Special Rapporteur Riphagen observed,

---

[50] YbILC (2001), vol. I, 35, para. 2 (Mr. Brownlie). See also ibid., 45, para. 22 (Mr. Sreenivasa Rao); YbILC (2000), vol. I, 305, para. 31 (Mr. Simma).

[51] Brownlie (1986), 491 at 500.   [52] YbILC (2000), vol. I, 305, para. 31 (Mr. Simma).

[53] Dupuy (1983), 542. Compare Leben (1982), 76.

[54] Hannum (1989), 137–138; Crawford, First Report, 16, para. 59; YbILC (2000), vol. I, 304, para. 18 (Mr. Kateka), 312, para. 4 (Mr. Goco). See also Cassese (2005), 269.

[55] Koskenniemi (2001), 344 (emphasis in original). See also Akehurst (1970), 15–16; Petman (2004), 314.

[56] See e.g. UN Doc. S/PV.2362 (22 May 1982), 9, paras. 102–105 (Soviet Union) regarding Western States' adoption of third-party countermeasures against Argentina over the Falklands crisis, but (at least initially) demonstrating a reluctance to do the same against South Africa to counter apartheid. Similarly: UN Doc. A/37/PV.53 (3 Nov. 1982), 916, para. 188 (Albania), 918, paras. 207–208 (Byelorussian Soviet Socialist Republic). Compare 'The Declaration of the Russian Federation and the People's Republic of China on the Promotion of International Law' (25 June 2016), para. 6, http://www.mid .ru/en/foreign_policy/news/-/asset_publisher/cKNonkJE02Bw/content/id/2331698.

[57] See e.g. GA Res. 36/103 (9 Dec. 1981), Principle II(l); and Section 1.2.

'the practice of States in relation to counter-measures is (also) dictated to a large extent by political factors'.[58]

In the words of the ICJ in the *Asylum* case, it thus seems that State practice was not sufficiently 'constant and uniform' to form the basis of a general rule of custom.[59] There was apparently 'so much uncertainty and contradiction, so much fluctuation and discrepancy ... so much inconsistency ...'[60] that it was simply not possible to discern any clear and legally relevant pattern in the practice concerning third-party countermeasures. However, the type of inconsistency referred to here is largely inconsequential. It would be very surprising if third-party countermeasures had been adopted in response to every serious breach of international law in the last half-century. Still, as Special Rapporteur Crawford himself recognized, third-party countermeasures have been adopted in response to 'some of the major political crises of recent times'.[61] Indeed, in addition to the examples identified by the ILC, the third-party countermeasures adopted against Burundi, Sudan, Burma, Zimbabwe, Belarus, Libya, Syria and Russia, among many others, may be recalled.

It may seem rather trite to observe that the criterion of uniformity is not a political or moral requirement but a legal one. But it is nevertheless worth emphasizing. The very notion of third-party countermeasures is based on a legal entitlement or power: there is no obligation to take such action in response to violations of communitarian norms. Recourse to third-party countermeasures is optional: the enforcement of international law is but one factor among many others that will determine their application in a given case. In the context of the third-party countermeasures adopted against Argentina during the Falklands crisis, the following statement by the United Kingdom provides an illustration:

> [T]he Government have always considered that, *in the appropriate circumstances*, economic measures can play a useful role in encouraging observance of international law.[62]

It seems that what matters is not whether third-party countermeasures have sometimes not been adopted 'in the appropriate circumstances' –

---

[58] Riphagen, Preliminary Report, 129, para. 97.
[59] *Asylum* case, ICJ Rep. (1950), 266 at 276–277.   [60] Ibid.
[61] Crawford, Third Report, 105, para. 399. See also e.g. Tams (2005), 234–235.
[62] Marston BYIL (1982), 517 (statement by the FCO Minister of State, Lord Belstead) (emphasis added).

but whether, once actually adopted, they meet the requirement of uniformity. As Mendelson explains:

> [E]ach State whose conduct is under consideration must have behaved in the same way on virtually all of the occasions on which it engaged in the conduct in question.[63]

The argument of selectivity considered here therefore does not call into question the existence of the right to resort to third-party countermeasures.[64] The real question – alluded to by Mendelson above, but hardly addressed by the ILC – which merits more careful scrutiny concerns the degree of uniformity of actual conduct and statements by States on the matter.

State practice is rarely (if ever) uniform in any absolute sense. The practice concerning third-party countermeasures is no exception. As the ICJ has repeatedly explained, it is sufficient that the relevant practice is 'virtually uniform'.[65] In the same vein, the ICJ has further specified that 'too much importance need not be attached to the few uncertainties or contradictions, real or apparent ... [which] may be easily understood';[66] in sum, practice need not be 'perfect' in the sense of being 'in absolutely rigorous conformity' with the relevant rule.[67] Minor inconsistencies do not matter; major ones do.

Unsurprisingly, the practice examined in Chapters 3 and 4 does indeed demonstrate some contradictions, but the question is whether practice is fatally riddled with contradictions. These contradictions provide an intriguing and even striking feature of practice: in reality, actual practice is far more nuanced than the debate in the Sixth Committee taken in isolation would otherwise suggest. For present purposes, the following examples from Chapters 3 and 4 will suffice to illustrate the point.

Argentina and Costa Rica opposed the adoption of third-party countermeasures during the Falklands crisis on the basis that they were deemed an instrument of abuse favouring powerful States and incompatible with the

---

[63] Mendelson (1998), 212. Compare Alland (2002), 1239; Tams (2005), 234–235; Villalpando (2005), 411.

[64] Compare Alland (2002), 1239; Tams (2005), 235.

[65] *North Sea Continental Shelf,* ICJ Rep. (1969), 3 at 43, para. 74.

[66] *Fisheries* case, ICJ Rep. (1951), 116 at 138.

[67] *Nicaragua* case, ICJ Rep. (1986), 14 at 98, para. 186. Generally: Wood, Second Report, 41–45, paras. 55–59 (his Draft Conclusion 9); as provisionally adopted by the ILC Drafting Committee, UN Doc. A/CN.4/L.869 (14 July 2015) (Draft Conclusion 8).

enforcement authority of the Security Council under Chapter VII UNC.[68] Still, they nevertheless found the concept 'acceptable' in the Sixth Committee.[69] For its part, Costa Rica also later expressed support for the adoption of third-party countermeasures against the FRY and Burma.[70] Likewise, Botswana, Cameroon and Tanzania opposed third-party countermeasures on similar grounds in the Sixth Committee but seemingly expressed support for their adoption against Nigeria, Burundi and Zimbabwe; Tanzania even itself adopted third-party countermeasures against South Africa and Burundi.[71] Zimbabwe (and later, SADC and the Non-Aligned Movement) opposed the adoption of third-party countermeasures against it based on the same rationale, but had previously seemingly supported their adoption against South Africa, Nigeria and Burundi.[72] In the Sixth Committee, South Africa (on behalf of SADC, including Zimbabwe) expressed support for third-party countermeasures, albeit in rather cautious terms.[73] India expressed grave reservations in the Sixth Committee but (as a Commonwealth Member State) seemingly supported the adoption of third-party countermeasures against South Africa, Nigeria and Zimbabwe.[74]

The Czech Republic and Greece opposed third-party countermeasures in the Sixth Committee but have repeatedly supported their adoption within the EU context; the former already expressing such support against the FRY, Burma and Zimbabwe prior to its EU membership.[75] The FRY may have protested the adoption of third-party countermeasures against it during the Kosovo crisis but Serbia and Montenegro have both supported their adoption against Burma, Zimbabwe, Belarus and Syria.[76] Japan characterized third-party countermeasures as a 'revolutionary development of international law'[77] during the debate in the Sixth Committee and yet Japan has presumably itself taken part in that 'revolutionary development' by expressing support for or taking such action against Iraq, the FRY, Syria and

---

[68] See Section 4.2.9 (nn. 204, 223).   [69] See Section 3.2.1.3(ii) (nn. 174–175).

[70] See Sections 4.2.15 (nn. 490–491); 4.2.16 (n. 561).

[71] See Sections 3.2.1.3(ii) (nn. 197, 213–214); 4.2.1 (n. 23); 4.2.12 (nn. 340, 343–344); 4.2.13 (nn. 384–385); 4.2.17 (n. 601).

[72] See Sections 4.2.10 (n. 281); 4.2.12 (n. 340); 4.2.13 (n. 406); 4.2.17 (nn. 616–617, 619–621).

[73] See Section 3.2.1.3(ii) (nn. 179–180).

[74] See Sections 3.2.1.3(ii) (n. 209); 4.2.10 (n. 281); 4.2.12 (n. 340); 4.2.17 (n. 601).

[75] See Sections 3.1.3 (n. 76); 3.2.1.3(ii) (n. 185); 4.2.15–4.2.17 (nn. 469, 471, 522–524).

[76] See Sections 4.2.15–4.2.18; 4.2.20 (nn. 461–463, 585, 639, 686).

[77] See Section 3.2.1.3(ii) (n. 216).

Russia.[78] The United Kingdom stressed before the Sixth Committee that the use of third-party countermeasures would be 'potentially highly destabilizing of treaty relations'.[79] The numerous examples of third-party countermeasures, including but not limited to violations of the GATT/WTO, adopted by the United Kingdom (as well as at its own request) need not be repeated here. The statement by the United States that the enforcement of fundamental norms was 'better left to the Security Council'[80] is likewise seemingly at variance with its actual conduct in practice.

On balance, having attributed appropriate weight to this occasionally conflicting practice, it becomes apparent that these contradictions, in the aggregate, in fact decidedly point to a 'virtually uniform' practice in support of a permissive rule on third-party countermeasures. This conclusion is further reinforced by the uniform and widespread affirmative practice of the many other States examined in Chapters 3 and 4.

5.1.3   The Absence of a Practice Accepted as Law

Finally, the ILC concluded that there appeared to be 'no clearly recognised entitlement' to take third-party countermeasures.[81] Special Rapporteur Crawford observed that it was 'unclear' whether the practice on third-party countermeasures was accepted as law – that is, whether any *opinio juris* was associated with it.[82] The view was expressed in the ILC that practice was 'too close to politics than [sic] it was to law to demonstrate that any such right existed'.[83] As already observed, States appeared to have an implied preference for concepts other than third-party countermeasures and did not always officially designate their actions by reference to countermeasures.[84] With the Kosovo example in mind, Special Rapporteur Crawford added a further element of ambiguity:

> Different inferences could be drawn from the Yugoslav experience, which also showed that, very often in that type of intervention, the measures

---

[78] See Sections 4.2.11 (n. 312); 4.2.15 (nn. 455, 474); 4.2.20 (nn. 691, 720, 726–727); 4.2.21 (n. 758).

[79] See Section 3.2.1.3(ii) (n. 217).   [80] See Section 3.2.1.3(ii) (n. 206).

[81] ARSIWA Commentary, Art. 54, §6.

[82] ILC Report (2000), UN Doc. A/55/10, 58, para. 356; YbILC (2000), vol. I, 303, para. 7 (Mr. Crawford). Generally: Wood, Second Report, 45–70 paras. 60–80 (his Draft Conclusions 10 and 11); as provisionally adopted by the ILC Drafting Committee, UN Doc. A/CN.4/L.869 (14 July 2015) (Draft Conclusions 9 and 10).

[83] YbILC (2000), vol. I, 333, para. 20 (Mr. Rodríguez Cedeño).   [84] See above nn. 49–50.

taken were condemned or legitimated retrospectively, depending on the results. Hence, the extreme difficulty in defining the subject-matter of article 54 in any detail.[85]

Brownlie suggested that third-party countermeasures were a 'neologism' – a 'completely invented' legal category based on practice that had been 'classified *ex post facto*'.[86] By contrast, Simma argued that 'it was an exercise in futility to demand an *opinio juris* on the question: clearly, the *opinio juris* of a State taking countermeasures could not be that of the target State'.[87] Still, in the words of the ICJ in the *Asylum case*, practice on third-party countermeasures was apparently 'so much influenced by considerations of political expediency'[88] that it was not possible to discern any *opinio juris*.

It is certainly important to distinguish between legal and political justifications for State conduct. The distinction may not always be straightforward. But this is part of a wider problem with the assessment of State practice. As Wood (a former FCO legal adviser) has explained:

> There is often considerable difficulty in ascertaining State practice. Governments do not indicate publicly, clearly, or at all, the legal basis for each and every thing that they do or refrain from doing.[89]

Lowe has likewise observed that

> States do not usually assert explicitly that their actions are (or are not) consistent with international law: explicit statements of *opinio juris* are rare.[90]

This is also a general feature of the practice concerning third-party countermeasures. As Tzanakopoulos has observed:

> States reacting to a violation of international law will 'only reluctantly' officially qualify their reaction as a countermeasure or a 'reprisal', as it was called in the past . . . a State may justify its action as a countermeasure in substance, without, however, officially proclaiming it to qualify as belonging to that legal category.[91]

---

[85] YbILC (2001), vol. I, 36, para. 8 (Mr. Crawford).

[86] Ibid., 35, para. 5 (Mr. Brownlie); and compare Brownlie (1963), 220. There is in any event no *a priori* reason to dismiss practice based solely on an *ex post facto* classification: see Lowe (2000), 934.

[87] YbILC (2001), vol. I, 35, para. 4 (Mr. Simma).

[88] *Asylum* case, ICJ Rep. (1951), 266 at 277.

[89] Wood (2010), para. 9. See already Lauterpacht (1958), 380–381; Waldock (1962), 46.

[90] Lowe (2007), 40.

[91] Tzanakopoulos (2011), 188–189. See already to the same effect Tomuschat (1973), 186–187; Malanczuk (1985), 297; Dawidowicz (2006), 350, 414–415. Compare Thirlway (2009),

It seems that it was essentially for the foregoing reason that Judges Tanaka and Sørensen in the *North Sea Continental Shelf* cases stressed that it was often 'extremely difficult' – if not 'practically impossible' – to get concrete evidence of *opinio juris* 'in view of the manner in which international relations are conducted'.[92] A few observations are warranted to demystify the seemingly 'mysterious phenomenon'[93] of *opinio juris*.

The question that must be addressed squarely is whether practice concerning third-party countermeasures can really be said to have any significance in legal terms if States do not explicitly refer to the concept as a basis for their conduct. It seems that if any State practice motivated by political considerations were dismissed *a priori*, there would not be much potential for law to make a contribution to international affairs. A politically motivated practice is still susceptible to legal analysis and evaluation, and can constitute valuable evidence of a rule of custom.[94] It may well be that third-party countermeasures belong to 'an area in which the borderline between international law per se and foreign relations [is] fairly indistinct',[95] but this does not vitiate the law-making capacity of the relevant practice. The key question is whether practice is motivated solely by extra-legal considerations.[96] A negative answer must be provided to this question. Even if States have not explicitly invoked the concept of third party countermeasures, the practice examined in Chapter 4 nevertheless demonstrates that they have relied on it in substance. In other words, States have adopted *prima facie* unlawful unilateral coercive measures based on an explicit legal rationale; namely, the enforcement of obligations *erga omnes (partes)*. This rationale neatly corresponds to third-party countermeasures as a legal category.

149–150 (discussing conduct which – even if not primarily presented as a countermeasure – the ICJ in the *Gabčíkovo Nagymaros Project* case (ICJ Rep. (1997), 7 at 55–56, paras. 82–83) nevertheless determined bore all the hallmarks of a countermeasure).

[92] *North Sea Continental Shelf*, ICJ Rep. (1969), 3 at 176 (Diss. Op. Judge Tanaka), 246 (Judge Sørensen). The discovery of concrete evidence of *opinio juris* (if any) may require a 'prolonged search' and 'a certain amount of good fortune': Lauterpacht (1958), 385. Insofar as it does exist, it often forms part of the 'secret life of international law': Bethlehem (2012), 24.

[93] Lauterpacht (1950), 395; Waldock (1962), 41; Lowe (2007), 50–51; Crawford (2013b), 49. See further Wood, Second Report, 51–53, para. 66 (for a summary of the debate on the 'paradox' of *opinio juris*).

[94] See e.g. Lauterpacht (1958), 380; Waldock (1962), 47; Baxter (1970), 68; Tams (2005), 239.

[95] YbILC (2000), vol. I, 296, para. 46 (Mr. Opertti Badan).

[96] See Wood, Second Report, 46–47, 56, para. 61.

It is true that the ICJ has looked for concrete evidence of *opinio juris* in instances where practice was deemed inconclusive and in doing so has applied an exacting standard.[97] However, in the absence of evidence of non-normative intent (*opinio non juris*), the ICJ has often presumed that consistent practice is accompanied by normative intent (*opinio juris*).[98] There has long been support for such a presumption of *opinio juris* in the literature.[99] It appears to apply *a fortiori* in the case of conduct based on a permissive rule. As Akehurst has explained:

> In the case of a permissive rule, it may be possible to find express statements that States are permitted to act in a particular way. But express statements are not necessary to establish a permissive rule; a claim that States are entitled to act in a particular way can be inferred from the fact that they do act in that way.[100]

Lowe has made a very similar point emphasizing that in the case of conduct based on a permissive rule '*opinio juris* is presumed to exist'.[101] ILC Special Rapporteur Wood has also made a distinction based on cases involving the assertion of a legal right and those acknowledging a legal obligation.[102]

By parity of reasoning, it may be presumed that the sheer adoption of a third-party countermeasure by a State entails recognition of the legal power to do so, whereas *opinio juris* on the obligatory safeguards governing its use might be more difficult to establish.[103] This presumption may of course be rebutted by a statement to the contrary. The statement made by the United Kingdom during the Kosovo crisis provides a rare example of *opinio non juris*: the immediate suspension of its air services agreement with the FRY was only exceptionally justified on 'moral and political

---

[97] See e.g. *S.S. 'Lotus'* (1927), PCIJ Ser. A, No. 10, 28; *North Sea Continental Shelf*, ICJ Rep. (1969), 3 at 43–45, paras. 75–81; *Ahmadou Sadio Diallo*, ICJ Rep. (2007), 582 at 614–615, paras. 88–90.

[98] See e.g. *Barcelona Traction*, ICJ Rep. (1970), 3 at 42, para. 70; *Gulf of Maine*, ICJ Rep. (1984), 246 at 293–294, 299, paras. 91–93, 111; *Pulp Mills on the River Uruguay*, ICJ Rep. (2010), 14 at 82–83, para. 204. Also: *North Sea Continental Shelf*, ICJ Rep. (1969), 3 at 176 (Diss. Op. Judge Tanaka), 231 (Diss. Op. Judge Lachs), 242 (Diss. Op. Judge Sørensen); *Nuclear Tests*, ICJ Rep. (1974), 253 at 305–306 (Sep. Op. Judge Petrén); *Responsibilities and Obligations of States Sponsoring Persons and Entities with Respect to Activities in the Area*, ITLOS Case No. 17 (Adv. Op., 1 Feb. 2011), para. 135.

[99] See e.g. Sørensen (1946), 88–111; Lauterpacht (1958), 380; Waldock (1962), 49; Wolfke (1964), 155–156; Guggenheim (1967), 103–105; Baxter (1970), 69; Kirgis (1987), 146; Tams (2005), 238; Crawford (2012), 26–27.

[100] Akehurst (1974–1975), 38.   [101] Lowe (2007), 51.

[102] Wood, Second Report, 58, 70, paras. 71, 80 (his Draft Conclusion 11).

[103] The safeguards regime is discussed in Chapter 6.

grounds'.[104] And yet the United Kingdom made no such caveat regarding rights withheld under customary international law when freezing internationally protected State assets in the same case – or in any other instance of practice for that matter, irrespective of whether the source of the violation emanated from treaty or custom.

Statements expressing *opinio juris* in the field of third-party countermeasures are equally rare, but they do exist. For example, the Council of the European Union in 2004 released a policy statement on the use of sanctions (known in EU parlance as 'restrictive measures' or 'autonomous sanctions'), which in relevant part provides:

> If necessary, the Council will impose autonomous sanctions [i.e. acts of retorsion and/or third-party countermeasures][105] in support of efforts to . . . uphold human rights, democracy, the rule of law and good governance. We will do this in accordance with our common foreign and security policy, as set out in Article 11 TEU, and in full conformity with our obligations under international law.[106]

Indeed the European Commission in 2008 observed that autonomous sanctions 'have been *frequently* imposed by the EU in recent years . . . to bring about a change in activities or policies such as violations of international law or human rights, or policies that do not respect the rule of law or democratic principles'.[107] In the opinion of EU Member States, the freezing of assets, including those belonging to Heads of State and central banks, among other unilateral coercive measures adopted by way of third-party countermeasures, are evidently a frequent tool of enforcement used in full conformity with international law.

In conclusion, the ILC's argument that *opinio juris* is 'unclear' is ultimately unconvincing – it is not borne out by international practice. The category of third-party countermeasures is needed to explain this

---

[104] See Section 4.2.15 (n. 485); and also above n. 79. By contrast, it is 'somewhat surprising' that the United Kingdom expressed no such doubts about the legality of its humanitarian intervention in Kosovo: Simma (1999), 2.

[105] See Sections 1.4.3–1.4.4 (for a discussion of terminology).

[106] Council of the European Union, Basic Principles on the Use of Restrictive Measures (Sanctions) (2004), para. 3, http://register.consilium.europa.eu/doc/srv?l=EN&f=ST%2010198%202004%20REV%201. See also European Commission, EU Guidelines on Implementation and Evaluation of Restrictive Measures (2008), 6 ('The introduction and implementation of restrictive measures must always be in accordance with international law'), http://eeas.europa.eu/cfsp/sanctions/docs/index_en.pdf.

[107] European Commission, EU Guidelines on Implementation and Evaluation of Restrictive Measures (2008), 1 (emphasis added), http://eeas.europa.eu/cfsp/sanctions/docs/index_en.pdf.

practice in legal terms. It is not possible to determine with any degree of certainty at what precise moment in time in the last half-century of practice a nascent *opinio juris* on third-party countermeasures matured into a fully fledged legal entitlement – custom is formed gradually through an untidy mass of activity in constant motion, with inevitable ebbs and flows.[108] Big bangs are normally not the stuff of international law. Often, as Fisher Williams once put it: 'The Rubicon which divides custom from law is crossed silently, unconsciously and without proclamation'.[109] And so it is for third-party countermeasures – the Rubicon has been crossed, silently and without fanfare.

5.2 Other Salient Considerations

A number of other salient considerations that emerge from the examination of practice in previous chapters also merit attention. This section will in turn examine: the relationship between third-party countermeasures and enforcement measures taken by the UN Security Council (5.2.1); the communitarian norms that have triggered adoption of third-party countermeasures (5.2.2); the modalities for the ascertainment of wrongful conduct (5.2.3); the requirement of a 'serious' breach (5.2.4); the role of a directly injured State (5.2.5); the indeterminacy of communitarian norms (5.2.6); and the effectiveness of third-party countermeasures (5.2.7). This will be followed by some concluding observations (5.3).

5.2.1 *The Relationship between Third-Party Countermeasures and Security Council Enforcement Measures*

It may be recalled from Chapter 3 that the relationship between third-party countermeasures and the UN Security Council was the source of some controversy in the ILC and Sixth Committee debate. Indeed one of the general objections that prompted the adoption of the saving clause in Article 54 ARSIWA was the unclear relationship between third-party countermeasures and enforcement measures taken by the Security Council under Chapter VII UNC – a natural consequence of the general lack of clarity between the law of State responsibility and the law of

---

[108] Compare McDougal (1955), 357. See also Wood, Fourth Report, 6, para. 17 (with further references).
[109] Fisher Williams (1939), 44.

collective security expressed in Article 59 ARSIWA.[110] The boundary between these areas of law is a porous one where complex questions of coexistence and coordination are bound to arise.[111] This was deemed to raise highly controversial issues in a field already controversial enough.[112]

There was concern among some members of the ILC and Sixth Committee that the use of third-party countermeasures would threaten – even violate – the collective security system based on Chapter VII UNC by creating overlapping enforcement regimes which would impinge on the powers of the Security Council.[113] It was recognized that the UN Charter was silent on this point but it was nevertheless suggested that 'by analogy with Article 51 of the Charter concerning the right of self-defence, a State should cease its own countermeasures once the Security Council had ordered collective economic sanctions'.[114] Article 59 ARSIWA raises – but does not explicitly answer – the question whether the monopoly on the use of force afforded to the Security Council under the UN Charter also applies to third-party countermeasures.[115] Commentators have noted that the relationship between third-party countermeasures and Security Council enforcement measures remains unclear.[116]

Specifically, it has been suggested that the triggering of enforcement action by the Security Council under Chapter VII UNC entails an implied obligation to suspend third-party countermeasures already adopted, in so far as they are different or incompatible with UN sanctions, or at least to adapt them to ensure harmonization with the

---

[110] See e.g. ILC Report (2000), UN Doc. A/55/10, 60, para. 366; Topical Summary of Government Comments in the Sixth Committee, UN Doc. A/CN.4/513 (2000), 33, para. 176; Sicilianos (2010), 1144; Crawford (2013a), 706. Generally: Section 3.2.1.3.

[111] See e.g. Gowlland-Debbas (2012), 225–297. Further: Forteau (2006).

[112] Crawford, Fourth Report, 18, para. 71.

[113] See e.g. Topical Summary of Government Comments in the Sixth Committee, UN Doc. A/CN.4/513 (2000), 33, para. 176; YbILC (2001), vol. I, 35, para. 2 (Mr. Brownlie); Sicilianos (2010), 1137. Also: YbILC (1992), vol. I, 144, para. 8 (Mr. Pellet).

[114] UN Doc. A/C.6/55/SR.11, 7, para. 39 (Morocco). For proposals to this effect see UN Docs. A/C.6/55/SR.17, 14, para. 85 (Greece); A/CN.4/515, 87 (Netherlands).

[115] See e.g. YbILC (2001), vol. I, 36, para. 8 (Mr. Crawford); Gowlland-Debbas (2010), 124. Also: UN Docs. A/C.6/55/SR.18, 4, para. 15 (Jordan); A/CN.4/515, 91–92 (Austria), 92 (Spain); A/CN.4/515/Add.2, 18 (Poland); A/C.6/56/SR.14, 10, para. 62 (Cameroon); A/C.6/56/SR.16, 2, para. 4 (Brazil).

[116] See e.g. Gowlland-Debbas (2010), 122, 124; Sicilianos (2010), 1140–1142; Crawford (2013a), 709; Palchetti (2014), 1234–1236; Jazairy, Report of the Special Rapporteur on the negative impact of unilateral coercive measures on the enjoyment of human rights, UN Doc. A/HRC/30/45 (10 Aug. 2015), 17–18.

institutional action taken. Put simply, enforcement action under Chapter VII UNC effectively ends any entitlement to adopt third-party countermeasures.[117] The limited question that will be examined here is whether this proposition finds support in practice.

The extensive examination in Chapter 4 demonstrates that practice provides only a handful of genuine examples of potential conflict. In November 1977, after unrelenting pressure from the UN General Assembly for a more resolute stance against apartheid, the Security Council, acting under Chapter VII UNC, finally imposed an arms embargo against South Africa.[118] In July 1985, a draft resolution under Chapter VII UNC which proposed more comprehensive sanctions against South Africa had been vetoed by the United Kingdom and the United States.[119] The Security Council instead adopted a resolution under Chapter VI UNC by which it 'commended' those States that had already adopted unilateral coercive measures against South Africa and recommended that others follow suit.[120] The UN arms embargo was lifted in May 1994 following the establishment of democratic rule in South Africa.[121] During the relevant period, the third-party counter-measures adopted by a large number of States against South Africa remained in force. At least prior to July 1985, these third-party counter-measures were not explicitly approved by the Security Council (though their adoption had been strongly encouraged by the General Assembly since the early 1960s). In any event, the fact that the Security Council belatedly commended the use of third-party countermeasures against South Africa demonstrates that their use was not considered to encroach on the powers of the Council under the UN Charter.[122]

On 3 April 1982, in response to Argentina's invasion of the Falkland (Malvinas) Islands, the Security Council adopted a resolution under Chapter VII UNC by which it demanded that Argentina immediately

---

[117] See e.g. Frowein (1994), 370–371; Sicilianos (2010), 1142; Dupont (2012), 332–334; Crawford (2013a), 709; Jazairy, Report of the Special Rapporteur on the negative impact of unilateral coercive measures on the enjoyment of human rights, UN Doc. A/HRC/30/45 (10 Aug. 2015), 17–18. Also: ILC Report (1992), UN Doc. A/47/10, 28, para. 185; YbILC (2001), vol. I, 40, para. 41 (Mr. Economides); UN Docs. A/C.6/55/SR.17, 14, para. 85 (Greece); A/CN.4/515, 87 (Netherlands).

[118] SC Res. 418 (4 Nov. 1977); SC Res 558 (13 Dec. 1984); SC Res. 591 (28 Nov. 1986). See further Section 4.2.10.

[119] UN Docs. S/17363 (26 July 1985) (Burkina Faso et al.); Report of the Security Council (1985–1986), A/41/2, 55–56.

[120] SC Res. 569 (26 July 1985).   [121] SC Res. 919 (25 May 1994).

[122] Similarly Sicilianos (2010), 1140–1141.

withdraw its occupying forces and called on the parties to seek a diplomatic solution to the conflict.[123] A week later, EC Member States, followed by other Western States, adopted third-party countermeasures against Argentina. EC Member States noted that the invasion was 'a matter of serious concern for the international community as a whole' and justified, *inter alia*, 'in order to ensure, within the shortest possible time, the full implementation of Security Council resolution 502'.[124] Several Latin American States and Eastern European States protested that the Security Council enjoyed a monopoly on sanctions; the third-party countermeasures adopted against Argentina had not been authorized by the said resolution.[125] However, Belgium (on behalf of EC Member States) dismissed the notion that the Security Council had a 'monopoly on sanctions' as 'an entirely new idea'.[126] At least in the view of EC Member States, the use of third-party countermeasures was clearly not incompatible with Chapter VII UNC and the diplomatic resolution of the conflict called for by the Security Council.

On 6 August 1990, in response to Iraq's invasion of Kuwait, the Security Council took enforcement action against Iraq under Chapter VII UNC by way of a trade embargo and an asset freeze.[127] Several States had at that time already taken the same action against Iraq by way of third-party countermeasures. Japan declared that 'for its part, [it] will faithfully respect this resolution, *in addition to carrying out its own measures*, as it announced earlier on 5 August'.[128] It seems unlikely that these additional unilateral coercive measures, in the trade and financial sectors, albeit not expressly mentioned in the relevant resolution, could be deemed in conflict with the UN sanctions regime.

In April 1996, in response to acts of State-sponsored terrorism involving violations of the principles of non-use of force and non-intervention, the Security Council took enforcement action against Sudan under Chapter VII UNC in the form of travel bans and diplomatic sanctions.[129] In August 1996, the UN sanctions regime was broadened to include an

---

[123] SC Res. 502 (3 Apr. 1982).
[124] See UN Doc. S/14976 (14 Apr. 1982) (Belgium on behalf of EC Member States); and further Section 4.2.8.
[125] See Section 4.2.8 (nn. 204, 209–216).
[126] UN Doc. S/PV.2363 (23 May 1982), 12, paras. 131–132 (Belgium on behalf of EC Member States).
[127] SC Res. 661 (6 Aug. 1990). See further Section 4.2.11.
[128] UN Doc. S/21461 (8 Aug. 1990) (Japan) (emphasis added).
[129] SC Res. 1054 (26 Apr. 1996). See further Section 4.2.14.

aviation embargo.[130] The United States expressed general support for the enforcement action taken against Sudan, but stressed that it was insufficient:

> We do not believe that the sanctions outlined in this resolution are sufficient . . .
> We favour the steps the Council is taking today, but we must say again that they are not big enough. We believe that firmer measures should be taken, not against the people of Sudan, but against their unresponsive Government.[131]

It later added:

> Continued Sudanese non-compliance with the demands of the international community not only will bring these measures into force [i.e. the aviation embargo], but will compel consideration of further steps.[132]

In November 1997, the United States adopted several unilateral coercive measures against Sudan, including third-party countermeasures by way of asset freezes.[133] This action was clearly not contemplated by the limited sanctions regime adopted by the Security Council, which was terminated in September 2001.[134]

The United States has nevertheless maintained its third-party countermeasures against Sudan in response to continuing human rights violations. In September 2004, the United States broadened the rationale for the continuation of its third-party countermeasures by reference to alleged acts of genocide in Darfur. In March 2005, the Security Council again adopted sanctions against Sudan in response to the humanitarian crisis in Darfur, including by referring the situation to the ICC.[135] The current UN sanctions regime continues to operate in parallel with the one initially adopted by the United States in 1997, which still remains in force based on a distinct and broader rationale.

In March 1998, in response to grave violations of human rights and humanitarian law in Kosovo, the Security Council took enforcement action under Chapter VII UNC by imposing an arms embargo against the

---

[130] SC Res. 1070 (16 Aug. 1996).
[131] UN Doc. S/PV.3660 (26 Apr. 1996), 20, 22 (United States).
[132] UN Doc. S/PV.3690 (16 Aug. 1996), 10 (United States).
[133] President Clinton's Executive Order 13067 (3 Nov. 1997), 'Blocking Sudanese Government Property and Prohibiting Transactions with Sudan', www.treasury.gov /resource-center/sanctions/Documents/13067.pdf.
[134] SC Res. 1372 (28 Sept. 2001).
[135] SC Res. 1591 (29 March 2005); SC Res. 1593 (31 March 2005).

FRY.[136] In September 1998, the Security Council adopted a further resolution under Chapter VII UNC by which, *inter alia*, it demanded that the parties (with international involvement) enter into meaningful negotiations to find a political solution to the Kosovo issue.[137] Soon thereafter, EU Member States, the United States and a large number of other States adopted (or expressed support for) a host of third-party countermeasures against the FRY. In September 1998, the Security Council (in the above-mentioned resolution) took note 'with appreciation' of the third-party countermeasures adopted against the FRY, notwithstanding the otherwise limited sanctions regime it had itself adopted. This expression of appreciation also suggests that the Security Council did not consider the adoption of third-party countermeasures against the FRY to contradict its sanctions regime or its efforts to seek a negotiated political settlement to the situation in Kosovo.

In early 2011, the Security Council took enforcement action under Chapter VII UNC against Libya by, *inter alia*, freezing the assets of its Head of State, Colonel Gaddafi.[138] Switzerland and the United States had at that time already taken the same action by way of third-party countermeasures. In addition, they had also unilaterally taken action to freeze the assets of the Central Bank of Libya.[139] For its part, the Arab League had suspended Libya's membership in the organization by way of third-party countermeasures – a decision 'welcomed' by the Security Council.[140] This expression of support suggests that the use of third-party countermeasures by the Arab League was not considered to impinge on the powers of the Security Council.

Finally, in September 2013, the Security Council adopted a resolution against Syria in response to a heinous chemical weapons attack outside Damascus that killed a large number of innocent civilians. The resolution

---

[136] SC Res. 1160 (31 March 1998). See further Section 4.2.15.

[137] SC Res. 1199 (23 Sept. 1998).

[138] SC Res. 1970 (26 Feb. 2011); SC Res. 1973 (17 March 2011). See further Section 4.2.19.

[139] See Swiss Federal Council, 'Ordonnance instituant des mesures à l'encontre de certaines personnes originaires de la Libye' (21 Feb. 2011), www.admin.ch/opc/fr/classified-compilation/20110418/201103110000/946.231.149.82.pdf; President Obama's Executive Order 13566 (25 Feb. 2011), 'Blocking Property and Prohibiting Certain Transactions Related to Libya', www.treasury.gov/resource-center/sanctions/Programs/Documents/2011_libya_eo.pdf.

[140] See 'Arab League Bars Libya From Meetings', *The Wall Street Journal*, 23 February 2011, http://blogs.wsj.com/dispatch/2011/02/23/arab-league-bars-libya-from-meetings; Security Council Press Statement on Libya (22 Feb. 2011), www.un.org/News/Press/docs/2011/sc10180.doc.htm. Also: GA Res. 65/265 (1 March 2011) (preamble); and similarly, HRC Res. S-15/1 (25 Feb. 2011) (preamble).

was not formally adopted under Chapter VII UNC but was nevertheless explicitly made binding under Article 25 UNC; it provided for the dismantling of Syrian stockpiles of chemical weapons subject to on-site verification by international inspectors. Moreover, the resolution provided that enforcement action under Chapter VII UNC would follow in case Syria failed to cooperate.[141] The extensive use of third-party countermeasures against Syria has continued with undiminished force. Still, as the rationale for the use of third-party countermeasures against Syria is much broader than the limited response by the Security Council to a specific event, it does not seem to encroach on the powers of the Security Council under the UN Charter, at least not in any meaningful way.

The example above involving Iraq does not shed any further light on the relationship between third-party countermeasures and enforcement action taken by the Security Council under Chapter VII UNC. By contrast, the examples of South Africa, Argentina, Sudan, the FRY and Libya suggest that third-party countermeasures can be maintained in parallel with enforcement action taken by the Security Council. In the cases of South Africa, the FRY and Libya, the Security Council has even expressed its support for concurrent action. The Syria example provides some further (albeit more limited) support for the same conclusion. It should be noted that the relevant enforcement action taken by the Security Council in the above examples was mostly limited. This serves as an apt reminder that the rationale for the use of third-party countermeasures is at its strongest in cases where the Security Council fails to act or its actions are ineffective in enforcing communitarian norms.[142]

In sum, as a minimum, practice suggests that the use of third-party countermeasures will remain available (subject to overall compliance with their safeguards regime, notably necessity and proportionality) to the extent that Chapter VII UNC action by the Security Council is ineffective. Put differently, enforcement action under Chapter VII UNC does not *per se* end any entitlement to adopt third-party countermeasures. A Security Council resolution may certainly limit or even extinguish the entitlement to use third-party countermeasures in a given case,

---

[141] SC Res. 2118 (27 Sept. 2013). See further Section 4.2.20.

[142] Dawidowicz (2006), 335; Crawford (2013a), 709. See also generally the unilateral action taken by the United States and EC Member States against Iran during the Tehran hostage crisis in 1979–1980 in line with a vetoed Chapter VII UNC resolution: *United States Diplomatic and Consular Staff in Tehran*, ICJ Rep. (1980), 3 at 15–17, paras. 28–30; EC Bull. No. 4 (1980), paras. 1.2.6–1.2.9; and Section 2.1.3.

but this is largely a question of interpretation that is difficult to assess in the abstract.[143] The matter does not seem to have arisen so far in practice and this is in itself noteworthy: the power of the Security Council to limit or rule out the use of third-party countermeasures is not in doubt, but the Council is yet to exercise that power.

In any event, contrary to the views of some commentators, there is no indication in practice (including under Article 31(3)(b) VCLT) to suggest that the concurrent use of third-party countermeasures is contrary to 'the spirit of the Charter' or 'distorts the institutional balance envisioned by the Charter'.[144] This is so irrespective of whether the Council is inactive, actively seized of an issue or has actually taken some enforcement action[145] – a conclusion that is in part corroborated by Article 52(3) ARSIWA.[146] The principle of proportionality may however operate as a substantive limitation on the use of third-party countermeasures in cases where the Security Council has also taken action.[147]

5.2.2   Communitarian Norms Triggering Resort to Third-Party Countermeasures

Third-party countermeasures have been adopted in response to a very large number of obligations erga omnes *(partes)*. It is however not always

---

[143] Compare Tams (2005), 264–268; Villalpando (2005), 448–450; Forteau (2006), 468–481; Hillgruber (2006), 287–288; Gaja (2013), 94–96; Palchetti (2014), 1235–1236. See also Draft Articles Commentary, Art. 39, §2 ('[T]he maintenance of international peace and security *may* [in the opinion of the competent UN organ] require that countermeasures in response to a particular internationally wrongful act are not to be taken for the time being') (emphasis in the original); and to the same effect, UN Doc. A/CN.4/488, 95 (United States); 'The Declaration of the Russian Federation and the People's Republic of China on the Promotion of International Law' (25 June 2016), para. 6, http://www.mid .ru/en/foreign_policy/news/-/asset_publisher/cKNonkJE02Bw/content/id/2331698.

[144] Sicilianos (2010), 1141–1142. A study has suggested that in 82 per cent of cases, UN sanctions were preceded or supplemented by a variety of unilateral coercive measures (whether by regional organizations or individual States): see Designing United Nations Targeted Sanctions: Initial Findings of the Targeted Sanctions Consortium Evaluating Impacts and Effectiveness of UN Targeted Sanctions (2012), 13, www.graduateinstitute .ch/files/live/sites/iheid/files/sites/internationalgovernance/shared/PSIG_images/ Sanctions/Designing UN Targeted Sanctions.pdf.

[145] See Dawidowicz (2006), 415–417; Hillgruber (2006), 287–288; Calamita (2009), 1437–1441; Gaja (2013), 95–96; Palchetti (2014), 1235. Compare Klein (2002), 1253–1255; Frowein and Krisch (2002), 714 MN 37; Tsagourias and White (2013), 225–228.

[146] ARSIWA Commentary, Art. 52, §8. See further Section 6.4.1 (on the relationship between procedural conditions and the Security Council).

[147] See further Section 6.3.

possible to determine with confidence exactly which of the often many breaches of such obligations that have actually motivated the adoption of third-party countermeasures in a particular instance. Two factors nevertheless provide some useful guidance. First, States contemplating the use of third-party countermeasures have regularly co-sponsored (or otherwise expressed support for) resolutions repeatedly adopted by various international organizations. These resolutions have condemned the responsible State for a multitude of breaches of communitarian norms and called for a prompt return to legality. Second, the trigger statements – i.e. the statements by which the target State has been notified of the imminent adoption of third-party countermeasures against it – often make a generic reference to violations, for example, 'widespread and systematic violations of human rights', before occasionally inserting the adverb 'including' or 'in particular' by which certain violations are singled out for specific mention.[148] Thus it seems reasonable to conclude that the adoption of third-party countermeasures has normally been based on the broader rationale expressed in the preceding joint statements of institutional *sommation*.[149]

Third-party countermeasures have most frequently been adopted in response to the following breaches of conventional and/or customary international law: (1) the prohibition of torture, the right to a fair trial, arbitrary arrest and freedom of expression;[150] (2) right to life;[151] (3) freedom of assembly and the principle of non-use of force;[152] (4) freedom of association;[153] (5) war crimes and crimes against

---

[148] See e.g. Common Position 96/635/CFSP (28 Oct. 1996), OJ 1996 L 287/1 (8 Nov. 1996); President Clinton's Executive Order 13067 (3 Nov. 1997), 'Blocking Sudanese Government Property and Prohibiting Transactions with Sudan', www.treasury.gov /resource-center/sanctions/Documents/13067.pdf; Council Decision 2012/122/CFSP (27 Feb. 2012), OJ 2012 L 54/14 (28 Feb. 2012). See further Sections 4.2.14 (Sudan); 4.2.16 (Burma); 4.2.20 (Syria).

[149] On the practice of joint statements and institutional *sommation* see further below Section 5.2.3 and Section 6.4.2.

[150] See Sections 4.2.2 (Greece); 4.2.4 (Central African Republic); 4.2.5 (Liberia); 4.2.7 (Poland); 4.2.12 (Nigeria); 4.2.14 (Sudan); 4.2.15 (FRY); 4.2.16 (Burma); 4.2.17 (Zimbabwe); 4.2.18 (Belarus); 4.2.19 (Libya); 4.2.20 (Syria).

[151] See Sections 4.2.4 (Central African Republic); 4.2.5 (Liberia); 4.2.12 (Nigeria); 4.2.14 (Sudan); 4.2.15 (FRY); 4.2.16 (Burma); 4.2.17 (Zimbabwe); 4.2.19 (Libya); 4.2.20 (Syria).

[152] See Sections 4.2.1 and 4.2.10 (South Africa); 4.2.2 (Greece); 4.2.6 (Soviet Union); 4.2.7 (Poland/Soviet Union); 4.2.8 (Argentina); 4.2.9 (Soviet Union); 4.2.11 (Iraq); 4.2.14 (Sudan); 4.2.16 (Burma); 4.2.17 (Zimbabwe); 4.2.18 (Belarus); 4.2.19 (Libya); 4.2.20 (Syria); 4.2.21 (Russia).

[153] See Sections 4.2.2 (Greece); 4.2.7 (Poland); 4.2.12 (Nigeria); 4.2.14 (Sudan); 4.2.16 (Burma); 4.2.17 (Zimbabwe); 4.2.18 (Belarus); 4.2.19 (Libya); 4.2.20 (Syria).

humanity;[154] (6) non-discrimination and various violations of international humanitarian law;[155] (7) the principle of self-determination and freedom of religion;[156] (8) genocide, minority rights, freedom of movement and non-intervention;[157] (9) slavery and forced labour;[158] and (10) apartheid.[159]

It is not surprising that third-party countermeasures have often been adopted in response to human rights violations. Leaving aside acts of torture, it is interesting to note however that third-party countermeasures have most often been adopted in response to arbitrary arrests, denials of freedom of expression and the right to a fair trial. Third-party countermeasures have also commonly been adopted in response to extra-judicial killings and in order to ensure protection of the rights to freedom of assembly and association. In short, it appears that third-party countermeasures are most often resorted to in an effort to ensure compliance with obligations *erga omnes partes* (or at least not core obligations *erga omnes*) under human rights treaties. This conclusion should be emphasized: it represents a key aspect of State practice that has not always been well understood.[160]

5.2.3   The Ascertainment of Wrongful Conduct

A key criticism of third-party countermeasures concerns the inherent risk of abuse arising from the auto-interpretation of wrongful conduct. International law remains an essentially decentralized system in which 'each State establishes for itself its legal situation vis-à-vis other States'.[161] This entails the risk that one or more States could individually resort to third-party countermeasures contrary to the obligations incumbent

---

[154] See Sections 4.2.1 and 4.2.10 (South Africa); 4.2.15 (FRY); 4.2.16 (Burma); 4.2.19 (Libya); 4.2.20 (Syria).

[155] See Sections 4.2.2 (Greece); 4.2.12 (Nigeria); 4.2.14 (Sudan); 4.2.15 (FRY); 4.2.16 (Burma); 4.2.17 (Zimbabwe); 4.2.19 (Libya); 4.2.20 (Syria).

[156] See Sections 4.2.1 and 4.2.10 (South Africa); 4.2.2 (Greece); 4.2.6 (Soviet Union); 4.2.7 (Soviet Union); 4.2.8 (Argentina); 4.2.14 (Sudan); 4.2.16 (Burma); 4.2.17 (Zimbabwe).

[157] See Sections 4.2.3 (Uganda); 4.2.6 (Soviet Union); 4.2.7 (Soviet Union); 4.2.12 (Nigeria); 4.2.13 (Burundi); 4.2.14 (Sudan); 4.2.15 (FRY); 4.2.16 (Burma); 4.2.20 (Syria); 4.2.21 (Russia).

[158] See Sections 4.2.12 (Nigeria); 4.2.14 (Sudan); 4.2.16 (Burma); 4.2.20 (Syria).

[159] See Sections 4.2.1 and 4.2.10 (South Africa).

[160] Compare Tams (2005), 233–234; 2005 IDI Krakow Resolution (Arts. 1 and 5). See also Section 3.2.1.3 (n. 147).

[161] *US-France Air Services Agreement* (1978), RIAA, vol. XVIII, 417 at 443, para. 81. See also *Affaire du Lac Lanoux* (1957), RIAA, vol. XII, 281 at 310, para. 16.

upon them on the basis of the mere assertion of wrongful conduct by the target State.[162] Special Rapporteur Crawford observed that the risk of abuse clearly involves an important issue of 'due process'[163] for the target State:

> ... since at the time collective countermeasures are taken, its responsibility for the breach may be merely asserted, not demonstrated, and issues of fact and possible justifications are likely to have been raised and left unresolved. Some formula such as a 'gross and reliably attested breach' is called for.[164]

The ILC has likewise stressed that the legitimate adoption of countermeasures 'presupposes an objective standard' – i.e. an actual breach – in terms of Article 49(1) ARSIWA.[165]

The concerns associated with the arrogation of coercive powers based on auto-interpretation help explain the 'extreme sensitivity'[166] of the topic in the ILC and Sixth Committee. Indeed there was serious concern that the category of third-party countermeasures would provide a further pretext for power politics, intervention and even the use of force.[167] In particular, it was feared that third-party countermeasures would merely provide 'a superficial legitimacy for the bullying of small States on the claim that human rights must be respected'.[168] In practice, much will turn on the extent to which the adoption of third-party countermeasures is based on well-established serious breaches of communitarian norms. Their legitimacy largely depends on 'credible evidence' of wrongful conduct.[169]

It was observed in Chapter 3 that the various proposals made in the ILC to involve UN organs in the prior establishment of breaches of communitarian norms were resoundingly rejected on the basis that they were considered unrealistic and contrary to the UN Charter. In any event, the ILC noted the likely involvement of competent

---

[162] Alland (2010), 1129.   [163] Crawford, Third Report, 37, para. 115.

[164] Ibid. Compare Riphagen, Fourth Report, 8–9, para. 37.

[165] ARSIWA Commentary, Art. 49, §3. See also Crawford, Third Report, 105, para. 399 (n. 808).

[166] Crawford, Fourth Report, 14, para. 55.

[167] See e.g. Topical Summary of Government Comments in the Sixth Committee, UN Doc. A/CN.4/513 (2000), 29, 33, paras. 149, 175.

[168] YbILC (2001), vol. I, 35, para. 2 (Mr. Brownlie).

[169] UN Doc. A/C.6/55/SR.15, 3, para. 16 (Iran). Compare UN Doc. A/C.6/55/SR.16, 10, para. 72 (Croatia) ('[T]he fundamental precondition for taking countermeasures should be borne in mind, namely being *certain* that an internationally wrongful act has indeed occurred') (emphasis added).

international organizations, including the Security Council and the General Assembly, in dealing with alleged breaches of communitarian norms.[170] For its part, the Institut de Droit International concluded in its 2005 Krakow Resolution that third-party countermeasures were only permissible 'should a widely acknowledged grave breach of an *erga omnes* obligation occur'.[171] Rapporteur Gaja explained:

> [T]he reference to the wide acknowledgment of the existence of a breach is designed to limit the risk of unilateral assessment ... diminish the risk of abuses and ensure that States genuinely seek to protect an interest of the international community.[172]

Gaja added that this position found support in practice on third-party countermeasures which has 'generally related to infringements of obligations *erga omnes* that were indeed widely acknowledged'.[173]

State practice does indeed indicate that third-party countermeasures are normally adopted in response to 'widely acknowledged' grave breaches of obligations *erga omnes (partes)*. In fact, it is striking that, in all instances of practice examined in Chapter 4, breaches of communitarian norms have (often repeatedly) been established through the adoption of resolutions in major UN organs, including the General Assembly, the Security Council and the Human Rights Council (and its predecessor, the Commission on Human Rights), prior to the adoption of third-party countermeasures. In most of these cases, several regional international organizations (in addition to individual States) will in parallel have denounced the same wrongful conduct and called for a return to legality. It has already been observed that States subsequently adopting third-party countermeasures have regularly co-sponsored the said resolutions.[174]

The role of UN Special Rapporteurs, fact-finding missions and commissions of inquiry in establishing breaches also merits attention. The examples involving Burundi, Burma, Belarus, Libya and Syria[175] suffice to demonstrate that, prior to the adoption of relevant resolutions and subsequent third-party countermeasures, breaches of communitarian norms are often well documented within international

---

[170] See Section 3.1.3.
[171] See 2005 IDI Krakow Resolution (Art. 5). It should be noted that obligations *erga omnes partes* were included within the definition of obligations *erga omnes* (Art. 1).
[172] Gaja (2005), 149, 199.   [173] Ibid., 200. See already Sicilianos (1990), 176.
[174] See above Section 5.2.2.
[175] See Sections 4.2.13 (Burundi); 4.2.16 (Burma); 4.2.18 (Belarus); 4.2.19 (Libya); 4.2.20 (Syria).

organizations (notably the UN) through the work of Special Rapporteurs and various fact-finding missions or commissions of inquiry.[176] For example, in the case of Burundi, the UN Security Council established a commission of inquiry to investigate the massacres taking place in that country. The commission concluded based on a detailed report that acts of genocide attributable to Burundi had been committed.[177] Likewise, successive UN Special Rapporteurs have repeatedly found Burma responsible for massive violations of international human rights and humanitarian law.[178] The UN Human Rights Council has relied on similar fact-finding mechanisms in the cases of Belarus, Libya and Syria.[179] A full and independent inquiry into alleged breaches of communitarian norms conducted by an international monitoring body provides an especially strong and credible basis for the subsequent adoption of third-party countermeasures.[180]

It may be noted that the ICJ, whose docket increasingly includes fact-intensive cases,[181] has itself placed decisive importance on fact-finding by UN monitoring bodies – in lieu of its own findings of fact[182] – in order to establish whether wrongful conduct has been committed. For example, the ICJ in the *Armed Activities* case found reports from UN Special Rapporteurs and the UN Secretary General sufficient to convince it that Uganda was responsible for massive violations of international human rights law and grave breaches of humanitarian law on the territory of the DRC.[183] Most international disputes are settled without recourse to judicial means of settlement. Crucially, judicial settlement is not necessarily required in every circumstance to bestow authority and legitimacy on pronouncements of State responsibility.[184] Tanzania's observation in the Sixth Committee that 'an objective appreciation [of wrongful conduct] could presumably *only* be attained through a judicial process'[185] is unpersuasive.

---

[176] An early example of this practice includes the judicial inquiry set up by the Sixth Franco-African Summit in April 1979 to determine issues of responsibility following a massacre of school children in the Central African Republic: see Section 4.2.4. Generally: van den Herik (2014), 507.

[177] See Section 4.2.13. [178] See Section 4.2.16. [179] See Sections 4.2.18–4.2.20.

[180] See already Schachter (1982), 184. [181] See Higgins (2006).

[182] For criticism see Halink (2007).

[183] *Armed Activities (DRC v. Uganda)*, ICJ Rep. (2005), 168 at 239–242, paras. 205–212. The ICJ in that case based its findings on 'the coincidence of reports from credible sources' (ibid., para. 207).

[184] See e.g. Higgins (1994), 248.

[185] UN Doc. A/C.6/55/SR.14, 9, para. 47 (Tanzania) (emphasis added). Indeed Tanzania (together with other East African States) had itself adopted third-party countermeasures against Burundi, most notably in order to stop the genocide taking place there. This action was taken less than a week after a commission of inquiry established by the

Whatever the specific modalities for the prior establishment of breach by international bodies, practice suggests that third-party countermeasures have (with two possible limited exceptions)[186] invariably met the 'objective standard' required by Article 49(1) ARSIWA insofar as they have been adopted in response to well-established and 'widely acknowledged' grave violations of communitarian norms. States do not seem inclined to resort to third-party countermeasures without good reason. The adoption of joint statements on alleged serious illegalities has significantly (if not entirely, as discussed further below)[187] reduced the risk of abuse.[188]

5.2.4   The Seriousness of the Breach

A closely related issue of auto-interpretation and 'due process' for the target State concerns the threshold question of whether third-party countermeasures may only be adopted in response to a *serious* breach of an obligation *erga omnes (partes)*. A 'serious' breach may be defined as one that involves a 'gross or systematic failure of the responsible State to fulfil the obligation [*erga omnes (partes)*] in question'.[189] There is no reason of principle or logic to limit third-party countermeasures – a possible means of invocation of State responsibility, among others – to 'serious' breaches of such obligations. Indeed this much is suggested by even a cursory reading of Articles 48 and 54 ARSIWA.[190]

Security Council had concluded that acts of genocide were attributable to Burundi (see above n. 177). Also: Arangio-Ruiz, Fourth Report, 6, para. 2.

[186] In the cases of Uganda and Sudan, the United States alone determined that genocide had been committed for which State responsibility was invoked: see Sections 4.2.3 and 4.2.14. In the former case, Ugandan President Binaisa subsequently shared this conclusion: see UN Doc. A/34/PV.14 (28 Sept. 1979), 270, para. 13. In the latter case, the ICC's subsequent prosecution of Sudanese President Al-Bashir also suggests that this determination was not without foundation.

[187] See below Section 5.2.6.

[188] The separate question of whether third-party countermeasures may *only* be adopted when the breach of a communitarian norm has been 'widely acknowledged' largely concerns the procedural safeguards regime under Article 52(1) ARSIWA and as such is considered in Sections 6.4.1–6.4.2.

[189] ARSIWA Commentary, Art. 40, §7. In essence, the term 'gross' refers to the intensity of the breach or its effects whereas the term 'systematic' concerns violations carried out in an organized or deliberate way. Relevant factors to establish a 'serious' breach would notably include the scope and number of individual violations, and the gravity of their consequences for the victims (ibid., §8). Further: Gaeta (2010), 421; Damrosch (2011).

[190] See Gaja (2010), 962; Sicilianos (2010), 1139–1140.

There was nevertheless overwhelming support in the ILC and the Sixth Committee for the proposition that only a serious breach of an obligation *erga omnes* could potentially justify resort to third-party countermeasures.[191] The ILC concluded that

> Some such limitation is supported by State practice. For example, when reacting against breaches of international law, States have often stressed their systematic, gross, or egregious nature.[192]

For his part, Special Rapporteur Crawford likewise concluded that third-party countermeasures had not been adopted in response to isolated or minor violations of obligations *erga omnes*: in practice, it appeared that their use had been limited to serious violations arising from 'major political crises'.[193] The ILC commentary to Article 54 ARSIWA (perhaps unsurprisingly) provides no further guidance on this point.[194]

The ILC's conclusion about State practice on this point is essentially correct: third-party countermeasures have normally been adopted in response to alleged serious breaches of obligations *erga omnes (partes)*. It should be understood that third-party countermeasures taken in defence of certain peremptory norms, most notably the prohibitions of aggression and genocide, will necessarily be predicated on the notion of a serious breach within the meaning of Article 40 ARSIWA.[195] More broadly, references to 'serious', 'massive', 'gross', 'grave', 'severe', 'egregious', 'flagrant', 'blatant', 'widespread' or 'systematic' violations of communitarian norms are common in practice.[196] This is hardly surprising: these adjectives 'reflect judgments made on political and prudential grounds'.[197] Third-party countermeasures are highly controversial and it is only natural then that States will, in attempting to justify their otherwise unlawful conduct, stress the serious nature of the breach motivating the exceptional action taken.

The threshold condition of a serious breach is a rather subjective criterion that affords responding States a large degree of discretion and

---

[191] See generally Section 3.2.1.3. Compare 1989 IDI Santiago de Compostela Resolution (Art. 2); 2005 IDI Krakow Resolution (Art. 5).

[192] ARSIWA Commentary, Art. 40, §7.

[193] Crawford, Third Report, 105, paras. 398–399.

[194] See Gaja (2013), 131 (noting that it would have added little to elaborate on this point in a 'without prejudice' clause).

[195] See ARSIWA Commentary, Art. 40, §8; Gaeta (2010), 421. See however GA Res. 3314 (XXIX) (14 Dec. 1974) (Annex, Art. 2). Compare 1989 IDI Santiago de Compostela Resolution (Art. 2).

[196] See e.g. above n. 148; and generally Chapter 4. Also: Gaja (2013), 131.

[197] Schachter (1982), 330.

may invite abuse as a mere rhetorical device.[198] The possible character-ization of wrongful conduct as 'serious' will to some extent inevitably involve value-judgments based on the 'moral intuitions'[199] of decision-makers, and especially so in hard cases. Still, the real question is whether widely shared perceptions of serious breaches are genuine and broadly correspond to the facts of the impugned conduct.

Given the multitude of breaches of communitarian norms that have seemingly triggered recourse to third-party countermeasures and the somewhat impressionistic and flexible nature of the criterion of serious-ness, it is difficult to answer this question with precision – especially in borderline cases.[200] In general terms, however, an affirmative answer can be provided. States have normally adopted third-party countermeasures in response to widely acknowledged serious breaches of communitarian norms. As Special Rapporteur Crawford observed:

> [T]he States taking [third-party countermeasures] asserted that they were justified on the basis – and by clear implication, only on the basis – that the grounds invoked were genuine, serious and, if established, warranted such a response.[201]

It is thus apparent that third-party countermeasures have developed in practice – no doubt, for good reason – as a *sui generis* form of invocation of State responsibility limited to serious breaches of communitarian norms. The ICJ in the *Nicaragua* case also appeared to suggest that – if at all – only a serious breach could justify recourse to third-party countermeasures.[202]

5.2.5   Third-Party Countermeasures on Behalf of an Injured State

It may be recalled from Chapter 3 that Special Rapporteur Crawford initially proposed to the ILC that third-party countermeasures should be

---

[198] Compare YbILC (2000), vol. I, 311, para. 83 (Mr. Brownlie); Koskenniemi (2001), 348, 353; Gaja (2005), 149. See also e.g. UN Doc. A/CN.4/515, 46 (United Kingdom), 48 (Austria), 53 (United States).

[199] Koskenniemi (2001), 349.

[200] To give but three examples, did the Soviet troop movements along Poland's eastern border in 1981 amount to a 'serious' violation of Article 2(4) UNC? Did the summary executions of thirteen Liberian ministers and other high-ranking public officials following sham trials amount to a 'serious' breach of international human rights law? Did the extra-judicial killing of 50–200 school children in the Central African Republic amount to a 'serious' breach of international human rights law? See further Sections 4.2.4; 4.2.5; 4.2.7.

[201] Crawford, Third Report, 105, para. 399 (n. 808).   [202] See Section 2.1.4.

permissible in response to any violation of an obligation *erga omnes* *(partes)*, i.e. irrespective of the seriousness of the breach, on condition that they were adopted at the request and on behalf of a directly injured State. The Drafting Committee in 2000 provisionally adopted his proposal as Draft Article 54(1) [2000].[203] Although practice has not developed in this direction, Special Rapporteur Crawford was correct to observe that it does not seem inconsistent with the principle embodied in Article 48 ARSIWA to recognize the use of third-party counter-measures in such circumstances, i.e. with the consent of the injured State.[204] Bilateral countermeasures strongly favour States that are more powerful. Unless interested third States are allowed to assist less powerful States by way of countermeasures breaches of communitarian norms may remain without redress – a point acknowledged by Japan.[205] Still, Japan was equally correct to observe that such a 'subrogation system of countermeasures' does not have an established basis in international law.[206] Practice suggests that States have little appetite to act as a 'surrogate'.[207]

5.2.6 The Indeterminacy of Communitarian Norms

Even where the breach of a communitarian norm is widely acknowledged, individual States may not have standing to adopt third-party countermeasures. This entails a further risk of abuse. Beyond a minimal core of obligations that can be readily identified, it has been observed that the precise identification of those international obligations that qualify as *erga omnes* is 'very mysterious'.[208] This is especially true in the field of human rights where there is no agreement – beyond a narrow compass of basic human rights – about the peremptory status and corresponding *erga omnes* validity of individual human rights

---

[203] See Section 3.2.1.3.

[204] Ibid. The limited examples of practice provided by the ILC are inconclusive on this point as they concern serious breaches: see Crawford, Third Report, 104–106, paras. 394, 400–402; ARSIWA Commentary, Art. 54, §§3, 5. The separate (albeit closely related) question of prior consent by the directly injured State as a possible precondition for the enforcement of claims for cessation and/or reparation by way of third-party counter-measures is discussed as an aspect of the safeguards regime in Section 6.1.3.1(i).

[205] UN Doc. A/CN.4/515, 79 (Japan). See also Dawidowicz (2006), 337; Crawford (2013a), 703–704.

[206] Ibid.   [207] Ibid.

[208] Brownlie (1988), 71; Reisman (1993), 170. See also YbILC (2000), vol. I, 81–82, paras. 15–23 (Mr. Hafner); Bianchi (2008), 491.

obligations.[209] For example, the United States has observed that 'there is no consensus ... as to what constitutes "fundamental human rights"'.[210] The United Kingdom has stated that the content of the category of obligations *erga omnes* is 'far from settled'.[211] It added:

> Given the significance of this category of *erga omnes* obligations in the context of countermeasures, this point has very considerable practical importance.[212]

It may be recalled from Chapter 2 that the ICJ in *Barcelona Traction* merely provided a list of examples of obligations *erga omnes*.[213] For its part, the ILC observed that, although all peremptory norms were by definition *erga omnes*, not all obligations *erga omnes* were necessarily peremptory in character.[214] Still, as Tams has noted, the existence of obligations *erga omnes* beyond peremptory norms largely remains 'unchartered territory'.[215]

The relative vagueness with which communitarian norms are postulated raises questions about possible abuse related to their enforcement. It was noted during the debate in the Sixth Committee that the concept of obligations *erga omnes* was 'indeterminate' and could give rise to 'serious abuses', notably in relation to the use of third-party countermeasures.[216] Indeed it was feared with respect to the category of obligations *erga omnes* that 'its lack of precision might lead to the justification of collective sanctions or collective interventions'.[217] Koskenniemi has likewise cautioned: 'Because the primary rules that govern the field [of third-party countermeasures] are insufficiently precise, the danger of abuse is great'.[218] It is this potential for abuse that will be examined here.

---

[209] See e.g. YbILC, vol. I (2000), 85, para. 52 (Mr. Momtaz); Tams (2005), 117–157; Orakhelashvili (2006), 53–60; Crawford (2013a), 365, 692.

[210] UN Doc. A/CN.4/515, 79 (United States). Compare UN Doc. A/CN.4/488, 132 (United States).

[211] UN Doc. A/CN.4/515, 46 (United Kingdom).   [212] Ibid.   [213] See Section 2.1.1.1.

[214] ILC Report (1998), UN Doc. A/53/10, 69, para. 279. See also ILC Report on Fragmentation of International Law, UN Doc. A/CN.4/L.682 (2006), 204, para. 404.

[215] Tams (2005), 151. See also ARSIWA Commentary, Art. 48, §9; Crawford (2011), 224.

[216] See e.g. UN Docs. A/C.6/55/SR.15, 5–6, para. 31, A/C.6/56/SR.14, 7, para. 40 (India); A/C.6/55/SR.18, 11, para. 59 (Cuba); A/C.6/56/SR.11, 10, paras. 59, 62 (China); A/C.6/56/SR.14, 3, para. 12 (Mexico); A/C.6/56/SR.15, 5, paras. 30–31 (Thailand); A/CN.4/515, 46 (United Kingdom). The notion of peremptory norms has also been described as 'radically indeterminate': see Crawford, Second Report, 77, para. 312 (with further references).

[217] See Topical Summary of Government Comments in the Sixth Committee, UN Doc. A/CN.4/513 (2000), 26–27, para. 137 (also ibid., paras. 140, 175).

[218] Koskenniemi (2001), 355. See also Petman (2004), 321.

A closer examination of practice reveals that third-party countermeasures have occasionally been adopted in circumstances where, for lack of standing, the justification provided by the breach of a conventional human rights obligation is unavailable and there is no obvious alternative justification available based on a corresponding violation of an obligation *erga omnes* under customary international law. In these cases, even if the breach is otherwise widely acknowledged, the absence of a treaty-based justification may be understood as an example of the abusive use of third-party countermeasures for lack of individual standing (i.e. the breached obligation is established in the collective interest and owed to a group of States, not including the responding State). But there is also another possibility. State practice on third-party countermeasures may constitute evidence – perhaps even 'particularly strong evidence' – of the putative *erga omnes* validity of a particular (human rights) obligation under customary international law.[219] Put differently, the adoption of third-party countermeasures in such circumstances may entail an indirect claim to *erga omnes* status. With this in mind let us now examine the most salient examples of possible abuse.

In 1978–1979, EC Member States and the United States adopted third-party countermeasures against Uganda and did so most notably in response to genocide, widespread extra-judicial killings and acts of torture.[220] The US action taken in response to genocide was undoubtedly based on a core obligation *erga omnes*. By contrast, the same could not be said with equal confidence in relation to the action taken by EC Member States motivated by extra-judicial killings and acts of torture. This conduct could potentially have been justified as a response to violations of Articles 6 and 7 of the ICCPR; however, Uganda was not a contracting party to the ICCPR at the time. The action taken by EC Member States against Uganda could accordingly only have been justified by reference to prior violations of obligations *erga omnes*.

In 1979, EC Member States also adopted third-party countermeasures in response to the extra-judicial killing of school children in the Central African Republic.[221] The Central African Republic was also not a contracting party to the ICCPR at the time. In 1980, the adoption of third-party countermeasures against Liberia raised similar questions of standing.[222] As it happened, EC Member States adopted the so-called

---

[219] See Tams (2005), 154–156, 232–234; Thirlway (2010), 120; Bird (2010), 896–899. To similar effect: Gaja (2005), 122.
[220] See Section 4.2.3.   [221] See Section 4.2.4.   [222] See Section 4.2.5.

Uganda Guidelines, which denounced a denial of 'basic human rights' in both Uganda and the Central African Republic. This use of language, reminiscent of the terminology espoused by the ICJ in *Barcelona Traction* a few years earlier, suggests that EC Member States considered obligations *erga omnes* to be at issue.

In December 1981, the United States, later followed by Switzerland, adopted third-party countermeasures against Poland. They did so primarily in response to arbitrary arrests, violations of the right to a fair trial and the rights to freedom of expression, assembly and association.[223] Poland was at the time a contracting party to the ICCPR (which includes the aforementioned human rights); however, the United States and Switzerland were not. It follows that their conduct, in contrast to the adoption of third-party countermeasures by Austria, the Netherlands and the United Kingdom, ostensibly based on ICCPR violations, could only have been justified by reference to violations of obligations *erga omnes*.

In May 2000, EU Member States, later followed by Switzerland, the United States, Australia and Canada, adopted third-party countermeasures against Burma.[224] They did so, *inter alia*, in response to numerous violations of human rights under the ICCPR, most notably the right to life, freedom from torture, freedom from arbitrary arrest, the right to a fair trial, freedom of expression, freedom of assembly, freedom of association, freedom of religion and freedom of movement. However, Burma is not (and has never been) a contracting party to the ICCPR. Thus the permissibility of the third-party countermeasures adopted against Burma (at least insofar as they relate to the ICCPR) will in the first instance likewise depend on the *erga omnes* status of the impugned conduct.

While there can be little doubt today that the conventional prohibition of torture also amounts to an obligation *erga omnes* under customary international law,[225] the situation is less certain regarding other human rights obligations under the ICCPR. There is certainly no indication in practice that all conventional human rights obligations possess such status.[226] It nevertheless seems clear that third-party countermeasures have largely been adopted in response to breaches of communitarian

---

[223] See Section 4.2.7.   [224] See Section 4.2.16.

[225] *Prosecutor v. Furundžija*, ICTY Case No. IT-95-17/1-T, Judgment, 10 Dec. 1998, para. 151. See also ARSIWA Commentary, Art. 40, §5; *Obligation to Prosecute or Extradite*, ICJ Rep. (2012), 422 at 457, para. 99.

[226] See e.g. Higgins (1976–1977), 282; YbILC (2000), vol. I, 73, paras. 11–12 (Mr. Simma), 74, para. 18 (Mr. Crawford), 85, para. 52 (Mr. Momtaz); and discussion in Section 6.2.1.2.

norms for which there is significant support in practice for *erga omnes* status.[227] This appears to be so at least in respect of the right to life, freedom from arbitrary detention and the right to a fair trial.[228]

Moreover, it is noteworthy that the UN General Assembly has in its annual resolutions against Burma consistently referred to the ICCPR and called on Burma to comply with the relevant obligations contained therein even though they are clearly not binding on it as a matter of treaty obligation.[229] Western States' adoption of third-party countermeasures against Burma may in these circumstances be understood as further support for a claim to the parallel *erga omnes* status of the aforementioned treaty obligations.

More broadly, it should be added that only limited guidance is provided by those instances in practice where there is a possible overlap and responsibility could have been – and indeed by reasonable inference appears to have been – invoked under the ICCPR.[230] Although the basis of the action (treaty or custom) in these cases is not 'entirely speculative',[231] the distinction in practice between obligations *erga omnes* and obligations *erga omnes partes* may admittedly sometimes be blurred.[232] In any event, the risk of abuse seems all but eliminated if there is a clear conventional basis for acting. As seen above, in the absence of such a basis, the examples of possible abuse are, in reality, rather limited. What is more, they are not obvious examples of abuse. Practice supports the conclusion that most of the conventional human rights obligations discussed above have attained (or are in the process of attaining) a separate *erga omnes* status for which there would be autonomous standing to adopt third-party countermeasures.[233] The relative vagueness with which obligations *erga omnes* are postulated may entail a concomitant risk of abuse, but it is not one that seems to have materialized in practice concerning third-party countermeasures.

---

[227] Similarly Tams (2005), 233.

[228] See e.g. General Comment No. 29, UN Doc. CCPR/C/21/Rev.1/Add.11 (31 Aug. 2001), para. 11; Report of the UN Working Group on Arbitrary Detention, UN Doc. HRC/22/44 (24 Dec. 2012), 17–20, paras. 42–51. Further: Orakhelashvili (2006), 53–60 (with many further references).

[229] See e.g. GA Res. 55/112 (4 Dec. 2000); GA Res. 68/242 (27 Dec. 2013).

[230] See Sections 4.2.12 (Nigeria), 4.2.15 (FRY), 4.2.17 (Zimbabwe), 4.2.18 (Belarus), 4.2.19 (Libya); 4.2.20 (Syria).

[231] *North Sea Continental Shelf*, ICJ Rep. (1969), 3 at 43–44, para. 76. See also discussion above in Section 5.2.2.

[232] Compare Sicilianos (2010), 1139.

[233] For a similar conclusion see Tams (2005), 233–234.

In fact, as Simma observed during the ILC debate, the problem seems to lie elsewhere:

> [T]he practice of States showed that not directly injured States were far from abusing countermeasures in the event of a breach of human rights and other obligations *erga omnes* and that they were in fact hardly concerned with such breaches, in respect of which selectivity was widespread.[234]

The risk of abusive third-party countermeasures certainly cannot be ignored. But there is a larger point. It is aptly made by Higgins:

> We must face the reality that we live in a decentralised international legal order, where claims may be made either in good faith or abusively. We delude ourselves if we think that the role of norms is to remove the possibility of abusive claims ever being made. The role of norms is the achievement of values for the common good. Whether a claim invoking any given norm is made in good faith or abusively will *always* require contextual analysis by appropriate decision-makers – by the Security Council, by the International Court of Justice, by various international bodies ... There are a variety of important decision-makers, other than courts, who can pronounce on the validity of claims advanced; and claims which may in very restricted circumstances be regarded as lawful should not *a priori* be disallowed because on occasion they may be unjustly invoked.[235]

The above observations were made in the context of humanitarian intervention; they apply *a fortiori* to third-party countermeasures. Germany has made a similar point with respect to the risk of abuse and the safeguards regime applicable to countermeasures:

> The overall approach should be to proceed from the assumption that a State choosing to initiate countermeasures will normally do so in good faith, because it actually seeks redress for an injury which it has suffered or is still suffering.[236]

---

[234] YbILC (2000), vol. I, 305, para. 31 (Mr. Simma). See also Tomuschat (1993), 366–367; Simma and Pulkowski (2010), 162. Compare Schachter (1982), 218 ('It is quite clear that the reluctance of many States to adopt enforcement measures against States condemned as violators can be attributed to their unwillingness to sacrifice their own immediate self-interest for the general interest. The gap between verbal condemnation and effective sanctions in case after case attests to that fact').

[235] Higgins (1994), 247–248 (emphasis in the original). To similar effect: Greenwood (2000), 931. A 'contextual analysis' of practice suggests that third-party countermeasures have overall been adopted in good faith.

[236] UN Doc. A/CN.4/488, 115 (Germany). See also Simma (1994b), 102.

5.2.7 The Effectiveness of Third-Party Countermeasures

During the debate in the Sixth Committee, the concept of countermeasures was regularly characterized as an 'effective instrument of law'.[237] The actual effectiveness of third-party countermeasures begs the question of the yardstick against which it should be measured. In principle, the answer seems clear: it should be measured against the instrumental function of countermeasures to ensure a return to legality within the meaning of Article 49(1) ARSIWA. Simply put, if third-party countermeasures do not ensure the cessation of serious breaches of communitarian norms they must surely be deemed ineffective.

Against this exacting standard, a cursory review of practice suggests that third-party countermeasures have overall not been very effective. To give but four examples, third-party countermeasures have been in place against Burma for over fifteen years and yet (despite historic democratic elections in 2015) serious illegalities persist. The same applies to Zimbabwe against which third-party countermeasures have remained in force for over a decade. Massive violations of international law are continuing in Syria despite the widespread adoption of third-party countermeasures against it over several years. Russia continues to violate international law with respect to Ukraine notwithstanding the adoption of third-party countermeasures against it. But this is a rather crude and deceptive yardstick.

Just as the effectiveness of a legal system cannot solely be measured by the length of the Austinian policeman's truncheon so too the effectiveness of third-party countermeasures cannot solely be assessed in a simple mono-causal relation between sanction and (continuing) violation.[238] In reality, the situation is more complex. The real question is not so much whether third-party countermeasures are effective in an ideal sense of full compliance but whether they are capable of being effective at all as a legal tool of enforcement. Several factors determine the ultimate effectiveness of third-party countermeasures, and they point to a more finely calibrated yardstick.

---

[237] Topical Summary of Government Comments in the Sixth Committee, UN Doc. A/CN.4/513 (2000), 28, 32, paras. 148, 174. See also UN Doc. A/C.6/55/SR.17, 8, para. 48 (Chile).

[238] Compare Crawford (2013b), 36. Also: Designing United Nations Targeted Sanctions: Initial Findings of the Targeted Sanctions Consortium Evaluating Impacts and Effectiveness of UN Targeted Sanctions (2012), 14 (concluding that UN targeted sanctions exclusively designed to coerce a change in behaviour are the least effective form of sanction), www.graduateinstitute.ch/files/live/sites/iheid/files/sites/internationalgovernance/shared/PSIG_images/Sanctions/Designing UN Targeted Sanctions.pdf.

First, the choice of individual third-party countermeasures is often rather modest. It has been noted that 'their actual effects were often rather trivial'.[239] This simply reflects the degree of political will to enforce communitarian norms: it says nothing about the potential of third-party countermeasures as a tool of law enforcement. It may be 'glaringly obvious'[240] that certain forms of third-party countermeasures will not be effective. For example, the suspension of an air services agreement is highly unlikely by itself to have a decisive effect on intransigent conduct involving violations of communitarian norms. The effect of asset freezes, including those belonging to Heads of State, will necessarily depend on the amount of assets actually available within the jurisdiction of the responding State(s).[241]

Second, the notion that third-party countermeasures alone, no matter how resolute, can stop genocide, acts of aggression or other massive violations of international law is unrealistic.[242] Moreover, even a total trade embargo against a target State may be a blunt instrument if participation is not universal (or at least includes major trading partners). But this does not obviate the need for third-party countermeasures. The coercive action taken against Syria provides a useful illustration.

---

[239] Tams (2005), 229. To the same effect: YbILC (1992), vol. I, 162–163, para. 42 (Mr. Sreenivasa Rao).

[240] Reisman (1995), 354.

[241] In June 2006, the United Kingdom reported that the amount of Zimbabwean assets frozen within its jurisdiction was approximately £160,000. See UK House of Lords Select Committee on Economic Affairs, Second Report of Session 2006–2007, The Impact of Economic Sanctions, Vol. II: Evidence, 3–4, www.publications.parliament.uk/pa/ld200607/ldselect/ldeconaf/96/96ii.pdf. President Mugabe still appears solvent and undeterred: see e.g. 'Zimbabwe: Robert Mugabe Buys £4m Apartment in Hong Kong', The Daily Telegraph, 15 February 2009, www.telegraph.co.uk/news/worldnews/africaan dindianocean/zimbabwe/4631148/Zimbabwe-Robert-Mugabe-buys-4m-apartment-in-Hong-Kong.html.

[242] Even so, third-party countermeasures may still perform an important symbolic function as a 'communication tool' by signalling disapproval of egregious conduct and reinforcing public commitment to communitarian norms: see Boisson de Chazournes (1995), 338; Reisman (1995), 354; Arangio-Ruiz, Seventh Report, 15, para. 59; Hakimi (2014), 128–129; Statement by the President of the European Council Herman Van Rompuy and the President of the European Commission in the Name of the European Union on the Agreed Additional Restrictive Measures against Russia (29 July 2014), www .consilium.europa.eu/uedocs/cms_data/docs/pressdata/en/ec/144158.pdf. Also: Report of the UN Secretary-General's High Level Panel on Threats, Challenges and Change, UN Doc. A/59/565 (2 Dec. 2004), 51, para. 179; Designing United Nations Targeted Sanctions: Initial Findings of the Targeted Sanctions Consortium Evaluating Impacts and Effectiveness of UN Targeted Sanctions (2012), 9–10, www.graduateinstitute.ch /files/live/sites/iheid/files/sites/internationalgovernance/shared/PSIG_images/ Sanctions/Designing UN Targeted Sanctions.pdf.

In a debate before the Security Council, France criticized the 'scandalous silence' of the Council. It added:

> Of course, we have continued our efforts despite the Council's silence. The European Union has 11 times increased the sanctions on the regime and its leaders ... However, the actions of the European Union or the Arab League, no matter how resolute, cannot replace action by the Council. By virtue of the legitimacy conferred on it by the United Nations Charter, it is the Council that can express authoritatively the will of the international community.[243]

France nevertheless cautioned the Security Council: 'We will continue to up the pressure [on Syria] by imposing further sanctions of the European Union'.[244] A 'concerted multinational effort'[245] involving a multitude of different actions will normally be required to effect any meaningful change in recalcitrant behaviour. This is also what usually happens in practice – with varying degrees of success.

Third, third-party countermeasures are rarely (if ever) adopted in isolation:[246] their effectiveness must be measured in contextual and incremental terms.[247] Although concurrent enforcement action under Chapter VII UNC is relatively uncommon,[248] third-party countermeasures are invariably accompanied by other forms of coercive measures against the target State, such as various means of diplomatic pressure (retorsion) and institutional action taken by international organizations at both regional and universal levels.[249] Quiet diplomacy will in many cases undoubtedly also play a key role.[250] It is within the broader context

---

[243] UN Doc. S/PV.6710 (31 Jan. 2012), 14–15 (France).

[244] UN Doc. S/PV.6711 (4 Feb. 2012), 4 (France).

[245] Statement by the Friends of the Syrian People International Working Group on Sanctions (Tokyo, 30 Nov. 2012), para. 8, www.government.nl/documents-and-publications/leaflets/2012/12/10/joint-statement-tokyo-30-nov-2012.html. To similar effect: Council of the European Union, 'EU Restrictive Measures – Factsheet' (29 Apr. 2014), 3, www.consilium.europa.eu/uedocs/cms_data/docs/pressdata/EN/foraff/135804.pdf.

[246] The United States may have been alone in adopting third-party countermeasures against Sudan, but institutional action (including under Chapter VII UNC) was taken in parallel: see Section 4.2.14 and above Section 5.2.1.

[247] Compare Designing United Nations Targeted Sanctions: Initial Findings of the Targeted Sanctions Consortium Evaluating Impacts and Effectiveness of UN Targeted Sanctions (2012), 13, www.graduateinstitute.ch/files/live/sites/iheid/files/sites/internationalgovernance/shared/PSIG_images/Sanctions/Designing UN Targeted Sanctions.pdf.

[248] See above Section 5.2.1.

[249] Compare Arangio-Ruiz, Seventh Report, 15, para. 59; Tams (2011), 392.

[250] Crawford (2013a), 68. The totality of such concerted action – including when combined with the 'hue and cry' effect of the finding of serious illegalities by international bodies

of this concerted multilateral effort that the discrete and incremental role of third-party countermeasures in an essentially decentralized system of communitarian law enforcement is best understood.[251]

For example, on the occasion of the lifting by the Security Council of its sanctions regime against South Africa, a handful of States noted the 'effective supportive role'[252] played by UN sanctions, as well as unilateral coercive measures, in ultimately eradicating apartheid.[253] More recently, the Group of Friends of the Syrian People has concluded that the adoption of unilateral coercive measures, including third-party countermeasures, against Syria by different States and international organizations – 'aimed at depriving the Syrian regime of the [financial] resources it and its supporters rely on to perpetuate the regime's repression of the people of Syria' – has 'seriously affected' the Assad regime and 'reduced its ability to crack down on the Syrian people'.[254] The conclusion was clear: 'The members of the Group have adopted effective, proportional and coordinated sanctions'.[255] In June 2006, the United Kingdom indicated, albeit more cautiously, that the use of unilateral coercive measures, including third-party countermeasures, against Zimbabwe 'appears to be impacting on the regime and may bring forward an end to the crisis'.[256]

Finally, practice suggests that the yardstick against which the effectiveness of third-party countermeasures should be measured is to some

and the 'moral condemnation' it entails – may constitute an effective 'deterrent' against wrongdoing: see Arangio-Ruiz, Seventh Report, 15, para. 59.

[251] See e.g. Council of the European Union, 'EU restrictive measures – Factsheet' (29 Apr. 2014), 1 ('Sanctions are one of the EU's tools to promote ... human rights and international law. They are always part of a comprehensive policy approach involving political dialogue and complementary efforts'), www.consilium.europa.eu/uedocs/ cms_data/docs/pressdata/EN/foraff/135804.pdf; Council of the European Union, Basic Principles on the Use of Restrictive Measures (Sanctions) (2004), para. 5, http://register .consilium.europa.eu/doc/srv?l=EN&f=ST%2010198%202004%20REV%201; Ukraine Freedom Support Act of 2014, Public Law 113–272 (18 Dec. 2014) (s. 3), https://www .congress.gov/113/plaws/publ272/PLAW-113publ272.pdf.

[252] UN Doc. S/PV.3379 (26 May 1994), 4 (Botswana).

[253] Ibid., 3 (South Africa), 14 (India), 26 (United States). See also Farrall (2007), 261.

[254] See Statement by the Friends of the Syrian People International Working Group on Sanctions (Doha, 19 July 2012 and The Hague, 20 Sept. 2012), www.state.gov/e/eb/tfs/ spi/syria/documents/211642.htm; www.government.nl/files/documents-and-publica tions/reports/2012/09/20/statement-by-the-friends-of-the-syrian-people-internationalworking-group-on-sanctions/statement-eng.pdf.

[255] Statement by the Friends of the Syrian People International Working Group on Sanctions (The Hague, 20 Sept. 2012), para. 7.

[256] UK House of Lords Select Committee on Economic Affairs, Second Report of Session 2006–2007, The Impact of Economic Sanctions, Vol. II: Evidence, 3–4, www .publications.parliament.uk/pa/ld200607/ldselect/ldeconaf/96/96ii.pdf.

extent subjective and depends on the broader purpose of the action. Simply put, the degree of incremental change required for the use of third-party countermeasures to be deemed successful in a given case is ultimately a matter of appreciation. The example of Burma is instructive. In 2012, in response to 'historic changes' and 'wide-ranging reforms',[257] EU Member States, the United States and Australia suspended the application of third-party countermeasures against Burma notwithstanding continuing serious breaches of international law. For its part, the United States could only have withdrawn its third-party countermeasures if Burma had made 'substantial and measurable progress to end violations of internationally recognized human rights'.[258]

By contrast, Switzerland and Canada still have third-party countermeasures in place against Burma. In response to Burma's improved compliance record, Canadian Foreign Minister Baird stated that 'this is probably one of the best examples in the modern era where sanctions have proven very effective' before adding that 'limited sanctions [including the continued freezing of Head of State assets] may be useful in pressuring for continued progress'.[259] For his part, Australian Foreign Minister Carr explained that, although human rights challenges in Burma still remained, following recent improvements 'lifting sanctions is the best way to promote further progress'.[260] As Brownlie has observed: 'Whether in a given situation the law is ultimately "effective" is a question of taste, in other words it is a matter of political and moral evaluation'.[261] The same observation appears to be equally valid for third-party countermeasures.

The use of third-party countermeasures has clearly not resulted in an ideal or full level of compliance with communitarian norms. Third-party countermeasures are no panacea for the ills of enforcement. However, the key point lies elsewhere: the concept of third-party countermeasures

---

[257] See Council of the European Union, 'Council Conclusions on Burma/Myanmar' (23 Apr. 2012), http://register.consilium.europa.eu/pdf/en/12/st09/st09008.en12.pdf.

[258] See Burmese Freedom and Democracy Act of 2003, Public Law 108–61 (28 July 2003), www.treasury.gov/resource-center/sanctions/Documents/bfda_2003.pdf.

[259] See Regulations Amending the Special Economic Measures (Burma) Regulations (SOR/2012–85) (24 Apr. 2012), http://www.gazette.gc.ca/rp-pr/p2/2012/2012-05-09/html/sor-dors85-eng.html; 'Canada to Lift Sanctions on Burma in Wake of Historic Vote', The Toronto Star, 24 April 2012, www.thestar.com/news/canada/2012/04/24/canada_to_lift_sanctions_on_burma_in_wake_of_historic_vote.html.

[260] Press Statement by Foreign Minister Carr, 'Australia to Lift Sanctions against Myanmar' (7 June 2012), http://foreignminister.gov.au/releases/2012/bc_mr_120607.html.

[261] Brownlie (1981), 8.

is *capable* of being an effective instrument of law enforcement. As EU institutions have implicitly observed, the use of third-party countermeasures (among other unilateral coercive measures) '*can* be a powerful tool' of enforcement.[262] In a similar vein, then President of the European Council, Mr. Van Rompuy, has stressed that third-party countermeasures may send a 'powerful signal' that serious illegalities will not be tolerated.[263] Indeed Denmark (on behalf of the Nordic countries) has observed that

> In particular cases, the risk of countermeasures may actually be the *only* effective deterrent to the commission of internationally wrongful acts.[264]

To conclude, the effectiveness of third-party countermeasures depends on several factors. Above all, their effectiveness depends on the political will and organization of States to enforce communitarian norms. Like politics, law enforcement is to some extent the art of the possible. Third-party countermeasures may not represent the best of all possible worlds, but they are nevertheless a necessary tool in an otherwise limited communitarian law enforcement toolbox.

5.3   Conclusion

It may sometimes be a difficult and delicate matter to determine with confidence whether a rule of customary international law has come into existence. Several difficult questions admittedly arise in the assessment of practice concerning third-party countermeasures. But these difficulties should not be overstated. The key points arising from the above analysis may now be summarized. First, the analysis of twenty-one examples in

---

[262] European Commission, EU Guidelines on Implementation and Evaluation of Restrictive Measures (2008), 4–5 (emphasis added), http://eeas.europa.eu/cfsp/sanctions/docs/index_en.pdf.

[263] Statement by the President of the European Council Herman Van Rompuy and the President of the European Commission in the Name of the European Union on the Agreed Additional Restrictive Measures against Russia (29 July 2014), www.consilium.europa.eu/uedocs/cms_data/docs/pressdata/en/ec/144158.pdf.

[264] UN Doc. A/CN.4/488, 114 (Denmark on behalf of the Nordic countries) (emphasis added). See also Riphagen, Fourth Report, 18, para. 96; Tomuschat (1994), 80–81; Arangio-Ruiz, Seventh Report, 15, para. 59; Kamto (2010), 1171. Compare the emphasis on deterrence in the statement by Mr. Van Rompuy (above n. 263) with respect to the EU's adoption of third-party countermeasures against Russia in July 2014: 'The [sanctions] package . . . is meant as a strong warning: illegal annexation of territory and deliberate destabilisation of a neighbouring sovereign country cannot be accepted in 21st century Europe'.

Chapter 4 suggests that practice cannot today be qualified as neither limited nor embryonic. Second, practice is also more subtle and complex than the debate in the Sixth Committee taken in isolation would otherwise suggest: it demonstrates some apparent contradictions – notably between statements made in the Sixth Committee and actual conduct – but overall decidedly points to a virtually uniform conduct capable of forming the basis of a general rule of custom. Third, although dominated by Western States, practice is considerably more widespread and diverse than the ILC had assumed. Indeed the sheer volume and diversity of practice is striking. In addition to Western States, a very large number of States from Eastern Europe, Eurasia, the Middle East, Asia and Africa have contributed to practice – many of them repeatedly – over the course of several decades. Latin American States may not have actually adopted third-party countermeasures but some of them have nevertheless expressed tentative support for the concept. Fourth, the relative absence of diplomatic protests against third-party countermeasures is also noteworthy.

Fifth, *opinio juris* may be somewhat obscure but it nevertheless exists. It is often very difficult to get concrete evidence of *opinio juris* in view of the manner in which international relations are conducted. This is especially true in the case of third-party countermeasures where States do not explicitly refer to the concept as a basis for their conduct. This phenomenon may be largely dictated by political considerations but it does not negate the law-making capacity of the practice. The category of third-party countermeasures is needed to explain practice in legal terms. In sum, there is considerable support for the conclusion that third-party countermeasures are permissible under international law.

A number of other salient observations also emerge from an examination of practice. First, in principle, it does not appear that the triggering of enforcement action under Chapter VII UNC ends any entitlement to adopt third-party countermeasures. Third-party countermeasures may (subject to overall compliance with their safeguards regime, notably necessity and proportionality) be adopted in parallel with enforcement action taken by the Security Council under Chapter VII UNC. The language of a Security Council resolution may undoubtedly limit or even proscribe the use of third-party countermeasures but this is largely a question of interpretation that does not seem to have arisen so far in practice. Second, third-party countermeasures are most often adopted to induce compliance with obligations *erga omnes partes* (or at least not well-established obligations *erga omnes*) in the field of human rights. Third, third-party countermeasures are normally adopted in response to widely acknowledged breaches of obligations *erga omnes (partes)* and this has significantly reduced the risk of abuse associated with the auto-interpretation of wrongful conduct. Fourth, third-party countermeasures have developed as a *sui generis* form of invocation of State responsibility limited to serious breaches of obligations *erga omnes (partes)*.

Fifth, it does not seem inconsistent with principle to allow States to adopt third-party countermeasures with the consent of a directly injured State, irrespective of the seriousness of the breach of a communitarian norm. Still, the absence of any practice sheds some doubt on this proposition and its relevance. Sixth, the relative vagueness with which obligations *erga omnes* are postulated may entail a concomitant risk of abuse but it is not one that seems to have materialized in practice. Examples of possible abuse for lack of standing are limited. Moreover, third-party countermeasures have mostly been adopted in response to violations of conventional human rights obligations for which there is considerable support in practice for a separate *erga omnes* status under customary international law.

Finally, the effectiveness of third-party countermeasures may have been less than ideal in terms of inducing full compliance with communitarian norms; but their real effectiveness is best measured in contextual and incremental terms. Against this yardstick, States have noted that they do appear to have had a measure of success and are capable of serving as a powerful tool of enforcement if circumstances permit. Having notably concluded that third-party countermeasures are permissible under international law, it is now finally convenient to assess the safeguards regime applicable to third-party countermeasures.

6

Third-Party Countermeasures and Safeguards against Abuse

It was concluded in the previous chapter that recourse to third-party countermeasures is permissible under international law; however, this is only so if they are strictly limited to the requirements of the situation. Prudence dictates that third-party countermeasures must be subject to appropriate conditions and limitations in order to minimize the risk of abuse and seek to ensure that they are 'kept within generally acceptable bounds'.[1] The concept of countermeasures expresses a basic tension between order and disorder in international relations. Tools of law enforcement aim to reinstate order, ruptured by illegality, but unilateral self-help measures (notably, countermeasures) entail a risk of disorder and further rupture. The ILC, largely relying on pre-existing customary international law, sought to balance these concerns by devising an operational system of safeguards for the taking of countermeasures in Articles 49–53 ARSIWA.[2]

It may be recalled from Chapter 3 that, having provisionally adopted Draft Article 54 [2000] which recognized the entitlement to adopt third-party countermeasures, the ILC Drafting Committee in 2000 simply added in its third paragraph: 'Where more than one State takes countermeasures, the States concerned shall cooperate in order to ensure that the conditions laid down by this Chapter [i.e. what became Articles 49–53 ARSIWA] for the taking of countermeasures are fulfilled'.[3] The inclusion of Article 54 ARSIWA in the chapter on countermeasures makes it clear

---

[1] ARSIWA Commentary, Introductory Commentary to Chapter II of Part Three, §2.

[2] For judicial affirmation of the customary law status of Articles 49–53 ARSIWA, see *Corn Products International Inc. v. Mexico*, ICSID Case No. ARB(AF)/04/01, Decision on Responsibility, 15 Jan. 2008, para. 145.

[3] ILC Report (2000), UN Doc. A/55/10, 71. See also YbILC (2000), vol. I, 399, para. 90 (Chairman of the Drafting Committee, Mr. Gaja) ('Like the Commission, the Drafting Committee did not think it would be possible to address that matter in detail ... All that could reasonably be required was that States should generally cooperate when they intended to take countermeasures, so that those measures, whether individually or collectively taken, complied with the conditions laid down in Chapter II for taking countermeasures').

that the ILC intended only to reserve its position with respect to the permissibility of third-party countermeasures. The term 'lawful' in Article 54 ARSIWA refers to the requirement that any third-party countermeasure would always have to comply with Articles 49–53 ARSIWA.[4] The 2005 IDI Krakow Resolution likewise affirms that third-party countermeasures are essentially permissible 'under conditions analogous to those applying to a State specifically affected by the breach'.[5] Thus the general safeguards regime for countermeasures, which applies *mutatis mutandis* to third-party countermeasures, is the subject of this final chapter. It will examine the object and limits of countermeasures in the intimately related Articles 49 and 53 ARSIWA (6.1); the scope of excluded countermeasures in Article 50 ARSIWA (6.2); the principle of proportionality in Article 51 ARSIWA (6.3); and the procedural conditions in Article 52 ARSIWA (6.4). This will be followed by some concluding observations (6.5).

6.1   The Object and Limits of Countermeasures

The object and limits of lawful countermeasures are set out in Article 49 ARSIWA:

Article 49
Object and limits of countermeasures
1. An injured State may only take countermeasures against a State which is responsible for an internationally wrongful act in order to induce that State to comply with its obligations under Part Two.
2. Countermeasures are limited to the non-performance for the time being of international obligations of the State taking the measures towards the responsible State.
3. Countermeasures shall, as far as possible, be taken in such a way as to permit the resumption of performance of the obligations in question.

In addition, Article 53 ARSIWA provides:

Article 53
Termination of countermeasures
Countermeasures shall be terminated as soon as the responsible State has complied with its obligations under Part Two in relation to the internationally wrongful act.

---

[4] See Gaja (2013), 130. Compare Ago, Eighth Report, 39, para. 80; Draft Articles Commentary, Art. 30, §2 (on the meaning of a 'legitimate' countermeasure).
[5] 2005 IDI Krakow Resolution (Art. 5).

These provisions describe the permissible object of countermeasures and place limits on their scope. Three issues merit closer examination: the existence of a prior breach of international law as a precondition to taking countermeasures (6.1.1); the relative effect of countermeasures in precluding wrongfulness (6.1.2); and the instrumental function of countermeasures (6.1.3).

6.1.1   The Existence of a Prior Breach of International Law

The existence of a prior breach of international law is a 'fundamental prerequisite' for any lawful countermeasure.[6] This cardinal principle has an ancient pedigree.[7] At the 1930 Hague Conference for the Codification of International Law, all States which responded on this point stated that a prior breach was an indispensable prerequisite for the adoption of countermeasures against the responsible State.[8] The application of this principle presupposes an 'objective standard' for the taking of countermeasures. It does not however mean that the existence of a wrongful act must have been established by a prior judicial procedure or of action taken by a political or fact-finding body. A State which resorts to countermeasures on the basis of its own unilateral assessment of the situation does so at its own peril and may incur responsibility for its own wrongful conduct in the event of an incorrect assessment.[9]

The Portugal/Germany Arbitral Tribunal, established during the inter-war period, affirmed this cardinal principle in two awards concerning the use of reprisals. The arbitral tribunal in the *Naulilaa* case stressed that 'the first requirement – *sine qua non* – of the right to take reprisals is a motive furnished by an earlier act contrary to the law of nations'.[10]

---

[6] ARSIWA Commentary, Art. 49, §2; Draft Articles Commentary, Art. 47, §1.

[7] See e.g. Grotius (1646), Book III, Chapter II, §4; Vattel (1758), Book II, Chapter XVIII, §§ 342–343; Phillimore (1857), Vol. III, 10; 1934 IDI Paris Resolution (Art. 1).

[8] League of Nations, Conference for the Codification of International Law, Bases of Discussion for the Conference drawn up by the Preparatory Committee, Vol. III: Responsibility of States for Damage caused in their Territory to the Person or Property of Foreigners (Doc. C.75.M.69.1929.V), 128 (discussed in ARSIWA Commentary, Art. 49, §2 (n. 745)).

[9] ARSIWA Commentary, Art. 49, §3; Draft Articles Commentary, Art. 47, §1. See also *Corn Products International Inc. v. Mexico*, ICSID Case No. ARB(AF)/04/01, Decision on Responsibility, 15 Jan. 2008, para. 187; and further below Section 6.4 (on procedural conditions for countermeasures).

[10] *Naulilaa (Responsibility of Germany for damage caused in the Portuguese colonies in the south of Africa) (Portugal/Germany)* (1928), RIAA, vol. II, 1011 at 1027. No previous wrongful act had in fact been committed in that case entitling recourse to reprisals (ibid.).

The arbitral tribunal in the *Cysne* case again emphasized that 'reprisals, which constitute an act in principle contrary to the law of nations, are defensible only in so far as they were *provoked* by some other act likewise contrary to that law'.[11] In the modern period, the tribunal in the *Air Services* arbitration reaffirmed the same point.[12] The ICJ in the *Gabčíkovo Nagymaros Project* case confirmed in unequivocal terms that

> In order to be justifiable, a countermeasure must meet certain conditions . . .
> In the first place it must be taken in response to a previous international wrongful act of another State and must be directed against that State.[13]

As already observed, the ILC codified this fundamental prerequisite in Article 49(1) ARSIWA. It has been recognized as an authoritative statement of customary international law by international tribunals.[14]

6.1.2   The Relative Effect of Countermeasures in Precluding Wrongfulness

The ICJ in the *Gabčíkovo Nagymaros Project* case affirmed a second basic condition of a lawful countermeasure, namely, that it 'must be directed against' the State responsible for the wrongful act.[15] Although incidental or collateral effects on third States may be unavoidable 'in an interdependent world where States are increasingly bound by multilateral obligations' a countermeasure cannot violate the individual rights of third States.[16] This is the equivalent in the law of countermeasures to the *pacta*

---

[11] *Cysne (Responsibility of Germany for acts committed subsequent to 31 July 1914 and before Portugal entered the war) (Portugal/Germany)* (1930), RIAA, vol. II, 1035 at 1056 (emphasis in the original).

[12] *US-France Air Services Agreement* (1978), RIAA, vol. XVIII, 417 at 443, para. 81. See also ARSIWA Commentary, Art. 49, §3 (n. 746) (pointing out that the remarks by the *Air Services* tribunal (at ibid.) have on occasion been wrongly interpreted as suggesting that a bona fide belief of wrongful conduct would suffice to justify recourse to countermeasures); and further Arangio-Ruiz, Third Report, 14, para. 37 (n. 65) (with further references).

[13] *Gabčíkovo Nagymaros Project* case, ICJ Rep. (1997), 7 at 55, para. 83.

[14] See e.g. *Mexico – Tax Measures on Soft Drinks and Other Beverages*, WT/DS308/R, Report of the Panel, 7 Oct. 2005, paras. 8.178–8.180; *Archer Daniels Midland Company and Tate & Lyle Ingredients Americas, Inc. v. Mexico*, ICSID Case No. ARB(AF)/04/05, Award, 21 Nov. 2007, paras. 125–126; *Corn Products International Inc. v. Mexico*, ICSID Case No. ARB(AF)/04/01, Decision on Responsibility, 15 Jan. 2008, paras. 145–146, 185–189; *Application of the Interim Accord of 13 September 1995*, ICJ Rep. (2011), 644 at 691–692, para. 164.

[15] *Gabčíkovo Nagymaros Project* case, ICJ Rep. (1997), 7 at 55, para. 83.

[16] Draft Articles Commentary, Art. 47, §7.

tertiis rule on the relative effect of treaties, and its equivalent also for obligations under general international law.[17]

The arbitral tribunal in the *Cysne* case first affirmed this basic principle and did so in clear terms.[18] In this case, Germany alleged that the United Kingdom had violated certain obligations laid down in the 1909 London Declaration concerning the Laws of Naval War; by way of reprisal, Germany unilaterally added several items to the list of absolute contraband (i.e. items exclusively used for war) in violation of Article 23 of the London Declaration. On 28 May 1915, a German submarine thereupon destroyed the neutral Portuguese merchant vessel *Cysne*, while en route to deliver its cargo in England, which was carrying such items.[19] The arbitral tribunal stressed that

> [R]eprisals, which constitute an act in principle contrary to the law of nations, are defensible only in so far as they were *provoked* by some other act likewise contrary to that law. *Only reprisals taken against the provoking State are permissible.* Admittedly, it can happen that legitimate reprisals taken against an offending State may affect the nationals of an innocent State. But that would be an indirect and unintentional consequence which, in practice, the injured State will always endeavour to avoid or to limit as far as possible.[20]

The *Cysne* principle finds expression in Article 49(1) ARSIWA, which in relevant part provides that 'an injured State may only take countermeasures against a State which is responsible for an internationally wrongful act'. The ILC commentary explains that the word 'only' is intended to convey that the wrongfulness of countermeasures is precluded solely as against the responsible State:

> In a situation where a third State is owed an international obligation by the State taking countermeasures and that obligation is breached by the countermeasure, the wrongfulness of the measure is not precluded as against the third State. In that sense the effect of countermeasures in

---

[17] Crawford (2013a), 687.

[18] *Cysne (Responsibility of Germany for acts committed subsequent to 31 July 1914 and before Portugal entered the war) (Portugal/Germany)* (1930), RIAA, vol. II, 1035. For widespread support of the principle see e.g. Ago, Eighth Report, 45–46, paras. 96–98; Draft Articles Commentary, Art. 30, §§18–19; Alland (1994), 227–229; Sicilianos (2005), 463–465.

[19] *Cysne (Responsibility of Germany for acts committed subsequent to 31 July 1914 and before Portugal entered the war) (Portugal/Germany)* (1930), RIAA, vol. II, 1052–1054.

[20] Ibid., 1056–1057 (emphasis in the original). The case dealt with the principle in the context of belligerent reprisals, but it is equally valid for non-forcible countermeasures: see ARSIWA Commentary, Art. 22, §5.

precluding wrongfulness is relative. It concerns the legal relations between the injured State and the responsible State.

This does not mean that countermeasures may not incidentally affect the position of third States or indeed other third parties ... Such indirect or collateral effects cannot be entirely avoided.[21]

The principle of the relative effect of countermeasures in precluding wrongfulness continues to be recognized by international tribunals.[22]

6.1.3   The Instrumental Function of Countermeasures

The ICJ in the *Gabčíkovo Nagymaros Project* case noted by way of dictum a third basic condition of a lawful countermeasure. The Court observed that the purpose of a countermeasure must be 'to induce the wrongdoing State to comply with its international obligations, and that the measure must therefore be reversible'.[23] Article 49 ARSIWA reflects the ICJ's observations. The ILC commentary explains that

> Countermeasures may only be taken to induce the responsible State to comply with its obligations under Part Two, namely, to cease the internationally wrongful conduct, if it is continuing, and to provide reparation to the injured State. Countermeasures are not intended as a form of punishment for wrongful conduct but as an instrument for achieving compliance with the obligations of the responsible State under Part Two.[24]

This explanation of the instrumental function of countermeasures prompts three observations.

First, at least in relation to third-party countermeasures, it is not obvious that practice supports such a wide instrumental function in

---

[21] ARSIWA Commentary, Art. 49, §4; Art. 22, §§4–5. Compare Draft Articles Commentary, Art. 30, §§18–19; Art. 47, §7. Recourse to countermeasures with extra-territorial application (such as the US Helms-Burton Act of 1996 or the Iran and Libya Sanctions Act of 1996, 35 ILM (1996), 357, 1273) provides a notorious example of countermeasures with potentially unlawful effects on third States: see e.g. Sicilianos (2005), 464; Report of the Secretary-General, UN Doc. A/70/120 (9 Oct. 2015); GA Res. 70/5 (27 Oct. 2015) (preamble).

[22] *Mexico – Tax Measures on Soft Drinks and Other Beverages*, Report of the Panel, WT/DS308/R, 7 Oct. 2005, para. 4.335 (n. 70); *Archer Daniels Midland Company and Tate & Lyle Ingredients Americas, Inc. v. Mexico*, ICSID Case No. ARB(AF)/04/05, Award, 21 Nov. 2007, para. 126, *Corn Products International Inc. v. Mexico*, ICSID Case No. ARB(AF)/04/01, Decision on Responsibility, 15 Jan. 2008, paras. 163–164, 176.

[23] *Gabčíkovo Nagymaros Project* case, ICJ Rep. (1997), 7 at 56–57, para. 87.

[24] ARSIWA Commentary, Art. 49, §1. To similar effect: Draft Articles Commentary, Art. 47, §2.

terms of remedial rights; i.e. that third-party countermeasures may be adopted to ensure both cessation and reparation. Second, the question arises as to whether any State may autonomously claim either of these remedies by way of third-party countermeasures or may only do so with the consent and on behalf of the directly injured State or the beneficiaries of the communitarian obligation breached. Third, the strictly instrumental function of countermeasures was not always made apparent by the ILC. This allowed some doubts to linger about the exclusion of a punitive aim of countermeasures and appears to have reinforced critical views about the true function of third-party countermeasures. But even if it were excluded, concern was expressed that the risk of abuse from punitive measures was still too great. It remains to be seen whether this concern is borne out by practice. Let us now examine in turn the legitimate aims of countermeasures, including the scope of remedial rights and the modalities of their exercise (6.1.3.1), and the intimately related requirement of reversibility (6.1.3.2).

6.1.3.1 The Legitimate Aims of Countermeasures

The formulation of the legitimate aims of countermeasures evolved in the course of the ILC's work as they were progressively dissociated from measures that are punitive rather than instrumental in character.[25] On first reading, there was some uncertainty as to whether the ILC actually intended countermeasures to exclude a punitive aim. Special Rapporteur Ago's proposed draft article 30 ('Legitimate application of a sanction'), which included both countermeasures under general international law and enforcement measures under Chapter VII UNC, defined a 'sanction' as 'an action the object of which is to inflict punishment or to secure performance and which takes the form of an infringement of what in other circumstances would be an international subjective right, requiring respect, of the subject against which the action is taken'.[26]

It may be recalled from Chapter 3 that the ILC in 1979 provisionally adopted Ago's proposal as Draft Article 30 [1996] ('Countermeasures in respect of an internationally wrongful act') with only a terminological change: the unitary term 'sanction' was replaced by the terms 'countermeasures' and 'measures' (or 'sanctions') in order to prevent any

---

[25] See e.g. Ago, Eighth Report, 39–47, paras. 78–99; Arangio-Ruiz, Third Report, 15–16, paras. 39–45; Arangio-Ruiz, Fourth Report, 6–8, paras. 3–5; Crawford, Third Report, 78–80, paras. 287, 290(d), 296.

[26] Ago, Eighth Report, 39, para. 79. See generally ibid., 39–47, paras. 78–99 (on his draft article 30).

misunderstanding between countermeasures under general international law and enforcement measures under Chapter VII UNC.[27] Following Ago's proposal, the ILC otherwise explained that

> The countermeasures with which this article is concerned are measures the object of which is, by definition, to inflict punishment or to secure performance – measures which, under different conditions, would infringe a valid and subjective right of the subject against which the measures are applied.[28]

This conception of countermeasures seemed difficult to reconcile with its later elaboration in Draft Article 47 [1996]. The ILC commentary to this provision stressed that State practice supported a strictly instrumental function of countermeasures; punitive action was explicitly ruled out.[29] This aspect of Draft Article 47 [1996] was widely supported in the Sixth Committee.[30] However, Singapore criticized the 'apparent contradictions' between Draft Articles 30 and 47 [1996].[31] For Tanzania, it was 'patently clear' that punitive countermeasures had been recognized.[32]

The ILC's ambiguous position on first reading concerning the legitimate aims of countermeasures appears to have influenced the critical position of those ILC and Sixth Committee members who opposed bilateral countermeasures, and especially those who opposed third-party countermeasures. In particular, it seems to have reinforced the suspicion among critics that third-party countermeasures were merely a fig leaf for power politics.[33] Tanzania provides a good example of a State whose grave reservations were based precisely on the impression that recognition of third-party countermeasures would legitimize punitive action. During the debate in the Sixth Committee in 2000, Tanzania stated:

> It could hardly be refuted that countermeasures were a threat to small and weak States. It was thus misleading to claim that their only purpose was to induce compliance by a wrongdoing State. It was patently clear from the commentary [as adopted by the ILC on first reading] that countermeasures could be punitive in order to satisfy the political and economic

---

[27] Draft Articles Commentary, Art. 30, §21; and further Section 3.1.1.

[28] Ibid., Art. 30, §3.   [29] Ibid., Art. 47, §2.

[30] See e.g. Topical Summary of Government Comments in the Sixth Committee, UN Doc. A/CN.4/504 (1999), 20, para. 74; UN Doc. A/CN.4/488, 114 (Denmark on behalf of the Nordic countries), 117 (United States), 118 (Ireland).

[31] UN Doc. A/CN.4/488/Add.3, 5–6, para. 14 (Singapore).

[32] UN Doc. A/C.6/55/SR.14, 9, para. 46 (Tanzania).

[33] See generally Sections 3.2.1.3(i)–(ii).

interests of the State claiming to be injured. The degree of subjectivity in the application of countermeasures must therefore be a matter of concern.[34]

On second reading, however, the unlawfulness of any punitive aim of countermeasures was not in doubt.[35] Unlike Draft Article 30 [1996], the ILC commentary to Article 22 ARSIWA makes no reference to a punitive function of countermeasures. There is instead a simple *renvoi* to the purely instrumental function of countermeasures as embodied in Article 49 ARSIWA.[36]

Still, if the exclusion of a punitive function of countermeasures was ultimately made clear, a more fundamental concern remained. It was suggested during the ILC debate that ruling out a punitive element provided merely an 'illusory guarantee against abuse' as it was difficult in practice to distinguish between punitive and instrumental aspects of countermeasures.[37] It was said that punitive intentions may usually be gleaned from the trigger statements that accompany the adoption of countermeasures; however, such intentions could often be 'skilfully concealed', notably by more powerful States.[38] Indeed it is not uncommon in practice for target States to protest that the adoption of third-party countermeasures against them – purportedly 'in the name of certain noble doctrines or ideals'[39] – is but a 'political tool'[40] based on 'invented'[41] and 'trumped-up claims'[42] motivated by 'unavowed

---

[34] UN Doc. A/C.6/55/SR.14, 9, para. 46 (Tanzania).

[35] See e.g. ILC Report (2000), UN Doc. A/55/10, 54, para. 318; Topical Summary of Government Comments in the Sixth Committee, UN Doc. A/CN.4/513 (2000), 29, para. 153. For the avoidance of any doubt, Ireland proposed (unsuccessfully) to add a sentence to Article 49(1) ARSIWA explicitly excluding a punitive function of countermeasures: see UN Doc. A/CN.4/488, 118 (Ireland).

[36] ARSIWA Commentary, Art. 22, §4.

[37] ILC Report (1992), UN Doc. A/47/10, 24, para. 154. See further YbILC (1992), vol. I, 158, para. 18 (Mr. Al-Khasawneh).

[38] Ibid.   [39] UN Doc. S/PV.3692 (28 Aug. 1996), 6 (Burundi). See further Section 4.2.13.

[40] UN Doc. A/66/138 (14 July 2011), 11 (Burma). Also: GATT Doc. L/5414 (12 Nov. 1982), 17 (Argentina protesting that the countermeasures adopted against it during the Falklands crisis were 'based on reasons of a political nature ... meant to exert political pressure on the sovereign decisions of Argentina ... '); UN Docs. A/HRC/20/G/3 (15 June 2012); A/68/211 (22 July 2013), 6 (Syria). See further Sections 4.2.8; 4.2.16; 4.2.20.

[41] 'Comment by the Russian Ministry of Foreign Affairs regarding the continuing anti-Russian sanctions of the United States' (30 July 2014), available at www.mid.ru/brp_4.nsf/main_eng. See further Section 4.2.21.

[42] UN Doc. S/2012/242 (Belarus). See further Section 4.2.18.

objectives'[43] contrary to the principle of non-intervention.[44] In short, as Botswana opined during the debate in the Sixth Committee, third-party countermeasures are 'open to abuse by powerful States against a weaker State that they might particularly dislike for other reasons'.[45]

For its part, Tanzania was correct to point out that inducing the responsible State to comply with international law may not be 'the *only* purpose' for which third-party countermeasures are adopted; 'political and economic interests', among others, may also motivate their use in a given case.[46] But this is hardly surprising; it should not without more be a cause for concern. It would be unrealistic to assume that States do not have any broader policy interests in mind – beyond mere law enforcement concerns – when taking coercive action. In fact, as justification for the third-party countermeasures taken against Burundi, Tanzania itself acknowledged before the UN Security Council that they were partly meant to ensure the restoration of constitutional order and 'the fundamental principles of democracy in the country' (i.e. as such an impermissible aim of third-party countermeasures); however, '*above all*, they are meant to stop genocide'.[47] As another example, EU Member States' adoption of third-party countermeasures against Burma was motivated not only by 'severe and systematic violations of human rights', but also by the concern that 'the Burmese authorities have taken no steps towards democracy and national reconciliation'.[48] The United States adopted third-party countermeasures against Burma based on a similar rationale.[49]

---

[43] UN Docs. S/PV.3692 (28 Aug. 1996), 3–5; S/1996/788, 2 (Burundi). See further Section 4.2.13.

[44] See generally Declaration on the Inadmissibility of Intervention and Interference in the Internal Affairs of States, GA Res. 36/103 (9 Dec. 1981), Principle II(l) ('The duty of a State to refrain from the exploitation and distortion of human rights issues as a means of interference in the internal affairs of States').

[45] UN Doc. A/C.6/55/SR.15, 10, para. 63 (Botswana).

[46] UN Doc. A/C.6/55/SR.14, 9, para. 46 (Tanzania) (emphasis added). See also YbILC (2000), vol. I, 277, para. 6 (Mr. Kateka); Topical Summary of Government Comments in the Sixth Committee, UN Doc. A/CN.4/513 (2000), 29, para. 149 ('Countermeasures ... often serv[ed] as a pretext for the adoption of unilateral measures such as armed reprisals and other types of intervention. Therefore, it was misleading to claim that their only purpose was to induce compliance by the wrongdoing State').

[47] UN Doc. S/PV.3692 (28 Aug. 1996), 10 (Tanzania) (emphasis added). It may be added that even Botswana considered that the coercive action taken against Burundi 'deserve[d] the commendation of the international community' (ibid., 16–17). See further Section 4.2.13.

[48] Common Position 2000/346/CFSP (26 Apr. 2000), Council Regulation (EC) No. 1081/2000, OJ 2000 L 122/29 (24 May 2000). See further Section 4.2.16.

[49] See Burmese Freedom and Democracy Act of 2003, Public Law 108–61 (28 July 2003), www.treasury.gov/resource-center/sanctions/Documents/bfda_2003.pdf. See further Section 4.2.16.

Whether these actions were used as a 'political tool' or were motivated by 'unavowed objectives', as alleged above by Burma and Burundi, is not necessarily decisive. As Schachter observed, in assessing State conduct, 'motivation and justification are analytically distinct'.[50] Brownlie has likewise noted that 'countermeasures had a multitude of purposes, not in the legal sense but in terms of the political behaviour of States'.[51] The ICJ made a similar point in the *Nicaragua* case in distinguishing between political motive and legal justification for State action.[52] This point applies *mutatis mutandis* to the legitimate aims of third-party countermeasures. It is worth reproducing in full:

> Nicaragua claims that the references made by the United States to the justification of collective self-defence are merely 'pretexts' for the activities of the United States. It has alleged that the true motive for the conduct of the United States is unrelated to the support which it accuses Nicaragua of giving to the armed opposition in El Salvador, and that the real objectives of United States policy is to impose its will upon Nicaragua and force it to comply with United States demands. In the Court's view, however, if Nicaragua has been giving support to the armed opposition in El Salvador, and if this constitutes an armed attack on El Salvador and the other appropriate conditions are met, collective self-defence could be legally invoked by the United States, even though there may be the possibility of an additional motive, one perhaps even more decisive for the United States, drawn from the political orientation of the present Nicaraguan Government. The existence of an additional motive, other than that officially proclaimed by the United States, could not deprive the latter of its right to resort to collective self-defence. The conclusion to be drawn is that special caution is called for in considering the allegations of the United States concerning conduct by Nicaragua which may provide a sufficient basis for self-defence.[53]

By parity of reasoning, it is only in circumstances where third-party countermeasures are incapable of legal justification because punitive or ulterior aims totally eclipse instrumental ones that their use must be deemed unlawful. Conversely, as the ICJ suggested in the above passage, so long as the 'officially proclaimed' position of a State (even if implied) could be justified by reference to third-party countermeasures, it does not really matter, legally speaking, that ulterior political motives – 'perhaps

---

[50] Schachter (1982), 59. Compare Lowe (2007), 57; Lowe and Tzanakopoulos (2011), para. 34.
[51] YbILC (2000), vol. I, 301, para. 90 (Mr. Brownlie).
[52] For a useful discussion see Kritsiotis (2004), 235–241.
[53] *Nicaragua* case, ICJ Rep. (1986), 14 at 70–71, para. 127.

even more decisive' than law enforcement considerations – may have prompted the action. Indeed, as Simma has rightly noted, it is 'self-interested political motives' that in part propel the actual adoption of third-party countermeasures; they form part of the 'legitimate regime' governing their use.[54] The examples of Burundi and Burma mentioned above – albeit partially influenced by motivations extraneous to law enforcement – were clearly justified by instrumental aims and as such were lawful. However, in line with Article 53 ARSIWA, it should be stressed that the lawfulness of the action will only endure for as long as the illegality remains. It is only if the action continues to remain in place after the illegality has ceased that it would become unlawful.

It should also be noted that third-party countermeasures are rarely adopted in isolation; they are almost invariably accompanied by several acts of retorsion. The latter are inherently lawful measures and as such may be motivated by considerations unrelated to cessation and/or reparation for wrongful conduct – that is, they may include a punitive element.[55] A single trigger statement will often precede the adoption of both forms of unilateral coercive measures with an integrated rationale for the action. Although mixed motivations are not an uncommon feature of practice, references to widely acknowledged breaches of com-munitarian norms, and calls for a return to legality, provide a clear indication that the use of third-party countermeasures is permissible notwithstanding the presence of a punitive element for the action as a whole.

However, as the ICJ noted in the above *Nicaragua* passage, 'special caution' is sometimes called for. Albeit in relation to bilateral counter-measures, a rare recent example can be found in the *Application of the Interim Accord* case.[56] It provides an apt reminder that the risks of abuse certainly cannot be ignored. In that case, Greece had sought to justify certain wrongful conduct vis-à-vis FYROM under the Interim Accord of

---

[54] Simma (2007), 380–381.   [55] Compare Elagab (1999), 126; Crawford (2013a), 677.

[56] *Application of the Interim Accord of 13 September 1995*, ICJ Rep. (2011), 644. See also *United States Diplomatic and Consular Staff in Tehran*, ICJ Rep. (1980), 3 at 37–41, paras. 80–87 (Iran's action by way of countermeasures against US diplomatic and consular staff in Tehran indicated that its real motivation was unconnected with any aim of remedying alleged US breaches of diplomatic law); *Archer Daniels Midland Company and Tate & Lyle Ingredients Americas, Inc. v. Mexico*, ICSID Case No. ARB(AF)/04/05, Award, 21 Nov. 2007, paras. 152–153, 156. In the latter case, a NAFTA tribunal found (at ibid.) that Mexico's adoption of a sugar tax by way of countermeasure against the United States had not been intended to induce compliance with US obligations under NAFTA but was, in reality, designed to protect the domestic Mexican sugar industry.

13 September 1995 (involving steps taken to object to FYROM's admission to NATO), *inter alia*, by invoking countermeasures as a defence. The ICJ summarily dismissed this argument. It found that the countermeasures defence was unavailable since the impugned wrongful conduct had already ceased; and, in any event, the action taken by Greece was not actually intended to induce FYROM to comply with the relevant obligation.[57] For his part, Judge Simma did not mince his words:

> I have difficulties to view Greece's 2008 action as anything but a politically motivated attempt at coercing the FYROM to back down on the name issue. After having been brought before the Court, what the Respondent then tried *ex post facto* was to hide, somewhat desperately and with a pinch of embarrassment, this show of political force amounting to a treaty breach behind the three juridical fig leaves [including countermeasures], presented as 'subsidiary defences' by very able counsel (but *ad impossibilia nemo tenetur*). In the Judgment, these arguments got the treatment they deserved.[58]

In short, even assuming a prior breach of international law, a unilateral coercive measure that is motivated purely as a 'show of political force' is incapable of legal justification as a countermeasure.[59] If covered in such a 'juridical fig leaf', it would be punitive in nature and as such unlawful. Thus countermeasures clearly cannot be legitimized if they serve as 'a tactic motivated by purely political considerations'.[60] There is little evidence in modern practice of punitive third-party countermeasures.[61]

6.1.3.1(i) The Scope of Remedial Rights and the Modalities of their Exercise The scope of remedial rights for countermeasures and the modalities of their exercise raised more difficult questions. The ILC recognized that the injured State will, in many cases, be primarily

---

[57] *Application of the Interim Accord of 13 September 1995*, ICJ Rep. (2011), 644 at 690–692, paras. 161, 163–164.

[58] Ibid., 696, para. 3 (Sep. Op. Judge Simma). Compare *Oil Platforms*, ICJ Rep. (2003), 161 at 265, para. 62 (Sep. Op. Judge Kooijmans), 333–334, paras. 15–16 (Sep. Op. Judge Simma).

[59] Compare UN Doc. A/C.6/55/SR.18, 11, para. 62 (Cuba). Also: Elagab (1999), 126; and below Section 6.3.1 (n. 443) (on proportionality as a possible limitation on punitive countermeasures).

[60] Ibid.

[61] By contrast, the US trade embargo against Cuba provides a well-known example of a punitive bilateral countermeasure which has repeatedly been widely denounced by UN Member States: see generally US Dept. of the Treasury, www.treasury.gov/resource-center/sanctions/Programs/pages/cuba.aspx; Report of the Secretary-General, UN Doc. A/71/91 (21 July 2016), esp. at 27–59 (Cuba); GA Res. 71/5 (26 Oct. 2016). Further: White (2015). See also Section 4.2 (n. 8) (regarding EU action against Iran).

concerned with the cessation of the wrongful act by the responsible State, as opposed to reparation in a broad sense.[62] Cessation will often be the central issue arising from unlawful conduct. This is especially so for the enforcement of communitarian norms where cessation is frequently requested, notably through the adoption of resolutions by international organizations.[63] As the ILC has explained, unlike reparation, the general function of cessation is to safeguard the continuing validity and effectiveness of the underlying primary rule. Thus the obligation of cessation of the unlawful act 'protects both the interests of the injured State[s] and the interests of the international community as a whole in the preservation of, and reliance on, the rule of law'.[64]

Still, although a right to claim cessation and reparation has been recognized for communitarian norms, involving a measure of progressive development embodied in Article 48(2) ARSIWA,[65] the fact is that it has very rarely been enforced by judicial or quasi-judicial means, especially in relation to claims for reparation. And this is so even where there is a treaty-based institutional mechanism allowing States to take remedial action.[66] Only two such inter-State cases, involving requests for cessation and satisfaction, respectively, have ever been brought before the European Commission and European Court of Human Rights.[67] The *Obligation to Prosecute or Extradite* case before the ICJ involving a claim for cessation of wrongful conduct under the Torture Convention (and belatedly under customary international law) may also be mentioned.[68] As for the inter-State complaint procedure available in many UN human rights treaties

---

[62] ARSIWA Commentary, Art. 49, §8. See also Sicilianos (1990), 60; Alland (1994), 188, 255; YbILC (2000), vol. I, 5, para. 22 (Mr. Crawford).

[63] ARSIWA Commentary, Art. 30, §4; Art. 48, §11.

[64] ARSIWA Commentary, Art. 30, §5. See also Corten (2010a), 545, 548–549.

[65] See e.g. ARSIWA Commentary, Art. 48, §§11–12; *Responsibilities and Obligations of States Sponsoring Persons and Entities with Respect to Activities in the Area*, ITLOS Case No. 17 (Adv. Op., 1 Feb. 2011), para. 180; *Obligation to Prosecute or Extradite*, ICJ Rep. (2012), 422 at 449–450, paras. 68–69. Also: 2005 IDI Krakow Resolution (Art. 2); *Armed Activities (DRC v. Uganda)*, ICJ Rep. (2005), 168 at 347, para. 35 (Sep. Op. Judge Simma).

[66] See Gaja (2010), 962; Simma (2013), 321; Crawford (2013a), 374.

[67] See *'The Greek Case'* (*Denmark, Norway, Sweden and the Netherlands v. Greece*), Report of the European Commission of Human Rights, 12 YbECHR (1969), 1 (cessation); *Denmark v. Turkey*, Friendly Settlement, ECtHR (Application No. 34382/97), Judgment, 5 Apr. 2000, paras. 20, 23 (satisfaction). On *'The Greek Case'* see further Section 4.2.2.

[68] *Obligation to Prosecute or Extradite*, ICJ Rep. (2012), 422 at 428–429, 449–450, paras. 12–14, 68–69. See further Section 2.1.

(e.g. under Article 41 ICCPR), it has never been used[69] – a stillborn baby still awaiting the kiss of life. The compromissory clauses found in many UN human rights treaties (allowing the possibility of referring treaty disputes involving a community interest to the ICJ) have, with rare exception,[70] likewise remained a dead letter. In particular, it seems that the inter-State enforcement mechanism under the ICCPR is in serious need of CPR.[71]

The enforcement of communitarian norms by way of third-party countermeasures has been much more common. From the extensive State practice examined in Chapter 4, it appears that third-party countermeasures have almost always been adopted to ensure cessation of wrongful conduct. With the possible exception of the KAL 007 flight incident,[72] third-party countermeasures have simply not been adopted to obtain any form of reparation. As a member of the ILC, Gaja reached essentially the same conclusion: in most (if not all) cases, States had adopted third-party countermeasures simply to ensure cessation of wrongful conduct. Even if, as a matter of principle, States were entitled to seek reparation, practice seemed to justify the use of third-party countermeasures only in relation to cessation. Thus Gaja suggested that the instrumental function of third-party countermeasures should be limited to cessation.[73] Poland made the same point.[74] For its part, Japan limited itself to observing that practice on bilateral countermeasures was usually limited to claims for cessation.[75] In more general terms, France and the United Kingdom proposed to limit the

---

[69] See 'Human Rights Bodies – Complaints Procedures', Office of the High Commissioner for Human Rights, www.ohchr.org/EN/HRBodies/TBPetitions/Pages/HRTBPetitions.aspx #interstate. Compare *Obligation to Prosecute or Extradite*, ICJ Rep. (2012), 422 at 484, para. 20 (Sep. Op. Judge Skotnikov).

[70] See above n. 68.   [71] See e.g. Henkin (2003), 383.

[72] See Section 4.2.9. During the debate before the Security Council, South Korea demanded that the Soviet Union provide a mixture of compensation, satisfaction and guarantees of non-repetition to all directly injured States. The Soviet Union vetoed a draft resolution (otherwise widely supported) that explicitly recognized the demands for compensation and satisfaction. A number of States therefore adopted third-party countermeasures against the Soviet Union. Since the Soviet action amounted to an instantaneous wrongful act (and in the absence of clear justifying statements), it seems reasonable to assume that those third-party counter-measures were primarily intended to ensure the effective implementation of the demands for reparation embodied in the vetoed draft resolution. For the South Korean demands see UN Doc. S/PV.2470 (2 Sept. 1983), 3, paras. 17–21; and for the vetoed resolution largely adopting those demands, UN Doc. S/15966/Rev.1 (12 Sept. 1983). Also: Alland (1994), 188–189.

[73] YbILC (2000), vol. I, 308, para. 58 (Mr. Gaja). See also ILC Report (2000), UN Doc. A/55/10, 60, para. 370.

[74] UN Docs. A/C.6/55/SR.18, 9, para. 48; A/CN.4/515/Add.2, 18–19 (Poland).

[75] UN Doc. A/CN.4/515, 78 (Japan). Similarly: Sicilianos (1990), 60; Alland (1994), 188.

invocation of responsibility for breaches of communitarian norms to requests for cessation.[76]

Special Rapporteur Crawford agreed that third-party countermeasures were in practice essentially limited to claims for cessation. While sympathetic to a more stringent remedial limitation for third-party countermeasures, Crawford nonetheless decided against it as cessation may be indistinguishable from restitution, for example in cases where the wrongful act had ceased but its consequences continued to exist.[77] The ILC Drafting Committee in 2001 expressly rejected the possibility of limiting the instrumental function of (bilateral) countermeasures to cessation. State practice did not support such a restrictive conception of countermeasures. Moreover, reparation was necessary in situations where damage had already been done[78] The ILC explained that (bilateral) countermeasures taken to ensure reparation must be permissible since any other conclusion would 'immunize' the responsible State from countermeasures if the wrongful act had ceased, irrespective of the seriousness of the breach or its consequences.[79] Article 49(1) ARSIWA provides accordingly. Likewise, it may be recalled from Chapter 3 that Draft Article 54 [2000] (as provisionally adopted by the Drafting Committee based on Special Rapporteur Crawford's proposal)[80] recognized claims for both cessation and reparation on behalf of the injured State or the beneficiaries of the communitarian obligation breached to be enforced by way of third-party countermeasures.[81] However, the ILC's position was ultimately reserved in Article 54 ARSIWA. Thus the question remains as to the precise scope of remedial rights and the modalities of their exercise in case of third-party countermeasures.

As Gaja himself implicitly acknowledged, the fact that States have rarely (if ever) demanded reparation by way of third-party countermeasures does not necessarily mean that they are not entitled to do so.[82] The same could be said for practice on bilateral countermeasures: it

---

[76] UN Docs. A/CN.4/515, 72–73 (United Kingdom); A/CN.4/515/Add.2, 15–16 (France).

[77] YbILC (2000), vol. I, 308, para. 59 (Mr. Crawford). See also ARSIWA Commentary, Art. 30, §§7–8; Corten (2010a), 548. Further: Crawford (2013a), 465–469.

[78] YbILC (2001), vol. I, 111, paras. 50–51 (Chairman of the Drafting Committee, Mr. Tomka). To the same effect: Draft Articles Commentary, Art. 47, §2 (with further references).

[79] ARSIWA Commentary, Art. 49, §8.

[80] Crawford, Third Report, 108, para. 413 (his draft articles 50 A and 50 B); ILC Report (2000), UN Doc. A/55/10, 70.

[81] See Sections 3.2.1.2–3.2.1.3.

[82] YbILC (2000), vol. I, 308, para. 58 (Mr. Gaja). See also Gaja (2010), 962.

likewise demonstrates that States have only rarely made claims for reparation.[83] And yet the entitlement to demand reparation by way of bilateral countermeasures is not in doubt.[84] The rationale for the use of countermeasures may occasionally be directed towards the future, but they are mostly situated in the present.[85] It is significant that almost all cases of third-party countermeasures examined in Chapter 4 refer to situations where the wrongful act was continuing. Indeed third-party countermeasures are most often adopted in response to continuing human rights violations for which cessation is the crucial issue.[86] It is only natural then that the State(s) adopting third-party countermeasures would normally prioritize cessation. However, albeit rare, it seems that claims for reparation are sometimes made. The KAL 007 flight incident[87] provides a rare example of an instantaneous wrongful act in response to which States appear to have demanded reparation by way of third-party countermeasures. The key point is that States may, in principle, freely elect the remedies they wish to pursue without prejudice to their putative legal rights. In short, the existence of a possible entitlement to obtain reparation by way of third-party countermeasures is distinct from its actual exercise in a given case.

As the United Kingdom observed in the Sixth Committee, it must however be admitted that the right for third States to obtain reparation on behalf of the injured State or the beneficiaries of the communitarian obligation breached is 'novel' and still controversial.[88] It is also not entirely clear how such claims for reparation would operate in practice[89] – the KAL 007 flight incident provides little guidance. For its part, the ILC recognized that Article 48(2) ARSIWA involved 'a measure of progressive development', but nevertheless concluded that '[it] is justified since it provides a means of protecting the community or collective interest at stake'.[90] The ILC added that, in the absence of

---

[83] Compare Sicilianos (1990), 60; Alland (1994), 188, 255; UN Doc. A/CN.4/515, 78 (Japan).

[84] Draft Articles Commentary, Art. 47, §2; YbILC (2001), vol. I, 111, paras. 50–51 (Chairman of the Drafting Committee, Mr. Tomka).

[85] Sicilianos (1990), 60–61.   [86] Compare UN Doc. A/CN.4/515, 73 (United Kingdom).

[87] See above n. 72. Also: Gaja (2013), 108 (discussing the establishment of the UNCC and SC Res. 687 (3 Apr. 1991), op. para. 16).

[88] UN Doc. A/CN.4/515, 72–73 (United Kingdom).

[89] Ibid. See also YbILC (2000), vol. I, 192, para. 3 (Mr. Simma).

[90] ARSIWA Commentary, Art. 48, §12. See also to the same effect 2005 IDI Krakow Resolution (Art. 2) (adding the following sentence: 'Restitution should be effected unless materially impossible'). The added sentence was apparently based on the ICJ's advisory opinion in the Wall case: see ICJ Rep. (2004), 136 at 198, para. 153; Gaja (2013), 108–109.

a directly injured State, it would be 'highly desirable' for States to be in a position to claim reparation (notably, restitution).[91] All that can be said with confidence is that third-party countermeasures have in practice effectively been limited to claims for cessation.

By contrast, examples of claims for reparation in the enforcement of communitarian norms – whether by way of judicial proceedings[92] or third-party countermeasures – are extremely rare. Unlike claims for cessation, there is no clearly recognized entitlement to obtain reparation by way of third-party countermeasures. Practice is too limited to reach any firm conclusions. Still, a sound analytical basis, as embodied in Article 48(2)(b) ARSIWA, nevertheless exists to suggest that the instrumental function of third-party countermeasures may develop to also include reparation. Such an entitlement would be especially significant in the context of human rights violations and claims for restitution.[93] In sum, it appears that the instrumental function of third-party countermeasures may be more limited than under the traditional regime applicable to bilateral countermeasures. It is now convenient to consider whether the modalities for the exercise of claims of cessation (and possibly, reparation) by way of third-party countermeasures demonstrate any distinct features.

Special Rapporteur Crawford had proposed to the ILC that, in case of a breach of a communitarian norm involving a directly injured State, claims for cessation and reparation enforced by way of third-party countermeasures could only be adopted with its prior consent. However, in provisionally adopting Draft Article 54 [2000], the Drafting Committee did not fully endorse that proposal. It concluded that, insofar as serious breaches of obligations *erga omnes* involving a directly injured State were concerned, no such consent was required.[94] The relevant practice is sparse and inconclusive. At least in relation to claims for cessation, several Western States adopted third-party

---

[91] ARSIWA Commentary, Art. 48, §12.

[92] It should be noted that the only such claim to date for satisfaction before the ECtHR (above n. 67) was expressly authorized by Article 41 ECHR; as such, its relevance for the position under customary international law is limited.

[93] Compare *Wall* case, ICJ Rep. (2004), 136 at 198, para. 153 (on restitution as a primary form of reparation in remedying serious breaches of communitarian norms); Gaja (2013), 109.

[94] See Crawford, Third Report, 108, para. 413 (his draft articles 50 A and 50 B); YbILC (2000), vol. I, 399, para. 89 (Chairman of the Drafting Committee, Mr. Gaja); and further Section 3.2.1.3.

countermeasures against Argentina and Iraq following specific requests by the United Kingdom and Kuwait, respectively.[95] By contrast, no such requests (perhaps unsurprisingly) were made by the Soviet puppet regimes in Afghanistan or Poland in relation to the adoption of third-party countermeasures by Canada, New Zealand and the United States against the Soviet Union.[96]

In the absence of clear guidance from practice, the key issue here concerns the potential loss of the right to invoke responsibility through waiver; i.e. whether (and if so, to what extent) a directly injured State may validly waive the breach of a communitarian norm and all of its remedial consequences, and thereby bar the adoption of third-party countermeasures. In line with the general principle embodied in Article 45 ARSIWA, the directly injured State, as the individual right-holder, may certainly waive its claim to cessation and/or reparation – this is the principle of disposability.[97] But this does not necessarily mean that its waiver will prevent other States from invoking responsibility, including by way of third-party countermeasures.

As an illustration, can State A, the victim of an armed aggression by State B, having validly waived all its claims to cessation and reparation, bar States C-Z from adopting third-party countermeasures against the aggressor, State B? Article 48(2) ARSIWA suggests that the answer will depend on whether cessation or reparation is claimed. Article 48(2)(b) ARSIWA is authority for the proposition that claims for reparation by way of third-party countermeasures (assuming *arguendo* that this remedial right exists) will not be possible in cases where it has been validly waived by the directly injured State.

By contrast, in line with the basic principle affirmed in Article 48(2)(a) ARSIWA, the situation is different regarding claims for cessation (and assurances and guarantees of non-repetition), in which case, by extension, third-party countermeasures may be adopted irrespective of the

---

[95] Crawford, Third Report, 105, para. 400; ARSIWA Commentary, Art. 54, §§3, 5. In supporting the United States at its request, Western States also adopted several acts of retorsion against Iran in response to the hostage crisis at the US Embassy in Tehran in 1979–1980. The European Parliament and the Council of Ministers also made statements implying a right to resort to third-party countermeasures. See EC Bull. No. 4 (1980), paras. 1.2.6–1.2.9; Crawford, Third Report, 104–105, paras. 394, 400. Further: Frowein (1987), 74–75; Sicilianos (1990), 159–160; Frowein (1994), 416–417; Tams (2005), 226–227; Dawidowicz (2006), 402–403.

[96] See Sections 4.2.6–4.2.7; ARSIWA Commentary, Art. 54, §3.

[97] Tams (2010), 1039; Crawford (2013a), 563–564. For waiver to be valid it must be clear and unequivocal: see ARSIWA Commentary, Art. 45, §5.

wishes of the directly injured State.[98] This is so because a State cannot validly waive a right which it does not hold: *nemo plus dare potest quam ipse habet*. By parity of reasoning, even if a directly injured State decides to waive its own right to invoke State responsibility for the breach of an obligation *erga omnes (partes)*, it cannot prevent other States from claiming cessation – a point repeatedly affirmed by the ILC.[99] At the normative level, this accords with the wider function of cessation[100] and the minimum required to operationalize the enforcement of communitarian norms as part of the construction of a system of 'multilateral public order'[101] expressed in Article 48 ARSIWA.

Finally, in cases where the direct injury is not allocatable to a particular State (notably, human rights violations of nationals of the responsible State), waiver will in reality not be an issue – except in the most unlikely scenario that all States with a right to make claims under Article 48 ARSIWA agree to the waiver.[102] Practice clearly demonstrates that claims for cessation have been enforced by way of third-party countermeasures in the interest of the beneficiaries of the communitarian obligation breached, irrespective of possible waiver or acquiescence by individual States.

6.1.3.2   The Reversibility of Countermeasures

The ICJ affirmed another 'very substantial element'[103] of countermeasures in the *Gabčíkovo Nagymaros Project* case: the principle of reversibility.[104] As the Court suggested, reversibility is an intrinsic element of the instrumental function of countermeasures insofar as it must be possible to revert to a situation of legality after the occasion for taking them has ceased; i.e. once the responsible State has complied with its

---

[98] YbILC (2000), vol. I, 308, para. 58 (Mr. Gaja). Similarly: Villalpando (2005), 337–343; Gaja (2013), 104; Crawford (2013a), 563–565; Palchetti (2014), 1232–1234. See however Tams (2010), 1039–1042. Also: Hillgruber (2006), 289–291.

[99] ARSIWA Commentary, Art. 45, §4; Art. 41, §9; Art. 26, §6. See also UN Doc. A/CN.4/515, 67 (Netherlands), 68 (Republic of Korea); Crawford (2013a), 71. Compare *Gabčíkovo Nagymaros Project* case, ICJ Rep. (1997), 7 at 117–118 (Sep. Op. Judge Weeramantry) (making the same point with respect to estoppel but seemingly overlooking the issue of special injury).

[100] See above n. 64.

[101] YbILC (2000), vol. I, 311, para. 78 (Mr. Brownlie). Also: ILC Report (2000), UN Doc. A/55/10, 60, para. 365.

[102] Tams (2010), 1040; Crawford (2013a), 564.

[103] YbILC (2000), vol. I, 265, para. 68 (Mr. Crawford).

[104] *Gabčíkovo Nagymaros Project* case, ICJ Rep. (1997), 7 at 56, para. 87.

obligations of cessation and reparation.[105] The requirement of reversibility reinforces the notion that countermeasures must have an essentially temporary or remedial character, not a punitive one.[106] Countermeasures are permitted only for as long as the circumstances justifying their use obtain. Once the responsible State has complied with its obligations of cessation and reparation, countermeasures must be terminated forthwith and the performance of the obligation suspended must be resumed.[107] Thus Article 53 ARSIWA provides:

Article 53
Termination of countermeasures
Countermeasures shall be terminated as soon as the responsible State has complied with its obligations under Part Two in relation to the internationally wrongful act.[108]

On first reading, the ILC conveyed the essence of the entitlement to take countermeasures in Draft Article 47 [1996] by the words not to 'comply with one or more of its obligations towards the State which has committed the internationally wrongful act'.[109] On second reading, Special Rapporteur Crawford criticized this wording as it suggested the possibility of a definite termination of an obligation.[110] In Crawford's view, this was an extremely broad formulation which 'seemed to raise a very serious problem', namely, the prospect of punitive or irreversible countermeasures.[111] Crawford strongly supported the principle of

---

[105] See YbILC (2000), vol. I, 265, paras. 68–69 (Mr. Crawford). Further: Kamto (2010), 1174–1175.

[106] Sicilianos (1990), 57; ARSIWA Commentary, Art. 49, §§7, 9.

[107] ARSIWA Commentary, Art. 49, §7; Art. 53, §§1–2.

[108] For the drafting history of the provision see UN Doc. A/CN.4/488, 133 (the French proposal); Crawford, Third Report, 94, 96, paras. 361, 367 (his draft article 50 *bis*); YbILC (2000), vol. I, 400, para. 92 (Chairman of the Drafting Committee, Mr. Gaja); Crawford, Fourth Report, 18, para. 75; YbILC (2001), vol. I, 112, para. 63 (Chairman of the Drafting Committee, Mr. Tomka). For judicial recognition of Article 53 ARSIWA see *United States – Continued Suspension of Obligations in the EC – Hormones Dispute*, WT/DS320/AB/R, Report of the Appellate Body, 16 Oct. 2008, para. 382; *Canada – Continued Suspension of Obligations in the EC – Hormones Dispute*, WT/DS321/AB/R, Report of the Appellate Body, 16 Oct. 2008, para. 382. See already *Naulilaa (Responsibility of Germany for damage caused in the Portuguese colonies in the south of Africa) (Portugal/Germany)* (1928), RIAA, vol. II, 1011 at 1026; 1934 IDI Paris Resolution (Art. 6(6)).

[109] For the drafting history on first reading see Riphagen, Fourth Report, 17, paras. 92–94; Riphagen, Sixth Report, 10–11; Arangio-Ruiz, Fourth Report, 23, para. 52; YbILC (1993), vol. I, 141, para. 5 (Chairman of the Drafting Committee, Mr. Mikulka); Draft Articles Commentary, Art. 47, §3. Compare Draft Articles Commentary, Art. 30, §7.

[110] YbILC (2000), vol. I, 265, para. 67 (Mr. Crawford).

[111] Ibid.; Crawford, Third Report, 87–88, paras. 326, 331. See however Draft Articles Commentary, Art. 47, §2 (excluding punitive countermeasures).

reversibility but stressed that it was not absolute. Although a counter-measure may be reversible (assets can be unfrozen, civil aviation can be resumed, etc.), its effects will rarely be entirely reversible, since consequential losses will normally have been suffered by the target State and third parties during the period in which the countermeasure was in force.[112] A balance had to be struck.

Crawford observed that an absolute application of the principle of reversibility would effectively preclude the use of countermeasures in many cases. However, irreversible damage done to the target State would 'amount to punishment [which was] not a countermeasure as conceived in the Draft articles'.[113] Crawford proposed a solution inspired by Article 72(2) VCLT: a countermeasure should not 'preclude the resumption of performance' of the obligation to the responsible State.[114] The ILC Drafting Committee in 2000 qualified Crawford's proposal by adding the proviso that countermeasures should only 'as far as possible' have reversible effects.[115] In 2001, influenced by the debate in the ILC, the Drafting Committee proposed that the temporary and remedial nature of countermeasures should instead be emphasized by the notion that they entailed 'the non-performance for the time being of international obligations'.[116] Article 49 ARSIWA in relevant part accordingly provides that

2. Countermeasures are limited to the non-performance for the time being of international obligations of the State taking the measures towards the responsible State.
3. Countermeasures shall, as far as possible, be taken in such a way as to permit the resumption of performance of the obligations in question.[117]

Practice confirms that third-party countermeasures, such as asset freezes and various suspensions of treaty rights, have typically involved actions that could relatively easily be reversed.[118] There is also no

---

[112] Crawford, Third Report, 88, para. 330 (providing the example of an airline forced into liquidation as a result of the suspension of an air services agreement).

[113] Ibid., 88, 96, paras. 331, 367 (for Crawford's draft article 47).   [114] Ibid., 88, para. 331.

[115] YbILC (2000), vol. I, 396–397, paras. 64–65 (Chairman of the Drafting Committee, Mr. Gaja).

[116] YbILC (2001), vol. I, 111, paras. 52–53 (Chairman of the Drafting Committee, Mr. Tomka).

[117] See ARSIWA Commentary, Art. 49, §§6, 7 and 9.

[118] Similarly: YbILC (2000), vol. I, 265, para. 71 (Mr. Crawford). For an example of a potentially irreversible act, the suspension of environmental obligations may be mentioned: see *Gabčíkovo Nagymaros Project* case, ICJ Rep. (1997), 7 at 134, para. 52 (Sep. Op. Judge Bedjaoui); Boisson de Chazournes (2010), 1212.

indication in practice that third-party countermeasures have remained in force once the wrongful act has ceased. In fact, expiry or review clauses are a common feature of practice providing for the repeal of third-party countermeasures once their objectives have been met.[119]

6.2   Obligations Not Affected by Countermeasures

Countermeasures by definition involve the suspension of performance of an international obligation. A State entitled to take countermeasures has broad discretion in deciding which obligation to suspend. It would be 'absurd' however if a State could choose to suspend any obligation.[120] Indeed, as the ILC explains, 'considerations of good order and humanity' strongly militate in favour of some limitation on the types of obligations that may be suspended by way of countermeasures.[121] The arbitral tribunal in the *Naulilaa* case emphasized that the use of countermeasures was 'limited by the requirements of humanity and the rules of good faith applicable in relations between States'.[122] During the debate in the Sixth Committee, States widely recognized that 'the interests of the international community required that certain categories of

---

[119] See e.g. European Commission, EU Guidelines on Implementation and Evaluation of Restrictive Measures (2008), 6, http://eeas.europa.eu/cfsp/sanctions/docs/index_en.pdf ('Another fundamental element of EU restrictive measures is either an expiry or a review clause, in order to ensure that restrictive measures are repealed or adapted in response to developments. All EU autonomous measures are kept under continual review'); Council of the European Union, Basic Principles on the Use of Restrictive Measures (Sanctions) (2004), para. 9, http://register.consilium.europa.eu/doc/srv?l=EN&f=ST%2010198% 202004%20REV%201 ('In all cases, our objectives should be clearly defined in the enabling legal instruments. Sanctions should be regularly reviewed, in order to ensure they are contributing to their stated objectives. Sanctions should be lifted according to their objectives being met'). Compare GA Res. 60/1 (16 Sept. 2005) (2005 World Summit Outcome), para. 107 ('Sanctions should be implemented and monitored effectively with clear benchmarks and should be periodically reviewed, as appropriate, and remain for as limited a period as necessary to achieve their objectives and should be terminated once the objectives have been achieved').

[120] Crawford (2013a), 688.

[121] ARSIWA Commentary, Introductory Commentary to Chapter II of Part Three, §5. See also Crawford, Third Report, 87, para. 328.

[122] *Naulilaa (Responsibility of Germany for damage caused in the Portuguese colonies in the south of Africa) (Portugal/Germany)* (1928), RIAA, vol. II, 1011 at 1026. See also 1934 IDI Paris Resolution (Art. 6(4)) (countermeasures must not involve 'any harsh measure which would be contrary to the laws of humanity or the demands of the public conscience'); *Prosecutor v. Kupreškić*, ICTY Case No. IT-95-16-T, Judgment, 14 Jan. 2000, para. 528 ('barbarous means of seeking compliance with international law' are unlawful).

countermeasures be prohibited'.[123] However, beyond references to 'the requirements of humanity' or 'the interests of the international community', these formulas do not provide a clear basis for identifying the obligations whose performance may not be suspended by way of countermeasures.

It is certainly clear on the basis of Article 26 ARSIWA that countermeasures cannot derogate from peremptory norms. As the ILC explains, 'it is obvious that a peremptory norm, not subject to derogation as between two States even by treaty, cannot be derogated from by unilateral action in the form of countermeasures'.[124] Evidently 'a genocide cannot justify a counter-genocide'.[125] While Article 50 ARSIWA excludes peremptory norms, it also provides that countermeasures shall not affect certain other obligations whose peremptory status is less clear. The basis for the exclusion of these obligations accordingly requires clarification. For his part, Special Rapporteur Crawford was 'particularly unhappy' with the ILC's treatment of prohibited countermeasures: the 'essential problem' was that it appeared to embody 'no clear principle'.[126] This critique finds support in the list of excluded countermeasures in Article 50 ARSIWA, which provides:

Article 50
Obligations not affected by countermeasures[127]
1. Countermeasures shall not affect:
   (a) the obligation to refrain from the threat or use of force as embodied in the UN Charter;
   (b) obligations for the protection of fundamental human rights;

---

[123] Topical Summary of Government Comments in the Sixth Committee, UN Doc. A/CN.4/496 (1999), 18, para. 121; UN Doc. A/CN.4/488, 128 (Czech Republic and Ireland). Also: Ago, Eighth Report, 39, para. 80; Draft Articles Commentary, Art. 30, §§4–5.

[124] ARSIWA Commentary, Art. 50, §9; Crawford, Third Report, 90, para. 342. See already Gaja (1981), 297.

[125] ARSIWA Commentary, Art. 26, §4.

[126] YbILC (2001), vol. I, 6, para. 36 (Mr. Crawford); Crawford, Fourth Report, 16, para. 64. Similarly: YbILC (2001), vol. I, 113, para. 70 (Mr. Pellet). A similar absence of principle in terms of what amounts to permissible responses to treaty breaches by way of suspension or termination also underpins Article 60 VCLT: see Simma and Tams (2011), 1369, 1377.

[127] For criticism of the term 'prohibited countermeasures', as adopted in Draft Article 50 [1996], see e.g. YbILC (2000), vol. I, 275, para. 81 (Mr. Simma) (preferring the term 'prohibited effects of countermeasures'), 281, para. 38 (Mr. Kamto) (noting the 'logical impossibility' of prohibited countermeasures which 'by definition ... could not be prohibited'), 288, para. 45 (Mr. Pambou-Tchivounda) (the term 'contained a contradiction because, once a countermeasure has been authorized, it could not be prohibited').

    (c) obligations of a humanitarian character prohibiting reprisals;

    (d) other obligations under peremptory norms of general international law.

2. A State taking countermeasures is not relieved from fulfilling its obligations:

    (a) under any dispute settlement procedure applicable between it and the responsible State;

    (b) to respect the inviolability of diplomatic or consular agents, premises, archives and documents.

The ILC explains with respect to Article 50(1) ARSIWA that 'by reason of their character ... [these obligations] are sacrosanct'.[128] Irrespective of their peremptory status, the ILC considered it essential to specify that these sacrosanct obligations were excluded in view of their importance.[129] A separate justification was provided for the excluded obligations in Article 50(2) ARSIWA, which concern 'not so much the substantive character of the obligation[s] but [their] function in relation to the resolution of the dispute between the parties which has given rise to the threat or use of countermeasures'.[130]

There is a simple explanation for the seemingly unprincipled approach in Article 50 ARSIWA: beyond the unifying principle of peremptory norms,[131] it was not possible in the ILC and Sixth Committee to find agreement on a stronger analytical basis.[132] The Drafting Committee in 2001 stated that Article 50 ARSIWA 'had been drafted with a view to State practice, and accordingly it contained specific provisions, not general principles that could be subjected to different interpretations by practitioners or academics'.[133] Thus the list of exclusions in that provision was adopted without the ILC pronouncing itself on the peremptory status of each individual obligation.[134] A general category of peremptory

---

[128] ARSIWA Commentary, Art. 50, §§1–2.   [129] Ibid.   [130] Ibid., §§2, 11 and 15.

[131] Notwithstanding agreement on this basic point of principle, the indeterminacy of peremptory norms (especially regarding the lack of consensus on the human rights standard) was controversial: see e.g. Crawford, Second Report, 77, para. 312; Crawford, Third Report, 85–86, 90, paras. 317–318, 342; UN Docs. A/CN.4/488, 133 (France, Ireland and the United States); A/CN.4/515, 78 (United Kingdom), 79 (United States). See further Section 5.2.6; and below Section 6.2.1.2.

[132] Crawford (2013a), 690.

[133] YbILC (2001), vol. I, 117, para. 26 (Chairman of the Drafting Committee, Mr. Tomka). Compare YbILC (2000), vol. I, 397, para. 75 (Chairman of the Drafting Committee, Mr. Gaja).

[134] YbILC (2001), vol. I, 117, para. 26 (Chairman of the Drafting Committee, Mr. Tomka). For a similar approach on first reading see Draft Articles Commentary, Art. 50, §1. Compare the commentary to what became Article 53 VCLT: YbILC (1966), vol. II, 248 (deciding against the inclusion of a general list of *jus cogens* norms).

norms was nevertheless included in Article 50(1)(d) ARSIWA in order to safeguard possible future developments and strengthen the basic principle enshrined in Article 26 ARSIWA that countermeasures derogating from such norms were unlawful *per se*.[135] Finally, the ILC stressed in uncontroversial terms that the use of countermeasures may also be excluded by *lex specialis* based on normal principles of treaty interpretation.[136]

Although the ILC did not elaborate a general theory of prohibited countermeasures, a key principle can arguably be identified to determine whether a given obligation is capable of being suspended by way of countermeasures: the principle of reciprocity. In line with ILC Special Rapporteur Fitzmaurice's influential structural analysis of obligations embodied in Article 60 VCLT (at least with respect to obligations deriving from humanitarian law)[137] it seems clear as a matter of principle that countermeasures can only be taken in relation to reciprocal or synallagmatic obligations. Put differently, as Gaja suggested on second reading, only a bilateralizable obligation capable of suspension can be the subject of a countermeasure.[138] It even seems possible to explain Article 50 ARSIWA on that basis.[139] In fact, the ILC recognized in Article 50(2)(a) ARSIWA the 'well-established principle', consonant with the principle of *lex specialis*, that dispute settlement provisions in a treaty are not

---

[135] Crawford, Third Report, 90, para. 342; YbILC (2000), vol. I, 397, paras. 73, 75 (Chairman of the Drafting Committee, Mr. Gaja); YbILC (2001), vol. I, 111, para. 55 (Chairman of the Drafting Committee, Mr. Tomka); ARSIWA Commentary, Art. 40, §§4–6; Art. 50, §9. A similar position had been adopted on first reading: see YbILC (1993), vol. I, 145, para. 33 (Chairman of the Drafting Committee, Mr. Mikulka); Draft Articles Commentary, Art. 50, §§1, 26.

[136] ARSIWA Commentary, Introductory Commentary to Chapter II of Part Three, §9; Art. 50, §10 (with further references); Art. 55, §§1, 4. See also Draft Articles Commentary, Art. 37, §§1–3; Crawford, Third Report, 90–91, para. 343. Further: Simma and Pulkowski (2010), 139. As an example, third-party countermeasures may be excluded under treaties (such as the ECHR) to the extent that they have their own effective enforcement mechanisms: see further Tams (2005), 120–128, 252–299 (esp. at 286–299); Simma and Pulkowski (2010), 139; and Section 2.1.4.

[137] It has been noted that Article 60 VCLT 'depart[s]' from Fitzmaurice's 'logic of reciprocity' by seemingly allowing suspension and termination of those absolute (non-reciprocal) obligations not covered by its fifth paragraph: see Simma and Tams (2011), 1369, 1377–1378. Still, Fitzmaurice's analysis remains normatively desirable and analytically sound. Further: Fitzmaurice, Fourth Report, 46 (his draft article 18(3)(e) excluding countermeasures in cases of absolute or non-reciprocal obligations).

[138] YbILC (2000), vol. I, 279, para. 34 (Mr. Gaja). See also ibid., 295, para. 34 (Mr. Economides).

[139] To the same effect: YbILC (2000), vol. I, 279, para. 22 (Mr. Crawford).

capable of suspension.[140] The ILC recognized the same basic point in Article 50(2)(b) ARSIWA in relation to aspects of diplomatic and consular law.[141]

Article 50(1) ARSIWA concerns integral obligations, i.e. obligations *erga omnes (partes)*, whose performance is not undertaken on a *quid pro quo* basis. It was for this reason that the ICJ in the *Bosnian Genocide* case observed that 'in no case could one breach of the [Genocide] Convention serve as an excuse for another'.[142] Moreover, the structure of performance of such communitarian obligations is 'legally indivisible' in the sense that they require an integral application by each and every State with respect to all the others.[143] A violation of an integral obligation affects the legal interests of all States to which the infringed norm applies.

These considerations provided the rationale for Special Rapporteur Arangio-Ruiz's proposal to explicitly prohibit countermeasures in violation of obligations *erga omnes (partes)*.[144] On second reading, Gaja insisted (with good reason) that any other conclusion would be 'strange'.[145] Gaja's conclusion was clear: there should be a general rule prohibiting countermeasures in such circumstances.[146] Only 'bilateral obligations', i.e. obligations owed solely to the responsible State, could be breached by way of countermeasures.[147] Special Rapporteur Crawford seemed to agree: 'Possibly the Commission should bite the bullet and say plainly that countermeasures must ... relate to obligations only as between the injured State and the target State'.[148] Already on first reading, however, the ILC had rejected Arangio-Ruiz's proposal as it was viewed as 'too sweeping in an interdependent world where States

---

[140] ARSIWA Commentary, Art. 50, §13. See further below Section 6.2.1.4.
[141] ARSIWA Commentary, Art. 50, §15. See also YbILC (2000), vol. I, 276, para. 84 (Mr. Tomka). Compare YbILC (1985), vol. I, 116–117, para. 7 (Mr. Sinclair). See further below Section 6.2.1.5.
[142] *Application of the Convention on the Prevention and Punishment of the Crime of Genocide*, Counter-claims, Order of 17 Dec. 1997, ICJ Rep. (1997), 243 at 258, para. 35.
[143] Arangio-Ruiz, Fourth Report, 34, para. 92.
[144] Ibid., 34–35, paras. 92–93, 96 (his draft article 14(1)(b)(iv)); Draft Articles Commentary, Art. 47, §7. See also Riphagen, Fifth Report, 3–4; Riphagen, Sixth Report, 12–13 (his draft article 11(1)).
[145] YbILC (2000), vol. I, 279, para. 19 (Mr. Gaja).
[146] Ibid. See already Gaja (1981), 297; and Gaja (1989), 156.
[147] YbILC (2000), vol. I, 279, para. 24 (Mr. Gaja).
[148] Ibid., 299, paras. 73–74 (Mr. Crawford). Compare Crawford, Third Report, 96, para. 367 (his draft article 50(b)).

were increasingly bound by multilateral obligations'.[149] The ILC did not revisit the issue on second reading. Still, the proposal remains both normatively desirable and analytically sound.[150] It is also consistent with State practice, which has invariably been limited to the suspension of reciprocal obligations. In sum, it appears that obligations *erga omnes (partes)* may not be suspended by way of countermeasures. Based on a similar rationale, obligations requiring integral performance within the meaning of Article 42(b)(ii) ARSIWA (e.g. disarmament obligations) would also be excluded.[151]

Two other non-reciprocal obligations that seemingly cannot be suspended by way of countermeasures should also be mentioned. During the ILC debate, Special Rapporteur Crawford proposed that the obligation to respect the territorial integrity of a State was a 'permanent attribute of the State and is not subject to measures of suspension'.[152] The same applied to the principle of non-intervention.[153] Thus Crawford's draft article 50(a) provided that countermeasures must not 'endanger the territorial integrity or amount to intervention in the domestic jurisdiction of the responsible State'.[154] There is some support for these exclusions in resolutions adopted by the UN General Assembly.[155]

---

[149] YbILC (1993), vol. I, 141, para. 8 (Chairman of the Drafting Committee, Mr. Mikulka). The ILC explained (at ibid.) that the wrongfulness of countermeasures in violation of obligations *erga omnes (partes)* was not precluded as against third States. In other words, the *Cysne* principle applied and 'served as an invitation to the injured State to pause before resorting to such measures and to take such precautionary steps as consulting with the third States concerned, weighing the consequences of alternative courses of action and ascertaining that no other choice was available on account of an instant overwhelming necessity'.

[150] See e.g. Gaja (1981), 297; Lattanzi (1983), 314; YbILC (2000), vol. I, 270, para. 31 (Mr. Simma); Borelli and Olleson (2010), 1178–1182; Leben (2010), 1199–1201; Boisson de Chazournes (2010), 1212–1213.

[151] For an explicit proposal to this effect see Riphagen, Sixth Report, 12 (his draft article 11(1)(a)). Also: Schachter (1982), 177; Arangio-Ruiz, Fourth Report, 34–35, paras. 94–96 (his draft article 14(1)(iv)).

[152] Crawford, Third Report, 83–84, 93, paras. 312(b), 352. To similar effect: UN Doc. A/C.6/55/SR.18, 2, para. 4 (Algeria).

[153] Crawford, Third Report, 93, para. 354.

[154] Ibid., 96, para. 367 (his draft article 50(a)). Also: YbILC (2000), vol. I, 274, para. 66 (Mr. Pellet). See however Talmon (2004), 148–153, 163–167 (suggesting that such obligations can, in principle, be suspended by way of third-party countermeasures); and to the same effect YbILC (1992), vol. I, 190, para. 36 (Mr. Arangio-Ruiz).

[155] See notably, Declaration on Principles of International Law concerning Friendly Relations and Cooperation among States in accordance with the Charter of the United Nations, GA Res. 2625 (XXV) (24 Oct. 1970) (Principles 3 and 6(d)); Declaration on the Inadmissibility of Intervention and Interference in the Internal Affairs of States, GA Res.

The above two exclusions – which it should be stressed address real concerns, especially among developing States[156] – were proposed by Crawford as a way of disaggregating the key elements of the otherwise elusive (and rather ill-conceived) notion of 'economic coercion'.[157] On first reading, based on a proposal by Special Rapporteur Arangio-Ruiz, the ILC had adopted Draft Article 50(b) [1996] which provided that an injured State could not resort by way of countermeasures to 'extreme economic or political coercion designed to endanger the territorial integrity or political independence of the State which has committed the internationally wrongful act'.[158] In practice, target States frequently protest that the use of third-party countermeasures against them violates the principle of non-intervention and (albeit to a somewhat lesser extent) amount to a form of 'economic coercion'.[159] But these protests – in response to widely acknowledged serious breaches of communitarian norms – are largely without merit. As Special Rapporteur Crawford explained:

> Evidently, whether that State [i.e. the responsible State] complies with its international obligations of cessation and reparation is not a matter of its domestic jurisdiction, but countermeasures must not be taken as an excuse to intervene in other issues internal to the responsible State, distinct from the question of its compliance with its international obligations; such issues continue to be protected by the principle of domestic jurisdiction.[160]

36/103 (9 Dec. 1981) (Principle II (esp. (b) and (k)). Generally: Draft Declaration on Rights and Duties of States, GA Res. 375 (IV) (6 Dec. 1949).

[156] The matter has been debated for several decades in the UN General Assembly under the heading 'Unilateral economic measures as a means of political and economic coercion against developing countries': see e.g. Report of the Secretary-General, UN Doc. A/68/218 (29 July 2013); GA Res. 70/185 (22 Dec. 2015). Also: Crawford, Third Report, 93, para. 354; Topical Summary of Government Comments in the Sixth Committee, UN Doc. A/CN.4/513 (2000), 30–31, para. 160.

[157] Crawford, Third Report, 92–93, paras. 352–354. See also Boisson de Chazournes (2010), 1209–1211 (with further references).

[158] This proposed exclusion (which was ultimately not adopted in Article 50 ARSIWA) generated a lot of debate in the ILC and strongly divided opinion among States. See Arangio-Ruiz, Third Report, 31–32, paras. 101–102; Arangio-Ruiz, Fourth Report, 28–30, paras. 70–77 (his draft article 14(2)); Draft Articles Commentary, Art. 50, §§ 5–12; Crawford, Third Report, 83–85, 92–93, 96, paras. 312(b), 315, 352–354, 367 (for his draft article 50(a)); ILC Report (2000), UN Doc. A/55/10, 55, para. 325; YbILC (2000), vol. I, 397, para. 70 (Chairman of the Drafting Committee, Mr. Gaja). For a brief assessment see Leben (2010), 1203–1204; Boisson de Chazournes (2010), 1209–1211.

[159] See e.g. UN Docs. S/PV.3692 (28 Aug. 1996), 5 (Burundi) (discussed in Section 4.2.13); S/2012/242 (Belarus) (discussed in Section 4.2.18). Also: UN Doc. S/2008/199 (Cuba on behalf of the Non-Aligned Movement).

[160] Crawford, Third Report, 93, para. 354. See also 1989 IDI Santiago de Compostela Resolution (Art. 2) ('A State acting in breach of its obligations in the sphere of human

This must surely be correct.

Crawford's draft article 50(a) finds support in the *Corfu Channel* case in which the ICJ held that such countermeasures (especially if forcible) 'cannot . . . find a place in international law'.[161] The ICJ stated 'with the utmost emphasis'[162] in this context that 'respect for territorial sovereignty is an essential foundation of international relations'.[163] In the same case, the ICJ also famously recalled an ignominious past in which such (forcible) countermeasures had led to 'most serious abuses'.[164] For its part, the ILC observed on first reading that countermeasures of the kind discussed here 'may have consequences as serious as those arising from the use of armed force'.[165] With few possible exceptions,[166] modern practice confirms that the obligations related to non-intervention and respect for territorial integrity have not been suspended by way of (third-party) countermeasures. They should be added to the list of obligations excluded from the operation of countermeasures.[167]

---

rights cannot evade its international responsibility by claiming that such matters are essentially within its domestic jurisdiction').

[161] *Corfu Channel*, ICJ Rep. (1949), 4 at 35. See also *Nicaragua* case, ICJ Rep. (1986), 14 at 106, para. 202; and for the (doubtful) suggestion that the principle of non-intervention qualifies as a peremptory norm see ibid., 199 (Sep. Op. Judge Sette-Camara).

[162] Waldock (1962), 240.

[163] *Corfu Channel*, ICJ Rep. (1949), 4 at 35. In the *Gabčíkovo Nagymaros Project* case (ICJ Rep. (1997), 7), Hungary argued that ' . . . as a result of the diversion [of the Danube], the internationally agreed character of the border line of the two countries has been unilaterally modified. This blow to Hungary's territorial jurisdiction is contrary to the substantive rules limiting the use of countermeasures'. See ibid., Hungary's Memorial, vol. I (2 May 1994), 241, para. 7.115. The ICJ did not pronounce itself on this issue instead holding that the unilateral diversion of the Danube amounted to a disproportionate countermeasure: see further below Section 6.3.

[164] *Corfu Channel*, ICJ Rep. (1949), 4 at 35.

[165] Draft Articles Commentary, Art. 50, §5. Also: Arangio-Ruiz, Fourth Report, 35, para. 96 (his draft article 14(2), which assimilated the use of force and economic coercion). It may be recalled that a Brazilian proposal to prohibit economic coercion under Article 2(4) UNC was explicitly rejected at the San Francisco Conference: see Draft Articles Commentary, Art. 50, §§6–7; Randelzhofer (2002), 118 MN 18 (both with further references).

[166] See Tams (2005), 211–213, 236; Sicilianos (2010), 1147–1148 (qualifying G77 States' supply of arms and other materials in support of struggles for national liberation and self-determination during the Cold War as third-party countermeasures).

[167] In any event, countermeasures taken in violation of the basic principles of territorial integrity and non-intervention would likely be deemed disproportionate and unlawful on that basis: see e.g. YbILC (1992), vol. I, 153, para. 22 (Mr. Bowett); Topical Summary of Government Comments in the Sixth Committee, UN Doc. A/CN.4/513 (2000), 30, para. 160. For example, a boundary treaty (or a treaty involving cession of territory) could presumably not be suspended by way of countermeasures: see e.g. YbILC (1992),

6.2.1   Excluded Obligations under Article 50 ARSIWA

Leaving aside the general exclusion of peremptory norms (already discussed above), the following subsections will in turn assess each of the exclusions in Article 50 ARSIWA, namely: the obligation to refrain from the threat or use of force (6.2.1.1); obligations for the protection of fundamental human rights (6.2.1.2); obligations of a humanitarian character prohibiting reprisals (6.2.1.3); the separability of dispute settlement provisions (6.2.1.4); and obligations safeguarding diplomatic and consular inviolability (6.2.1.5).

6.2.1.1   The Obligation to Refrain from the Threat or Use of Force

The exclusion of forcible countermeasures in Article 50(1)(a) ARSIWA is firmly established. This is hardly surprising as the primary rules embodied in the UN Charter relating to the use of force are widely recognized as peremptory norms.[168] There is considerable authority in support of a prohibition of forcible countermeasures. In 1949, the ICJ affirmed this prohibition with 'vigour and clarity'[169] in the *Corfu Channel* case.[170] In that case, the United Kingdom attempted to justify 'Operation Retail' – a Royal Navy operation designed to secure evidence

---

vol. I, 190, paras. 32–33 (Messrs. Al-Khasawneh and Arangio-Ruiz); UN Doc. A/CN.4/ 515, 81 (Spain). Compare *Construction of a Road in Costa Rica along the San Juan River (Nicaragua v. Costa Rica)*, ICJ, Judgment, 16 Dec. 2015, Costa Rica's Counter-Memorial, vol. I (19 Dec. 2013), 135–142, paras. 6.15–6.26 (denying that Nicaragua was entitled to suspend its right of navigation – closely linked with a territorial settlement in a treaty of limits – on the San Juan river as a lawful countermeasure). Also: Akande and Gillard (2016), 55, para. 156 (humanitarian relief operations conducted by States or international organizations without the consent of the territorial State may only 'in the most extreme cases' be justified by way of (third-party) countermeasures). On proportionality see further below Section 6.3.

[168] See e.g. §§1 and 3 of the commentary to what became Article 53 VCLT, YbILC (1966), vol. II, 247–248; YbILC (1993), vol. I, 145, para. 33 (Chairman of the Drafting Committee, Mr. Mikulka); Draft Articles Commentary, Art. 50, §3; ARSIWA Commentary, Art. 40, §4 (with further references). For judicial support see *Nicaragua* case, ICJ Rep. (1986), 14 at 100–101, 127, 153 (Sep. Op. President Nagendra Singh), 199 (Sep. Op. Judge Sette-Camara); *Oil Platforms*, ICJ Rep. (2003), 161 at 269 (Diss. Op. Judge Al-Khasawneh), 291 (Diss. Op. Judge Elaraby), 327–328, 329–330 (Sep. Op. Judge Simma,); *Wall* case, ICJ Rep. (2004), 136 at 254 (Sep. Op. Judge Elaraby); *Armed Activities (DRC v. Uganda)*, ICJ Rep. (2005), 168 at 223–227. Further: Leben (2010), 1197; Crawford (2013a), 690–691; Darcy (2015), 879.

[169] *Oil Platforms*, ICJ Rep. (2003), 161 at 327 (Sep. Op. Judge Simma).

[170] *Corfu Channel*, ICJ Rep. (1949), 4.

of minelaying in Albanian territorial waters in order to submit it to the ICJ – as a forcible countermeasure:

> The Court cannot accept such a line of defence. The Court can only regard the alleged right of intervention as the manifestation of a policy of force, such as has, in the past, given rise to most serious abuses and such as cannot, whatever be the present defects in international organization, find a place in international law. Intervention is perhaps still less admissible in the particular form it would take here; for, from the nature of things, it would be reserved for the most powerful States, and might easily lead to perverting the administration of international justice itself.[171]

Since the 1950s, the UN Security Council has repeatedly affirmed the prohibition of forcible countermeasures.[172] In 1970, the UN General Assembly spelled out the prohibition in the Friendly Relations Declaration, which proclaimed that 'States have a duty to refrain from acts of reprisal involving the use of force'.[173]

In 1978, the *Air Services* tribunal stated:

> If a situation arises which, in one State's view, results in the violation of an international obligation by another State, the first State is entitled, within the limits set by the general rules of international law pertaining to the use of armed force, to affirm its rights through 'counter-measures'.[174]

In 1986, the ICJ explained in the *Nicaragua* case that '[w]hile an armed attack would give rise to an entitlement of collective self-defence, a use of force of a lesser degree cannot ... produce any entitlement to take collective counter-measures involving the use of force'.[175] In 1996, the ICJ in *Nuclear Weapons* likewise observed that 'armed reprisals in time of peace ... are considered to be unlawful'.[176] It was on the basis of these

---

[171] Ibid., 35.

[172] See ARSIWA Commentary, Art. 50, §5 (n. 758) which refers to the following examples: SC Res. 111 (19 Jan. 1956); SC Res. 171 (9 Apr. 1962); SC Res. 188 (9 Apr. 1964); SC Res. 316 (26 June 1972); SC Res. 332 (21 Apr. 1973); SC Res. 573 (4 Oct. 1985); and SC Res. 1322 (7 Oct. 2000). Also: Corten (2010b), 234–236. The prohibition of forcible counter-measures was also affirmed in the early work of the ILC: see already Fitzmaurice, Fourth Report, 67–68, paras. 85–86(a) (discussing his draft article 18 on reprisals).

[173] Declaration on Principles of International Law concerning Friendly Relations and Cooperation among States in accordance with the Charter of the United Nations, GA Res. 2625 (XXV) (24 Oct. 1970), Principle 1, §6. See also *Nicaragua* case, ICJ Rep. (1986), 14 at 101, para. 191 (for recognition of the resolution as customary law); and Draft Articles Commentary, Art. 30, §10; Art. 50, §2; ARSIWA Commentary, Art. 50, §5.

[174] *US-France Air Services Agreement* (1978), RIAA, vol. XVIII, 417 at 443, para. 81.

[175] *Nicaragua* case, ICJ Rep. (1986), 14 at 127, para. 249. See also ARSIWA Commentary, Art. 50, §5 (n. 757); and further Section 2.1.4.

[176] *Legality of the Threat or Use of Nuclear Weapons*, ICJ Rep. (1996), 226 at 246, para. 46.

authorities that the ILC in 2001 adopted the prohibition in Article 50(1)(a) ARSIWA, which excludes 'the obligation to refrain from the threat or use of force as embodied in the UN Charter'.[177]

Notwithstanding the unequivocal prohibition of forcible countermeasures, it may be recalled from Chapter 3 that many members of the ILC and the Sixth Committee still opposed third-party countermeasures. Based on the worrying precedent of NATO's intervention in Kosovo, they feared that recognition of third-party countermeasures would endanger the UN collective security system and add a new and dangerous category of justification that might eventually extend to the use of force (notably in the form of unilateral humanitarian intervention).[178] For this risk to actually materialize, it would be necessary as a bare minimum to demonstrate that States have attempted to justify their occasional resort to forcible unilateral coercive measures on humanitarian grounds by reference to the rationale of third-party countermeasures as a legal category. This would require a demonstration that States have primarily sought to ensure a return to legality rather than act in a protective manner in order to 'prevent an overwhelming humanitarian catastrophe . . . and save lives'.[179] But there is simply no such indication in practice: States have not attempted to justify their use of forcible unilateral coercive measures on humanitarian grounds by reference to third-party countermeasures. To the extent that such action is justified in legal (as distinct from political and moral) terms, it is done by reference to the primary norms regulating the use of force embodied in the UN Charter.

In reality, States make a clear distinction between forcible humanitarian intervention and non-forcible third-party countermeasures in response to grave humanitarian crises. The rather curious statements made by the United Kingdom to justify its actions in Kosovo underline this point: forcible humanitarian intervention was 'legally justifiable' as

---

[177] For a summary of the drafting history see Ago, Eighth Report, 42, para. 89; Draft Articles Commentary, Art. 30, §10; Riphagen, Fourth Report, 15, para. 81; Riphagen, Fifth Report, 4 (his draft article 12(b)); Arangio-Ruiz, Third Report, 29–32, paras. 97–102; Arangio-Ruiz, Fourth Report, 23–28, 35, paras. 58–69, 96 (his draft article 14(1)(a)); YbILC (1993), vol. I, 143–144, para. 26 (Chairman of the Drafting Committee, Mr. Mikulka); Draft Articles Commentary, Art. 50, §§2–4; Crawford, Third Report, 89, 96, paras. 335–336, 367 (his draft article 47 bis); YbILC (2000), vol. I, 397, para. 70 (Chairman of the Drafting Committee, Mr. Gaja); ARSIWA Commentary, Art. 50, §§4–5.

[178] See generally Sections 3.2.1.3(i)–(ii).

[179] UN Doc. S/PV.3988 (23 March 1999), 12 (United Kingdom).

a protective measure to 'save lives' but non-forcible third-party counter-measures – as a law enforcement action – were merely permissible on 'political and moral grounds'.[180] States use non-forcible third-party countermeasures cautiously and are remarkably reluctant to openly justify their use in legal terms. *A fortiori*, it seems that States would be extremely reluctant (and rightly so)[181] to rely on third-party counter-measures as justification for unilateral forcible measures on humanitar-ian or other grounds.[182]

This impression is reinforced by the United Kingdom's explicit reaffirmation in 2013 of the legality of forcible humanitarian interven-tion against Syria – following a large-scale chemical weapons attack on its civilian population – and its concurrent use of non-forcible third-party countermeasures against that country based on a distinct rationale.[183] In other words, the United Kingdom did not seek to justify a possible armed intervention against Syria as a forcible third-party countermeasure.[184] It may also be noted that the seemingly unlawful action taken in 2013 by eleven States, as members of the Group of Friends of the Syrian People, to provide military assistance to Syrian rebels was not justified as a forcible third-party countermeasure.[185] In fact, these States explained that this support was motivated by 'the right to self defense of the Syrian people and the need to change the

---

[180] Ibid; Marston (1998), 581. See further Section 4.2.15.

[181] Contra: Joyner (2013) (seemingly expressing support for forcible third-party counter-measures as the 'holy grail' of international law). Such a prospect would truly engender a risk of a Hobbesian *bellum omnium contra omnes* – quite apart from possibly unravelling the entire regime of non-forcible unilateral enforcement of communitarian norms. Compare Cassese (1999), 23, 791.

[182] Compare YbILC (2001), vol. I, 35, para. 4 (Mr. Simma).

[183] See 'Chemical Weapon Use by Syrian Regime: UK Government Legal Position' (29 Aug. 2013), www.gov.uk/government/publications/chemical-weapon-use-by-syrian-regime-uk-government-legal-position/chemical-weapon-use-by-syrian-regime-uk-government-legal-position-html-version. In the event, military action was aborted but its express purpose would have been to 'deter and degrade the capacity for the further use of chemical weapons by the Syrian regime' (ibid.).

[184] For the suggestion *per contra* that the rationale offered by Western States for the possible use of force against Syria in September 2013 was best understood as an exercise of law enforcement by way of (unlawful) forcible third-party countermeasures, see Darcy (2013).

[185] See Joint Statement of the Participating Countries in the Istanbul Meeting on Syria (20 Apr. 2013), www.mfa.gov.tr/joint-statement-of-the-participating-countries-in-the-İstanbul-meeting-on-syria_-20-april-2013.en.mfa. Further: Akande (2013); Wezeman (2013), 271–273.

balance of power on the ground'[186] – hardly suggestive of a law enforcement rationale akin to third-party countermeasures.

To conclude, as Iran emphasized in *Oil Platforms*, the exclusion of forcible countermeasures under Article 50(1)(a) ARSIWA is 'absolutely clear ... [and] that rule knows of no exception – except possibly self-defence'.[187] The prohibition embodied in that provision was expressly reaffirmed in the *Guyana/Suriname* arbitration.[188] Although the ILC could simply have excluded forcible countermeasures based on the prohibition on the use of force as a cardinal peremptory norm, its explicit treatment in a separate provision is still important as it serves to underline the peaceful character of countermeasures[189] – an integral attribute which States have respected in practice.

6.2.1.2 Obligations for the Protection of Fundamental Human Rights

The impact of countermeasures on human rights is a complex issue which raises a range of concerns. Humanitarian considerations initially dictated the development in international humanitarian law to gradually limit the use of belligerent reprisals.[190] The 1880 IDI Oxford Resolution declared that the use of belligerent reprisals in land warfare was subject to 'the laws of humanity and morality'.[191] Two decades later, the so-called 'Martens Clause' was famously introduced for the first time in the preamble to the 1899 Hague Convention (II) on the Laws and Customs of War on Land which aimed to subject the conduct of hostilities to 'the laws of humanity and the requirements of the public conscience'.[192] It was recognized early on that humanitarian limitations on belligerent reprisals in wartime should apply *a fortiori* in time of peace.[193] As already noted, during the inter-war period, similar (if not

---

[186] Joint Statement of the Participating Countries in the Istanbul Meeting on Syria (20 Apr. 2013).

[187] *Oil Platforms*, ICJ Rep. (2003), 161, Verbatim Record, 3 March 2003, CR/2003/16 (translation), 16, paras. 11–12 (Mr. Pellet on behalf of Iran).

[188] *Guyana/Suriname*, Award, 17 Sept. 2007, RIAA, vol. XXX, 1 at 126, para. 446. See also *Oil Platforms*, ICJ Rep. (2003), 161 at 294 (Sep. Op. Judge Elaraby), 332 (Sep. Op. Judge Simma).

[189] Compare YbILC (2001), vol. I, 111, para. 55 (Chairman of the Drafting Committee, Mr. Tomka); Alland (2010), 1130.

[190] See e.g. Draft Articles Commentary, Art. 50, §§17–19; Bederman (2001), 242–249; Gardam (2004), 32–38 (with many further references).

[191] See 1880 IDI Oxford Resolution (Art. 86). Also: Draft Articles Commentary, Art. 50, §17.

[192] 187 CTS 429.   [193] Arango-Ruiz, Third Report, 32 (with further references).

identical) humanitarian formulas found expression in the *Naulilaa* case and the 1934 IDI Paris Resolution, which excluded those counter-measures which did not meet 'the requirements of humanity' or 'the demands of the public conscience'.[194] In the modern period, the development of international human rights law has ensured that these traditional formulas have become firmly established in international law. Such formulas may appeal to the better angels of our nature, but there remains ambiguity as to the precise extent of limitations dictated by humanitarian concerns.

It is certainly clear from Articles 22 and 50(1)(d) ARSIWA that a State cannot adopt countermeasures in violation of those human rights obligations that qualify as peremptory norms. And so the question is whether the entire body of human rights law or only a part of it has attained peremptory status. The former view – sometimes associated with Judge Tanaka in *South West Africa* – has only received limited support.[195] In fact, beyond a few well-established basic human rights, the peremptory status of individual human rights obligations is contested.[196] The ILC commentary to what became Article 53 VCLT limited itself to 'some of the most obvious and best settled rules of *jus cogens*'.[197] The same is true for the ILC commentaries to Articles 26 and 40 ARSIWA.[198] As Crawford has observed, the question for the ILC was accordingly whether, beyond a few well-established human rights obligations of a peremptory character, other human rights obligations should in principle also be excluded by way of countermeasures.[199] The ILC ultimately reserved its answer to this question.

6.2.1.2(i) The ILC's Contribution on First Reading

On first reading, Special Rapporteur Riphagen proposed to exclude the use of counter-measures for all human rights obligations deriving from treaties.[200]

---

[194] See above n. 122.

[195] *South West Africa*, ICJ Rep. (1966), 6 at 298 (Diss. Op. Judge Tanaka). See Crawford (2013a), 692 (nn. 103–104, for some examples of support for this minority view).

[196] See e.g. Orakhelashvili (2006), 53–60 (with many further references); Crawford (2013a), 692; and also above n. 131.

[197] See YbILC (1966), vol. II, 248 (citing the examples of non-use of force, genocide, piracy and generally acts criminal under international law).

[198] ARSIWA Commentary, Art. 26, §5; Art. 40, §§4–5 (noting the prohibitions on aggression, genocide, slavery, racial discrimination, crimes against humanity and torture, and the obligation to respect the right to self-determination). See also ibid., Art. 48, §9 (for the same approach to obligations *erga omnes*).

[199] Crawford (2013a), 692.

[200] Riphagen, Fifth Report, 3–4 (his draft article 11); Riphagen, Sixth Report, 12–13 (for the accompanying commentary). Also: Riphagen, Preliminary Report, 127, para. 91.

However, Riphagen did not address the issue of human rights obligations under customary international law. Under Riphagen's proposal, the suspension of human rights under customary international law was accordingly only prohibited by way of countermeasures insofar as it involved a breach of a peremptory norm.[201] For his part, Special Rapporteur Arangio-Ruiz proposed to prohibit countermeasures in relation to conduct 'not in conformity with the rules of international law on the protection of fundamental human rights'.[202] As to the meaning of the phrase 'fundamental human rights', Arangio-Ruiz based his approach on the notion of derogation in human rights treaties. He accordingly proposed to make a distinction between 'core' or 'essential' (non-derogable) human rights – the *minimum irréductible des droits de la personne humaine* – and 'less essential' (derogable) human rights.[203] Arangio-Ruiz did not consider it appropriate to enumerate the core human rights that could not be suspended by way of countermeasures; however, he suggested that they were those which had become part of customary international law, irrespective of their individual peremptory status.[204] However, this did not mean that less essential human rights could be suspended by way of countermeasures. Arangio-Ruiz's general exclusion of obligations *erga omnes (partes)* ruled out that possibility.[205]

Arangio-Ruiz also briefly noted the tendency in practice for States to make allowance for humanitarian exemptions with respect to items necessary for basic subsistence (i.e. food and medicines) in the adoption of unilateral coercive measures. This raised the broader issue of whether countermeasures should be excluded in respect of 'any rules intended in any way to protect human beings', i.e. indirect breaches of human rights.[206] Although Arangio-Ruiz considered the practice of humanitarian exemptions as 'significant',[207] he discarded the specific suggestion

---

[201] Riphagen, Fifth Report, 4 (his draft article 12(b)); Riphagen, Sixth Report, 13 (for the accompanying commentary).

[202] Arangio-Ruiz, Fourth Report, 35, para. 96 (his draft article 14(1)(b)(i)). Further: Arangio-Ruiz, Third Report, 32–34; Arangio-Ruiz, Fourth Report, 30–32.

[203] Arangio-Ruiz, Fourth Report, 31, paras. 80–82.   [204] Ibid.

[205] Ibid. (n. 213); and also ibid., 33–34, paras. 89–95. For criticism see notably YbILC (1992), vol. I, 167, para. 9 (Mr. Tomuschat) (suggesting that a State could suspend Article 12 ICCPR on the freedom of movement of persons by way of so-called 'reciprocal counter-measures'). Such action is 'inconceivable' and has no place in international law: ARSIWA Commentary, Introductory Commentary to Chapter II of Part Three, §5. Also: Crawford, Third Report, 87, para. 328.

[206] Arangio-Ruiz, Fourth Report, 30, 32, paras. 79, 82.

[207] Ibid., 31, para. 79. For a useful analysis, see generally Tehindrazanarivelo (2005), 137–186.

advanced by some commentators to the effect that it would be impermissible to suspend the performance of a development assistance treaty by way of countermeasures insofar as it indirectly affected nationals of the target State.[208] Practice did not support such a limitation; and at the normative level, the need not to substantially deprive States of the possibility to respond to breaches of international law militated against such a rule.[209]

The Drafting Committee, in order to better convey Arangio-Ruiz's intention, and drawing on the judgment of the ICJ in *Barcelona Traction*, decided to replace the phrase 'fundamental human rights' with the phrase 'basic human rights'.[210] It explained:

> The intention of that phrase was to prohibit any infringement of the right of every individual to life, liberty and security of person. Also prohibited were infringements of the rules of the humanitarian law on the protection of war victims and massive violations of human rights, particularly in the form of racial discrimination.[211]

The Drafting Committee also rejected the exclusion of countermeasures in violation of obligations *erga omnes (partes)* as 'too sweeping'.[212] With broader humanitarian concerns in mind, it added that an important factor to be taken into consideration in determining the lawfulness of a countermeasure derogating from basic human rights was that 'countermeasures should remain essentially a matter between States and have minimal effects on private individuals lest they amount to collective punishment'.[213]

The ILC on first reading provisionally adopted the modified proposal as Draft Article 50(d) [1996], which prohibited the use of countermeasures in relation to 'any conduct which derogates from basic human rights'.[214] The ILC commentary explained that the phrase 'basic human rights' limited the scope of prohibited countermeasures to the non-derogable 'core' of human rights, without prejudice to their individual

---

[208] Arangio-Ruiz, Third Report, 33, para. 109 (with further references).
[209] Arangio-Ruiz, Fourth Report, 32, para. 82. For the suspension of development assistance treaties by way of third-party countermeasures see Sections 4.2.2 (Greece); 4.2.3 (Uganda); 4.2.4 (Central African Republic); 4.2.5 (Liberia).
[210] YbILC (1993), vol. I, 145, para. 32 (Chairman of the Drafting Committee, Mr. Mikulka). Also: YbILC (1992), vol. I, 166, para. 8 (Mr. Tomuschat).
[211] YbILC (1993), vol. I, 145, para. 32 (Chairman of the Drafting Committee, Mr. Mikulka).
[212] Ibid., 141, para. 8.
[213] Ibid., 145, para. 32. Also: Draft Articles Commentary, Art. 50, §22.
[214] Draft Articles Commentary, Art. 50.

peremptory status.[215] In other words, albeit by implication, counter-measures remained possible in respect of less essential human rights obligations. To reinforce this notion, the ILC added that it preferred the phrase 'basic human rights' over the phrase 'fundamental human rights', found in Article 1(3) UNC, 'the interpretation of which might be undesirably influenced by its use in the present context'.[216]

Although there was broad agreement in the Sixth Committee that the phrase 'basic human rights' 'strikes a sympathetic chord',[217] some States nevertheless criticized this language as unclear and difficult to grasp.[218] As the United States observed, 'the language of subparagraph (d) provides only limited guidance for there are very few areas of con-sensus, if any, as to what constitutes "basic human rights"'.[219] Even so, a proposal by Ireland to add clarity by basing the exclusion on the list of non-derogable human rights enumerated in Article 4 ICCPR proved unsuccessful.[220]

Finally, the ILC commentary also made the important basic point that inhumane consequences of countermeasures could arise either as a direct result of action taken by a State against foreign nationals within its territory or as the indirect result of action aimed at the target State. With respect to the latter, the commentary referred to the practice of trade embargoes and other unilateral coercive measures which had regularly exempted 'articles intended to relieve human suffering' or activities 'directly aimed at humanitarian assistance'.[221] Again, the ILC stressed that countermeasures were essentially a matter between the States concerned and as a consequence they should avoid collective punishment of individuals.[222]

6.2.1.2(ii) The ILC's Contribution on Second Reading

On second reading, Special Rapporteur Crawford was critical of the ILC's rationale

---

[215] Ibid., §§23–24, 26.   [216] Ibid., §24.
[217] UN Doc. A/CN.4/488, 132 (United Kingdom).
[218] See UN Docs. A/CN.4/492, 16 (Japan); A/CN.4/488, 131–132 (United States, United Kingdom, Ireland). Also: Crawford, Third Report, 85, para. 317.
[219] UN Doc. A/CN.4/488, 132 (United States).
[220] Ibid., 131–132 (Ireland) ('Countermeasures involving a derogation from any of the rights specified in article 4, paragraph 2, of the International Covenant on Civil and Political Rights as well as countermeasures which are discriminatory on any of the grounds mentioned in article 4, paragraph 1, should be expressly prohibited'). Compare Draft Articles Commentary, Art. 50, §23; ARSIWA Commentary, Art. 50, §6.
[221] Draft Articles Commentary, Art. 50, §§20–22.   [222] Ibid., §22.

for excluding basic human rights as embodied in Draft Article 50(d) [1996]. In Crawford's view, the 'problem' was that

> [C]ountermeasures against a State by definition cannot permit the violation of non-derogable human rights, the beneficiaries of which are by definition third parties in relation to the target State, even if they are its nationals ...
>
> [H]uman rights obligations are not, in the first instance at least, owed to particular States, and it is accordingly difficult to see how a human rights obligation could itself be the subject of legitimate countermeasures.[223]

This statement of the problem endorsed comments made earlier by the United Kingdom.[224] As a result, it was clear to Crawford that human rights obligations could not themselves be suspended by way of counter-measures. He concluded that

> The position with respect to human rights is at one level the same as the position with respect to third States. Evidently, human rights are not owed to States as the primary beneficiaries, even though States are entitled to invoke those obligations and to ensure respect for them. Moreover, human rights obligations have their own regime of qualifications and derogations which takes into account considerations such as national emergency. Thus it is obvious that human rights obligations (whether or not qualified as 'fundamental' or 'basic') may not themselves be the subject of countermeasures, in other words, that human rights obligations may not be suspended by way of countermeasures, and that conduct inconsistent with human rights obligations may not be justified or excused except to the extent provided for by the applicable regime of human rights itself.[225]

Put simply, consistent with the definition of countermeasures in what became Article 49(1) ARSIWA, '[a] countermeasure was taken against a State and not a human being'.[226] It followed that only 'State-to-State obligations' could be the subject of countermeasures.[227]

Crawford noted that the 'real problem' did not concern direct breaches of human rights but was a different one: the consequential effects of countermeasures on individuals (or indeed the population as a whole) in the target State and the legal justification for excluding indirect breaches

---

[223] Crawford, Third Report, 84, 90, paras. 312(d), 340.
[224] UN Doc. A/CN.4/488, 132 (United Kingdom).
[225] Crawford, Third Report, 92, para. 349.
[226] YbILC (2000), vol. I, 266, paras. 73, 77 (Mr. Crawford).
[227] Ibid., 271, para. 41 (Mr. Crawford).

of human rights.[228] Crawford observed (quite rightly) that the practice of making allowance for humanitarian exemptions in the adoption of unilateral coercive measures did not necessarily correspond to conduct by the reacting State which was required of it under international human rights law.[229]

The issue of secondary effects of coercive action was the subject of intense debate in the 1990s in the context of the negative impact on the civilian population of UN sanctions against Iraq – perhaps most famously culminating in the innovative but ill-fated so-called 'Oil-for-Food Programme'.[230] In 1997, the Human Rights Committee noted that 'the effect of sanctions and blockades has been to cause suffering and death in Iraq, especially to children'.[231] In its General Comment No. 8 (1997), the CESCR noted the traditional (if often flawed) practice of the Security Council to include humanitarian exemptions in its sanctions regimes and indicated that such exemptions were equally relevant to the debate on countermeasures.[232] In short, Crawford considered that the ILC's legal basis for dealing with the impact of human rights on countermeasures was somewhat unpersuasive.

In order to avoid the suggestion that human rights obligations as such could be suspended by way of countermeasures, Crawford's proposed solution to the problem was to focus on the notion of third-party rights and the inter-State aspect of countermeasures. Crawford, recalling the ILC commentary to Draft Article 50(d) [1996],[233] agreed that countermeasures were 'essentially a matter for the States concerned' and that such measures should have 'minimal effects on private parties

---

[228] Crawford, Third Report, 92, para. 349 (and ibid., 84, para. 312(d)).

[229] Ibid., 84, para. 312(d).

[230] See e.g. SC Res. 986 (14 Apr. 1995); UN Docs. S/1996/356; S/1996/636. See generally Tehindrazanarivelo (2005), 137–205; Farrall (2007), 108–109, 141–144, 223–227, 268–271; Verdirame (2011), 306–310 (all with many further references).

[231] UN Doc. CCPR/C/79/Add.84 (5 Nov. 1997), para. 4.

[232] UN Doc. E/C.12/1997/8 (4 Dec. 1997), paras. 4, 11; Crawford, Third Report, 92, para. 350. Already the first Chapter VII UNC sanctions regime against Southern Rhodesia included humanitarian exemptions: see SC Res. 253 (29 May 1968). Compare GA Res. 51/242 (15 Sept. 1997) (Supplement to an Agenda for Peace), Annex II, para. 4; GA Res. 60/1 (16 Sept. 2005) (2005 World Summit Outcome), para. 106; Council of the European Union, Basic Principles on the Use of Restrictive Measures (Sanctions) (2004), para. 6, http://register.consilium.europa.eu/doc/srv?l=EN&f=ST%2010198%202004%20REV% 201; European Commission, EU Guidelines on Implementation and Evaluation of Restrictive Measures (2008), 6, http://eeas.europa.eu/cfsp/sanctions/docs/index_en.pdf.

[233] Draft Articles Commentary, Art. 50, §22; and discussion above n. 213.

in order to avoid collective punishment'.[234] In Crawford's view, this understanding of countermeasures provided 'a more persuasive justification' for the exclusion of indirect breaches of human rights.[235]

More specifically, Crawford proposed to distinguish between obligations the suspension of which was not subject to the regime of countermeasures and obligations which must not be infringed in the course of taking countermeasures. Put differently, Crawford made a distinction between the subject of countermeasures and their effect.[236] Based on this distinction, Crawford proposed two separate provisions dealing with 'Obligations not subject to countermeasures' and 'Prohibited countermeasures'.[237] By definition, it was obvious that human rights obligations could not be the subject of countermeasures. But the effect of countermeasures on human rights was a different matter. Crawford's draft article 50(b) dealt with prohibited countermeasures and accordingly provided that 'countermeasures must not ... impair the rights of third parties, in particular basic human rights'.[238] Finally, Crawford took note of the criticisms by some States regarding the lack of clarity as to the definition of 'basic' or 'fundamental' human rights but noted that this was a matter which required a foray into the territory of primary norms and as such it was not an issue that the ILC could resolve.[239]

As it happened, Crawford's proposed solution was not adopted. In fact, as he readily acknowledged, it had been 'a complete failure' and was perceived as an 'excess of human rights-ism' insofar as it regarded the beneficiaries of human rights as being third parties vis-à-vis the State.[240] In particular, Simma was critical of the rationale put forward by Crawford to justify the exclusion of human rights from the operation of countermeasures. He explained:

> The idea was that, with regard to human rights obligations, the primary beneficiaries were not other States, but human beings. That idea was fine, but it was dangerous to relieve States of the responsibility to secure performance of human rights obligations on the part of other States, thereby de-emphasizing the inter-State aspect of human rights obligations.[241]

---

[234] Crawford, Third Report, 84, para. 312(d).   [235] Ibid.

[236] Ibid., 88, para. 334. Also: YbILC (2000), vol. I, 266, para. 73 (Mr. Crawford).

[237] Crawford, Third Report, 96, para. 367 (his draft articles 47 *bis* and 50).   [238] Ibid.

[239] Ibid., 92, para. 351.

[240] YbILC (2000), vol. I, 271, 299, paras. 41, 71 (Mr. Crawford). For criticism see e.g. ibid., 273, para. 57 (Mr. Pellet) who 'utterly rejected the idea that individuals could be "third parties" in the context of inter-State responsibility'.

[241] Ibid., 270, para. 31 (Mr. Simma).

Furthermore:

> [H]e wished to underline the view that it was dangerous to 'privatize' human rights obligations by saying that they were obligations not owed to other States. He thought human rights obligations, especially those laid down in treaties, had a double nature: they were obligations between States parties which, like other obligations, justified the exercise of countermeasures in the event that they were breached. That aspect was important and should not be overshadowed by the other aspect of human rights brought out by the European Court of Human Rights in the sense that the obligations arising from treaties were not just obligations among States, but were also, and perhaps in the first instance, obligations vis-à-vis individuals.[242]

Based on the above 'double nature'[243] of human rights obligations, Simma proposed a different justification for their exclusion from the regime on countermeasures:

> His own rationale was that, while it was true that human rights must not be an object of countermeasures, human rights obligations, whether derived from treaty or grounded in customary international law, were by definition 'integral obligations' ... Performance of those obligations could accordingly not be bilateralized because that would impair the right of other States parties to the obligation to see the human right respected.[244]

This rationale recalled the one advanced by Arangio-Ruiz on first reading. It also accorded with Gaja's proposal on second reading to limit the operation of countermeasures to bilateral obligations.[245] The ILC ultimately favoured the rationale provided by the 'double nature' argument by placing emphasis on the inter-State enforcement aspect of human rights obligations (as distinct from the notion of third-party rights and individual remedies); however, it stopped short of extending it to obligations *erga omnes (partes)*. Again, the issue was simply whether human rights obligations below the threshold of peremptory norms were also excluded.

---

[242] Ibid., 271, para. 42 (Mr. Simma).

[243] For a brief analysis see Borelli and Olleson (2010), 1182–1185 (with further references).

[244] YbILC (2000) vol. I, 270, para. 31 (Mr. Simma). See also Simma (1994a), 370 ('Human rights treaties are "built" like all other multilateral treaties. They, too, create rights and obligations between their parties to the effect that any State party is obliged as against any other State party to perform its obligations and that, conversely, any party has a correlative right to integral performance by all the other contracting States').

[245] See above text accompanying nn. 145–147.

The Drafting Committee in 2000 explained its concern that 'given the wide meaning acquired by the concept of human rights, resort to countermeasures would be severely limited unless the reference to human rights was qualified'.[246] It added that '[a]s in the text adopted on first reading, the important thing was that the effects of countermeasures should essentially be limited to the injured State and the responsible State and should have only minimal effects on individuals'.[247] The Drafting Committee evidently referred to State practice, which appeared to have respected certain humanitarian limitations in cases where the use of countermeasures might have had indirect consequences on the nationals of the target State. In short, collective punishment of the population of the target State should be avoided.[248] A change in language was also proposed. The Drafting Committee replaced the term 'basic human rights' with the largely identical term 'fundamental human rights'.[249] It explained that the qualifier 'fundamental' referred to 'the category of human rights that were protected from any derogation by virtue of their peremptory nature'.[250]

The Drafting Committee in 2000 had adopted its proposal despite concerns expressed by some ILC members about any attempt to draw a distinction between 'fundamental' (or 'basic') human rights and other human rights: such a distinction would be difficult to apply in practice and would be contrary to a unified approach to human rights.[251] Opinion in the Sixth Committee was divided along similar lines. Some States opined that even derogable human rights could not be infringed by way of countermeasures.[252] Others proposed that only the peremptory core of non-derogable human rights, i.e. 'those designed to protect the life and physical integrity of the human person', should be excluded.[253]

---

[246] YbILC (2000), vol. I, 397, para. 71 (Chairman of the Drafting Committee, Mr. Gaja).

[247] Ibid.

[248] See Draft Articles Commentary, Art. 50, §§20–22. Also: Crawford, Third Report, 83–84, para. 312(d).

[249] YbILC (2000), vol. I, 397, para. 71 (Chairman of the Drafting Committee, Mr. Gaja).

[250] Ibid., 397, para. 75. See however YbILC (2001), vol. I, 116, para. 13 (Mr. Hafner), 117, para. 22 (Mr. Dugard).

[251] ILC Report (2000), UN Doc. A/55/10, 31, para. 122. See further YbILC (2000), vol. I, 278, para. 14 (Mr. Kateka), 286, para. 25 (Mr. Goco), 287, para. 34 (Mr. Momtaz), 297, para. 50 (Mr. Opertti Badan), 298, para. 61 (Mr. Galicki). Contrast Article 53(1)(b) DARIO ('Countermeasures shall not affect ... obligations for the protection of human rights'), DARIO Commentary, Art. 53, §3.

[252] Topical Summary of Government Comments in the Sixth Committee, UN Doc. A/CN.4/513 (2000), 30, para. 157.

[253] Ibid., 30, paras. 158–159.

Special Rapporteur Crawford noted that it was 'controversial' to what extent the phrase 'fundamental human rights' covered peremptory norms since 'the phrase "fundamental human rights" has no settled meaning'.[254] As a result, Crawford advised the ILC to 'reserve its position on whether there were fundamental [human] rights from which counter-measures could derogate in certain circumstances and other [human] rights which were non-derogable'.[255] For its part, the Drafting Committee in 2001 explained:

> [Article 50 ARSIWA] had been drafted with a view to State practice, and accordingly it contained specific provisions, not general principles that could be subjected to different interpretations by practitioners or aca-demics. The Drafting Committee had adopted it *without taking a position* as to whether or not obligations for the protection of fundamental human rights and obligations of a humanitarian character prohibiting reprisals were peremptory norms. No one disputed the fact that the obligation to refrain from the threat or use of force was a peremptory norm, however.[256]

The ILC commentary confirms that these humanitarian exclusions are not necessarily based on the peremptory status of individual norms.[257] Although the matter is not free from ambiguity, it appears that the ILC intended only to exclude non-derogable human rights without prejudice to their individual peremptory status.[258] In any event, the matter was evidently best left to be decided by State practice which would elucidate the meaning of the phrase 'fundamental human rights'.

Moreover, to emphasize that Article 50(1)(b) ARSIWA deals not only with direct violations of human rights obligations but also with indirect breaches, the provision provides that 'countermeasures shall not *affect* obligations for the protection of fundamental human rights'.[259]

---

[254] Crawford, Fourth Report, 16, para. 64.

[255] YbILC (2000), vol. I, 286, para. 28 (Mr. Crawford). Also: ibid., 275, para. 76 (Mr. Crawford).

[256] YbILC (2001), vol. I, 117, para. 26 (Chairman of the Drafting Committee, Mr. Tomka) (emphasis added).

[257] ARSIWA Commentary, Art. 50, §9 ('The reference to "other" obligations under per-emptory norms makes it clear that subparagraph (d) does not qualify the preceding subparagraphs, *some of which* also encompass norms of a peremptory character. In particular, subparagraphs (b) and (c) stand on their own') (emphasis added).

[258] ARSIWA Commentary, Art. 50, §6 (which refers 'in particular' to non-derogable human rights under relevant human rights treaties). Compare O'Keefe (2010), 1164–1165.

[259] Emphasis added. On the introduction of the word 'affect' see YbILC (2001), vol. I, 111, para. 54 (Chairman of the Drafting Committee, Mr. Tomka); and compare YbILC (2000), vol. I, 397, paras. 68–69 (Chairman of the Drafting Committee, Mr. Gaja).

The commentary to this provision explains that both non-derogable human rights obligations under relevant human rights treaties as well as indirect human rights violations causing 'collateral infliction of suffering upon the most vulnerable groups within the targeted country' are excluded from the range of permissible countermeasures.[260] In particular, the commentary stresses that 'whatever the circumstances, [countermeasures] should always take full account of the provisions of the International Covenant on Economic, Social and Cultural Rights'.[261] This clarification was widely supported by States.[262] The ILC's approach to countermeasures and human rights merits a few observations.

6.2.1.2(iii) Evaluation   It is somewhat unclear from the ILC's approach to what extent human rights obligations are actually excluded from the operation of countermeasures as a matter of international law. It was noted above that the ILC concluded that the answer was best left to State practice rather than divined by general principle. As it happens, it seems that both elements point towards the same conclusion: human rights obligations cannot themselves be suspended by way of countermeasures. Based on general principle, two possible rationales may be advanced in support of this conclusion. In line with Special Rapporteur Crawford's proposal, it is certainly possible to explain such a general exclusion of human rights based on the notion of third-party rights.[263] The better rationale however appears to be that human rights obligations are excluded based on the *erga omnes (partes)* structure of their performance.

---

[260] See ARSIWA Commentary, Art. 50, §§6–7 (citing CESCR General Comment No. 8 (4 Dec. 1997), UN Doc. E/C.12/1997/8, para. 4).

[261] Ibid., citing para. 1.

[262] Topical Summary of Government Comments in the Sixth Committee, UN Doc. A/CN.4/513 (2000), 28, para. 146.

[263] See e.g. Paparinskis (2008), 331–334. Also: Lowenfeld (2010), 747; Parlett (2015), 394–404. The case law on the analogous issue of the possible exclusion of countermeasures in the field of international investment law is sparse and contradictory: see *Corn Products International Inc. v. Mexico*, ICSID Case No. ARB(AF)/04/01, Decision on Responsibility, 15 Jan. 2008, paras. 153–191; *Cargill, Incorporated v. Mexico*, ICSID Case No. ARB(AF)/05/2, Award, 18 Sept. 2009, paras. 420–430 (countermeasures cannot apply to investor rights as these are autonomous); *Archer Daniels Midland Company and Tate & Lyle Ingredients Americas, Inc. v. Mexico*, ICSID Case No. ARB(AF)/04/05, Award, 21 Nov. 2007, paras. 161–180 (countermeasures can apply, in principle, to investor rights as these are derivative). In any event, the suspension of investment protections owed to foreign investors by way of countermeasures may well be deemed disproportionate: see below Section 6.3.

The ILC's basic position embodied in Article 50(1)(b) and (c) ARSIWA should be understood as 'the direct descendant and logical extension' in the law of State responsibility of the humanitarian principle in the law of treaties contained in Article 60(5) VCLT.[264] This provision excludes the possibility of suspension or termination of a treaty, or part thereof, in case of

> provisions relating to the protection of the human person contained in treaties of a humanitarian character, in particular to provisions prohibiting any form of reprisals against persons protected by such treaties.

The provision may not have been included in the ILC's Draft Articles on the Law of Treaties, as adopted in 1966,[265] but Special Rapporteur Fitzmaurice had nevertheless foreshadowed its rationale. Fitzmaurice had proposed to exclude suspension or termination, and even non-performance, 'where the juridical force of the obligation is inherent, and not dependent on a corresponding performance by the other parties to the treaty ... so that the obligation is of a self-existent character, requiring an absolute and integral application and performance under all conditions ... '.[266] Notable examples of such obligations could be found in international human rights and humanitarian law.[267]

In the event, the provision was belatedly added at the Vienna Conference in May 1969 following a proposed amendment by Switzerland, which 'for humanitarian reasons' was anxious to remove any justification for the suspension or termination of the 1949 Geneva Conventions and other international humanitarian law treaties in response to a breach by another party.[268] However, Switzerland further explained that 'the protection of human rights in general' was 'equally important' and accordingly also intended to be covered by the exclusion in what became Article 60(5) VCLT.[269] The Swiss amendment was duly adopted with widespread support.[270]

---

[264] Borelli and Olleson (2010), 1178.

[265] See YbILC (1966), vol. II, 184, 253–255 (draft article 57, with accompanying commentary).

[266] Fitzmaurice, Second Report, 31 (his draft article 19(1)(iv)).

[267] Ibid., 54–55, paras. 125–128 (his commentary to draft article 19(1)(iv)).

[268] See the oral statement by the Swiss delegate, Mr. Bindschedler, UN Docs. A/CONF.39/11, 354, para. 12; and the subsequent written statement by Switzerland, A/CONF.39/11/Add.1, 112, paras. 20–21.

[269] Ibid. Further: Schwelb (1973–1975), 14–26; Barile (1987), 3; Sicilianos (1990), 352–358; Gomaa (1996), 109–111; Provost (2002), 169–171; Borelli and Olleson (2010), 1178–1179; Simma and Tams (2011), 1366–1368.

[270] For the text of the Swiss proposal and its adoption by the Vienna Conference see UN Docs. A/CONF.39/L.31; A/CONF.39/SR.21, 115, para. 68.

As observed above, Special Rapporteurs Riphagen and Arangio-Ruiz on first reading both proposed to extend the rationale of Article 60(5) VCLT to the law of State responsibility and the relationship between countermeasures and human rights. In particular, the combined effect of Arangio-Ruiz's proposal was to completely exclude obligations in the field of human rights – being obligations *erga omnes (partes)* – from the operation of countermeasures. Arangio-Ruiz expressly invoked Article 60(5) VCLT and Fitzmaurice's notion of 'integral' obligations in support of his approach.[271] On second reading, Gaja and Simma notably expressed support for such an exclusion based on the same rationale. They likewise did so by reference to the integral or non-bilateralizable structure of performance of human rights obligations, whether derived from treaty or custom, relying on Fitzmaurice's influential analysis.[272] For his part, it may be recalled that Gaja noted that it would be 'strange' if countermeasures adopted in violation of obligations *erga omnes (partes)* were considered lawful.[273]

In the case of treaty-based human rights obligations, it may be that countermeasures are also excluded by *lex specialis*. Major human rights treaties allow contracting parties to derogate from certain human rights obligations.[274] Such derogation can however only occur subject to strict substantive and procedural limitations on the power to derogate. As Special Rapporteur Crawford observed, it therefore seems obvious that conventional human rights obligations (whether derogable or not) cannot be suspended by way of countermeasures. As a matter of treaty interpretation, conduct inconsistent with human rights obligations seemingly cannot be justified or excused except to the extent provided for in the human rights treaty itself.[275] Simply put, the derogation clause in a human rights treaty cannot itself be suspended by way of countermeasures.[276] In short, the exclusion of human rights obligations

---

[271] Arangio-Ruiz, Third Report, 25, paras. 81–83; Arangio-Ruiz, Fourth Report, 34, paras. 92–95.

[272] See above nn. 145–147, 244. Compare Crawford, Third Report, 90, para. 341; Crawford, Fourth Report, 16, para. 64.

[273] See above n. 145.

[274] See e.g. Article 15 ECHR; Article 27 ACHR; Article 4 ICCPR; and Article 4 ICESCR. No derogation is possible in the absence of a derogation clause: see e.g. Crawford, Third Report, 90, para. 343.

[275] See above n. 225. Also: YbILC (2000), vol. I, 272, para. 45 (Mr. Crawford). Compare Boisson de Chazournes (1992), 154; Alland (1994), 270–271.

[276] Compare HRC General Comment No. 24, UN Doc. CCPR/C/21/Rev.1/Add.6 (2 Nov. 1994), para. 10; Topical Summary of Government Comments in the Sixth

from the operation of countermeasures is both normatively desirable and analytically sound.

There is also no clear indication that States (unlike the ILC on first reading) would consider such a general exclusion as 'too sweeping'.[277] The practice examined in Chapter 4 demonstrates that States have not purported to directly suspend human rights obligations by way of countermeasures.[278]

The real problem – indirect breaches of human rights in the target State
This brings us back to the real problem, which concerns indirect breaches of human rights obligations. Target States, as well as other States, have regularly protested that third-party countermeasures are unlawful, *inter alia*, on the basis that they adversely affect the enjoyment of human rights of civilian populations. A particularly controversial example is provided by the trade embargo adopted in July 1996 by several East African States against Burundi. In August 1996, Burundi protested against its adoption by denouncing 'the cruel consequences of the economic blockade on the entire people of Burundi' which it alleged amounted to a violation of the African Charter on Human and Peoples' Rights.[279] Worse still, Burundi even denounced a 'possible genocide by Draconian economic sanctions'.[280] For his part, the UN Special Rapporteur on the human rights situation in Burundi criticized the trade embargo for its 'serious impact on the food security of the Burundi people', which adversely affected the right to an adequate standard of living and the right to health under relevant provisions of the ICESCR.[281]

As it happened, the embargoing East African States soon made gradual allowance for humanitarian exemptions, including food products and medicines, 'in order to alleviate the suffering of the people of Burundi'[282] – a decision welcomed by the Security Council.[283] Ultimately, Kenya nevertheless stated:

Committee, UN Doc. A/CN.4/513 (2000), 30, para. 157. See however Provost (1994), 440–442.
[277] See above n. 149.   [278] Similarly Borelli and Olleson (2010), 1182.
[279] UN Doc. S/PV.3692 (28 Aug. 1996), 5–6 (Burundi). See further Section 4.2.13.
[280] Ibid.
[281] Second Report on the Human Rights Situation in Burundi, UN Doc. E/CN.4/1997/12, 16, para. 65. See also Interim Report on the Human Rights Situation in Burundi, UN Doc. A/52/505, 12, para. 51 (on the 'disastrous effect' of the trade embargo on the provision of health services in Burundi).
[282] UN Doc. S/1997/319, 3, para. 8 (Tanzania).   [283] S/PRST/1997/32 (30 May 1997).

> Although the Government of Kenya recognizes that the innocent citizens
> of Burundi may suffer as a result of the imposition of economic sanctions,
> we in Kenya view these sanctions as unavoidable sacrifices needed to
> arrest further deterioration of the situation of Burundi.[284]

The UN Special Rapporteur considered that, notwithstanding the easing of the trade embargo, it was still having a 'disastrous effect' on the civilian population.[285] In December 1998, the OAU urged the East African States to lift the trade embargo, notably because of its adverse effects on the civilian population.[286] The trade embargo was lifted shortly thereafter.[287] In 2000, a report commissioned by the UN Sub-Commission on the Promotion and Protection of Human Rights concluded that the trade embargo against Burundi had violated international law as it was contrary to 'the principles of humanity and the dictates of the public conscience'.[288]

In other examples, Sudan has protested that the unilateral coercive measures adopted against it by the United States since 1997 has had 'long-term harmful consequences on the human rights of the Sudanese population ... [making it] impossible for the Sudan to ensure the right and access to food and basic needs of its population'.[289] The FRY protested that 'the normal economic development and lives of millions of people [were] hampered' by the (non-forcible) unilateral coercive measures adopted against it in the late 1990s.[290] In a similar vein, Zimbabwe has protested that the unilateral coercive measures adopted against it since 2003 have 'brought much suffering to the people of Zimbabwe'.[291] In August 2013, the SADC called for the lifting of these measures as

---

[284]   UN Doc. S/1996/651, 2 (Kenya).
[285]   Third Report on the Human Rights Situation in Burundi, UN Doc. E/CN.4/1998/72, 18, para. 80.
[286]   UN Doc. S/1998/1229.
[287]   'World: Africa Burundi Sanctions Lifted', *BBC News*, 23 January 1999, http://news.bbc .co.uk/1/hi/world/africa/261258.stm. The lifting of the trade embargo was particularly welcomed by international aid agencies, including the UN World Food Programme (ibid.).
[288]   'The adverse consequences of economic sanctions on the enjoyment of human rights', Working Paper prepared by Mr. Marc Bossuyt, UN Doc. E/CN.4/Sub.2/2000/33, 12, 19–22, paras. 47, 74–86.
[289]   UN Doc. A/68/211 (22 July 2013), 6 (Sudan). Also: Final Communiqué of the Twenty-Fifth Session of the Islamic Conference of Foreign Ministers (Doha, 15–17 March 1998), UN Doc. S/1998/311, 26–27, para. 103 (denouncing the 'harmful effects' of the US action). See further Section 4.2.14.
[290]   UN Doc. S/PV.3868 (31 March 1998), 16 (FRY). See further Section 4.2.15.
[291]   UN Doc. S/PV.5933 (11 July 2008), 3 (Zimbabwe). See further Section 4.2.17.

Zimbabweans, in the words of Malawian President Banda, had 'suffered enough'.[292] Belarus has protested on similar grounds against the unilateral coercive measures adopted against it since 2004.[293] Syria has likewise protested against the adverse effect on the civilian population of the multitude of unilateral coercive measures adopted against it since 2011.[294] For its part, Brazil has expressed reservations about the effectiveness of the action taken against Syria and its 'devastating humanitarian impact' on the civilian population.[295]

In Brazil's view, such devastating effects underlined a 'recurring paradoxical situation' in which the persons who were most affected by the adoption of unilateral coercive measures in the promotion of international human rights and humanitarian law were frequently the same civilians who were supposed to be protected by such measures.[296] In its General Comment No. 8 (1997), the CESCR stressed that such a paradoxical situation must be avoided:

> Just as the international community insists that any targeted State must respect the civil and political rights of its citizens, so too must that State and the international community itself do everything possible to protect at least the core content of the economic, social and cultural rights of the affected peoples of that State . . .
>
> Lawlessness of one kind should not be met by lawlessness of another kind which pays no heed to the fundamental rights that underlie and give legitimacy to any such collective [enforcement] action.[297]

The question of the adverse effect of unilateral coercive measures on the enjoyment of human rights in target States is a controversial topic of particular concern to developing States that has been on the agenda of the

---

[292] 'Zimbabwe's Mugabe Should Not Face Sanctions, SADC Says', *BBC News*, 19 August 2013, www.bbc.co.uk/news/world-africa-23754623.

[293] See e.g. UN Docs. A/66/272 (5 Aug. 2011), 4–5; A/67/181 (25 July 2012), 3–4; A/68/211 (22 July 2013), 3 (Belarus). See further Section 4.2.18.

[294] See e.g. UN Docs. A/HRC/20/G/3 (15 June 2012); A/68/211 (22 July 2013), 6 (Syria) for wide-ranging criticisms; and further Section 4.2.20.

[295] UN Doc. A/68/211 (22 July 2013), 4 (Brazil). See however Chairman's Conclusions of the International Conference of the Group of Friends of the Syrian People (Tunis, 24 Feb. 2012), paras. 10, 14–16 (regarding humanitarian assistance), www.state.gov/r/pa/prs/ps/2012/02/184642.htm.

[296] UN Doc. A/68/211 (22 July 2013), 4 (Brazil). See also UN Doc. A/68/218 (29 July 2013), 5 (Brazil). Many other States have expressed similar criticisms: for recent examples see UN Docs. A/64/219 (3 Aug. 2009), 2 (Algeria); A/66/272 (5 Aug. 2011), 12–14 (Guyana); A/67/181 (25 July 2012), 3 (Andorra), 5 (Bosnia-Herzegovina), 5–7 (Cuba), 8–9 (Iran), 10 (Jamaica and Kuwait); A/68/211 (22 July 2013), 5 (Egypt, Iraq and Jordan).

[297] UN Doc. E/C.12/1997/8, paras. 7, 16.

UN Commission on Human Rights (now the Human Rights Council) and the UN General Assembly for decades. In 1993, the Vienna World Conference on Human Rights called on States to refrain from the use of any unilateral coercive measure which impeded the full realization of human rights, in particular the rights of individuals under Articles 11 and 12 ICESCR to a standard of living adequate for their health and well-being.[298] In its General Comment No. 8 (1997), the CESCR stated that 'sanctions ... almost always have a dramatic impact on the rights recognized in the [ICESCR]'.[299] It explained:

> Thus, for example, they often cause significant disruption in the distribution of food, pharmaceuticals and sanitation supplies, jeopardize the quality of food and the availability of clean drinking water, severely interfere with the functioning of basic health and education systems, and undermine the right to work. In addition, their unintended consequences can include reinforcement of the power of oppressive élites, the emergence, almost invariably, of a black market and the generation of huge windfall profits for the privileged élites which manage it, enhancement of the control of the governing élites over the population at large, and restriction of opportunities to seek asylum or to manifest political opposition. While the phenomena mentioned in the preceding sentence are essentially political in nature, they also have a major additional impact on the enjoyment of economic, social and cultural rights.[300]

The UN General Assembly has considered the matter on an annual basis since 1996 under the heading 'Human rights and unilateral coercive measures'.[301] The General Assembly has repeatedly condemned the practice of unilateral coercive measures and its negative impact on the full realization of human rights in target States.[302] It has notably stressed that the use of unilateral coercive measures should exempt essential goods such as food and medicines, and should under no circumstances deprive people of their own means of subsistence in accordance with Article 1(2) common to the ICCPR and ICESCR.[303] But mere allowance

---

[298] UN Doc. A/CONF.157/24 (Part I), chap. III, para. 31.

[299] UN Doc. E/C.12/1997/8, para. 3.

[300] Ibid. Compare Supplement to an Agenda for Peace, UN Doc. A/50/60-S/1995/1, 16, para. 70.

[301] See GA Res. 51/103 (12 Dec. 1996).

[302] See e.g. GA Res 70/151 (17 Dec. 2015). Compare HRC Res. 27/21 (26 Sept. 2014) (by which, *inter alia*, the UN Human Rights Council decided to appoint a Special Rapporteur on the topic). Generally: GA Res. 51/242 (15 Sept. 1997) (Supplement to an Agenda for Peace), Annex II, para. 4; GA Res. 60/1 (16 Sept. 2005) (2005 World Summit Outcome), para. 106.

[303] GA Res. 70/151 (17 Dec. 2015), op. para. 8. Compare ARSIWA Commentary, Art. 50, §7.

for humanitarian exemptions would be insufficient. The General Assembly's proposed solution has been to repeatedly call on States to 'commit themselves to their obligations and responsibilities arising from the international human rights instruments to which they are parties by revoking such measures at the earliest possible time'.[304]

States adopting third-party countermeasures have sought to mitigate adverse consequences by regularly making allowance for humanitarian exemptions. The East African trade embargo against Burundi has already been mentioned. In a similar vein, EU Member States have introduced humanitarian exemptions in the case of asset freezes and trade embargoes.[305] The United States has also done so.[306] Still, the CESCR has noted that humanitarian exemptions are generally insufficient to ensure basic respect for the ICESCR.[307] Albeit less drastic than the UN General Assembly, the CESCR has therefore stated that 'whatever the circumstances . . . sanctions [including third-party countermeasures] should always take full account of the provisions of the International Covenant on Economic, Social and Cultural Rights'.[308] This is certainly a fine policy prescription, but it is somewhat problematic in legal terms.

As already noted, the problem is that the practice of humanitarian exemptions – as indeed any effort to take full account of the ICESCR or other human rights treaties – does not necessarily correspond to conduct by the State taking countermeasures which is required of it under international human rights law.[309] Human rights obligations are primarily meant to operate between a State and the inhabitants of its own territory. As the ECtHR held in *Banković*, the concept of 'jurisdiction' within the

---

[304] GA Res. 70/151 (17 Dec. 2015), op. para. 9.

[305] See e.g. Common Position 2007/750/CFSP (19 Nov. 2007), OJ 2007 L 308/1 (24 Nov. 2007) (Burma); Council Decision 2011/101/CFSP (15 Feb. 2011), OJ 2011 L 42/6 (16 Feb. 2011) (Zimbabwe); Council Decision 2011/273/CFSP (9 May 2011), OJ 2011 L 121/11 (10 May 2011); Council Decision 2012/739/CFSP (29 Nov. 2012), OJ 2012 L 330/21 (30 Nov. 2012); Council Decision 2013/186 (22 Apr. 2013), OJ 2013 L 111/101 (23 Apr. 2013) (Syria). Also: Rousseau (1980), 364; and Section 4.2.4 (Central African Republic) (regarding the French suspension of development assistance to the Central African Republic, with exemptions for health, education and foodstuffs).

[306] See e.g. Tom Lantos Block Burmese JADE (Junta's Anti-Democratic Efforts) Act of 2008, Public Law 110–286 (29 July 2008), s. 5(f)(1).

[307] CESCR General Comment No. 8 (4 Dec. 1997), UN Doc. E/C.12/1997/8, paras. 4–5. For a contemporaneous critical assessment of humanitarian exemptions in the context of UN sanctions see e.g. Craven (2002), 43; O'Connell (2002), 63; von Sponeck (2002), 81.

[308] CESCR General Comment No. 8 (4 Dec. 1997), UN Doc. E/C.12/1997/8, para. 1; see also ibid., paras. 11–12.

[309] See above n. 229.

meaning of Article 1 ECHR, and by extension the spatial scope of application of human rights obligations thereunder, is 'primarily territorial'; they may apply extra-territorially but only in exceptional circumstances.[310] Similarly, the ICJ in the *Wall* case held that the ICCPR and ICESCR both applied to acts done by a State in the exercise of its jurisdiction outside its own territory – a prime example being the case of territories under belligerent occupation.[311] The ICJ reached this conclusion notwithstanding the fact that the ICESCR guarantees rights that are 'essentially territorial'; and unlike Article 2(1) ICCPR, contains no express provision on its scope of application. It thus seems clear that even the extraterritorial application of the ICESCR cannot be excluded.[312]

However, leaving aside the exceptional circumstances of occupation (or even the extraterritorial presence of State organs),[313] the State(s) taking countermeasures would not normally exercise any jurisdiction in the territory of the target State. As a result, contrary to the above suggestion by the UN General Assembly, it is far from clear that human rights obligations are even applicable to the adverse effects of countermeasures on individuals in the target State.[314] In the absence of an obligation, let alone a breach, such action presumably cannot 'affect' human rights norms within the meaning of Article 50(1)(b) ARSIWA. The CESCR's indirect reference to Article 2(1) ICESCR in this respect, with its perfunctory obligation on each State party to provide 'international assistance and co-operation', does not take matters much further.[315] In short, it seems that countermeasures that have an adverse effect on the enjoyment of human rights in the target State will normally not be excluded under international law.[316]

The basic problem still remains. The use of countermeasures may affect the ability of the target State to comply with its own human rights

---

[310] *Banković v. Belgium* (Application No. 52207/99), Admissibility Decision of 12 Dec. 2001, para. 59.

[311] *Wall* case, ICJ Rep. (2004), 136 at 178–181, paras. 107–112. The ICJ also found that the Convention on the Rights of the Child applied extraterritorially to the Occupied Palestinian Territories (ibid., para. 113).

[312] Ibid., 180, para. 112.   [313] See e.g. Meron (1995), 78.

[314] See e.g. Craven (2002), 54–57; Borelli and Olleson (2010), 1187.

[315] CESCR General Comment No. 8, UN Doc. E/C.12/1997/8, para. 14. Further: CESCR General Comment No. 3 (1990), UN Doc. E/1991/23, 83–87; Karimova (2014), 163. Under Article 2(1) ICESCR, States parties commit themselves to take steps, to the maximum of available resources, to achieve progressively the full realization of ICESCR rights.

[316] Borelli and Olleson (2010), 1187.

obligations insofar as they put a strain on its resources and its ability to ensure relevant protections for its population.[317] While it would be an overstatement to suggest that countermeasures 'almost always have a dramatic impact'[318] on individuals in the target State and the enjoyment of their rights under the ICESCR, many countermeasures will likely – if not 'inevitably'[319] – have some adverse effect on them. This is especially so in the case of third-party countermeasures in the form of trade embargoes, the freezing of State assets or the suspension of development assistance, when taken by a large number of States, including important institutional actors such as the EU. The adverse effect on human rights will be further compounded when such action is taken against a weak State which may already find itself in a precarious situation – as illustrated by the East African trade embargo against Burundi.

As will be further discussed in Section 6.3 below, the problem identified here can, however, be legally addressed by the principle of proportionality which forms an integral part of the law of countermeasures.[320] For example, *in extremis*, countermeasures resulting in starvation or serious malnutrition of the population in the target State would clearly be disproportionate and as such unlawful.[321] In that sense, the CESCR was correct to stress that States parties to the ICESCR have an obligation to respond to 'any disproportionate suffering experienced by vulnerable groups within the targeted country'.[322] That said, it may be difficult to establish the necessary causal link between the use of countermeasures and their adverse impact on the enjoyment of human rights.[323] The example of Burundi, engaged in massive inter-ethnic violence during the period of the East African trade embargo, underlines this difficulty. More recently, the widespread adoption of unilateral coercive measures against Syria, including third-party countermeasures, notwithstanding Brazil's reservations about their allegedly 'devastating humanitarian impact'[324] on the civilian population, is indicative of the same problem.[325]

---

[317] Compare CESCR General Comment No. 8, UN Doc. E/C.12/1997/8, para. 9.
[318] Ibid., para. 3.   [319] YbILC (2000), vol. I, 284, para. 6 (Mr. Dugard).
[320] See e.g. O'Connell (2002), 74–79 (discussing the application of the proportionality test in the law of countermeasures to UN sanctions regimes); O'Keefe (2010), 1164–1165.
[321] Compare the approach by analogy in ARSIWA Commentary, Art. 50, §7.
[322] CESCR General Comment No. 8, UN Doc. E/C.12/1997/8, para. 14.
[323] Compare Craven (2002), 56; Borelli and Olleson (2010), 1187–1188; Crawford (2013a), 693 (n. 112); UN Doc. A/HRC/27/32 (10 July 2014), 7, para. 18 (Mr. Tzanakopoulos).
[324] See above n. 295.
[325] It should also be borne in mind that 'whatever the difficulties' the target State remains responsible for complying with its human rights obligations vis-à-vis its own

In spite of the many difficulties observed above, the ILC endorsed the CESCR's position that countermeasures should 'whatever the circumstances ... always take full account of the provisions of the International Covenant on Economic, Social and Cultural Rights'.[326] More broadly, the ILC seemingly extended this rationale by excluding any countermeasures under Article 50(1)(b) ARSIWA which 'affect' human rights obligations; that is to say, even if the adverse effect on human rights is situated outside the territory or jurisdiction of the State(s) taking countermeasures. For the reasons stated, it seems that this rationale essentially amounted to a laudable endorsement of policy motivated by humanitarian concerns – and an appeal to the better angels of our nature – rather than a statement of contemporary international human rights law.[327]

6.2.1.3   Obligations of a Humanitarian Character Prohibiting Reprisals

The relationship between countermeasures and obligations under international humanitarian law is relatively straightforward.[328] There appears to be widespread agreement that the basic rules of international humanitarian law are peremptory in character.[329] Their suspension by way of countermeasures would accordingly be excluded under Article 26 ARSIWA. In addition, Article 50(1)(c) ARSIWA, which is modelled on Article 60(5) VCLT, excludes 'obligations of a humanitarian character prohibiting reprisals'. In other words, the provision is simply a *renvoi* to the widely accepted rules of international humanitarian law prohibiting belligerent reprisals against individuals.[330] It has been noted that the

population – a point stressed by the Human Rights Committee in 1997 in relation to Iraq notwithstanding the crippling UN sanctions regime adopted against it: see UN Doc. CCPR/C/79/Add.84 (5 Nov. 1997), para. 4. This is especially so where target States are endemically corrupt and divert scare budgetary resources away from human rights protection within their own jurisdictions.

[326]   ARSIWA Commentary, Art. 50, §7 (citing CESCR General Comment No. 8, UN Doc. E/C.12/1997/8, para. 1).

[327]   For the same conclusion, see Borelli and Olleson (2010), 1188.

[328]   See generally Borelli and Olleson (2010), 1188–1195 (with many further references). Also: Crawford (2013a), 693–694.

[329]   See *Legality of the Threat or Use of Nuclear Weapons*, ICJ Rep. (1996), 226 at 257, para. 79; and 273 (Dec. President Bedjaoui), 496 (Diss. Op. Judge Weeramantry), 574 (Sep. Op. Judge Koroma). Also: *Prosecutor v. Kupreškić*, ICTY Case No. IT-95-16, Judgment, 14 Jan. 2000, para. 520; ARSIWA Commentary, Art. 40, §5; *Wall* case, ICJ Rep. (2004), 136 at 199, para. 157.

[330]   See Crawford, Fourth Report, 16, para. 64; YbILC (2001), vol. I, 111, para. 54 (Chairman of the Drafting Committee, Mr. Tomka); ARSIWA Commentary, Art. 50, §8. Also: Draft Articles Commentary, Art. 50, §§17–18.

purpose of this 'somewhat abstract and metaphysical layering of prohibition upon prohibition' is to make clear that countermeasures cannot be invoked to justify non-compliance with rules of international humanitarian law prohibiting belligerent reprisals against individuals.[331] The explicit mention of this principle in Article 50(1)(c) ARSIWA is consistent with the ILC's broader ambition to minimize the adverse effects of countermeasures on individuals.[332]

6.2.1.4   The Separability of Dispute Settlement Provisions

It seems clear that the availability of binding third-party dispute settlement procedures must limit (if not entirely exclude) recourse to countermeasures. It is precisely when difficulties arise with respect to alleged wrongful conduct that dispute settlement provisions in treaties assume their greatest importance. They cannot be disregarded in those very circumstances, following the 'well-established' principle of the separability of dispute settlement provisions.[333]

These provisions are not undertaken on a *quid pro quo* basis and the non-reciprocal structure of their performance is recognized in Article 60(4) VCLT, which provides that 'the foregoing paragraphs are without prejudice to any provision in the treaty applicable in the event of a breach'.[334] The ICJ has repeatedly affirmed the principle of separability. In *Appeal Relating to the Jurisdiction of the ICAO Council*, the Court said:

> Nor in any case could a merely unilateral suspension *per se* render jurisdictional clauses inoperative, since one of their purposes might be, precisely, to enable the validity of the suspension to be tested. [. . .]
>
> The acceptance of such a proposition would be tantamount to opening the way to a wholesale nullification of the practical value of jurisdictional clauses . . . Such a result, destructive of the whole object of adjudicability, would be unacceptable.[335]

---

[331] Borelli and Olleson (2010), 1194–1195.

[332] Crawford (2013a), 694. For judicial affirmation see *Prisoners of War – Eritrea's Claim 17 (Eritrea/Ethiopia)*, Partial Award, 1 July 2003, RIAA, vol. XXVI, 23 at 69–70, paras. 159–160.

[333] ARSIWA Commentary, Art. 50, §13.

[334] The uncontroversial character of this provision is clear from the brief commentary to what became Article 60(4) VCLT: see YbILC (1966), vol. II, 255. Further: Simma and Tams (2011), 1357. See also Scelle, Fourth Report on the Law of Arbitral Procedure, YbILC (1958), vol. II, 3; and the ILC Model Rules on Arbitral Procedure (preamble) at ibid., 83.

[335] *Appeal Relating to the Jurisdiction of the ICAO Council*, ICJ Rep. (1972), 46 at 53, 64, paras. 16(b), 32. See also the *Namibia* case, ICJ Rep. (1971), 16 at 47, para. 94 (for an affirmation of the customary law status of Article 60 VCLT).

In *Tehran Hostages*, the Court affirmed that

> In any event, any alleged violation of the Treaty [of Amity] by either
> party could not have the effect of precluding that party from invoking the
> provisions of the Treaty concerning the pacific settlement of disputes ...
> It is precisely when difficulties arise that the treaty assumes its greatest
> importance.[336]

In short, there is strong support under general international law for
the principle of the separability of dispute settlement provisions and
its application to countermeasures.[337] Based on a proposal by Special
Rapporteur Crawford, Article 50(2)(a) ARSIWA essentially reaffirms this
principle by providing that '[a] State taking countermeasures is not
relieved from fulfilling its obligations ... under any dispute settlement
procedure applicable between it and the responsible State'.[338] In other
words, an obligation relating to dispute settlement cannot itself be suspended by way of countermeasures.[339] The apparent absence of any
relevant practice confirms the largely uncontroversial character of this
exclusion.

6.2.1.5   Obligations Safeguarding Diplomatic and Consular Inviolability

It has been recognized since ancient times that the maintenance of
a basic level of diplomatic communication is essential for the promotion
of friendly relations among States. This is particularly so in situations
involving allegations of unlawful conduct, which by definition are likely
to cause strain in relations between them.[340] As the ICJ stressed in *Tehran Hostages*:

> [T]he institution of diplomacy [is] an instrument essential for effective
> co-operation in the international community, and for enabling States,

---

[336] *United States Diplomatic and Consular Staff in Tehran*, ICJ Rep. (1980), 3 at 28, paras. 53–54.

[337] See e.g. Crawford (2013a), 694–696.

[338] For a summary of the drafting history see Crawford, Third Report, 89, para. 339; YbILC (2000), vol. I, 397, para. 76 (Chairman of the Drafting Committee, Mr. Gaja); YbILC (2001), vol. I, 111, para. 56 (Chairman of the Drafting Committee, Mr. Tomka); ARSIWA Commentary, Art. 50, §§11–13. For the treatment of the issue on first reading see Draft Articles Commentary, Art. 48, §6.

[339] This exclusion is further reinforced by the procedural safeguard in Article 52(3) ARSIWA: see further below Section 6.4.

[340] See Draft Articles Commentary, Art. 50, §14; Barnhoorn (1994), 63; Crawford, Third Report, 89, para. 337; Denza (2008), 2; Simma and Pulkowski (2010), 151.

irrespective of their differing constitutional and social systems, to achieve mutual understanding and to resolve their differences by peaceful means.[341]

The institution of diplomacy would be severely undermined if diplomatic or consular personnel could be targeted by countermeasures. It thus seems clear that the use of countermeasures must entail some limitation in the field of diplomatic law on functional grounds.[342]

Indeed, the exclusion of diplomats from the operation of countermeasures is firmly rooted in international law. For example, Bynkershoek noted 'the reasoning of all time and the practice of all nations [which] have established the immunity of ambassadors from reprisals'.[343] Grotius and Vattel both made statements to the same effect.[344] Twiss noted that diplomatic agents 'cannot be the subject of reprisals, either in their persons or in their property, on the part of the Nation which has received them in character of envoys (*legati*), for they have entrusted themselves and their property in good faith to its protection'.[345]

The modern debate in the ILC on this issue mostly focussed on a rather infelicitous passage in the ICJ's judgment in *Tehran Hostages*. The Court in this case was concerned with the issue of whether Iran's violations of diplomatic law could be justified as a countermeasure in response to alleged US violations of diplomatic law towards Iran. The Court rejected the Iranian argument that 'special circumstances'[346] justified its actions, stating that 'diplomatic law itself provides the necessary means of defence against, and sanction for, illicit activities by members of diplomatic or consular missions'.[347] It added:

> The rules of diplomatic law, in short, constitute a self-contained régime which, on the one hand, lays down the receiving State's obligations regarding the facilities, privileges and immunities to be accorded to diplomatic missions and, on the other, foresees their possible abuse by members of the mission and specifies the means at the disposal of the

---

[341] *United States Diplomatic and Consular Staff in Tehran*, Provisional Measures, 15 Dec. 1979, ICJ Rep. (1979), 7 at 19, para. 39. Similarly: *United States Diplomatic and Consular Staff in Tehran*, ICJ Rep. (1980), 3 at 43, para. 92.

[342] ARSIWA Commentary, Art. 50, §15.   [343] Bynkershoek (1744), Chapter XXII, 120.

[344] Grotius (1646), Book II, Chapter XVIII, §7; Vattel (1758), Book IV, Chapter VII, §102.

[345] Twiss (1884), 39. See also Cahier (1962), 22; Dominicé (1981), 547.

[346] *United States Diplomatic and Consular Staff in Tehran*, ICJ Rep. (1980), 3 at 37, paras. 80–81. Iran alleged that the United States had been complicit in the 1953 *coup d'état* which had resulted in the overthrow of Prime Minister Mossadegh and the restoration of the Shah to the throne of Iran (see ibid., 8–9, para. 10).

[347] Ibid., 38, para. 83.

receiving State to counter any such abuse. These means are, by their nature, entirely efficacious.[348]

The above passage suggests that the ICJ completely excluded the use of countermeasures in response to violations of diplomatic law. However, it is widely agreed that such a conclusion is unwarranted.[349] The ICJ in *Tehran Hostages* sought to make a more limited point; namely, that non-compliance with certain core obligations under diplomatic law cannot be justified by way of countermeasures.[350]

The ICJ's reference in *Tehran Hostages* to diplomatic law as a self-contained regime caused some confusion in the ILC debate. On first reading, Special Rapporteur Riphagen proposed to completely exclude diplomatic and consular immunities from the remit of legitimate countermeasures.[351] But his proposal was widely criticized in the ILC as too sweeping.[352] For his part, Special Rapporteur Arangio-Ruiz considered it obvious that countermeasures should not be entirely excluded. It would however be necessary to ensure basic respect for the *ne impediatur legatio* principle by excluding those rules of diplomatic law with which it was essential to comply in order to preserve the normal operation of diplomatic channels.[353] Thus Arangio-Ruiz proposed to exclude only those countermeasures which could result in 'serious prejudice to the normal operation of bilateral and multilateral diplomacy'.[354]

Arangio-Ruiz's proposal received a mixed reception in the ILC. The terms 'serious prejudice' and 'the normal operation of diplomacy' were considered too vague; it was deemed preferable to focus on the prohibition of countermeasures threatening the inviolability of persons or premises protected by diplomatic law. In short, recourse to countermeasures in the area of diplomatic law should be limited but not entirely

---

[348] Ibid., 40, para. 86.

[349] See e.g. YbILC (1984), vol. I, 264, para. 30 (Mr. Reuter), 304, para. 9 (Mr. Sinclair); Zemanek (1987), 40; Sicilianos (1990), 350–351; YbILC (1992), vol. I, 159, para. 24 (Mr. Al-Khasawneh); Crawford, Third Report, 89, para. 337; Cannizzaro (2001), 897–898; Simma and Pulkowski (2010), 151.

[350] See e.g. Simma and Pulkowski (2010), 151; Crawford (2013a), 697.

[351] Riphagen, Second Report, 86, para. 59; Riphagen, Fourth Report, 18, para. 97; Riphagen, Sixth Report, 13 (his draft article 12(a) with accompanying commentary).

[352] ILC Report (1984), UN Doc. A/39/10, 103–104, para. 374.

[353] Arangio-Ruiz, Fourth Report, 33, para. 87. See generally YbILC (1985), vol. I, 150, para. 21 (Mr. Arangio-Ruiz); Arangio-Ruiz, Third Report, 34, para. 116; Arangio-Ruiz, Fourth Report, 32–33, 39, paras. 86–87, 108–110.

[354] Arangio-Ruiz, Fourth Report, 35, para. 96 (his draft article 14(b)(ii)).

excluded.[355] The Drafting Committee in 1993 rejected Arangio Ruiz's proposal as it could be construed as effectively prohibiting all counter-measures in the diplomatic field. Instead the Drafting Committee proposed to limit the scope of excluded countermeasures to the inviolability of diplomatic and consular persons, premises, archives and documents.[356] The ILC on first reading adopted this proposal as Draft Article 50(c) [1996], and in doing so explicitly acknowledged that coun-termeasures that did not affect diplomatic and consular inviolability remained permissible.[357]

On second reading, Special Rapporteur Crawford expressed support for Draft Article 50(c) [1996] and noted that no government in the Sixth Committee had proposed its deletion.[358] Crawford accordingly pro-posed to make the same exclusion in almost identical terms.[359] The Drafting Committee in 2001 likewise expressed its approval; however, unlike the approach on first reading, it proposed to deal with the exclusion of diplo-matic and consular inviolability in a separate paragraph. The purpose of this change was to clarify that the rules on diplomatic and consular inviolability were not peremptory in character and that their exclusion was justified on functional grounds.[360] Article 50(2)(b) ARSIWA accordingly prohibits any countermeasure which does not 'respect the inviolability of diplomatic or consular agents, premises, archives and documents'.[361] The ILC commen-tary to this provision explains that jurisdictional immunity is an aspect of inviolability covered by the prohibition.[362] Conversely, any countermeasure that does not concern inviolable obligations under diplomatic and consular law remains permissible.[363]

---

[355] See ILC Report (1992), UN Doc. A/47/10, 34, paras. 236–239.
[356] YbILC (1993), vol. I, 144, paras. 29–30 (Chairman of the Drafting Committee, Mr. Mikulka).
[357] See Draft Articles Commentary, Art. 50, §§13–16.
[358] Crawford, Third Report, 89, paras. 337–338. See also YbILC (2001), vol. I, 111, para. 54 (Chairman of the Drafting Committee, Mr. Tomka).
[359] See Crawford, Third Report, 96, para. 367 (his draft article 47 *bis* (b)).
[360] YbILC (2001), vol. I, 111, para. 54, (Chairman of the Drafting Committee, Mr. Tomka). For the suggestion that these inviolable obligations have a peremptory character see e.g. YbILC (2000), vol. I, 286, para. 31 (Mr. Momtaz); UN Doc. A/CN.4/515/Add.1, 10 (Mexico).
[361] This includes any countermeasure inconsistent with Articles 22, 24, 29, 44 and 45 VCDR. See further Denza (2008), 135–179, 189–199, 256–269, 481–483, 484–496.
[362] See ARSIWA Commentary, Art. 50, §14. Also: YbILC (2001), vol. I, 283, paras. 38–39 (Messrs. Economides and Crawford).
[363] ARSIWA Commentary, Art. 50, §14. Further: Sicilianos (1990), 344–351; Boisson de Chazournes (2010), 1206–1208; Crawford (2013a), 696–697.

Practice indicates that EU Member States regularly exempt from the remit of legitimate unilateral coercive measures any travel bans on representatives of the target State insofar as they would contradict their obligations as a host country to an international organization or a diplomatic conference held under UN auspices, or otherwise depart from a multilateral agreement conferring privileges and immunities.[364] EU Member States have also exempted payment for current expenses, including salaries of local staff employed by embassies and consulates of the target State, from the freezing of State assets.[365] For its part, the United States has excluded from trade embargoes the importation of any items the prohibition of which would be contrary to the VCDR, the VCCR, the UN Headquarters Agreement and other legal instruments providing equivalent privileges and immunities.[366] To conclude, there is no indication in practice that States have suspended any obligations under diplomatic or consular law by way of third-party countermeasures.

6.3 Proportionality

The principle of proportionality is firmly established as an essential substantive limitation on the right to take countermeasures.[367] It is one of the fundamental conditions to be met if the use of countermeasures is to be legitimate. Proportionality is relevant in determining both the type of countermeasure that may be adopted and its degree of intensity.[368] In so doing, proportionality aims to 'put a brake on the injured State's reaction' in order to avoid 'escalating cycles of transactional violence'.[369]

---

[364] EU Member States regularly do so in standard terms: see e.g. Common Position 2004/661/CFSP (24 Sept. 2004), OJ 2004 L 301/67 (28 Sept. 2004) (Belarus); Council Decision 2011/273/CFSP (9 May 2011), OJ 2011 L 121/11 (10 May 2011) (Syria). See further Sections 4.2.18; 4.2.20.

[365] See e.g. Common Position 98/326/CFSP (7 May 1998), OJ 1998 L 143/1 (14 May 1998), Council Regulation (EC) No. 1295/98 (Arts. 3 and 7), OJ 1998 L 178/33 (23 June 1998) (FRY/Serbia). See Section 4.2.15.

[366] See e.g. President Bush's Executive Order 13310 (28 July 2003), 'Blocking Property of the Government of Burma and Prohibiting Certain Transactions', www.treasury.gov/resource-center/sanctions/Documents/13310.pdf. See further Section 4.2.16.

[367] See e.g. *Naulilaa (Responsibility of Germany for damage caused in the Portuguese colonies in the south of Africa) (Portugal/Germany)* (1928), RIAA, vol. II, 1011 at 1028; 1934 IDI Paris Resolution (Art. 6(2)); *US-France Air Services Agreement* (1978), RIAA, vol. XVIII, 417 at 443, para. 83; *Nicaragua* case, ICJ Rep. (1986), 14 at 127, para. 249; *Gabčíkovo Nagymaros Project*, ICJ Rep. (1997), 7 at 56, para. 85; ARSIWA Commentary, Art. 51, §2. Further: O'Keefe (2010), 1157.

[368] See ARSIWA Commentary, Art. 51, §1.

[369] YbILC (1993), vol. I, 143, para. 22 (Chairman of the Drafting Committee, Mr. Mikulka); Franck (2008), 715. See also O'Keefe (2010), 1160; Crawford (2013a), 698.

The fact that responsibility could arise from disproportionate counter-measures provides target States with a 'measure of assurance'[370] while at the same time encouraging the State(s) taking them to act in 'a spirit of . . . moderation'.[371]

Although the basic principle of proportionality has long been estab-lished as a key constraint on the use of countermeasures, it remains a flexible standard and the exact criteria on the basis of which it should be measured in a given case are somewhat elusive. In essence, propor-tionality requires 'some degree of equivalence'[372] between the wrongful act and the countermeasure; however, as the ILC has stressed, 'what is proportionate is not a matter which can be determined precisely'.[373] The assessment of the proportionality of countermeasures is accordingly 'not an easy task and can best be accomplished by approximation'.[374] Put differently, it can only be achieved 'with a certain degree of subjectivity'.[375] This is especially so in the case of third-party counter-measures where the role of reciprocity is much reduced (if not entirely excluded) and the requirement of equivalence between breach and response provides a rather crude yardstick against which to measure proportionality.[376] The proportionality calculus for third-party counter-measures will generally require reconciliation or balancing of incom-mensurable interests. Quantitative factors must be weighed against qualitative ones. Simply put, the adoption of third-party countermea-sures in response to, for example, aggression, genocide or other massive violations of international human rights and humanitarian law will likely require 'an awkward balancing of apples and oranges'.[377]

Partly for this reason, ILC member Al-Khasawneh, among others, stressed that the principle of proportionality was 'difficult to apply in

---

[370] ARSIWA Commentary, Art. 51, §1. See also Draft Articles Commentary, Art. 49, §2.

[371] *US-France Air Services Agreement* (1978), RIAA, vol. XVIII, 417 at 445, para. 91.

[372] Ibid., 443, para. 83.

[373] ARSIWA Commentary, Art. 51, §5 (see also ibid., §7). Countermeasures affecting the performance of several obligations may be proportionate even if taken in response to a single wrongful act: see ARSIWA Commentary, Art. 49, §6.

[374] *US-France Air Services Agreement* (1978), RIAA, vol. XVIII, 417 at 443, para. 83. See also YbILC (1992), vol. I, 159, para. 20 (Mr. Al-Khasawneh); ILC Report (1992), UN Doc. A/47/10, 30, para. 209; UN Doc. A/CN.4/488, 127 (United States).

[375] *Gabčíkovo Nagymaros Project*, ICJ Rep. (1997), 7 at 224 (Diss. Op. Judge Vereshchetin). See also O'Keefe (2010), 1165.

[376] Compare YbILC (1992), vol. I, 159, para. 20 (Mr. Al-Khasawneh); ILC Report (1992), UN Doc. A/47/10, 30, para. 209; UN Doc. A/CN.4/488, 126 (Ireland); ARSIWA Commentary, Introductory Commentary to Chapter II of Part III, §5.

[377] Franck (2008), 716.

practice' and cautioned against its 'inadequacy ... as an effective limit to the scope of countermeasures'.[378] Still, despite its indeterminacy, the principle of proportionality does have a practical effect on the conduct of interstate relations.[379] As Austria emphasized in the Sixth Committee, 'the mere fact that the element of proportionality may be invoked by a State against which countermeasures are taken already provides a regulating effect'.[380] For its part, Cameroon stated that 'any State against which countermeasures were taken was likely to consider them disproportion-ate'.[381] It is however unusual in practice for explicit reference to be made to proportionality as a substantive limitation on countermeasures.[382] Reference to allegedly disproportionate countermeasures is often made in general and implicit terms; notably, in the form of protests against their adverse effects on the enjoyment of human rights in the target State.[383] States taking countermeasures are sensitive to accusations concerning their disproportionate effects, especially as they relate to the enjoyment of human rights by the civilian population in the target State. For example, the decision by several East African States to modify (and ultimately lift) the third-party countermeasures they had adopted against Burundi, fol-lowing requests by the OAU and others to do so on humanitarian grounds, may be recalled.[384] More generally, it may likewise be recalled that States adopting third-party countermeasures regularly make allowance for humanitarian exemptions even if international human rights law does not strictly require them to do so.[385]

The requirement of proportionality in the law of countermeasures has evolved over time. It assumed a more precise content in the twentieth century following the First World War, a development associated with the outlawing of the use of force. In the 1920s, the tribunal in the *Naulilaa* arbitration was given an opportunity to address the matter.[386] This arbitration arose out of an incident on 19 October 1915 in which, following a series of misunderstandings caused in part by an incompetent

---

[378] YbILC (1992), vol. I, 158, para. 19 (Mr. Al-Khasawneh); ILC Report (1992), UN Doc. A/47/10, 30, para. 209.

[379] Franck (2008), 717–718; Crawford (2013a), 698. See also Tehindrazanarivelo (2005), 365.

[380] UN Doc. A/CN.4/488, 124 (Austria).

[381] UN Doc. A/C.6/55/SR.24, 10, para. 61 (Cameroon).

[382] See Arangio-Ruiz, Fourth Report, 22, para. 54; Draft Articles Commentary, Art. 49, §5. Also: Kolb (2004), 407–410.

[383] See above Section 6.2.1.2(iii).   [384] Ibid.   [385] Ibid.

[386] *Naulilaa (Responsibility of Germany for damage caused in the Portuguese colonies in the south of Africa) (Portugal/Germany)* (1928), RIAA, vol. II, 1011.

German interpreter,[387] three German nationals were killed by members of the Portuguese frontier post at Naulilaa in Portuguese South West Africa (now Angola). Two others were wounded and taken prisoner. In response, by way of forcible countermeasures, the Governor of German South West Africa (now Namibia) ordered the attack and destruction of several forts in the Portuguese colony. With respect to the proportionality of the German action, the *Naulilaa* tribunal stated:

> The most recent doctrine, notably the German doctrine ... does not require that the reprisal be proportioned to the offence. On this point, authors, unanimous for some years, are now divided in opinion. The majority considers a certain proportion between offence and reprisal a necessary condition of the legitimacy of the latter. International law in process of formation as a result of the last war tends certainly to restrain the notion of legitimate reprisals and to prohibit their abuse.[388]

In a well-known dictum, it continued:

> [E]ven if one were to admit that the law of nations does not require that the reprisal should be approximately in keeping with the offence, one should certainly consider as excessive and therefore unlawful reprisals out of all proportion to the act motivating them. In the present case ... there was an evident disproportion between the incident at Naulilaa and the six acts of reprisal which have followed it.[389]

The extent to which this negative requirement of proportionality actually reflected the contemporaneous practice of States in the field of countermeasures is unclear. The use of gunboat diplomacy was certainly not known for its moderation.[390] For her part, Colbert concluded that the *Naulilaa* dictum on proportionality 'although reflecting the opinions of international lawyers, has little or no support in the practice of states'.[391] In any event, the issue of the proportionality of forcible countermeasures largely became moot with the UN Charter prohibition on the use of force.

In the *Air Services* arbitration, the issue of proportionality was examined in some detail. In that case, France had refused to allow a change of gauge in London on Pan Am flights from the west coast of the United

---

[387] Ibid., 1020. For the relevant facts of the incident see further ibid., 1019–1025.
[388] Ibid., 1026.
[389] Ibid., 1028. For a stricter test see 1934 IDI Paris Resolution (Art. 6(2)) ('Dans l'exercice des représailles, l'Etat doit ... [p]roportionner la contrainte employée à la gravite de l'acte dénonce comme illicite et à l'importance du dommage subi').
[390] Compare Hall (1890), 368. See further Section 1.2.
[391] Colbert (1948), 76–77. See also e.g. Brownlie (1963), 220–222; Gardam (2004), 47–49; Kolb (2004), 429.

States bound for Paris and ultimately suspended its landing rights. The United States responded by threatening to suspend Air France flights to Los Angeles altogether by way of countermeasures seemingly in order to induce France to agree to arbitration on certain procedural terms. Having achieved their apparent objective,[392] following the signature of an arbitration agreement on the day before the said US countermeasures were supposed to take effect, they were never implemented.[393] For its part, France challenged the proposed US action on the basis that, if implemented, it would be disproportionate.[394]

The *Air Services* tribunal (chaired by Riphagen) held that the proposed US countermeasures would have been consistent with the principle of proportionality because they 'do not appear to be clearly disproportionate when compared to those taken by France'.[395] In particular, the majority stated:

> It is generally agreed that all counter-measures must, in the first instance, have some degree of equivalence with the alleged breach: this is a well-known rule ... It has been observed, generally, that judging the 'proportionality' of counter-measures is not an easy task and can at best be accomplished by approximation. In the Tribunal's view, it is essential, in a dispute between States, to take into account not only the injuries suffered by the companies concerned but also the questions of principle arising from the alleged breach. The Tribunal thinks that it will not suffice, in the present case, to compare the losses suffered by Pan Am on account of the suspension of the projected services with the losses which the French companies would have suffered as a result of the counter-measures; it will also be necessary to take into account the importance of the positions of principle which were taken when the French authorities prohibited changes of gauge in third countries. If the importance of the issue is viewed within the framework of the general air transport policy adopted by the United States Government and implemented by the conclusion of a large number of international agreements with countries other than France, the measures taken by the United States do not appear to be clearly disproportionate when compared to those taken by France. Neither Party has provided the Tribunal with evidence that would be

---

[392] See *US-France Air Services Agreement* (1978), RIAA, vol. XVIII, 417 at 442, para. 78.

[393] Ibid., 419–421, paras. 1–9 (see also ibid., 426–427, paras. 15–16). Thus ARSIWA Commentary, Art. 51, §3 should not be understood as suggesting that the United States actually adopted countermeasures against France: it only threatened to do so. See also Nash (1980), 769 et seq. (for extracts of the US pleadings).

[394] *US-France Air Services Agreement* (1978), RIAA, vol. XVIII, 417 at 422, 427, paras. 9, 17. France also alleged that the US action failed to meet certain procedural conditions (on which see below Section 6.4).

[395] Ibid., 443, para. 83.

sufficient to affirm or reject the existence of proportionality in these terms, and the Tribunal must be satisfied with a very approximative appreciation.[396]

This double negative formulation of proportionality ('not ... clearly disproportionate'), which referred to both quantitative ('the losses suffered') and qualitative criteria ('the questions of principle'), afforded considerable leeway to the injured State in the adoption of countermeasures.[397]

In the *Gabčíkovo Nagymaros Project* case, the ICJ, while also taking account of both quantitative and qualitative factors, adopted a more rigorous positive formulation of proportionality. The Court stated that in its view 'the effects of a countermeasure must be commensurate with the injury suffered, taking account of the rights in question'.[398] In that case, Hungary and Czechoslovakia had entered into a treaty in 1977 concerning the construction and operation of a barrage system on the Danube. In 1989, mainly motivated by environmental concerns, Hungary suspended and subsequently abandoned its works in violation of its obligations under the treaty. Czechoslovakia immediately responded that it would be compelled to take unilateral action in case Hungary did not resume performance of its obligations under the treaty. Prolonged and ultimately fruitless negotiations ensued and, in 1992, Czechoslovakia put into operation a provisional, substitute solution (subsequently known as 'Variant C') which entailed the unilateral diversion of water from the Danube into a bypass canal located entirely on its territory, allegedly in order to ensure an approximate application of the treaty. In practice, the operation of 'Variant C' led Czechoslovakia (and later Slovakia, as the successor State) to appropriate, essentially for its own use and benefit, between 80 and 90 per cent of the waters of the Danube before returning them to the main bed of the river.[399]

Slovakia argued before the ICJ that the action taken was lawful based on the principle of approximate application and in any event could be justified as a countermeasure.[400] For its part, Hungary argued that the action did not satisfy the conditions for lawful countermeasures and in particular the condition of proportionality.[401] The ICJ concluded that the

---

[396] Ibid. See also ibid., 448 (Diss. Op. Mr. Reuter).
[397] For criticism see e.g. Greenwood (1979), 237–238; Zoller (1984a), 133–136; Sicilianos (1990), 277; Focarelli (1994), 392–393.
[398] *Gabčíkovo Nagymaros Project*, ICJ Rep. (1997), 7 at 56, para. 85.
[399] Ibid., 25–26, 50–51, 53–54, paras. 22–23, 65, 67, 75, 78.
[400] Ibid., 51–53, paras. 67, 69, 75.   [401] Ibid., 52, para. 71.

operation of 'Variant C' violated the treaty.[402] More specifically, with respect to the countermeasures defence, it stated:

> Czechoslovakia, by unilaterally assuming control of a shared resource, and thereby depriving Hungary of its right to an equitable and reasonable share of the natural resources of the Danube – with the continuing effects of the diversion of these waters on the ecology of the riparian area of the Szigetköz – failed to respect the proportionality which is required by international law ...
>
> The Court thus considers that the diversion of the Danube carried out by Czechoslovakia was not a lawful countermeasure because it was not proportionate.[403]

These partly divergent judicial pronouncements were reflected in the ILC debate on the proportionality test applicable to countermeasures.

6.3.1   The ILC's Contribution

In 1995, two years before the ICJ's judgment in the *Gabčíkovo Nagymaros Project* case, the ILC observed that

> There is no uniformity ... in the practice or the doctrine as to the formulation of the principle, the strictness or flexibility of the principle and the criteria on the basis of which proportionality should be assessed.[404]

The precise content of the principle of proportionality thus required clarification; namely, the rigour with which it should be applied, and the criteria by which it should be assessed. Different views on these matters were expressed in the ILC and Sixth Committee. On first reading, Special Rapporteur Riphagen proposed that countermeasures 'shall not, in its effects, be manifestly disproportional to the seriousness of the internationally wrongful act committed'.[405] For his part, Special Rapporteur Arangio-Ruiz likewise favoured a more flexible negative formulation of proportionality. However, noting the concerns expressed by several States in the Sixth Committee concerning Riphagen's use of the term 'manifestly', Arangio-Ruiz agreed that such a formulation introduced an

---

[402] Ibid., 54, para. 78.

[403] Ibid., 56, paras. 85, 87. For a different conclusion see ibid., 223–226 (Diss. Op. Judge Vereshchetin).

[404] Draft Articles Commentary, Art. 49, §3. See also Arangio-Ruiz, Third Report, 21, para. 65.

[405] Riphagen, Sixth Report, 11 (his draft article 9(2) with accompanying commentary).

element of excessive uncertainty which could result in abuse on the part of the State(s) taking countermeasures.[406]

Arangio-Ruiz also agreed with the *Air Services* tribunal and Riphagen that proportionality should be assessed by taking into account not only the purely 'quantitative' element in terms of the material injury caused but also 'qualitative' factors such as the importance of the interest protected by the rule infringed and the seriousness of the breach.[407] The instrumental function of countermeasures was, despite the views of some ILC members, not a relevant qualitative factor to be taken into account.[408] Arangio-Ruiz accordingly proposed that countermeasures 'shall not be out of proportion to the gravity of the internationally wrongful act and of the effects thereof'.[409]

The Drafting Committee in 1993 adopted Arangio-Ruiz's proposal but added the concluding phrase 'on the injured State'. In doing so, it made the important clarification that, consistent with the bilateral conception of injury embodied in Draft Article 40 [1996], this was not intended to have the effect of 'unduly restricting a State's ability to take effective countermeasures in respect of certain wrongful acts involving obligations *erga omnes*, such as violations of human rights'.[410] On first reading, the ILC repeated the same point in adopting the Drafting Committee's proposal as Draft Article 49 [1996]. At the same time, however, the ILC noted in the commentary to the provision that a legally injured State, as compared to a materially injured State, could be more limited in its choice of the type and the intensity of the countermeasures that would be proportional to the legal injury suffered.[411] The ILC also explained that the purpose of countermeasures, i.e. to induce the wrongdoing State to return to legality, was not a relevant consideration in the assessment of proportionality.[412]

As for comments by States on first reading, Ireland questioned the distinction drawn in the ILC commentary between a legal and a material injury which might unduly restrict the effectiveness of third-party countermeasures. In particular, both Ireland and the United States criticized

---

[406] Arangio-Ruiz, Fourth Report, 23, para. 54 (his n. 127 for further references).
[407] Ibid., 23, para. 55.
[408] Ibid., 23, para. 56; ILC Report (1992), UN Doc. A/47/10, 31, para. 212.
[409] Arangio-Ruiz, Fourth Report, 35, para. 96 (his draft article 13).
[410] YbILC (1993), vol. I, 143, para. 21 (Chairman of the Drafting Committee, Mr. Mikulka). For a summary of the debate on Arangio-Ruiz's proposal, see ILC Report (1992), UN Doc. A/47/10, 30–31.
[411] Draft Articles Commentary, Art. 49, §§8–9.   [412] Ibid., §10.

the fact that the purpose of countermeasures had not been taken into account as an additional qualitative element in the assessment of proportionality.[413] In other words, according to the United States, the proportionality of countermeasures should 'principally' be assessed on the basis of whether they were 'tailored to induce the wrongdoer to meet its obligations under international law'.[414] For its part, the Czech Republic expressed support for Draft Article 49 [1996] which suggested that the principle of proportionality in the case of third-party counter-measures should be applied 'by each State individually'.[415] In sum, the ILC had on first reading completely assimilated the proportionality test for bilateral and third-party countermeasures.

On second reading, Special Rapporteur Crawford proposed that the principle of proportionality should be more strictly formulated. The negative formulation 'not be out of proportion' required reconsideration and Crawford proposed to replace it with the positive formulation of proportionality adopted by the ICJ in the *Gabčíkovo Nagymaros Project* case. In Crawford's view, a positive formulation was clearly preferable; it would generally be consistent with other areas of international law where proportionality was relevant (e.g. self-defence) even though what was proportionate could still not be determined with precision.[416] In terms of the criteria by which proportionality should be assessed, Crawford essentially agreed with the ILC's approach on first reading subject to one caveat: the reference to 'injured State' in Draft Article 49 [1996] was unduly restrictive insofar as the wrongful act and its effects on the victim did not necessarily involve a State.[417]

With respect to what Crawford called the 'inducement factor',[418] he noted that the purpose of countermeasures had some relevance in that a clearly disproportionate measure may well be judged not to have been necessary to induce compliance either.[419] That said, the proportionality

---

[413] UN Doc. A/CN.4/488, 125–126 (Ireland), 127 (United States).
[414] Ibid., 127 (United States).   [415] Ibid., 124 (Czech Republic).
[416] Crawford, Third Report, 91, para. 346.   [417] Ibid.
[418] Crawford, Fourth Report, 16, para. 65.
[419] Crawford, Third Report, 91, para. 346. For example, the use of countermeasures *sub judice* may, in accordance with Article 52(3)(b) ARSIWA, be considered disproportionate. Likewise, the ILC has recognized that, given the subsidiary role of satisfaction in the spectrum of reparation, requests for satisfaction by way of countermeasures would be 'highly unlikely' to be deemed proportionate. Similar considerations apply to assurances and guarantees of non-repetition. However, the breach of a communitarian norm would presumably qualify as an exceptional case in which satisfaction could rightly be enforced by way of countermeasures. See ARSIWA Commentary, Art. 49, §8; Art. 52, §8; O'Keefe

of a countermeasure had 'a function partly independent of the question whether the countermeasure was necessary to achieve a particular result'.[420] Put differently, the proportionality of a countermeasure constituted a restriction over and above that implied by its stated object. Crawford accordingly proposed that '[c]ountermeasures must be commensurate with the injury suffered, taking into account the gravity of the internationally wrongful act and its harmful effects on the injured party'.[421] Thus Crawford removed the previous reference to 'injured State'; countermeasures were instead required to be commensurate with the broader notion of 'injury suffered'.

Already on first reading, Crawford had been critical of the ILC's bilateral conception of injury in Draft Article 40 [1996] and the implication in Draft Article 49 [1996] that the proportionality of third-party countermeasures should be assessed on an individual rather than a collective basis.[422] On second reading, Crawford proposed to modify the proportionality test applicable to third-party countermeasures by cumulatively taking into account the conduct of each individual State engaging in such action.[423] Put differently, third-party countermeasures 'should not, taken together, infringe the requirement of proportionality'.[424] This requirement of overall proportionality was, however, never explicitly made in the proposed provision itself – a point mainly criticized by Chile in the Sixth Committee.[425] The requirement instead implicitly followed from Crawford's proposal that States would generally be obligated to coordinate the adoption of third-party countermeasures: 'Where more than one State takes countermeasures ... those States shall cooperate in order to ensure that the conditions laid down ... for the taking of countermeasures [notably, proportionality] are fulfilled'.[426]

The Drafting Committee in 2000 adopted Crawford's proposal with a minor drafting change to more closely reflect the language of the ICJ in

---

(2010), 1158, 1163. Requests for satisfaction would in any event be limited by Article 37(3) ARSIWA: 'Satisfaction shall not be out of proportion to the injury and may not take a form humiliating to the responsible State' (see ARSIWA Commentary, Art. 37, §8). On procedural safeguards see below Section 6.4.

[420] Crawford, Third Report, 91, para. 346.   [421] Ibid., 96, para. 367 (his draft article 49).

[422] YbILC (1992), vol. I, 89–90, para. 38 (Mr. Crawford).

[423] Crawford, Third Report, 106, para. 402.

[424] Ibid., 106, para. 406. See also Crawford, Second Report, 91, para. 373. To the same effect: Gaja (2005), 149.

[425] UN Doc. A/C.6/55/SR.17, 8, para. 48 (Chile). See also Topical Summary of Government Comments in the Sixth Committee, UN Doc. A/CN.4/513 (2000), 33, para. 177.

[426] Crawford, Third Report, 108, para. 413 (his draft article 50(B)(2)).

the *Gabčíkovo Nagymaros Project* case. The revised proposal accordingly provided that 'countermeasures must be commensurate with the injury suffered, taking into account the gravity of the wrongful act and the rights in question'.[427] The Drafting Committee explained that the words 'taking into account' were not intended to be exhaustive and that other factors (in addition to the gravity of the wrongful act and the rights in question) might also be relevant in the assessment of proportionality. Those factors could not, however, be determined in the abstract but would have to be identified in the particular context of each case. It was nevertheless made clear that the purpose of countermeasures was not a relevant factor – a position consistent with the ICJ in *Gabčíkovo Nagymaros Project*.[428] Furthermore, it was explained that the reference to the 'rights in question' had a broad meaning and was intended to include not only the effect of a wrongful act on the injured State but also on the rights of the responsible State. In addition, the position of any other affected States could also be taken into account.[429] Finally, the Drafting Committee also expressed support for Crawford's proposal concerning an obligation of cooperation in order to ensure the overall proportionality of third-party countermeasures; however, it did not elaborate further on this putative requirement.[430]

Although States generally accepted the Drafting Committee's proposal on proportionality, some reservations were nevertheless expressed as to its exact formulation.[431] In particular, several States doubted whether the obligation of cooperation in case of third-party countermeasures could have any real effect given its vagueness and generality.[432] A small

---

[427] YbILC (2000), vol. I, 397–398, para. 77 (Chairman of the Drafting Committee, Mr. Gaja); ILC Report (2000), UN Doc. A/55/10, 70 (Draft Article 52 [2000]).

[428] YbILC (2000), vol. I, 398, paras. 77–78 (Chairman of the Drafting Committee, Mr. Gaja). See also ILC Report (2000), UN Doc. A/55/10, 56, para. 334. For support with respect to the inducement factor see further YbILC (2000), vol. I, 278, para. 18 (Mr. Gaja), 297, para. 56 (Mr. Yamada); YbILC (2001), vol. I, 38, para. 23 (Mr. Simma).

[429] YbILC (2000), vol. I, 398, paras. 77–78 (Chairman of the Drafting Committee, Mr. Gaja). See also ARSIWA Commentary, Art. 51, §6.

[430] YbILC (2000), vol. I, 398, paras. 77–78 (Chairman of the Drafting Committee, Mr. Gaja), 399, paras. 86, 90; ILC Report (2000), UN Doc. A/55/10, 70 (Draft Article 54(3) [2000]).

[431] See Topical Summary of Government Comments in the Sixth Committee, UN Doc. A/CN.4/513 (2000), 31, paras. 162–163. For a summary of the ILC debate see ILC Report (2000), UN Doc. A/55/10, 56, paras. 333–334.

[432] See e.g. UN Docs. A/C.6/55/SR.17, 8, para. 48 (Chile); A/C.6/55/SR.17, 13, para. 79 and A/CN.4/515, 72, 90 (Austria); A/C.6/55/SR.18, 4, para. 17 (Jordan). Some States nevertheless supported the flexibility of the proposed obligation of cooperation: see e.g. UN Doc. A/C.6/55/SR.16, 5, para. 28 (Italy). Also: Topical Summary of Government

minority even doubted whether third-party countermeasures were at all compatible with the principle of proportionality.[433] Some States also continued to stress the relevance of the inducement factor.[434] For its part, the United States specifically proposed that proportionality should, *inter alia*, take into account 'the degree of response necessary to induce the State responsible for the internationally wrongful act to comply with its obligations'.[435]

The Drafting Committee in 2001 considered the issue again but remained unconvinced.[436] The ILC accordingly adopted the principle of proportionality unchanged as Article 51 ARSIWA:

> **Article 51**
> **Proportionality**
> Countermeasures must be commensurate with the injury suffered, taking into account the gravity of the internationally wrongful act and the rights in question.

The ILC commentary to this provision reiterates that proportionality is a limitation even on countermeasures which may be justified under Article 49 ARSIWA: the function of proportionality is partly independent of the question whether a countermeasure is necessary to achieve the result of ensuring compliance.[437] In sum, in line with *Air Services* and *Gabčíkovo Nagymaros Project*,[438] proportionality, as embodied in Article 51 ARSIWA, is a factor mitigating the instrumental function of countermeasures and is assessed not purely on quantitative grounds but also on qualitative ones.

The process of taking into account the gravity of the wrongful act and the rights in question as part of the proportionality analysis in Article 51 ARSIWA is meant to ensure that the countermeasures adopted are

---

Comments in the Sixth Committee, UN Doc. A/CN.4/513 (2000), 34, para. 182; Crawford, Fourth Report, 18, para. 73.

[433] See UN Docs. A/C.6/55/SR.18, 4, para. 17 (Jordan), 11, para. 61 (Cuba); A/CN.4/515, 69 (China). Also: Topical Summary of Government Comments in the Sixth Committee, UN Doc. A/CN.4/513 (2000), 33, para. 177.

[434] See UN Docs. A/C.6/55/SR.14, 12, para. 69, A/CN.4/515, 80 (Japan); A/C.6/55/SR.18, 2, para. 5, A/C.6/56/SR.16, 8, para. 49 (Algeria); A/C.6/55/SR.17, 11, para. 65 (Costa Rica); A/C.6/55/SR.23, 2, para. 4 (Colombia on behalf of the Rio Group). Also: Topical Summary of Government Comments in the Sixth Committee, UN Doc. A/CN.4/513 (2000), 31, paras. 162–163.

[435] UN Doc. A/CN.4/515, 83 (United States). See also UN Doc. A/C.6/56/SR.14, 12, para. 75 (United States).

[436] YbILC (2001), vol. I, 112, para. 57 (Chairman of the Drafting Committee, Mr. Tomka).

[437] ARSIWA Commentary, Art. 51, §7.   [438] Ibid., Art. 51, §4.

compared against the proper function of the action of self-redress. As Cannizzaro explains:

> Proportionality requires not only that the means chosen are appropriate to the subjective aim of the respondent state, but also, and primarily, that the aim in itself be reasonable and appropriate in the context of the structure of the breached norm and of the legal consequences deriving from the breach. In other words, the essence of proportionality resides in comparing the measures adopted with the proper function of the action of self-redress.[439]

For example, in *ADM and Tate & Lyle v. Mexico*, a NAFTA tribunal found the imposition of a Mexican sugar tax, an action allegedly taken in response to US breaches of certain NAFTA obligations, to amount to a disproportionate countermeasure as it adversely affected US investors in Mexico.[440] The arbitral tribunal concluded that Mexico's action was not necessary or reasonably connected to its stated aim of ensuring US compliance; this aim could have been attained by other measures not impairing obligations owed to US investors.[441] By parity of reasoning, aside from obligations owed to foreign investors, countermeasures adversely affecting the enjoyment of human rights in the target State may well be judged disproportionate.[442] The same applies to countermeasures with a marked punitive aim or with potentially irreversible effects.[443] Countermeasures affecting the principles of territorial integrity and non-intervention, or even, *in extremis*, endangering international peace and security, may also fall into the same category.[444] Article 51 ARSIWA has thus been recognized by international tribunals as an authoritative statement of customary international law.[445]

---

[439] Cannizzaro (2001), 899. See also *Archer Daniels Midland Company and Tate & Lyle Ingredients Americas, Inc. v. Mexico*, ICSID Case No. ARB(AF)/04/05, Award, 21 Nov. 2007, para. 154; Crawford (2013a), 699.

[440] *Archer Daniels Midland Company and Tate & Lyle Ingredients Americas, Inc. v. Mexico*, ICSID Case No. ARB(AF)/04/05, Award, 21 Nov. 2007, paras. 152–160.

[441] Ibid.

[442] See e.g. O'Keefe (2010), 1164–1165. Compare CESCR General Comment No. 8, UN Doc. E/C.12/1997/8, para. 14.

[443] See e.g. Arangio-Ruiz, Fourth Report, 7, para. 4; ARSIWA Commentary, Art. 51, §7; Sicilianos (2005), 467; Tzanakopoulos (2011), 186. Also: ARSIWA Commentary, Art. 49, §9.

[444] See Topical Summary of Government Comments in the Sixth Committee, UN Doc. A/CN.4/513 (2000), 30, para. 160. Compare ILC Report (1992), UN Doc. A/47/10, 29–30, paras. 203, 205; Cannizzaro (2001), 911–912.

[445] See e.g. *United States – Transitional Safeguard Measure on Combed Cotton Yarn from Pakistan*, WT/DS192/AB/R, Report of the Appellate Body, 8 Oct. 2001, paras. 119–120;

In line with the ILC debate, the proportionality test for third-party countermeasures appears to be largely the same subject to the separate condition of overall proportionality. Chile rightly criticized that the requirement of overall proportionality was not explicitly stated, but the issue largely became moot with the adoption of the saving clause in Article 54 ARSIWA.[446] The assessment of the proportionality of third-party countermeasures, as required by Article 51 ARSIWA, raises some difficult questions. As Austria observed:

> There are problems relating to article 54, paragraph 3 [2000], concerning cooperation between several States in taking countermeasures. Such countermeasures must also comply with the principle of proportionality laid down in article 52 [i.e. what became Article 51 ARSIWA]. The application of this rule is difficult enough if one State takes countermeasures and it is unclear how it should be applied if several States do so, let alone if they are applying different countermeasures. A possible solution could be to redraft article 53 [i.e. what became Article 52 ARSIWA], envisaging an obligation of all States intending to take countermeasures to negotiate joint countermeasures prior to taking them.[447]

Cameroon raised a more specific problem:

> Equally important was the relationship between countermeasures taken by one or more States and measures decided upon by the Security Council under Article 41 of the Charter of the United Nations. Article 59 did not resolve that problem, since the Charter itself did not establish whether Council-mandated measures automatically entailed the cessation of

---

United States – Definitive Safeguard Measures on Imports of Circular Welded Carbon Quality Line Pipe from Korea, WT/DS202/AB/R, Report of the Appellate Body, 15 Feb. 2002, paras. 258–259; *United States – Tax Treatment for 'Foreign Sales Corporations'*, WT/DS108/ARB, Decision of the Arbitrator, 30 Aug. 2002, para. 5.26; *Archer Daniels Midland Company and Tate & Lyle Ingredients Americas, Inc. v. Mexico*, ICSID Case No. ARB(AF)/04/05, Award, 21 Nov. 2007, para. 152; *Corn Products International Inc. v. Mexico*, ICSID Case No. ARB(AF)/04/01, Decision on Responsibility, 15 Jan. 2008, para. 146(5); *United States – Subsidies on Upland Cotton, Recourse to Arbitration by the United States under Article 22.6 of the DSU and Article 4.11 of the SCM Agreement*, WT/DS267/ARB/1, Decision by the Arbitrator, 31 Aug. 2009, para. 4.113; *United States – Subsidies on Upland Cotton, Recourse to Arbitration by the United States under Article 22.6 of the DSU and Article 7.10 of the SCM Agreement*, WT/DS267/ARB/2, Decision by the Arbitrator, 31 Aug. 2009, para. 4.61. See further O'Keefe (2010), 1167 (his n. 70 with many further references to WTO case law).
[446] See above n. 425.
[447] UN Doc. A/CN.4/515, 90 (Austria). Compare UN Doc. A/CN.4/488, 116 (United Kingdom).

countermeasures by States or whether the two types of measures could be implemented simultaneously without violating the principle of proportionality.[448]

As already suggested, the Drafting Committee in 2000 did not, aside from a vague reference to the putative obligation of cooperation, consider these issues further.[449] It is now convenient to briefly examine them.

6.3.2   Evaluation

It seems that three closely related issues concerning the assessment of proportionality of third-party countermeasures merit examination. First, it must be examined whether the proportionality test in Article 51 ARSIWA applies on an individual basis to each State separately against the wrongdoer or to all third-party countermeasures taken together (i.e. overall proportionality). Second, it must be examined whether States are under an obligation to cooperate with respect to third-party counter-measures in order to ensure proportionality. Third, taking into account the particular importance attached to the integrity of communitarian norms, it must be examined whether the inducement factor may excep-tionally be considered a relevant criterion to assess proportionality. These issues will be considered in turn.

As a minimum, it is clear from practice that third-party countermea-sures are not as such incompatible with the principle of proportionality. Beyond this conclusion, practice concerning third-party countermea-sures provides only limited guidance. It nevertheless suggests that overall proportionality is required. For example, in a rare judicial pronounce-ment, the Brussels Court of Appeal in *JAT v. Belgium* held that the EU flight ban adopted by way of third-party countermeasures against the FRY in response to the Kosovo crisis was proportionate overall.[450] More recently, the Group of Friends of the Syrian People have noted that, taken together, 'the members of the Group have adopted effective, proportional

---

[448] UN Doc. A/C.6/56/SR.14, 10, para. 62 (Cameroon). See also e.g. UN Docs. A/CN.4/515, 91–92 (Austria); Topical Summary of Government Comments in the Sixth Committee, A/CN.4/513 (2000), 33, para. 176.

[449] See YbILC (2000), vol. I, 399–400, paras. 90–91 (Chairman of the Drafting Committee, Mr. Gaja).

[450] *Jugoslovenski Aerotransport c. l' État Belge*, Cour d'appel de Bruxelles (9ème chambre), Decision of 10 June 1999 (No. 1998/KR/528), Journal des tribunaux (1999), 693. See further Paasivirta and Rosas (2002), 214–215; d'Argent (2003), 588–589, 622–624; Tzanakopoulos (2011), 188–189.

and coordinated sanctions', including third-party countermeasures, against Syria.[451]

Protests against the adverse humanitarian consequences of third-party countermeasures on the civilian population in a target State likewise generally seem to refer to a yardstick by which proportionality is measured in cumulative terms.[452] Practice further indicates that Security Council enforcement measures and third-party countermeasures may operate in parallel consistent with the principle of overall proportionality. However, as part of the assessment of the overall proportionality of third-party countermeasures, any relevant action taken by the Security Council under Chapter VII UNC must be taken into account.[453] Aside from its basis in practice, it seems that the putative requirement of overall proportionality would be consistent with the rationale of Article 48 ARSIWA and also normatively desirable.[454]

In reality, some form of cooperation and coordination between States will normally be required to ensure the overall proportionality of third-party countermeasures. However, it is doubtful whether, contrary to the suggestion by the Drafting Committee in 2000, this amounts to a legal requirement. As the ILC itself observed with respect to Article 41(1) ARSIWA:

> What is called for in the face of serious breaches is a joint and coordinated effort by all States to counteract the effects of these breaches. It may be open to question whether general international law at present prescribes a positive duty of cooperation, and paragraph 1 in that respect may reflect the progressive development of international law. But in fact such cooperation, especially in the framework of international organizations, is carried out already in response to the gravest breaches of international law and it is often the only way of providing an effective remedy.[455]

---

[451] See Statement by the Friends of the Syrian People International Working Group on Sanctions (The Hague, 20 Sept. 2012), para. 2, www.government.nl/files/documents-and-publications/reports/2012/09/20/statement-by-the-friends-of-the-syrian-people-international-working-group-on-sanctions/statement-eng.pdf. See further Section 4.2.20.

[452] See above Section 6.2.1.2(iii).   [453] See Section 5.2.1.

[454] For support in the literature see e.g. de Guttry (1985), 314–315; Hutchinson (1988), 206–207 (n. 236); Sachariew (1988), 286; Annacker (1994a), 161; Zemanek (1997), 267; Kolb (2004), 413–415; Gaja (2005), 149; Villalpando (2005), 376. It is a separate matter that States, having at a minimum an autonomous entitlement to demand cessation of breaches of communitarian norms under Article 48 ARSIWA, can, in principle, do so individually by way of third-party countermeasures. As already discussed, proportionality may act as a substantive limitation even on otherwise lawful third-party countermeasures. On procedural conditions, see below Section 6.4.

[455] ARSIWA Commentary, Art. 41, §3. See also e.g. YbILC (2001), vol. I, 52, para. 16 (Mr. Galicki); Topical Summary of Government Comments in the Sixth Committee, UN Doc. A/CN.4/513 (2000), 24, para. 118. Further: Jørgensen (2010), 695.

Indeed, States generally seek to coordinate the adoption and implementation of unilateral coercive measures, including third-party countermeasures, and especially do so in the framework of international organizations. Practice does not however suggest that such cooperation is predominantly motivated by legal considerations. Quite simply, as the ILC itself recognized in the above passage, it is often the only way of providing an effective remedy for serious breaches of communitarian norms. The recent action taken by the Group of Friends of the Syrian People against Syria may again serve as a useful illustration:

> The Group reiterated its resolve to ensure that sanctions against the Syrian regime and its designated supporters are coordinated, effective and implemented robustly in order to hasten the end of the regime's oppression of the Syrian people.[456]

A 'continued concerted multinational effort'[457] is clearly essential in order to achieve this objective. In more general terms, the EU guidelines on the use of autonomous sanctions explain:

> The Council will work to enlist the support of the widest possible range of partners in support of EU autonomous sanctions which will be more effective when they are reinforced by broad international support.[458]

In short, States will for pragmatic reasons normally cooperate to maximize the effectiveness of third-party countermeasures. Crucially, they do not appear to be under any obligation to do so in order to ensure their overall proportionality.

Finally, as for the inducement factor as a relevant criterion to assess proportionality, it may be recalled that it was explicitly rejected by the ILC. During the course of the debate, several ILC members nevertheless

---

[456] Statement by the Friends of the Syrian People International Working Group on Sanctions (The Hague, 20 Sept. 2012), para. 2, www.government.nl/files/documents-and-publications/reports/2012/09/20/statement-by-the-friends-of-the-syrian-people-international-working-group-on-sanctions/statement-eng.pdf.

[457] Statement by the Friends of the Syrian People International Working Group on Sanctions (Tokyo, 30 Nov. 2012), para. 8, www.government.nl/documents-and-publications/leaflets/2012/12/10/joint-statement-tokyo-30-nov-2012.html.

[458] Council of the European Union, Basic Principles on the Use of Restrictive Measures (Sanctions) (2004), para. 4, http://register.consilium.europa.eu/doc/srv?l=EN&f=ST%2010198%202004%20REV%201. See also Council of the European Union, 'EU restrictive measures – Factsheet' (29 Apr. 2014), 3 ('EU candidate countries are systematically invited to align themselves with EU restrictive measures'), www.consilium.europa.eu/uedocs/cms_data/docs/pressdata/EN/foraff/135804.pdf.

expressed their support.[459] Several States in the Sixth Committee likewise expressed support.[460] There is also some (albeit limited) support for the inducement factor in State practice concerning third-party countermeasures. During the Falklands crisis, Belgium (on behalf of EC Member States) stated before the Security Council that the action taken against Argentina, including third-party countermeasures, was not 'disproportionate to what was at stake'; namely, to induce Argentina to cease its unlawful use of force in the South Atlantic.[461] More recently, EU Member States have stressed that resort to unilateral coercive measures, including third-party countermeasures, 'must always be proportionate to their objective'.[462]

Cannizzaro has noted that normative considerations of effectiveness militate in favour of taking the instrumental function of third-party countermeasures into account in the overall assessment of proportionality, as otherwise 'the practical consequence would be that serious offences to collective interests could remain unprocessed'.[463] Such considerations must, however, be counterbalanced against the risks of abusive third-party countermeasures, especially as they relate to possible adverse humanitarian consequences on individuals in target States. Practice does not provide a clear answer. In any event, it seems that the basic proportionality test, as embodied in Article 51 ARSIWA, is already sufficiently flexible to satisfactorily take into account the discrete issues raised by the enforcement of communitarian norms by way of third-party countermeasures.

To conclude, the assessment of the proportionality of countermeasures is 'an inexact science'.[464] To complicate matters further, some uncertainty still remains with respect to the assessment of the proportionality of third-party countermeasures. Still, the basic requirement of

---

[459] See ILC Report (1992), UN Doc. A/47/10, 31, para. 212; ILC Report (2000), UN Doc. A/55/10, 56, para. 334.

[460] See above nn. 413–414, 434.

[461] See UN Doc. S/PV.2363 (23 May 1982), 12, paras. 128–129 (Belgium on behalf of EC Member States). For affirmation of the proportionality of the third-party countermeasures adopted against Argentina see e.g. Dewost (1982), 231; Kuyper (1983), 155; de Guttry (1984), 402–406. See further Section 4.2.8.

[462] European Commission, EU Guidelines on Implementation and Evaluation of Restrictive Measures (2008), 6, http://eeas.europa.eu/cfsp/sanctions/docs/index_en.pdf.

[463] Cannizzaro (2001), 915. See also e.g. Fitzmaurice, Fourth Report, 67, para. 85 (commenting on his draft article 18 on reprisals); Sicilianos (1990), 279–280; Kolb (2004), 421–424; Cassese (2005), 306. Contra: Alland (1994), 304–305; Villalpando (2005), 375 (his n. 1301).

[464] O'Keefe (2010), 1165.

proportionality appears to have had a regulating effect on practice concerning third-party countermeasures by injecting a degree of moderation. Despite its indeterminacy, the principle of proportionality thus serves as a useful tool by which to temper the use of third-party countermeasures.

6.4 Procedural Conditions

Countermeasures may only legitimately be taken in response to an actual breach of international law. The special importance of procedural conditions for countermeasures is readily apparent: the wrongfulness of the act of the target State that triggered them will not normally have been objectively determined at the time they are taken – at least not by a judicial body.[465] Countermeasures are a form of decentralized law enforcement which operate 'in an international system in which the impartial settlement of disputes through the due process of law is not yet guaranteed'.[466] Recourse to compulsory third-party dispute settlement may not be available, immediately or at all. At the same time, where recourse is available and has been invoked by either party to the dispute, it seems reasonable that it should be taken into account in the assessment of the necessity of taking countermeasures to resolve the dispute.[467] Countermeasures should be 'a wager on the wisdom, not the weakness of the other Party . . . and be accompanied by a genuine effort at resolving the dispute'.[468]

It also seems clear that a State cannot take countermeasures *ex nihilo* without any prior explanation or advance warning to the target State: such action would invariably invite abuse and exacerbate the dispute.[469] The target State must be given an opportunity to explain, for example, that it has committed no wrongful act or that the wrongful act is not attributable to it. By initiating a dialogue and assessing the response of the target State before taking countermeasures, the State contemplating coercive action may itself avoid committing a wrongful act based on erroneous or incomplete information. In other situations, countermeasures may even be avoided altogether if the target State accepts

---

[465] See Iwasawa and Iwatsuki (2010), 1149; Crawford (2013a), 700. It should be noted that the wrongfulness of conduct is normally ascertained by various international bodies, including the UN General Assembly: see further Section 5.2.3.

[466] ARSIWA Commentary, Art. 52, §2.   [467] Ibid.

[468] *US-France Air Services Agreement* (1978), RIAA, vol. XVIII, 417 at 445, para. 91.

[469] See already Vattel (1758), Book II, Chapter XVIII, §343.

responsibility for its unlawful conduct and decides to revert to legality.[470] Put differently, 'the necessity of countermeasures diminishes in inverse proportion to the achievement of their legitimate aims'.[471] Prudence thus dictates that countermeasures must comply with certain basic procedural conditions. These appear to be generally guided by the principles of necessity and non-aggravation of disputes.[472]

There is support in international jurisprudence for at least certain minimum procedural safeguards for countermeasures. The arbitral tribunal in the *Naulilaa* case stressed that countermeasures were only lawful if they had been preceded by an unfulfilled demand for redress.[473] In the *Air Services* arbitration, the issue of procedural conditions was closely examined. In that case, it may be recalled that France had taken certain action against a US carrier in violation of the 1946 US-France Air Services Agreement. The United States responded by threatening France with similar countermeasures unless it agreed to resolve the treaty dispute on certain procedural terms not all of which were envisaged by the compromissory clause in Article X of the 1946 Agreement.[474] The US posture was maintained as the parties negotiated a separate *compromis*.[475] Aside from the issue of proportionality,[476] France alleged that the US action was unlawful on the following grounds:

> [R]eprisals may be resorted to only in case of necessity, *i.e.* in the absence of other legal channels to settle the dispute; plainly this condition was not met for such channels were available under Article X of the 1946 Agreement. Furthermore, the retaliation procedure should have been preceded by an unsuccessful formal request, as required by international law.[477]

---

[470] See e.g. Draft Articles Commentary, Art. 47, §§5–6; UN Doc. A/CN.4/488, 121 (Czech Republic). Also: Kamto (2010), 1171 (noting that such a dialogue 'certainly has a psychological effect and may be used as a means of exerting pressure on the State in question to induce it to cooperate. And this is, in the end, the purpose of countermeasures').

[471] Draft Articles Commentary, Art. 47, §6.

[472] Iwasawa and Iwatsuki (2010), 1152–1155; Crawford (2013a), 700–702. Waiver and extinctive prescription within the meaning of Article 45 ARSIWA may provide an additional rationale: see e.g. UN Doc. A/CN.4/488, 120 (United Kingdom); Crawford, Third Report, 64–65, paras. 234–238; Peel (2010), 1030.

[473] *Naulilaa (Responsibility of Germany for damage caused in the Portuguese colonies in the south of Africa) (Portugal/Germany)* (1928), RIAA, vol. II, 1011 at 1026 (a condition Germany had failed to meet in this case). Also: 1934 IDI Paris Resolution (Art. 6(1)).

[474] *US-France Air Services Agreement* (1978), RIAA, vol. XVIII, 417 at 422, 426–427, 429, paras. 9, 15–16, 23 (n. 63).

[475] Ibid., 421, paras. 8–9.   [476] See above Section 6.3.

[477] *US-France Air Services Agreement* (1978), RIAA, vol. XVIII, 417 at 427, para. 17. The *Air Services* tribunal only implicitly pronounced itself on the issue of a prior demand for redress: see ibid., paras. 85–87. Also: ARSIWA Commentary, Art. 52, §3.

For its part, the United States rejected the French argument that 'no countermeasures may be taken where alternative means of satisfaction exist'.[478] The *Air Services* tribunal stated:

> [T]he arbitral tribunal does not believe that it is possible, in the present state of international relations, to lay down a rule prohibiting counter-measures during negotiations, especially where such counter-measures are accompanied by an offer for a procedure affording the possibility of accelerating the solution of the dispute.
>
> . . .
>
> With regard to the machinery of negotiations, the actions by the United States Government do not appear, therefore, to run counter to the international obligations of that Government.[479]

It continued:

> However, the lawfulness of such counter-measures has to be considered still from another viewpoint. It may indeed be asked whether they are valid in general, in the case of a dispute concerning a point of law, where there is arbitral or judicial machinery which can settle the dispute. Many jurists have felt that while arbitral or judicial proceedings were in progress, recourse to counter-measures, even if limited by the proportionality rule, was prohibited. Such an assertion deserves sympathy but requires further elaboration. If the proceedings form part of an institutional framework ensuring some degree of enforcement of obligations, the justification of counter-measures will undoubtedly disappear, but owing to the existence of that framework rather than solely on account of the existence of arbitral or judicial proceedings as such.
>
> [T]he situation during the period in which a case is not yet before a tribunal is not the same as the situation during the period in which that case is *sub judice*. So long as a dispute has not been brought before the tribunal . . . the period of negotiation is not over and the rules mentioned above remain applicable.
>
> The situation changes once the tribunal is in a position to act. To the extent that the tribunal has the necessary means to achieve the objectives justifying the counter-measures, it must be admitted that the right of the Parties to initiate such measures disappears. In other words, the power of a tribunal to decide on interim measures of protection . . . leads to the disappearance of the power to initiate counter-measures and may lead to an elimination of existing counter-measures to the extent that the tribunal so provides as an interim measure of protection. As the object and scope of the power of the tribunal to decide on interim measures of protection may be defined quite narrowly, however, the power of the Parties to

---

[478]   *US-France Air Services Agreement* (1978), RIAA, vol. XVIII, 417 at 428, para. 18.
[479]   Ibid., 445, paras. 91, 93.

maintain or initiate counter-measures, too, may not disappear completely.[480]

In the *Gabčíkovo Nagymaros Project* case, the ICJ emphasized a fundamental condition which must be fulfilled before taking countermeasures: '[T]he injured State must have called upon the State committing the wrongful act to discontinue its wrongful conduct or to make reparation for it'.[481] This requirement of a prior demand for redress is sometimes referred to as *sommation*.[482] In the said case, it also included a notification that countermeasures would be adopted in case of continued non-compliance.[483] The ILC built on this case law in laying down procedural conditions for countermeasures in Article 52 ARSIWA.

6.4.1 The ILC's Contribution

The extent to which procedural conditions, and especially compliance with dispute settlement procedures, should be a prerequisite for taking countermeasures was a highly controversial issue in the ILC. A balance had to be struck between maintaining the effectiveness of countermeasures and ensuring appropriate safeguards against premature and unlawful countermeasures. On first reading, Special Rapporteur Arangio-Ruiz proposed that no countermeasures could be adopted prior to the injured State having made an unfulfilled demand for redress and provided an appropriate and timely communication of its intention to do so.[484] Beyond these minimum procedural preconditions, Arangio-Ruiz considered prior recourse to dispute settlement procedures an indispensable guarantee against unfounded or unreasonable claims enforced by way of countermeasures. To this effect, Arangio-Ruiz initially introduced a far-

---

[480] Ibid., 445–446, paras. 94–96. To the same effect: 1934 IDI Paris Resolution (Art. 5).

[481] *Gabčíkovo Nagymaros Project*, ICJ Rep. (1997), 7 at 56, para. 84. See also 1934 IDI Paris Resolution (Art. 6(1)).

[482] ARSIWA Commentary, Art. 52, §3.

[483] *Gabčíkovo Nagymaros Project*, ICJ Rep. (1997), 7 at 47, paras. 61 et seq. The ICJ did not consider the possible requirement of prior negotiations. It may be recalled that the adoption of countermeasures in the case (by way of 'Variant C') had been preceded by exhaustive and fruitless negotiations and so the point did not arise. See however ibid., 221 (Diss. Op. Judge Vereshchetin). It may also be noted that 'Variant C' (as well as the illegality to which it was a response) remained in place while the dispute was pending before the ICJ. For a summary of the facts of the case see above Section 6.3.

[484] Arangio-Ruiz, Fourth Report, 22 (his draft articles 11 and 12(1)(b)); Arangio-Ruiz, Sixth Report, 15–17, paras. 67–72, 81, 85 (for his revised draft articles 11 and 12). Compare Riphagen, Seventh Report, 4–6 (his drafts articles 1–5 of Part Three, with accompanying commentary).

reaching and cumbersome proposal: the adoption of countermeasures by an injured State should be preceded by the exhaustion 'of all the amicable settlement procedures available under general international law, the Charter of the United Nations or any other dispute settlement instrument to which it is a party' – a proposal he subsequently limited to an obligation to seek a settlement under a binding third-party dispute settlement procedure or, in the absence of such a possibility, to offer to resolve the dispute by such means.[485]

In order to protect the injured State, Arangio-Ruiz's proposal exempted 'interim measures of protection' – i.e. the most readily reversible forms of countermeasures (such as asset freezes) likely to be ineffectual unless taken immediately – and cases where the target State did not cooperate in good faith in selecting and implementing available dispute settlement procedures.[486] Arangio-Ruiz also proposed an elaborate system for post-countermeasures dispute settlement under a possible future convention on State responsibility.[487] However, as already observed in Chapter 3, Arangio-Ruiz proposed a separate procedural safeguards regime for third-party countermeasures involving pronouncements by the UN General Assembly or the Security Council and the ICJ – an unrealistic proposal that was firmly rejected in the ILC.[488]

Arangio-Ruiz's proposals concerning the preconditions of prior demand for redress and notification of countermeasures were widely supported in the ILC.[489] By contrast, his proposed requirement to exhaust all available dispute settlement procedures prior to the adoption of countermeasures was strongly criticized as unrealistic and unworkable.[490] On first reading, the ILC adopted Draft Article 47 [1996], which in very brief and implicit terms dealt with the preconditions of prior demand and notification.[491] With respect to dispute settlement procedures there was

---

[485] Arangio-Ruiz, Fourth Report, 22 (his draft article 12(1)); Arangio-Ruiz, Sixth Report, 17, para. 82 (for his revised draft article 12(1)). See further Arangio-Ruiz (1994), 20. Compare Riphagen, Sixth Report, 11–12 (his draft article 10, with accompanying commentary).

[486] Arangio-Ruiz, Fourth Report, 22 (his draft article 12(2)).

[487] Arangio-Ruiz, Fifth Report, 28–30 (for his proposed draft articles and dispute settlement annex). Compare Riphagen, Seventh Report, 6 (for his dispute settlement annex).

[488] Arangio-Ruiz, Seventh Report, 12–13, 29, 31, paras. 41–45, 140 (his draft article 17), 147 (his draft article 7 of Part Three); YbILC (1996), vol. I, 178–180, paras. 63–65, 70–73 (Chairman of the Drafting Committee, Mr. Calero Rodrigues); and Section 3.1.3.

[489] ILC Report (1992), UN Doc. A/47/10, 26, 29, paras. 171–173, 197.

[490] Ibid., 28–29, paras. 188–196. Further: Simma (1994b), 102.

[491] Draft Articles Commentary, Art. 47, §§5–6. See also YbILC (1993), vol. I, 142–143, paras. 9–19 (Chairman of the Drafting Committee, Mr. Mikulka).

a central disagreement in the ILC. While it was generally agreed that such procedures should be pursued, there was disagreement concerning the extent to which this should be a necessary precondition for taking counter-measures. The possibilities for a State to postpone the settlement of the dispute and engage in dilatory tactics needed to be balanced against the fact that some forms of countermeasures (such as asset freezes) were only effective if taken promptly.[492]

Following an extensive debate, the ILC resolved this tension by adopting Draft Article 48 [1996] which required the initiation of only one pre-dispute settlement procedure: the injured State would be under an obligation to seek to settle the dispute by negotiation prior to taking countermeasures. The obligation to negotiate was not subject to any specific time limit other than a criterion of reasonableness.[493] Notwithstanding this requirement, the injured State was nevertheless entitled to adopt 'interim measures of protection' (i.e. 'interim counter-measures') in order to preserve its rights pending the outcome of the negotiation. It was only following an unsuccessful attempt to resolve the dispute by negotiation that an injured State would be entitled to adopt 'full-scale countermeasures'.[494]

In any event, if a State decided to take countermeasures, it would be under an obligation to resort to post-countermeasures dispute settlement procedures under a future convention on State responsibility (notably, compulsory arbitration) or any other binding dispute settlement procedure in force between itself and the target State. Put differently, in taking countermeasures under this treaty-based scheme, the injured State effectively offered the target State the opportunity to resolve the dispute by arbitration.[495] In other respects, Draft Article 48 [1996] was inspired by remarks of the *Air Services* tribunal concerning the suspensive effect of countermeasures once the dispute was submitted to a court or tribunal with the power to order interim measures of protection provided that the target State acted in good faith and the breach was not a continuing one.[496] In sum, the ILC's procedural safeguards regime

---

[492] Draft Articles Commentary, Art. 48, §2.

[493] Draft Articles Commentary, Art. 48, §5. See further YbILC (1996), vol. I, 156, 171, paras. 55, 57 (Mr. Bennouna) (for the compromise proposal).

[494] Draft Articles Commentary, Art. 48, §§3–4. See further YbILC (1996), vol. I, 171–176 (for the debate on the compromise solution of 'interim countermeasures').

[495] Draft Articles Commentary, Art. 48, §7. See also Draft Articles Commentary, Art. 58(2) (linking countermeasures to compulsory arbitration).

[496] Draft Articles Commentary, Art. 48, §§8–11.

for countermeasures on first reading sought to ensure that the inherent risks of abuse associated with the auto-interpretation of wrongful conduct were minimized. A judicial body would ultimately rule on the legality of countermeasures.

In the Sixth Committee, States expressed differing, even conflicting, views on Draft Article 48 [1996].[497] Some States expressed support for the provision while others considered that it should be substantially amended, if not omitted altogether. With respect to the obligation of negotiation as a precondition to taking countermeasures, some States expressed support on the basis that countermeasures should be considered only as 'a last resort, once the various methods of peaceful settlement of disputes, and above all the obligation to negotiate, have been exhausted'.[498] Others strongly disapproved mainly on the basis that the obligation to negotiate prior to taking countermeasures did not form part of customary international law, unlike the requirement of a prior demand for redress. For example, the United Kingdom observed that

> Customary international law does not require that States negotiate prior to taking countermeasures, or even that States abandon countermeasures while negotiations are in process. Paragraph 1 [of Draft Article 48] proposes a novel and unjustified restraint upon States which is impractical and utopian in the fast-moving modern world.[499]

The United States, invoking the *Air Services* arbitration, raised the same objection.[500] For its part, Germany expressed 'some doubts' on the matter adding that, as recently confirmed by the ICJ in the *Gabčíkovo Nagymaros Project* case, '[i]t would rather seem that under customary international law only a demand for cessation or reparation must precede the imposition of countermeasures'.[501] Moreover, '[i]t would also be quite unreasonable to expect the injured State to refrain from taking (peaceful) countermeasures until it has exhausted all means to settle the dispute amicably'.[502]

As for the notion of interim measures of protection, many States expressed strong reservations, as it would be difficult in practice to

---

[497] For a useful summary of the debate see Crawford, Third Report, 81–82, paras. 298–305.
[498] UN Doc. A/CN.4/488/Add.1, 7 (Argentina). See also e.g. UN Doc. A/CN.4/488, 120 (Switzerland), 120–121 (Austria), 121 (Czech Republic and France). Further: Topical Summary of Government Comments in the Sixth Committee, UN Docs. A/CN.4/496 (1998), 18, para. 121; A/CN.4/504 (2000), 20–21, para. 76.
[499] UN Doc. A/CN.4/488, 122 (United Kingdom).   [500] Ibid. (United States).
[501] Ibid., 121 (Germany). Compare UN Doc. A/C.6/55/SR.14, 10, para. 55 (Germany).
[502] Ibid.

distinguish them from countermeasures proper – a situation which could lead to abuse and merely serve to fuel further disagreement between States.[503] In addition, the United Kingdom vigorously denounced the reference to interim measures of protection as 'an unfortunate use of language which may suggest a conceptual link, which it considers entirely misconceived, with interim measures in the International Court of Justice'.[504] The organic link between countermeasures and post-dispute settlement procedures in the form of compulsory arbitration was also strongly criticized as it was heavily balanced in favour of the target State. Indeed it was suggested that a system of binding post-dispute settlement procedures would inhibit widespread acceptance of the draft articles among States.[505] By contrast, there was broad agreement in the Sixth Committee concerning the principle that countermeasures should be suspended once a dispute settlement procedure had been engaged in good faith before a court or tribunal with the power to order interim measures of protection.[506]

On second reading, the debate in the ILC proceeded on the basis that the link between countermeasures and post-dispute settlement procedures would not be retained.[507] In other respects, Special Rapporteur Crawford believed that the essential balance struck in Draft Article 48 [1996] was an appropriate one even if it should be expressed in clearer language.[508] Based on a French proposal, Crawford proposed that prior to taking countermeasures an injured State was required to 'submit a reasoned request to the responsible State, calling on it to fulfil its obligations; notify that State of the countermeasures it intends to take; [and] agree to negotiate with that State'.[509] Notwithstanding the

---

[503] See e.g. UN Docs. A/CN.4/488, 119–120 (Ireland), 121–122 (Germany), 122–123 (United States); A/CN.4/492, 15 (Japan). Also: Topical Summary of Government Comments in the Sixth Committee, UN Doc. A/CN.4/504 (1999), 20–21, para. 76.

[504] UN Doc. A/CN.4/488, 122 (United Kingdom).

[505] See e.g. ibid., 122 (United Kingdom), 123 (Czech Republic), 123–124 (United States), 142 (Austria), 143 (France). Also: Topical Summary of Government Comments in the Sixth Committee, UN Doc. A/CN.4/496 (1998), 20, para. 126. As one ILC member explained: 'It was not for a handful of experts to revolutionize international law'. See YbILC (2001), vol. I, 15, para. 40 (Mr. Pellet).

[506] See however UN Doc. A/CN.4/488, 124 (United States). France and Japan suggested specific drafting improvements: see UN Docs. A/CN.4/488, 119 (France); A/CN.4/492, 15–16 (Japan).

[507] See Crawford, Third Report, 93, para. 355 (with further references).

[508] Ibid., 93–94, paras. 355–360.

[509] Ibid., 81, 94, 96, paras. 301 (n. 581), 358, 367. For the French proposal see UN Doc. A/CN.4/488, 119.

obligation to negotiate, the injured State was entitled, as from the date of notification, to adopt 'provisional countermeasures' to protect its rights. It was only if 'within a reasonable time' the negotiations had failed to resolve the dispute that the injured State could adopt 'full-scale countermeasures'.[510] A separate provision dealt with the suspensive effect of countermeasures in the event that the dispute was submitted to third-party settlement.[511] The Drafting Committee in 2000, having attempted to reconcile wide differences of opinion in the ILC, provisionally adopted Crawford's proposal albeit with some minor changes.[512] However, opinion remained polarized especially concerning the relationship between dispute settlement and countermeasures and the risks of abuse associated with auto-interpretation of wrongful conduct.

In the Sixth Committee, States continued to express concern with respect to the requirement of a prior demand for redress and the possibility of unilateral determinations on the part of the State taking countermeasures.[513] For example, Iran expressed regret that it was left to the State taking countermeasures to determine for itself whether an act was unlawful: 'A party to the dispute could not also be the judge'.[514] If recourse to compulsory dispute settlement procedures was not required, Iran proposed an amendment to at least make it clear that allegations of wrongful conduct would have to be substantiated by 'credible evidence'.[515] Croatia stressed that 'the fundamental precondition for taking countermeasures should be borne in mind, namely, being certain that an internationally wrongful act had indeed occurred', and questioned whether it was justified in all cases to rely on the unilateral assessment of the State taking countermeasures.[516]

---

[510] Crawford, Third Report, 94, 96, paras. 358, 360, 367 (his draft article 48).

[511] Ibid., 94, 97, paras. 359–360, 367 (his draft article 50 bis). See also Crawford, Fourth Report, 17, para. 69.

[512] YbILC (2000), vol. I, 398–399, paras. 79–85 (Chairman of the Drafting Committee, Mr. Gaja). For a summary of the debate see also ILC Report (2000), UN Doc. A/55/10, 55–56, paras. 328–332, 335–337.

[513] See e.g. Topical Summary of Government Comments in the Sixth Committee, UN Doc. A/CN.4/513 (2000), 28, para. 147.

[514] UN Doc. A/C.6/56/SR.16, 4, para. 12 (Iran). Similarly: UN Doc. A/CN.4/488/Add.1, 7 (Argentina).

[515] UN Docs. A/C.6/55/SR.15, 3, para. 16 (Iran); A/C.6/56/SR.16, 4, para. 12 (Iran). See also Topical Summary of Government Comments in the Sixth Committee, UN Doc. A/CN.4/513 (2000), 31, para. 164.

[516] UN Doc. A/C.6/55/SR.16, 10, para. 72 (Croatia). See also Topical Summary of Government Comments in the Sixth Committee, UN Doc. A/CN.4/513 (2000), 31, para. 164.

For Tanzania '[i]t was of little comfort that ... shared perceptions of egregious breaches corresponded to the facts ... an objective apprecia- tion could presumably only be attained through a judicial process'.[517] Similarly, Poland proposed that countermeasures could only be used 'after a prior reference to the procedures in force in accordance with all the relevant rules of international law in force between the States concerned (and not only to negotiations, as mentioned in article 53(2) [2000])'.[518] To similar effect, the Netherlands proposed to add a subpar- agraph indicating that countermeasures were not permitted or should be suspended 'if the Security Council has taken a binding decision with regard to the dispute'.[519] Greece went even further by proposing to add a provision excluding third-party countermeasures as soon as the Security Council was seized of the matter.[520] Austria tentatively proposed that States intending to take third-party countermeasures should be under an obligation to negotiate 'joint countermeasures' prior to taking them.[521] Support also continued to be expressed for the requirement of prior negotiations subject to the possibility of 'provisional and urgent' countermeasures.[522] To forego this requirement would be 'a retrograde step'.[523] The principle that countermeasures should be suspended in case the dispute was submitted to third-party settlement received broad support.[524]

Other States continued to strongly believe that the proposed proce- dural safeguards regime for countermeasures included restrictions that

---

[517] UN Doc. A/C.6/55/SR.14, 9, para. 47 (Tanzania).

[518] UN Doc. A/CN.4/515/Add.2, 16–17 (Poland). To the same effect see also e.g. UN Docs. A/C.6/55/SR.17, 14, para. 85 (Greece); A/C.6/55/SR.24, 10, paras. 60–62 (Cameroon); A/ C.6/56/SR.16, 4, para. 12 (Iran).

[519] UN Doc. A/CN.4/515, 87 (Netherlands).

[520] UN Doc. A/C.6/55/SR.17, 14, para. 85 (Greece). To similar effect: UN Docs. A/C.6/55/ SR.15, 3, para. 17 (Iran); A/C.6/55/SR.20, 5, paras. 35–36 (Mexico); A/C.6/55/SR.24, 11, para. 64 (Cameroon); A/C.6/56/SR.11, 7, para. 39 (Morocco); A/C.6/56/SR.16, 2, para. 4 (Brazil). Also: Crawford, Fourth Report, 18, para. 73.

[521] UN Doc. A/CN.4/515, 83, 90 (Austria). See also UN Doc. A/C.6/55/SR.17, 13, para. 79 (Austria); and above n. 432.

[522] See Topical Summary of Government Comments in the Sixth Committee, UN Doc. A/CN.4/513 (2000), 31, para. 167. Some States argued that not even 'urgent' counter- measures should be permissible during negotiations: see e.g. UN Docs. A/C.6/55/SR.15, 3, para. 16 (Iran); A/C.6/55/SR.17, 14, para. 85 (Greece); A/C.6/55/SR.19, 14, para. 87 (Bahrain). Compare UN Docs. A/C.6/56/SR.14, 4, para. 18 (Mexico); A/CN.4/515/ Add.3, 9 (Argentina).

[523] UN Doc. A/CN.4/515, 84 (Netherlands).

[524] See e.g. Topical Summary of Government Comments in the Sixth Committee, UN Doc. A/CN.4/513 (2000), 32, paras. 171–172.

did not reflect customary international law. It was suggested that no rule of customary international law required either that the existence of a wrongful act should be determined by a third party before taking countermeasures or that prior negotiations should be pursued.[525] The notion of 'urgent and provisional' countermeasures was again rejected as artificial and unreal.[526] The United Kingdom stressed that, in any event, negotiations were not required with respect to the enforcement of communitarian norms by way of third-party countermeasures – for example, in the face of genocide, it would clearly be unacceptable to require negotiations (which the target State would no doubt accept with alacrity) prior to taking countermeasures.[527] While otherwise supportive of the requirement of prior negotiations, Chile and Costa Rica also proposed to exclude its application in such cases.[528] Finally, some criticism was also expressed against the principle that countermeasures should be suspended once the dispute had been submitted to binding third-party settlement.[529] As on first reading, aside from the critical observations noted above, the minimum procedural requirements of prior demand and notification remained, *faute de mieux*, largely uncontroversial.

The Drafting Committee in 2001 proposed only minor changes to the basic requirements of prior demand and notification.[530] By contrast, it partly reconsidered the delicate relationship between dispute settlement and countermeasures. To address that difficulty, it now proposed to omit altogether the requirement that countermeasures should essentially be excluded while negotiations were being pursued in good faith. Although an injured State should be required to 'offer to negotiate' with the target State it could still adopt (or maintain) countermeasures in seeking to ensure its remedial rights to cessation and reparation.

---

[525] See UN Doc. A/CN.4/515, 84 (Slovakia), 85 (United Kingdom), 85 (United States), 87 (Republic of Korea). Also: Topical Summary of Government Comments in the Sixth Committee, UN Doc. A/CN.4/513 (2000), 28, para. 148.

[526] See e.g. Topical Summary of Government Comments in the Sixth Committee, UN Doc. A/CN.4/513 (2000), 32, paras. 168–170.

[527] UN Doc. A/CN.4/515, 85 (United Kingdom).

[528] UN Doc. A/C.6/55/SR.17, 9, para. 50 (Chile), 11, para. 65 (Costa Rica). See also Topical Summary of Government Comments in the Sixth Committee, UN Doc. A/CN.4/513 (2000), 31–32, paras. 165, 168.

[529] See UN Doc. A/CN.4/515, 84–85 (United Kingdom), 86–87 (United States). Also: Topical Summary of Government Comments in the Sixth Committee, UN Doc. A/CN.4/513 (2000), 32, para. 173.

[530] YbILC (2001), vol. I, 112, para. 59 (Chairman of the Drafting Committee, Mr. Tomka).

'Urgent countermeasures' could be adopted without an offer to negotiate or even any prior notification to the target State albeit subject to the basic requirement of a prior demand for redress. In exchange, the Drafting Committee proposed to retain the principle that countermeasures should, subject to certain exceptions, be excluded where the dispute was before a tribunal with the power to make binding decisions on the parties.[531] It explained:

Article 53 [i.e. what became Article 52 ARSIWA] had been redrafted along the lines of the *Air Service Agreement* case and other case law, based on an understanding which the Special Rapporteur had reported to the Commission in plenary. The major criticism had been that, when a case was the subject of judicial proceedings or negotiations, that did not [sic] have the effect of preventing a State from taking countermeasures. That position was not supported by case law, however. ICJ [sic] had [in *Gabčikovo Nagymaros Project*] considered the question of whether a certain measure undertaken by a State was or was not a countermeasure. The measure had continued to be taken during judicial proceedings, and at the same time, negotiations between the parties to settle the matter out of court had been ongoing. The Court had not rejected the notion that the measure might be a countermeasure on the grounds that judicial proceedings were in progress and there was no possibility of the parties negotiating in good faith.[532]

The Drafting Committee concluded: 'One might dream of a better world, but article 53 had been drafted to reflect customary international law'.[533]

The ILC adopted the Drafting Committee's proposal as Article 52 ARSIWA. It reads:

Article 52
Conditions relating to resort to countermeasures
1. Before taking countermeasures, an injured State shall:
   (a) call on the responsible State, in accordance with article 43, to fulfil its obligations under Part Two;
   (b) notify the responsible State of any decision to take countermeasures and offer to negotiate with that State.

---

[531] Ibid., 112, paras. 58–60.
[532] Ibid., 117, para. 27. For the same interpretation of the case law, notably *Gabčikovo Nagymaros Project*, see also ibid., 54, para. 24 (Mr. Tomka) (advising that the ILC should 'not continue in its efforts to revolutionize the law of countermeasures on those points, and should instead base itself on customary law on the question'); UN Doc. A/CN.4/515, 84 (Slovakia); and the comments by Germany, above n. 501.
[533] YbILC (2001), vol. I, 117, para. 27 (Chairman of the Drafting Committee, Mr. Tomka).

2. Notwithstanding paragraph 1(b), the injured State may take such urgent countermeasures as are necessary to preserve its rights.
3. Countermeasures may not be taken, and if already taken must be suspended without undue delay if:
   (a) the internationally wrongful act has ceased, and;
   (b) the dispute is pending before a court or tribunal which has the authority to make decisions binding on the parties.
4. Paragraph 3 does not apply if the responsible State fails to implement the dispute settlement procedure in good faith.

The ILC commentary explains that Article 52 ARSIWA builds upon the observations of the *Air Services* tribunal.[534]

The requirement of a prior demand for redress in Article 52(1)(a) ARSIWA finds support not only in the case law but it also appears to reflect a general practice.[535] Still, although embodying an important underlying principle, its relevance may be limited in practice:

> [T]here are usually quite extensive and detailed negotiations over a dispute before the point is reached where some countermeasures are contemplated. In such cases the injured State will already have notified the responsible State of its claim in accordance with article 43, and it will not have to do it again in order to comply with paragraph 1(a).[536]

There is no strict temporal relationship between the basic (and cumulative) preconditions in Article 52(1) ARSIWA.[537] The 'urgent countermeasures' referred to in Article 52(2) ARSIWA (previously 'interim' or 'provisional' countermeasures')[538] are justified on the basis that the target State may otherwise seek to immunize itself from coercive action, for example, by withdrawing assets from banks in the injured State. Thus the ILC commentary notably mentions the freezing of assets as an example of 'urgent countermeasures'.[539]

With respect to Article 52(3) ARSIWA, the ILC commentary explains that 'where a third-party procedure exists and has been invoked by either

---

[534] ARSIWA Commentary, Art. 52, §3. To very similar effect, see already 1934 IDI Paris Resolution (Art. 5).

[535] ARSIWA Commentary, Art. 52, §3.

[536] ARSIWA Commentary, Art. 52, §4. Compare *Application of the Interim Accord of 13 September 1995*, ICJ Rep. (2011), 644, Greece's Rejoinder (27 Oct. 2010), 201–203, paras. 8.37–8.40.

[537] ARSIWA Commentary, Art. 52, §5.

[538] The change in terminology was explained by the provisional and reversible character of all countermeasures: see YbILC (2001), vol. I, 112, para. 60 (Chairman of the Drafting Committee, Mr. Tomka).

[539] ARSIWA Commentary, Art. 52, §6.

party to the dispute, the requirements of that procedure, e.g. as to interim measures of protection, should substitute as far as possible for countermeasures ... [as it] ... will perform a function essentially equivalent to that of countermeasures'.[540] Notwithstanding the proposals in the Sixth Committee noted above, the reference to 'court or tribunal' in Article 52(3)(b) ARSIWA is intended to cover any third-party dispute settlement procedure, whatever its designation; however, it does not refer to political organs such as the UN Security Council.[541] Article 52(3)(a) ARSIWA makes clear that countermeasures can still be taken in such cases if the wrongful act has not ceased; by contrast, claims for reparation seemingly cannot be enforced by way of countermeasures.[542] The remedy of countermeasures revives under Article 52(4) ARSIWA in case the responsible State does not implement the dispute settlement procedure in good faith.[543] Several procedural conditions in Article 52 ARSIWA have thus been explicitly recognized by international tribunals as forming part of customary international law.[544]

6.4.2 Evaluation

The basic requirements of prior demand and notification in Article 52(1) ARSIWA are firmly established in practice concerning third-party countermeasures. As observed in Section 5.2.3, the UN General Assembly (among other institutional actors) normally calls on the responsible State to comply with its obligations under international law prior to individual States taking third-party countermeasures against it. In case of an unfulfilled demand for redress, this form of institutional *sommation* is usually followed by a trigger statement (for

---

[540] ARSIWA Commentary, Art. 52, §§2, 8. See also ibid., Art. 52, §7 (on the meaning of 'pending before a court or tribunal'). This safeguard is reinforced by the exclusion in Article 50(2)(a) ARSIWA (on which see above Section 6.2.1.4).

[541] ARSIWA Commentary, Art. 52, §8.

[542] See however the comments by Mr. Tomka who during the ILC debate pointed to some 'inconsistency' between the instrumental function of countermeasures in what became Article 49 ARSIWA and its apparent limitation in Article 52(3)(a) ARSIWA and 'wondered whether it was a correct reflection of international law': YbILC (2001), vol. I, 54, para. 25.

[543] ARSIWA Commentary, Art. 52, §9.

[544] See *United States – Continued Suspension of Obligations in the EC – Hormones Dispute*, WT/DS320/AB/R, Report of the Appellate Body, 16 Oct. 2008, para. 382; *Canada – Continued Suspension of Obligations in the EC – Hormones Dispute*, WT/DS321/AB/R, Report of the Appellate Body, 16 Oct. 2008, para. 382. Also: *Application of the Interim Accord of 13 September 1995*, ICJ Rep. (2011), 644 at 710 (Dec. Judge Bennouna).

example, an EU Council Decision)[545] by which the target State is notified of any decision to take third-party countermeasures and the corrective action required of it. Albeit not formally included in Article 52(1) ARSIWA, as Iran proposed, the regular involvement of institutional actors in adopting joint statements arguably provides 'credible evidence'[546] of actual breaches of international law in that they are – in the words of the 2005 IDI Krakow Resolution – 'widely acknowledged'[547] by the international community. Tanzania, as well as others, may still find 'little comfort'[548] in this non-judicial process of establishing responsibility but in practice it appears to provide an adequate safeguard against abuse.

This is not to say, however, that customary international law necessarily requires a breach of an obligation *erga omnes (partes)* to have been 'widely acknowledged' prior to the adoption of third-party countermeasures. Practice does not seem to indicate that States have adopted joint statements out of a sense of legal obligation.[549] Nor does practice appear to bear out Austria's proposal in the Sixth Committee that States should be required to negotiate 'joint countermeasures' prior to taking them.[550]

Although the risk of abuse associated with auto-interpretation has not materialized in practice, a related concern nevertheless merits brief comment. As already observed in Section 5.2.2, the link between institutional *sommation* and notification is not always readily apparent. To assess the necessity of countermeasures under Article 49(1) ARSIWA, as well as the requirement to notify the target State of 'any decision' to take countermeasures under Article 52(1)(b) ARSIWA, the 'decision' communicated to the target State must be sufficiently precise to enable it to make an adequate response. The target State is entitled to know exactly which international obligations have triggered the adoption of third-party countermeasures against it.[551] As Special Rapporteur Arangio-Ruiz cautioned, 'vague and undefined charges' may thus in

---

[545] See e.g. Council Decision 2011/273/CFSP (9 May 2011), OJ 2011 L 121/11 (10 May 2011) (notification of third-party countermeasures against Syria); and further Section 4.2.20.

[546] See above n. 515. ARSIWA 'do not deal with issues of evidence or the burden of proof': see ARSIWA Commentary, Introductory Commentary to Chapter V of Part One, §8.

[547] See 2005 IDI Krakow Resolution (Art. 5). Further: Section 5.2.3.

[548] See above n. 517.

[549] Compare Dawidowicz (2015), 359–360. See also Gaja (2013), 132 ('The wide acknowledgment of the existence of a serious breach could represent an additional procedural condition, which has not yet taken firm root').

[550] Compare the discussion above (text accompanying nn. 455–458).

[551] Compare ILC Report (1992), UN Doc. A/47/10, 26, para. 171.

some cases be a source of concern.[552] Notifications, including those by key actors such as the EU, prior to the adoption of unilateral coercive measures would sometimes benefit from being more precise.

As for the requirement to 'offer to negotiate' with the target State, practice concerning third-party countermeasures demonstrates (perhaps unsurprisingly) that their adoption is normally accompanied by a flurry of parallel diplomatic activity aimed at resolving the dispute; as such, it broadly conforms with the principle established in Article 52(1)(b) ARSIWA. In terms of the possible exception of 'urgent countermeasures' in Article 52(2) ARSIWA, it should be recalled that it was merely introduced in the ILC as a compromise solution between sharply opposing positions on the suspensive effect of negotiations: it had (and continues to have) no clear basis in customary international law.[553] A brief glance at practice suffices to demonstrate that most third-party countermeasures involve asset freezes and as such clearly qualify as 'urgent countermeasures'. However, such action (even if implemented promptly) appears to be preceded by a notification to the target State (or affected individuals) in the normal way.[554] Put differently, there does not appear to be any example in practice of the adoption of 'urgent third-party countermeasures' without prior notification to the target State. The possibility of 'urgent third-party countermeasures' thus seems to be of limited relevance in practice.

Finally, it should be noted that practice concerning third-party countermeasures is non-existent with respect to the specific situation envisaged in Article 52(3) and (4) ARSIWA: third-party countermeasures have simply not been adopted in parallel with attempts to resolve the dispute before an international court or tribunal. It is nevertheless worth reiterating a broader point. As the ILC commentary to this provision explains,[555] it was not intended to apply to political organs such as the UN Security Council – a position that is confirmed by practice.[556]

6.5 Conclusion

Third-party countermeasures aim to reinstate international public order, ruptured by illegality, but they entail a risk of disorder and further rupture. Prudence thus dictates that the entitlement to resort to third-

---

[552] Ibid., 26, para. 173.
[553] Crawford, Fourth Report, 17, para. 69 (with further references).
[554] For an example (among many others) see above n. 545.
[555] See ARSIWA Commentary, Art. 52, §8.   [556] See Section 5.2.1.

party countermeasures should be subject to several safeguards designed to minimize the risk of abuse and seek to ensure that they are kept within generally acceptable bounds. In the *Interim Accord* case, Judge Bennouna opined that 'it is yet to be established that the legal régime of counter-measures, as set forth in Articles 49 to 54 [ARSIWA], is of a customary nature'.[557] This general conclusion seems overly cautious. Admittedly, even if the sheer adoption of a third-party countermeasure arguably entails recognition of the legal power to do so, it is more difficult to establish *opinio juris* concerning the applicable safeguards regime. The following main conclusions can nevertheless be drawn from practice.

Third-party countermeasures are almost always adopted in response to continuing internationally wrongful acts with the aim of inducing their cessation. Claims for reparation are extremely rare. Still, a sound analytical basis (as embodied in Article 48(2)(b) ARSIWA) exists to suggest that the instrumental function of third-party countermeasures may develop to also include reparation. Such an entitlement would be especially significant in the context of human rights violations and claims for restitution. All that can be said with confidence is that there is no clearly recognized entitlement to obtain reparation by way of third-party countermeasures. The instrumental function of third-party countermeasures thus appears to be limited to claims for cessation. In line with Article 48(2)(a) ARSIWA, such claims can be enforced independently of the wishes of the directly injured State.

The adoption of third-party countermeasures will normally be motivated by a range of policy interests which go beyond mere law enforcement concerns. Mixed motivations are not in themselves a cause for concern and simply reflect the manner in which international relations are conducted. Third-party countermeasures are rarely adopted in isolation; they are almost always accompanied by inherently lawful acts of retorsion. Such action is generally based on an integrated rationale that is extremely difficult to disentangle. Trigger statements that refer to widely acknowledged breaches of communitarian norms, and call for a return to legality, provide a clear indication that the use of third-party counter-measures is permissible notwithstanding the presence of a punitive element for the action as a whole. By contrast, a unilateral coercive measure that is incapable of legal justification as a countermeasure should be

---

[557] *Application of the Interim Accord of 13 September 1995*, ICJ Rep. (2011), 644 at 710 (Dec. Judge Bennouna).

deemed punitive and as such unlawful. The prohibition against punitive countermeasures is reinforced by the principle of reversibility and the obligation to terminate countermeasures once their lawful objectives have been achieved. The principle of proportionality provides an additional substantive limitation on punitive countermeasures.

The adoption of third-party countermeasures is further limited by certain international obligations the suspension of which is excluded from the operation of countermeasures. It is clear that third-party countermeasures cannot derogate from peremptory norms. However, other obligations whose peremptory status is less clear are also excluded. Article 50 ARSIWA is not based on any clear principle but on the kind of pragmatism that characterizes the international law-making process. Although the ILC did not elaborate a general theory of prohibited countermeasures, a key principle can nevertheless be identified to determine whether a given obligation is capable of being suspended by way of countermeasures: the principle of reciprocity. It seems clear as a matter of principle that countermeasures can only be taken in relation to reciprocal or synallagmatic obligations which are undertaken on a *quid pro quo* basis. Put differently, only a bilateralizable obligation capable of suspension can be the subject of a countermeasure. Obligations *erga omnes (partes)* cannot be suspended by way of countermeasures. The same applies to obligations which require integral performance (e.g. disarmament obligations) and are performed on an all-or-nothing basis. Both types of obligations require an integral performance. This conclusion seems to be both normatively desirable and analytically sound. Practice also does not suggest that such an exclusion would be considered too sweeping.

Based on this rationale, it is suggested that human rights obligations are completely excluded from the operation of third-party countermeasures. The principles of non-intervention and respect for territorial integrity likewise seem excluded. In terms of human rights obligations, it should be stressed that they do not normally apply extra-territorially. The problems raised by the adverse effects of third-party countermeasures on the civilian population in the target State are, *faute de mieux*, best addressed by the principle of proportionality.

Even if it is established that the adoption of third-party countermeasures is intended to ensure a return to legality and does not involve the suspension of an inviolable obligation, the right to take such action is not unlimited. The principle of proportionality is firmly established as an essential substantive limitation on the right to take countermeasures.

Still, it is a flexible and somewhat elusive standard. Despite its indeterminacy, the mere fact that the element of proportionality may be invoked by a State against which third-party countermeasures are taken already provides a regulating effect. States are sensitive to accusations concerning the disproportionate effect of third-party countermeasures, especially as they relate to the enjoyment of human rights by the civilian population in the target State. The proportionality test for third-party countermeasures appears to be largely the same as for bilateral countermeasures subject to the separate condition of overall proportionality. It is doubtful whether the purpose of third-party countermeasures in inducing a return to legality is a relevant consideration in the assessment of proportionality. In any event, it seems that the basic proportionality test, as embodied in Article 51 ARSIWA, is already sufficiently flexible to satisfactorily take into account the discrete issues raised by the enforcement of communitarian norms by way of third-party countermeasures.

Finally, the adoption of third-party countermeasures is subject to certain procedural conditions intended to reduce the inherent risk of abuse associated with the auto-interpretation of wrongful conduct. As it happens, this risk has not materialized in practice. Various UN bodies (among other institutional actors) normally call on the responsible State to comply with its obligations under international law prior to individual States taking third-party countermeasures against it. In case of an unfulfilled demand for redress, this form of institutional *sommation* is usually followed by a joint trigger statement by which the target State is notified of any decision to take third-party countermeasures and the corrective action required of it. This practice – albeit not necessarily required under customary international law – ensures that breaches of international law are widely acknowledged before the adoption of third-party countermeasures. In short, it appears to provide an adequate safeguard against abuse. Thus the main features of the safeguards regime governing third-party countermeasures have crystallized in practice and form part of the emerging law of third-party countermeasures.

~

Conclusion

This study has examined modern practice at length in order to answer the question of whether States are entitled to take third-party counter-measures under contemporary international law and, if so, whether there are adequate safeguards against abuse. I hope to have demonstrated that there is strong support for an affirmative answer. Still, for the reasons identified at the outset, the question is a difficult and extremely contro-versial one.

The light which history shines on the topic is a lantern on the stern that continues to colour the whole approach to it – and perhaps understand-ably so. After all, the topic of third-party countermeasures raises a serious normative dilemma. There is an inherent tension between the need for a more effective legal order in spite of decentralization, and the risks of abuse relating to the allocation of enforcement authority to individual States, even if limited to the most serious illegalities. There is no point in repeating the conclusions reached in earlier chapters with respect to the position of third-party countermeasures in international law. All that remains is to briefly comment on what light practice sheds on the main normative arguments raised in the fraught debate on third-party countermeasures.

Two points merit particular attention with respect to the risk of abuse. First, there was concern in the Sixth Committee that third-party counter-measures were 'open to abuse by powerful States against a weaker State that they might particularly dislike for other reasons'.[1] Several target States have protested that the adoption of third-party countermeasures against them – supposedly 'in the name of certain noble doctrines or ideals'[2] – is merely a thinly veiled 'political tool'[3] based on 'trumped-up

---

[1] UN Doc. A/C.6/55/SR.15, 10, para. 63 (Botswana).
[2] UN Doc. S/PV.3692 (28 Aug. 1996), 6 (Burundi).
[3] UN Docs. A/66/138 (14 July 2011), 11 (Burma); A/HRC/20/G/3 (15 June 2012) (Syria); A/68/211 (22 July 2013), 6 (Syria).

claims'[4] and 'unavowed objectives'.[5] Practice shows that States have used third-party countermeasures cautiously: they have not been used for ulterior motives on the pretext that human rights or other communitarian norms must be respected.[6] In particular, the fear that third-party countermeasures might facilitate 'the exploitation and distortion of human rights issues as a means of interference in the internal affairs of States'[7] has not materialized.

An important reason for this seems to be that breaches of communitarian norms have generally been widely acknowledged through the adoption of resolutions in major UN organs, including the General Assembly, the Security Council and the Human Rights Council, prior to the adoption of third-party countermeasures. Several regional international organizations (in addition to individual States) will normally also have denounced the same wrongful conduct and called for a return to legality. In addition, breaches of communitarian norms are often well documented within international organizations, notably through the work of UN Special Rapporteurs and various fact-finding missions or commissions of inquiry – as witnessed by the examples of Burundi, Burma, Belarus, Libya and Syria. In short, the adoption of third-party countermeasures has on the whole been preceded by credible evidence of wrongful conduct. This has greatly reduced the risk of abuse arising from the auto-interpretation of wrongful conduct and the pursuit of ill-founded or even spurious claims based on objectives distinct from the enforcement of the law.

Second, there was also concern in the Sixth Committee that the category of third-party countermeasures might be used as a pretext to justify otherwise unlawful unilateral uses of force, especially on humanitarian grounds, in violation of the collective security system established under the UN Charter.[8] But there is no such indication in practice: States have not attempted to justify their occasional use of forcible unilateral coercive measures on humanitarian or other grounds by reference to third-party countermeasures. To the extent that such action is justified in legal (as distinct from political and moral) terms, it is done by reference

---

[4] UN Doc. S/2012/242 (Belarus). See also UN Doc. S/2008/199 (Cuba on Behalf of the Non-Aligned Movement).
[5] UN Docs. S/PV.3692 (28 Aug. 1996), 3–5; S/1996/788, 2 (Burundi).
[6] For such concerns see notably YbILC (2001), vol. I, 35, para. 2 (Mr. Brownlie).
[7] GA Res. 36/103 (9 Dec. 1981), Principle II(l).
[8] See e.g. Topical Summary of Government Comments in the Sixth Committee, UN Doc. A/CN.4/513 (2000), 29, para. 149. Also: YbILC (2001), vol. I, 35, para. 2 (Mr. Brownlie).

to the primary norms regulating the use of force embodied in the UN Charter. In sum, there is little indication in practice that the fears raised with respect to third-party countermeasures have been substantiated.

With respect to the effectiveness of third-party countermeasures, it bears repeating that they are no panacea for the ills of enforcement afflicting multilateral public order. The heavy weight of expectation sometimes placed on them cannot be sustained. A more cautious and nuanced assessment of their contribution to the integrity of multilateral public order is warranted. Third-party countermeasures may have been less than ideal in terms of inducing full compliance with communitarian norms, but this is a rather crude yardstick with which to measure their effectiveness. Several factors point to a more finely calibrated yardstick. For their part, States have affirmed that third-party countermeasures can be a powerful tool in defence of multilateral public order. In a world order wrought by an unequal distribution of power, third-party counter-measures may not represent the best of all possible worlds, but they nevertheless increasingly appear to be viewed as a necessary tool in an otherwise limited communitarian law enforcement toolbox.

BIBLIOGRAPHY

Abi-Saab G., (2001) 'The Concept of Sanctions in International Law', in Gowlland-Debbas V. (ed.), *United Nations Sanctions and International Law* (The Hague: Kluwer Law International), 29.

Ago R., (1989) 'Obligations *Erga Omnes* and the International Community', in Weiler J.H.H., Cassese A. and Spinedi M. (eds.), *International Crimes of State: A Critical Analysis of the ILC's Draft Article 19 on State Responsibility* (Berlin: Walter de Gruyter), 237.

Akande D., (2013) 'Would It Be Lawful for European (or Other) States to Provide Arms to the Syrian Opposition?', EJIL: *Talk!* (17 Jan.), www.ejiltalk.org /would-it-be-lawful-for-european-or-other-states-to-provide-arms-to-the-syr ian-opposition.

and Gillard E.C., (2016) 'Oxford Guidance on the Law Relating to Humanitarian Relief Operations in Situations of Armed Conflict', https:// docs.unocha.org/sites/dms/Documents/Oxford%20Guidance%20pdf.pdf.

Akehurst M., (1970) 'Reprisals by Third States', 44 *BYIL*, 1.

(1974–1975) 'Custom as a Source of International Law', 47 *BYIL*, 1.

Alland D., (1994) *Justice privée et ordre juridique international* (Paris: Pedone).

(2002) 'Countermeasures of General Interest', 13 *EJIL*, 1221.

(2010) 'The Definition of Countermeasures', in Crawford J., Pellet A. and Olleson S. (eds.), *The Law of International Responsibility* (Oxford: Oxford University Press), 1127.

Amerasinghe C.F., (2005) *Principles of the Institutional Law of International Organizations* (Cambridge: Cambridge University Press, 2nd ed.).

Angelet N. (ed.), (2003) 'Pratique du pouvoir exécutive et contrôle des chambres législatives en matière de droit international (1995–1999)', 35 *RBDI*, 5.

Annacker C., (1994a) 'The Legal Regime of *Erga Omnes* Obligations in International Law', 46 *AJPIL*, 131.

(1994b) *Die Durchsetzung von erga omnes-Verpflichtungen vor dem Internationalen Gerichtshof* (Hamburg: Kovac).

Arangio-Ruiz G., (1994) 'Counter-Measures and Dispute Settlement: The Current Debate within the ILC', 5 *EJIL*, 20.

Arts K., (1995) 'European Community Development Cooperation, Human Rights, Democracy and Good Governance: At Odds or Ease with Each Other?', in Ginther K., Denters E. and de Waart P. (eds.), *Sustainable Development and Good Governance* (Dordrecht/London: Martinus Nijhoff), 259.

(2000) *Integrating Human Rights into Development Cooperation: The Case of the Lomé Convention* (The Hague/London: Kluwer Law International).

Aust A., (2013) *Modern Treaty Law and Practice* (Cambridge: Cambridge University Press, 3rd ed.).

Azevedo D., (1984) 'The US Measures against Argentina Resulting from the Malvinas Conflict', 78 *AJIL*, 323.

Barile G., (1987) 'The Protection of Human Rights in Article 60 Paragraph 5 of the Vienna Convention on the Law of Treaties', in *International Law at the Time of Its Codification. Essays in Honour of Roberto Ago*, Vol. II (Milano: Guiffrè), 3.

Barnhoorn L.A.N.M., (1994) 'Diplomatic Law and Unilateral Remedies', 25 *NYIL*, 39.

Bartels L., (2005) *Human Rights Conditionality in the EU's International Agreements* (Oxford: Oxford University Press).

Basdevant J., (1904) 'L'Action coercitive anglo-germano-italienne contre le Venezuela (1902–1903)', 12 *RGDIP*, 362.

Bastid S., (1985) *Les traités dans la vie internationale: conclusions et effets* (Paris: Economica).

Baxter R.R., (1970) 'Treaties and Customs', 129 *RdC*, 25.

Bederman D., (1998) 'Article 40(2)(E) & (F) of the ILC Draft Articles on State Responsibility: Standing of Injured States under Customary International Law and Multilateral Treaties', 92 *ASIL Proc.*, 291.

(2001) *International Law in Antiquity* (Cambridge: Cambridge University Press).

(2002) 'Counterintuiting Countermeasures', 96 *AJIL*, 817.

Benedek W., (2007) 'The Drago-Porter Convention', in *Max Planck Encyclopedia of Public International Law*, http://opil.ouplaw.com/home/EPIL.

Bernhardt R., (2002) 'Article 103', in Simma B. (ed.) *The Charter of the United Nations: A Commentary* (Oxford: Oxford University Press, 2nd ed.), 1292.

Bethlehem D. and Lauterpacht E. (eds.), (1991) *The Kuwait Crisis: Sanctions and Their Economic Consequences*, Vol. I (Cambridge: Grotius Publications).

(2012) 'The Secret Life of International Law', 1 *CJICL*, 23.

Bianchi A., (2008) 'Human Rights and the Magic of Jus Cogens', 19 *EJIL*, 491.

Bird A., (2010) 'Third State Responsibility for Human Rights Violations', 21 *EJIL*, 883.

Bluntschli J.C., (1868) *Das moderne Völkerrecht der civilisirten Staaten als Rechtsbuch dargestellt* (Nördlingen: C.H. Beck).

Boisson de Chazournes L., (1992) *Les contre-mesures dans les relations internationales économiques* (Paris: Pedone).
(1995) 'Economic Countermeasures in an Interdependent World', 89 *ASIL Proc.*, 337.
(2004) 'Qu'est-ce que la pratique en droit international?', in Société Française pour le droit international: Colloque de Genève, *La pratique et le droit international* (Paris: Pedone), 13.
(2010) 'Other Non-Derogable Obligations', in Crawford J., Pellet A. and Olleson S. (eds.), *The Law of International Responsibility* (Oxford: Oxford University Press), 1205.
Bollecker-Stern B., (1973) *Le préjudice dans la théorie de la responsabilité internationale* (Paris: Pedone).
Borchard E.M., (1915) *The Diplomatic Protection of Citizens Abroad* (New York: Banks Law).
Borelli S. and Olleson S., (2010) 'Obligations Relating to Human Rights and Humanitarian Law', in Crawford J., Pellet A. and Olleson S (eds.), *The Law of International Responsibility* (Oxford: Oxford University Press), 1177.
Bowett D.W., (1972) 'Economic Coercion and Reprisals by States', 13 *VJIL*, 1.
Bradford J.C. (ed.), (2006) *International Encyclopedia of Military History* (London: Routledge).
Brandtner B. and Rosas A., (1998) 'Human Rights and the External Relations of the European Community: An Analysis of Doctrine and Practice', 9 *EJIL*, 468.
de la Brière Y., (1928) 'Evolution de la doctrine et de la pratique en matière de représailles', 22 *RdC*, 237.
Brierly J.L., (1932) 'International Law and Resort to Armed Force', 4 *CLJ*, 308.
Brownlie I., (1963) *International Law and the Use of Force by States* (Oxford: Clarendon Press).
(1981) 'The Reality and Efficacy of International Law', 52 *BYIL*, 1.
(1983) *System of the Law of Nations: State Responsibility, Part 1* (Oxford: Clarendon Press).
(1986) 'The U.N. Charter and the Use of Force, 1945-1985', in Cassese A. (ed.), *The Current Legal Regulation of the Use of Force* (Dordrecht: Martinus Nijhoff), 491.
(1988) 'To What Extent Are the Traditional Categories of Lex Lata and Lex Ferenda Still Viable?', in Cassese A. and Weiler J.H.H. (eds.), *Change and Stability in International Law-Making* (Berlin: Walter de Gruyter), 66.
and Apperley C.J., (2000) 'Kosovo: House of Commons Foreign Affairs Committee 4th Report, June 2000: Kosovo Crisis Inquiry: Memorandum on the International Law Aspects', 49 *ICLQ*, 878.
(2008) *Principles of Public International Law* (Oxford: Oxford University Press, 7th ed.).

Buergenthal T., (1968) 'Proceedings against Greece under the European Convention of Human Rights', 62 *AJIL*, 441.

von Bulmerincq A., (1889) 'Die Staatstreitigkeiten und ihre Entscheidung ohne Krieg', in von Holtzendorff F. (ed.), *Handbuch des Völkerrechts: auf Grundlage europäischer Staatspraxis*, bd. 4 (Berlin: Habel), 3.

Byers M., (1997) 'Conceptualizing the Relationship between *Jus Cogens* and *Erga Omnes* Rules', 66 *Nordic JIL*, 1.

van Bynkershoek C., (1737/1930) *Quaestionum Juris Publici Libri Duo* (English trans. T. Frank, Oxford: Clarendon Press).

(1744/1946) *De foro legatorum liber singularis* (English trans. G.J. Laing, Oxford: Clarendon Press).

Cahier P., (1962) *Le droit diplomatique contemporain* (Geneva: E. Droz).

Calamita N.J., (2009) 'Sanctions, Countermeasures and the Iranian Nuclear Issue', 42 *VJTL*, 1393.

Cannizzaro E., (2001) 'The Role of Proportionality in the Law of International Countermeasures', 12 *EJIL*, 889.

Carish E. and Rickard-Martin L., (2011) 'Global Threats and the Role of United Nations Sanctions', http://library.fes.de/pdf-files/iez/08819.pdf.

Carmody C., (1996) 'On Expelling Nigeria from the Commonwealth', 34 *CYIL*, 273.

Carter B., (1988) *International Economic Sanctions: Improving the Haphazard U.S. Legal Regime* (Cambridge: Cambridge University Press).

(2009) 'Economic Coercion', in *Max Planck Encyclopedia of Public International Law*, http://opil.ouplaw.com/home/EPIL.

Cassese A, (1995) *Self-Determination of Peoples: A Legal Reappraisal* (Cambridge: Cambridge University Press).

(1999) 'Ex iniuria ius oritur: Are We Moving towards International Legitimation of Forcible Humanitarian Countermeasures in the World Community?', 10 *EJIL*, 23.

(1999) 'A Follow-Up: Forcible Humanitarian Countermeasures and *Opinio Necessitatis*', 10 *EJIL*, 791.

(2005) *International Law* (Oxford: Oxford University Press, 2nd ed.).

Charney J., (1989) 'Third State Remedies in International Law', 10 *Michigan JIL*, 57.

Charpentier J., (1970) 'Cour internationale de Justice: Affaire de Barcelona Traction: arrêt du 5 février 1970', 16 *AFDI*, 307.

(1982) 'Pratique française concernant le droit international', 28 *AFDI*, 1017.

Chesterman S., (2001) *Just War of Just Peace? Humanitarian Intervention and International Law* (Oxford: Oxford University Press).

Chinkin C., (1996) 'The East Timor Case (Portugal v. Australia)', 45 *ICLQ*, 712.

Clark G., (1933) 'The English Practice with regard to Reprisals by Private Persons', 27 *AJIL*, 694.

Cohen S.B., (1982) 'Conditioning US Security Assistance on Human Rights Practices', 76 *AJIL*, 246.

Colbert E.S., (1948) *Retaliation in International Law* (New York: King's Crown Press).

Corten O., (2010a) 'The Obligation of Cessation', in Crawford J., Pellet A. and Olleson S. (eds.), *The Law of International Responsibility* (Oxford: Oxford University Press), 545.

  (2010b) *The Law against War: The Prohibition on the Use of Force in Contemporary International Law* (Oxford: Hart).

Cortright D., Lopez G.A. and Gerber-Stellingwerf L., (2007) 'Sanctions', in Weiss T.G. and Daws S. (eds.), *The Oxford Handbook on the United Nations* (Oxford: Oxford University Press), 349.

Coufoudakis V., (1977–1978) 'The European Economic Community and the "Freezing" of the Greek Association 1967-1974', 16 *Journal of Common Market Studies*, 114.

Craven M., (2002) 'Humanitarianism and the Quest for Smarter Sanctions', 13 *EJIL*, 43.

Crawford J., (1996) 'The General Assembly, the International Court and Self-Determination', in Fitzmaurice M. and Lowe A.V. (eds.), *Fifty Years of the International Court of Justice* (Cambridge: Cambridge University Press), 585.

  (2000) 'The Standing of States: A Critique of Article 40 of the ILC's Draft Articles on State Responsibility', in Andenas M. and Fairgrieve D (eds.), *Judicial Review in International Perspective. Liber Amoricum in Honour of Lord Slynn of Hadley*, Vol. II (The Hague: Kluwer Law International), 23.

  (2001a) 'Responsibility to the International Community as a Whole', 8 *Indiana Journal of Global Legal Studies*, 303.

  (2001b) 'The Relationship Between Sanctions and Countermeasures', in Gowlland-Debbas V. (ed.), *United Nations Sanctions and International Law* (The Hague: Kluwer Law International), 57.

  (2002) 'Introduction', in Crawford J. (ed.), *The International Law Commission's Articles on State Responsibility: Introduction, Text and Commentaries* (Cambridge: Cambridge University Press), 1.

  (2006a) *The Creation of States in International Law* (Oxford: Clarendon Press, 2nd ed.).

  (2006b) 'Multilateral Rights and Obligations in International Law', 319 *RdC*, 325.

  (2010) 'International Crimes of States', in Crawford J., Pellet A. and Olleson S. (eds.), *The Law of International Responsibility* (Oxford: Oxford University Press), 405.

(2011) 'Responsibility for Breaches of Communitarian Norms: An Appraisal of Article 48 of the ILC Articles on Responsibility of States for Internationally Wrongful Acts', in Fastenrath U. et al. (eds.), *From Bilateralism to Community Interest. Essays in Honour of Bruno Simma* (Oxford: Oxford University Press), 224.

(2012) *Brownlie's Principles of Public International Law* (Oxford: Oxford University Press, 8th ed.).

(2013a) *State Responsibility: The General Part* (Cambridge: Cambridge University Press).

(2013b) 'Chance, Order, Change: The Course of International Law', 365 *RdC*, 1.

Dale W., (1982) 'Is the Commonwealth an International Organisation?', 31 *ICLQ*, 451.

Damrosch L.F., (2011) 'Gross and Systematic Human Rights Violations', in *Max Planck Encyclopedia of Public International Law*, http://opil.ouplaw.com /home/EPIL.

Darcy S., (2013) 'Military force against Syria would be a reprisal rather than humanitarian intervention, but that doesn't make it any more lawful', EJIL: *Talk!* (1 Sept.), http://www.ejiltalk.org/military-force-against-syria -would-be-a-reprisal-rather-than-humanitarian-intervention-but-that -doesnt-make-it-any-more-lawful.

(2015) 'Retaliation and Reprisal', in Weller M. (ed.), *The Oxford Handbook of the Use of Force in International Law* (Oxford: Oxford University Press), 879.

d'Argent P., (2003) 'Jurisprudence belge relative au droit international public (1993–2003)', 36 *RBDI*, 575.

d'Aspremont J., Dopagne F. and van Steenberghe R., (2005) 'Article 39', in Cot J.-P., Pellet A. and Forteau M. (eds.), *La Charte des Nations Unies: Commentaire article par article* (Paris: Economica, 3rd ed.), 1131.

David E., (1984–1985) 'Les sanctions économiques prises contre l'Argentine dans l'affaire des Malouines', 18 *RBDI*, 150.

Dawidowicz M., (2006) 'Public Law Enforcement without Public Law Safeguards? An Analysis of State Practice on Third-Party Countermeasures and Their Relationship to the UN Security Council', 77 *BYIL*, 333.

(2010) 'The Obligation of Non-Recognition of an Unlawful Situation', in Crawford J., Pellet A. and Olleson S. (eds.), *The Law of International Responsibility* (Oxford: Oxford University Press), 677.

(2015) 'Third-Party Countermeasures: Observations on a Controversial Concept', in Chinkin C. and Baetens F. (eds.), *Sovereignty, Statehood and State Responsibility. Essays in Honour of James Crawford* (Cambridge: Cambridge University Press), 340.

(2016) 'Third-Party Countermeasures: A Progressive Development of International Law?', 29 *QIL, Zoom-In*, 3, http://www.qil-qdi.org/third -party-countermeasures-progressive-development-international-law.

Delbrück J., (1995) 'The Impact of the Allocation of International Law Enforcement Authority on the International Legal Order', in Delbrück J. (ed.), *Allocation of Law Enforcement Authority in the International System* (Berlin: Dunker & Humblot), 152.

Denza E., (2008) *Diplomatic Law: A Commentary on the Vienna Convention on Diplomatic Relations* (Oxford: Oxford University Press, 3rd ed.).

Desierto D., (2014) 'The EU/US v. Russia Trade Wars: Revisiting GATT Article XXI and the International Law on Unilateral Economic Sanctions', EJIL: *Talk!* (22 Sept.), http://www.ejiltalk.org/the-euus-v-russia-trade-wars -revisiting-gatt-article-xxi-and-the-international-law-on-unilateral-eco nomic-sanctions.

Dewost J.-L., (1982) 'La communauté, les Dix et les "sanctions" économiques: de la crise iranienne à la crise des Malouines', 28 *AFDI*, 215.

Dickinson E. De Witt, (1920) *The Equality of States in International Law* (Cambridge, Mass.: Harvard University Press).

Dominicé C, (1981) 'Reprisals and Diplomatic Law', in *Recht als Prozess und Gefüge – Festschrift für Hans Huber* (Bern: Stämpfli), 547.

Dopagne F., (2010) *Les contre-mesures des organisations internationales* (Paris: LGDJ).

Drago L.-M., (1907) 'State Loans in Their Relation to International Policy', 1 *AJIL*, 692.

Dugard J., 'The South West Africa Cases, Second Phase', 83 *South African Law Journal* (1966), 429.

(1967) 'The Organisation of African Unity and Colonialism: An Inquiry Into the Plea of Self-Defence as a Justification for the Use of Force in the Eradication of Colonialism', 16 *ICLQ*, 157.

(1973) *The South West Africa/Namibia Dispute: Documents and Scholarly Writings on the Controversy between South Africa and the United Nations* (Berkeley: University of California Press).

(1996) '1966 and All That. The South West Africa Judgment Revisited in the East Timor Case', 8 *AJCIL*, 549.

Dupont P.-E., (2012) 'Countermeasures and Collective Security: The Case of the EU Sanctions against Iran', 17 *JCSL*, 301.

Dupuy P.-M., (1983) 'Observations sur la pratique récente des "sanctions" de l'illicite', 87 *RGDIP*, 505.

Dutheil de la Rochère J., (1983) 'L'affaire de l'accident du Boeing 747 de Korean Airlines', 29 *AFDI*, 749.

Duxbury A., (1997) 'Rejuvenating the Commonwealth – The Human Rights Remedy', 46 *ICLQ*, 344.

(2011) *The Participation of States in International Organisations: The Role of Human Rights and Democracy* (Cambridge: Cambridge University Press).

Dzida B., (1997) *Zum Recht der Repressalie im Heutigen Völkerrecht* (Frankfurt am Main: Peter Lang).

Elagab O.Y., (1988) *The Legality of Non-Forcible Countermeasures in International Law* (Oxford: Clarendon Press).

(1999) 'The Place of Non-Forcible Countermeasures in International Law', in Goodwin-Gill G. and Talmon S. (eds.), *The Reality of International Law: Essays in Honour of Ian Brownlie* (Oxford: Clarendon Press), 125.

Farrall J.M., (2007) *United Nations Sanctions and the Rule of Law* (Cambridge: Cambridge University Press).

Fauchille P., (1926) *Traité de droit international public* (Paris: Librairie A. Rousseau, 8th ed.).

Fawcett J., (1963) *The British Commonwealth in International Law* (London: Stevens).

de La Fayette L., (1996) 'Access to Ports in International Law', 11 *IJMCL*, 1.

Fierro E., (2003) *The EU's Approach to Human Rights Conditionality in Practice* (The Hague: Martinus Nijhoff).

Fisher P. and Hafner G., (1982) 'Aktuelle österreichische Praxis zum Völkerrecht', 33 *ÖZÖR*, 389.

Focarelli C., (1993) 'Le contromisure pacifiche collettive e la nozione di obblighi *erga omnes*', 76 *RDI*, 52.

(1994) *Le contromisure nel diritto internazionale* (Milano: Guiffrè).

Forteau M., (2006) *Droit de la sécurité collective et droit de la responsabilité internationale de l'État* (Paris: Pedone).

Fox H., (2005) 'Reply of Lady Fox', 71 *Ann. IDI*, 156.

Franck T.M., (2002) *Recourse to Force: State Action against Threats and Armed Attacks* (Cambridge: Cambridge University Press).

(2008) 'On Proportionality of Countermeasures in International Law', 102 *AJIL*, 715.

Fredman S., (1979) 'US Trade Sanctions against Uganda: Legality under International Law', 11 *Law and Policy in International Business*, 1149.

Freeman A.V., (1938) *The International Responsibility of States for Denial of Justice* (London/New York: Longman).

Frowein J., (1983) 'Die verpflichtungen *erga omnes* im Völkerrecht und ihre Durchsetzung', in *Völkerrecht als Rechtsordnung Internationale Gerichtsbarkeit Menschenrechte: Festschrift für Hermann Mosler* (Berlin: Springer), 241.

(1987) 'Collective Enforcement of International Obligations', 47 *ZaöRV*, 67.

(1994) 'Reactions by Not Directly Affected States to Breaches of Public International Law', 248 *RdC*, 345.

and Krisch N., (2002) 'Introduction to Chapter VII', in Simma B. (ed.), *The Charter of the United Nations: A Commentary* (Oxford: Oxford University Press, 2nd ed.), 701.

and Krisch N., (2002) 'Article 39', in Simma B. (ed.), *The Charter of the United Nations: A Commentary* (Oxford: Oxford University Press, 2nd ed.), 717.

and Krisch N., (2002) 'Article 41', in Simma B. (ed.), *The Charter of the United Nations: A Commentary* (Oxford: Oxford University Press, 2nd ed.), 735.

Gaeta P., (2010) 'The Character of the Breach', in Crawford J., Pellet A. and Olleson S. (eds.), *The Law of International Responsibility* (Oxford: Oxford University Press), 421.

Gaja G., (1981) '*Jus Cogens* beyond the Vienna Convention', 172 *RdC*, 271.

(1989) 'Obligations *Erga Omnes*, International Crimes and *Jus Cogens*: A Tentative Analysis of Three Related Concepts', in Weiler J.H.H., Cassese A. and Spinedi M. (eds.), *International Crimes of State: A Critical Analysis of the ILC's Draft Article 19 on State Responsibility* (Berlin: Walter de Gruyter), 151.

(2005) 'Obligations and Rights *Erga Omnes* in International Law', 71 *Ann. IDI*, 119.

(2010) 'The Concept of an Injured State', in Crawford J., Pellet A. and Olleson S (eds.), *The Law of International Responsibility* (Oxford: Oxford University Press), 941.

(2010) 'States Having an Interest in Compliance with the Obligation Breached', in Crawford J., Pellet A. and Olleson S. (eds.), *The Law of International Responsibility* (Oxford: Oxford University Press), 957.

(2013) 'The Protection of General Interests in the International Community', 364 *RdC*, 9.

Gardam J., (2004) *Necessity, Proportionality and the Use of Force by States* (Cambridge: Cambridge University Press).

Gattini A., (2002) 'A Return Ticket to "Communitarisme", Please', 13 *EJIL*, 1181.

Giegrich T., (2011) 'Retorsion', in *Max Planck Encyclopedia of Public International Law*, http://opil.ouplaw.com/home/EPIL.

Gomaa M., (1996) *Suspension or Termination of Treaties on Grounds of Breach* (The Hague: Martinus Nijhoff).

Gowlland-Debbas V., (2010) 'Responsibility and the United Nations Charter', in Crawford J., Pellet A. and Olleson S. (eds.), *The Law of International Responsibility* (Oxford: Oxford University Press), 115.

(2012) 'The Security Council and Issues of Responsibility under International Law', 353 *RdC*, 185.

Grabher O'Brien J., (2002) 'In Defense of the Mystical Body: Giovanni da Legnano's Theory of Reprisals', 1 *Roman Legal Traditions*, 25, http://roman legaltradition.org/contents/2002/RLT-OBRIEN1.PDF.

Graefrath B., (1984) 'Responsibility and Damages Caused: Relationship between Responsibility and Damages', 185 RdC, 9.

(1989) 'International Crimes – A Specific Regime of International Responsibility of States and its Legal Consequences', in Weiler J.H.H., Cassese A. and Spinedi M. (eds.), International Crimes of State: A Critical Analysis of the ILC's Draft Article 19 on State Responsibility (Berlin: Walter de Gruyter), 161.

Gray C., (1990) Judicial Remedies in International Law (Oxford: Clarendon Press).

(2008) International Law and the Use of Force (Oxford: Oxford University Press, 3rd ed.).

Greenwood C., (1979) 'The US/French Air Service Arbitration', 38 CLJ, 233.

(2000) 'Kosovo: House of Commons Foreign Affairs Committee 4th Report, June 2000: International Law and the NATO Intervention in Kosovo', 49 ICLQ, 926.

Grewe W.G., (2000) The Epochs of International Law (English trans. M. Byers, Berlin: Walter de Gruyter).

Grotius H., (1646/1925) De Jure Belli ac Pacis (English trans. F.W. Kelsey, Oxford: Clarendon Press).

Grove R., (1979) 'International Trade: Lifting of Uganda Trade Restrictions', 20 HILJ, 704.

Guggenheim P., (1967) Traité de droit international public, Vol. I (Geneva, 2nd ed.).

de Guttry A., (1984) 'Le contromisure adottate nei confronti dell'Argentina da parte delle communità Europee e dei terzi Stati ed il problema de la lore liceità internazionale', in Ronzitti N. (ed.), La questione delle Falkland-Malvinas nel diritto internazionale (Milano: Guiffrè), 343.

(1985) Le rappresaglie non comportanti la coercizione militare nel diritto internazionale (Milano: Guiffrè).

(1986–1987) 'Some Recent Cases of Unilateral Countermeasures and The Problem of Their Lawfulness in International Law', 7 IYIL, 169.

Hahn M.J., (1990–1991) 'Vital Interests and the Law of GATT: An Analysis of GATT's Security Exception', 12 Michigan JIL, 573.

(1996) Die einseitige Aussetzung von GATT-Verpflichtungen als Repressalie (Berlin: Springer).

Hailbronner K., (1992) 'Sanctions and Third Parties and the Concept of International Public Order', 30 ARV, 2.

Hakimi M., (2014) 'Unfriendly Unilateralism', 55 HILJ, 105.

Halink S., (2007) 'All Things Considered: How the International Court of Justice Delegated Its Fact-Assessment to the United Nations in the Armed Activities Case', 40 NYJILP, 13.

Hall W.E., (1890) A Treatise on International Law (Oxford: Clarendon Press, 3rd. ed.).

Halleck H.W., (1861) *International Law: or Rules Regulating the Intercourse of States in Peace and War* (San Francisco: H.H. Bancroft & Co.).

Hannum H., (1989) 'International Law and Cambodian Genocide: The Sounds of Silence', 11 *HRQ*, 82.

Heffter A.G., (1857) *Le Droit International Public de l'Europe* (Paris: Cotillon).

Henkin L., (2003) 'Inter-State Responsibility for Compliance with Human Rights Obligations', in Vohrah L.C. et al. (eds.), *Man's Inhumanity to Man – Essays on International Law in Honour of Antonio Cassese* (The Hague: Kluwer Law International), 383.

van den Herik L.J., (2014) 'An Inquiry into the Role of Commissions of Inquiry in International Law: Navigating the Tensions between Fact-Finding and Application of International Law', 13 *Chinese JIL*, 507.

Hernández G.I., (2013) 'A Reluctant Guardian: The International Court of Justice and the Concept of "International Community"', 83 *BYIL*, 13.

Hershey A.S., (1907) 'The Calvo and Drago Doctrines', 1 *AJIL*, 26.

Higgins R., (1966) 'The International Court and South West Africa: The Implications of the Judgment', 42 *International Affairs*, 573.

(1976–1977) 'Derogation under Human Rights Treaties', 48 *BYIL*, 281.

(1994) *Problems and Process. International Law and How We Use It* (Oxford: Clarendon Press).

(1995) 'Fundamentals of International Law', in Jasentuliyana N. (ed.), *Perspectives on International Law. Essays in Honour of Judge Manfred Lachs* (The Hague: Kluwer Law International), 3.

(2006) 'Speech by H.E. Judge Rosalyn Higgins, President of the International Court of Justice, at the 58th session of the International Law Commission' (25 July), http://www.icj-cij.org/court/index.php?pr=1272&pt=3&p1=1&p2=3&p3=1.

Hillgruber C., (2006) 'The Right of Third States to Take Countermeasures', in Tomuschat C. and Thouvenin J.-M. (eds.), *The Fundamental Rules of the International Legal Order: Jus Cogens and Obligations Erga Omnes* (Leiden: Martinus Nijhoff), 265.

Hindmarsh A.E., (1932) 'Self-Help in Time of Peace', 26 *AJIL*, 315.

(1933) *Force in Peace. Force Short of War in International Relations* (Cambridge: Harvard University Press).

Hoffmeister F., (1998) *Menschenrechts- und Demokratieklauseln in den vertraglichen Außenbeziehungen der Europäischen Gemeinschaft* (Berlin: Springer).

Hogan A.E., (1908) *Pacific Blockade* (Oxford: Clarendon Press).

de Hoogh A., (1991) 'The Relationship between *Jus Cogens*, Obligations *Erga Omnes* and International Crimes: Peremptory Norms in Perspective', 42 *AJPIL*, 183.

(1996) *Obligations Erga Omnes and International Crimes: A Theoretical Inquiry into the Implementation and Enforcement of the International Responsibility of States* (The Hague: Kluwer Law International).

Hufbauer G.C., Schott J.J. and Elliott K.A., (1985/1990) *Economic Sanctions Reconsidered: History and Current Policy* (Institute for International Economics: Washington, DC).

Hutchinson D.N., (1988) 'Solidarity and Breaches of Multilateral Treaties', 59 *BYIL*, 151.

Iwasawa Y. and Iwatsuki N., (2010) 'Procedural Conditions', in Crawford J., Pellet A. and Olleson S. (eds.), *The Law of International Responsibility* (Oxford: Oxford University Press), 1149.

Jahn I.L., (1984) 'Applying International Law to the Downing of Korean Air Lines Flight 007 on September 1, 1983', 27 *GYIL*, 444.

Jamnejad M. and Wood M., (2009) 'The Principle of Non-Intervention', 22 *LJIL*, 345.

Jennings R., (1961) 'State Contracts in International Law', 37 *BYIL*, 156.

and Watts A. (eds.), (1996) *Oppenheim's International Law*, Vol. I: Peace (London/New York: Longman, 9th ed.).

Jiménez de Aréchaga E., (1978) 'International Law in the Past Third of a Century', 159 *RdC*, 1.

Jørgensen N.H.B., (2010) 'The Obligation of Non-Assistance to the Responsible State', in Crawford J., Pellet A. and Olleson S. (eds.), *The Law of International Responsibility* (Oxford: Oxford University Press), 687.

(2010) 'The Obligation of Cooperation', in Crawford J., Pellet A. and Olleson S. (eds.), *The Law of International Responsibility* (Oxford: Oxford University Press), 695.

Joyner D., (2013) 'Iran's Nuclear Programme and International Law', 2 *Penn State Journal of Law and International Affairs*, 237.

(2013) 'On Syria and the Use of Force', *Arms Control Law* (2 Sept.), http://armscontrollaw.com/2013/09/02/2047.

Kagan D., (1969) *The Outbreak of the Peloponnesian War* (Ithaca: Cornell University Press).

Kamminga M.T., (1992) *Inter-State Accountability for Violations of Human Rights* (Philadelphia: University of Pennsylvania Press).

Kamto M., (2010) 'The Time Factor in the Application of Countermeasures', in Crawford J., Pellet A. and Olleson S. (eds.), *The Law of International Responsibility* (Oxford: Oxford University Press), 1169.

Karimova T., (2014) 'The Nature and Meaning of "International Assistance and Cooperation" under the International Covenant on Economic, Social and Cultural Rights', in Riedel E., Giacca G. and Golay C. (eds.), *Economic, Social and Cultural Rights in International Law: Contemporary Issues and Challenges* (Oxford: Oxford University Press), 163.

Katselli Proukaki E., (2010) *The Problem of Enforcement in International Law: Countermeasures, the Non-Injured State and the Idea of International Community* (London: Routledge).

Kawasaki K., (2000) 'The "Injured State" in the International Law of State Responsibility', 28 *Hitotsubashi Journal of Law and Politics*, 17.

Kelsen H., (1950) *The Law of the United Nations: A Critical Analysis of Its Fundamental Problems* (Praeger: New York).

(1952) *Principles of International Law* (Rinehart: New York).

(1961) *General Theory of Law and State* (Russell & Russell: New York).

(1967) *Pure Theory of Law* (2nd ed., trans. by Max Knight, University of California Press: Berkeley).

King T., (1997) 'Human Rights in the Development of the European Community: Towards a European World Order?', 28 *NYIL*, 51.

Kirgis F., (1987) 'Custom on a Sliding Scale', 81 *AJIL*, 146.

Klabbers J., (2009) *An Introduction to International Institutional Law* (Cambridge: Cambridge University Press, 2nd ed.).

Klein E., (1981) 'South West Africa/Namibia (Advisory Opinions and Judgments)', in Bernhardt R. (ed.), *Max Planck Encyclopedia of Public International Law* (Amsterdam), Vol. II, 260.

Klein P., (2002) 'Responsibility for Serious Breaches of Obligations Deriving from Peremptory Norms of International Law and United Nations Law', 13 *EJIL*, 1249.

Kolb R., (2001) *Théorie du Jus Cogens International* (Paris: PUF).

(2004) 'La proportionnalité dans le cadre des contre-mesures et des sanctions – essai de clarification conceptuelle', in Picchio Forlati L. and Sicilianos L.-A. (eds.), *Economic Sanctions in International Law* (Leiden: Martinus Nijhoff), 379.

(2010) *An Introduction to the Law of the United Nations* (Oxford: Hart).

(2013) 'L'article 103 de la Chartre des Nations Unies', 367 *RdC*, 9.

Koskenniemi M., (2001) 'Solidarity Measures: State Responsibility as a New International Order?', 72 *BYIL*, 337.

Kritsiotis D., (2004) 'Arguments of Mass Confusion', 15 *EJIL*, 233.

Kuyper P.-J., (1982) 'Community Sanctions against Argentina: Lawfulness under Community and International Law', in O'Keeffe D. and Schermers H.G. (eds.), *Essays in European Law and Integration* (Deventer: Kluwer Law), 141.

Lachs M., (1980) 'The Development and General Trends of International Law in Our Time', 169 *RdC*, 9.

(1986) 'Jessup: Memorials and Reminiscences', 80 *AJIL*, 896.

Lakehal D.-E., (1984–1985) 'Les sanctions à la destruction du Boeing Sud-Coréen, Le 1er Septembre 1983', 18 *RBDI*, 171.

Lattanzi F., (1983) *Garanzie dei diritti dell'uomo nel diritto internazionale generale* (Milano: Guiffrè).

Lauterpacht H., (1933) 'Boycott in International Relations', 14 *BYIL*, 125.

(1950) 'Sovereignty over Submarine Areas', 27 *BYIL*, 376.

(1958) *The Development of International Law by the International Court* (London: Stevens & Sons).

Lawrence T.J., (1911) *The Principles of International Law* (Boston: D.C. Heath and Co., 4th ed.).

Leben C., (1982) 'Les contre-mesures inter-étatique et les réactions à l'illicite dans la société internationale', 28 *AFDI*, 9.

(2010) 'Obligations Relating to the Use of Force and Arising from Peremptory Norms of International Law', in Crawford J., Pellet A. and Olleson S. (eds.), *The Law of International Responsibility* (Oxford: Oxford University Press), 1197.

da Legnano G., (1360/1917) *Tractatus De Bello, De Represaliis et De Duello* (ed. T.E. Holland, English trans. J.L. Brierly, Oxford: Oxford University Press).

Leir M., (1999) 'Canadian Practice in International Law 1998-99', 37 *CYIL*, 317.

Lesaffre H., (2010) 'Circumstances Precluding Wrongfulness in the ILC Articles on State Responsibility: Countermeasures', in Crawford J., Pellet A. and Olleson S. (eds.), *The Law of International Responsibility* (Oxford: Oxford University Press), 469.

Lindemann H.H., (1984) 'Die Völkerrechtliche Praxis der Bundesrepublik Deutschland im Jahr 1982', 44 *ZaöRV*, 495.

Linsi C., (1994) *Gegenmassnahmen in der Form des Embargos zur Durchsetzung elementarer Völkerrechtsverpflichtungen in der schweizerischen Aussenpolitik: die Bedeutung der Praxisänderung vom August 1990 aus der Sicht der Staatenverantwortlichkeit und der Neutralität* (Basel: Helbing Lichtenhahn).

Lowe A.V., (1977) 'The Right of Entry into Maritime Ports in International Law', 14 *San Diego Law Review*, 597.

(1995) 'The International Court in a Timorous Mood', 54 *CLJ*, 484.

(2000) 'Kosovo: House of Commons Foreign Affairs Committee 4th Report, June 2000: International Legal Issues Arising in the Kosovo Crisis', 49 *ICLQ*, 937.

(2007) *International Law* (Oxford: Clarendon Press).

and Tzanakopoulos A., (2011) 'Humanitarian Intervention', in *Max Planck Encyclopedia of Public International Law*, http://opil.ouplaw.com/home/ EPIL.

and Tzanakopoulos A., (2013) 'Economic Warfare', in *Max Planck Encyclopedia of Public International Law*, http://opil.ouplaw.com/home/ EPIL.

Lowenfeld A., (2010) 'Countermeasures, Diplomatic Protection and Investor-State Arbitration', in Fernández Ballesteros M.A. and Arias D. (eds.), *Liber Amicorum Bernardo Cremades* (Madrid: La Ley), 747.

Maccoby S., (1924) 'Reprisals as a Means of Redress Short of War', 2 *CLJ*, 60.

Magliveras K., (1999) *Exclusion from Participation in International Organisations: The Law and Practice behind Member States' Expulsion and Suspension of Membership* (The Hague: Kluwer Law International).

Malamut M., (1983) 'Aviation: Suspension of Landing Rights of Polish Airlines in the United States', 24 *HILJ*, 190.

Malanczuk P., (1983) 'Countermeasures and Self-Defence as Circumstances Precluding Wrongfulness in the International Law Commission's Draft Articles on State Responsibility', 43 *ZaöRV*, 705.

(1985) 'Zur Repressalie im Entwurf der International Law Commission zur Staatenverantwortlichkeit', 45 *ZaöRV*, 293.

Manning W., (1839) *Commentaries on the Law of Nations* (London: S. Sweet).

Marek K., (1978–1979) 'Criminalizing State Responsibility', 14 *RBDI*, 481.

Marston G., (1982) 'United Kingdom Materials on International Law 1982', 53 *BYIL*, 337.

(1983) 'United Kingdom Materials on International Law 1983', 53 *BYIL*, 361.

(1995) 'United Kingdom Materials on International Law 1995', 66 *BYIL*, 583.

(1998) 'United Kingdom Materials on International Law 1998', 69 *BYIL*, 433.

(1999) 'United Kingdom Materials on International Law 1999', 70 *BYIL*, 517.

von Martens G.F., (1864) *Précis du droit des gens moderne de l'Europe*, tome 2 (Paris: Guillaumin, 2nd ed.).

Martin M.F., (2013) 'U.S. Sanctions on Burma: Issues for the 113th Congress' (Washington, DC: Congressional Research Service).

de Mas Latrie R., (1875) *Du droit de marque ou droit de représailles au Moyen-Age, suivi de pièces justificatives* (Paris: Bauer).

Mavroidis P., (2005) *The General Agreement on Tariffs and Trade: A Commentary* (Oxford: Oxford University Press).

Mbaye K., (1988) 'L'intérêt pour agir devant la Cour Internationale de Justice', 209 *RdC*, 223.

McCaffrey S., (1989) '*Lex Lata* or the Continuum of State Responsibility', in Weiler J.H.H., Cassese A. and Spinedi M. (eds.), *International Crimes of State: A Critical Analysis of the ILC's Draft Article 19 on State Responsibility* (Berlin: Walter de Gruyter), 242.

McDougal M.S., (1955) 'The Hydrogen Bomb Tests and the International Law of the Sea', 49 *AJIL*, 356.

McWhinney E., (1995) *Judge Manfred Lachs and Judicial Law-Making: Opinions on the International Court of Justice, 1967–1993* (The Hague: Martinus Nijhoff).

Mendelson M.H., (1998) 'The Formation of Customary International Law', 272 *RdC*, 155.

Meron T., (1986) 'On a Hierarchy of International Human Rights', 80 *AJIL*, 1.

(1995) 'Extraterritoriality of Human Rights Treaties', 89 *AJIL*, 78.

(2003) 'International Law in the Age of Human Rights', 301 *RdC*, 9.

de Mestral A., (1983) 'Canadian Practice in International Law during 1982', 21 *CYIL*, 327.

Möldner M., (2011) 'European Community and Union, Mixed Agreements', in *Max Planck Encyclopedia of Public International Law*, http://opil.ouplaw.com/home/EPIL.

Moyer E. and Mabry L., (1983) 'Export Controls as Instruments of Foreign Policy: The History, Legal Issues and Policy Lessons of Three Recent Cases', 15 *Law and Policy in International Business*, 1.

Müller D., (2010) 'The Work of García-Amador on State Responsibility for Injury Caused to Aliens', in Crawford J., Pellet A. and Olleson S. (eds.), *The Law of International Responsibility* (Oxford: Oxford University Press), 69.

Nash M., (1980) *Digest of United States Practice in International Law 1978* (Washington, DC: Office of the Legal Adviser, Department of State).

  (1982) 'Contemporary Practice of the United States Relating to International Law', 76 *AJIL*, 374.

  (1984) 'Contemporary Practice of the United States Relating to International Law', 78 *AJIL*, 244.

  (1986) *Digest of United States Practice in International Law 1980* (Washington, DC: Office of the Legal Adviser, Department of State).

  (1987) 'Contemporary Practice of the United States Relating to International Law', 81 *AJIL*, 197.

  (1990) 'Contemporary Practice of the United States Relating to International Law', 84 *AJIL*, 536.

  (1997) 'Contemporary Practice of the United States Relating to International Law', 91 *AJIL*, 697.

Neff S.C., (2005) *War and the Law of Nations: A General History* (Cambridge: Cambridge University Press).

Nolte G., (2002) 'From Dionisio Anzilotti to Roberto Ago: The Classical International Law of State Responsibility and the Traditional Primacy of a Bilateral Conception of Inter-State Relations', 13 *EJIL*, 1083.

Noortmann M., (2005) *Enforcing International Law: From Self-Help to Self-Contained Regimes* (Aldershot: Ashgate).

Nys E., (1894) *Les origines du droit international* (Bruxelles: Castaigne).

O'Connell M., (2002) 'Debating the Law of Sanctions', 13 *EJIL*, 63.

Oestreich G., (1990) *Menschenrechte als Elemente der dritten AKP-EWG-Konvention von Lomé* (Berlin: Dunker & Humblot).

O'Keefe R., (2010) 'Proportionality', in Crawford J., Pellet A. and Olleson S. (eds.), *The Law of International Responsibility* (Oxford: Oxford University Press), 1157.

Okowa P., (2014) 'Issues of Admissibility and the Law on International Responsibility', in Evans M. (ed.), *International Law* (Oxford: Oxford University Press, 4th ed.), 477.

Ollivier A., (2010) 'International Criminal Responsibility of the State', in Crawford J., Pellet A. and Olleson S. (eds.), *The Law of International Responsibility* (Oxford: Oxford University Press), 703.

Oppenheim L., (1905) *International Law: A Treatise*, Vol. II: War and Neutrality (London: Longmans, Green & Co.).

Orakhelashvili A., (2006) *Peremptory Norms in International Law* (Oxford: Oxford University Press).

(2011) *Collective Security* (Oxford: Oxford University Press).

Paarlberg R.L., (1980) 'Lessons of the Grain Embargo', 59 *Foreign Affairs*, 144.

Paasivirta E. and Rosas A., (2002) 'Sanctions, Countermeasures and Related Actions in the External Relations of the European Union: A Search for Legal Frameworks', in Cannizzaro E. (ed.), *The European Union as an Actor in International Relations* (The Hague: Kluwer Law International), 207.

Palchetti P., (2002) 'Reactions by the European Union to Breaches of *Erga Omnes* Obligations', in Cannizzaro E. (ed.), *The European Union as an Actor in International Relations* (The Hague: Kluwer Law International), 219.

(2014) 'Consequences for Third States as a Result of an Unlawful Use of Force', in Weller M. (ed.), *The Oxford Handbook of the Use of Force in International Law* (Oxford: Oxford University Press), 1224.

Paparinskis M., (2008) 'Investment Arbitration and the Law of Countermeasures', 79 *BYIL*, 264.

Parlett K., (2015) 'The Application of the Rules on Countermeasures in Investment Claims: Visions and Realities of International Law as an Open System', in Chinkin C. and Baetens F. (eds.), *Sovereignty, Statehood and State Responsibility: Essays in Honour of James Crawford* (Cambridge: Cambridge University Press), 389.

Parry C., (1938) 'British Practice in Some Nineteenth Century Pacific Blockades', 8 *ZaöRV*, 672.

Paulsson J., (2005) *Denial of Justice in International Law* (Cambridge: Cambridge University Press).

Peel J., (2010) 'Notice of Claim by an Injured State', in Crawford J., Pellet A. and Olleson S. (eds.), *The Law of International Responsibility* (Oxford: Oxford University Press), 1029.

Peles-Bodson S., (1984–1985) 'Les sanctions économiques prises par les états membres et la C.E.E. contre L'U.R.S.S. en raison de son intervention en Afghanistan', 28 *RBDI*, 202.

Pellet A., (2010) 'The ILC Articles on State Responsibility for Internationally Wrongful Acts and Related Texts', in Crawford J., Pellet A. and Olleson S. (eds.), *The Law of International Responsibility* (Oxford: Oxford University Press), 75.

and Miron A., (2011) 'Sanctions', in *Max Planck Encyclopedia of Public International Law*, http://opil.ouplaw.com/home/EPIL.

Penny C., (1998) 'Parliamentary Declarations in 1997-98', 36 *CYIL*, 421.

Petman J., (2004) 'Resort to Economic Sanctions by Not Directly Affected States', in Picchio Forlati L. and Sicilianos L.-A. (eds.), *Economic Sanctions in International Law* (Leiden: Martinus Nijhoff), 309.

Phillimore R., (1857) *Commentaries upon International Law*, Vol. III (Philadelphia: T. & J.W. Johnson).

Phillipson C., (1911) *The International Law and Custom of Ancient Greece and Rome*, Vol. II (London: Macmillan).

Picone P., (2013) *Comunità Internazionale e Obblighi 'erga omnes': Studi Critici di Diritto Internazionale* (Napoli: Jovene, 3rd ed.).

Pillitu A.P., (2003) 'Le sanzioni dell'Unione e della Comunità Europea nei confronti dello Zimbabwe e di esponenti del suo governo per gravi violazioni dei diritti umani e dei principi democratici', 86 *RDI*, 55.

Politis N., (1924) 'Les représailles entre les Etats membres de la Société des Nations', 31 *RGDIP*, 5.

(1934) 'Le régime des représailles en temps de paix', 38 *Ann. IDI*, 1.

Porges A., (1994) *Guide to GATT Law and Practice: Analytical Index* (Geneva: WTO, 6th ed.).

Provost R., (1994) 'Reciprocity in Human Rights and Humanitarian Law', 65 *BYIL*, 383.

(2002) *International Human Rights and Humanitarian Law* (Cambridge: Cambridge University Press).

Ragazzi M., (1997) *The Concept of International Obligations Erga Omnes* (Oxford: Clarendon Press).

Ralston J.H., (1929) *International Arbitration from Athens to Locarno* (Stanford: Stanford University Press).

Randelzhofer A., (2002) 'Article 2(4)', in Simma B. (ed.), *The Charter of the United Nations: A Commentary* (Oxford: Oxford University Press, 2nd ed.), 112.

Rapisardi-Mirabelli A., (1914) 'La retorsion. Etude de droit international', 16 *RDILC*, 223.

Raub G. and Malanczuk P., (1985) 'Die Völkerrechtliche Praxis der Bundesrepublik Deutschland im Jahr 1983', 45 *ZaöRV*, 714.

Reisman W.M., (1980) 'The Legal Effect of Vetoed Resolutions', 74 *AJIL*, 904.

(1993) 'Comment', in Delbrück J. (ed.), *The Future of International Law Enforcement. New Scenarios – New Law?* (Berlin: Dunker & Humblot), 168.

(1995) 'Assessing the Lawfulness of Non-Military Enforcement: The Case of Economic Sanctions', 89 *ASIL Proc.*, 350.

Reiterer M., (1997) 'Article XXI GATT – Does the National Security Exception Permit Anything under the Sun?', 2 *Austrian Review of International and European Law*, 191.

Riedel H. and Will M., (1999) 'Human Rights Clauses in External Agreements of the EC', in Alston P. (ed.), *The EU and Human Rights* (Oxford: Oxford University Press), 723.

Rivier A., (1896) *Principes du droit des gens* (Paris: Librairie A. Rosseau, 2nd ed.).

Ronen Y., (2011) *Transition from Illegal Regimes under International Law* (Cambridge: Cambridge University Press).

Rosenstock R., (1994) 'Crimes of State – An Essay', in *Völkerrecht zwischen normativem Anspruch und politischer Realität. Festschrift für Karl Zemanek zum 65. Geburtstag* (Berlin: Dunker & Humblot), 319.

Rousseau C., (1960) 'Chronique des faits internationaux', 64 *RGDIP*, 771.

(1979) 'Chronique des faits internationaux', 83 *RGDIP*, 361.

(1980) 'Chronique des faits internationaux', 84 *RGDIP*, 351 and 1068.

(1982) 'Chronique des faits internationaux', 86 *RGDIP*, 543.

(1984) 'Chronique des faits internationaux', 88 *RGDIP*, 413.

(1986) 'Chronique des faits internationaux', 90 *RGDIP*, 945.

Rucz C., (1992) 'Les mesures unilatérales de protection des droits de l'homme devant l'institut de droit international', 38 *AFDI*, 604.

Ruys T., (2010) *'Armed Attack' and Article 51 of the UN Charter* (Cambridge: Cambridge University Press).

Sachariew K., (1988) 'State Responsibility for Multilateral Treaty Violations: Identifying the "Injured State" and Its Legal Status', 35 *NILR*, 273.

Sands P. and Klein P., (2001) *Bowett's Law of International Institutions* (London: Sweet & Maxwell, 5th ed.).

Schachter O., (1977) 'Les aspects juridiques de la politique américaine en matière des droits de l'homme', 23 *AFDI*, 53.

(1982) 'International Law in Theory and Practice: General Course in Public International Law', 178 *RdC*, 1.

(1986) 'Phillip Jessup's Life and Ideas', 80 *AJIL*, 878.

Schiavone G., (1997) *International Organizations: A Dictionary* (London: Macmillan, 4th ed.).

Schwelb E., (1973–1975) 'The Law of Treaties and Human Rights', 16 *ARV*, 1.

Sicilianos L.-A., (1990) *Les réactions décentralisées à l'illicite: des contre-mesures à la légitime défense* (Paris: LGDJ).

(1993) 'The Relationship between Reprisals and Denunciation or Suspension of a Treaty', 4 *EJIL*, 341.

(2002) 'The Classification of Obligations and the Multilateral Dimension of the Relations of International Responsibility', 13 *EJIL*, 1127.

(2004) 'Sanctions institutionnelles et contre-mesures: tendances récentes', in Picchio Forlati L. and Sicilianos L.-A. (eds.), *Economic Sanctions in International Law* (Leiden: Martinus Nijhoff), 3.

(2005) 'La codification des contre-mesures par la commission du droit international', 38 *RBDI*, 447.

(2010) 'Countermeasures in Response to Grave Violations of Obligations Owed to the International Community', in Crawford J., Pellet A. and Olleson S. (eds.), *The Law of International Responsibility* (Oxford: Oxford University Press), 1137.

Simma B., (1970) 'Reflections on Article 60 of the Vienna Convention on the Law of Treaties and Its Background in General International Law', 20 ÖZÖR, 5.

(1989) 'International Crimes: Injury and Countermeasures. Comments on Part 2 of the ILC's Work on State Responsibility', in Weiler J.H.H., Cassese A. and Spinedi M. (eds.), *International Crimes of State: A Critical Analysis of the ILC's Draft Article 19 on State Responsibility* (Berlin: Walter de Gruyter), 283.

(1994a) 'From Bilateralism to Community Interest in International Law', 250 RdC, 217.

(1994b) 'Counter-Measures and Dispute Settlement: A Plea for a Different Balance', 5 EJIL, 102.

(1999) 'NATO, the UN and the Use of Force: Legal Aspects', 10 EJIL, 1.

(2007) 'Human Rights and State Responsibility', in Reinisch A. and Kriebaum U. (eds.), *The Law of International Relations – Liber Amicorum Hanspeter Neuhold* (Utrecht: Eleven), 359.

and Pulkowski D., (2010) *'Leges Speciales* and Self-Contained Regimes', in Crawford J., Pellet A. and Olleson S. (eds.), *The Law of International Responsibility* (Oxford: Oxford University Press), 139.

and Tams C., (2011) 'Article 60: Convention of 1969', in Corten O. and Klein P. (eds.), *The Vienna Conventions on the Law of Treaties: A Commentary* (Oxford: Oxford University Press), 1351.

(2013) 'Human Rights before the International Court of Justice: Community Interest Coming to Life?', in Tams C. and Sloan J. (eds.), *The Development of International Law by the International Court of Justice* (Oxford: Oxford University Press), 301.

Simpson G., (2004) *Great Powers and Outlaw States: Unequal Sovereigns in the International Legal Order* (Cambridge: Cambridge University Press).

Skubiszewski K., (2005) 'Reply of Mr. Skubiszewski', 71 Ann. IDI, 179.

Sørensen M., (1946) *Les sources du droit international: étude sur la jurisprudence de la Cour Permanente de Justice Internationale* (Copenhague: E. Munskgaard).

(1960) 'Principes de droit international public', 101 RdC, 1.

Spiegel H.W., (1938) 'Origin and Development of Denial of Justice', 32 AJIL, 63.

Spinedi M., (1989) 'International Crimes of State: A Legislative History', in Weiler J.H.H., Cassese A. and Spinedi M. (eds.), *International Crimes of State: A Critical Analysis of the ILC's Draft Article 19 on State Responsibility* (Berlin: Walter de Gruyter), 7.

von Sponeck H., (2002) 'Sanctions and Humanitarian Exemptions: A Practitioner's Commentary', 13 *EJIL*, 81.

Stahn C., (2007) 'Responsibility to Protect: Political Rhetoric or Emerging Legal Norm?', 101 *AJIL*, 99.

Stein T., (1982) 'Contempt, Crisis and the Court: The World Court and the Hostage Rescue Attempt', 76 *AJIL*, 499.

Stowell E.C., (1921) *Intervention in International Law* (Washington, DC: J. Byrne).

Strupp K., (1924) 'L'incident de Janina entre la Greece et l'Italie', 31 *RGDIP*, 255.

Talkington H., (1979) 'International Trade: Uganda Trade Embargo', 20 *HILJ*, 206.

Talmon S., (2004) 'The Constitutive versus the Declaratory Theory of Recognition: *Tertium Non Datur*?', 75 *BYIL*, 101.

Tams C., (2002a) 'All's Well That Ends Well: Comments on the ILC's Articles on State Responsibility', 62 *ZaöRV*, 759.

    (2002b) 'Do Serious Breaches Give Rise to Any Specific Obligations of the Responsible State?', 13 *EJIL*, 1161.

    (2005) *Enforcing Obligations Erga Omnes* (Cambridge: Cambridge University Press).

    (2010) 'Waiver, Acquiescence, and Extinctive Prescription', in Crawford J., Pellet A. and Olleson S. (eds.), *The Law of International Responsibility* (Oxford: Oxford University Press), 1035.

    and Tzanakopoulos A., (2010) '*Barcelona Traction* at 40: The ICJ as an Agent of Legal Development', 23 *LJIL*, 781.

    (2011) 'Individual States as Guardians of Community Interests', in Fastenrath U. et al. (eds.), *From Bilateralism to Community Interest. Essays in Honour of Bruno Simma* (Oxford: Oxford University Press), 379.

    (2014) 'Countermeasures against Multiple Responsible Actors', in Nollkaemper A. and Plakokefalos I. (eds.), *Principles of Shared Responsibility in International Law: An Appraisal of the State of the Art* (Cambridge: Cambridge University Press), 312.

Tehindrazanarivelo D.L., (2005) *Les sanctions des Nations Unies et leurs effets secondaires: Assistance aux victimes et voies juridiques de prévention* (Paris: PUF).

Thirlway H., (1989) 'The Law and Procedure of the International Court of Justice 1960–1989 – Part One', 60 *BYIL*, 1.

    (2009) 'The Law and Procedure of the International Court of Justice 1960–1989: Supplement, 2009 – Parts Seven and Eight', 80 *BYIL*, 10.

    (2010) 'The Sources of International Law', in Evans M. (ed.), *International Law* (Oxford: Oxford University Press, 3rd ed.), 95.

    (2014) *The Sources of International Law* (Oxford: Oxford University Press).

Thouvenin J.-M., (2005) 'Article 103', in Cot J.-P., Pellet A. and Forteau M. (eds.), *La Chartre des Nations Unies: Commentaire article par article* (Paris: Economica, 3rd ed.), 2133.

Tomaševski K., (2000) *Responding to Human Rights Violations 1946–1999* (Leiden: Martinus Nijhoff).

Tomuschat C., (1973) 'Repressalie und Retorsion: Zu einigen Aspekten ihrer innnerstaatlichen Durchfürung', 33 *ZaöRV*, 179.

(1993) 'Obligations Arising for States without or against Their Will', 241 *RdC*, 195.

(1994) 'Are Counter-Measures Subject to Prior Recourse to Dispute Settlement Procedures?', 5 *EJIL*, 77.

(2005) 'Reply of Mr. Tomuschat', 71 *Ann. IDI*, 159.

and Thouvenin J.-M. (eds.), (2006) *The Fundamental Rules of the International Legal Order: Jus Cogens and Obligations Erga Omnes* (Leiden: Martinus Nijhoff).

Torelli M., (1995) 'Chronique des faits internationaux', 99 *RGDIP*, 236.

(1996) 'Chronique des faits internationaux', 100 *RGDIP*, 197.

Tsagourias N. and White N.D., (2013) *Collective Security: Theory, Law and Practice* (Cambridge: Cambridge University Press).

Twiss T., (1884) *The Law of Nations Considered as Independent Political Communities: On the Rights and Duties of Nations in Time of Peace* (Oxford: Clarendon Press).

Tzanakopoulos A., (2011) *Disobeying the Security Council: Countermeasures against Wrongful Sanctions* (Oxford: Oxford University Press).

(2015) 'Sanctions Imposed Unilaterally by the European Union: Implications for the European Union's International Responsibility', in Marozzi A.Z. and Bassett M.R. (eds.), *Economic Sanctions under International Law: Unilateralism, Multilateralism, Legitimacy and Consequences* (Berlin: Springer), 145.

Ullman R.H., (1977–1978) 'Human Rights and Economic Power: The United States versus Idi Amin', 56 *Foreign Affairs*, 529.

de Vattel E., (1758/1805) *Le droit des gens ou principes de la loi naturelle* (English trans., Northampton (Mass.): Printed by T.M. Pomroy for S&E Butler).

Verdirame G., (2011) *The UN and Human Rights: Who Guards the Guardians?* (Cambridge: Cambridge University Press).

Villalpando S., (2005) *L'émergence de la communauté internationale dans la responsabilité des Etats* (Paris: PUF).

(2013) 'Some Archeological Explorations on the Birth of Obligations *Erga Omnes*', in Kamga M. and Mbengue M.M. (eds.), *Liber Amicorum Raymond Ranjeva: L'Afrique et le droit international: variations sur l'organisation internationale* (Paris: Pedone), 623.

de Visscher C., (1924) 'L'interprétation du Pacte au lendemain du Différend Italo-Grec', 5 *RDILC*, 213–230, 377–390.

(1968) *Theory and Reality in Public International Law* (English trans. P.E. Corbett, Princeton, NJ: Princeton University Press).

Voeffray F., (2004) *L'actio popularis ou la défense de l'intérêt collectif devant les juridictions internationales* (Paris: PUF).

Waldock H., (1952) 'The Regulation of the Use of Force by Individual States in International Law', 81 *RdC*, 455.

(1962) 'General Course on Public International Law', 106 *RdC*, 1.

Weil P., (1983) 'Towards Relative Normativity in International Law?', 77 *AJIL*, 413.

(1992) 'Le droit international en quête de son identité', 237 *RdC*, 9.

Weller M., (1999) *The Crisis in Kosovo 1989–1999: From the Dissolution of Yugoslavia to Rambouillet and the Outbreak of Hostilities* (Cambridge: Documents & Analysis Publishing).

Weschke K., (2001) *Internationale Instrumente zur Durchsetzung der Menschenrechte* (Berlin: Berlin Verlag Spitz).

Westlake J., (1913) *International Law*, Part II: War (Cambridge: Cambridge University Press, 2nd ed.).

Wezeman P.D., (2013) 'Arms Transfers to Syria', in *SIPRI Yearbook (2013): Armaments, Disarmament and International Security*, 269, http://www.sipri.org/yearbook/2013/files/sipri-yearbook-2013-chapter-5-section-3.

Wheaton H., (1936) *Elements of International Law* (Oxford: Clarendon Press, 5th ed. 1866, by R.H. Dana).

White N.D. and Abass A., (2014) 'Countermeasures and Sanctions', in Evans M. (ed.), *International Law* (Oxford: Oxford University Press, 4th ed.), 537.

(2015) *The Cuban Embargo under International Law: El Bloqueo* (London: Routledge).

Wibaux D., (1998) 'A propos de quelques questions juridiques posées par l'interdiction des vols des compagnies yougoslaves', 44 *AFDI*, 262.

Widdows K., (1982) 'Unilateral Denunciation of Treaties Containing No Denunciation Clause', 53 *BYIL*, 83.

Williams J.F., (1939) *Aspects of Modern International Law* (London/New York: Oxford University Press).

Winthrop W., (1894) 'The United States and the Declaration of Paris', 3 *Yale LJ*, 116.

Wittich S., (2007) 'Barcelona Traction Case', in *Max Planck Encyclopedia of Public International Law*, http://opil.ouplaw.com/home/EPIL.

(2010) 'Punitive Damages', in Crawford J., Pellet A. and Olleson S. (eds.), *The Law of International Responsibility* (Oxford: Oxford University Press), 667.

Wolfke K., (1964) *Custom in Present International Law* (Wroclaw: Ossolineum).

Wood M., (2010) 'State Practice', in *Max Planck Encyclopedia of Public International Law*, http://opil.ouplaw.com/home/EPIL.

Wright Q., (1924) 'Opinion of Commission of Jurists on Janina-Corfu Affair', 18 *AJIL*, 536.

Wyler E., (2002) 'From "State Crime" to Responsibility for "Serious Breaches of Obligations under Peremptory Norms of General International Law"', 13 *EJIL*, 1147.

Zemanek K., (1987) 'The Unilateral Enforcement of International Obligations', 47 *ZaöRV*, 32.

(1997) 'The Legal Foundations of the International System', 266 *RdC*, 9.

(2000) 'New Trends in the Enforcement of *Erga Omnes* Obligations', 4 *Max Planck Yearbook of United Nations Law*, 1.

Ziegler K.S., (2012) '*Domaine Réservé*', in *Max Planck Encyclopedia of Public International Law*, http://opil.ouplaw.com/home/EPIL.

Zifcak S., (2014) 'The Responsibility to Protect', in Evans M. (ed.), *International Law* (Oxford: Oxford University Press, 4th ed.), 509.

Zoller E., (1980) 'L'affaire du personnel diplomatique et consulaire des Etats-Unis à Téhéran. Arrêt du 24 mars 1980', 84 *RGDIP*, 973.

(1984a) *Peacetime Unilateral Remedies: An Analysis of Countermeasures* (Dobbs Ferry/New York: Transnational Publishers).

(1984b) 'Quelques réflexions sur les contre-mesures en droit international public', in *Droit et libertés à la fin du XXe siècle. Etudes offertes à C.A. Colliard* (Paris: Pedone), 361.

(1985) *Enforcing International Law through U.S. Legislation* (Dobbs Ferry/ New York: Transnational Publishers).

INDEX

CAMBRIDGE STUDIES IN INTERNATIONAL AND COMPARATIVE LAW

Books in the series